The Hardball Times Baseball Annual 2011

Featuring contributions by THT's staff writers:

Richard Barbieri • John Beamer • Brian Borawski
Josh Fisher • Brandon Isleib • Chris Jaffe
Brad Johnson • Max Marchi • Anna McDonald
Harry Pavlidis • Nick Steiner • Dave Studenmund
Steve Treder • Tuck • John Walsh • Geoff Young

With additional contributions by guest writers:

Rob Neyer • Craig Wright • John Dewan
Craig Calcaterra • Ben Jedlovec • Jon Daly
Tom Tango • Jeremy Greenhouse • Sean Smith
Larry Granillo • Vince Gennaro • Dave Cameron
David Golebiewski • Greg Rybarczyk • Kate McSurley

Produced by Dave Studenmund
Edited by Joe Distelheim, Bryan Tsao,
Jeremiah Oshan and Carolina Bolado Hale

ACTA SPORTS

The Hardball Times Baseball Annual 2011

New articles daily at www.hardballtimes.com

Edited by Joe Distelheim, Bryan Tsao, Jeremiah Oshan and Carolina Bolado Hale
Stats developed by Dave Studenmund and Bryan Donovan
Cover design by Tom Wright
Typesetting by Dave Studenmund

Published by: ACTA Sports
                 4848 North Clark Street
                 Chicago, IL 60640
                 1-800-397-2282
                 info@actasports.com
                 www.actasports.com

ISBN: 978-0-87946-440-0
ISSN: 1940-4484
Printed in the United States of America by McNaughton & Gunn, Inc.
Year: 16 15 14 13 12 11 10 09
Printing: 10 9 8 7 6 5 4 3 2 1

What's Inside

Welcome to Our Book........................... 5

The 2010 Season

The American League East View............. 9
by Brad Johnson
The American League Central View 12
by Josh Fisher
The American League West View...........15
by Geoff Young
The National League East View 19
by John Beamer
The National League Central View 22
by Harry Pavlidis
The National League West View 26
by Steve Treder

Commentary

The Year in Frivolity 31
by Craig Calcaterra
The Year in Taters..............................38
by Larry Granillo
The Year in a Single Number.................42
by Dave Studenmund
The Annotated 2010 in Baseball History ..47
by Richard Barbieri
The Booms and Busts of 2010...............51
by David Golebiewski
The Leaders of 2011...........................57
by Oliver
The Business of Baseball......................60
by Brian Borawski
At the Ballpark in the 21st Century.........65
by Larry Granillo
What Were They Really Worth? 68
by Vince Gennaro
How to Handle a Pitcher.......................76
by Craig Wright
A Perfect Summer Dream 91
by Anna McDonald

The Future of Fielding

Defense Matters 96
by Dave Cameron
The Pitching and Defense Splits 100
by John Dewan
The Next Frontier in Fielding Analysis ... 106
by Ben Jedlovec
Everything is About to Change............. 111
by Rob Neyer
An Introduction to FIELDf/x................. 114
by Kate McSurley and Greg Rybarczyk

History

2010: Year of the Pitcher? 120
by Steve Treder
The Best and Worst Benches of All Time 125
by Chris Jaffe
A Gentleman Remembered.................. 129
by Craig Wright
Bully for the Yankee Clipper................. 133
by Jon Daly

Analysis

Scouting by Numbers 136
by Jeremy Greenhouse and Nick Steiner
Do Catchers Have an ERA?.................. 143
by Sean Smith
That Was a Strike? 147
by John Walsh
The Curious Case of Barry Zito 152
by Max Marchi
Three Things I Wanted to Research 159
by Tom M. Tango
Ultimate Home Run Park Factors.......... 164
by Greg Rybarczyk

Statistics

As Much Fun as Doing Your Taxes........ 172
by Dave Studenmund

What's Inside (cont.)

American League Team Stats 178

National League Team Stats 183

Arizona Diamondbacks 188

Atlanta Braves................................. 192

Baltimore Orioles 196

Boston Red Sox 200

Chicago Cubs 204

Chicago White Sox 208

Cincinnati Reds................................ 212

Cleveland Indians............................. 216

Colorado Rockies 220

Detroit Tigers.................................. 224

Florida Marlins................................. 228

Houston Astros................................ 232

Kansas City Royals............................ 236

Los Angeles Angels of Anaheim............ 240

Los Angeles Dodgers 244

Milwaukee Brewers 248

Minnesota Twins 252

New York Mets................................. 256

New York Yankees............................. 260

Oakland Athletics............................. 264

Philadelphia Phillies 268

Pittsburgh Pirates 272

San Diego Padres............................. 276

San Francisco Giants 280

Seattle Mariners 284

St. Louis Cardinals 288

Tampa Bay Rays 292

Texas Rangers................................ 296

Toronto Blue Jays............................. 300

Washington Nationals 304

The Hardball Times Glossary 308

Trivia Answers................................. 312

Who are These People?...................... 313

Welcome to Our Book

This is the seventh time we've published a baseball annual, and each one has included something special. Our very first *Annual*, way back in 2004, included a new idea from Robert Dudek: measuring the "hang time" of each batted ball to determine what its likely outcome would be. Six years later, we now have a baseball statistics company, Baseball Info Solutions, collecting that information and reporting about it in these pages.

In fact, this year's *Annual* has a special section devoted to the current and future state of fielding stats, including commentary from well-known baseball writers Rob Neyer and Dave Cameron and fielding studies from well-known statisticians John Dewan, Ben Jedlovec and Greg Rybarczyk.

We even show you what the graphical future of fielding analysis could look like, courtesy of Sportvision, the same folks who post those graphical strike zones on your TV. Whether you're a stat nerd or just someone who enjoys watching a game at the ballpark, you will be intrigued by what you see.

Even if you aren't, there's plenty more to read. We begin with our review of the 2010 season, organized by division. Unfortunately, we rushed to get our book to the printer before the postseason was over (the sooner to get it to you, after all), so you'll have to download our postseason coverage from the Internet. I'll give you the instructions for that in a minute.

After the 2010 season section, you'll find lots of general baseball commentary, written by staff and friends of the Hardball Times. One of our friends is Craig Wright, who has written a 15-page magnum opus on the handling of pitchers and pitch counts. 20 years ago, Craig was one of the very first people to study this issue in depth, and he still has plenty to say about the subject.

Another good friend of THT (that's short for The Hardball Times) is Larry Granillo, of wezen-ball.com, who took the time to watch video of every 2010 home run to measure how long it took each batter to circle the bases. There's also the aforementioned Greg Rybarczyk, who also watched video of each home run to measure its distance, speed off the bat and other physical properties of the ball. Two guys, watching the same thing with stopwatches in hand, for two entirely different reasons. There is room in the *Hardball Times Annual* for virtually every kind of baseball nut.

Our book contains baseball history and baseball analysis, too. You may have heard of PITCHf/x, Sportvision's remarkable system that collects intricate detail of every pitch. Well, we have several people who specialize in PITCHf/x studies, such as Jeremy Greenhouse. Jeremy has devised a system for measuring the location and "stuff" of all major league pitchers.

We even have a contribution from our good friend "Oliver," the system behind THT Forecasts. Oliver has generously donated leaderboard projections for the 2011 season. You can access updated projections all year long by signing up for THT Forecasts at our website.

There's more, of course, and I've just insulted many good friends by not naming them in this intro. But keep in mind that commentary and articles are only half the book. We've also got 2010 statistics for you to pore over. Many of the stats are standard fare, but we've also included our patented "batted ball" stats. These aren't available anywhere on the Internet and you can glean insights about players you won't discover other places.

Tuck has drawn baseball 'toons for the book and Brandon Isleib has planted his aggravating yet wildly entertaining trivia quizzes throughout. Yes, the *Hardball Times Annual* is a veritable cornucopia of baseball bliss.

Oops. I always tell myself to start thanking people early, and I never do. But let me say that Baseball Info Solutions and ACTA Sports are tremendous partners. Thank you, Andrew Yankech, Damon Lichtenwalner and John Dewan. Greg, Ben, Mary and Donna too.

Fangraphs is a fantastic website and a lifelong friend of ours. Thank you, David Appelman, for your support and the stats. A big thanks, too, to Tom Tango, who has always been a huge supporter of ours. If you haven't read *The Book*, read it as soon as you're done with the *Annual*.

The Hardball Times website posts new content virtually every day of the year. Thanks to all of the THT writers, past, present and future, for making it go. And the biggest thanks goes to our editors—particularly our new chief editor Joe Distelheim—but also to Bryan Tsao, Jeremiah Oshan and Carolina Bolado Hale for their huge help with the *Annual*.

Doh! I knew I'd run out of room. Those download instructions can be found in the introduction to our statistics, "As Much Fun as Doing Your Taxes."

Happy Baseball,

Dave Studenmund

Welcome to my World

If you're like me (or actually me), you enjoy British panel shows, where comedians and personalities of all sorts talk about random things—often politics or just news generally. We at Hardballtimesia, a land as fair and utopian as its denizens, are no strangers to the real world, and in honor of a newsy time since our last *Annual* (sort of like rangy, but with more potential to be applied to David Eckstein), we bring you a news quiz.

Well … not really, but sorta. Our real world happens to have a ton of baseball, so when we see a timely piece of news (sort of like a timely piece of hitting, but with more potential to be applied to David Eckstein), it inspires trivia themes. This book contains three news stories of the last 12 months, with six baseball questions each. (Trivia warm-up: Did you know that if you multiplied that together, you'd have 216 months-questions-stories?) The first one is below—you'll find the others cleverly hidden inside. The answers to the quizzes are way in the back.

If there isn't a stated connection, some detail in my narrative might help you. I've ensured that every question connects to something I actually mentioned in the story; no previous knowledge is necessary. Okay, some baseball knowledge might help, but if you stumbled across this Annual and the trivia herein without baseball knowledge, then I'm as stumped as you'll be.

Your friend,
Brandon Isleib

Trivia Sidebar #1: Bye?

Six-year-old Coloradan Falcon Heene was the subject of a massive search and outpouring of sympathy when he was presumed fallen from a hot air balloon in October 2009. Granted, he was in his parents' attic the whole time, he outed his parents on national television (proving ultimately unhelpful in the family's attempt to get a reality show), and his dad pled guilty in November for attempting to influence a public servant, but the kid was all the rage for a few days.

I don't have the faintest idea what reality show gets based around kids getting lost in balloons, but I don't know who would want to risk their reputations and their freedom to be on a reality show either. Maybe I'm just not cut out for it.

1. No one's ERA ballooned quite like this fellow's. An 1880s southpaw who died two years after his playing days were done, he has the best single-season adjusted ERA out of anyone with only one season above 100.

2. Not counting the Union Association (else the answer would be Buster Hoover), who's the adjusted OPS counterpart of our man above? If we must be technical, he had an OPS+ of 103 one year after his big season of .378/.386/.458. But in the two seasons prior to his big year, he batted .191/.195/.247 and went 1-21 as a pitcher, while in the eight years after he batted .237/.266/.299.

3. In the bottom rounds of the 1967 draft, the Braves drafted a shortstop who would become a Pro Bowl quarterback, while the Falcons drafted a quarterback whose namesake, born seven months away from the shortstop, would become an All-Star first baseman. What were the names of these fellows?

4. Speaking of birds, who's the only player to have spent his career exclusively with all three current bird teams?

5. Two teams that play in some hot air, the Rangers and Braves, nearly broke their home winning percentage record this year (the Braves tied their record, while the Rangers missed by a game). What was the last year where two teams older than 10 years broke their home winning percentage record?

6. What is this a leaderboard of?

Barry Bonds	26
Eric Karros	21
Sammy Sosa	21
Jeff Kent	20
Ryan Klesko	20

The 2010 Season

The American League East View

by Brad Johnson

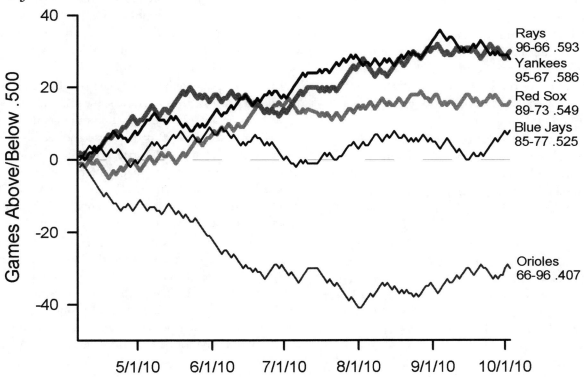

Head to Head Records

Team	BAL	BOS	NYA	TB	TOR	TOT
BAL		9	5	7	3	24
BOS	9		9	7	12	37
NYA	13	9		8	8	38
TB	11	11	10		10	42
TOR	15	6	10	8		39

To find wins, read across; losses are read from the top.

Play Against Other Divisions

Division	W	L	Win%
AL Central	103	83	.554
AL West	103	71	.592
NL East	17	22	.436
NL Central	6	3	.667
NL West	22	20	.524
Total	251	199	.558

In the so-called year of the pitcher, the American League East featured many of the most intriguing young arms in the game. The Rays, Blue Jays, and Orioles relied heavily on their young guns over the course of the 2010 season, while the Red Sox and Yankees mixed youth with pricier, upper-crust veteran hurlers.

The division was expected to be a dog fight between the Yankees, Red Sox, and Rays while the Blue Jays and Orioles battled for last. Of course things didn't turn out quite as expected. The Blue Jays were surprisingly good and might have made the postseason in another division despite finishing fourth in the AL East. The Rays and Yankees lived up to their hype with the Rays winning a down-to-the-wire division race. Meanwhile, the Red Sox felt the sting of injury early and often, hampering their

efforts to keep pace. The Orioles were supposed to take a step forward in 2010 but failed to do so, winning only 66 games.

The Tampa Bay Rays relied on their impressive young talent en route to the division title. With a rotation anchored by battle-tested veterans James Shields (age 28) and Matt Garza (26), the perennial emphasis on youth paid off yet again. Although the emerging ace-like dominance of David Price (24) stole the show, strong performances from sophomore Jeff Neimann (27), rookie Wade Davis (24), and rookie-of-the-future Jeremy Hellickson (23) proved crucial.

The Rays benefitted from impressive continuity in 2010, using only seven different starters. All but eight starts went to the original rotation of Shields, Garza, Price, Niemann, and Davis, with Hellickson and Andy Sonnanstine each taking four turns.

The top performer by any measure was Price, who posted a strong 2.73 ERA in 207.2 innings to go along with 187 strikeouts and 79 walks. His breakout campaign included an ERA that was third best in the American League and his 19 wins were tied for second.

Rookie Wade Davis allayed fears among some scouts that he wouldn't stick in the starting rotation, performing admirably given the tough atmosphere of the AL East. His 4.07 ERA ranked third best of the staff's regular starters and his 113 strikeouts and 62 walks in 168 innings indicate that he should remain useful going forward.

Jeremy Hellickson, who has yet to gain rookie status after hurling only 26.1 Major League innings, put together a spectacular season, earning himself a spot in the rotation going forward. The "Baseball America Minor League Player of the Year" won three games for the Rays while punching out 25 and walking merely four.

Guarding the rear of the rotation was 2009 success story Jeff Niemann. Although not technically a young gun since he's already 27, Niemann remains young in Major League service time. In his second major league season, Niemann slipped a little but remained serviceable. His 4.39 ERA is more than acceptable from a back-of-the-rotation starter in the AL East. While throwing 173.1 IP, he made modest improvements in his strikeout rate, raising it over half a strikeout per inning, but a few extra walks and home runs outweighed the positives.

Prior to the season, many analysts picked the Toronto Blue Jays as the AL East cellar dwellers. Several reasons were cited, although one stood prominent: It was assumed that a Roy Halladay-less rotation would flounder in a division that features some of the most explosive offenses in baseball. Instead, the Blue Jays' rotation thrived.

The Jays never really nailed down the fifth slot in their rotation, giving turns to Dana Eveland, Marc Rzepczynski, Jesse Litsch, Brian Tallet, Shawn Hill, and Kyle Drabek. But the top four mitigated that back-end churn, providing strong performances throughout the year. Shawn Marcum (age 28) returned from Tommy John surgery to post a quality 3.64 ERA in 195.1 innings.

Second year veteran and de facto ace Ricky Romero (25) built on his breakout 2009 with an even stronger 2010. His 3.73 ERA trailed only Marcum among regular Jays starters while his 210 innings pitched led the staff. On Aug. 14, Romero and the Blue Jays agreed to a five-year, $30.1 million contract extension. The deal buys out his final four seasons of team control plus his first free agent eligible season. There is also an option for 2016.

Brandon Morrow (25), acquired over the offseason from the Mariners in exchange for set-up man Brandon League, put together another mercurial season. However, Jays fans have reason to be pleased with his progress. In his first season as a rotation regular, Morrow pieced together a career-best strikeout rate, an impressive 10.95 strikeouts per nine innings in 146.1 innings. He also improved his walk rate considerably, cutting his year-to-year walk rate per nine innings from 5.68 to 4.06. Control remains an issue, but Morrow appears poised for a potential breakout season in 2011.

Brett Cecil put together a commendable age-23 season, leading the Blue Jays with 15 wins. He showed a consistent approach all year, eating up 172.2 innings while striking out 117 and walking 54. Prior to his 2009 debut, Cecil showed some ability to strike batters out at a higher rate, so he has plenty of room to grow in the future. The Jays may want to be careful in how they handle him though. He threw 41.1 more innings in 2010 than 2009. Research shows that in players under 25, increased workloads of that magnitude can lead to greater injury risk.

The team that was supposed to finally climb out of the cellar at the Blue Jays expense was the Baltimore Orioles. And they were supposed to do it on the back of emerging young pitching and a solid offense. Instead the Orioles crawled out of the gate and only picked things up once Buck Showalter took the helm. Their 66 wins were fourth worst in baseball and 19 behind the fourth place Blue Jays in the AL East.

While veterans Kevin Millwood and Jeremy Guthrie munched innings, combining for 400 nondescript innings, future rotation mainstays Brian Matusz, Jake Arrieta, and Chris Tillman got the chance to learn under fire.

Matusz was the best of the trio, taking 32 turns at the major league level and putting together a respectable season. While no facet of his game was particularly impressive, his 4.30 ERA and 143 strikeouts in 175.2 innings were great for a 23-year-old. He put together a dominant run over his final eight starts. In 46 innings, he struck out 43 and allowed only 8 earned runs (1.57 ERA). While that finish should give O's fans reason for hope, it's worth noting that it was also the difference between a solid and disappointing season for Matusz.

In his 18 starts, Arrieta (age 24) showed some cause for worry. In 100.1 innings, he struck out a meager 52 while walking 48. His 4.66 ERA wasn't terrible, but could get worse if those walk and strikeout rates don't improve. Thankfully for the Orioles, their prospect has a much better track record in the minors. His minor league walk rate has been marginally better in years past while his strike out rate has never been below 7.66 strikeouts per nine innings.

The youngest of the trio, 22-year-old Chris Tillman, managed to claim 11 starts. He struggled in his 53.2 innings, allowing a 5.87 ERA backed by 31 strikeouts and 31 walks. The long ball plagued him as he gave up nine, about 1.5 home runs per nine innings. Like Arrieta, patience is advisable. Tillman is just 22 after all. There's reason to believe that the walks should plummet as 2010 was his first year with the yips. In his 121.1 innings at Triple-A, he walked only 30 batters. He also managed a no-hitter while down on the farm.

The Boston Red Sox were supposed to rely on a strong rotation anchored by veterans Josh Beckett, Jon Lester, and John Lackey. Support was to be provided by Daisuke Matsuzaka, Clay Buchholz, and the ageless Tim Wakefield. What the Red Sox got was dominance from their youngest arms, Lester and Buchholz, while the rest of the unit was thoroughly mediocre.

The 25-year-old Clay Buchholz has seemingly been a perennial top prospect since 2006. No more. Though he finally lost his prospect status last season, the results were fairly disappointing and forgettable outside of New England. Buchholz responded in 2010 by putting together a career season. His 2.33 ERA led the staff by over a run (Lester, 3.25) and trailed only the untouchable Felix Hernandez (2.27) for top mark in the AL. His 17 wins tied for sixth best in the AL. There were some blemishes beneath the glory. The most notable were his strikeouts, only 120 in 173.2 innings. Rarely do pitchers with strikeout rates as low as Buchholz's sustain ERA's below 3.00. Like so many other youngsters in this column, Buchholz had much stronger strikeout rates in the minors, so there is a chance he'll improve at getting the swing-and-miss.

I would be remiss to exclude Jon Lester (26) just because he is a well-known veteran. His considerable talent allowed him to post a mirror season to his fantastic 2009 campaign despite a rough April. While his walk rate took a minor step back, he continued to strike out more than a batter per inning, and increased his ground ball rate by about 6 percent, proving himself to be a true ace in the process.

Much like the Red Sox, the Wild Card-winning New York Yankees went into the season determined to rely on veteran hurlers and a potent lineup to power their way to the postseason. While lefty ace CC Sabathia put together a fine showing including a league-best 21 wins along with a 3.18 ERA in 237.2 innings, the rest of the veteran crew can only be described as disappointing.

Sure, Andy Pettitte (11-3, 3.28 ERA, 129 innings) was great when healthy, but a groin injury suffered in July dogged him for much of the season. Javier Vazquez imploded in his return to New York, vindicating observers who claim that he can't handle pressure. AJ Burnett was his usual baffling self. Startlingly, his strikeout rate dipped below seven per nine innings for the first time since 2001, which partially explains the career-worst 5.26 ERA.

And that leaves Phil Hughes. The winner of a preseason rotation battle with Joba Chamberlain, Hughes put together a memorable 2010 campaign despite a second-half fade. After authoring an 11-2 record with a 3.65 ERA in the first half, Hughes was named to his first All Star team (he got the loss). He ended the year at 17-8 with a 4.23 ERA in 174.1 innings. Altogether, Yankees fans have to be pleased with Hughes' transition from the bullpen to the rotation. He was able to sustain all the skills he demonstrated out of the bullpen except for his exceptional strikeout rate.

Young pitching can't tell the whole story of the AL East. There are some details beyond pitching that simply *must* be covered.

First, Jose Bautista deserves all the praise and plaudits in the world. In a single season, he transformed his middling, platoon-fielder career into that of a potential superstar. His 54 home runs were 12 more than second place Albert Pujols. Hit Tracker Online, a great website for analyzing home runs, classified 13 of Jose's home runs as "Just Enough." These are the home runs that might otherwise go for doubles if conditions were just slightly different. For comparison's sake, Pujols had 13 of his own in the "Just Enough" category despite having fewer total home runs. Bautista's power is real, though don't be surprised if pitchers make some major adjustments to him in 2011.

Finally, the injuries in Boston cannot be ignored. Back in the preseason, the Red Sox looked like they might be the favorites to win the AL East. Things quickly unraveled for the Sox as the injuries started to pile up. Perhaps the most poignant example was the Jacoby Ellsbury saga. After colliding with Adrian Beltre on April 11, Ellsbury struggled to get back on the field. What was at first considered to be a day-to-day injury stretched into weeks and then months. Diagnoses changed. Players questioned Ellsbury's grit. Things got messy.

The true load of injuries was crippling. Players like Darnell McDonald and Ryan Kalish were able to patch holes in the outfield and miraculously, the oft-injured J.D. Drew stayed healthy all season. The loss of Dustin Pedroia halfway through the season was devastating. Later, Kevin Youkilis hit the shelf after 101 games and remained out for the stretch. Victor Martinez and Jason Varitek suffered nearly simultaneous injuries, forcing the Sox to scrape together some weak patches behind the plate. Mike Cameron was too frequently injured to perform adequately. Even Marco Scutaro played through injury for a considerable part of the season.

2010 was a fun year to follow the AL East. Young pitching played a critical role for every team in the division. Eventually, the Yankees and Rays stole the show, but it was injuries that stole the show in Boston. Meanwhile, a certain home run basher by the name of Jose Bautista entertained the faithful in Toronto.

The American League Central View

by Josh Fisher

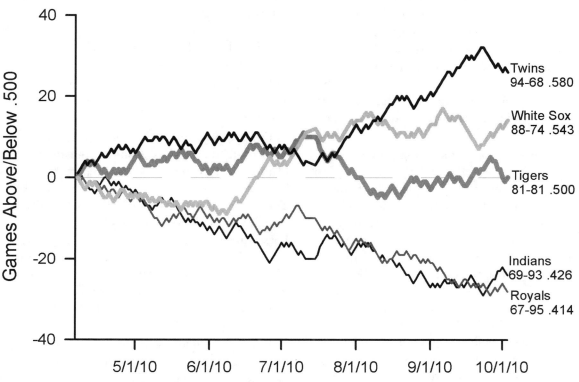

Head to Head Records

Team	CHA	CLE	DET	KC	MIN	TOT
CHA		9	8	10	5	32
CLE	9		9	10	6	34
DET	10	9		10	9	38
KC	8	8	8		5	29
MIN	13	12	9	13		47

To find wins, read across; losses are read from the top.

Play Against Other Divisions

Division	W	L	Win%
AL East	83	103	.446
AL West	89	85	.511
NL East	20	22	.476
NL Central	21	15	.583
NL West	6	6	.500
Total	**219**	**231**	**.487**

Minnesota Twins

Despite a disappointing first-round flameout against the New York Yankees, the Minnesota Twins might have had the most important year in the majors. By opening Target Field and selling nearly every available seat over the course of the year, the Twins made a bold move toward becoming the St. Louis Cardinals of the American League. The organization's new clout surfaced before a pitch was even thrown in 2010, appearing in the form of catcher Joe Mauer's contract extension. The new pact, which makes Mauer a Twin through 2018, will pay him $23 million annually beginning next spring. Such a commitment would not have been possible without the additional revenue flowing in via sparkling Target Field,

estimated to provide the Twins with about $60 million more each year than the Metrodome.

On the field this season, though, Mauer was hardly the story. While the All-Star catcher rebounded from a slow start to finish with a .327/.402/.469 line, Justin Morneau, Jim Thome, and Francisco Liriano provided the talking points.

Morneau was off to the best start in the majors before suffering a concussion in July. He never returned to game action, and, while the offseason is long and conducive to healing, the unpredictability of recovery from concussions means he'll start 2011 with a question mark. Thome did nothing but make history this season; he tied and passed Twins legend

Harmon Killebrew on the all-time home run list, doing so at Target Field on the same day, no less. And, while he is unlikely to garner any Cy Young buzz due to misleading ERA and wins figures, Liriano reemerged as one of the premier left-handed starters in the game. For a Twins staff long on strikes but short on strikeouts, Liriano is just the sort of pitcher the Twins need to be relevant in October.

Unfortunately for the Twins, one such power pitcher just might not be enough. The club's long-term outlook is clouded by its remarkable run of October failures. The Twins have lost 12 consecutive postseason games, including back-to-back sweeps at the hands of the hated Yankees. The problem seems to be that October baseball is fundamentally different from the regular season variety; rotation depth is largely tossed out the window. Given the short series and frequent off days, teams can effectively trim their rotations to their three best pitchers. For the Twins this year, that meant Liriano, Carl Pavano, and Brian Duensing. That's just not going to get it done most years.

The Twins have more of the usual on the way in recent first-round picks Kyle Gibson and Alex Wimmers—guys you can absolutely win 95 games with, but will not match up well in a short series against teams loaded with front-end, top-shelf talent. Whether the Twins can add some sizzle to the rotation over the offseason will determine how they should be evaluated as a serious contender in the spring.

Chicago White Sox

The Chicago White Sox nobly hung in the division race until mid-September, finishing 88-74, six games behind the first-place Twins. Still, though, in a year that saw the Twins emerge as a financial powerhouse, there is a sense of window-closing on the South Side of Chicago. In 2010, the White Sox were led by several strong performances. Alex Rios made Kenny Williams look like a genius, posting a quite-respectable .284/.334/.457 line. Andruw Jones and Carlos Quentin also combined for a little over a full season's worth of solid performance. The star of the show on offense was, without question, Paul Konerko, who had a career year at age 34. Fortunately for Konerko, he couldn't have picked a better time to post the best on-base and slugging percentages of his time in the majors: He's a free agent.

On the mound, John Danks led the charge for the White Sox. Still just 25, Danks bears all the hallmarks of a guy you can plug into a major league rotation and forget about for a half-decade or more. There's a ton of value in that. His performance, though, was countered by an average year from Mark Buehrle and a disappointing campaign from Jake Peavy. Buehrle, 31, can't be written off yet, but he just doesn't strike out enough batters to remain among the game's best starters.

Peavy was, in some ways, exactly what the White Sox should have expected: He was able to start just 17 games. However, he was not nearly as good in those starts as the White Sox might have hoped. The change in leagues and ballparks was not kind to Peavy, who had spent his entire pre-2010 career in San Diego. He recorded about two fewer strikeouts per game and allowed home runs twice as often than he did in his 2007 Cy Young year, and the performance dip combined with his durability issues make the two years and $33 million left on his contract foreboding figures.

In a division populated with an emerging powerhouse (the Minnesota Twins) and a loaded farm system (the Kansas City Royals), there is a sense that the rest of the teams had better get busy living, or get busy dying. The White Sox have some young talent—Alexei Ramirez and Gordon Beckham still very much qualify—but some retooling might be in order should the team wish to compete at the top of the division over the next several years. General manager Kenny Williams isn't afraid to take risks, and he's certainly pulled rabbits from the hat before. The White Sox aren't going away, but they have to get younger and healthier. It's a good thing those two often go together.

Detroit Tigers

Finishing an even 81-81, the Detroit Tigers might be best-positioned to wrest the division away from the Twins in 2011 and 2012. It all starts, of course, with a man building a great case for the Hall of Fame, and still just 27: Miguel Cabrera. There's no need to spend a ton of time on Cabrera; he did what he always does—hits and hits and walks and hits some more—he just did it better this year than any other in his career. Cabrera is probably a clear notch below the Cardinals' Albert Pujols, but it must not be disregarded that Cabrera plies his trade in the more-difficult American League. The Tigers' attack was led by Cabrera and Magglio Ordonez, with outfielders Johnny Damon, Ryan Raburn and Austin Jackson offering solid contributions as well.

Boiled down to just one moment, the 2010 Tigers will be remembered not for any of Cabrera's 38 home runs or Justin Verlander's 219 strikeouts, but for Armando Galarraga's perfect game that wasn't. Indeed, that near-perfecto, spoiled by a blown call from first base umpire Jim Joyce, might leave a more permanent legacy than anything else that happened in the division this year. Certainly, once baseball finally implements instant replay in some form, Galarraga's lost chance at history will be one of the reasons for a historic change to the way the game is officiated. And good for Galarraga; otherwise, his year was relatively forgettable.

Justin Verlander was Justin Verlander once again—a ton of strikeouts, a ton of innings. The best development on the mound for the Tigers was Max Scherzer's performance. There was never any question about Scherzer's stuff; that he struck out nearly a batter per inning is not surprising. The key is that he was able to make 31 starts. Due to an unusual delivery, Scherzer has long been considered an injury risk, but his 2010 effort suggests he should probably be regarded as no more volatile than any other young, hard-throwing pitcher. If Rick Porcello rebounds from a disappointing 2010, the 2011 Tigers have the makings of a good staff. Add that to a solid offensive nucleus, and the Tigers are well-situated to make a run at the Twins in 2011.

Cleveland Indians

As October reached its midpoint, Cliff Lee and CC Sabathia were preparing for the ALCS—for the Texas Rangers and New York Yankees, respectively. Unfortunately for Indians fans, that might be as close as the Indians get to representing the American League in the World Series for some time to come. Cleveland, which finished 25 games out of first place, doesn't have young studs in the pipeline to compare with fellow cellar-dweller Kansas City, so it might find itself alone at the bottom before long. Very little went according to plan in 2010 for the Indians. Grady Sizemore came to the plate just 140 times. Fausto Carmona was their best starter, and his year was no better than average. And top prospect Carlos Santana went down with an injury far too soon into a promising rookie season.

That's not to say there weren't bright spots. Shin-Soo Choo is quietly among the game's best overall players, Chris Perez looks like a bullpen fixture for several years to come, and Travis Hafner even returned from the grave to post an excellent season in nearly 500 plate appearances. The problem is that there's just not enough talent in or near the majors to expect the Indians to be a factor in the division any time soon. The task for Cleveland's front office now is to turn that seeming crisis into an opportunity.

The club needs to stick with Matt LaPorta, Michael Brantley, Jason Donald, Mitch Talbot and Justin Masterson. Will all those guys live up to their potential? Of course not. But they're young and talented enough to be considered possible pieces of the next competitive Indians team. The farm system is deep, and can likely be counted on to produce several solid major leaguers over the next few seasons. While the Indians' outlook may be bleak, one only needs to look at the Twins (nearly contracted in 2002) and Rays (61 wins in 2006) to see that things can turn around quickly.

Unfortunately for the Indians, the next entry to that list might just be the Royals, traditionally an AL Central doormat but hoping to compete at a high level in coming years. With the Twins flexing newfound muscle and the worst team in the division sitting on a gold mine of prospects, the AL Central is becoming tougher every year. The Indians are facing a long, uphill battle back toward competitiveness.

Kansas City Royals

The Royals won 67 games in 2010, finishing 27 games behind first place Minnesota. Alex Gordon edged closer to bust status, Zack Greinke took a big step back, Billy Butler didn't take a big step forward, and the ghost of Jason Kendall recorded nearly 500 plate appearances. It was a pretty dismal year for Kansas City, all things considered. So why did the organization have the second-best 2010 in the division? Omaha, Northwest Arkansas, and Wilmington.

The Royals farm system, a strong candidate to be ranked No. 1 by the several outlets concerned with these things, is bursting at the seams with solid hitters, interesting relievers, and—most of all—a remarkable wealth of left-handed starting pitching.

Some of the names are more familiar than others; Mike Montgomery is the most talked-about of the bunch. And among minor league hitters, there might not be a more promising pair in the same organization than Mike Moustakas and Eric Hosmer. The problem, of course, is that Royals fans have been in a similar spot before. For the last 20 years, the story was always the talent waiting in the wings. So what's different this time? Redundancy. For the first time in several talent generations, the Royals can absolutely afford a few failures. There are far fewer what-ifs; prospects abound, and not all of them will hit. It seems likely that, by 2013, enough will to make the Royals a true threat in the American League.

One uncertainty still hovers, however: Can general manager Dayton Moore handle that talent once it is major league-ready? While Moore has proven quite adept at developing talent in the minors, his major league roster construction is a running joke. Exhibit A is probably Gordon, who was league-average as a rookie, better than that his second season, and then suffered an injury in early 2009. After struggling in a brief reappearance late that year, he was given all of 38 plate appearances in 2010 before the club essentially gave up, demoting Gordon and directing him to learn a new position.

Truly, Gordon is the can't-miss prospect who, well, missed. And management is as responsible as anything else. While the stars appear to be aligning for the Royals, it remains to be seen whether Moore will have the patience to allow the talent to develop once it reaches Kansas City. If nothing else, the Royals have the luxury of time, and they must use it to the organization's long-term advantage.

The American League West View

by Geoff Young

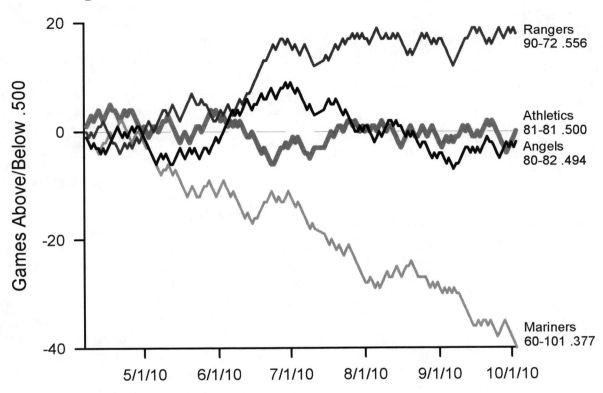

Head to Head Records

Team	LAA	OAK	SEA	TEX	TOT
LAA		11	15	9	35
OAK	8		13	9	30
SEA	4	6		7	17
TEX	10	10	12		32

To find wins, read across; losses are read from the top.

Play Against Other Divisions

Division	W	L	Win%
AL East	71	103	.408
AL Central	85	89	.489
NL East	3	0	1.000
NL Central	27	21	.563
NL West	12	9	.571
Total	198	222	.471

In American history and folklore, the West was frontier land. Settlers used whatever resources and strategies might be available to make, or lose, their fortune.

The AL West isn't a literal frontier, but innovation lives there. Each of its four teams has adopted a distinct approach to attaining, or trying to attain, sustainable success.

After enjoying a strong run in the early-'70s and another in the late-'80s, the Oakland A's fell on hard times before re-emerging in the early 2000s. The A's used techniques championed by Bill James and popularized by Michael Lewis' *Moneyball* to exploit market inefficiencies and gain a competitive advantage over richer competitors.

Playing in the shadows of Dodger Stadium and Disneyland, the Angels have spent much of their existence seeking a unique identity. Despite moderate success from the late-'70s through the mid-'80s, the Angels were an afterthought in the Southern California market. In 2002, emphasizing "small ball"—executing fundamentals, taking the extra base—the franchise won its first World Series. The Angels broke three million in attendance the following year. They have ranked among baseball's elite on the field and at the gate ever since.

The Mariners arrived in 1977, but didn't start winning until 1991. They hit their stride under manager Lou Piniella in the late-'90s and peaked with a remarkable 116-win season

15

in 2001. More recently in 2009, the Mariners won by emphasizing defense in their spacious home ballpark.

As for the Rangers, the once cellar-dwelling Washington Senators moved to Texas in 1972. After sporadic success throughout the '70s and '80s, they won their first division title in 1994 (with a losing record, in a season robbed of its postseason by labor strife). Later (1996-1999), they reached the playoffs three times in four years. The Rangers have slipped since those glory years under the late Johnny Oates, but now there is cause for renewed optimism.

Bay Area Arms

In the post-*Moneyball* era, it isn't always as easy to uncover hidden value as it once was. Other teams have caught on and are doing the same.

Expectations were justifiably low in the wake of consecutive 75-win seasons. That didn't keep Billy Beane and company from making moves to help support a young pitching staff. They traded for San Diego third baseman Kevin Kouzmanoff to replace the oft-injured Eric Chavez and signed free agent Ben Sheets to take pressure off the kids.

Although neither move worked as well as hoped, the A's held their own thanks to an embarrassment of capable young arms. Oakland's starting pitchers led the league with a 3.47 ERA.

From the left side, Gio Gonzalez (age 24) and Dallas Braden (26) led the way, with Braden tossing a perfect game in May. Brett Anderson (22) made an impact in more limited time. From the right side, Vin Mazzaro (23) showed promise, but the best was Trevor Cahill (22). As a sophomore, Cahill improved his hit and walk prevention en route to his first All-Star appearance and 18 wins. His strikeout rate remains uncomfortably low (5.40), although Mark Buehrle, Aaron Cook and Jon Garland have demonstrated that this isn't always a problem.

From an offensive standpoint, there wasn't much to celebrate. The A's finished 11th in the AL in runs scored, with no single player scoring as many as 80. Veterans Coco Crisp and Jack Cust rejuvenated their careers, Rajai Davis and Cliff Pennington ran but didn't hit, and Mark Ellis provided his usual steadying influence. Young first baseman Daric Barton (24) established himself as an offensive threat (albeit without the power expected at his position), leading the AL with 110 walks.

A's fans may be disappointed that their team finished with its fourth straight losing season. However, Oakland endured a similar stretch (six years in that case) before embarking on the journey that led to *Moneyball*. Despite the team's gaping offensive holes, young pitching and Beane's track record make its medium- to long-term prognosis promising.

Anaheim's Arrested Development

The Angels won in 2008 with great pitching and below-average hitting; the next year, they won by being above average at both. In 2010, the Angels' hitting returned to 2008 levels but the pitching plateaued, and so the club from Anaheim suffered its first losing season since 2003.

One frustrating aspect of the Angels' existence over the past several years has been their inability to consistently convert young position prospects into productive big-leaguers: Casey Kotchman, Jeff Mathis and Brandon Wood are among the players who have failed to fulfill their promise.

Particularly troublesome is the stagnation of Wood, who hit 43 homers in High-A ball at age 20. He popped 20 or more each of the next four years but has hit .169/.198/.260 in a season's worth of big-league games, with an 11-to-1 strikeout-to-walk ratio. Making consistent contact was never Wood's strong suit, but as a shortstop with power, he was considered a top-shelf prospect not long ago. Now he is clinging to the hope of a career.

Although Wood's case is the most extreme, he isn't alone. Middle infielders Eric Aybar and Howie Kendrick have become serviceable players, but not the stars some people envisioned.

Still, it isn't all bad. Catcher/first baseman Mike Napoli is developing into Mickey Tettleton-lite. Cuban-born first baseman Kendry Morales emerged in 2009 and was enjoying a fine follow-up season when he broke his leg jumping onto home plate after hitting a walk-off grand slam on May 29.

The Angels have had better luck developing pitchers, and if they are to succeed in 2011, much will depend on the right arms of Jered Weaver and Ervin Santana. Both took steps forward in 2010, with Weaver leading the AL with 233 strikeouts.

The Angels also acquired right-hander Dan Haren from Arizona in July despite being six games out of first place. In the NL East, the Phillies trailed Atlanta by the same margin, acquired Roy Oswalt, and ran away with the division. The Angels followed a different path, going 20-33 in July and August, but gave little to acquire a front-line pitcher who should give them John Lackey-type production.

Like the A's, the Angels are a mixed bag. The outfield is old and the bullpen is filled with forgettable flingers, but a rotation headed by Weaver, Santana and Haren could be formidable. Napoli and a healthy Morales provide a solid offensive nucleus, and if Aybar and/or Kendrick step up their games, this team could contend sooner rather than later.

Seattle's Defensible Disaster

Expected to build on their success of 2009, the Mariners instead lost 101 games. They went 17-40 within the division. Remarkably, the Mariners finished above .500 in only one month, June. More remarkably, they did so despite being outscored, 114-86.

A year after earning praise for guiding the Mariners to 85 wins with defense, GM Jack Zduriencik saw his team take a nasty tumble. A series of well-intentioned (and seemingly sensible) moves backfired.

First, Zduriencik shipped right-hander Carlos Silva to the Cubs for outfielder Milton Bradley. The previous regime signed Silva to an ill-advised four-year, $48 million contract in December 2007 and was rewarded with a 5-18, 6.81 ERA performance. Bradley, meanwhile, flopped in Chicago after hitting .321/.436/.563 for the Rangers in 2008. He should have helped a team that needed offense but didn't, hitting just .205/.292/.348.

Next, the Mariners let Adrian Beltre leave for Boston as a free agent. They brought in former Angels infielder Chone Figgins to play second base and moved incumbent Jose Lopez to third. Here's how the respective players fared in 2009:

Player	Age	PA	BA	OBP	SLG
Beltre	30	477	.265	.304	.379
Figgins	31	729	.298	.395	.393
Lopez	25	653	.272	.303	.463

And in 2010:

Player	Age	PA	BA	OBP	SLG
Beltre	31	641	.321	.365	.553
Figgins	32	702	.259	.340	.306
Lopez	26	622	.239	.270	.339

Beltre went from mediocrity to MVP candidate, Figgins from catalyst to afterthought, and Lopez from power threat at a defense-first position to Punch-and-Judy hitter at one that demands offense. This wasn't the sole cause of Seattle's struggles in 2010, but it served as a painful reminder that reasonable decisions can have disastrous consequences.

The Mariners also sent young right-hander Brandon Morrow to Toronto for reliever Brandon League. Although Morrow has some rough edges, he showed promise for the Blue Jays in his first season as a full-time rotation starter. League, meanwhile, continued to toil as a forgettable bullpen cog.

The Mariners got decent pitching for much of the year, fronted by perennial Cy Young contender Felix Hernandez and off-season acquisition Cliff Lee. Relative unknowns Jason Vargas and Doug Fister also contributed.

But too much went wrong. Ken Griffey Jr. retired at the end of May. Lee was traded to division rival Texas in July. Figgins and manager Don Wakamatsu tussled in the dugout that same month, with Wakamatsu being canned a few weeks later.

Seattle's offense misfired on all cylinders. Ichiro Suzuki became the third player in history (Moises Alou, 1968; Kirby Puckett, 1989) to score 75 runs or fewer while collecting at least 210 hits. Russell Branyan led the club with 15 homers, and he didn't arrive until June 26.

Zduriencik and the Mariners may have won with defense in 2009, but without anyone other than a couple of guys in their mid-30s to help produce runs, Hernandez et al. are in for frustration if changes aren't made. And if there's anyone the Mariners want to keep happy, it's Hernandez.

Where Did They Go Right in Arlington?

In 2009, Tom Hicks and company found themselves in a tight financial situation that forced the Rangers to file for Chapter 11 bankruptcy in May 2010. With a lack of money already on everyone's minds, the Rangers hardly needed further distractions.

Naturally they got some when it was revealed that manager Ron Washington tested positive for cocaine during the 2009 season. Rather than rip the team apart, Washington's troubles galvanized the Rangers.

General manager Jon Daniels helped. Where the A's once emphasized on-base percentage and the Mariners emphasized defensive utility, Daniels and the Rangers found a new value play in injury risk and uncertainty.

Daniels signed the once-dangerous but aging and health-challenged Vladimir Guerrero to a one-year deal at a bargain price. Guerrero responded by providing a productive middle-of-the-order bat to accompany Josh Hamilton and Nelson Cruz.

The Rangers also gambled on right-handers Rich Harden and Colby Lewis. Harden, who pitched well for Oakland between DL stints in the mid-2000s, didn't pan out, but Lewis did.

After failing to impress in several attempts at the big-league level, the former Rangers first-round pick spent two years in Japan. Texas wooed him back to North America with a two-year, $5 million deal. Lewis gave the Rangers 32 starts and a 3.72 ERA (respectable in that ballpark), pitching like Ted Lilly, but for a fraction of the cost.

Meanwhile, Washington made bold moves of his own. He slid former closer C.J. Wilson into the rotation and inserted

22-year-old rookie Neftali Feliz into the role shared by Wilson and Frank Francisco a year earlier. Wilson responded with 15 wins and a 3.35 ERA (10th in the AL). Feliz held opposing batters to a .176/.246/.269 line and notched 40 saves, becoming the youngest pitcher to reach that mark.

During the season, Daniels continued to make moves. In the span of four weeks, he acquired catcher Bengie Molina, pitchers Cliff Lee and Mark Lowe, and infielders Jorge Cantu and Cristian Guzman. He added outfielder Jeff Francoeur in August.

Not all the moves worked (Molina and Cantu were lousy, Guzman was worse), but they indicated a commitment to players and fans. It's impossible to know how (or if) such commitment translates into on-field results, but at worst, it leaves people with a good feeling about their team, which presumably fosters loyalty.

Fourth outfielder David Murphy continued to excel in his role. First baseman Mitch Moreland came up from the minors in July and supplied power. Right-hander Tommy Hunter won 13 games despite making his season debut on June 5. Feliz's supporting cast did a terrific job (only Tampa Bay had a better bullpen ERA among AL clubs than the Rangers' 3.38).

Cruz missed a third of his team's games but played at All-Star levels when healthy. And no story of the Rangers would be complete without mentioning Hamilton, who rebounded from a troubled 2009 to do a nice Albert Pujols impression, leading the league in batting average and slugging percentage.

The Rangers took calculated risks, got value from unexpected sources, and overcame adversity to win the AL West. For the first time since 1998-1999, they enjoyed consecutive winning seasons. The key to their future success will be in how well they adapt to ever-changing circumstances. Isn't that true for all of us?

The National League East View

by John Beamer

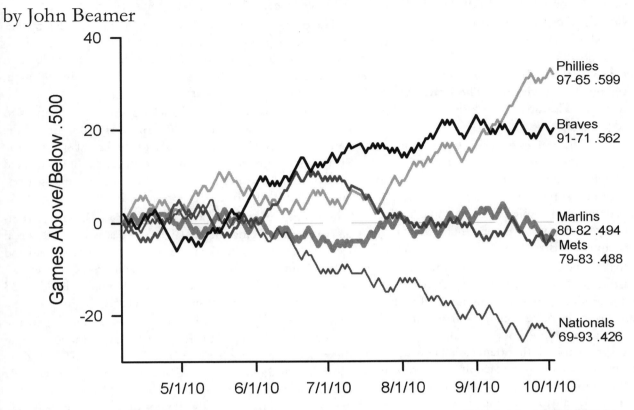

Head to Head Records

Team	ATL	FLA	NYN	PHI	WAS	TOT
ATL		11	11	8	8	38
FLA	7		12	5	13	37
NYN	7	6		9	9	31
PHI	10	13	9		12	44
WAS	10	5	9	6		30

To find wins, read across; losses are read from the top.

Play Against Other Divisions

Division	W	L	Win%
AL East	22	17	.564
AL Central	22	20	.524
AL West	0	3	.000
NL Central	106	94	.530
NL West	86	80	.518
Total	236	214	.524

A screaming comes across the sky. It has happened before, but there is nothing to compare it to now.

Although the opening of Thomas Pynchon's *Gravity's Rainbow* is referring to German V2 rockets shooting across the London horizon, it is also a wonderful metaphor to describe Jason Heyward's Opening Day, first at-bat blast off Carlos Zambrano into the seats at Turner Field. Reflecting on the season, it was almost as if in that moment the Braves' division credentials were established and the rest of the division was playing catch-up.

And so it played out until early September, when the Braves ran out of gas and the surging Phillies recovered their health, posting a 23-7 record down the stretch that saw them crowned NL East Division Champions for the fourth consecutive year with half a dozen games to spare.

In slightly more dramatic fashion, the slumping Braves, who in August looked a shoo-in for the playoffs, entered the final game of the season tied for the Wild Card and needing a win against the Phillies, having lost the previous five encounters against their division archrivals. Atlanta came through 8-7 and Bobby Cox was able to celebrate his final season in charge of the Braves with another visit to the postseason.

The screaming into the sky apart, it all looked far bleaker in late April after the Braves lurched to a nine-game losing streak including consecutive series defeats by the Cardinals and Mets. Heyward's Opening Day blast was succeeded by a downturn in form. Put it down to the law of small numbers perhaps, but Heyward was Captain Inconsistent all year.

In late April, he was hitless in six of seven games, at which point his average slipped to .224. May was a good month for Heyward and the Braves. Not only did Heyward find the lumber and stretch his average to over .300, the aging Troy Glaus came alive with six long balls and a .942 OPS to rally Atlanta to the division lead by the month's end.

The Braves seemed to muster up runs out of nothing. In late May, they pounded seven runs in the ninth inning, including a spectacular Brooks Conrad pinch-hit, walk-off grand slam to overcome the Reds 10-9. The Braves would end up with a major league leading 25 walk-off wins and 46 come-from-behind victories.

All things considered, the Phillies made the best start in the NL East. The only blip in the opening six weeks was at the end of April, when a 11-9 defeat to the Giants saw the Phillies slip out of first place for the first time in 135 games. However, by May 17 the Phils had opened a comfortable five-game lead on a 24-13 record. In retrospect, it was a bit of a shock when they found themselves behind the Braves less than 15 games later.

Trying to rationalize such a slump in a game that is so in thrall of the statistical gods is folly. But a few factors were working against the Phillies. First, although the Phils had acquired Roy Halladay in the offseason, the starting pitching was still thin. Cliff Lee was shipped out following the arrival of Halladay to manage payroll. Other than Cole Hamels, the remainder of the Phillies' rotation struggled. It was a problem that would recur until GM Ruben Amaro dug into his team's pockets to bring Roy Oswalt to the ballclub, who went 7-1 down the stretch, posting a 1.74 ERA.

Second, the bats died spectacularly, epitomized by an unusual three-game shutout sweep by the Mets. The Phillies were scoreless in 47 of 48 innings—the first time the defending NL champion failed to score in a three-game series. It wasn't until the fourth inning in the next game, against the Orioles that the streak was finally broken.

By no means was the East a two-horse race. By June, the Mets had started to come alive. Although the Queensiders were seven games back in late May they clawed back the deficit to half a game by mid-June and at that point seemed the closest challengers to the then rampaging Braves. However, with Carlos Beltran unhealthy, Jeff Francoeur placed as the everyday right fielder and the pricey Jason Bay misfiring and then getting knocked out for the season, the offense was never going to be able to support a lengthy pennant race. It was little surprise when GM Willie Randolph and Manager Jerry Manuel both departed as the season ended—most Mets fans will argue it should have been sooner.

However, the biggest NL East story of 2010 wasn't about the Phillies, Braves or Mets—it was Stephen Strasburg of the Washington Nationals. Strasburg was the first pick in the 2009 draft and has been hyped as the best No. 1 pick since ever. After much hyperbole, Strasburg started his first game in a Nationals

uniform on June 8 against the Pirates. The hype appeared justified as he threw seven innings, giving up just two earned runs while striking out 14 in a jaw-dropping debut.

His pitch repertoire is phenomenal with four plus pitches (four-seamer, two-seamer, change, curve) that he is able to locate consistently. In his first start, he touched 100 mph on the gun twice, with 34 of 98 pitches exceeding 98 mph, almost unheard of for a starter.

In his next two starts, he struck out another 18 batters to set a major league record of 32 strikeouts in his first three games as a pro. Unfortunately one of the bright spots of the 2010 season came to a crashing end when Strasburg tweaked his elbow in August against the Phillies and required season-ending Tommy John surgery. Bring on 2012.

Strasburg or not, 2010 was never going to be the Nationals' year after having suffered a 103-loss season in 2009 and lacking punch with both bat and ball. Ryan Zimmerman and Adam Dunn were the two standout hitters—Zimmerman notching .307/.388/.510 and the Big Donkey clunking 38 dingers at the cost of 199 strikeouts, a career high.

Strasburg aside, the pitching wasn't any better than the hitting, with 35-year-old soft-tosser Livan Hernandez being the pick of the rotation with a 3.88 ERA and a 3.95 Fielding Independent Pitching ERA (FIP). The only other remotely decent pitching performance was by Matt Capps, whom the Nationals acquired from the Pirates on a one-year deal. He was the backbone of the bullpen in April, recording 10 saves for an 0.68 ERA and his good form continued as he helped the NL win the All-Star game for the first time in almost a generation. It was no surprise when the Nationals traded him to the Twins for catcher Wilson Ramos and southpaw Joe Testa.

After about a half a decade or so of grumbling about salary bills, the Florida Marlins have earned what is best described as grudging acceptance for the way they manage to play decent ball despite a miniscule payroll. The 2010 Marlins had a total salary outlay of $55 million—ranked 25th in the bigs—with Dan Uggla and Hanley Ramirez earning in excess of $7 million each.

The Fish got off to a solid start and were at .500 by the end of May, which was good enough to be within 3.5 games of first. However, behind the win-loss record the team was in turmoil and ended up parting company with manager Freddie Gonzalez halfway through the season.

The bad stuff started in mid-May, when Ramirez was benched for a couple of games for lollygagging on a play (after making an error, Ramirez jogged after the ball, allowing two runners to score)—the video evidence was damning and Hanley was asked apologize. On June 19 things went from bad to worse when the Marlins handed out vuvuzelas to its fans. The noise was so deafening that players and umps had to resort to earplugs. Later in the game the Marlins were caught batting out of turn and a spat ensued between the umps and Gonzalez as to whether a revised line-up card was submitted. Four days later Gonzalez was fired.

With that back story, the Marlins were never going to challenge for the division, but the Fish played some good baseball and for most of the season were within a few games of .500.

Slothfulness aside, Ramirez was probably the pick of the roster, hitting .300/.378/.475—to reaffirm his status as one of the best shortstops in the majors. However, by his own high standards Ramirez had a poor 2010—it being his worst season since his rookie year back in 2006.

On the pitching side, Anibal Sanchez and Josh Johnson anchored the rotation. Johnson was one of the best hurlers in the league with an ERA 2.30. That both Chris Volstad and Ricky Nolasco recorded more wins despite both sporting an ERA of around 4.50 shows how little attention W-L records are worth.

Perhaps the Marlins' season is best summed up by what happened to Chris Coghlan, NL Rookie of the Year 2009, who tore the meniscus in his knee after planting a shaving-cream pie in the face of Wes Helms, who had belted a walk-off home run to beat the Braves in late July. New manager Edwin Rodriguez banned face pies shortly after.

Unlike the Nationals, the Marlins have a young, growing side. The average age of the rotation is 25 and it will only improve. Ultimately, they ended up with a credible 80-82 record, which although a step back from recent seasons is a great platform to build from. Although the spine of the team—Johnson, Ramirez, Uggla—will get expensive, there is room in the payroll to accommodate such talent, at least for the next few years.

It was hardly a consolation that the Marlins had the best seat in the house as Roy Halladay threw the 20th perfect game in major league history against them, leading the Phillies to a 1-0 victory. Halladay was awesome striking out 11 batters in just 115 pitches and with no lucky outs. Don't feel too sorry for the Marlins, because in a blatant show of commercialism they decided to sell the remaining unused tickets for Halladay's perfecto at full price.

By late July, the division had largely become a two-horse race—the Braves versus the Phillies. Philadelphia struggled with injuries with Utley, Shane Victorino, Ryan Howard and Placido Polanco all spending a good chunk of time on the DL. Coming up to the trade deadline the Braves made a few moves to reinforce the lineup, adding Rick Ankiel, Alex Gonzalez and, when Chipper was injured, Derrek Lee to the roster.

On July 22, the Phils were seven games back. A week later it was a mere 2.5 games. And then for the month of August the Phillies and Braves moved more or less in lockstep. Amazingly, the gaps stayed between two and three games for all but one day of the month. During a mid-August stretch the gap was a constant 2.5 games for nine consecutive days.

Then the Phillies seemed to step up a gear and started to magic up runs from nowhere. Take the Sept. 2 game against Colorado, in which the Rockies sped out to a 7-3 lead before conceding nine runs in the seventh. At the start of the inning, the Phillies' win expectancy was 0.1. As Howard registered the last out—his second at-bat in the inning—it stood at 0.96.

Coming into September, many fans were pointing to the last fortnight of the season as when the division would be decided as the Braves and Phillies squared off in two of the last four regular season series. It wasn't to be: The Braves entered a September slump losing two games against each to Florida, St. Louis, Pittsburgh and Washington and found themselves three games back of Philadelphia with 12 to play entering the first series against their rivals.

The Phillies crushed the Braves on the back of some dominant pitching from Hamels, Halladay and Ryan Madson, conceding just four runs in the three game series.

As Chipper Jones and Martin Prado went on the DL, the Braves' lineup started to look thin and runs were hard to come by. J-Hey wasn't quite the threat he was hyped to be and the bats of Nate McLouth, Matt Diaz, Melky Cabrera, Alex Gonzalez, Rick Ankiel, Troy Glaus and Eric Hinske don't really strike fear into the opposition as, say, Howard, Utley, Jayson Werth and Rollins would.

With the division crown out of reach, it was left to the Braves to try to clinch the Wild Card. In the end it came down to the final game, when the Braves had to beat the Phillies in their 162nd game of the season to guarantee one more game. They did, 8-7, and watched as the Giants beat the Padres 3-0 to secure the NL West and dump the Friars out of the playoff picture.

It was a fitting end to Bobby Cox's career as Braves manager. The old warhorse deserved one final shot at glory after leading the Braves to 14 consecutive championships over a 20-year stretch. His stats as a manager will stand in history as among the greatest: 2,504 wins, 2,001 losses, .556 winning percentage, 158 ejections. And you know what? With five pennants and just the sole World Series ring in 1995, it could have been so much more.

And as Cox rides off into the sunset, the NL East has a strangely familiar feel to it. The Phillies won the division with a 97-65 record—the fourth consecutive year they've come out on top. Is Charlie Manuel building the NL East's second dynasty? Who knows … he's made a good start but has a long way to go to match Bobby Cox's record. Amen.

The National League Central View

by Harry Pavlidis

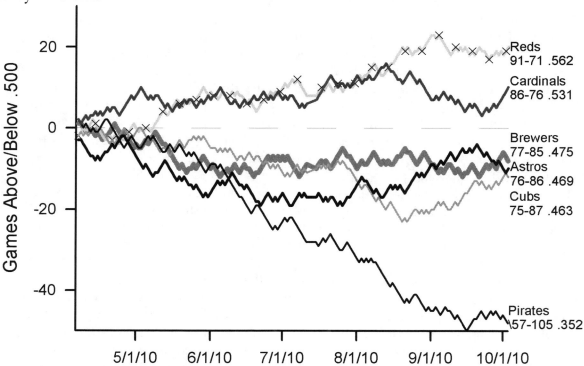

Head to Head Records

Team	CHN	CIN	HOU	MIL	PIT	STL	TOT
CHN		4	7	9	5	9	34
CIN	12		10	11	10	6	49
HOU	11	5		8	11	10	45
MIL	6	3	7		13	8	37
PIT	10	6	4	5		6	31
STL	6	12	5	7	9		39

To find wins, read across; losses are read from the top.

Play Against Other Divisions

Division	W	L	Win%
AL East	3	6	.333
AL Central	15	21	.417
AL West	21	27	.438
NL East	94	106	.470
NL West	94	115	.450
Total	227	275	.452

The winds of change that blew through the National League Central 2010 will swirl into the winter. For some teams it was a light zephyr, while others found themselves in the middle of a vortex.

The biggest change for the Central in 2010? The Reds won the division.

The last time a team other than the Cubs or Cardinals won the division was 2001. Even that year, the Astros had the same record as the Cardinals but owned the tiebreaker. 11 years ago was the last time the outright winner was not part of the I-57 rivalry, when the Astros beat the Reds by 1.5 games.

Some things didn't change. For example, the Pirates occupied the cellar for the fourth straight season. The Brewers finished third again, their fourth season in a row stuck in second or third. The Astros were also treading water.

For the Cubs, 2010 was a trip down to fifth place with erstwhile manager Lou Piniella. Sweet Lou led the Cubs to a pair of division crowns and one second place, but handed the reins to Mike Quade in August with the team more than 20 games under .500.

Despite what amounted to a disappointing season, the Cardinals managed to secure a second-place finish, but at season's end there were questions about who will be at their helm in 2011.

Managers on the Move

Leading into a busy winter changing managers, the Cubs got in on the act early. In the final year of a four-year contract, Piniella started to show the same signs of wear exhibited by his predecessor. Dusty Baker's fourth year in Wrigley Field was one of "I don't know, what am I supposed to tell you?" and a tired visage. Piniella was singing that familiar song in 2010.

While Piniella's tenure was filled with enough "Cubbie Occurrences" to last him a lifetime, he was facing challenges in a far more important arena. Piniella took leaves of absence when his uncle died and again when his mother fell ill. As his mother's health took another turn for the worse, he hung up his cleats and returned to Tampa. Already set to retire at the end of the season, Piniella said goodbye to the Wrigley faithful, tears in his eyes as he handed over his final line-up card.

Long-time minor league skipper Quade was given the helm and the team played its best ball of 2010 the rest of the way. Named interim manager, Quade did nothing to shake his hold on the permanent job by posting a 24-13 record and getting more out his young bullpen than his one-time boss. Bench coach Alan Trammell was told he would not be a candidate. Despite reports that the Cubs would sound out Yankees manager Joe Girardi after the postseason, despite their having groomed Hall of Fame Cub Ryne Sandberg for the job, they named Quade manager for 2011 while the Yanks were still playing.

While the Cubs' managerial situation may be the most unusual in the division, they are now far from alone in their search for a new leader. As 2010 drew to a close, the axe was sharpened and ready to fall.

The Brewers parted ways with Ken Macha and the Pirates dismissed John Russell within 24 hours of the last pitch of 2010. In three years calling the shots in PNC Park, Russell racked up 299 losses. No matter how deep the problems may run in Pittsburgh, no manager can expect job security after compiling such a dubious record.

Macha's record didn't scream "goodbye," but he lost his job in Oakland after four years of .568 ball, so he can't be too shocked after a .485 mark with the Brew Crew. But Macha's record was probably a moot point. As he alluded to after the Brewers declined his option, Macha had lost the clubhouse. Even if Prince Fielder won't be a Brewer in 2011, Macha's inability to communicate effectively with him, and others, was his ultimate undoing.

As more successful teams battled in the postseason, Baker, Houston's Brad Mills and the Cardinals' Tony La Russa received contract extensions. Macha, among others, was interviewing with the Pirates. The Brewers were connected briefly to Bob Brenly, but the former Arizona manager and current Cubs broadcaster did not appear to be headed up north.

Discord in St. Louis

Nothing like having a spat through the media to set the tone, and trend, for your season. It started in the offseason with former Cardinal Jack Clark taking issue with the club's new hitting coach. Mark McGwire, once the darling of Busch Stadium, emerged from his quasi-self-imposed exile, much to the disgust of "purists" like Clark. Using terms like "liar, faker, whimpering boy," Clark didn't serve himself well in this attack. But he wasn't done.

With the Cardinals tumbling toward elimination in mid-September, Clark called out La Russa for a lack of leadership and the entire team for having "poopy in their pants." Well, you try to lead a bunch of grown men who aren't potty trained.

Okay, maybe he had something on the leadership issues. Filthy trousers aside, La Russa and two of his best offensive players were making the wrong kinds of headlines. One player was rumored to have demanded a trade, and another was actually traded.

Making headlines with some fairly sharp words for Ryan Ludwick, La Russa made it clear the power-hitting outfielder wasn't in his everyday plans. Next thing you knew, Ludwick was gone in a three-way deal, landing in San Diego. Sure, Jake Westbrook was a nice pitcher to have down the stretch, but trading Ludwick when the offense was starting to sputter seemed like cutting off your nose to spite your face.

Talking about outfielders who don't get along with La Russa … Colby Rasmus wants out?! He's denied it up and down, but Rasmus' relationship with La Russa allegedly prompted him to request a trade. La Russa may be maxing out on "pissed-off starting (sic) outfielders." Both La Russa and Rasmus say they can co-exist, but the friction—fictional or otherwise—was still being discussed after the season had ended.

Don't Call it a Machine

While everyone else was either sinking or stalling, Dusty Baker's boys turned on the heat and ended up winning the division crown by a solid margin. The urge to call them "The New Red Machine" should have subsided after they were swept from the playoffs. The mid-'70s Reds were one of the best teams in history, but these Reds have a ways to go. Still, they broke the I-57 stranglehold and put together an impressive season. It's already tempting to look forward to the 2011 Reds, who could be primed to repeat as division champions.

One way to gauge the future success of a club is to look at its stock of young pitchers. Several youngsters made a mark with the Reds in 2010, particularly in the pitching department. First, the Reds drafted Mike Leake out of Arizona State in the June 2009 draft. Leake pitched in the Arizona Fall League, but made his major league debut in 2010 without ever being assigned to the minor leagues.

Leake earned his rotation spot during the Cactus League, and he kept himself there most of the season. As he either wore out or failed to make adjustments, Leake's performance tailed off and he found himself in the bullpen briefly before being shut down.

Leake's decline was blunted by the return of Homer Bailey—who spent a chunk of the season on the DL—and the emergence of Travis Wood. Johnny Cueto pitched well—including a one-hitter in May—and Edinson Volquez came back from the DL/suspended list to make a dozen starts.

Despite the glut of young starters, the most exciting rookie pitcher for the Reds was Cuban defector Aroldis Chapman. Armed with a fastball that has reached 105 mph, Chapman was strong in relief down the stretch. He had struggled as a starter in Triple-A, but moving to the Louisville bullpen was the first big step toward pitching in the majors in 2010. The Reds are certain to try Chapman as a starter in 2011.

Other than veteran Bronson Arroyo baffling opponents with his high leg kick and myriad arm angles, the Reds move into 2011 with a solid, young rotation. Aaron Harang—stalwart of the Cincy rotation for what seems like a long time—won't be back. Arroyo should be joined by some combination of Leake, Wood, Bailey, Cueto, Volquez and Chapman. Considering the Reds had the National League's most productive offense in 2010—led by MVP candidate and emerging superstar Joey Votto—maybe there is a machine revving up.

Letting the Kids Play

The Reds weren't the only team leaning on rookies in 2010. Far from it. The Cubs used six rookie pitchers in one game—a record for a non-September game. Starlin Castro and Tyler Colvin were regulars, with Castro taking over shortstop in May and never letting go. Colvin was part of a large group of outfielders seeking playing time, and his season was cut short when a broken bat pierced his chest and collapsed a lung. Darwin Barney emerged as a utility infielder, effectively replacing Mike Fontenot, who was sent to the Giants. Ryan Theriot and Ted Lilly were shipped to Los Angeles, Derrek Lee to Atlanta and suddenly an already young team was even younger.

About those rookie pitchers … the Cubs leaned hard on them as a group, including two individuals in particular. Andrew Cashner settled in as Carlos Marmol's set-up man under Quade

and Casey Coleman settled into a rotation spot. Both Cashner and Coleman will be considered for the 2011 rotation, but the Cubs seem to be driving Cashner to the bullpen.

James Russell, Thomas Diamond, Marcus Mateo and Justin Berg all saw time on the bump for the Northsiders. Diamond, a former No. 1 pick by the Rangers, was given a chance to start after a solid Triple-A season but ended up performing better after swapping roles with Coleman.

The Reds and Cubs didn't corner the market on rookie pitchers. If anything, the Cardinals had the gem of the bunch. Jamie Garcia's rookie season was a major surprise and boost for the Red Birds. Garcia's 28 starts and 163.1 innings put him third behind co-aces Adam Wainwright and Chris Carpenter. More importantly, Garcia was highly effective, finishing with 13 wins and a 2.70 ERA. Sure, he didn't go 230-plus innings like Carpenter and Wainwright, but that's a lot of good work out of a rookie. Given the lack of healthy innings from Kyle Lohse and Brad Penny, Garcia meant a lot to the 2010 Cardinals.

The Pirates gave Daniel McCutchen two shots at starting in 2010, and eventually shuffled him into the bullpen. Brad Lincoln was in the rotation for a couple of months, but had mixed results. A variety of midseason acquisitions, including rookies Chris LeRoux and Joe Martinez, got a few starts as well. Lincoln will be given a shot in 2011; the rest of the kids will be scrambling.

Neil Walker, Jose Tabata and Pedro Alvarez were called up into everyday roles during the season. None made the Pirates out of spring training, but Walker and Alvarez ended up with two of the best offensive seasons on the club. Tabata wasn't as impressive, but his .299/.346/.400 shouldn't crush anyone's optimism.

Walker and Alvarez were both first-round draft picks, and Tabata was a top amateur free agent signed by the Yankees. Tabata was acquired a trade with the Yankees (along with McCutchen). There's plenty of upside here, so keep an eye on the Pirates' offense the next couple years.

Alcides Escobar became the Brewers' full-time shortstop late in 2009, and he held the position throughout his age-23 season. Unlike his fellow rookie shortstop down the road, Escobar didn't hit a lick. His .235/.288/.326 season was actually worse than JJ. Hardy's abysmal 2009. The Cubs' Castro, meanwhile, hit .300/.347/.408 with less experience and at 20 years old. Calibrate your Midwestern shortstop expectations accordingly.

Hey, you know who hit better than Escobar? A weak-hitting rookie catcher on his own team. Jonathan LuCroy made his big league debut just a few weeks before the Giants called up Buster Posey, so perhaps he flew a bit under the radar. His performance at the plate did nothing to help. Barely better than Escobar, LuCroy managed to do something pretty neat for a catcher—steal as many bases as he hit home runs (four).

If the Brewers didn't get much pop out of their rookie hitters, they got a bit more out of their bullpen. Some good innings from Zach Braddock and Mike McClendon were the smallest contributions by staff rookies. That's probably a good thing, because the future may not hold much more for either.

When Trevor Hoffman came to Milwaukee from San Diego, Brewer fans figured they had their closer situation settled for 2009 and 2010, and possibly 2011. Not so much. When late May 2010 rolled around, Hoffman was replaced by John Axford and moved into a set-up role.

Axford racked up 24 saves for the Brewers, keeping Hoffman out of save situations until mid-August, when the veteran picked up saves 597 through 601. Axford's success is a surprise, and repeating it could be a stretch. He'll be 28 years old in 2011, so his time is now.

If the all-time saves leader working set-up for a non-contending team seemed strange, it actually fit in with some other 2010 National League Central oddities.

This Just Doesn't Seem Right

Carlos Zambrano in relief? With the bullpen struggling early, Piniella and company hit the panic button and moved their one-time ace into the set-up role. It did not go well. Zambrano was given another chance to start, but lost his cool in a game against the White Sox and was yanked after one inning.

Zambrano ended up being taken off the active roster and put into anger management. When the Cubs finally decided to put him back in the rotation, he looked like an ace again.

Big Z wasn't the only star pitcher in the division who found himself unhappy with his circumstances.

The Astros' anemic offense was driving Roy Oswalt to the brink. With slugging left fielder Carlos Lee leading the way with no home runs in April, Oswalt and his fellow pitchers were being victimized by the team's inability to score runs. Oswalt had no interest in being there for a rebuilding, and his desire, or willingness, to be traded was leaked to the press.

Oswalt started backing off his remarks, but before long he waived his no-trade rights and was sent to Philadelphia. Shortly thereafter, fellow veteran Lance Berkman was sent to the Yankees. The Astros were suddenly a bunch of no-names, after Hunter Pence and Lee. Rookie third baseman Chris Johnson stepped up and got some attention, but the Astros finished 2010 with their two most recognizable players in new uniforms.

Talking about strange uniforms: After a year off, Jim Edmonds returned to the NL Central. The former Cardinals star found himself without a job last year, despite a solid 2008 season with the Cubs. The Brewers gave him a shot in 2010 and traded him to the Reds in August. We all had the bizarre experience of seeing Jimmy Ballgame in two more incongruous jerseys.

Out of Sorts is the New Order

The Reds look like they're loading up for a run of good seasons. The Cubs, despite their struggles, seem to have a wealth of young pitchers, some of whom actually stayed in the minors in 2010. The Cardinals may be entering a period of flux as the days of Albert Pujols' contract are numbered. The Pirates and the Astros are struggling to find themselves, and the Brewers are looking for quality pitching. Okay, so maybe things didn't change that much.

The National League West View

by Steve Treder

Head to Head Records

Team	ARI	COL	LAN	SD	SF	TOT
ARI		9	5	8	5	27
COL	9		7	12	9	37
LAN	13	11		8	8	40
SD	10	6	10		12	38
SF	13	9	10	6		38

To find wins, read across; losses are read from the top.

Play Against Other Divisions

Division	W	L	Win%
AL East	20	22	.476
AL Central	6	6	.500
AL West	9	12	.429
NL East	80	86	.482
NL Central	115	94	.550
Total	**230**	**220**	**.511**

Faithful readers of this annual tome may recall that in last year's edition, in this space we offered a bold prediction. We asserted that the strong performance of the 2009 National League West Division, relative to other divisions, was no fluke, and would be sustained in 2010 and beyond.

Well, here it is a year later, and we can test the accuracy of that prediction: Was the NL West indeed a strong division again in 2010? The answer is yes—the aggregate winning percentage of 2010 NL West teams when playing outside their division (both intra- and interleague) was .511. Granted, this wasn't as robust a showing as their .533 mark of 2009, but it remained comfortably above .500. The NL West has in fact sustained its net positive performance, at least for one year beyond 2009. (Now, would we be bringing this up if our prediction had proved wrong? No comment.)

You may recall as well that the reasoning we presented in support of this piercingly brilliant (okay, sorry) prediction was simply this: The primary strength of every NL West team in 2009 was heavily represented by young players, and young players are less likely to decline, and more likely to improve, than old players. This year we'll take a closer look at each of the rosters deployed by the NL West teams in 2010, and consider how they compare with one another along the young/old and improving/declining scales.

A central issue when considering the relative ages of the talent on rosters is payroll. Young players may or may not be better than older players, but they're unquestionably cheaper than older players. Part of this is just sample selection bias: No one is allowed to become an older player unless he's a good player (or at least, used to be a good player), and other things being equal, good players demand more salary for their services than not-so-good players.

But, of course, in the real world other things aren't always equal. While there's a positive correlation between salary and performance in baseball, it's far from absolute. By itself, MLB's system of service time limitations on free agency introduces a significant degree of distortion, and beyond that, the judgment of teams determining the worth of each free agent is flawed, as are all human judgments. So, while to some extent "you get what you pay for" in terms of the price-performance relationship, by no means are there any guarantees.

Southern California Dollars and Sense

For a demonstration of this, we need look no further than the 2010 payrolls of the Los Angeles Dodgers and the San Diego Padres. The Dodgers spent approximately $122.5 million on major league salaries this year, by far the largest amount in the division; their payroll was third-largest in the National League and seventh-largest among the 30 major league teams. Meanwhile, the Padres spent just $48.6 million on payroll, the least of any NL West franchise, the second-least among the 16 teams in the league (only Pittsburgh's was lower), and the third-least in all of baseball (in the AL, only Cleveland's was lower).

Most preseason prognosticators (yours truly among them—I guess not all of my predictions are so hot) picked the back-to-back defending-champ Dodgers as the team to again win this division, and the Padres, 75-87 in 2009, were expected by nearly all of us to be contending for third at best, and most likely fourth or fifth. Yet it was the Padres who led the division nearly all season long, at several points by a comfortable margin, before finishing a very close second at 90-72, and it was the Dodgers who fell apart after a competitive first half, and wound up in fourth, at 80-82. San Diego got vastly more bang for its payroll buck.

Realistically, Padres general manager Jed Hoyer was likely as surprised as everyone else at the Padres' sudden success. But while sudden improvements of this magnitude are rare (that's why they're surprising), they aren't unprecedented, and when one does occur it's usually achieved by a young team, which certainly is what the Padres were.

San Diego's best player was its still-fairly-young superstar first baseman, 28-year-old Adrian Gonzalez, whose salary of $4.75 million (in the fourth year of a four-year contract) was a tremendous bargain. Yet bargains were abundant for the Padres, as among key contributors such as third baseman Chase Headley, catcher Nick Hundley and pitchers Mat Latos, Clayton Richard, Luke Gregerson and Tim Stauffer, none made as much as $500,000; all were relatively inexperienced players in the pre-free agency phase of their careers.

Even among the few veterans deployed by the Padres were a couple of sweet deals: 35-year-old second baseman David Eckstein at $1 million, and 31-year-old catcher Yorvit Torrealba at $750,000. San Diego's highest-paid player was the only one who could be truly considered a wasted expense: 31-year-old pitcher Chris Young made $6.25 million and spent nearly all season on the disabled list.

The contrast with the Dodgers is stark. Their highest-paid player was 38-year-old left fielder Manny Ramirez, who pocketed $20 million and also, as it turned out, spent a good deal of the year sidelined with injuries before Los Angeles cut him loose at the end of August. Two of the Dodgers' starting pitchers who were solid but hardly star-quality, 35-year-old Hiroki Kuroda and 34-year-old Ted Lilly, held contracts calling for $13 million and $12 million respectively. It is the case that Lilly was only with Los Angeles for about half the season, but it remains a dramatic point that on a full-year basis, those three contracts alone added up to very close to the entire San Diego payroll, and the Dodgers spent some $80 million on salaries in addition to those.

Accounting in the North

The late-charging 2010 division champion San Francisco Giants carried a slightly high payroll, at $99.7 million. But few of their most expensive properties were the ones propelling them to victory, as they spent $18.5 million on 32-year-old back-of-the-rotation starter Barry Zito, and $12 million, $9 million and $6 million respectively on three veterans who all failed to hold their starting jobs: 32-year-old center fielder Aaron Rowand, 33-year-old shortstop Edgar Renteria and 35-year-old left fielder Mark DeRosa.

Like the Padres, the Giants received significant contributions from several youngsters paid less than half a million dollars each, including catcher Buster Posey and third baseman Pablo Sandoval (each 23 years old) and reliever Sergio Romo (27). And like the Padres, a few of the key San Francisco veterans were bargains, including 33-year-old first baseman Aubrey Huff at $3 million, 30-year-old shortstop Juan Uribe at $3.25 million and 33-year-old left fielder Pat Burrell, to whom the Giants paid only the pro-rated major-league-minimum portion of his $9 million contract after salvaging him from the scrap heap in late May. The sweetest bargain was 32-year-old late-blooming center fielder Andres Torres, at $426,000.

The Colorado Rockies presented an odd season in several regards. Expected to strongly contend after a Wild Card-winning 2009, the Rockies spent much of the early season fighting to stay above .500, but caught a hot streak beginning in late June that lifted them to second place, just one game back of the Padres right before the All-Star break. Colorado then dropped 12 of its next 14 to fall back to fourth, nine games out, before July was over.

By mid-to-late August the Rockies were trailing San Diego by 11 and their season appeared as good as done. But, no, a 20-6 Colorado run reduced the deficit back down to a single game on Sept. 18—at which point the Rockies suddenly and thoroughly collapsed yet again, losing 13 of their final 14 games.

This see-saw ride of a performance was still enough to place the Rockies ahead of the tail-spinning Dodgers. And the Colorado payroll was a peculiar mix as well. At $84 million it was neither high nor low (it was nearly equal to the division-average figure of $82 million, and the league-average of $85 million), but similar to the case in San Francisco, what the Rockies paid their players bore little relation to how well they played.

By far the best Rockies were exceptionally cost-effective: 25-year-old superstar shortstop Troy Tulowitzki at $3.5 million, 26-year-old dominant ace pitcher Ubaldo Jimenez at $1.25 million, and the greatest bargain in all of baseball in 2010, 24-year-old breakout star outfielder Carlos Gonzalez at the major league minimum of just over $400,000.

Colorado's largest expenditure by far was on veteran first baseman Todd Helton, at $16.6 million, but at the age of 36 Helton was able to deliver only a dreary, punchless performance. Another $9 million was largely wasted on ineffective 31-year-old starting pitcher Aaron Cook. Two additional bad deals were $7.5 million paid to slumping 31-year-old outfielder Brad Hawpe and $5.75 million to struggling 29-year-old pitcher Jeff Francis.

Where to Go in Arizona?

The Arizona Diamondbacks witnessed all of this from far below, in dead last nearly wire-to-wire, completing their second straight last-place finish. GM Josh Byrnes was fired in midseason as he struggled with rebuilding a ball club that's rapidly fallen apart after capturing the division title as recently as 2007.

The D-backs didn't spend a lot of money to occupy the cellar in 2010; their payroll of $56.9 was fifth-lowest in the National League. Arizona's ride to the bottom has been accompanied by a steady shedding of hefty salaries, as conspicuous by their absence this season were figures such as the $15.1 million that was paid to 44-year-old pitcher Randy Johnson in 2008, and the 2009 expenditures of $11.7 million on 33-year-old outfielder Eric Byrnes and $8.75 million on 33-year-old pitcher Doug Davis.

The 2010 Snakes were a young ball club, with only a few key performers as old as 30. As was typical in the division, Arizona's best players were all 20-somethings carrying relatively modestly salaries: 27-year-old shortstop Stephen Drew at $3.4 million, 28-year-old second baseman Kelly Johnson at $2.35 million, and 26-year-old center fielder Chris Young at $3.25 million. Two terrific bargains were 26-year-old third baseman Mark Reynolds at $833,000, and 25-year-old starting pitcher Ian Kennedy at $403,000.

By contrast, Arizona's highest-paid player didn't play at all; 31-year-old former ace pitcher Brandon Webb pocketed $8.5 million to sit out the season with a bum shoulder. The Diamondbacks also paid most of the $12 million salary of another one-time ace, 28-year-old Dontrelle Willis, who was dreadful in just six appearances for Arizona. Thirty-year-old first baseman Adam LaRoche made $6 million while providing a solid but unexciting performance.

The lesson seems clear for incoming GM Kevin Towers as he endeavors to restore competitiveness in the Diamondbacks: Adding well-known veteran names to the roster would appear unlikely to yield a lot of wins. All across the NL West, not just the most cost-effective performances, but a large proportion of the best performances in an absolute sense, are being delivered by young and otherwise inexpensive players.

Obviously, it's far easier said than done to find the best young talent. But the competitive advantage to be gained by focusing on it, not just economically but in the sheer just-the-on-field-facts realm, seems as clear in 2010 as it's ever been.

The Bigger Picture

And this pattern isn't limited to the National League West. The only NL playoff team carrying a particularly large payroll was Philadelphia at $143 million, as neither Atlanta ($90 million) nor Cincinnati ($73 million) was a big spender. Meanwhile the 2010 Dodgers were far from the only team to spend lavishly and nevertheless fall short of the postseason. Other examples were the Cardinals ($113 million to go 86-76), the Mets ($118 million and 79-83), and the league's biggest underachiever, the Cubs ($125 million and 75-87).

It was little different in the American League. There are always the Yankees, of course, hefting their gargantuan $225 million payroll into the playoffs, but the other three AL qualifiers ranged from a moderately high spender (Minnesota at $99 million) to one in the middle of the pack (Texas at $87 million) to a downright low payroll (Tampa Bay at $63 million). There was no postseason baseball for the White Sox ($106 million and finishing 88-74), the Angels ($125 million and 80-82), the Tigers ($136 million and 81-81), or the Red Sox ($161 million and 89-73).

In baseball as in all businesses, the profit margin is a function of finding and maintaining the optimal leverage between resource investment and consequent revenue. But in today's baseball, the challenge of discovering the proper resource investment is particularly complex. Especially in the National League West, a dynamic of "not getting what you pay for" seems ascendant.

All figures in this article were taken from a single source, the "Payroll, Roster & Uniforms" team pages at Baseball Reference

Commentary

The Year in Frivolity

by Craig Calcaterra

This book is chock full of information about the 2010 baseball season. If you read even a portion of it and don't know who won, who lost, and why, there's no helping you.

But you can be forgiven if you forgot the year's ephemeral, trivial, embarrassing and pathetic events. That stuff doesn't stick in a fan's mind like who won the MVP. That's why I'm here. So, I give you an overview of all things funny, sad, stupid and ignominious of the 2010 baseball season!

February

In the wake of Mark McGwire's hiring as the St. Louis hitting coach, ex-Cardinals Whitey Herzog and Jack Clark criticize the organization for tacitly condoning steroid use. Hall of Fame Pitcher Bob Gibson differs, however, saying that McGwire should not be criticized. Since Bob Gibson is a man who once told Tim McCarver to shut up in the middle of a baseball game, observers agree to defer to his obviously superior judgment when it comes to matters of character.

Sam Donnellon of the *Philadelphia Inquirer* says that the Atlanta Braves "screwed up" by keeping Greg Maddux, Tom Glavine and John Smoltz together for so long, and warns the Phillies that, rather than keep their stars together, the team should trade some of them to become more versatile. His closing sentence: "Maybe we can't be the Yankees, but we sure don't want to be the Braves for the next decade either." Phillies fans agree that winning the NL East every single year for 14 years running would be a horrifying fate.

Manny Ramirez tells reporters that he seriously considered opting out of his contract with the Dodgers during the offseason and testing free agency rather than exercising his $20 million player option. He goes on say that he hadn't considered anything as seriously as this since he decided to invest his entire salary for the 1996 season in stock for the Hypercolor T-Shirt Company.

Reports suggest the Mets were having great difficulty negotiating with free agents because they insisted on taking each vacancy on their roster one-by-one, filling the spot, and then moving on to the next vacancy. Anonymous agents fume that the team is "far too linear" in its approach to player signings, and needs to "think in three dimensions." Mets Chief Operating Officer Jeff Wilpon is stung by such criticism, saying that it's the worst thing that's been said about him since he left his last job as the head of battle tactics on the U.S.S. Reliant under the command of Khan Noonien Singh.

Following a trend in which ballplayers are creating Twitter accounts to connect more directly with their fans, Cardinals outfielder Matt Holliday begins tweeting. Among his first tweets is one saying how much he loves the new Creed album. This is quickly determined to be the second most obnoxious thing ever said on Twitter. First on the list: the hundreds of nearly identical tweets from snotty, indie rock-loving hipsters telling Holliday why Creed sucks.

Former Mets general manager Steve Phillips, still reeling from revelations of an extra-marital affair with an ESPN staffer, issues a public apology for his actions and says he has entered a rehabilitation program for sex addicts. Such programs are modeled after Alcoholics Anonymous-style 12-step groups. One of the steps involves making amends for past transgressions, be they related to the addiction or not. To fulfill this step, Phillips spends the remainder of 2010 calling Mets fans and apologizing for the Mo Vaughn, Roberto Alomar, Pedro Astacio, Mike Bordick, Bobby Bonilla, Rickey Henderson, Kenny Rogers and Jeromy Burnitz deals.

The Milwaukee Brewers announce that they have commissioned a statue of Bud Selig that will be unveiled at Miller Park during the season. Several hours later, millions of baseball fans announce that they have converted to Hinduism in the hope that, after they die, they can be reincarnated as pigeons.

Citing a dearth of home runs hit in Citi Field during its debut season, the Mets announce that they are lowering the center field wall of their new ballpark from 16 to eight feet. The team is undecided, it announces, about how to address the Mets' dearth of home runs in the 15 other National League parks.

Scott Boras, when asked why client Johnny Damon still has not signed with a team despite being a free agent since November, says that at least four or five teams have offered Damon a contract, that "Johnny Damon has many opportunities to play," and that he's "not worried about where." When questioned further, Boras says "'Tis but a scratch," "I've had worse," "It's just a flesh wound" and "I'm invincible!"

The sale of the Texas Rangers to Pittsburgh businessman Chuck Greenberg—first announced in December 2009—hits a snag relating to the amount of cash existing creditors of the team would receive when the deal closes. Greenberg assures the public that there's nothing to worry about and that the deal will be finalized within "two to three weeks."

March

President Obama, in defending the chief executives of JP Morgan and Goldman Sachs for taking home astronomical year-end bonuses despite the ruin in which the nation's financial sector finds itself, says "there are some baseball players who are making more than that and don't get to the World Series either." Many take issue with the comparison for a number of reasons. Among them: Unlike the bank executives, baseball players get punished if they're caught gambling.

Journeyman reliever Matt Herges—who was named in the Mitchell Report—gives an interview in which he says that steroids made him "superhuman." Herges is then fined $100 by the Players' Association for straying from the "steroids just help me stay in the lineup" talking point everyone had agreed upon.

Despite suffering a serious injury to a testicle as a result of a bad-hop grounder while playing third base for the Seattle Mariners in 2009, Adrian Beltre admits that he does not wear a protective cup while playing. Upon learning this, an almost immediate consensus emerges: Adrian Beltre is friggin' nuts.

Mets great Darryl Strawberry is asked about Braves rookie Jason Heyward, a player who is frequently compared to the tall, lanky, powerful Strawberry. Strawberry says "He's going to go through some highs and lows. That's just what the game is all about for everybody." Politeness dictates that those in the room not point out that, no, not everyone's highs are the same as Strawberry's.

Nick Johnson is scratched from one of the Yankees' first spring training games. Yankees beat reporters are overjoyed because it gives them a chance to relive their youth by playing Mad Libs. They already have the cards: "Designated hitter Nick Johnson (type of injury) his (body part) while (any activity) today. A team spokesman says that results from (a type of medical examination) aren't known yet, but that the team expects Johnson to be ready to play (a date no earlier than June 4, 2019).

Torii Hunter, in an interview with *USA Today*, says that players from the Dominican Republic aren't really black—"they're imposters." Jose Reyes immediately realizes that his charade is over and removes his mask. Turns out that he really isn't a black baseball player. He's Old Man McGinnity, the caretaker of the old amusement park, who was trying to scare away people so they wouldn't catch on to the real estate scam he had cooking. And he would have gotten away with it, too, if weren't for that meddling Torii Hunter.

The Red Sox sign Nomar Garciaparra to a one-day contract, after which he is to retire from baseball. Unfortunately, he tears several ligaments in his right hand while reaching for the pen and is placed on the disabled list, thereby postponing his retirement until he can be moved to the 60-day DL when another roster move becomes necessary.

As the divorce case of Dodgers owners Frank and Jamie McCourt wears on, more and more strange information leaks out. The latest: a December 2008 email in which Dodgers executive Charles Steinberg presented Jamie McCourt with a seven-page action plan called "Project Jamie," which had as its purpose to have Jamie elected President of the United States. Which is patently ridiculous, of course, as there is no way that a vapid woman with scant expertise in any field and no coherent policy positions whatsoever could make herself a serious contender for the presidency on the power of celebrity alone.

ESPN's Buster Olney makes waves when he reports that unnamed Philadelphia Phillies executives had discussed the possibility of a blockbuster trade with the Cardinals in which Ryan Howard and Albert Pujols would be exchanged. After an uproar and denials by all involved, Olney defends his story, but then quickly moves on to other things. Afterwards, unnamed Philadelphia Phillies executives give each other high-fives, exchange the money they had wagered with one another and then try to go double or nothing with a "can we get Ken Rosenthal to bite on a Lincecum-for-Sabathia deal."

Negotiations relating to the sale of the Texas Rangers continue to experience complications due to an increasingly hostile relationship between Pittsburgh businessman Chuck Greenberg and team creditors. Greenberg assures the public that there's nothing to worry about and that the deal will be finalized within "two to three weeks."

April

Opening Day pits the New York Yankees against the Boston Red Sox. In a first, the game is broadcast to mainland China, where Major League Baseball is attempting to make marketing inroads. U.S.-China relations are subsequently chilled, however, when 300 million viewers' first exposure to Major League Baseball is a turgid, three and a half-hour slugfest.

The Mets open their season with a lineup in which Alex Cora leads off, Mike Jacobs bats cleanup, $66 million offseason acquisition Jason Bay hits fifth, Gary Matthews Jr. hits sixth and Angel Pagan is on the bench. This is where I'd normally put a little joke, but I really don't think I need to.

President Obama throws out the first pitch at the Nationals-Phillies game. The biggest surprise: the President—a noted White Sox fan—takes the mound wearing a Nationals warm-up jacket. Just before the first pitch, however, he removes the jacket to reveal a Paul Konerko jersey, picks up a metal folding chair, slams it over Pudge Rodriguez's head, grabs a microphone and barks "just when they think they have all the answers, *I change the questions!*"

Oakland Athletics pitcher Dallas Braden is enraged when Alex Rodriguez jogs across the pitcher's mound on his way back to first base following a foul ball during a Yankees-A's game at the Oakland Coliseum. In response, Braden repeatedly yells for A-Rod to "get off my mound." The controversy is resolved after the game when accountants determine that, thanks to tens of millions of revenue sharing dollars paid by the Yankees to low payroll teams over the years, A-Rod actually owns 4 percent of the pitcher's mound in Oakland.

Umpire Joe West, expressing his frustration over ever-longer baseball games, calls the Yankees and the Red Sox "embarrassments" and "a disgrace" for their dilatory in-game tactics. Later that day, Glenn Beck lashes out at his political foes for being alarmists and Lady Gaga accuses Katy Perry of being an attention whore.

In an interview, Hank Aaron says that players shouldn't concentrate on hitting home runs. Rather, they should "learn how to hit the ball to the opposite field and do the little things to help their ballclub win championships." Later that day Nolan Ryan releases a statement in which he implores pitchers to "relax, all right? Don't try to strike everybody out. Strikeouts are boring! Besides that, they're fascist. Throw some ground balls—it's more democratic."

Though he goes out of his way to avoid using the word "racism," Twins' second baseman Orlando Hudson suggests that racism is the reason why his friend Jermaine Dye does not have a job with a major league team while other aging, one-dimensional hitters such as Jim Edmonds and Mike Sweeney do. Hudson then announces plans to release a scholarly treatise about how Edmonds' and Sweeney's willingness to accept non-roster invites and salaries of $850,000 and $650,000 for 2010 while Dye has rejected several offers in excess of $2 million a year is an inevitability given our nation's racist heritage.

A man is arrested during a Phillies game for intentionally vomiting on an 11-year-old girl. Phillies fans are predictably mortified, as local tradition holds that only members of the crowd who are 16 or older are to be vomited upon.

The Cubs move pitcher Carlos Zambrano to the bullpen. When asked why they would turn a starting pitcher making nearly $18 million a year into a middle reliever, the Cubs respond by saying that Zambrano's history of exhibiting grace under pressure and demonstrating the ability to let go of setbacks moments after they happen make him perfectly suited for work as a relief pitcher.

Bud Selig and Major League Baseball step into the negotiations relating to the sale of the Texas Rangers to Pittsburgh businessman Chuck Greenberg, exerting pressure on team creditors to accept the deal that's on the table or face serious consequences. Greenberg assures the public that there's nothing to worry about and that the deal will be finalized within "two to three weeks."

May

A man jumps onto the field during a game at Citizens Bank Park. Unable to run him down, a police officer fires a taser at him, incapacitating the suspect. This ignites a firestorm of controversy, in which concerned Philadelphia citizens want to know why the usual method of stopping trespassers in the city—vomiting upon them—was not employed.

In an interview, Dallas Braden laments that the "get off my mound" incident between him and Alex Rodriguez kicked off a silly little war of words. Specifically, Braden says "we don't do much talkin' in the 209." His statement provides a moment of clarity for most observers because, while previously some people thought that A-Rod was unprofessional and some people thought that Braden was being way too touchy, *everyone* agrees that referring to where you come from as "the (area code)" is impossibly lame.

The United States Senate holds a reception honoring retiring Atlanta Braves manager Bobby Cox. The ceremony leads to some discomfort, however, when a cake is presented with the words "thanks for 50 Great Years Bobby Cocks" in a beautiful, flowing script. Cox takes it all in stride. The Senate, however, commissions a review to determine whether its "hire 13-year-old boys as cake decorators" policy is a prudent one.

Phillies reliever Ryan Madson has surgery on his big toe. While Madson won't comment on it, it is well-known that he broke the toe by kicking a chair in the Phillies' clubhouse following a blown save. At least, that's what everyone wants you to think. Brad Lidge "Truthers" would have you believe that Madson's toe was intentionally broken by Lidge supporters, worried that their man would forever lose the Phillies' closer job if Madson was not stopped.

An article in the *Tacoma Tribune* reveals that Ken Griffey Jr. was unavailable to pinch hit in the middle of a recent game because he was asleep on a recliner in the clubhouse. Not surprisingly, the article causes a considerable amount of controversy. Most people were under the impression that Griffey didn't fall asleep until late in Mariners games.

Dallas Braden and Roy Halladay throw the 19th and 20th perfect games in baseball history during the month of May. After his game, Halladay, who makes his offseason home in Odessa, Fla., says that "we don't do a lot of walkin' or hit-allowin' in the 813." Actually, he says no such thing because that would be a profoundly dumb thing to say.

On May 11, Royals general manager Dayton Moore says manager Trey Hillman is "exactly what our organization needs at this point in time." On May 13, Hillman is fired. In Moore's defense, it was, technically speaking, a different point in time.

Bud Selig is given "The Taylor Award," which is presented by the Taylor Hooton Foundation to "an individual who has made a major impact on efforts to educate and protect American youth from the dangers of using performance-enhancing drugs." The Taylor Hooton Foundation receives a majority of its funding from Major League Baseball. People who need people are the luckiest people in the world.

Dodgers minor leaguers Rafael Ynoa and Elisaul Pimentel are late to a game. The reason: While driving to the ballpark a motorcyclist in front of them hit a turkey, which caused him to crash. Ynoa and Pimentel are hailed as heroes for performing CPR on the man, who eventually recovered despite serious injuries. The turkey was transported to a local butcher in critical but delicious condition.

With negotiations to sell the Texas Rangers to Pittsburgh businessman Chuck Greenberg at an impasse, Major League Baseball seizes control of the team and threatens to invalidate the debt held by team creditors. In response, the creditors sue to force the team into bankruptcy. Greenberg assures the public that there's nothing to worry about and that the deal will be finalized within "two to three weeks."

June

On June 2, Detroit Tigers pitcher Armando Galarraga sets down the first 26 Cleveland Indians he faces in order, but is robbed of a perfect game when first base umpire Jim Joyce mistakenly calls Indians batter Jason Donald safe at first base. Joyce admits that night that he made a terrible call and the baseball world is moved by his genuine contrition over the missed call. A native of Toledo, Joyce says "we don't do a lot of denyin' reality in the 419."

On the same night as the Joyce/Galarraga game, Ken Griffey Jr. announces his retirement. A native of Donora, Pa., Griffey says "we don't do a lot of hangin' on past our prime in the 724." OK, that's just a lie. He didn't say anything, as he was sleeping at the time his agent announced that he was retiring. It was after 6 p.m., after all.

Despite an unprecedented uproar following the blown call in the Galarraga game, Bud Selig declines to consider expanding instant replay. When asked why, he says that he's talked to numerous people in and around the game and no one really wants it. This seems inexplicable given the public mood, but it makes sense later when it is revealed that Bud broached the subject of replay with these people by saying

"If you could have instant replay or a fresh pizza delivered to you by an amorous supermodel every night, which would you choose?"

While enjoying a drink at an upscale restaurant, Giants pitcher Barry Zito is approached by a long-haired young man in scruffy attire. A restaurant staffer intercedes, telling the interloper, "I'm sorry, please don't bother Mr. Zito. No autographs tonight." The widely reported punch line: the scruffy looking guy was actually Tim Lincecum. The actually *funny* punch line: The restaurant staff assumed someone would want Barry Zito's autograph.

Nationals phenom Stephen Strasburg makes his major league debut, and it's an impressive one as he strikes out 14 Pittsburgh Pirates en route to a 5-2 victory. After the game Strasburg arrogantly proclaims himself to be super-human and boldly predicts that he cannot be stopped by God or man.

Arizona Diamondbacks pitcher Edwin Jackson throws a no-hitter against the Tampa Bay Rays. It's the fourth no-hitter of the 2010 season, which has been increasingly called "the year of the pitcher." People stopped calling it that once the otherwise undistinguished Jackson threw his no-no, however, and went with the more sensible "year of the totally random occurrence."

Mariners first baseman Casey Kotchman sets the record for most consecutive defensive chances at first base without an error, with 2,008. The next night he sets the record for most consecutive plate appearances for a first baseman without presenting even a minor offensive threat.

The Florida Marlins fire manager Fredi Gonzalez. When asked why Gonzalez was let go, Marlins owner Jeff Loria says, "Everyone knows how I feel about winning." Given that the answer to that is "Based on his experience with the Marlins, he obviously feels that it's totally optional and is probably worth doing as long as it doesn't interfere with his turning a tidy profit," Loria's answer in no way explains why Gonzalez was fired.

Due to the G-20 international economic summit in Toronto, a three-game series between the Blue Jays and the Phillies is moved from Rogers Centre to Citizens Bank Park in Philadelphia, with the Blue Jays being designated as "the home team." The reason for the relocation: Baseball did not want a repeat of what took place during 2009's G-20 meeting in Pittsburgh, when a September series between the Pirates and the Reds led to the lowest attendance in the history of PNC Park. Though their arguments ultimately fall on deaf ears, Blue Jays fans make an excellent point when they note that such a scenario would not be repeated due to the fact that this is not a late September series between the Pirates and the Reds.

The bankruptcy judge overseeing the litigation relating to the sale of the Texas Rangers to Pittsburgh businessman Chuck Greenberg reprimands Greenberg and his attorneys in open court for their litigation strategy, and says the outcome of the case will be decided by the law and not the public relations concerns of Greenberg and his investors. The judge further threatens that if the bankruptcy plan proposed by Greenberg does not pass legal muster, the sale "will be back to square one." Greenberg assures the public that there's nothing to worry about and that the deal will be finalized within "two to three weeks."

July

The band U2 is scheduled to play concerts in Angels Stadium, the Oakland Coliseum, Toronto's Rogers Centre and Florida's Landshark Stadium. Because U2 requires several days to load and unload before and after each concert, the Angels, A's, Blue Jays and Marlins find themselves in the midst of unusually long road trips. An Anaheim man is found burning a copy of the band's "How to Dismantle an Atomic Bomb" album in the street. When asked if his protest is based on his anger that the concert schedule and attendant road trip could cause the Angels to miss the playoffs, he replies, "Who are the Angels?"

Dustin Pedroia suffers broken bones when he fouls a ball off his foot. A few days later he hobbles out to the infield before a game, sets his crutches down and takes ground balls from his knees. He is hailed as a gutsy and gritty gamer for doing so. That same day, Alex Rodriguez breaks into dilapidated warehouse and, armed with only a baseball bat and his own fearlessness, rescues two dozen children from slavery in a secret sweatshop labor operation run by the Russian mafia. After A-Rod secures the last child in a mobile hospital transport he paid for out of his own pocket, the Russians open fire. He escapes by running—literally running—across the East River to safety. The headline in the *Daily News* the next morning: "A-Rod can't swim!"

Astros utilityman Geoff Blum injures his elbow while getting dressed following a game against the Padres. As a result, manager Brad Mills declares a zero-tolerance policy regarding pants in the Astros clubhouse.

In anticipation of the Athletics-Yankees series, the A's sell t-shirts with the words "Get off my mound" printed on them. Dallas Braden, the author of that now-famous phrase, is not pleased with this, calling it "not cool" and saying it's "a serious, gross lack of tact." Braden adds "we don't do a lot of self-awareness in the 209."

Yankees owner George Steinbrenner dies. Ten minutes later Billy Martin is fired. Twenty minutes later Billy Martin is re-hired. Right after that Thurman Munson busts into God's office and demands to be sent to Hell where he can get some freakin' peace and quiet. Meanwhile, Yogi Berra announces that he's converting to Hinduism because, while Swarga Loka is not where he had been hoping to go upon his death, he'd prefer it to dealing with Steinbrenner and Martin's nonsense again.

Political pundit Rush Limbaugh says of Steinbrenner: "That cracker made a lot of African-American millionaires … He fired a bunch of white guys as managers left and right." Few remember that Rush Limbaugh once worked as director of promotions for the Kansas City Royals, but those who do take comfort in the idea of Willie Wilson, Willie Aikens and Frank White treating him like an annoying lackey and—if they allow their imaginations to run wild—giving him atomic wedgies on the first Tuesday of every month.

The All-Star Game is played. As has been the case for several years now, the game "counts," inasmuch as the outcome determines home field advantage for the World Series. All-Star managers Charlie Manuel and Joe Girardi show just how much that means to them by (a) lifting Roy Halladay for Matt Capps despite the fact that Halladay had only thrown 17 pitches; and (b) refusing to pinch-run Alex Rodriguez for David Ortiz late in the game, leading to Ortiz being thrown out at second base on a single to the outfield. But hey, it's not like home field in the World Series is of any consequence for the Phillies or the Yankees, so why should Manuel or Girardi care?

Super agent Scott Boras, reacting to negative comments about his client, Prince Fielder, in a news story, says "I'm tired of unnamed sources. No one put his name on those comments … I'm tired of negative comments about players from unnamed sources." Boras then had to end the interview to take phone calls from five "mystery teams" and to respond to a text from *Sports Illustrated's* Jon Heyman asking "got anything good for me?"

The sale of the Texas Rangers to Pittsburgh businessman Chuck Greenberg is in disarray. Intense fighting among creditors and Greenberg has opened the door for a previous bidder—Houston businessman Jim Crane—to make a new push to buy the team. Dallas Mavericks owner Mark Cuban also throws his hat into the ring. The court overseeing matters decides that Greenberg's original offer is inadequate and that an auction must be held, and it is almost certain that the sale price will skyrocket, threatening to cause Greenberg's investors to pull up stakes and his entire bid to become no longer viable. Greenberg assures the public that there's nothing to worry about and that the deal will be finalized within "two to three weeks."

August

The Orioles reassign interim manager Juan Samuel to vague scouting duties and replace him with Buck Showalter. At the press conference introducing him, Showalter politely evades questions about his reputation for being a micromanager. Those of us beta-testing Apple's new "iInnerMonologueMonitor" hear him loud and clear, however: "Yeah, I am a micromanager. And if you can find a team in greater need of micro-managing than the 2010 Baltimore Orioles, by all means, point me in that direction."

Ozzie Guillen creates controversy when he says that baseball treats Asian players better than Latino players. Two days later he attempts to defuse the controversy by saying his comments were taken out of context. Observers see right through this evasion, however, noting that Guillen has never said anything *in* context in his professional life.

The Yankees have their team picture taken. Everyone is in it except for Alex Rodriguez, who missed it for some reason. Joe Girardi laughs it off and says that Rodriguez will likely be fined by the team's "kangaroo court." A-Rod's a step ahead, however: He plans to bag the court date.

A former Tropicana Field beer vendor tells ESPN that his fellow concession workers were told by supervisors to wash and reuse discarded beer cups. Embarrassed Rays officials offer a profuse apology, making it clear that their policy of reusing things that should have been trashed ended when they released Pat Burrell back in May.

David Ortiz complains about what he perceives to be a strike zone that is far, far too large: "Swinging at all kinds of (stuff). That's what you've got to do. Swing, swing, swing, swing and good luck," Ortiz says. He adds: "it's killing the game." Immediately after these comments, Ortiz is jumped and beaten with bags full of doorknobs by Hank Aaron, Willie Mays and a bunch of other 1960s sluggers who had to deal with knees-to-the-armpits zones and somehow managed not to whine about it.

The Reds' Brandon Phillips and the Giants' Jonathan Sanchez each boldly predict victory in upcoming series against the Cardinals and Padres, respectively. Neither is able to back up his smack talk, however, and their teams post poor showings against division rivals. Those who disapprove of such braggadocio note that Karma has a way of making fools of the bold, and the sentiments of Phillips' and Sanchez's critics are truly borne out when the Cardinals and Padres go on to win their divisions.

Andy Martino of the New York *Daily News* thinks he has figured out the Mets' problem: "It all adds up to a 'F-you' edge that the Mets lack. From the general manager to the coaching staff to the star players to Chris Carter and Jesus Feliciano, they are almost all nice people. Maybe too nice." This hypothesis is proven incorrect a few days later when Francisco Rodriguez assaults an old man in the Mets' clubhouse and yet the team does not improve in any appreciable way.

After eight months of controversy, acrimony, litigation and tumult, the Texas Rangers are auctioned off. The winning bidder: Pittsburgh businessman Chuck Greenberg. Greenberg issues a statement to the public: "Dudes—I told you I had this one in the bag all along."

Mets right fielder Jeff Francoeur is traded to the Texas Rangers. Francoeur is reflective, saying "I had a great three months of the season, and it fell off for me and the team." Given that he had a first half OPS of .695 and hit .211/.262/.274 in the month of May, that "great three months" part may be open for interpretation. David Lennon of *Newsday* is reflective as well, writing "bottom line: Francoeur helped change clubhouse climate for his brief period here." Given that a teammate punched out an old man mere days before, and given that Francoeur himself had instigated a media campaign to get more playing time, the "change the clubhouse climate" part may be open for interpretation as well.

September

Mets pitcher Oliver Perez says on the radio that the Mets are treating him "unfairly" by rarely if ever using him. This causes quite a controversy until it is revealed that, in the part of Mexico he's from, the term "unfairly" means "with more deference and latitude than any person in his situation has any right to be treated."

Eric Chavez tells the *San Francisco Chronicle* that he is contemplating retirement. The article is held back a day, however, as it takes that long for *Chronicle* fact-checkers to determine that, yes, Chavez is still considered an active player.

A Cincinnati auto dealer runs a "buy a Chevy, have dinner with Pete Rose" promotion. It seems like a good idea until multiple Chevy purchasers report being stuck with the tab after Rose blew the money the dealership gave him on a three-team parlay. On preseason football, no less. Still, the promotion is far more successful than a competitor's "buy a Kia, have a late lunch with Ron Oester" promotion.

Darryl Strawberry opens a restaurant bearing his name not far from Citi Field. Everyone agrees: It's the best restaurant named after a former ballplayer with substance abuse problems in that particular part of Queens.

It is revealed that in 2009, Frank McCourt was turned down at least thee times in his efforts to secure additional financing for the Dodgers' day-to-day operations. The lenders: Citibank, an unnamed Chinese investment group and someone identified only as "a Southern California infomercial king." The Dodgers did manage to stay solvent during that period, however, so it is assumed that McCourt must have obtained loans from *someone*. In other news, Ned Colletti warns Dodgers beat writers not to look too deeply into how shortstop Rafael Furcal injured his kneecap.

Louisville Bats pitching coach Ted Power says that Aroldis Chapman may need to figure out how to throw an offspeed pitch that isn't a change-up because his hands are too big to effectively grip one. Chapman announces that he's going to switch to the knuckleball, which experts suspect he could throw at 95 miles per hour. Every single left-handed hitter in the majors files a grievance with the league.

The Arizona Diamondbacks shut down Kris Benson for the season. In other news, Kris Benson was apparently pitching for the Arizona Diamondbacks.

More controversy dogs the New York Mets when Carlos Beltran, Oliver Perez and Luis Castillo elect not to join the rest of the team to visit wounded veterans at Walter Reed Hospital during a trip to Washington. In an effort to defuse the situation, the wounded veterans sign a joint statement saying "No, really, it's cool. None of us particularly want to see Oliver Perez."

Indians manager Manny Acta is displeased with his pitchers' inability to get the final out in the inning. Acta worries that when his pitchers get two out, they tend to lose focus and concentration. Acta says "when you have two out, you're three-fourths of the way there. You need to zero in, make a pitch and get out of there." In other news, Indians coaches no longer let Acta be the banker during their weekly games of Monopoly.

Bud Selig allows Pete Rose to participate in ceremonies at Great American Ballpark marking the 25th anniversary of Rose's breaking of Ty Cobb's all-time hits record. This leads former Commissioner Fay Vincent to sharply criticize Selig. Pete Rose springs to Selig's defense, saying that Fay Vincent, of all people, should not "bash" the commissioner of baseball. Rose adds "It's okay to lie to the commissioner, to sue the commissioner, to repeatedly break the rule which is the very reason why there is a commissioner in the first place and to drive the commissioner into an early grave, but by gum, no one should ever *bash* the commissioner of baseball."

Derek Jeter fakes getting hit by a pitch in a game against the Tampa Bay Rays. While the incident ends up being harmless, some members of the Tampa media think that the Rays should retaliate for Jeter's poor sportsmanship by throwing at him in the following week's rematch. Joe Maddon shoots down such suggestions. Not because intentionally throwing at someone is in itself poor sportsmanship, but because, based on the way Jeter has been hitting all year, plunking him in the ribs and awarding him first base is to do him a favor.

October-November

The division winners are the Phillies, the Reds, the Giants, the Rays, the Twins and the Rangers. The wild card teams are the Braves and the Yankees. After several exciting weeks of playoffs during which umpires' calls come under fire, new heroes are born, goats created, and promos for new FOX and TBS television series get more air time than the actual shows they're promoting will actually receive, a World Series winner is crowned. And I think we can all agree that the best team won.

Right?

The Year in Taters

by Larry Granillo

Note from the author: When I started the Tater Trot Tracker back in April, my goal was only to watch every home run in the majors this year and to time how long an average player took to round the bases. I hoped that it would give people a fun new way to watch the game and help fans settle arguments about whose superstar slugger was more of a showboat. What I didn't expect was for it to give me a new appreciation for the art of the home run or for it to reveal so many nuances I had been missing in the game for years. Take it from someone who has watched 4,500+ home runs this year: There's a lot more to see than you ever thought possible.

The 2010 season was popularly called the "Year of the Pitcher" by broadcasters, sportswriters and pundits. And while that moniker may not be very accurate when you consider the season as a whole, when it comes to the big fly, it isn't exactly wrong either.

Across the major leagues, there were a grand total of 4,613 home runs hit by 494 different players. That is the fewest number of home runs hit in the majors since the league expanded to 30 teams in 1998, and by a good margin. The next smallest league-wide total in the 30-team era came in 2008, when 4,878 home runs were socked.

This is also presumably the shortest amount of time ball-players have spent rounding the bases in celebratory home run trots over that same period. With an average home run trot length of 22 seconds—and considering the 11 home runs that were ruled as such thanks to replay—ballplayers spent more than 28 hours this year fist-pumping and high-fiving their way around the basepaths. As few as they were, the home runs and their ensuing trots provided many memorable moments for the season.

North of the Border

With all of the stories in 2009 about the "home run haven" the new Yankee Stadium was, and with the historically inflated home run totals in ballparks like Coors Field, Minute Maid Park and Citizens Bank Park, one could understand if a team like the Yankees or Rockies or Phillies were considered the favorite to take the team home run crown at the start of the season. So when the Blue Jays wiped the floor with the rest of the majors in team home runs in 2010, it surprised everyone.

Toronto hit 257 home runs as a club, the third highest total in baseball history. The other two leaders—the 1997 Mariners (264 home runs) and the 2005 Rangers (260 home runs)—got there in years offense was unusually high, very unlike these Blue Jays. The only other two squads to hit even

200 home runs this year were the Red Sox, with 211, and the Yankees, with 201. Toronto's lead over second-place Boston is so large that, even if Jose Bautista, the team- and major league-leader with 54 home runs, were to have all his home runs removed, the Jays would be in second place by only seven home runs.

Bautista was certainly something. The only other major leaguer to hit even 40 home runs in 2010 was Albert Pujols, who finished the year with 42. Yet somehow, Bautista, who had never hit more than 16 home runs in a single year, managed to reach a total that would even impress fans from the 1998 season. Who said baseball was predictable?

Consistent Trotters

The most amazing thing about Bautista's season—besides the raw total, of course—was just how consistent he was in running out his home runs. Aside from a few notable exceptions—a spite-filled 29-second trot against the Yankees in August and two inside-the-park home runs come to mind— Bautista averaged an almost perfect 21.46-second per trot. Forty-seven of his 54 trots were clocked between 20.0 and 23.0 seconds. No one was more consistent.

If anyone could challenge Bautista in consistency, it would be David Ortiz. Big Papi started the season off slowly, with loud calls in the media for his ouster as the Red Sox's every-day DH. He turned things around in May, though, hitting seven home runs in the last two weeks of the month. In five of those seven home runs, Ortiz rounded the bases in 28.94 seconds or slower (including the season's only 30-second trot not due to injury), ending up on May's top 10 slowest chart with each one. By the end of the season, Ortiz had seven of the 10 slowest trots of the year (and 10 of the top 14). Talk about consistency.

Inside the Park

On May 19, the Mets' Angel Pagan hit a long fly ball to straightaway center field in Nationals Park. Nyjer Morgan jumped for the ball, but it eluded him, bouncing off the wall behind him and caroming back into center field. Left fielder Josh Willingham picked it up and threw it in to the shortstop, whose relay throw was slightly behind Pagan at the plate. If the throw had been even two feet to the left, the ball would have beaten Pagan and he would have been nailed at the plate. This is particularly amazing when you consider that Pagan's inside-the-park home run was the single fastest circuit of the year, coming in at a blazing 14.48 seconds. At that pace, Pagan could have rounded the bases twice in the time it took Ortiz to run out even one of his May homers. If Pagan had been even a quarter-of-a-second slower, he never would have been able to score.

As it is, Pagan became the fourth player to hit an inside-the-park home run in 2010. By the end of May, there were six inside-the-parkers. At the All-Star break, there had already been 11. Before the season was over, 17 different players would hit 18 inside-the-park home runs, the most in a single season since 20 were hit in 1997.

Of course, the beauty of inside-the-park home runs is their utter randomness. Derek Jeter, for example, hit only the second inside-the-park home run of his long career this summer, and he managed that only because Kansas City center fielder David DeJesus was unable to make a play on the ball after he collided with the wall, tearing a ligament in his thumb and ending his season.

Some other circumstances that led to inside-the-park home runs in 2010:

- DeJesus himself was credited with an inside-the-park home run this year when the ball bounced off of the top of the right field scoreboard/wall in Kauffman Stadium and Minnesota right fielder Michael Cuddyer just let it sit there, thinking that it had cleared the fence. Replays showed that it had indeed gone over the wall before bouncing back onto the field. The umpires never called it a home run, however, so DeJesus was forced to run it out at full speed.

- In the same vein, Bautista hit what appeared to be his second inside-the-parker of the year in August, when Oakland left fielder Conor Jackson missed the ball at the wall and refused to give chase. However, in Bautista's case, a post-game decision ruled the ball over the fence; thus Bautista is credited with only one inside-the-park home run this year despite hustling around the bases for two.

- Jhonny Peralta, a notoriously slow baserunner, came all the way around to score when Detroit center fielder Ryan Raburn fell through the bullpen fence in Progressive Field after trying to catch his fly ball.

- On July 4, the Yankees' Brett Gardner and the Giants' Andres Torres both hit inside-the-park home runs. Gardner was the beneficiary of a friendly scoring decision, when Dewayne Wise lost the ball in the sun and let it squirt out of his mitt. Torres hit a sharp ground ball down the first-base line in Coors Field that bounced far from Colorado right fielder Ryan Spilborghs after he made an ill-advised dive. Both were able to leg out inside-the-park home runs on balls that seemed destined to much more benign fates.

- Tony Gwynn Jr., became the only player to earn two inside-the-park home runs this year when he hustled around the horn after Arizona's Rusty Ryal made a poor dive attempt on Gwynn's line-drive in mid-July. The two inside-the-parkers, coupled with Gwynn's speedy trot on his only "regular" home run of the year, give Gwynn the single best average home run trot time in the majors at 16.41 seconds. Oakland's Adam Rosales, whose fastest single trot on a "regular" home run" was quicker than nine different inside-the-park circuits, has the second-fastest average overall time at 16.69 seconds. If inside-the-park home runs are ignored, Rosales moves to the top of the list.

- Baltimore's Adam Jones earned his inside-the-parker when the ball bounced off Nyjer Morgan's head after he jumped up for the ball at the same center field wall that helped Angel Pagan. Morgan was certain that the ball had bounced over the fence and he angrily threw his mitt to the ground in reaction. He was wrong, and Jones took advantage of that fact.

There really is nothing quite so unique as an inside-the-park home run.

Walking Off

But while an inside-the-park home run may be the "most exciting play in baseball" and something those in attendance are likely not to forget anytime soon, it's not the only type of home run that keeps fans talking long after the game is over. The game-ending, walk-off home run may happen a bit more often than an inside-the-park home run, but its very nature—the home team dramatically winning a game with one swing in its final at-bat—means that fans are more invested in it than just about any other single plate appearance.

Plus, walk-off home runs aren't exactly common. In 2010, 73 games ended with a home run. That may seem like a lot (it means that there was a walk-off home run around the league, on average, once every two or three nights), but it gets pretty thin when spread across 30 clubs. In the entire year, a full season-ticket holder for an average team could expect to see only two or three walk-off home runs.

If there was ever any doubt about just how exciting these events are, one need only watch the way the players on the field celebrate. The typical celebration sees the 20-plus players in the dugout of the winning team swarm onto the field and collect around home plate, leaving only a small mouth in the circle for the batter to run through. As the batter reaches the circle—through a hard run, a slow crouch, or an emphatic leap—it closes in as his teammates jump up and down with congratulatory slaps on the back and head.

It's a mini-mosh pit of joy.

Even a team in the dog days of a futile and disappointing year celebrates a walk-off as if it had just reached the playoffs. On Aug. 7, the 38-71 Pirates, 23 games out of first place, were hosting the third-place Rockies. After frittering away a three-run lead in the top of the ninth, Pittsburgh allowed Colorado to take the lead in the 10th with a two-run home run from Todd Helton. Down to their last out in the bottom of the inning, the Pirates looked ready to lose another game. With two runners on, Pedro Alvarez would not let that be. He crushed the second pitch from Huston Street into the right field bleachers to give the sell-out crowd its second, and final, walk-off home run of the season. Teammates mobbed the young rookie at the plate and lingered on the field afterward giving him hugs and congratulations. Listening to the broadcasters and the fans in the park, it was as if this early-August tilt was the biggest game of the year.

But not all celebrations are the same. When Nate McLouth, for example, beat the Phillies with a leadoff home run in the bottom of the 10th inning in April, his Atlanta teammates jumped off their seats and, instead of running out onto the field, ran deep into the tunnel to hide from him. The expression on McLouth's face as he rounded the bases and saw an empty plate waiting for him was priceless.

The walk-off celebration at home plate was threatened for a short while after the Angels' Kendry Morales broke his leg in the midst of one. After slugging a 10th-inning grand slam off Seattle's Brandon League on May 29, Morales rounded the bases in a normal fashion. As he approached the plate, Morales did the hop-skip-and-a-jump move that is so common on walk-off celebrations, but this time something happened. Morales landed wrong on the plate, twisting his ankle and breaking his leg. His season was over.

Players reacted to the accident by tempering their walk-off celebrations over the next few weeks. Some players, like Carlos Lee, even made a joke about it while running out their walk-offs. The subdued celebrations lasted only a few weeks, though. By July, the standard home plate celebration had returned, and scenes like the Pedro Alvarez mob were free to happen again.

Freak Accidents

The Kendry Morales "broken leg while celebrating a walk-off grand slam" may have been the most shocking and scary home run-related injury of the year, but, surprisingly, it was not the only one.

In June, Baltimore's Luke Scott followed a seventh-inning, game-tying home run from Ty Wigginton with a home run of his own. The opposite field shot did not look like a homer off the bat, so Scott ran hard out of the box. The ball reached the front row of the left-center field seats at the same time

that Scott touched first base. As Scott began to slow into a nice, normal home run trot, he reached for his left leg—he had pulled his hamstring. With nearly 270 feet still to run on the basepaths, Scott had a long, painful home run trot ahead of him. He toughed it out, but not before giving everyone the single longest home run trot of the year at 35.76 seconds.

The second-longest was also the result of an injury, though this one happened on the pitch prior to the home run pitch. On Sept. 18, the Mets' Luis Hernandez fouled the second pitch of his at-bat off the instep of his front foot, just below his shin/foot guard. He immediately crumpled to the ground in pain, looking like he'd be coming out of the game. After a two-and-a-half minute delay as the Mets trainers looked at him, Hernandez stepped back into the box to face Tim Hudson. Hernandez connected with that very next pitch, depositing it over the right field wall. But his foot was still in pain from the foul ball and, as he reached first base, it became apparent that he would trot out his home run on, essentially, one foot. He eventually reached home 33.08 seconds after making contact.

The surprise with the Scott, Hernandez and Morales injuries is that, at age 32, Luke Scott is the oldest of the three. When a player gets injured running out a home run, the joke tends to be that the player might be getting a little old. While that wasn't the case for Scott and the others, it certainly seemed to be with Jim Edmonds. The 40-year-old Edmonds hit a home run off of Milwaukee's Dave Bush on Sept. 21, only a few days after returning to the Reds' lineup from injury. As Edmonds approached third, he shuffled his feet to get in proper step and felt something pop. He took a few hops favoring his leg on the final approach home, but seemed to be okay. He did not come out to the field in the bottom of the inning, however, and did not play again for the rest of the year.

You Always Remember the First One

If Jim Edmonds does not make a roster for the 2011 season, he will join the likes of Mickey Cochrane, Ted Williams, Albert Belle, and Todd Zeile as players who hit a home run in their final career at-bat. He would be the first person in six years to make that claim.

On the flip side, five players in 2010 hit a home run in their first major league at-bat. The most heralded was Jason Heyward, who socked one in the first inning on Opening Day after earning his spot there with a powerful spring. Starlin Castro, the first player born in the 1990s to make it to The Show, was another. Luke Hughes, J.P. Arencibia and Daniel Nava were the last three. Nava's home run was a grand slam on the first pitch he ever saw in the major leagues, making him only the second player ever known to have accomplished that feat. In 188 plate appearances on the season, that was the only home run Nava hit.

Seventy-plus other players hit their first major league home run in the 2010 season. Many were top-flight prospects who scouts and other talent-observers expect to have long careers ahead of them. There was Heyward, as mentioned above, as well as Ike Davis, Mike Stanton, Domonic Brown, Austin Jackson, Justin Smoak, Carlos Santana and Buster Posey, to name only a few.

But they weren't all highly touted prospects. The 27-year-old Nava, for example, had more than 1,000 plate appearances in the minor leagues before he hit that first-pitch grand slam in June. Oakland's Steve Tolleson had nearly 2,500 minor league plate appearances before he hit his first major league shot. And Jai Miller, a right fielder for the Royals who appeared in 20 games this year, had more than 3,000 minor league plate appearances before he sent one over the wall at the big league level. Heyward, Stanton, Posey, et al have many home runs to look forward to in their career; Nava, Tolleson, Miller and their like may be happy to hit one or two more.

Pitchers, on the other hand, are impossible to figure out. Are the first career home runs from youngsters Mat Latos and Travis Wood the sign of long, "productive" careers at the plate, or just flukes the likes of which they'll be lucky to see again? Are either of them the next Mike Hampton and Carlos Zambrano, or are they the next Ben Sheets?

One thing is for certain: When Johan Santana (or even Gustavo Chacin) hit his first career home run this year after 200 career plate appearances, he was not exactly announcing himself as the second coming of Don Drysdale.

Helping Your Own Cause

In total, 13 pitchers hit a total of 16 home runs in 2010. Twelve pitchers hit only one home run apiece. The 13th—Milwaukee's Yovani Gallardo—hit four. In the four games that Gallardo went yard, the Brewers went 3-1, with Gallardo receiving the decision in all of them. In the three victories, Gallardo's homer played a key role in securing the win: in two, Gallardo's home run gave the Brewers the lead, while in the other, his home run tied the game. It'd be tough to find a pitcher who helped his own cause with the bat more than Gallardo.

There are always a few pitchers who are well-known for their hitting prowess. Gallardo is one. Livan Hernandez, Micah Owings and Carlos Zambrano are each celebrated for their power, and they did not disappoint this year. Owings

hit one in relief, joining Gustavo Chacin as the only two to achieve that feat in 2010. Zambrano hit his late in the year, about three starts after re-joining the rotation for good. It was the 21st home run of his career, the most career home runs of any pitcher in the last 40 years.

Overall, teams in 2010 were 11-5 in games in which their pitcher hit a home run. The pitchers themselves were 10-2 in their 12 decisions.

Wrapping Up

The 2010 season saw the home-run-per-game average dip below 2.0 for the first time since the expansion year of 1998. The one-year dip, from 2.07 per game in 2009 to 1.90 per game in 2010, helped justify the "year of the pitcher" story-line that writers and broadcasters have touted all year.

And while a 400+ drop in total home runs is certainly not insignificant, it doesn't really affect fans, or even players, on a game-to-game basis. Fans can still expect to see about two home runs per game and can still expect players to take about 22 seconds to round the bases. Inside-the-park home runs are still random, clumsy, and exciting all at the same time, rivaled only by the drama and excitement of a walk-off home run. Rookies, both young and old, continue to hit home runs, unfazed by their lack of experience, and sluggers will always be around. Jose Bautista may be the next Brady Anderson or Luis Gonzalez—or the next Roger Maris—but, for 2010 at least, he was the undisputed king of the long ball.

The game of baseball is so complex and layered that people of all stripes and personalities can find something in it to love. Hard-throwing pitchers like Justin Verlander, gritty throwbacks like David Eckstein, three-true-outcome masters like Adam Dunn, statistical oddities like Ichiro, freaks of nature like Tim Lincecum, and all-around greats like Albert Pujols all have a place in the hearts and minds of true baseball fans. And one thing all these fans can agree on is the beauty, excitement and majesty of a big home run.

The 2010 season offered slightly fewer opportunities to enjoy home runs than years past, but it was no less of a year for it. In fact, with everything that Jose Bautista, Jason Heyward, David Ortiz, Adam Rosales, Luke Scott, Daniel Nava, Angel Pagan, Pedro Alvarez, Derek Jeter and the roughly 500 other players to hit home runs this year did—including Alex Rodriguez's 600th home run and Jim Thome's pleasantly surprising run at the plateau—fans might find it hard for 2011 or 2012 to top it.

The Year in a Single Number

by Dave Studenmund

Let's start with a story, a little personal history mixed with a lot of baseball history. The story takes place in a bookstore about 25 years ago. I was browsing through the sports section and came across an edition of *The Hidden Game of Baseball*, an early sabermetric classic. I was grabbed by the introduction and never put it back.

You see, the introduction to this "revised and updated" paperback version had a radical claim: that Cal Ripken had just posted the fourth-best season in baseball history. The authors (Pete Palmer and John Thorn) weren't talking about 1983, Ripken's first MVP year. They were talking about 1984, when he finished 27th in MVP voting.

This was Palmer's way of introducing a new statistic—one that included the impact of both batting and fielding—that came to be known as "linear weights." Of course, he was also trying to shake our minds, get us to look at baseball in a new way. At that he was successful. The book, along with Bill James' *Abstracts* of the same time, shook up lots of folks.

The idea was to express a baseball player's value as the single most important number of all: the number of wins he contributes to his team. It was a radical idea at the time though it may seem old hat now. These days, we have several win statistics, such as James' Win Shares and Tom Tango's WAR (Wins Above Replacement) to choose from. (Actually we have two versions of WAR—thank you, FanGraphs and Baseball Reference—but let's not worry about that right now.)

At the time I didn't realize that there had been an earlier attempt at player win calculations. In 1970, the Mills brothers published a little-known classic called *Player Win Averages: A Computer Guide to Winning Baseball Players,* and started a statistical revolution that would slumber for about 30 years before reawakening this decade. In their little book, they laid the groundwork for something we now call Win Probability Added (WPA; also called Win Expectancy).

The Mills brothers (their given first names were Eldon and Harlan, which might explain why they were evidently computer nerds even back in 1970) designed an absolutely brilliant but simple way to tally up the events of a game and give appropriate credit to individual players.

Think of it this way. With two outs in the bottom of the ninth, runner on third, we can make a pretty darn good estimate of how many times an average team will score a specific number of runs the rest of the inning, like zero (74 percent), one (19 percent), two (5 percent), three or more (whatever is left percent). We know this sort of thing through the use of advanced mathematics such as Markov Chains or perhaps just plain old historical data, but we are pretty confident about the numbers.

So if the score is tied, then there is a 74 percent average probability that the home team will score no runs and the game will go into extra innings and a 26 percent average probability that the home team will score at least one run and win the game in the ninth. If you assume that each team has a 50 percent chance of winning in extra innings, that means that its Win Probability at that moment is 0.74 times 0.5, plus 0.26—or 63 percent.

I know that was hard to get through, but that was the end of it. That was all the math you need to understand WPA. The beauty of the system is that you can "chain" all of these probabilities backward through the game—all the way back to the very first batter in the very first inning—and determine the win probability at any point of a game.

Let me give you an example. On June 24 of this year, the Red Sox and Rockies played a wild one in Colorado. The Rockies jumped out to a 2-0 lead in the early innings, thanks to some walks and singles (the key one delivered by Brad Hawpe) but the Red Sox took a 4-2 lead in the fourth inning (key double by Mike Cameron) and built their lead to 6-2 an inning later (thanks to an Adrian Beltre homer).

The Rockies singled seven times in the sixth, however, and took the lead back, 7-6 (Ian Stewart had the single with the greatest impact). The Red Sox came right back in the next inning (key hit: a Jason Varitek double) to take a 9-8 lead and Dustin Pedroia padded the lead in the eighth with a two-run home run. 11-8.

The Rox were not happy about this. They chipped away with one run in the eighth to make it 11-9 and then posted a dramatic comeback in the bottom of the ninth to tie the game. The key hit was, once again, a single by Hawpe.

Yet it was not meant to be for Colorado. Pedroia hit another two-run homer in the top of the 10th, Jonathan Papelbon retired the Rockies in order (after he had given up the lead in the ninth) and the Red Sox won this seesaw battle, 13-11. If you were to graph the play-by-play win probability of the game (and why wouldn't you?), this is what it would look like…

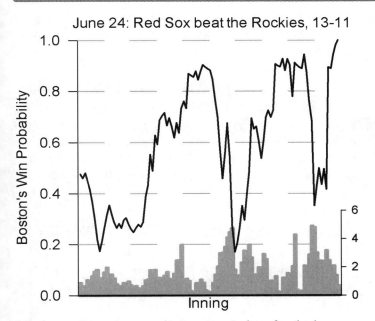

June 24: Red Sox beat the Rockies, 13-11

(Those gray lines represent the Leverage Index of each play; more about that later.)

By our calculation, this was the Most Exciting Game of the Year. To qualify for THT's special award, a game has to have the greatest number of Win Probability swings from play to play, divided by the number of innings in the game. No other game was so swingy. If this game had been a tennis match, the Colorado crowd would have had whiplash.

The hero of the game was obviously Pedroia. When you add up all the increases and decreases of Win Probability that occurred in his plate appearances, it turns out he contributed 0.9 "wins" to the cause. Hawpe was the Rockies' top contributor, with 0.25 "wins." In such a high-scoring game, the player with the most "losses" was naturally a pitcher, Boston's Hideki Okajima.

Parenthetical aside: I put "wins" in quotation marks, because those numbers aren't really wins. Each team begins a game with a 50 percent probability of winning—the winning team gains 50 percent throughout the ups and downs of the game and the losing team loses 50 percent by the end of the game. So, if a player has 0.9 WPA points, he's actually contributed almost two whole wins in just one game. That may not make sense to you, but what if all the other players on his team gave up a whole lot of losses in the same game? Someone's got to make up for them.

In fact, Pedroia's WPA total in this game was the sixth-highest of the year. The leader in single-game WPA was the Braves' remarkable rookie Jason Heyward, who led the Braves to a 4-3 comeback win over the Rockies (them again?) on April 18. Heyward didn't light up fireworks a la Pedroia; he only walked twice and singled in three at-bats. But he singled

with two outs, bases loaded and the Braves trailing 3-2 in the bottom of the ninth. That one hit was good for 0.74 WPA all by itself. Coupled with a bases-loaded walk earlier in the game and a couple of other plays, Heyward posted an astronomic total of 1.03 WPA in just one game.

That single of Heyward's, by the way, was the eighth-biggest hit of the year. The biggest single hit was Pedro Alvarez's two-out 10th-inning home run against—wait for it—the Rockies on Aug. 7. The Pirates were down by two runs at the time with runners on first and second. Alvarez's blast off Huston Street was worth 0.91 WPA points all by itself.

You know that walk-off home run by Kendry Morales on May 29? The one in which he broke his leg in the celebration at home, forcing him to sit out the rest of the year? That was worth only 0.16 WPA points, because the Angels had already loaded the bases with just one out in a tie game. Seems like a waste of an injury, doesn't it?

The best pitching performance of the year was turned in by Roy Halladay, of course. On May 29, he didn't just pitch a perfect game. He pitched a perfect game in a 1-0 win. The Marlins technically had a decent probability of winning in the ninth inning even though they hadn't reached base against Halladay. That's awesome pitching, yes, awesome pitching in a tight game.

Edwin Jackson's eight-walk no-hitter also occurred in a 1-0 game, against the Rays, and that performance ranks as the second-best pitching performance of the year.

WPA stats and graphs are available all year long at both Fangraphs.com and Baseball-Reference.com. At Baseball Reference, you can also see how well each player has performed in "high leverage" situations. You may have an intuitive sense of what high leverage means (basically, the most critical situations) but, thanks to WPA, we can quantify exactly how critical a specific situation is.

The trick to Leverage Index is to quantify the range of potential win probability outcomes of a specific play; the bigger the range of outcomes, the higher the criticality (or leverage). An average Leverage Index is 1.0 and most plays in a season are less critical than that. But many plays are very high leverage. For instance, when Heyward grounded that single to left on April 18, down by a run with the bases loaded and two out, the Leverage Index was 10.72—about as high as the Index goes.

Leverage Index gives us a tool to establish "clutch" play. When LI is high, the game is on the line and you can say that players who deliver have delivered in the clutch. I don't know if Heyward is a "clutch" batter, but his single on the 18th was certainly a clutch play. So let's see who delivered the most in the clutch in 2010.

I'm going to arbitrarily use a Leverage Index of 2.0 as a cutoff point for clutch play. About 10 percent of all plays have an LI of 2.0 or more, which makes them rare enough, but not too rare, to matter. Here are the 10 batters who contributed the most in high-leverage plays.

Batter	Plays	WPA
Rodriguez, Alex	64	3.3
Cabrera, Miguel	85	3.2
Votto, Joey	69	3.0
Cruz, Nelson	57	2.8
Bourn, Michael	74	2.4
Conrad, Brooks	38	2.3
Choo, Shin-Soo	68	2.2
Youkilis, Kevin	47	2.0
Hart, Corey	67	1.9
Lee, Carlos	64	1.9

This list includes the usual array of top-notch sluggers mixed in with some surprises. Astros leadoff man Michael Bourn performed very well in high-leverage situations, as did their cleanup hitter, the otherwise execrable Carlos Lee.

A few years ago, you heard a lot about Alex Rodriguez not being a clutch batter. Some of the WPA stats even seemed to back this up. Well, A-Rod did a fine job in the clutch this year. In seven different plays with a Leverage Index over 4.0, A-Rod walked, singled, doubled, homered, hit a sacrifice fly, advanced on a wild pitch and hit into a fielder's choice. His total WPA in those seven situations was 1.2. No one is going to start calling him A-Clutch, but give the guy his due.

Let's ratchet this up a notch. About one percent of plays have a Leverage Index of more than 4.0. Who were the leaders in those situations?

Batter	Plays	WPA
Conrad, Brooks	8	1.62
Lee, Carlos	6	1.50
Heyward, Jason	12	1.34
Cabrera, Miguel	14	1.32
Torres, Andres	12	1.25
Rodriguez, Alex	7	1.21
Kotchman, Casey	10	1.09
Berkman, Lance	8	1.04
Gonzalez, Adrian	9	0.96
Ortiz, David	10	0.94

The Braves' Brooks Conrad came to bat only 177 times last year, but he sure made his plate appearances count. In eight really-high-leverage appearances, he homered three times, singled, walked, sacrificed, flied out and struck out. That is a terrific record. Did I mention three home runs in eight plate appearances?

Oh, and Carlos Lee.

I hope you see that WPA gives you an entirely different way of judging batters. To show you what I mean, here are two lists. One is a list of the top 10 batters in the majors according to Base Runs, the best standard "run estimator" (a stat that tabulates the general impact of all individual batting events into a total number of runs created). The other list contains the leaders in batting WPA.

Batter	Base Runs	Batter	WPA
Pujols, Albert	130	Votto, Joey	7.0
Bautista, Jose	127	Cabrera, Miguel	6.9
Cabrera, Miguel	121	Hamilton, Josh	5.7
Gonzalez, Adrian	119	Pujols, Albert	5.4
Votto, Joey	119	Heyward, Jason	4.9
Crawford, Carl	118	Gonzalez, Adrian	4.9
Holliday, Matt	116	Holliday, Matt	4.1
Werth, Jayson	115	Choo, Shin Choo	4.0
Cano, Robinson	114	Bautista, Jose	3.7
Hamilton, Josh	114	Cano, Robinson	3.5

The two lists are mostly similar, but not entirely. Heyward was 28th in Base Runs, for example, but fifth in batting WPA. Cleveland's Shin-Soo Choo stepped it up a notch. There are several reasons the rankings differ, but situational hitting is probably the biggest one. WPA rewards hitting in high-leverage situations; Base Runs doesn't. Which list is more legitimate? You decide.

What about pitchers, you ask? Well, as you can imagine, the list of "clutch" pitchers is dominated by closers, since they are given the most opportunities in high-leverage situations. Still, you may find some surprises among the top 10 (Leverage Index higher than 2.0):

Pitcher	Plays	WPA
Soria, Joakim	137	6.11
Bell, Heath	133	4.50
Soriano, Rafael	101	3.86
Wilson, Brian	144	3.67
Marmol, Carlos	151	3.51
Lyon, Brandon	130	3.43
Feliz, Neftali	103	2.80
Pelfrey, Mike	85	2.61
Perez, Chris	119	2.51
Kuo, Hong-Chih	63	2.38

This list verifies the great (and somewhat overlooked) season that Joakim Soria had in Kansas City. One starter did make our list, the Mets' Mike Pelfrey. Color me surprised.

There's a natural extension to Win Probability, something that both Sky Andrecheck and I explored last year. Sky called it Championship Leverage Index. Once again, the concept is pretty simple. If you assume that all teams are fundamentally .500 teams, it's pretty easy to calculate each team's probability of making the postseason or winning the World Series at any point during the year (although the wild card makes the math kind of hairy).

A lot of websites do this sort of thing, and they even improve upon the concept by factoring in each team's strengths, weaknesses and schedule.

The real fun comes when you combine each team's championship probability with the number of games left in the season to determine its most crucial games; "Championship Leverage Index," naturally enough. You find, for instance, that...

- Some teams, such as Baltimore and Kansas City, had their "most critical" games on the first day of the season. Their tires went flat immediately.
- The most critical point for any teams in the American League belonged to Chicago and Minnesota in Aug. 10-12. Both teams' Championship Leverage Index stood around 3.0 (three times the criticality of a normal regular season game), but the Twins took two of three from the ChiSox in Chicago, and that was that.
- Meanwhile, in the National League, the Central competitors were in a very similar situation. The Reds and Cardinals were locked in a tight race after St. Louis swept the Reds in early August. On Aug. 11, both teams had Championship Leverage Indices around 3.0, but the Reds went on to win their next seven straight and the Cards lost five in a row. Drama over.
- The real drama came at the end of the season, when the Giants, Braves and Padres were fighting for two postseason slots. On the very last day of the season, the Padres' and Braves' Championship Index was over 12.0, meaning that the final game of the season was 12 times more critical for them than an average regular season game!
- The Giants' Championship Leverage Index that day was much lower—3.5—because they had more options to make the postseason. In fact, their Index had been higher (4.7) just a week before, but they took six of seven

before meeting the Pads, which gave them a bit of breathing room even after losing the first two games of the San Diego series.

In our Statistics section, where we graph the progress of each team during the season, you'll find their Championship Leverage Index plotted along their wins, losses, runs and runs allowed. We think it paints a full graphical picture of each team's season.

The "ultimate number" comes about when you combine the Championship Leverage Index with WPA. For example, Miguel Tejada's second-best WPA day of the year was on Sept. 24, when his Padres were in a dogfight in the NL West and playing the Reds. Tejada hit two RBI singles in crucial situations, the Padres won, 4-3, and Tejada's WPA for the day was 0.52.

Since the game was crucial for the Padres, their Championship Index that day was 4.26. If you multiply Tejada's WPA by the Padres' Championship Index, you get 2.23, which we'll call Championship WPA. Tejada's performance that day was the biggest single-game Championship WPA performance of the entire year. No batter contributed more to his team's chances of success in a single game.

In contrast, Tejada's best WPA game of the year was 0.71 on April 30 for the Orioles, who never really had a critical game all year. As a result, his Championship WPA that day was only 0.14—just one-seventeenth of the contribution he made to the Padres on September 24.

See how it works? Consider the case of the Giants' Pat Burrell, who played in 51 games with a Championship LI of more than 2.0, and compiled a total of 2.1 WPA. That is the highest WPA total in critical games of any player in the majors last year. Burrell's big pennant-producing performances included a key two-run homer in the bottom of the eighth against the Dodgers on July 31 and two more critical home runs against the Cubs on Aug. 11 and 12. Not bad for a guy dumped by the Rays earlier in the season.

The Twins' Jim Thome played in just four games with a Championship LI of 2.0 or more, but he did the job when it counted. Those four games included one against the White Sox on Aug. 18, when he belted a game-winning home run in the bottom of the tenth.

And let's not forget about the aforementioned Brooks Conrad, who not only hit in the clutch, but hit in the clutch in the critical games. His solid performance in the last week of the Braves' season helped them get into the playoffs.

These are just some of the plays and players that stand out when you look at the season this way, through the lens of the "ultimate number." To close this part of our discussion, let's take the natural step and simply multiply the two figures—WPA and Championship Leverage Index—for all batters and all games. Here's the top 10 in Championship WPA:

Batter	Champ WPA
Votto, Joey	8.13
Heyward, Jason	7.08
Cabrera, Miguel	6.74
Hamilton, Josh	6.27
Pujols, Albert	6.09
Conrad, Brooks	6.08
Gonzalez, Adrian	5.74
Holliday, Matt	4.95
Huff, Aubrey	4.65
Burrell, Pat	4.17

Look at that. The usual suspects, to be sure, but also some real surprises. I've touched on most of the surprise batters already, but let's take a moment to give a guy his due. Joey Votto had a great year (37 home runs and 113 RBIs), batted well in the clutch (a .355 batting average and 1.098 OPS with the game leverage at 1.5 or more) and continued to do it while the Reds played some tough games and ultimately made the postseason. National League MVP? You could do worse.

I've called Championship WPA the "ultimate number," but of course it isn't. For one thing, the current implementation of WPA doesn't include the impact of fielding, which (as you'll find elsewhere in these pages) is a tremendously important part of a ballplayer's value equation. I simply wanted to use WPA to give you some of the highlights of the year. That's really the value of WPA, why I like to call it the "story stat."

As I said upfront, we have a plethora of win-based statistics these days. So the question still nagged at me. How good was Cal Ripken in 1984? I decided to try to figure it out.

Let's step through the systems one-by-one. According to Win Shares, he was really, really good. I've created a modification that I consider an improvement over Bill James' original Win Shares system, called Win Shares Above Bench (WSAB). I won't go into the details, but WSAB thinks that Ripken was

indeed the MVP of the league in 1984, even better than he was in 1983. In fact, WSAB ranks Ripken's 1984 as the best year of his career. But it's still only 238th on the list of all seasons by position players since 1900.

According to Win Shares (and WSAB), the greatest individual season since 1900 among position players was turned in by another shortstop, the legendary Honus Wagner in 1908. Wagner was 47 Wins Shares Above Bench in that memorable year. In 1984, Ripken was 24 Win Shares Above Bench. Big difference.

Wins Above Replacement (WAR) is essentially the original linear weights system updated and abetted by computing power and the fantastic Retrosheet database. Sean Smith has done the calculating and generously made the results available to all at his website (http://www.baseballprojection.com/). According to Sean's WAR, Ripken's 1984 ranks more highly—the 132nd best season of all time—and higher than his 1983 season. However, WAR really likes Ripken's other MVP year, 1991, ranking it 36th among all seasons.

Ripken had three MVP-type years. In 1983, his first MVP year, he "created" 43 runs above average at bat (according to Sean's approach) and was nine runs above average in the field. The next year, his offensive output declined a bit (36 runs above average) but his fielding runs jumped up to 20. In 1991, he put both sides of his excellent game together: 48 batting runs and 20 fielding runs. His MVP selection that year was a no-brainer, though Cecil Fielder did receive nine first-place votes. According to WAR, Fielder was almost eight wins worse than Ripken.

In the WAR files, Wagner's 1908 is the 20th-best year of all time. In first place is the Babe, in 1923.

WPA provides another reason to exalt Ripken's 1984. He batted .381 in high-leverage situations (LI of 1.5 or more) that year, with a .979 OPS. Overall, his bat contributed 3.7 WPA in '84. But several players ranked more highly. The American League leader was Ripken's teammate Eddie Murray, who had a 1.107 OPS in high-leverage situations (and he had more of them, too). Murray finished with 7.3 WPA, three-and-a-half more than Ripken.

In fact, if you replace the "runs created" portion of WAR with WPA, Murray has a higher WAR than Ripken in 1984. That's right. If you think of it this way, Ripken's 1984 wasn't even the best year on his own team.

There are many ways to skin this cat. Always will be. Don't let anyone tell you otherwise.

The Annotated 2010 in Baseball History

by Richard Barbieri

On our site each week, I pick an event from the annals of baseball history and try to establish its proper context. While it's not hard to find a historic topic each week, each season has a number of historically interesting stories in its own right. Here are 12 stories from the last year in baseball, with the history each one represents.

November 2009: Yankees Win World Series

One of the reasons—besides practicalities in our publishing schedule—that I write the year in review from November through October is, in baseball terms, that is a year. The World Series ends in October closing the book on the previous year and free-agent season starts in November, beginning the Hot Stove for the next year.

Owing to the postseason schedule established this season, however, the World Series ended in November, tying the record for the latest ending ever, with the 2001 Series which was delayed by the Sept. 11 attacks.

This does give me a chance to comment on an interesting phenomenon, albeit one that is, with a little thought, an obvious one: teams that win the World Series play really well. In theory, a team could win a World Series with an 11-8 record, which is a good record, but not outstanding. (It would be roughly equivalent to a 93-win team in the regular season.)

But those teams that achieve World Series glory have never needed so many games to win the title, indeed, they typically need far fewer. Since the 11-game format began in 1995, no team has lost more than six games in their playoff run and only two (the '03 Marlins and '01 Diamondbacks) lost that many, the same number that went 11-1 on their run. Indeed, the average record by a World Series winning team comes to a nearly .750 winning percentage.

Although that is an astonishingly high winning percentage when considering the competition, it is a logical one. To win a Series, a team has to be playing well. And when a team is playing well, in a small sample, they will win a high percentage of their games, even against excellent opponents. We are going to press too soon for me to know how many games the World Series winner will lose this year, but the smart money is on four or less.

December 2009: Italian Baseball League Announces Changes

You might have missed this story, being that it was not exactly big news in the United States, even among the truly baseball-mad. The Italian league, Serie A1, chose to abandon the traditional European relegation and promotion model (where the highest finishing teams from lower leagues replace the lowest finishing teams in the next league up) in favor of the American "fixed" model.

But while news like this rarely draws coverage, especially when compared to the leagues of the United States and Japan, it is worth remembering that each year also sees champions crowned in leagues all around the world.

In addition to MLB and Nippon Professional Baseball, there are active leagues virtually everywhere, ranging from the Netherlands' Honkbal Hoofdklasse to the China Baseball League. In Europe, teams qualifying from each league played in a European Cup, which saw teams from Italy, Germany and, improbably, San Marino qualify for the "Final Four."

Italy's Fortitudo Bologna won the European Cup this season, its first title but Italy's third consecutive victory in the "Final Four." It may be some years—if ever—before an Italian team could hope to compete with the best of Major League Baseball. But it may be sooner than we think that teams are seriously scouting Europe for young talent.

January 2010: Pirates Unveil Bill Mazeroski Statue

As you might have guessed from the date, this was not the unveiling of the actual full-sized statue—January in Pittsburgh not being the time of year to stand around and think of warm summer days—but rather of a model of the statue. The statue, which was eventually unveiled on its subject's 74th birthday, is modeled on Mazeroski's trip around the bases after hitting his World Series-winning home run in 1960. It also stands, appropriately enough, on Mazeroski Way outside PNC Park.

Pittsburgh has a long history of honoring their players with statues. In addition to Mazeroski's, the team has statues of Honus Wagner, Roberto Clemente and Willie Stargell around its park. The statue of Wagner dates back to 1955 and stood outside of Forbes Field, Three Rivers Stadium and now PNC Park.

While honoring legends with statues is hardly a new tradition, in recent times it has grown increasingly popular. This sometimes leads to an air of unintentional farce, such as this year when the Cubs rededicated their statue of Harry Caray after moving it to a new location so they could make room for a different statue, one of Billy Williams. Even Bud Selig was honored with a statue, now standing outside Miller Park next to tributes to Hank Aaron and Robin Yount.

Whether the popularity of statues will continue is hard to judge—one would think teams will eventually run out of deserving figures—right now we are living in the glory days of seeing the game's greats immortalized in bronze.

February 2010: Nationals Sign Livan Hernandez

Anyone with an even passing familiarity with the Bible knows the story of Lazarus, resurrected by Jesus after being dead for four days. Lazarus comparisons are so frequent as to almost be cliché, but the literary device survives in no small part because the metaphor is often just so apt.

In 2010, the Lazarus pitcher of the season was Livan Hernandez. And even more impressive than the Biblical Lazarus, Hernandez found himself restored again, after having his career seeming dead, or nearly so, many times before.

While Hernandez made his mark in his rookie season, winning nine games in the regular season and four more in the playoffs (along with the NLCS and World Series MVP awards) by the 2002 off-season he seemed on the decline. Although just entering his age-28 season, Hernandez's previous two seasons were mediocre at best with a combined ERA near 5.00. In 2002, despite pitching for the NL Champions, he managed to lead the league in losses.

Traded to Montreal for Jim Brower and Matt Blank, Hernandez immediately posted the two best seasons of his career, with a WAR (Wins Above Replacement) over five both years. Hernandez slowly declined thereafter, and by the 2009 off-season he had spent the three prior seasons with five different teams and posted a combined ERA of nearly 5.50.

The Nationals brought Hernandez back on a minor league contract and once again Livan proved himself worthy of Lazarus comparisons. The big Cuban pitched more than 200 innings and led all Nats starters in wins, innings, ERA and strikeouts.

Other players in baseball history earned comparisons to Lazarus but Hernandez—now on his third resurrection—unquestionably deserves the association.

March 2010: Stephen Strasburg Makes Spring Training Debut

I have a lot of faith in the abilities of the various Hardball Times stat gurus, along with those with names like MGL and the staff at Baseball Prospectus, to measure almost anything that takes place during a baseball game. Some things connected to baseball cannot be measured, no matter how much effort or skill is applied. One such thing is hype, which will always be at least partially subjective.

Having said that, and conceding many players have been hyped over the years (as a Yankees fan I remember the build-up for Hideki Irabu's first start) it seems likely that Stephen Strasburg's spring training debut was as widely hyped as any spring performance in baseball history.

Two hundred people went to watch Strasburg warm up in the bullpen—including Ivan Rodriguez, who wasn't playing in the Nationals game that day. Across both the DC press and Twitter potential names were tossed around for the start, with "Strasburgeddon" apparently emerging as the winner.

Of course, a spring training start, especially the first one, is inevitably anti-climatic. Strasburg pitched two scoreless innings, allowed two hits (both singles) and struck out two on 27 pitches. There was more of Strasburg's story to come, including his 14-strikeout debut in a regular season game and the season-ending Tommy John surgery. On this day in March, it was all about Strasburgeddon and, even if there's no number to measure it, what was surely the most hyped spring training debut ever.

April 2010: Joe Maddon Receives Permission to Wear Hoodie

This was, even by the low standards for what constitutes news over a long baseball season, not really news. Like Bill Belichick and drug dealers around the world, Maddon likes to wear a hooded sweatshirt when he works. But Major League Baseball briefly ruled that Maddon could not wear the hoodie, instead telling him to wear "official team jackets or Majestic brand tops" instead. Shortly thereafter, MLB reversed itself, so Maddon and his sweatshirts were reunited.

Maddon is representative of an unusual trend, that of managers who are almost never seen in uniform tops. Others who follow this pattern include Terry Francona, whose pullovers were themselves a source of controversy when a Major League Baseball official demanded verification Francona had a uniform top on in the midst of a Yankees-Red Sox game. Joe Torre, meanwhile, also a fan of wearing such garments, described a warning letter he received from the Commissioner's office about it as "Mickey Mouse stuff."

That baseball managers are the only coaches who wear uniforms is a well-known (and much discussed) idea so it is perhaps no surprise that some managers have sought to work around the edges of the policy. Of course, none look as dapper as Connie Mack who famously wore a suit—and straw hat!—in the dugout during games. Sadly, we are unlikely to ever see a manager so stylishly attired again, as (excluding medical personnel) anyone taking the field must be in uniform per Major League rules. We are thus left with Maddon's hoodies as the farthest one can go from a straight uniform in managerial garb.

May 2010: Oliver Perez Makes Last Start of Season

In past editions of these articles, I have written about notable starting pitchers' contracts which have turned into busts. Those include recent deals like Carl Pavano, and those a bit farther back in history like Jamie Navarro.

Some contracts turned into busts simply owing to the huge amount of money paid out, like Barry Zito, who is 40-57 during his time in San Francisco and still has more than $60 million left on his deal. Other contracts turn into busts because the pitcher simply cannot stay healthy, like Mike Hampton who earned $121 million over eight years while throwing fewer than 900 innings and missing two full seasons.

When compared to numbers like that, it seems hard to imagine that Oliver Perez—whose deal was signed before the 2009 season and is for "just" three years and $36 million—might be the biggest bust of all. But in a situation almost never seen, the Mets gave up on Perez—he pitched just six times after returning from the DL on July 21—but nonetheless kept him on the Major League roster. This was in part owing to Perez's apparent refusal to go to the minor leagues and attempt to improve his performance, but also the Mets' own stubbornness in refusing to release Perez and eat his remaining contract.

Of course, on a performance level Perez did not deserve to pitch much. In his last five starts before the Mets pulled him for the rotation, he went 0-2 with a 7.17 ERA while walking an astounding 21 in 21.1 innings. Whether bad or injured, few starting pitcher busts have compelled their team to play with a 24-man roster for much of a season. With that in mind, Perez may be the biggest bust of all.

June 2010: Armando Galarraga Pitches "Almost" Perfect Game

Alright, all together now, one last time for nostalgia's sake: I can't believe he blew that call! Arguably Galarraga's "Imperfect Game" was the most discussed, most widely covered game of the year, in part because of the reactions on both sides. But while the story of how Jim Joyce and Galarraga turned a bad situation into a positive one on the values of accountability and sportsmanship is well-known, less so is the history that would have been made if not for Joyce's call.

Roy Halladay had thrown his perfect game just days before, and Galarraga would have set a new record for the shortest period between two perfect games—a record that had just been set by Halladay when he pitched his game 20 days after Dallas Braden's.

Although Halladay's perfect game was the third perfecto in a calendar year (with Mark Buehrle throwing one in July the previous year) Galarraga would have made it four in a calendar year—a new record—along with the first time three perfect games had ever been thrown in a single season. It would also have been the first time three consecutive no-hitters were perfect games.

Finally, Galarraga would have given the Tigers their first perfect game in their more than 100 years of history.

July 2010: Roy Oswalt Traded to Phillies

Who is the best pitcher in Astros history? For pure single-season dominance, it would be either Mike Scott's 1986 season (18-10, 2.22 ERA, 306 strikeouts, 275 innings) or Larry Dierker's 1969 (20-13, 2.33 ERA, 305 innings). The best pitchers to spend any significant time in Houston are surely Nolan Ryan and Roger Clemens, but both pitched more innings for other teams. When considering all of these factors, the best Astros pitcher can only really be one man: Roy Oswalt.

During his time in Houston, Oswalt twice won 20 games, led the league in ERA, winning percentage, strikeout-to-walk ratio and placed in the top five in Cy Young voting five times while making three All-Star teams. But despite this series of accomplishments—and a host of others not mentioned—there is one prominent Astros record not held by Oswalt. But it is also not held by Dierker, or Ryan, or Scott or Clemens.

That record is the most wins in Astros' franchise history, and it belongs to Joe Niekro. Niekro spent 11 years pitching for the Astros, and like Oswalt twice won 20 games for the team. All said, the knuckleballer picked up 144 of his career 221 wins in an Astros uniform.

When Oswalt left for Philadelphia in July, he was sitting on 143 wins, just two away from taking over the record. Oswalt is contracted to the Phillies through at least the 2012 season, but will still be under age 35 when that deal expires. It remains possible that he could return to Houston and claim his place on top of the wins list. But for now, Joe Niekro stands tall.

August 2010: Bobby Thomson Dies

Like a lot of people—both in baseball and the wider world—Bobby Thomson was a man whose entire life was inevitably summed up in one line describing one moment. *The New York Times* obituary for example, ran the headline "Bobby Thomson dies at 86, hit epic home run." Elsewhere in his obituary, Thomson's "Shot Heard Round the World" is described as both the "most famous home run in baseball history" and "perhaps the most dramatic moment in baseball history."

Just as it would overshadow the rest of his life, Thomson's glorious last at-bat overshadowed his play in the entire three-game series with the Dodgers. He was the hitting star for the Giants, batting .500 with six RBIs in the series, including a two-run homer off Ralph Branca in the first game of the series that gave the Giants a lead they would never relinquish.

His heroics also pushed to the background the quality of his play in 1951. Thomson finished the year with a 150 OPS+, and was among the team's most valuable players. He never repeated that level of hitting again, and spent much of the end of his career bouncing from team to team, playing for five teams in his final four years.

With Thomson's passing, it probably falls to Bucky Dent to carry the title—or burden, perhaps—of being the living player whose life is all about one moment. Of course, there are worse things than to be known for one moment of glory.

September 2010: Rangers Clinch Playoff Spot

This was no doubt an exciting moment for Rangers fans, being the team's first playoff appearance since 1999, when they were swept out by the Yankees. But surely the happiest person when the Rangers secured their spot in October was Michael Young. When Young made his playoff debut, it removed him from an unfortunate list: players with the most games played without a playoff appearance. For the brief period between the end of the Rangers' regular season and beginning of the postseason, Young had more than 1,500 games without October glory.

In general, this was a good year for players looking to end that streak. In addition to Young, Aubrey Huff—who had to wait until the season's very last day to qualify—and Mike Sweeney both celebrated postseason berths this year. For both men, who had played more than 1,400 games without a taste of the playoffs, this was extra sweet.

Moreover, while pitchers cannot rack up the huge numbers of games played, postseason debutantes Roy Halladay and Francisco Cordero had played more than 10 years in the major leagues without being on a playoff team. Halladay in

particular must have appreciated his postseason appearance, being that he helped orchestrate a trade to Philadelphia for just that purpose.

Of course, some are not so lucky. Especially unlucky this year was Randy Winn. Winn started his year with the Yankees—who did qualify for the postseason—but was released early in the season. Winn caught on with St. Louis, but the Cards fell short, leaving Winn with more than 1,700 games played and no postseason appearances.

October 2010: Chan Ho Park Sets Record

Like most people, when I think of successful Asian-born pitchers, Chan Ho Park does not come to mind quickly. Despite a 17-year career, he has long been overshadowed by other names. Though Park actually debuted a season before Hideo Nomo, it was "The Tornado" who burst on to the scene most spectacularly, winning the Rookie of the Year award and finishing in the top four in the Cy Young voting his first two years in the league.

That was just the beginning for Park in being overshadowed by other Asian-born pitchers. Park's "big accomplishments" never matched those of players like Kaz Sasaki, who also won a Rookie of the Year award and saved more than 100 games. Or Chien-Ming Wang, who led the league in victories and finished as a runner-up in Cy Young voting. Even Daisuke Matsuzaka, who has been a pedestrian pitcher much of his time in the major leagues, comes to mind first, owing to his enormous posting fee and World Series ring.

But despite his seeming lack of fame, it is Park who holds the record for most major league wins by an Asian-born pitcher. He topped Nomo's 123 this month by pitching three perfect innings of relief in Pittsburgh's 5-1 win over the Marlins. I would not necessarily argue that Park is the best of the Asian-born pitchers—though he definitely belongs in the conversation—but his longevity should not go unnoticed. It seems fitting that while the greater honors eluded Park, he nonetheless earned a place in baseball history, one that should be his for the near future.

The Booms and Busts of 2010

by David Golebiewski

Before the season begins, a great deal of time and effort is expended trying to figure out just what the heck is going to happen from Opening Day through the final pitch and dog pile of the postseason. An alphabet soup of projection systems—CHONE, Oliver, PECOTA, ZiPS—use past major and minor league production, historical precedent, age and regression to forecast player performance for the upcoming year.

These projections are immensely useful, keeping us from making the lazy assumption that whatever a guy did last season, he'll probably do again this year. But even with so many trying to play baseball's Nostradamus, some hitters and pitchers far exceed our expectations, while others fall woefully short of preseason prognostications. The inherent unpredictability of baseball is a major part of what both attracts and aggravates fans of the sport. No matter how much time we spend studying and quantifying the game, we can never say with certainty what's going to happen from April through October (er, November).

I'd like to embrace that unpredictability, celebrating some of the players who zipped past their preseason projections and somberly noting the slackers who caused much teeth-gnashing and grumbling amongst fans. What better way to honor the players who so drastically and unexpectedly altered their teams' fortunes than by having them form their own squads?

Using preseason projections from Brian Cartwright's Oliver system (included in THT Forecasts), I selected a starting lineup and a starting pitcher for both 2010's over- and under-achievers. Oliver takes a simple weighted mean of a player's past three seasons, then applies aging factors and regression to the mean. The guys on the "Boom" team greatly outperformed their preseason Oliver projections, while the poor souls on the "Bust" team disappointed Oliver and might appear in an upcoming episode of *Eastbound & Down*. Well, maybe things aren't *that* bad. But they're probably not feeling like bulletproof tigers right about now.

Before we get to the teams, here's a brief explanation of the main offensive statistic referenced. Weighted On-Base Average (wOBA) is a linear weight formula set as a rate statistic and scaled to mirror On-Base Percentage. The average wOBA will equal the average OBP. wOBA assigns a run value for every outcome on the field (a home run, a triple, a double, etc.), thus properly weighing each event in the game. A home run, for example, is worth about twice as much as a single.

wOBA is preferable to, say, On-Base Plus Slugging percentage (OPS), because it more accurately reflects the value of each outcome. OPS weighs slugging percentage too heavily relative to OBP. For instance, with the slugging percentage formula, a homer is considered four times as valuable as a single. Two players can have similar OPS figures, yet the value of their offensive contributions may vary significantly. Chase Utley, a highly patient hitter, had an .832 OPS in 2010. Delmon Young, a free swinger, had an .826 OPS. While both were above-average hitters, Utley holds a more than 20-point wOBA advantage (.373 to .352) because he gets on base far more than Young.

Now, on to the teams. First, the "Booms." These guys made fans all warm and fuzzy inside in 2010.

Booms!

Catcher: Carlos Ruiz, Philadelphia Phillies

"Chooch" had what was then the best offensive season of his career in 2009, batting .255/.355/.425 (Batting Average/On-Base Percentage/Slugging Percentage) with a .337 wOBA. Oliver was skeptical that he could keep it up, calling for less pop in 2010. Ruiz was projected for a .235/.330/.356 line and a .309 wOBA. Instead of regressing, Ruiz upped his production to .302/.400/.447, good for a .366 wOBA. His batting average on balls in play (BABIP) was lofty at .335, though Ruiz did increase his line drive rate and hit fewer pop ups. It's highly unlikely that he keeps a BABIP more than 50 points above his career average, but Ruiz's bat (and glove) aided the Phillies in overcoming a plethora of up-the-middle injury problems to clinch the NL East.

First Base: Aubrey Huff, San Francisco Giants

The Giants reportedly pursued Adam LaRoche heavily last winter, supposedly offering him a sizable multi-year deal at one point. Instead, they serendipitously signed Huff. At the time, some (this author included) rolled their eyes at the transaction. Typical Brian Sabean move, right? Sign a generic, geriatric position player whose best days are in the past. Huff was fresh off an abysmal 2009 season split between Baltimore and Detroit in which he batted .241/.310/.384 with a sub-.300 wOBA, played poor defense and was well below replacement-level. Oliver predicted a moderate bounce back to .264/.324/.433 (.330 wOBA), but that's still tepid for a player down the defensive spectrum.

Evidently, someone forgot to tell Huff he was cooked. Drawing more walks than ever before and reclaiming his power stroke, Huff hit .290/.385/.506 and helped lead the Giants to their first playoff appearance since 2003. His .388 wOBA was the best of his career, just beating out his big 2008 campaign with the O's, and Oliver had the long-time defensive butcher saving some runs with the glove between first base and the corner outfield spots. Sometimes Plan B is much, much better than Plan A.

Second Base: Kelly Johnson, Arizona Diamondbacks

Non-tendered by the Braves after a superficially poor 2009, Johnson latched on with the D-Backs last offseason. Despite few changes in his walk and power numbers, Johnson's wOBA dipped from .346 in 2008 to .306 in 2009 due to a 90-plus point freefall in his BABIP. Oliver anticipated a comeback, with a projected .263/.336/.432 line and a .335 wOBA. Johnson bested that by a considerable margin, slashing .284/.370/.496 with a career-best .377 wOBA. Hitting more line drives and fewer pop ups, Johnson had a near-.340 BABIP and posted a .212 ISO that dwarfed his .169 projection. Chase Field surely helped, but Johnson is a solid hitter in a neutral environment and he's adequate afield. He'll remain an asset for Arizona (either as a starter or trade bait) in 2011 as well, as he's got a year of arbitration eligibility left.

Shortstop: Rafael Furcal, Los Angeles Dodgers

Little went right in the land of the McCourts in 2010, but Furcal provided some positive news in the sports pages while owner and marital acrimony dominated the tabloids. Furcal was projected to bat .270/.335/.374 and post a .317 wOBA, yet he raked for a .300/.366/.460 line and a .366 wOBA. The switch-hitter did miss considerable time with hamstring and back maladies, but his wOBA ranked third among shortstops taking at least 400 trips to the plate. Also, he swiped 22 bases in 26 tries (an 85 percent success rate) while getting picked off just once. Furcal is still one of the more talented shortstops in the game, though his lack of durability is troubling.

Third Base: Adrian Beltre, Boston Red Sox

Hitting relatively well considering the power-sapping tendencies of Safeco Field and playing world-class 'D' at third base, Beltre was worth every penny of his free-agent deal with the Mariners that spanned the 2005-2009 seasons. But coming off an injury-plagued 2009, Beltre settled for a one-year deal with the Red Sox last winter in hopes of re-establishing his value and hitting the market again. Suffice it to say, Beltre won't have to settle this offseason. He bashed to the tune of a .321/.365/.553 line and a .390 wOBA, making a mockery of his Oliver projection (.266/.313/.433, .324 wOBA).

Fastballs, curveballs, sliders, changeups, Jacoby Ellsbury, Jeremy Hermida ... you name it, Beltre hit it. Chances are he's not this good of a hitter, but Beltre's a guy with a career .339 wOBA and a sterling defensive reputation. He's one of the more underrated players of the new millennium.

Outfielder: Jose Bautista, Toronto Blue Jays

Prior to 2010, Jose Bautista was Joe Average. Left off the Pirates' 40-man roster after the 2003 season and subsequently taken in the Rule 5 Draft, Bautista pinballed from Baltimore to Tampa Bay, Kansas City to Queens and finally back to the 'Burgh. The Pirates cast him off last August, trading him to Toronto for Robinzon Diaz. From 2004-2009, Bautista had a .320 wOBA and booted his share of balls at third base and the corner outfield spots. Oliver projected a non-descript .318 wOBA and a .233/.326/.396 line in 2010. For a guy who was dubbed "Joey Bats" in Pittsburgh, Bautista's lumber wasn't exactly legendary.

But then, Bautista went bonkers. Batting .260/.378/.617, Bautista pieced together a .422 wOBA that trailed just Josh Hamilton, Joey Votto and Miguel Cabrera among qualified big league hitters. His 54 home runs placed 12 ahead of his closest competitor, Albert Pujols. Bautista's .357 ISO was over 60 points ahead of Cabrera.

Fans sat in the left field bleachers at their own peril, as Bautista bopped 47 of his homers to the pull side. And they got there fast: according to Greg Rybarczyk's Hit Tracker Online, Bautista's average speed of the bat on his big flies was 106.6 mph, compared to the 103.3 mph MLB average. "Joey Bats," indeed.

Per Hit Tracker Online, Bautista led the majors with 19 "No Doubt" home runs, defined as balls that clear the fence by at least 20 vertical feet and land at least 50 feet beyond the fence. But Bautista also had the most "Just Enough" round-trippers, with 13. "Just Enough" home runs are balls that clear the fence by less than 10 vertical feet or land less than one fence height past the fence. Will Bautista remain the most powerful hitter in the game? I have my doubts. But don't dismiss his season, either: Changes in home run rate become significant at about 300 plate appearances, and changes in ISO become significant at about 550 plate appearances. Chances are he retains some these offensive gains. Bautista, eligible for free agency after 2011, should be an interesting arbitration case this winter.

Outfielder: Andres Torres, San Francisco Giants

Torres took a circuitous route to big league playing time. He had two tours of duty in the Detroit organization, passed through both sides of Chicago and also spent a season each with Texas and Minnesota. The fleet-footed switch-hitter had a .379 wOBA in limited time with the Giants last season and he pummeled minor league pitching between the Tigers' and Cubs' affiliates in 2007 and 2008, but he entered 2010 as a 32-year-old with no sustained track record of success.

Oliver adored Torres' center field defense, to the extent that it projected him as nearly an average everyday player despite a punchless .239/.300/.380 (.295 wOBA) offensive prediction. Instead, Torres did his best Carlos Beltran impression. Torres lived up to the billing with the glove, with Oliver claiming he added well over a win in value defensively, but he also hit .268/.343/.479 and had a .363 wOBA. He walked in nearly 10 percent of his plate appearances and popped enough extra-base hits to put up a .211 ISO.

On the bases, Torres was called safe in 26 of his 33 steal attempts (a 79 percent success rate). He was adept at taking the extra base, too. Baseball Reference shows that Torres took an extra base (defined as the rate at which a runner advances more than one base on a single or more than two bases on a double, when possible) 57 percent of the time, compared to the 40 percent NL average. Torres' all-around brilliance made him one of the most valuable players in the game.

Outfielder: Josh Hamilton, Texas Rangers

Hampered by a strained rib cage, a torn abdominal muscle and a pinched nerve in his back in 2009, Hamilton's bat barely made a whimper. He put up a .321 wOBA, batting .268/.315/.426 while rarely showing the top-shelf power of years past. Oliver threw out a .277/.341/.468 projection, with a .350 wOBA. He beat that wOBA by nearly 100 points. In 2010, Hamilton eviscerated pitchers for a MLB-leading .447 wOBA, owning a .359/.411/.633 triple-slash. He got through the 2010 season relatively unscathed until September, when he suffered a rib cage injury that nearly cost him the rest of the regular season.

Hamilton matched his 2008 home run total by going deep 32 times, and established a new career best in ISO (.274). While Bautista was all about the pull power, Hamilton hit 19 of his homers to center field. Some of them might not have landed yet: According to Hit Tracker, Hamilton's jacks had an average "Standard Distance" of 419.1 feet. Standard Distance estimates the distance a home run would travel after factoring out wind, temperature and altitude. The MLB average was 393.6 feet. Hamilton also holds the distinction of hitting the longest Standard Distance homer of the year—485 feet off of Roy Oswalt during a June 27 game at Rangers Ballpark.

No doubt, Hamilton got some fortuitous bounces: his .390 BABIP was second-highest in the majors. But he is a high BABIP hitter (.344 career), with a career line drive rate near 22 percent and a pop up rate below 3 percent (the MLB average is 7-8 percent). The only thing that can stop Hamilton from being a championship-caliber player on a yearly basis is health.

Designated Hitter: Jim Thome, Minnesota Twins

Thome switched AL Central allegiances over the winter, leaving the White Sox to sign a skimpy one-year deal with the Twins. And, despite turning 40 years old late in the season, Thome thumped pitchers like few others in the game. Oliver thought the gregarious slugger would continue a downward slide in 2010, projecting a .348 wOBA and a .231/.347/.447 line. OK, but nothing special for a guy whose only job is to mash. Well, Thome harkened back to his halcyon days with the Indians by slashing .283/.412/.627 and putting up a .437 wOBA, helping to ease the sting of losing Justin Morneau to post-concussion syndrome during the summer. Meanwhile, the South Siders often turned to Mark Kotsay (.297 wOBA) at the DH spot before acquiring Manny Ramirez. Oops.

Starting Pitcher: Francisco Liriano, Minnesota Twins

Back in 2006, Liriano annihilated batters with a sinister upper-80's slider and a tumbling mid-80's changeup. At just 22 years old, the lefty did everything you could ask of a pitcher: He racked up the strikeouts, issued few walks and he kept the ball on the ground. And then, his elbow gave out. Liriano's post-Tommy John pitching in 2008 and 2009 was better than his bloated ERA suggested. But he wasn't the same upper-echelon talent, with solid strikeout rates but diminished control and fewer grounders. In 2010, though, Liriano re-emerged as an ace.

Oliver forecast a shrug-inducing line for Liriano, including these rates per nine innings: 7.7 K/9, 4 BB/9, 1.15 HR/9 and a 4.91 ERA in fewer than 160 innings pitched. A sharp, fully healthy Liriano zoomed by that with a 3.62 ERA, 9.4 K/9, 2.72 BB/9 and 0.4 HR/9 in 191.2 innings. Liriano's ground-ball tendencies returned, as he got batters to smack the ball into the grass 53.6 percent of the time. Stuff-wise, Liriano showed those Tommy John scars are a distant memory. The lefty's fastball climbed from 91-92 mph to nearly 94 mph, and his slider and changeup were sublime. Fangraphs shows that per 100 pitches thrown, Liriano's slider was worth about 1.9 runs above average and his changeup was 0.4 runs above average. The Twins have long been known for having starting staffs with pinpoint control, but Liriano's power arm played a prominent role in clinching the AL Central title.

Now, on to the "Busts." These guys might need a Kenny Powers-style highlight tape to remember the good old days, because 2010 certainly wasn't a year to cherish.

Busts!

Catcher: Bengie Molina, San Francisco Giants/Texas Rangers

The oldest Molina brother frustrated two fan bases this season, drawing the ire of Giants fans as a result of not being Buster Posey and then failing to provide an upgrade behind the plate for the Rangers after a mid-season trade. Always a hacker, Bengie had been a reasonably effective hitter by catching standards by virtue of above-average pop. In 2010, however, those extra-base hits dried up.

Oliver projected Molina for a .269/.294/.431 triple-slash and a .162 Isolated Power, but he limped to a .249/.297/.326 line, with a .077 ISO. As a result, his wOBA, projected to be .311, nosedived to .275. Some might point to Bengie's .259 batting average on balls in play as part of the reason for his struggles. But his career mark is .275, and really, Molina runs like tree sap in winter. He's not beating out many dribblers down the third base line.

First Base: Casey Kotchman, Seattle Mariners

Outside of his 2007 season with the Angels, Kotchman has disappointed his employers with weak offensive showings. That trend continued in a big way with the M's, as his .217/.280/.336 line and .269 wOBA were a far cry from even his lukewarm .266/.333/.407 (.326 wOBA) pre-season Oliver forecast. Known for hitting an infuriatingly high number of power-killing ground balls (more than 53 percent for his career), Kotchman hit the ball downward more than 55 percent of the time in 2010. His BABIP on those grounders was just .155, compared to a career mark of .181, and his line drive BABIP fell to .508 (.685 career average). Consequently, his overall .229 BABIP was nearly 40 points worse than his career average. Unlucky? Maybe. An inadequate hitter for his position either way? You betcha. Kotchman's a skilled fielder, but unless you think his leather saves scads of runs and can find a cure for cancer between innings, he's not starting material.

Second Base: Chone Figgins, Seattle Mariners

Seattle inked Figgins to a four-year deal last offseason, with the long-time Angel coming off the best season of his career. Oliver didn't expect Figgins to reach his offensive heights of 2009, when he hit .298/.395/.393 with a .358 wOBA. But Chone was projected to bat .284/.372/.358, good for a .334 wOBA. Add in quality defense, and Seattle seemed to have added a comfortably above-average starter.

That was the plan, anyway. Figgins' batting line was .259/.340/.306 (.302 wOBA). It has always been rare to see the switch hitter slap the ball for more than a single, but Figgins'

.047 ISO fell short of even his modest .074 projection. After moving from third base to the keystone spot, Figgins rated as below-average defensively to boot.

It's easy to criticize the Mariners' decision to sign Figgins in retrospect, but there was good reason to think he would be a quality starter for the club. I'm not convinced that he's finished, and I'd be surprised if he rates so poorly with the glove again next season. The M's will surely hope for a bounce back from the soon-to-be 33-year-old, who is owed a decent sum of cash through at least 2013.

Shortstop: Derek Jeter, New York Yankees

Put down the pitch forks and torches, Yankees fans. Remember, this isn't a team of the worst players, or even necessarily bad players. Rather, it's a team of those who didn't come close to meeting their preseason Oliver projections. And while Jeter was by no means poor in 2010, he didn't play as well as expected. Coming off a brilliant 2009 campaign, The Captain was projected for a .356 wOBA and a .309/.377/.422 line. But, for the first time in his career, Jeter's bat was below-average. He hit .270/.340/.370, with a .320 wOBA.

Why? His BABIP was nearly 50 points lower than his career average. Jeter has always hit lots of ground balls (57 percent since 2002), but he scorched the earth a major league high 65.7 percent of the time in 2010. Fewer of those ground balls found holes: his BABIP on grounders, .260 since '02, was .239 this past year. Jeter grounded into a double play in 18 percent of his chances, tied for the highest mark of his big league tenure and well above the 11 percent MLB average. The question now becomes, are these figures just a blip on the radar, or are they indicative of a player slowing down as he approaches his late thirties?

Third Base: Jose Lopez, Seattle Mariners

It was a bad year to be a Mariners infielder. Lopez has always been a batter who swings first and asks questions later, but he managed to be an average offensive player in 2008 (.328 wOBA) and 2009 (.325) because of increasing power production. Oliver gave him a .318 wOBA projection for 2010, with a .276/.303/.440 line.

In 2010, he shifted from second base to third to make room for Figgins and became a prime example of the all-glove, no-hit archetype. Oliver shows that Lopez added the better part of a win defensively at his new position. However, his batting line was ghastly: .239/.270/.339, with a .268 wOBA that was second-worst among qualified MLB hitters (thanks, Cesar Izturis!) Lopez continued to swing liberally, but he didn't lash many extra-base hits. His ISO was a career-worst .099, well below Oliver's .163 prediction. Lopez's .254 BABIP may bounce, back, but only relatively. Hitting a below-average number of line drives and popping the ball up more than most, Lopez holds a career .280 BABIP.

Outfielder: Carlos Lee, Houston Astros

The Astros owe Lee stacks-o-cash between now and 2012, and things began to get ugly in 2010. "El Caballo" has long been a liability in the field, but he at least bopped enough to retain some value to his club. That changed this past season. Lee, of whom Oliver expected a .350 wOBA on a .288/.337/.477 line, compiled a paltry .308 wOBA and a .246/.291/.417 triple-slash.

His .238 batting average on balls in play was quite low, but so was his sub-16 percent line drive rate. While some BABIP bounce back should be expected, the larger concern is Lee's fading secondary skills: his walk rate declined for a third straight season to under 6 percent, and his Isolated Power dropped for a third consecutive year as well, down to .170. Add in stationary defense (he got some starts at first base late in the year) and a huge financial commitment, and Houston has the baseball player equivalent of a subprime mortgage.

Outfielder: Nyjer Morgan, Washington Nationals

Morgan was a defensive darling last season, adding well over a win in value in the outfield between Pittsburgh and Washington according to Oliver. The system thought he'd do the same this year, while regressing at the plate as fewer balls put in play evaded gloves (.282/.335/.353, .309 wOBA Oliver projection for 2010, compared to 2009's actual .307/.367/.388 and .340 wOBA). Morgan still rated pretty well defensively, but his bat was even worse than anticipated. He hit .253/.319/.314 with a .287 wOBA in 2010, as his BABIP fell about 50 points.

Morgan was also a wreck stealing bases, serving as a prime example of why we need to look at more than gross stolen base totals to evaluate base thieves. Sure, he swiped 34 bags. But he was caught stealing 17 times and was picked off a staggering 11 times. Morgan did take the extra base 49 percent of the time and grounded into a double play in just 3 percent of his opportunities, making him roughly average overall as a base runner.

Still, Morgan rated as a replacement-level player in 2010. Ironically, the relievers involved in last summer's Morgan-Lastings Milledge trade, Joel Hanrahan and Sean Burnett, provided far more value to the Pirates and Nats than the pair of flailing outfielders.

Outfielder: Jason Bay, New York Mets

Bay, the Mets' big-ticket free agent acquisition, pretty much summed up the season in Queens when he smashed, Wile E. Coyote style, into the Dodger Stadium outfield fence in late July. Unfortunately, Bay suffered a concussion on the play and took the field for the final time in 2010 a few nights later. The collision ended a season in which he hit a mild .259/.347/.402 with a .336 wOBA, far from Oliver's projection of .259/.358/.487 with a .366 wOBA.

Bay's power was conspicuously absent. Forecast for a .228 ISO, he had a .144 ISO that was one point under the big league average. Nothin' much happened when Bay pulled the ball: his wOBA to left field was .351, compared to a career .470 average and a near .420 average for MLB right-handed hitters. Bay's not known for defensive prowess, he's now 32 and he's got at least three years left on his contract. The Mets have to hope this deal doesn't blow up on them like a cheap Acme bomb.

Designated Hitter: Adam Lind, Toronto Blue Jays

Lind scuffled in stints with the Jays in 2007 and 2008, displaying mid-range pop and expanding his strike zone far too often. He seemingly revamped his plate approach in 2009, however, hitting for excellent power (.257 ISO) while raising his walk rate from the 4-5 percent range to nearly 9 percent. Lind's wOBA rocketed to .394 as he hit .305/.370/.562. Oliver didn't expect him to keep all of those gains, projecting a .349 wOBA on a .280/.334/.476 line, but Lind finished the 2010 season a full 40 points below that wOBA figure.

Oliver pretty much nailed his power output, predicting a .196 ISO compared to Lind's actual .188. So, why was Lind's offensive production similar to that of a middle infielder? One of the biggest reasons for the fall was his relapse into hackery: Lind's rate of swinging at pitches out of the strike zone was 2 percent lower than the MLB average in '09, but it spiked to 18 percent over the big league average this year. Consequently, his walk rate dipped to slightly over 6 percent. Lind probably was a bit unlucky—despite little change in his batted ball profile, his batting average on balls in play was 26 points below his career average—but a little patience would go a long way for this lefty hitter.

Starting Pitcher: Javier Vazquez, New York Yankees

No one should have expected Vazquez to replicate his 2009 season with the Braves in the Bronx, not when you consider that '09 was arguably the pinnacle of his career and that he was transitioning back to the DH league. But the well-traveled Vazquez was a shell of his former self during his second stint in pinstripes. Oliver projected that Vazquez would post a 3.65 ERA with 8.8 K/9, 2.2 BB/9 and 1.1 HR/9 in over 200 innings of work. In reality, he had a 5.32 ERA with 6.9 K/9, 3.7 BB/9, 1.8 HR/9 in 157.1 frames. Never a pitcher to wage a ground assault, Vazquez generated grounders just 35.5 percent of the time. That's a problem when home starts are made in a park that, according to StatCorner, increased dinger production by 24 percent for left-handed batters and 10 percent for righties. Vazquez coughed up 2.44 home runs per nine innings at New Yankee Stadium.

Strangely, Vazquez's fastball vanished. He averaged 91-92 mph with the pitch in recent seasons, but he fell to the 88-89 mph range this year. While the veteran righty has never been overly reliant on his fastball, perhaps that loss of zip had a damaging effect on the rest of his repertoire. According to Fangraphs' Pitch Type Run Values, Vazquez's slider was over a run below average per 100 pitches thrown, his curve was -0.8 runs/100 pitches and his changeup was two-tenths of a run below average per 100 tosses. Add in diminished fastball at -0.25 runs/100, and you have a pitcher who was banished from the postseason rotation. He gets the starting assignment here, though.

Conclusion

While looking at these teams, it's important to keep in mind that one year of performance, no matter how great or lousy, should not be taken as a player's new talent level. A player's most recent work is weighed more heavily in future projections, but we can't just ignore how that player hit, fielded and pitched in previous years. Some of the guys on the "Boom" team likely had career-best seasons and will come back to earth to some extent in 2011. The reverse can be said for some of the "Busts": 2010 was hardly a year to remember for these guys, but that doesn't necessarily mean their careers are doomed.

So, who will appear on the "Boom" and "Bust" teams in 2011? I don't know. And that's one of the reasons I love baseball.

The Leaders of 2011

by Oliver

Oliver is The Hardball Times' projection system, developed by Brian Cartwright. It uses a simple weighted mean of the previous three seasons, with aging factors and regression to the mean. Adding extra complication hasn't added any accuracy—what really makes the system shine is the quality of its minor league and international translations.

Unlike other systems, which construct their Major League Equivalencies (MLEs) based on changes in players' statistics from one level to the next, Oliver builds its translations based on how players from any given level perform once they reach the major leagues. The result is a significantly more accurate set of projections for minor league and international players, as well as a greater breadth of forecasts—almost 10,000 forecasts for 2011.

So we're willing to go on record and say that Florida's Mike Stanton, who has just 400 major league at-bats, will finish second in the National League in home runs next year. Here is a list of the ten major league batters we feel will hit the most home runs in 2011:

Batter	HR
Pujols, Albert	40
Stanton, Mike	39
Reynolds, Mark	37
Cabrera, Miguel	36
Dunn, Adam	35
Gonzalez, Adrian	35
Howard, Ryan	35
Fielder, Prince	34
Uggla, Dan	31
Pena, Carlos	29

In case you're wondering, Jose Bautista is just below the top ten with 27 home runs.

Are we certain that Mike Stanton will hit exactly 39 home runs next year? No, of course not. But we are certain that the young right fielder will be high on this list at the end of the 2011 season as long as he stays healthy. We haven't figured out how to predict injuries. Yet.

This past year, Oliver took some flak for predicting that Stephen Strasburg would post a 2.86 ERA when he made the majors. His final ERA? 2.91. I'm just sayin'.

Oliver projects all kinds of baseball stats for all of these players. Here is our prediction for next year's top ten RBI leaders:

Batter	RBI
Pujols, Albert	120
Cabrera, Miguel	114
Stanton, Mike	107
Gonzalez, Adrian	106
Howard, Ryan	103
Fielder, Prince	103
Dunn, Adam	100
Braun, Ryan	99
Teixeira, Mark	98
Uggla, Dan	96

This list looks a lot like the home run list. There's that Stanton kid again.

If you play in a fantasy league, for instance, you may also be interested in next year's leaders in stolen bases. Here's the top ten:

Batter	SB
Bourn, Michael	46
Upton, B.J.	37
Crawford, Carl	36
Pierre, Juan	35
Ellsbury, Jacoby	32
Figgins, Chone	30
Gardner, Brett	29
Andrus, Elvis	28
Davis, Rajai	28
Reyes, Jose	27

No surprises there. There don't appear to be any Mike Stantons among young base stealers.

Oliver goes beyond the standard stats and projects many sabermetric stats as well. For instance, here are the projected top ten batters in weighted On-Base Average (wOBA), a construct of Tom Tango's that measures the overall impact of a batter:

Batter	wOBA
Pujols, Albert	.440
Cabrera, Miguel	.413
Votto, Joey	.400
Mauer, Joe	.397
Gonzalez, Adrian	.395
Fielder, Prince	.391
Ramirez, Hanley	.389
Youkilis, Kevin	.385
Morneau, Justin	.385
Holliday, Matt	.384

Mike Stanton is a fine young hitter, but his specialty is the home run. These are the best overall batters in the majors.

We even have Wins Above Replacement (WAR) projections for all players. WAR is an important stat because it includes the impact of each's player's fielding performance and it also factors in the position that he plays. Here's the top ten list for batters...

Batter	WAR
Pujols, Albert	6.4
Mauer, Joe	6.2
Ramirez, Hanley	5.2
Longoria, Evan	5.2
Cabrera, Miguel	4.4
Holliday, Matt	4.2
Tulowitzki, Troy	4.1
McCann, Brian	4.1
Heyward, Jason	4.0
Stanton, Mike	4.0

...and the top ten list for pitchers:

Pitcher	WAR
Hernandez, Felix	5.8
Halladay, Roy	5.6
Jimenez, Ubaldo	5.3
Wainwright, Adam	5.2
Lincecum, Tim	5.1
Lee, Cliff	5.0
Sabathia, CC	4.8
Greinke, Zack	4.7
Haren, Dan	4.6
Kershaw, Clayton	4.6

Of course, we have all the standard stats for pitchers, too. These are our projected ERA leaders for next year, assuming they qualify by reaching our projected number of innings:

Pitcher	IP	ERA
Kershaw, Clayton	184.0	3.17
Hernandez, Felix	234.8	3.18
Wainwright, Adam	209.2	3.18
Jimenez, Ubaldo	214.0	3.21
Hanson, Tommy	188.8	3.25
Lincecum, Tim	216.9	3.29
Bumgarner, Madison	163.0	3.32
Lewis, Colby	186.8	3.32
Halladay, Roy	241.4	3.34
Johnson, Josh	173.4	3.37

And a strikeout leaderboard:

Pitcher	SO
Lincecum, Tim	248
Haren, Dan	220
Verlander, Justin	216
Hernandez, Felix	204
Greinke, Zack	204
Jimenez, Ubaldo	203
Lester, Jon	199
Halladay, Roy	194
Kershaw, Clayton	192
Sabathia, CC	190

Oliver also extends its projections six years into the future, so not only can we see that Cliff Lee is projected to post a 3.39 ERA next season, but that his ERA will rise half a point by 2015. Moreover, Oliver calculates an error bar around its projection, since no forecast is ever perfect. So while Oliver projects a 1.098 OPS from Albert Pujols next season, it also acknowledges that there's a 25 percent chance it will be below 1.044 and a 25 percent chance it will be above 1.152.

We offer Oliver projections year-round at THT Forecasts (hardballtimes.com/forecasts), along with a slew of other great features, including playing time projections, player comments, injury data, and a fantasy value calculator that can be suited to your league's specific scoring and roster settings. And best of all, we update everything weekly throughout the year.

What this means is that not only will THT Forecasts help you have the best possible fantasy draft this winter, but when, come May, you decide to make some moves, you won't have to rely on dated projections and intuition to figure out who the best available players are. Instead, you'll have updated Oliver forecasts and depth chart projections to help you make the right move all season long.

So visit hardballtimes.com/forecasts, and take a look at everything we offer. It's free to peruse the player cards of the World Series winner, and $14.95 to sign up for everything else. It's a small price to pay for winning your fantasy league.

CARDS' SEASON, 2010

The Business of Baseball

by Brian Borawski

Major League Baseball entered the second year of the Great Recession with a ton of question marks. Would the leagues be able to make gains on their tepid attendance in 2009? Would Minor League Baseball show further signs of resilience? How would a divorce disrupt one of the game's storied franchises? Would teams like the Tampa Bay Rays and the Oakland Athletics make inroads toward getting new stadiums? And what unexpected developments would turn the league on its head?

Here's what happened.

Attendance: Another Notch Down

In 2009, MLB's attendance reached a low it hadn't seen since 2004 with 73.4 million tickets sold. In 2010, there was good news and bad news. The good news was that the 2004 low in attendance stood. The bad news was attendance was down from 2009 to 73 million. This barely beat out 2004 and it's a far cry from the record of 79.5 million tickets sold set back in 2007.

The New York Yankees once again led baseball in attendance in 2010 with 3.8 million. This was up from when they opened their new ballpark and, with a smaller seating capacity, their years of consistently having four million in attendance may be behind them. This also marked the second straight year in which no team topped four million in attendance. Nine teams surpassed the three million mark in 2010—the same as in 2009. Twenty teams topped the two million mark in 2010, up from 19 in 2009.

The Philadelphia Phillies led the National League in attendance and finished second overall with a team record 3.6 million tickets sold. The Los Angeles Dodgers, who led MLB in attendance in 2009, fell to third with just over 3.5 million and the St. Louis Cardinals (fourth) and Los Angeles Angels of Anaheim rounded out the top five. The Minnesota Twins opened Target Field, bringing a boon at the ticket booth. They finished sixth in baseball with 3.2 mililon tickets sold, the team's highest attendance figure since moving to the Twin Cities.

At the bottom of the pile were the Cleveland Indians, who drew just 17,395 fans a game. It's sad to see how far Cleveland has fallen. When the stadium was still called Jacobs Field and the Indians were perennial contenders in the 1990s, they set the record (which has now been broken by the Boston Red Sox) for consecutive sellouts.

Second to last were the Oakland Athletics, who have been clamoring for a new stadium. The lowest National League team was the Florida Marlins at 28th and there's hope that they'll see a boost next year leading up to their new stadium opening in 2012. Many teams see gains the year before a new stadium opens, with ticket buyers seeking season ticket privileges heading into the season with the new ballpark.

The lowest attendance by a playoff team was by the Tampa Bay Rays at 22nd place. In fact the low attendance eventually wore on the players and there was a media outburst regarding the small crowds at the end of the season when the team was ready to clinch a playoff spot. Just ahead of them were the Cincinnati Reds at 20th. The Seattle Mariners, who struggled out of the gate in 2010, still managed to sell more tickets than either of those playoff teams.

The Yankees were first in road attendance with 34,939 tickets sold per game. This is the first time they've been in first place since 2006. The Los Angeles Dodgers were in second place, leading the National League with 33,802 tickets sold per game. The worst road draw was the Chicago White Sox with 26,311 per game—due in part to having both Cleveland and Kansas City in their division.

With attendance still declining, you have to wonder whether teams will start slashing prices. When times are good, teams are almost able to name their price. In this recessionary economy, winning usually sells and the teams that don't win have to get creative. My bet is we'll see more promotions and lower tickets prices across the board in 2011.

Minor League Baseball Holds its Ground

In 2009, Minor League Baseball weathered the recessionary storm a lot more favorably then did the majors. Attendance was down just slightly, and that was off of a record year in 2008. In 2010, we saw the same downward trend, but once again, the decrease was very small. In 2010, Minor League Baseball sold 41,432,456 tickets, an average of 3,992 per game. In 2009, attendance was 41,644,518 with a 4,055 average; that's less then a 0.5 percent decrease.

The Lehigh Valley IronPigs led the minors in attendance in 2010 with 9,227 tickets sold per game. This was after a number two showing the year before. The Sacramento River-Cats came in second at 9,137 tickets sold per game and the Columbus Clippers, who opened a new ballpark and led in attendance in 2009, fell to number three with 8,945. The Gwinnet Braves, who also opened a new ballpark in 2009, saw their attendance decline dramatically in 2010 from 5,965 in 2009 to 4,817.

All teams in the top 10 were Triple-A teams except for one, the Single-A Dayton Dragons. The Dragons have sold out every one of their games since the team began in Dayton; the sellout streak now sits at 774 games. Their 597,433 tickets sold in 2010 broke the Single-A record that they set back in 2004.

The Florida State League, Eastern League and Midwest Leagues all broke records in 2010. In addition, 21 individual teams set new attendance records in 2010. Once again, value rules in Minor League Baseball, which has seen only these slight decreases in tickets sold across the board. With their more family friendly and intimate atmosphere as well as much lower prices, minor leagues are attracting families looking for a night out at a bargain.

An even-numbered year means some affiliations change. Four came about mostly because the Texas Rangers were sold to an ownership group that included two people who owned minor league teams themselves. The Round Rock Express, owned by Ryan-Sanders Baseball, became a Rangers affiliate and the Myrtle Beach Pelicans, who are owned by a group led by Chuck Greenberg, also entered the Rangers' fold. The Houston Astros then effectively swapped Triple-A affiliates with the Rangers and signed on with the Oklahoma City RedHawks while the Braves, who lost the Pelicans as their affiliate, signed on with the Lynchburg Hillcats.

The year also marked the end of the longest affiliation to date. The Baltimore Orioles, deciding not to field an Appalachian League team after 2010, dropped the Bluefield Orioles and ended their 53-year relationship. The Toronto Blue Jays then took on Bluefield. That leaves a tie for the longest affiliation: the Detroit Tigers and their Lakeland Flying Tigers and the Philadelphia Phillies and Reading Phillies. These relationships began in 1967.

Balancing the Books

In November 2009, as the free agent signing period began, super agent Scott Boras contended that baseball was still in a golden age and that some team owners were pocketing many tens of millions of dollars. Boras seemed almost sage-like after what happened in August 2010 when Deadspin.com released a set of leaked financial statements for the Pittsburgh Pirates, Tampa Bay Rays, Florida Marlins, Los Angeles Angels of Anaheim, Seattle Mariners and Texas Rangers.

There was a lot of outrage over some of the teams' financials, especially the Marlins and Pirates. Many speculated that the disclosures would cause a war between the big market teams and the small market teams in the next round of collective bargaining negotiations when the current contract expires at the end of 2011. Others wondered whether it would throw off the free agent signing season for the next couple of years. MLB seemed more concerned about finding out who leaked the financials than what was actually in them.

First off, the teams that pocketed the revenue sharing money did nothing wrong—at least in a legal sense. They're running businesses and decisions are made each year as to what they're going to do with any excess funds. If the owners choose to give the money back to themselves, they are within their rights. Of course these teams also have to answer to their fans and that's where we'll see whether this leak has any effect. Teams like the Pirates, who haven't had a winning team since 1992, have blamed economics, but now it's being revealed that they have more money then they'd indicated.

The Marlins came under fire because they cried "poor" to get a new ballpark only to have it revealed that they too were making a profit. This caused many to want to delve deeper into what the Marlins told the city of Miami to get their ballpark deal and it also resulted in some talks over a renegotiation, but to date, nothing has come of this.

The reaction to the Marlins, and the general reaction to the leaked financial statements, was swift and loud but turned quiet shortly thereafter. The big market teams probably already knew what was going on, so the case for a rift over the collective bargaining agreement was moot. As far as free agent signings, my guess is that we will hear some initial noise, but once the deals start happening, it'll die down again.

Stadium Games

In 2010, one new ballpark opened, another continued its progress and three more struggled to get off the ground. The Minnesota Twins opened Target Field on April 12 to a sellout crowd that was an indicator of things to come. Not only did the Twins go on to win the American League Central, but they also were sixth in overall attendance, selling nearly 40,000 tickets a game.

In October 2009, the Marlins won a lawsuit over local businessman Norman Braman that could have stopped the construction of their new ballpark set to open in 2012. The Marlins then ran into a minor snag when their stadium bond issue was held up by the Securities and Exchange Commission. This put them under audit but in April 2010, they were cleared to sell $75 million in bonds to begin the construction of a parking site near the stadium. This would later become an issue once the Marlins' financial statements were leaked and it was shown that they were profitable.

Las Vegas' mayor, Oscar Goodman, has made it a crusade to bring a major league team to his city. While his term is coming to an end and he's not going to see that happen while he's in office, Goodman proclaimed in late August that the city is closer then ever to picking up a team. He said the city was in talks to build a 45,000-seat stadium and that Vegas had been designated an American League city. With two American League teams looking for ballparks—the Tampa Bay Rays and Oakland Athletics—you wonder if Goodman is just acting as leverage for those teams or if something might actually happen in Sin City.

After giving up on moving to Fremont early in 2009, the Athletics began their quest for a new stadium site. Their main focus was San Jose, but that city is designated as San Francisco Giants territory. It's going to be hard to get anything done without giving some major concessions to the Giants. MLB formed a task force to analyze the A's stadium situation and there was a lot of activity in 2010 despite the fact that the commission still hasn't issued an opinion. Both Oakland and Fremont made further proposals that the A's dismissed. Then in late August, San Jose mayor Chuck Reed made a push to put a stadium proposal on the November ballot. He eventually pulled that proposal back when he got some backlash from the league.

The Rays' push for a new stadium reached a new level of tension as groups began to form to try to move the team to their respective regions. For now, the big issue is that the Rays are bound to Tropicana Field for another 17 years. Stuart Steinberg, the owner of the Rays, has said he'd consider selling the team if he doesn't get a new ballpark and it was announced not too long before the Rays clinched a playoff spot that the team would need to cut payroll next year. For now, the Rays and the city of St. Petersburg have agreed to put their talks on hold until the season is over.

Baseball Teams for Sale

In the fourth quarter of 2009, we had one baseball team sale close, one more kick off in a big way and another show the fruits of a potential sale.

After a bankruptcy, the Tribune Company was finally able to unload a 95 percent stake in the Chicago Cubs for the healthy price of $845 million to a group led by the Ricketts family, which made its money with the online brokerage firm TD Waterhouse. Tribune kept five percent to defer the gain on the sale. In a way, the Cubs sale and its exit from bankruptcy was a smooth precursor to what would happen to the Texas Rangers.

In 2009, rumors began to surface that Tom Hicks, the owner of the Texas Rangers, had missed some debt payments and that he was going to shop the team. By October 2009, things had been whittled down to three potential buyers. Chuck Greenberg was a minor league baseball team owner and Pittsburgh sports attorney. Jim Crane was a Houston businessman who made a run at buying the Cubs. Dennis Gilbert, a former player and sports agent, was the third candidate.

Then things got interesting. In late November, Hicks decided to put his own group of investors together to try to sell a piece of the team, yet keep his majority ownership. This didn't last long, though. Hicks' group started with Hall of Fame pitcher Nolan Ryan, but a rift developed between the two when Hicks tried to strike a deal with Gilbert. Under the terms, Hicks would have retained majority ownership but Gilbert would have taken over Ryan's job, which included control over day-to-day operations. Ryan then said that if Gilbert was involved, he was gone. Hicks eventually backed away from the plan.

In late December, Hicks entered into exclusive negotiations with the group led by Greenberg, which now included Ryan. After that, things moved pretty quickly and in late January, Hicks agreed to sell the team to Greenberg for $575 million. However, since Hicks was in bankruptcy, he needed his creditors' approval.

A couple of weeks after Hicks agreed to the sale, reports surfaced that some of Hicks' creditors didn't think he got full value from Greenberg. By late April, nothing had been resolved and it appeared that MLB might step in and take control of the team to push the sale through. In May, the ball club actually filed for bankruptcy to try to expedite the sale. In July, it was finally decided that there would be an auction for the team and if Greenberg's group didn't win it, he'd get $15 million for his troubles.

Then Mark Cuban entered the picture. Cuban, the owner of the Dallas Mavericks who had made a run at the Cubs, became a late entrant as a bidder for the Rangers. The auction was initially set for mid-July but the creditors were able to push it back into early August so they could drum up as much interest in the team as possible. The creditors tried to push it back even further but the bankruptcy judge wouldn't approve the extension, so late into the night on Aug. 4, the Rangers were sold to the highest bidder.

Cuban's largest bid of $581 million was topped by Greenberg's $593 million, and after months of legalities, the team was finally sold. MLB approval came quickly and Greenberg and Ryan began making plans for the team's future.

In other transaction news, Great Court Capital, a New York investment firm, expressed an interest in buying the Houston Astros from Drayton McLane in January, 2010 for a reported $650 million. McLane entered into a 30-day exclusive negotiating agreement with the firm, but the deadline came and went without a sale.

There were no other sales in 2010 but late in 2009, rumors began to swirl that Los Angeles Dodgers owner Frank McCourt and his wife, Jamie, had separated. This eventually led to Jamie being fired from her role with the team and things have been nasty ever since. While there was speculation that the team would be sold, nothing has happened on that front as we've gone to press. As for the divorce, that deserves its own section, courtesy of Josh Fisher:

Special Report of the Absurd: Dodgers Divorce

The McCourt divorce represents a perfect nexus between baseball, business and celebrity gossip. To really understand why it has become the saga it has, one must go back to 2003. The Los Angeles Dodgers were under Fox ownership, and hemorrhaging cash. Fox, which had acquired the club mainly to block a potential Disney bid, clearly had little interest in holding onto the team long-term. It put the Dodgers on the block, and Frank and Jamie McCourt bit.

Having failed on bids for the Red Sox and Angels, the McCourts' third attempt at ownership was indeed charmed. Without putting a dime of their own into the purchase, the McCourts acquired the Dodgers for close to $431 million, before generous rebates that Fox termed "training wheels." Fox, which kept the broadcast television rights to the Dodgers, would eventually accept as payment 24 acres of South Boston waterfront property. For the McCourts, it was something of a miracle: They had turned parking lots into one of the premier franchises in American sports.

The magic, though, was superficial. On the day they moved to Los Angeles, the McCourts together signed a marital property agreement that separated the couple's assets. The couple's considerable residential real estate holdings were allocated to Jamie, and the Dodgers to Frank. The point was to protect their homes in case the Dodgers acquisition failed: In theory, the agreement could keep creditors away from the homes.

This formula, as a McCourt financial advisor put it, enabled the couple to engage in risky business practices because the protected homes provided a nest egg. And there are few transactions riskier than buying a baseball team entirely on credit. In any case, the McCourts finally had their baseball team, and the Dodgers finally had family ownership again. And, in the beginning, it was good.

Stories, of course, have middles and ends, too. And things got ugly in the middle. The marriage became strained and, whether it was a cause or result of the strain, the couple began to look at their marital property agreement a little more closely. In 2008, Jamie and Frank consulted with an estate planning attorney who informed them that, in the context of a divorce, the Dodgers would be Frank's alone. After several months of consideration, Frank decided in the spring of 2009 that he would not change the agreement. This appears to have been the final straw: Jamie moved out shortly thereafter, and filed for divorce in October of that year. She claimed, at the time of her filing, that the agreement did not do what she thought it did when it was signed, and that it was never supposed to have this effect in case of divorce.

It must be noted that the world had changed considerably from 2004 to fall 2009. The Dodgers acquisition, once risky, had become incredibly profitable. Conservative estimates placed the Dodgers at nearly twice the price the McCourts paid in 2004. And the residential real estate market had ceased to exist. So the property agreement, which offered Jamie peace of mind and a sizable nest egg in 2004, worked much differently in 2009. Still, Frank said, Jamie got what she wanted in the agreement, and, as a lawyer, she should not be allowed to say she didn't understand the document. The relationship had so deteriorated that the couple missed a chance to save months and months of public scrutiny not just of themselves, but how the Dodgers operate under their watch.

Because the McCourts failed to settle the issue before it went public, Dodgers finances were exposed for all to see. It was reported that the McCourts took nearly $400 million out of the club over the years, all while paying no personal income taxes. Further, it became clear that the couple used the Dodgers as their personal credit card; what the team didn't pay for directly—private jet travel, luxury accommodations, hair stylists on demand—it subsidized by giving the McCourts a cut of the loan proceeds, some secured by future ticket sales. This largely outraged Dodgers fans, who suddenly noticed the team's failure to invest in young talent and consistent willingness to part with top prospects for veteran Band-Aids. It was an ugly, ugly winter.

It didn't get a whole lot better as the Aug. 30 trial date approached. Late in the game, it was disclosed to Jamie's attorneys that, among the six copies of the agreement the couple signed in 2004, three contained an exhibit completely opposite to the comparable exhibit on the other copies. Long story short: One copy gave the Dodgers to Frank, the other put the Dodgers in the couple's community property bucket.

To make matters worse, the attorney who drafted the agreement and gave it to the McCourts for their signatures switched out the "mistaken" exhibit days after it was signed and notarized without ever informing the McCourts. What's more, the same attorney was, in 2004, also engaged to represent Frank alone in his acquisition of the Dodgers.

Jamie's attorneys, at trial, offered the compelling argument that Jamie never had a fair shot when it came to the agreement. Frank's lawyers countered with evidence that Jamie never knew of the "mistaken" version and got exactly what she wanted in the "correct" one. With the parties unable to reach a settlement on the eve of final arguments, the case went to Judge Scott Gordon on Sept. 29, to be settled by the holiday season.

If the McCourts don't settle, Gordon's decision will inevitably lead to more litigation. Each party has other theories it will press in separate trials, and the loser will certainly appeal the judge decision. The litigation has the potential to go on for months, if not years, but the potential outcomes are not that difficult. Whether by settlement or his own victory, the Dodgers might end up in Frank's hands. Should Jamie win, the value of the Dodgers would have to be split, which would seemingly lead to a sale.

In any case, the McCourts' Hollywood story, with its superficially nice beginning and tumultuous middle, is heading toward an uncertain end. The Dodgers go into the offseason with several glaring issues, but perhaps none more important, and more difficult to fix, than the fractured relationship between the club's owners and its customers.

- Josh Fisher

Spring Training Wars

For the first time in a long time, there were no defections from Florida to Arizona, although that doesn't mean there wasn't any activity on the spring training front. In fact, now it looks like the battle is more within Arizona then between the Grapefruit and Cactus Leagues. In November 2009, the Arizona Diamondbacks and Colorado Rockies broke ground on Salt River Fields at Talking Stick near Phoenix. The facility will be the first on Native American soil and it leaves Tucson without a spring training team after having three teams just a few years ago.

At about the same time as the Rockies and Diamondbacks were breaking ground, the Cubs began shopping their spring training digs. The team had the option of buying out its contract with Mesa after the 2012 season, giving the Cubs a jump on either finding a new home or pushing for Mesa to upgrade the facilities there. Naples, Fla., became a point of interest initially and this noise prompted Mesa to move: In January 2010, the city released a proposal to spend $84 million to keep the Cubs there. A few weeks later, and despite some heavy courting by Naples, the Cubs decided to stay in Mesa, assuming the new facility.

Initially, the state tried to push a ticket surcharge on all spring training games in the state to pay for the facility. Most of the teams were very much for the Cubs staying in Mesa, but they also didn't want to pay for the team's new complex. The Diamondbacks proposed that the Cubs use Tax Increment Financing to fund the new stadium. In March, the Cubs proposed using a $1 surcharge on rental cars. By fall, this issue hadn't been resolved, and Mesa voters were to be asked on the November ballot to vote on a stadium initiative that didn't spell out how the stadium is going to be paid for.

There also was some infighting in Florida. The Cincinnati Reds moved into their new complex in Arizona, prompting Sarasota to begin looking for a team to replace them. After courting, then failing to bring in, the Red Sox, the city persuaded the Baltimore Orioles to abandon Fort Lauderdale for Sarasota.

George Steinbrenner

On July 13, 2010, New York Yankees owner George Steinbrenner died of a heart attack in his Tampa home. While Steinbrenner hadn't been heavily involved with the team the last couple of years as his health faltered, he will be remembered as one of the most successful and controversial owners in any sport. I'll probably take my knocks for saying this, but what George Steinbrenner built was good for baseball. The Yankees helped sell out even losing teams and the Yankees contributed more profit-sharing and luxury tax money to the leagues' pot then any other team.

The Yankees were either loved for their success or hated for it, but you have to have teams that people love to hate. The result of 37 years of Steinbrenner ownership was seven World Series titles and an increase in the value of the team of well over a billion dollars.

Parting Words

In a lot of ways, 2010 was a stabilizing year. The Cubs and Rangers should now be able to move forward without the ownership issues that have been plaguing them. Attendance fell, but not nearly as much as the past two years, and there's even been a slowdown in the activity within the spring training locations.

Still, it'll be interesting to see how the end of 2010 and 2011 play out. Who will win the McCourt divorce battle? Will the Athletics and Rays get their new stadiums moving? What kind of wrench will the economy throw the league heading into the next round of collective bargaining negotiations next year? In short, a lot got resolved but the theme remains unchanged: always stay tuned.

At the Ballpark in the 21st Century

by Larry Granillo

Depending on who you ask, the experience of going to a baseball game over the last half-century has either changed immensely or hardly changed at all. For those who value the finer details of the traditional experience, a ballgame in 2010 may be hard to appreciate with the constant stream of music, scoreboard games, trivia and public urgings to "Get loud!" But for those who experience a trip to the ballpark on the whole, who view the game on the field as the main attraction and the experience in the stadium as merely window dressing, a 2010 ballgame may be no different than a 1980 ballgame or a 1950 ballgame. After all, the essence of the game—nine guys on each side, the tension of the pitcher/batter confrontation, fans cheering for their heroes and booing their opponents—is still the same in any decade.

There is no doubt, however, that the details of a typical ballpark experience are changing. With expansion and relocation, Major League Baseball has seen new teams in roughly 12 new cities since 1969. Coupled with the new ballpark craze of the last 15 years, that's suddenly a lot of new tradition that needs to be created where there never was any before. Teams are bound to experiment with new ideas and copy those that they see succeed elsewhere until they find what works best for their fans.

Now that we're 10 years into the 21st century, it's worth asking how these new changes and refinements are working out, especially considering the way the Internet, mobile communications, and satellite/cable TV have seemingly shrunk the nation. Is there reason to worry about where the in-stadium experience is heading, or can we all take a cue from the holistic fans and relax about the future?

It's a beautiful day at Wrigley Field—peeking out from behind the clouds are the blue skies and sunny weather you come to expect in Chicago in early August. There's a nice breeze blowing out to center field. It's the eighth inning and starter Randy Wells has held the first-place Reds to only one run. Drew Stubbs steps to the plate, already one-for-two on the afternoon, and promptly deposits the 1-0 pitch into the left-field bleachers to break the tie and give Cincinnati the late lead. Heading back to your seats, you turn the corner to enter the tunnel and see Stubbs' home run ball take a funny bounce and come right at you. Excitedly, you grab the ball out of the air and begin to celebrate your good luck until you hear shouts of "Throw it back! Throw it back!" That's all the encouragement you need—after all, this is Wrigley Field and visiting team home runs don't belong in the bleachers. You quickly wind up and throw that ball

as hard as you can back onto the field as everyone in the crowd cheers you on. There will be no Cincinnati celebrations on your watch.

As the second-oldest park in the major leagues, there are a few things completely synonymous with Wrigley Field: brick walls, ivy, day baseball, Ferris Bueller, Old Style, snagging home runs out on Waveland Avenue, and throwing back any home run balls not slugged by the boys from the North Side. It's all part of the aura and tradition of that great venue, and each has been going on for decades.

It is reported that the tradition of throwing back "enemy" home run balls began in 1969, when one of the original "Bleacher Bums" threw a Hank Aaron home run ball back on the field on the spur of the moment. The accuracy of the story may be questionable—not only is it unverifiable that he was the first person ever to throw a ball back, it also seems a little suspicious that it was started by a semi-famous Cubs fan on a home run hit by one of the most famous home run hitters of all time—but it does give a pretty good time frame on the beginnings of the tradition.

Forty years later, it isn't only Cubs fans who are eager to reject souvenirs from their opponents. Fans in other cities have taken to the tradition with glee. And while it may not be something you see every night in every city, it is getting more and more popular. Fans in Philadelphia, Texas, and Detroit are the most common imitators of the tradition, while the new Target Field in Minneapolis and the new Yankee Stadium in New York also have their fair share. Other home teams that have seen the practice this year: Atlanta, Florida, Milwaukee, Kansas City, San Francisco, St. Louis and Tampa Bay. (And that's just what you find when you watch home run highlights. There are likely many more that the cameras ignore.)

It's fair to say that the practice is becoming more and more common throughout the league. Should fans be concerned that a Wrigley Field tradition is overtaking their home ballparks?

It's Thursday afternoon at Miller Park and the third-place Brewers are hosting the first-place Twins. It's now the middle of the sixth and Minnesota's Brian Duensing is busy getting ready to face the bottom of the Brewers lineup. But you're not interested in that—not now, not with the Miller Park Racing Sausages running onto the field. You rise to your feet along with the other 35,000 Brewers and Twins fans and start cheering loudly for your sausage of choice. Being of German ancestry yourself—and considering your deep love for a grilled brat—it's bratwurst all the way for you. As the sausages race pass the visitor's dugout on the third base side, you glance over to make sure that Randall Simon hasn't secretly signed on with the Twins. The race quickly ends, with bratwurst winning it all. You cheer and high-five your buddy. It's a good day, though you are a bit puzzled by how this can be only the brat's third win of the year when no other sausage has fewer than five wins. (And the Polish has 10!) You have no time to ponder it—you're off to find a brat.

The Klements Racing Sausages became a live-action staple at Brewers games in the mid-1990s. After running the sausage races on the video scoreboard between the bratwurst, Polish, and Italian sausages, the costumed meats began racing in person to the delight of the crowd in 1994. A fourth sausage, the hot dog, was added a little while later. Since then, the four sausages have raced in every Brewers home game at County Stadium and Miller Park. (A fifth sausage, the chorizo, was added in 2006.) If there's one tradition that Milwaukeeans can be proud to call their own, it's the Klements Sausage Race.

The Brewers are far from alone in holding costumed mascot races, though. Fans in Pittsburgh, for example, are treated on a nightly basis to four racing pierogies—Jalapeño Hannah, Cheese Chester, Sauerkraut Saul, and Oliver Onion. The Great Pierogi Race, Pittsburgh's shenanigans-free foot race of costumed local food items, is the closest thing to Milwaukee's Sausage Race in the major leagues.

In Washington, the Nationals delved into the city's history to treat their fans to a race between Mt. Rushmore's four presidents: George Washington, Thomas Jefferson, Abraham Lincoln, and Teddy Roosevelt. But the Nats give their fans a little twist: in five years of live racing, the Teddy Roosevelt mascot has never won a single race. Something similar occurs in Atlanta during the Home Depot Tool Race. The race—between a hammer, a paint brush, a saw, and a drill—always ends with the drill getting knocked down and taken out of the running.

In Phoenix, the Arizona Diamondbacks added their own little spice to the format this year. The newly debuted race features four mascots running the field, like every other team. For the Diamondbacks, though, the four mascots are 10-foot tall likenesses of some of the best players in Diamondbacks history. The four legends are: Randy Johnson, Luis Gonzalez, Matt Williams, and Mark Grace. Much like Teddy Roosevelt in Washington and the drill in Atlanta, the Mark Grace mascot gets to play the role of the "loser."

These aren't the only mascot races run today. A tradition that started in Milwaukee fifteen years ago is now replicated by at least half a dozen clubs. The fans in each city never seem to mind the duplication, though. They're always too busy cheering on their favorite racer.

The weather is a bit cool and you find yourself wondering why you didn't wear long pants to a Tuesday night game at Fenway Park in early May. At least the Red Sox are beating up on the Blue Jays pretty good, 6-1, as Aaron Hill grounds out to third to end the top of the eighth. You stand and cheer the out with the crowd as the Red Sox leave the field. But no one sits down. They all know what's coming next: the opening chords to Neil Diamond's "Sweet Caroline" make their way out of the ballpark's speakers. It isn't long before the crowd starts singing along with good ol' Neil. "Sweet Caroline! ... BUM BUM BUM ... Good times never seemed so good ... SO GOOD SO GOOD SO GOOD!" It's hard to disagree.

Singing at the ballpark is nothing new or unique. "Take Me Out to the Ballgame" has been a staple for over half a century, and other crowd-singing traditions are nearly as old. In Baltimore, for example, fans have been singing along to John Denver's "Thank God I'm a Country Boy" since Frank Cashen brought it to Memorial Stadium in 1975.

Clevelanders, who can visit the Rock and Roll Hall of Fame and Progressive Field in the same day, sing along to Ohio's own state rock song, "Hang On, Sloopy." Brewers fans zing, boom, and tar-rar-rel along to the "Beer Barrel Polka" on a nightly basis, while visitors to Minute Maid Park admire the stars at night "Deep in the Heart of Texas." "Build Me Up, Buttercup," "Louie, Louie," and "Shout!" are also popular staples at various major league ballparks.

But the in-stadium tradition that seems to resonate the most these days is a relatively young one. No doubt buoyed by the team's recent World Series success (and the increase in nationwide fans that breeds) and by being featured in major motion pictures, the eighth inning singalong to Neil Diamond's "Sweet Caroline" at Fenway Park is incredibly popular. On some nights, the sell-out crowd might never be louder than they are when "singing" the triple-note trumpet blast.

The fact that "Sweet Caroline" didn't become a nightly tradition until 2002 doesn't seem to detract from the experience. To many, it even feels timeless.

It's early September and the Mets are visiting Atlanta for the last time this year. At the start of the year, most pundits had predicted this series to mean something—for the Mets. No one expected the first-place Braves to be battling the fourth-place Mets, but that's how it is. As you walk around Turner Field before first pitch, you pause behind the left-field bullpen to watch the grounds crew finish up. While they do that, you pull out your phone and connect to Twitter. It's a Braves home game and that means the ballpark's organist is online telling Braves fans what tunes he's going to play for the various Mets batters as they walk to the plate. Last night, you learn, he alternated between "Camptown Races" and "Zip-a-Dee-Doo-Dah" for the appropriately named Lucas Duda. Tonight, it seems Johan Santana will get a smattering of Johann Sebastian Bach as his walkup music while Joaquin Arias will have to suffer through the "Age of Aquarius." You see that and smile. Sometimes it's awful fun to be a Braves fan in the twenty-first century.

Not everything is rooted in the past. Major League Baseball, making use of its excellent MLB Advanced Media, has done a lot to open itself up to the twenty-first century. Its flagship internet television product, MLB.tv, is an easy and affordable way to watch games across the league and Gameday shows pitch-by-pitch information, including pitch type, speed and batted-ball type, in nearly real time. After the games are over, nearly every meaningful play is highlighted and tagged for easy viewing the next day, week, or year. To top it off, all of this power is also available to the fan at the ballpark, provided he or she has access to a smartphone.

But it's not just Major League Baseball itself that is reaching out to the fans of today—clubs are finding ways to do so at the ballpark. Fans at Seattle's Safeco Field, for example, can connect to the "Nintendo Fan Network" with their portable Nintendo DS gaming systems and use them to order food right to their seats. In San Francisco, the Giants offer a similar service. The Giants WiFi Network gives fans the ability to watch in-game video highlights "moments after they occur," locate food options, or read captions of the public address announcements.

The most inventive initiative is happening in Atlanta, where the Braves are ingeniously mixing the old and new. For years, the trend has been for stadiums to move towards pre-recorded music for at-bat songs, closer entrances, mid-inning entertainment, etc. It's gotten to the point now that live organ music is almost quaint. But not at Turner Field, where the Braves' organist, Matthew Kaminski, solicits advice online from Braves fans on what humorous songs he can play for

opposing batters. On a given night, fans may hear anything from Beethoven to Hank Williams to Van Halen to Lady Gaga. The response has been overwhelmingly positive, proving the experiment to be a great success. It's only the first in what is sure to be a long line of online interactive experiences between fan and club.

In the 1970s and 1980s, traditionalists were complaining about the introduction of modern-day music to the ballpark experience. When the Orioles started playing "Thank God I'm a Country Boy" during the seventh-inning stretch, it did not sit well with everyone. Only 10 years later, when a new front office considered taking it away, the backlash was resounding. It didn't take long for fans to embrace a new change as a full-on tradition. The league caught on and the idea quickly (and successfully) spread to other ball clubs.

Things are no different today. Teams are always looking for something unique and new to bring to their fans. Some of the ideas will work out and be embraced for generations to come; others will die a quick and forgotten death. The only common thread among those that survive is that they will always be something that appeals to the local fans in a real and unique way. It is for that reason that one can see a Cubs game and a Red Sox game in the same week and not feel like the two are identical, no matter how similar the ballpark entertainment is. Somehow, the detailed traditionalist and the holistic fan are appeased at the same time. It's not easy, but ballclubs have figured out how to make it work for over a century. There's no reason to think that they won't be able to continue to do so no matter what conveniences (or "distractions") a new generation of fan brings with them.

What Were They Really Worth?

by Vince Gennaro

What defines a "good" versus "bad" free agent signing by a major league team? There is a temptation to immediately gravitate toward the outcome of a past deal as the primary criterion for success or failure. One might ask, "Did the player perform up to expectations, based on the value of his contract?" The Carl Pavano signing by the Yankees in 2005 is a good example of the outcome bias overwhelming the evaluation of a deal. Most would claim it was a terrible deal for the Yankees, based entirely on the fact that the Yankees got only 26 starts out of Pavano, whose injuries for most of his four years in pinstripes earned him the ignominious title, "American Idle."

While the outcome—in this example, actual performance—is one factor in judging the success of a past free agent signing, it's far too narrow to be used as the only measuring stick. It allows potentially unforeseen injuries to dominate judgment and tends to ignore the role of luck or chance. We can add more depth to the analysis by evaluating the quality of the signing decision, including the terms of the contract, which sheds light on something teams control completely—their decision processes. Doing so can sometimes lead to a very different conclusion about the merits of a contract. What constitutes a good decision to sign a free agent to a particular contract? Could the Pavano signing be a case of good decision/bad outcome? By separating decisions and outcomes, we can differentiate between deals that are "bad decision/good outcome" versus "good decision/bad outcome," and the full range of possibilities.

Evaluating a Free Agent Signing Decision

To do a thorough evaluation of a free agent signing decision, we would ideally know the data available to the decision-makers: medical reports on the player, the team's assumption about its level of competitiveness for the upcoming season, and the revenue opportunity that winning presents for the signing team. Short of having all of these details, I used my statistical analysis that models the behavior of the free agent market (see the sidebar "What Does the Market Value in Free Agency?") as a proxy for the market's fair valuation of any player. By running any player's stats and attributes through the model, we can estimate what the free agent market would pay in terms of average annual value (AAV) and contract length in the year the player reached free agency. To keep this simple, if the signing team paid the price dictated by the model (plus or minus 10 percent), we will call it a "fair

deal." If they overpaid in terms of dollars and years, we will call it a "bad deal," and if the team paid the player less than the model's estimate of his value, it's labeled a "good deal." But first, to be fair to the teams' decision-makers we need to make two adjustments to the model's estimates. Recognizing that the market value of players can be situational, we will adjust for whether a team could be reasonably expected to contend for the postseason, as well as the size of its revenue base.

One of the realities of major league baseball is that revenues are apt to rise when a team reaches the postseason. Contending teams stand to gain far more than a 75-win team when adding a key free agent. We can make the case that adding a big free agent to an 87-win team has a reasonable probability of vaulting the club into the postseason, thereby unlocking a $20-$50 million revenue stream. The same cannot be said of the free agent being added to the 75-win team. To incorporate this reality into our criteria we make an adjustment for contending teams. If a team that is expected to contend signs a free agent, we allow it to spend 10 percent over the model's estimated market value for any player and still rationalize it as a fair deal, as it's likely the increased revenues from being competitive will cover the premium salary paid.

Finally, we know that high revenue teams tend to pay additional dollars for the same quality of talent in the free agent market. This premium is often justified by their higher revenues. A contending New York Mets team is likely to have a bigger revenue gain than a contending Kansas City Royals team. In our evaluation of signing decisions, the Dodgers, Angels, Cubs, White Sox, Yankees, Mets, and Red Sox are permitted to spend an extra 10 percent premium for a player, before we consider it an overpay situation. To summarize our adjustments to the output of the free agent model, our criteria allows for a 10 percent premium to the model's estimate for each of two factors: the competitiveness of the team and the size of the revenue base.

Let's use Ryan Dempster's $13 million average annual value (AAV), four-year contract with the Cubs prior to the 2009 season as an example of how the adjustments work. The model estimates his value in the 2009 market to be $13.5 million per year. However, we can add $1.35 million (+10 percent) to the estimate because the Cubs were coming off a 97-win playoff season and were expected to once again be competitive in 2009, and another $1.35 million due to their standing as a high revenue team. The net result is the Cubs could pay up to $16.2 million AAV and still feel like they got a fair deal. The actual $13 million price tag yields a bargain, so this would be termed a good decision by the Cubs.

Conversely, let's look at Gil Meche, who signed a five-year $11 million AAV deal with the Kansas City Royals in 2007. The model estimates his worth at $8.5 million, with no additions, since the Royals were not expected to be competitive, nor are they a large market team. This would lead us to classify the Meche signing as a bad decision.

The contracts of Meche and Dempster are still in progress, set to expire after the 2011 and 2012 seasons, respectively, so let's focus on free agent contracts that are completed. That way, we can evaluate both the decision and the outcome of the deals. Continuing with the evaluation of the decision to sign a player (we will discuss the verdict on the outcome later), I chose 30 recent contracts (signed since 2004) that are split evenly among good, fair, and bad decisions. See the complete list below.

"Good" Signing Decisions by Teams

Free Agent	Team (Year)	Actual AAV (Years)	Estimated AAV	% Difference
Pedro Martinez	NYM (2005)	$ 13.3 (4)	$15.90	20%
JD Drew	LAD (2005)	$ 11.0 (5)	$15.10	37%
Jason Varitek	BOS (2005)	$ 10.0 (4)	$12.80	28%
Jason Schmidt	LAD (2007)	$ 15.7 (3)	$21.00	34%
Gary Sheffield	NYY (2004)	$ 13.0 (3)	$15.20	17%
Vicente Padilla	TEX (2007)	$ 11.3 (3)	$13.60	21%
Greg Maddux	CHC (2004)	$ 8.0 (3)	$9.50	19%
Brian Giles	SDP (2006)	$ 10.0 (3)	$11.90	19%
Mike Mussina	NYY (2007)	$ 11.5 (2)	$18.00	57%
Jeff Kent	LAD (2005)	$ 8.5 (2)	$10.70	26%

"Fair" Signing Decisions by Teams

Free Agent	Team (Year)	Actual AAV (Years)	Estimated AAV	% Difference
Billy Wagner	NYM (2006)	$ 10.8 (4)	$9.90	-8%
Vladimir Guerrero	LAA (2004)	$ 14.0 (5)	$13.50	-3%
Johnny Damon	NYY (2006)	$ 13.0 (4)	$13.20	2%
Carl Pavano	NYY (2005)	$ 10.0 (4)	$10.70	7%
Ivan Rodrgiuez	DET (2004)	$ 10.0 (4)	$10.50	5%
Derek Lowe	LAD (2005)	$ 9.0 (4)	$8.40	-7%
Bengie Molina	SFG (2007)	$ 5.3 (3)	$4.80	-9%
Andy Pettitte	HOU (2004)	$ 10.5 (3)	$10.50	0%
Omar Vizquel	SFG (2005)	$ 4.1 (3)	$4.40	-7%
Matt Clement	BOS (2005)	$ 8.5 (3)	$9.30	9%

"Bad" Signing Decisions by Teams

Free Agent	Team (Year)	Actual AAV (Years)	Estimated AAV	% Difference
Miguel Tejada	BAL (2004)	$12.0 (6)	$10.00	-17%
Jeff Suppan	MLW (2007)	$10.5 (4)	$5.70	-46%
Richie Sexson	SEA (2005)	$12.5 (4)	$7.20	-42%
Russ Ortiz	ARZ (2005)	$8.3 (4)	$4.50	-46%
Julio Lugo	BOS (2007)	$9.0 (4)	$5.70	-37%
Raul Ibanez	SEA (2004)	$4.4 (3)	$2.20	-50%
Adam Eaton	PHL (2007)	$8.2 (3)	$4.30	-48%
Ramon Hernandez	BAL (2006)	$6.9 (4)	$5.10	-26%
Kyle Farnsworth	KCR (2009)	$4.6 (2)	$1.30	-72%
Magglio Ordonez	DET (2005)	$15.0 (5)	$9.00	-40%

For example, Jason Varitek's four-year $40 million deal with the Red Sox, signed amidst the euphoria of their first world championship in 86 years, is judged to be a good decision. When the free agent model considered Varitek's position, age, durability, and past performance, it acknowledged the deal as fair. (Note: the free agent model implicitly assumes all players have medical clearance and are not carrying an injury into their contract negotiations.) When we add in the adjustments for competitiveness and market size, the deal rises a notch to good. A second example is the controversial case of the infamous Carl Pavano and his 2005 contract with the New York Yankees. The model judges Yankee general manager Brian Cashman's decision to settle on a four-year $40 million deal as a fair one. In other words, my analysis implies that any reasonable person in Cashman's shoes at the time would have viewed the deal favorably, as there were no red flags or glaring issues with which to contend. An example of a bad signing is Richie Sexson's 2005, four-year $50 million deal with Seattle Mariners. Based on the slugger's track record, age and other factors, a four-year $29 million deal would have been a fair value, suggesting the Mariners overpaid by about 42 percent, according to the model.

Sidebar: What Does the Market Value in Free Agency?

We can learn a lot about how general managers and owners think by studying the free agent market. Some might be inclined to say that every transaction is unique, so how much can we really glean from what goes on from November to March each year? However, by analyzing the 800+ free agent signings since November 2003, clear patterns and themes emerge—enough to draw some conclusions about which attributes and performance measures teams explicitly or implicitly value, and to quantify their impact on both a free agent's average annual value (AAV) and length of his contract.

My analysis starts by recognizing that the free agent market is not one market, but rather a combination of several markets. For example, following the 2003 season both Miguel Tejada and Miguel Cairo hit the free agent market, with Tejada securing a six-year, $72 million deal with the Orioles and Cairo signing a one-year, $900,000 deal with the Yankees. When teams sign long-term, high-value deals, they base their decisions on different factors and considerations than one-year, low-value deals. When signing a player to a high value, multi-year deal teams typically expect a high-impact player and must be keenly aware of the player's injury risk and durability and the potential for declining performance as the player ages. All of these issues carry relatively less importance on one-year, low-value deals. The driving factor is the amount of dollars at risk. Over the last seven years, the average one-year deal was worth about $2 million in guaranteed salary, while the average multi-year deal was a three-year, $19 million contract. This reality led me to segment free agent deals, analyzing multi-year deals separately from one-year deals.

I statistically analyzed the 800+ free agent transactions from November 2003 through March 2010, dividing them into four groups—multi-year versus one-year deals and pitchers versus position players. I used regression analysis to create separate models to explain the average annual value of free agent contracts for the four groups, as well as separate models to explain the length of the contracts. For pitchers and position players, I tested a wide range of factors before settling on the final model, which includes some obvious measures such as past performance (relying on FanGraphs' version of WAR), the year the contract was signed, left- or right-handedness, and the player's age. The model also includes some less-obvious measures: the variation in the number of games played over each of the previous four years and the impact of baseball's super-agent, Scott Boras. The pitcher's model has its own nuances, including estimating the difference in market value based on the pitcher's role as a starter, reliever, or closer. For position players the analysis includes consideration of the player's defensive performance.

From my ongoing study of this topic, I continue to believe that one additional important factor in determining a player's market value is his star power off the field—his marquee value, which I include in the model. The theory behind marquee value is simple. If brands like Pepsi and Nike pay star ballplayers millions of dollars to endorse their products and build their brands, it seems logical that these players can provide the same type of value to teams whose uniforms they wear every day. While the concept behind marquee value is straightforward, measuring it can be a hazardous endeavor. My solution is to develop a proprietary metric, which I continue to refine, to represent a player's popularity. The measure is an index that combines Internet metrics, including the number of hits when a player's name is searched and the number of Twitter followers, with his All-Star votes and several other factors.

The poster boy for a player's marquee value is the Yankees' Derek Jeter. As Jeter transitions to the later stages of his illustrious career, his contribution to the team's performance may be declining, but his star still shines brightly—maybe even with greater intensity than when he was at his peak performance. Later in this decade when Jeter's career inevitably wanes, thousands of fathers and mothers will rush their young child to Yankee Stadium to ensure they have a chance to see the once-great Yankee. Some will also buy his jersey and other Jeter-related merchandise. Over a career, the trajectory of a player's marquee status often differs from that of his on-field performance. The brightness of Jeter's star, like all marquee stars, is likely to shine long after his glove and bat fade.

At the heart of the free agent model is the way in which it accounts for a player's performance. In any advertisement for personal investments you will undoubtedly see the legally mandated caveat, "past performance is no guarantee of future results." The same warning label could accompany any free agent signing. One interesting aspect of the way in which general managers implicitly value performance is their heavy reliance on the player's most recent performance—his "walk year". While multiple past years are included in my model, the most recent season carries the most weight. The frequency of a player having a great walk year is higher than one might expect. For the 271 multi-year free agent contracts signed in the last seven years, 44 percent of the players had their highest WAR over the four years preceding free agency in their walk years.

The age of a free agent has little impact on the AAV of a one-year deal, but it does have a large effect on both the AAV and the length of multi-year contracts. According to my model, the impact is even greater for pitchers than for position players. C.C. Sabathia's deal with the Yankees is a good example of how a player's age might affect his contract. Sabathia signed his seven-year, $161 million deal as a 29-year-old. If Sabathia were five years older with the identical performance history, my analysis suggests he could have expected to land a five-year, $100 million deal in the context of the 2009 free agent market. The $3 million per year and the two fewer years represent the penalty for being a 34-year-old (versus a 29-year-old) ace.

For an MLB team, the length of a free agent contract can often place a greater financial burden on a team than its average annual value, as it compounds the risk of a player's injury and performance decline. During a long-term contract, each year is a roll of the dice to see if the player remains healthy and able to perform at the expected level implicit in his contract, while the team's financial obliga-

tion remains intact. Some of the same variables that go into determining the average annual value also impact contract length. Not surprisingly, a player's age is among the factors that most impact the number of years he is awarded.

Valuing Free Agents at the Team Level

Another factor to consider when studying the free agent market is how specific general managers or teams tend to value players. I analyzed each free agent transaction to see if there was any team effect that indicated that certain teams systematically paid a premium or discount for playing talent, versus the rest of the market. My results show that six teams seem to pay a premium to the market—the Yankees, Mets, Red Sox, Cubs, Angels, and Dodgers. The premium ranged from $250,000 to $600,000 per the previous year's WAR for each of the clubs.

Before we condemn these teams for mismanagement by overpaying for talent, let's acknowledge that this list includes the largest market teams whose revenues may support the premium the teams are paying. A way to evaluate a team's spending in the free agent market is to ask the question, "Did the team pay market rates for the talent, or does the team's revenue model justify the expenditure, from a return on investment standpoint?"

I estimate the financial value of reaching the postseason for the Red Sox to be twice that of the Kansas City Royals. If a player represents the last piece of the puzzle for either team, he represents a greater revenue opportunity to the Red Sox, giving them a reason to bid higher than the Royals in the free agent market. The teams that pay the premium may have a financial justification for their action.

The free agent market remains an enigma to MLB teams and analysts alike. Free agent deals can sometimes seem like they are drawn up in the heat of battle and even appear arbitrary. The reality is a lot of factors go into the way in which the market places a value on free agents. Teams are often processing this information, in their own individual ways with their own biases, in order to get to a reasoned value for each contract. There will always be examples of an owner or general manager doing whatever it takes to sign a key free agent. But when looking at the market in aggregate, transactions can be studied and conclusions can be drawn as to the factors that teams explicitly and implicitly value. While the free agent market may be a little easier to understand, it's no less interesting to watch unfold.

Evaluating the Outcome of the Free Agent Contract

The second part of the evaluation of a free agent contract is the outcome, the analysis to answer the question, "How did the player perform during the length of the agreement?" Since most MLB contracts represent a fixed cost to the team, a way to judge the outcome is the salary cost per win above replacement level (WAR). A "good outcome" is when a player's on-field performance delivers enough WAR to lower his cost per WAR below the average of what other free agents earned.

Before we see how our 30 free agents fared on the outcome scale, let's examine the primary metric we will use in our evaluation: the average cost per WAR in the free agent market over the last six years. We calculate this metric by simply dividing the average annual value of all free agent contracts signed in a given year by the actual WAR (FanGraphs version) these players produced each year. For all position players who signed free agent contracts for the 2004 season, their performance in the 2004 season led to an average cost per WAR of $2.7 million. For those who signed contracts for the 2008 season, the average cost per WAR was twice that level, at $5.5 million. For pitchers signed for the 2004 and 2008 seasons, the average cost was $2.5 million and $7.9 million, respectively. The following table lists the average cost per WAR for both position players and pitchers that correspond with each of the last seven free agent markets.

The Cost of Wins in the Free Agent Market (in Millions)

Year	Position Player Cost/WAR	Pitcher Cost/WAR
2004	$2.7	$2.5
2005	$3.1	$3.4
2006	$2.9	$4.5
2007	$5.3	$6.3
2008	$5.5	$7.9
2009	$3.7	$5.9
2010	$2.6	$5.9

As an example, let's examine Miguel Tejada's 2004 contract with the Orioles. We evaluate the outcome by determining Tejada's cost per WAR over the life of his contract versus the market cost per WAR during the same years. As you can see from the table, the wins above replacement that Tejada produced would have cost the Orioles $87 million if they had purchased them on an annual basis at fair market value, yet Tejada's contract called for only $72 million in salary. The outcome was a good one for Baltimore as they paid $15 million dollars less, or 17 percent less, over the life of his contract.

The Outcome of Miguel Tejada's Contract

Year	WAR	Market Cost
2004	6.8	$18.5
2005	4.7	$14.5
2006	5.3	$15.4
2007	2.3	$12.1
2008	3.1	$16.9
2009	2.6	$9.6
Total	24.8	$87.0

An example of a completed contract that did not fare as well as Tejada's deal is Pedro Martinez's 2005 contract with the Mets. Boston GM Theo Epstein allowed an aging Martinez to walk via free agency rather than give him a four-year deal. Martinez took his talents to New York where the Mets' GM, Omar Minaya, willingly paid Martinez $13.25 million per year for four years. After a solid first year, the $53 million deal began to haunt the Mets as arm injuries limited Martinez's contribution. After delivering an ace-like season in 2005 worth 5.9 WAR, the former Red Sox hero earned only 3.4 additional WAR over the final three years of his deal. The net result was a contract that cost the Mets $53 million, but yielded only $38 million in WAR (at fair market value) over the four years—a deficit of $15 million, more than enough to term this a bad outcome for the Mets.

The tables on the next page show the outcome for the same 30 free agent contracts—split between position players and pitchers—we discussed in the decision section of this analysis. (Note that while our 30 players fit neatly into three groups of 10 for the good, fair, and bad categories when we evaluated the signing decision, the breakout was not even for the outcome evaluation. Eleven players were in the good category, 10 in the fair category, and nine in the bad outcome category.)

Two contrasting free agent contract outcomes from our group are Derek Lowe and Adam Eaton. Lowe's 2005 contract with the Dodgers was an overwhelming success for the team, as they paid the right-hander $36 million over the four-year deal but received 15.4 WAR in return. Based on the prices for free agent wins in the years that Lowe delivered the goods, the Dodgers would have been expected to pay $89.6 million for the WAR—a cost of $5.8 million per WAR. Lowe provided the Dodgers with inexpensive wins at less than half the market rate.

Prior to the 2007 season, pitcher Adam Eaton signed a three-year $24.5 million deal with the Philadelphia Phillies.

"Outcome" of Free Agent Deals (Pitchers)

Player	Team (Year)	Total Value of Contract	$ Value of Actual WAR	Contract Value less WAR
Pedro Martinez	NYM (2005)	$53	$38	-$15
Jeff Suppan	MLW (2007)	$42	$10	-$32
Jason Schmidt	LAD (2005)	$47	$0	-$47
Russ Ortiz	ARZ (2005)	$33	$0	-$33
Greg Maddux	CHC (2004)	$24	$40	$16
Mike Mussina	NYY (2007)	$23	$60	$37
Adam Eaton	PHL (2007)	$25	$0	-$25
Billy Wagner	NYM (2007)	$43	$30	-$13
Kyle Farnsworth	KCR (2009)	$9	$9	$0
Carl Pavano	NYY (2005)	$40	$5	-$35
Derek Lowe	LAD (2005)	$36	$90	$54
Andy Pettitte	HOU (2004)	$31	$40	$9
Vicente Padilla	TEX (2007)	$34	$30	-$4
Matt Clement	BOS (2005)	$25	$16	-$10

"Outcome" of Free Agent Deals (Position Players)

Player	Team (Year)	Total Value of Contract	$ Value of Actual WAR	Contract Value less WAR
JD Drew (opted out after Yr 2)	LAD (2005)	$22	$22	$0
Jason Varitek	BOS (2005)	$40	$40	$0
Gary Sheffield	NYY (2004)	$39	$17	-$22
Brian Giles	SDP (2006)	$30	$44	$14
Jeff Kent	LAD (2005)	$17	$18	$1
Vladimir Guerrero	LAA (2004)	$70	$74	$4
Johnny Damon	NYY (2006)	$52	$54	$2
Ivan Rodriguez	DET (2004)	$40	$37	-$3
Bengie Molina	SFG (2007)	$16	$33	$17
Omar Vizquel	SFG (2005)	$12	$29	$16
Miguel Tejada	BAL (2004)	$72	$89	$17
Richie Sexson	SEA (2005)	$50	$13	-$37
Julio Lugo	BOS (2007)	$36	$8	-$28
Raul Ibanez	SEA (2004)	$13	$23	$10
Ramon Hernandez	BAL (2006)	$28	$31	$3
Magglio Ordonez	DET (2005)	$75	$88	$13

Over his injury-riddled years with the Phillies he won 14 games, but given the number of innings he worked and the way he pitched, he actually pitched at the level of a replacement player. In other words, before he was released prior to the final season of his contract, he contributed zero WAR to the Phillies. The net result is obvious—a bad outcome to his Phillies contract. As you can see in the table, nine of the 14 pitchers' contracts fell short of earning their value, with eight of the nine falling far short. Only four pitchers from our list—Mussina, Lowe, Pettitte, and Maddux—had good outcomes under their contracts.

The position player results yield a different story. First, there are a larger number of positive outcomes, with 10 of our list of 16 outperforming their contracts. Also, perhaps more importantly in terms of the big picture findings, the variability in the performance of position players was much less than that of pitchers. In other words, position players' performance beat (or fell short of) their contract by a much smaller amount, suggesting teams found it far easier to estimate the market value of position players than pitchers. In our database of free agents dating back to 2004, there are 91 position players and 90 pitchers who have completed multi-year contracts. The variability of their performance relative to their contract is twice as high for pitchers versus position players. For pitchers, teams seem to miss wildly, both on the positive side (Derek Lowe contributed performance that was worth more than twice his contract value) or on the negative side (Jason Schmidt delivered no value on a $47 million contract). Fewer pitching contracts are termed fair outcomes, with most being labeled good or bad, while position players have far more fair outcomes.

Combining Decisions and Outcomes

The analysis gets even more interesting when we integrate the rating of the signing decisions with the ratings for outcomes for our 30 free agent contracts. The table below shows the ratings in nine boxes on a grid, combining good, fair, and bad across both signing decisions and outcomes, with the top right box labeled as good-good and the bottom left box termed bad-bad. Mike Mussina's 2007 two-year $23 million deal with the Yankees falls into the good-good box. The deal the Yankees signed with the veteran starting pitcher was below market at the time of the contract and Mussina outperformed the contract in terms of the value of the wins above replacement he delivered to the Bronx Bombers. My free agent model suggested that Mussina's fair market value at the time of his signing was actually two years at $36 million (versus the $23 million he received), which is still far less than the $60 million in value that he ultimately produced over the two years.

An example at the other end of the scale is Richie Sexson. The Seattle Mariners' right-handed power hitter signed an over-valued four-year deal worth $50 million (versus my model's estimate of his value at $29 million) and then managed to drastically underperform against the contract by

providing on-field performance that yielded only $13 million in value over the four years. Of the 10 players in the bad outcome column, only Sexson and Julio Lugo did not have a major injury contribute to the shortfall in their performance under the contract analyzed. Each of the other bad outcomes missed playing time that curtailed their production. Of the 14 pitchers included in our list of 30, seven produced bad outcomes, three were fair, and four were good. The position players were concentrated in the good and fair categories, with only three of the 16 listed as bad outcomes.

Looking Forward

Current contracts to keep an eye on include some of the highest value contracts in MLB history, such as Alex Rodriguez's 10-year $275 million deal, or teammate Mark Teixeira's eight-year $180 million deal. While it will be years before we can assess the outcome of those deals, the verdict is becoming clear on some others. Alfonso Soriano just completed his fourth year of an eight-year $136 million deal with the Cubs, and while he is on track to deliver the full value of the contract, the trend line looks troublesome. For half the contract term, Soriano has delivered $70 million in value—about half the cost of his deal. Unfortunately for the Cubs, $60 million of his value came in the first two years of the deal. Soriano would need to return to being a 4 or 5 WAR player over the remaining four years for the contract to have a fair outcome for the Cubs. Carlos Beltran's health issues may prevent him from earning his seven-year $119 million deal with the Mets. Through his first six years, he has delivered about $106 million in value, which means he would need to be a 3 WAR player in 2011 if he is to add another $13 million in value in his final year of his contract. Another long-term deal that is in jeopardy of delivering its value is the six-year

Decision Rating:	Outcome Rating		
	Bad	Fair	Good
Good	Pedro Martinez 2005 Jason Schmidt 2007 Gary Sheffield 2004	Vicente Padilla 2007 Jason Varitek 2005 Jeff Kent 2005 JD Drew 2005	Mike Mussina 2007 Brian Giles 2006 Greg Maddux 2004
Fair	Carl Pavano 2005 Billy Wagner 2006 Matt Clement 2005	Vlad Guerrero 2004 Johnny Damon 2006 Ivan Rodriguez 2004	Derek Lowe 2005 Andy Pettitte 2004 Bengie Molina 2007 Omar Vizquel 2005
Bad	Richie Sexson 2005 Adam Eaton 2007 Russ Ortiz 2005 Julio Lugo 2007	Ramond Hernandez 2006 Jeff Suppan 2007 Kyle Farnsworth 2009	Miguel Tejada 2004 Magglio Ordonez 2004 Raul Ibanez 2004

$100 million contract given to Carlos Lee by the Houston Astros. At the halfway point (through 2009) of his contract he had provided the Astros with approximately $48 million in value, but his poor 2010 season places him far on the negative side of delivering the value of his contract, on a pro-rated basis.

Turning to pitchers with long-term deals, Barry Zito's seven-year $126 million contract, signed prior to the 2007 season, is problematic for the San Francisco Giants. In an evaluation of the signing decision, my analysis pegs the true market value of Zito at less than half the value of his seven-year $126 million contract with the Giants. Part of the driver of the gap is the model's unwillingness to rationalize a deal longer than five years for a player of Zito's caliber. Leading up to his 2007 contract signing, Zito's previous six years yielded 5.0 WAR, followed by 4.4, 4.3, 3.2, 3.0 and 2.1 WAR in succession. This gradual decline should have been enough to convince the Giants to value Zito as a mere mortal, say a solid No. 3 starter—the caliber of a Ryan Dempster. Instead, the Giants inked a contract at the time worthy of not only a staff ace, but a Cy Young contender. Zito has proved to be neither in his four years in San Francisco. In fact, until the hints of resurgence shown in his most recent 2010 season, Zito's high-water mark as a Giant was a modest 2.2 WAR in 2009. In terms of an evaluation of the outcome, he has delivered approximately $45 million in value over the first four years of his deal. Unless Zito returns to his near-Cy Young form of his Oakland days, it will likely be termed a bad contract when the deal finally comes to an end after the 2013 season.

I recognize that there are often factors that are not captured by this analysis that could account for the difference between the actual deal and the model's estimate. Perhaps the Giants calculated they would steal some Athletics fans by bringing Zito across the Bay, or that Zito's carefree image was a perfect fit with their fans. (Note: A measure of the player's marquee value is included in the free agent model.) Maybe they believed Zito could help cultivate a relationship with one of their sponsors to help financially justify the deal. Even

if that were the case, which is unlikely, the gap between fair value and the amount the Giants paid was too large for it to change the rating of the decision to sign him for $18 million per year for seven years.

CC Sabathia holds more promise. Through the first two years of his seven-year $161 million deal with the Yankees, the big lefty has delivered about $55 million in value, putting him on pace to earn his contract value. However, the reason pitchers often fall short is due to lost time from injuries rather than poor performance. Time will tell if Sabathia can stay healthy and earn his keep.

Occasionally we can declare a verdict on a contract even before it's over. Oliver Perez's 2009 deal with the Mets for three years, $36 million is a case in point. In his first two seasons, Perez performed below replacement level, which means, at least theoretically, he should have paid the Mets for the right to pitch. Even if Perez should miraculously contend for the Cy Young award in 2011, the final season of his contract, he will likely not avoid being classified as a bad outcome. His contract will also fall into the category of a bad decision, as my free agent model called for a two-year $4.9 million per year deal totaling $9.8 million, compared to the $36 million commitment made by the Mets. This is arguably the single worst signing decision (on a percentage basis) of any major league player in the last seven years, as my estimates suggest the Mets committed more than 3.5 times fair market value to the left-handed Perez.

Signing any free agent to a long-term deal is a slippery slope for teams. A lot can happen over four or five years. As players age, their skills erode, or injuries place them on the shelf, making them unable to earn the value of their contract. While it's reasonable to say that teams bear the greatest risk in long-term deals, the players also forgo the opportunity to capitalize on the upside of their performance. Just ask Derek Lowe, who might have netted considerably more dollars if he had chosen to sign successive one-year deals and performed at his same 2005 to 2008 levels. There are no easy answers when it comes to the free agent market.

How to Handle a Pitcher

by Craig Wright

Editor's Note: This is an expanded version of a column that appeared in Craig's The Diamond Appraised—*a regular column that is available by subscription at www.diamondappraised.com*

Part One: "Nolan Ryan's Crusade"

After an article appeared in *Sports Illustrated* (May 24, 2010) titled "Nolan Ryan's Crusade," I got several emails asking me to comment. Many were similar to the following.

Did you see the article in SI where Nolan Ryan disses pitch counts and talks about how his Rangers have stopped coddling their pitchers? I actually liked the sound of it, but it also sounds more like attitude than substance. More of a "When the going gets tough, the tough get going" thing, and "Look what I did back in my day." You've done a lot of work in this area; do you think he's wrong?

No, I don't think Ryan is wrong. I agreed with the majority of what he had to say. I believe he and Rangers pitching coach Mike Maddux are resisting some trends that fully deserve to be resisted, particularly in regard to pitch counts. But this is both a hugely important and complex topic, and there were elements in that article to which I would offer a cautionary voice of balance.

Probably more than any other area in baseball, this subject is closest to my point of expertise. I've been studying baseball from a scientific perspective for over 40 years now, and I've had a particular focus, dating back to the mid-1970s, of trying to make sense of the widely varied career curves of pitchers. While I wrote the pitching chapters in the book *The Diamond Appraised* back around 1987, those chapters mostly tell the story of theorizing and research I had done in the years prior to my baseball career, particularly in the 1974-79 period. That's certainly true for all of the chapter "Men-at-Arms through the Ages" and also for much of the following chapter titled "Learning How to Live to Pitch Another Day." My point is I've been dancing with this subject for a long time now and I suspect I have about as good a feel for it as anyone.

I had considerable success in my many years as a player acquisition consultant in directing my teams away from pitchers headed for trouble and toward pitchers who would be better bets for the future. That advice was directly based on the things I had learned about how to estimate the age of a pitcher's arm separately from his calendar age, and the shifts in risk of injury between certain groups of pitchers. What I did not get to do was to directly employ my work to enhance the durability of pitchers and manage the workloads of pitchers who already had experienced damaging abuse or actual arm injuries, in order to help them battle back to their best combination of effectiveness and durability. That was a "player enhancement" issue and I rarely got to do that kind of work. That sort of task was something that required a lot of cooperation among various people to make it work, and the atmosphere of the game at that time was simply not up to it.

But I find it impossible not to assume that similar practical value would have been demonstrated if I had been allowed to shape customized in-season guidelines for individual pitchers. The exact same principles are involved. Rather than using those principles looking backwards to get the right feel for the future of the subject pitchers, you are using those principles to help create the best atmosphere for the pitcher's consistent success. That is, to improve their future. And we have seen the impact of certain elements of my work that *did* become part of the mainstream of thought in managing the workloads of pitchers. (The current use of pitch counts is decidedly not one of them, and I will cover that later on.)

The one thought that really caught on from my research was the conclusion that: "… younger pitchers in their formative years need to be handled with exceptional care that eases to general monitoring in the prime seasons." I'm very glad to see that. I felt then, and feel even more strongly today, that the evidence for this guideline is overwhelming. That understanding and agreement quickly spread through the game. It is today such a commonly accepted principle in baseball that you would think everybody learned it at their grandfather's knee. I take great satisfaction that both baseball men—managers, pitching coaches, player development people—and analysts and sabermetricians, have embraced this principle to a point that when they look back at the recommendations I made so long ago based on that principle, that they now seem like statements of the obvious.

But of course, most of the baseball people from my generation remember a time when that wasn't obvious at all, and young pitchers were routinely pushed as hard as their effectiveness justified, just the same as physically mature veterans.

Denny McLain was leading the Tigers in complete games and innings per start by the time he was 21. This was not a singular oddity. Thirteen years later—even after watching

McLain's arm crash and burn after his 25th birthday—the Tigers did exactly the same thing with another 21-year-old pitcher, Mark Fidrych, and Mark even led the league in complete games. They let this kid pitcher have the highest complete game percentage (83 percent) since Bob Feller way back in 1946. The very next year, while Fidrych's arm blew out in mid-season, they let a *20-year-old* (Dave Rozema) lead the team in innings and complete games.

Gary Nolan got to lead the Reds in innings and complete games when he was still a *teenager*. During that season he topped 130 pitches in numerous games and twice his estimated pitch count went over 140.

Frank Tanana was allowed to throw 246.1 innings when he was just 19 years old. When he was 20 they let him throw an estimated 150 pitches in just his second start out of spring training. At 21 he was throwing over 250 innings and threw 288 at age 22. Just five weeks after his 22nd birthday he had the highest estimated pitch count of his career (189).

Dennis Eckersley was allowed to top 200 professional innings when he was just 18. When he was still only 21 he was allowed to throw an estimated 157 pitches in a big league game. At 22 they had him throwing 247.1 innings and bumped it to 268.1 the next year, along with throwing the second-most complete games in the league.

At age 20 Fernando Valenzuela led the league in innings pitched and complete games. At age 21 he had three games with estimated pitch counts of 140+ pitches, and easily led the Dodgers in innings and complete games. At age 21 Brett Saberhagen got to lead his team in complete games and innings per start. When Dwight Gooden was just 20 years he was allowed to lead the National League in both innings and complete games. At least three times that season his estimated pitch count went over 140.

And even when teams started moving away from this practice there were a few holdouts. The Atlanta Braves let Steve Avery top 130 pitches a few times when he was only 21 and allowed him to average 222.1 innings for ages 21-23. Even in this millennium, the Cubs let 22-year-old Mark Prior lead the majors in pitches per start.

All of these pitchers were seen as possible Hall of Fame starting pitchers in those early years. But they all ended up seeing the brilliance of their careers derailed by either outright shoulder injuries or a significant drop in their durability and effectiveness with symptoms consistent with what I called premature aging syndrome (PAS). Only Eckersley made it to the Hall, and even he experienced serious shoulder trouble that made it impossible to continue in a starting role. Even when he was used as a reliever his team had to exercise great care in managing his workload, such that he was among the most lightly used closers of his generation.

Because of the less impressive centers and ends of these careers, we sometimes forget how brightly these pitchers shone as youngsters. Two of them, Frank Tanana and Dwight Gooden, were the very best young pitchers I ever saw. And most of the rest would make my top 10.

Dwight Gooden is the only pitcher to lead the majors in strikeouts at ages 19 and 20. Gary Nolan had an even better season at age 19 than Gooden did. In fact, it was the best season by a teenager in the last 100 years. Gooden's and Rozema's seasons at age 20 are among the five best at that age in the last 100 years. Fidrych's season at age 21 was the sixth best at that age. Saberhagen's was the seventh best.

And then there is the remarkably strong overall beginning to Frank Tanana's career. He led the league in strikeouts when he was 21, and took an ERA title at age 23. During the period from his big league debut, which was a couple of months after his 20th birthday in 1973, until a couple weeks shy of his 25th birthday (1978), he was the best darn pitcher in all of baseball. His ERA in nearly 1200 innings was 30 percent below the league ERA. In the Live Ball era, which dates from 1920, you can count the number of pitchers who have done that before their 25th birthday on … *one finger*! That's right, Frank Tanana is the only one. The next closest is Bob freakin' Feller at .705!

But from there …

Frank's season ERA on June 19, 1978 was 2.53. It shot up well over 2 full runs (4.71) the rest of the year. Out of the blue Tanana's fabulous fastball suddenly vanished. Frank had great control and he was able to reinvent himself as a finesse pitcher who ended up having a long career, but he was never again a star pitcher. Years later I got to ask Frank about it and it was definitely a shoulder problem. He had found that after his fastball went south on him, that if he tried to throw really hard, he not only could not throw with his old velocity, it hurt his shoulder to even try. So, he simply stopped trying and found that by working hard on his conditioning, he could manage to work as a regular starter if he was content to throw

Frank Tanana	W-L	Win%	IP	ERA	Relative ERA	K%	Relative K%
1973 to June 19, 1978	76-52	0.597	1193.0	2.62	0.699	7.54	1.56
Thereafter	164-184	0.471	2995.1	4.06	1.000	5.33	1.00

his fastball in the 84-88 range with command and a variety of breaking balls.

As rough as the rest of his career was relative to that brilliant beginning, Tanana actually finished better than most of these young stars. Young Denny McLain won back-to-back Cy Young awards and set a record for the Live Ball era for most wins by his 25th birthday, but then he won only 21 more games in his career.

Fernando Valenzuela was the best pitcher in the majors at age 20, followed by five more good seasons, and then his career went into a stunning tailspin after age 25.

Valenzuela	W-L	Win%	ERA	Relative ERA
Thru age 25	99-68	0.593	2.94	0.814
Thereafter	74-85	0.465	4.96	1.253

Dwight Gooden in his early 20s was among the best ever, but when he got to what should have been his physical prime, Gooden had devolved into just an average pitcher. He ended up being pretty much washed up after age 28, averaging just 112 innings a year with an ERA worse than the league mark.

Gooden	W-L	Win%	ERA	Relative ERA
Ages 19-25	119-46	0.721	2.82	0.766
Ages 26-28	35-35	0.500	3.57	0.952
Ages 29-35	40-31	0.563	4.99	1.044

I sincerely hope that Nolan Ryan's crusade does not end up sending the Rangers back towards the Dark Ages, when being "too good too soon" meant a formative history that would greatly increase the risk of injury and eventually a radically premature decline in durability and effectiveness.

I am concerned about this happening for two reasons. First, the Rangers have a bushel load of fine young pitchers. Some say it is the best group of pitching prospects in the game today. Even after trading Blake Beavan and Josh Lueke for Cliff Lee, the Rangers are loaded with young pitching talent. On their big league club is 22-year-old Neftali Feliz and 23-year-olds Derek Holland and Tommy Hunter. At Triple-A there is a supplemental first-rounder from 2009, Tanner Scheppers (age 23) and 23-year-old Mike Kirkman, who was called up to the majors in late August. At Double-A is a hard throwing 22-year-old lefty, Kasey Kiker (the second high school pitcher taken in the nation in 2006), and 19-year-old Martin Perez, who had to be among the youngest pitchers starting off at Double-A this past summer. (Perez was rated the No. 17 prospect in all of the minors going into 2010.) And

21-year-old lefty Robbie Ross at A-ball has one of the highest rated sliders in their system.

I'd hate to see the futures of any of these prospects compromised by handling that does not appreciate that they are still in their formative years. My second point of concern is a more general one. I worry that Ryan's own experiences as a big league pitcher might color his judgment somewhat without understanding how his own formative workload contributed to his great durability and longevity.

Nolan Ryan started more games under the modern rules than any pitcher in major league history. He threw more innings than any non-knuckleballer in the history of the Live Ball era. In 1988 I told Ranger GM Tom Grieve that in my assessment the 41-year-old Nolan Ryan had surpassed Warren Spahn as having the best aging profile of any non-knuckle-baller in his 40s in the history of the game. I repeated that assessment in 1990 when Ryan was 43 years old.

I trust Ryan understands that this was true in part because (1) he was a great power pitcher who started out with one of the greatest fastballs ever, if not the greatest, (2) he had a solid physique and good mechanics, and (3) he worked on being an extremely well conditioned athlete. I wonder, though, if he appreciates the immense impact that his formative history had in helping his shoulder age remarkably well compared to the other great arms from his era?

Before detailing Ryan's unusual formative history, a refresher on the formative years:

1. The joints are the last part of the body to physically mature. It varies from person to person, but in the general population that maturation process tends to complete at age 25. My studies of pitchers suggests this may happen a little quicker among professional athletes, but not by a great deal.

2. The shoulder, like other joints, is more easily abused in the formative period. According to an article in *The Physician and Sports Medicine*, when such abuse builds up, "The simplest way and probably one of the most effective treatments is complete rest or modified activity in the shoulder."

3. The further you go back before the maturation process is complete, the more vulnerable the shoulder is to this type of abuse. That is, you can relax the protection of a 24-year-old arm compared to a 23-year-old. But you want to be even more careful with the arm of a pitcher who is 20 to 22, and extremely careful in the professional workload you give to a teenager.

Ryan began pitching professionally at age 18 and threw 78 innings. He threw 202 innings at age 19, which you didn't like to see in a teenager even back in that era, but then he spent almost all of age 20 fulfilling military obligations and threw just 11 professional innings at that age. Then he was rushed to the majors where he played a limited role due to his lack of control and being bothered for awhile with chronic finger blisters on his pitching hand. From age 21 to 24, his innings pitched went 134, 89.1, 131.2, and 152.

If you were to lay an analysis of Ryan's formative history next to those of other pitchers from his era, you would see that his formative workload stands out as remarkably light. If you were to lay it next to an analysis of the formative history of Ryan's old teammate Frank Tanana, it would hit you over the head like a sledge hammer just how radically different they were.

Tanana was worked harder at every single one of the seven formative ages. Frank had no recuperative break (like Ryan's near year off at age 20—or Warren Spahn's long break during ages 22-24 while he was serving in World War II). Frank threw over twice as many innings in his formative years as Ryan did. More relevant, Frank was consistently being pushed deeper in his starts, which tends to carry more risk because it indicates more frequently pushing the envelope where you can cross the line between work that strengthens the arm and on to a level of fatigue that starts to break the arm down.

Age	Ryan: Innings	Tanana: Innings	Ryan: Batters per Start	Tanana: Batters per Start
18	78.0	129.0	28.1	29.2
19	205.0	246.1	26.8	31.7
20	11.0	268.2	14.8	30.8
21	134.0	257.1	28.9	31.2
22	89.1	288.1	23.2	33.6
23	131.2	241.1	28.1	31.4
24	152.0	239.0	26.2	30.7
18-24	801.0	1670.0	26.9 in 118 starts	31.4 in 217 starts

I have a point version of positives and negatives I use for assessing formative history. Ryan's formative profile scored higher than any pitcher I have ever evaluated. Tanana's formative history was filled with danger signs. No pitcher who had scored as low had ever gone on to a normal aging pattern, much less a good one.

I hope the revolution going on in Texas will not include a departure from extra care given to their pitchers while still in their formative years. If it does, the results could drown out the good that exists in their new approach.

I have another small concern, perhaps totally unjustified, but I also wonder if the Rangers may read too much into the benefits of physical conditioning and think that this allows them to set aside some of the more common sense guidelines for reducing risk of arm strain. This was the key point of disagreement between my views on the handling of pitcher workloads and that of pitching coach Tom House. We shared a common belief that good pitching mechanics and a focus on proper physical conditioning enhanced a pitcher's durability, but Tom felt that I underestimated their impact and focused too much on what he called "mileage."

I in turn was concerned that House was overconfident in the benefits he ascribed to his special conditioning program. He felt that with proper conditioning of a pitcher one could ignore safeguards that I recommended and other general methods of pitcher protection common in the game. Someone who greatly valued House's conditioning program during his years in Texas was Nolan Ryan, and he even mentioned in his Hall of Fame induction speech how House's program had gotten him in the best shape of his career. I naturally wonder if Ryan might also have picked up House's overconfidence about the degree of protection that proper conditioning can provide a pitcher.

Just as I used Frank Tanana, an old teammate of Ryan's, to make the earlier point, let me use another of Ryan's teammates, this time from his Texas days, to make my point that even the best conditioning program can only do so much and does not warrant taking unnecessary risks with a pitcher in his formative years.

The big pitching prospect on the Rangers during House's tenure was Bobby Witt. He was the No. 1 pitcher in the nation in the 1985 amateur draft. He was a wonderful athlete, solidly built, and had fine mechanics that generated one of the best fastballs in the game. Early in Witt's career he had used a different off-season conditioning program than House's and ended up with a touch of a sore shoulder the next spring. After that, Witt abandoned the other program and became an enthusiastic follower of House's conditioning program.

Through the end of the 1987 season, the 23-year-old Witt had a pretty clean formative history. That had been his hardest working season thus far, but under my guidelines it was not potentially an abusive one, although it was getting close. His average workload per start was almost exactly the uppermost ceiling that I deemed age-appropriate. But considering that we were talking about a true power pitcher, it was not even a gray area to say it was not a season of concern.

Texas went into 1988 so close to getting Witt through his formative years without any significant seasonal abuse. They just needed to get him through one more year, age 24, without going overboard, and he'd have a solid positive base for his aging profile. My cautionary age-appropriate workload for a 24-year-old starting pitcher in that era was quite generous: keep his average pitches per start under 110 and use a maximum single game ceiling of 140 pitches. House knew my view on this and had even seen it in black and white the year before in the draft of the pitching chapters for the book.

One would also expect with a pitcher still in his formative period that the Rangers would also try to avoid other common stressors with Witt, such as stretching him out too quickly fresh out of spring training, or having several high-pitch games in a row, or failing to work in what I called the occasional "oasis game" in *The Diamond Appraised,* which is simply a game of lighter use in the midst of what would otherwise be a steady run of hard charging games.

But with Witt firmly in House's conditioning program for a good while now, it was decided to take the restraints off and work him shockingly hard. First off, the general maxim of easing a pitcher into his seasonal workload as he came out of spring training was thrown out the window. In Witt's first three starts his pitch counts went 103, 138, 128. That average of 123 pitches in his first three starts was the third most in the league, and was easily the highest of any pitcher still in his formative years.

That unwise use may have been responsible for a short-term negative response in his shoulder. Bobby's next three starts were horrendous (20 earned runs in 16 innings for an 11.25 ERA) and he got sent to Triple-A to straighten himself out. He was there for 11 starts and kept up his average of 123 pitches per start. Witt came back to the big leagues on July 10 and cranked out six straight starts that were all over 125 pitches and *averaged* 132.5. Then on Aug. 30 he had a 151-pitch game. On Sept. 9 he had a 147-pitch game immediately followed by two games of 130 or more, and finished off the season with his second 151-pitch game of the year. He was handled with anything but care in that formative season. It would end up being the hardest he was worked in any season of his whole career.

Witt threw 251 innings that year, and averaged 125.4 pitches in 33 starts. The average was 126.7 in his major league starts, *the most of any pitcher in baseball.* He had at least three starts where he was pushed seven pitches or more past my age-appropriate maximum. As far as mixing in an "oasis" start, I can't tell you what his low was in his 11 minor league starts, but I can tell you that he topped 100 pitches in every single one of his major league starts. A lot of folks were happy with his performance, which had shaved a full run off his

ERA from the previous year, and there were a lot of folks going "Way to go, Bobby." But I was saying this was no way to work a pitcher in a formative year.

Witt's arm did not respond well to that heavy use, which would be another indicator that he should be handled with care in his future. The next year his ERA relative to the league jumped 34 percent, or about a full run and a quarter. It was his worst mark since his rookie season. But at least he struggled so much that he wasn't worked hard. He pitched 29 fewer innings and had a much lighter workload in his starts (106.8 pitches per start). In fact, if Witt had been worked at age 24 the way he was worked at age 25, I think it's likely he would have been more effective both years, thrown as many or more innings combined, and he would have had a much better aging profile for his whole future.

Ryan was with the Rangers at this point, and he got to see Witt respond well to that lighter use. He bounced back in 1990 to have a pretty nice season, the best of his career. I bet that during that 1990 season Ryan even heard comparisons of Witt to himself at that age—a young fireballer starting to overcome control problems and blossoming in his mid-20s.

At age 26	W-L	Win%	Relative ERA	Relative K%	Relative BB%
Nolan Ryan	21-16	0.568	0.751	2.07	1.30
Bobby Witt	17-10	0.610	0.857	1.58	1.31

Witt averaged 116.2 pitches in his 1990 starts. With a power pitcher with a clean formative history and no hint of shoulder trouble in his past, that 116 average would not have been a concern at all, especially in that era. But Witt did not have a clean formative history. And his negative response at age 25 to his very heavy workload at age 24 suggested that his shoulder had a vulnerability to rotator cuff impingement. He had a compromised arm such that his workload probably needed to be managed with greater care than that of the average pitcher for, really, the rest of his career. He also needed to avoid in-season abuse situations that might set off extended periods ineffectiveness or even an arm injury.

But that was not the way it was going to work, in part because the Rangers believed Witt's mechanics and conditioning gave him an exemption from that profile. In 1991 Witt was treated as if he was a 27-year-old Nolan Ryan, a power pitcher with a perfect aging profile, which of course he was not. They let Witt throw 128 pitches in his first start out of spring training and then 136 in his second start, which was crazy, given how his actual profile should have been interpreted. He pitched very well in those two starts and was among the early leaders in ERA with a 1.12 ERA, but his effectiveness was completely thrown off by the abuse of being stretched out that much in his first two starts out of spring training. He didn't get out of the third inning in his next start for the first of four gruesome starts, allowing 17 ER in 23 innings (6.65 ERA).

Meanwhile, Witt had started another run of high-pitch games which went 123, 137, 121, 129, which also brought his season average to 120 pitches per start. His velocity was way off in his next start and he struck out just two of the 27 batters he faced. Witt's shoulder was very sore and when it didn't subside in a couple of days, he was put on the disabled list and was quoted in an AP story saying, "This is as sore as it's ever been." It was then discovered that he had torn his rotator cuff.

It was a small enough tear that rather than go with surgery, Witt did nine weeks of rehabilitation instead. He was still struggling badly when he came back. He could not get out of the fourth inning in his first four starts and had a 15.89 ERA in those games. He came out of the rotation again after seven starts, rested for 10 days, made a relief outing and was done for the year, finishing with a 6.09 ERA.

This ordeal was painful and costly for the Rangers as an organization. Witt went 3-7, and the best the pitching-thin Rangers were able to do to replace his missed 16 starts was to try a washed up Oil Can Boyd, who went 2-7 with a 6.68 ERA in his 12 starts with the Rangers. If Witt had been able to repeat his 17-10 season from the year before, the Rangers would likely have won the Western Division and even had the best record in the league. It was also expensive in that Witt had signed a lucrative three-year deal after the previous season. Pitching with a bum shoulder under that contract, he averaged only 167 innings a year with an ERA about half a run worse than the league average.

It was also painful just to watch it happen to Bobby Witt, who was a really good kid with great, great heart. The combination of a rotator cuff tear and rotator cuff impingement problems in your mid-20s is not the kind of thing that ever completely clears up. Witt pitched several more seasons but never with sustained success. He would have periods of pitching well, even brilliantly, but any time he was pushed for about half a season, his shoulder would act up and his effectiveness would go south for about a year or more.

With Oakland in 1993, Witt had a good season going through July 11 (3.77 ERA) but was working harder than his arm could handle (on pace for 230 innings) and his shoulder started acting up. His ERA jumped up about a full run in the second half and he had a miserable start to the next year as well, taking a 6.88 ERA into June. His shoulder started to come around in mid-season but then he threw three straight complete games—including his near perfect game—and his

arm rebelled again. He averaged only 3.7 innings in his next six starts, had a 5.60 ERA, and was shut down for the rest of the year after his Aug. 8 start.

The same sort of thing happened in 1997 when Witt was back with Texas. He had a good first half through July 13 (3.57 ERA) but again he was working too hard (on pace for 229 innings) and again his shoulder balked. The rest of the way he had a 6.72 ERA, and he continued to pitch poorly the next season (6.56 ERA). After his shoulder injury at age 27, Witt's career was a repeated story of one step forward and two steps back.

Bobby Witt was a well-conditioned athlete working in the best conditioning program for pitchers that probably had ever existed up to that point. I'm not saying that it wasn't good for him. I'm not saying it didn't benefit him. I'm sure that it did. I'm simply saying it was not enough to protect him.

I believe what *did* hurt Witt was the belief that the Rangers' special conditioning program gave Bobby a degree of invincibility, and that at a minimum it was used to dismiss cautionary guidelines for his last formative year as something that was necessary only for *other* pitchers.

There's no way to know that an appropriate workload for Witt in his last formative season—as opposed to the uncontrolled and extremely heavy workload he actually had—would have led to a better future for him. We're talking likelihoods here, not guarantees. But boy, with the *combination* of the modified workload *and* the special conditioning, I think he would have had a good chance to pull it off. We do know that relying on just the conditioning did not protect him from the ramifications of that serious abuse in his formative workload. His career became a cascading disaster that likely cost the Rangers at least one division title, wasted a boatload of money, and greatly damaged the career of a promising pitcher who deserved a lot better than he got.

It's an episode that shines an interesting light on Tom House's criticism of my guidelines for pitchers in their formative years. Writing in 1988 for *The Diamond Appraised*, House argued:

> *"This approach will slow down the development of pitching prospects who don't have a propensity for sore arms — and there are such people, and we can identify them."*

My reply was:

> *"I don't doubt there are such people, though I don't believe we can identify them with the certainty Tom suggests. But even if we had a confidence level of 90%, I'd still make the same recommendations.*

"The ceilings I suggest for a minor-leaguer in his early twenties are not going to hold back anyone's development. Those levels can produce a very normal season of work. I think the evidence is pretty clear that even those iron arms can benefit from lighter use in their formative years."

That super-arm stuff was the justification for Fernando Valenzuela being worked tremendously hard in his formative years, and we all saw how that came out: a radical decline that began for him at age 26 and worsened at age 27 when he should have been in his peak physical prime. Tom obviously thought Witt either had one of those unusual arms or that he had gained one through House's excellent conditioning program. He was mistaken.

I wholeheartedly approve of the conditioning program the Rangers are employing, including the extended long toss, which incidentally has roots in pitcher conditioning that stretch all the way back to 1884, when Hoss Radbourne would do warm-ups throwing from the outfield to home plate. I'm just cautioning the Rangers to keep in mind that conditioning is just one of the components in "building" durable pitchers.

So, where exactly is it that I agree with Nolan Ryan the *most*? It is with his most radical statement in the article, the one that has probably been dismissed the most as out of touch or an exaggeration.

"There's no reason kids today can't pitch as many innings as people did in my era."

You would be hard pressed to find anyone in baseball who agrees with Ryan on this more than I do, although I have to say I'm still only about 92 percent in agreement. The strike zone today is smaller than it was for the bulk of Ryan's era. Batters of the modern era both swing and miss more and take more pitches than the batters of Ryan's era. It does take slightly more pitches to get through the same number of innings. Compared to the heart of Ryan's career, it's about a 6 percent increase.

Smaller parks, bigger players, and an emphasis on power hitting has created a depth of hitters with long ball potential such that it is tougher to find moments in a game when a pitcher might coast for a batter or two. Orel Hershiser,

former star pitcher and later a pitching coach, says pitchers today have to work harder with each pitch they throw, and so they need to throw fewer pitches to stay healthy. I believe that is true to a certain extent, though I resist greatly taking it too far because of the following points:

- I think modern pitchers also have the pedal to the metal simply because they are taught not to pace themselves but to instead rely on the bullpen to be there for them when they tire. That's something that could be changed, and I think needs to be changed.

- Pitchers of today are larger, better conditioned, and more likely to be "mechanically optimized," as Tom House would say.

- We have better knowledge available for how to avoid work patterns that increase risk of injury, and a better understanding of how to give pitchers better aging profiles. A pretty poor job has been made of using that knowledge, but "there's no reason ..." not to use it.

So, I'll give Hershiser's point a measly weight of 2 percent. Add that to the 6 percent more pitches needed per inning, and you have my 92 percent agreement with Ryan. In my book I have a chapter titled "Bring Back the Four-Man Rotation," which is another point of agreement I have with Nolan, who has suggested this possibility several times, and a return to the four-man rotation would obviously be necessary for kids today to throw nearly as many innings as the pitchers of Ryan's era.

So, with a resurrection of the four-man rotation, how many innings do I think the most durable arms of the modern pitchers could safely throw in a season in their prime if they have an excellent aging profile behind them? I answered that question with "325" over a couple of decades ago, when pitches per inning were about 5 percent less than today. Add 2 percent for the "Hershiser Factor" and 93 percent of 325 is ... 302.

Three-hundred inning pitchers—*that's* how much I agree with Nolan Ryan. I invite you to walk to the edges of the major league kingdom to find someone other than Nolan and myself who believe "there's no reason" that isn't possible.

Part Two: Pitch Counts

I know that the book *The Diamond Appraised* has often been cited as a flash point in getting folks to think more about the workloads of pitchers and shaping them to best promote the durability and effectiveness of the pitchers, both short and long-term. In *The Neyer/James Guide to Pitchers*, Bill James wrote:

> *"For more than twenty years, momentum has been build-ing within the sabermetric community for the belief that having a pitcher throw an excessive number of pitches in a game is dangerous and counter-productive. This belief traces back essentially to the work of my longtime friend Craig Wright ... [and his] ... book The Diamond Appraised."*

In the book I actually focused more on the impact of *seasonal* workloads, but there was certainly stuff in there about the stressors of in-season abuse, particularly for vulner-able pitchers: youngsters in their formative years or mature pitchers who already had damaged shoulders. That a pitcher can be overworked to a point that is dangerous beyond just having a tired pitcher on the mound in those last few innings is certainly a key element in my studies. That was already a somewhat common belief in the 1980s and is essentially universal today.

But nothing I advocated in the book, or anywhere else for that matter, links to the current state in baseball in which many teams are employing fairly rigid and generic pitch limits on all their starting pitchers, and doing it in a remarkably dumb fashion that actually goes against the recommenda-tions and logic of what I brought out in my book.

But that doesn't mean such a link doesn't get assumed. There are people in baseball and the media who—while acknowledging that where we are today comes out of the work of other people—assume that this later work is a natural extension of my own. But if you were to compare the two, you'd see that with the one important exception of trying to treat younger pitchers with greater care, that these modern practices have distinct departures from my work and conclusions.

Just a couple of years ago the *Associated Press* ran a story that blamed my book for the present emphasis on pitch counts and declining workloads of pitchers. It was lost on the AP writer that my work was very much focused on how to *increase* the number of innings we got from our best pitchers, both in individual seasons and over their careers, and that I antici-pated that with the right approach we could return to the higher workloads that have been missing from the game for over 35 years now. The AP story also made the odd charge that the book helped kill the four-man rotation, which was a particularly strange criticism given that the four-man rota-tion vanished about a decade before *The Diamond Appraised* was published, and that in the book I specifically argued for the *return* of the four-man rotation and dedicated a whole chapter to it.

Bill James is one of the few to make a distinction between the things I was actually advocating and where others have since driven the bus. He wrote in 2004:

> *"If you look back to Craig Wright's ... writings on this issue, it is clear that Craig was concerned mostly with the effect of hard usage on young pitchers. Craig wrote ... that a 20-to-22-year-old pitcher should never throw more than 130 pitches in a game [but not to average anywhere near that]. ... I believe [Craig] suggests that pitch counts of 130 to 150 pitches may be perfectly OK for mature pitch-ers with no history of an impingement syndrome but they should be assiduously avoided for [physically] immature pitchers and for certain other "vulnerable" pitchers.*
>
> *"... The problem is that we have raced way past that, where now we are second guessing managers for giving 120, 125 pitches to a [physically] mature pitcher."*

That's fairly accurate though I didn't actually write that a pitcher at age 20-22 should *never* throw more than 130 pitches in a game. The use of that cautionary generic ceiling was introduced as recommendation to be adhered to in *player development* situations, in the *minor leagues*. I also wrote that I would raise the pitch ceiling to a maximum of 140 pitches for minor leaguers for ages 23-24 of the formative years. If I had a numbered concept of a pitch ceiling for healthy pitchers *after* the formative years, it would logically be more than that. I actually do think that there are pitchers who at the right points in their career, in the right spots in the season, and with the right pitching approach, could throw *over* 150 pitches in a game with very minimal risk.

There are many modern practices in controlling pitcher workloads that I disagree with, and none is bigger than this: I am amazed and dismayed over the crazy practice in the modern game of setting pitch limits right around where the *average* might normally be and not providing the option for the pitcher to stretch out beyond that. It seems to me that most people involved with this are quite capable of seeing that it is a huge mistake, and that this practice actually creates a lose-lose situation.

Where is the general line of a pitcher's durability—the point where you risk passing from work that builds up the shoulder to work that abuses the shoulder and tears it down? The maximum cap will vary from pitcher to pitcher, just like the ability to throw hard, and it will vary during the different stages of the career, and *in each season as well*. The latter case is the classic example of how we have a role in creating the "durability line" by how we work the pitcher. That understanding is basically second nature in baseball. That's why we have spring training and are still gradually stretching out pitcher's arms as we move into the regular season. We are working on raising the line of durability. We are essentially creating where it is and will be.

In the various versions of the "pitch limit" programs followed by so many teams, they begin by doing what teams have been doing forever. In spring training and in the first few weeks of the season, they steadily raise the bar for durability as part of getting the pitchers ready for his normal workload. But now they only raise it so far—say, to the point of being a 100-pitch pitcher—and then they stop cold. If you constantly hold a pitcher at, or close to, 100 pitches, that's the kind of pitcher you get: one whose durability is about 100 pitches. And from there the modern plan seems to be to get the pitcher to work as close to that line as many times as you can.

From my research and analysis, that's pretty crazy. On the one hand, this practice locks you into a limited durability situation that ends up taking innings away from your best pitchers and instead giving them to pitchers who, if not for the need to replace those innings, wouldn't even be good enough to make the roster. Further, the lack of flexibility in this practice makes it harder for the manager to work with his roster in pursuit of a win. With negatives like that, you better be getting something valuable in return.

The only reason I don't characterize this use of pitch limits as "jaw-dropping stupidity" is because I understand that some people sincerely believe this practice is safer for the pitcher's arms. My view is exactly the opposite. I believe that this practice creates a scenario that is less safe.

Look, raising the bar of durability always has risk. You can take the pitcher a little too far in stretching him out and damage his shoulder. But we go ahead and work through that process every spring with every pitcher. Why? Because we have to. We need the innings, and the risk relative to the reward makes it a no-brainer. A part of the reward that is often overlooked is that developing higher levels of durability is in itself a future form of protection for the arm.

A key concept for protecting the shoulder from abusive work is to reduce the number of times you risk crossing that line of durability. Is it safer to repeatedly press to the trained level of durability but never really stretch it out? Or is it safer to stretch past that line when you feel strongest and to back off it when you do not? All my research and thought on this subject has come down squarely on the side of the latter being safer. It does have the degree of risk inherent to building

durability, but it is acceptable relative to the reward of building durability as safely as possible.

This is a key point, so let me repeat it. A workload that has *less* consistency in the form of stretching out a pitcher when he is at his best and pulling back when he isn't, is healthier than a consistent workload pressing frequently against a pitch limit.

I suspect the current use of pitch limits involves *more risk*, not less, and if that is correct, then there is no balance of reward for its shortcomings. It is a lose-lose situation. No, it's actually a lose-lose-lose-lose situation: (1) greater risk of damaging the shoulder, (2) doesn't build durability, (3) makes it harder to manage in a winning manner, and (4) doesn't contribute to relatively safe growth of innings from our best pitchers.

When I have tried to explain the difference in my approach from the current practice of pitch limits, I often get asked, "What's the difference? You have a pitch ceiling, at least for pitchers in their formative years. Whether you call it a 'pitch limit' or a 'pitch ceiling,' isn't that the same thing?"

In the sense that each represents a number that you try to not pass, then, sure, "pitch ceiling" and "pitch limit" are the same thing. But I've never recommended a stand-alone "pitch ceiling." My guideline of a "pitch ceiling" has always been in conjunction with a seasonal average of pitches per start, estimating the "pitch ceiling" to be about 25 percent above the seasonal average, and narrowing the gap for the younger pitchers and also for those with compromised arms.

In my approach, the dominant focus is on not letting the "seasonal average" get out of hand, and that generally means the "pitch ceiling" itself becomes an issue in maybe two to four games a year. This current practice of "pitch limit" has that "limit" in play in the unfolding of nearly every start. It shackles the manager in the things he can do, and it shackles the development of the pitcher's durability.

The concept of pitch ceiling in conjunction with seasonal average is radically different. It creates the room to stretch out a pitcher while also encouraging looking for the right spots to back off as well.

My sharpest disagreement with the current use of pitch counts is with the concept of *generic* measures related to pitch counts. There is one single page in *The Diamond Appraised* where I touched on such a use, and it has ended up being so misunderstood that I wish I had never written it. I introduced that section as clearly being meant only for use in player development in the minor leagues, but it has been mistakenly interpreted over time as a sort of endorsement of the use of generic guidelines based on pitch counts. My actual introduction to that brief section says:

"The idea of establishing rigid measurements for cause and effect is unrealistic, and that is not the goal here. Given a young pitcher who could make an impact on a major-league race, the evidence is not there to justify firmly shackling the manager's use of that pitcher. For that situation, the goal is simply to make the manager aware of the potential effect on that pitcher's career if he is consistently pushed to his endurance limits.

"In the minor leagues, where the goal is player development, [emphasis added] cautious guidelines are more than acceptable. Some recommendations from this research are:"

And then I gave my cautionary generic guidelines for *minor leaguers* for three stages of the formative years (teenagers, ages 20-22, and ages 23-24). I would not have used generic guidelines even in that instance if it weren't for the logic of these points:

- Pitcher's arms are more vulnerable in the formative years, and abuse in those seasons can significantly alter their aging profiles for the rest of their careers. It's a situation that calls for general caution and not trying to fine tune workloads to maximize innings.

- Most young minor leaguers have unknown qualities that we are still learning about, making it hard to customize workload guidelines to the individual pitcher. Thus, you need to rely more on generic guidelines.

- Fewer arm problems have manifested at this point in their careers, particularly the kind of damage to the shoulder that often needs the most customized guidelines to avoid setting off lengthy negative reactions or even further injury. The greater uniformity in the health of young arms reduces the need to customize their workload. Generic guidelines come closer to the target with young arms than when dealing with the wide variety of health histories found with older pitchers.

- This is the minor leagues. The pressure to take risks to win ballgames is tempered by the player development goal of preparing the players to win big league games in the future. The caution of using a generic guideline is more tenable at this level.

With the exception of pitchers in their formative years in a player development situation, I think the use of *generic* guidelines based on pitch counts tends to be so ineffective as to be inappropriate. We've got ballgames to win and we need to do our very best to work out the risk/reward equations

that help the team the most. That should include fine-tuning and customizing the guidelines for each pitcher's workload. By the time most pitchers make the majors, we've had some time to get to know them and what kind of arm they have. We've had a chance to see how their arms respond in various situations and have a sense of whose arm is on the fragile side and whose arm tends to be rebound quickly. Most pitchers in the major leagues are not in their formative years, and we have a better sense of their aging profile and whether they should have restraints taken off or if we need to continue to monitor and modify their workloads consistent with potential vulnerabilities. We know who has had prior arm trouble or had strong symptoms of rotator cuff impingement.

The use of pitch counts can be helpful in the monitoring and assessment process in the older population of pitchers, but by that point it becomes increasingly ludicrous to take a stance of "one size fits all." Workloads that you would want to be cautious about with certain vulnerable pitchers would be perfectly fine and even unnecessarily restrictive for a physically mature pitcher with a good history and sound arm. Trying to pick a simplistic, middle-of-the-road workload and then systematically apply it to everyone would be a backwards combination of danger and waste. You are going to cause problems for the pitchers who should be worked shy of a normal workload, and you are going to unnecessarily hold back valuable pitchers and actually hurt them by interfering with the development of their durability to a higher level that they can safely reach.

Frankly, if an organization came to me and said, "We'd like you to come up with the best generic model you can for modifying a pitcher's workload to maximize return at minimal risk, and we'll use that for all of our pitchers across the board," I'd decline. I'd flatly tell them they would likely be better off following the old practice of playing it completely by ear, relying on the pitcher's self-report and the visual assessment of the manager, pitching coach, and catcher.

And that's exactly the point I would make to the vast majority of teams today. Good for you that you have embraced the idea that younger pitchers should not be pushed as hard as physically mature pitchers. And good for you that you *want* to do a better job of managing the workloads of all your pitchers. But the way you are going about it is so off the mark, that you would be better off returning to the practices of 15 years ago. And as far as dealing with pitchers who are past their formative years, you'd probably do as well or better to go back to the practices of 30-35 years ago.

That is my actual suggestion to the vast majority of the teams. Go back to the old ways, or at least stop cold this current practice of pitch limits and start over in trying to work in the things we have learned about enhancing the durability of pitchers with the least risk. Either option is preferable to what you are doing right now. The modern practice of pitch limits is bad enough as it is, and you only make it worse by applying the pitch limit in a generic fashion to every pitcher. It all strikes me as being a lot like the advent of the five-man rotation: all the right intentions, some distant ties to a few right ideas, but an actual practice that is simply a waste.

And why not return to the old ways and leave it at that? Why should we consider anything other than the pitcher's self-report and the judgment of the manager, pitching coach, and catcher?

Well, the old path hasn't been a walk in the park either. We are capable of doing better, and the rewards make it worthwhile to aspire to something better. I'm talking about greater success in pitcher development, and longer and better careers. I'm talking about getting considerably more success out of pitchers with compromised arms, who otherwise end up mostly frustrating teams and end up on the junk heap. And I'm talking about getting to a point where you are taking 150 to 200 innings a year away from the worst pitchers on your staff and replacing them with quality innings from the best pitchers on your staff.

I've written quite a bit in this chapter about the shortcomings of the misguided approaches used today in an attempt to improve the once traditional way of managing pitcher workloads. Let me balance that by enumerating some of the stumbling points of the older style of pitcher management. This will also bring out why the causes of those stumbles are largely hard-wired into the game, and that it would be hard to reduce the mistakes in that process without adding another perspective and layer to addressing the issue.

First, consider all the inherent problems in getting a reliable self-report out of a pitcher in regard to how his arm is holding up.

- Like the vast majority of professional baseball players, pitchers tend to be abnormally competitive people. It is easy with that type of mentality to misread pitching too far past your fatigue level as simply stretching yourself out.

- Both as competitors and creatures of habit, pitchers resist the idea of not being able to "do what I did before." If there comes a point during the season when the arm fatigues a little early, perhaps needing what I refer to as an "oasis" start, pitchers have a tendency to ignore that early onset of arm fatigue because they are thinking, "I should not be tired."

- The belief and drive to "do what I did before" can also cause a pitcher to mislead both himself and the manager and pitching coach in regard to less singular instances than the need for an "oasis" start. A pitcher may resist acknowledging a reaction to an in-season abuse problem that may last several weeks. (This happens a lot more frequently than commonly assumed, particularly among pitchers with compromised arms.) The pitcher may have an internal argument of, "That was a couple of starts ago. I've got to ignore what's going on, suck it up and get back to the level I was at."

- And that's just an in-season response. On a *seasonal* level in his career, a pitcher may resist acknowledging the signals related to the aging of his arm. The career of Robin Roberts provided a great example of a pitcher who could have had several more good seasons if he had accepted the need to modify his workload when he began experiencing premature aging syndrome in response to his previously ultra-heavy workloads. Instead, he kept trying to be the pitcher he *had* been, and that kept setting off long periods of ineffectiveness. This cycle went on for years, until he finally did modify his workload and then experienced a late resurgence in his career in his effectiveness.

- As competitors, pitchers also tend to look at themselves in relation to others, and have trouble acknowledging danger signs when they see someone else of a similar age, similar build, and similar raw skills being more durable than they are. Pitchers are particularly vulnerable to this, because it is not well understood that the aging process of the arm can easily derail from the common aging process related to calendar age. Because Joe Blow over there is the same age as you, it is hard to comprehend that your arm may be "older" than his arm.

- There are issues of subtle long-term impact—especially in the cases of young pitchers and those already with compromised arms—that often have no immediate manifestation in a single game, and that even the most self-aware pitcher is not going to be able to "feel" or recognize a need to dial things back.

- Many pitchers tend to associate the building of dangerous fatigue in their shoulder with a decline in velocity only. If they feel they are still able to throw their pitches with normal velocity, it is easy for them to imagine that they are still doing fine. Actually, for most pitchers the clearer sign of crossing the line into dangerous fatigue is a loss of command. When I watch a game on TV and I am looking for signs of whether a pitcher might need to come out, I pay some attention to the radar readings flashing on the screen, but what I look for most is whether his fastball is starting to miss the target, particularly jumping up, and I look for whether his breaking pitches are flattening out.

Try this. The next time you watch a game and see a pitcher get nailed by a few batters before he comes out, as you watch the replay of those hits, ask yourself if he suddenly started getting hit because of a failure of velocity or location. You'll quickly see it is far more often a matter of location. If you want to extend the exercise, start looking in other games for that decline of command when a pitcher might be tiring. When you see it, notice how often he gets into trouble if he stays in the game.

Understand that I am *not* saying that a pitcher's self-report of how he is feeling is useless. Far from it. It definitely deserves to be a factor, and it is not a mistake to encourage pitchers to work on improving their self-assessments. There are certain pitchers who have a knack for assessing how they are holding up, making their self-report especially helpful. (Their heightened self-awareness also helps them to make in-game adjustments, which is part of learning how to go deep in one's appearances with the most effectiveness and least risk.) And I'd say that *any* pitcher who tells you that he is starting to feel gassed has just given you a very important piece of information. For almost every pitcher that would definitely deserve to be a red flag.

What I *am* saying is that staying with a pitcher based almost exclusively on his report that he feels fine is a largely unreliable practice that has played a direct role in huge numbers of arm injuries and compromised arms in the long history of the game.

Moving on from the weaknesses of the pitcher's self-report, we have the stumbling points that can get in the way of the manager, pitching coach, and catcher when assessing the risk of removing a tiring pitcher versus the potential reward of leaving him in.

- "We want to win!" And added on top of that imperative is, "We want to win today!" These common competitive instincts cloud the ability to judge wisely, particularly in decisions to stretch out a pitcher not because they think he is strong but for reasons like: "I want to reduce the work of our bullpen which is either (A) dragging or (B) likely needed to be at full strength to pick up tomorrow's sad sack pitcher." And then there is the wicked temptation of: "Even a tired Joe Ace is better than who I've got to replace him."
- Sometimes it's just simply impossible to tell from the visual cues if the pitcher has crossed the line of durability to a point that it will affect his next outing. And if it

does, you know that you rolled the dice and lost. The only question is by how much.

Using Bobby Witt again, he had an interesting example of this point in his rookie year. His average workload per start that year was "age appropriate" but he had one start that year that clearly went past the pitch ceiling I would have recommended for him if he had been a minor leaguer. Witt was allowed to stay in one more inning because he was looking particularly strong that day, and he in fact did pitch great in that extra inning. He struck out the side and it was the heart of the opposing batting order.

But as it turned out, it did affect Witt who had nothing in his next start. It was literally his worst game of the year. He had no command, couldn't get out of the second inning, put seven of the 11 he faced on base, and he did not strike out a single batter. In fact, it was the only start during Witt's first six seasons that he failed to strike out a batter. I'm serious. In the first 163 starts of his big league career that is his only start without a strikeout.

The key point to this example is that Witt looked very strong and, based on that, the decision was made that it was worth the risk to leave him in. The extreme negative results of his next start suggest that the field personnel were fooled. The visual cues and Witt's self-report were not enough to pick up on the danger that likely resulted in his struggling so badly in his next start.

A secondary point is that this case offers a classic example of how a mixture of traditional judgment and the added scientific perspective might have resulted in a different decision with a better result. So let's change that scenario. Let's pretend this scenario comes up with the organization and manager following this idea of integrating the two approaches.

Let me point out again that if my program had been involved, the manager would not have been prevented or even faulted for leaving Witt in for that extra inning. As I've said before, I do not believe in following rigid guidelines based on pitch counts. The field personnel need the leeway to weigh in their judgment on whether the pitcher is working into a danger zone or not.

The difference in this case would be the added information that the manager would consider along with the visual cues and the pitcher's self-report. Now the manager's reasoning might go:

1. Witt says he feels fine and he's throwing great with 11 strikeouts in his seven innings.
2. I'm not picking up any concerning signs of fatigue, and neither is the pitching coach or our catcher.

3. This is a pretty young pitcher, just a couple of months past his 22nd birthday. Making mistakes with pitchers this young can have added long-term negative consequences, making it a greater risk if we misjudge this situation.

4. With pitchers this young, it is also easier to make a mistake in stretching them out too far.

5. He's a rookie and that limits our understanding of the qualities of his arm. If he were in the minor leagues, we would exercise caution at this point and not send him out for another inning.

6. He has already had a nice stretching out of his arm that will help build his durability. (Before that extra inning Witt was already about 25 percent ahead of his seasonal average of pitches per start.)

7. We are trailing by three runs after seven innings and we have a very small chance of winning, probably about 7 percent. If Bobby gives us a shutout inning in the top of the eighth, our chances of winning will only go up to about 9 percent.

I, the manager, am going to …

Now whatever decision the manager settled on, wouldn't you believe it was a better decision than if it were based solely on points No. 1 and No. 2? Let's do another case, a tougher one in which the manager has to really wrestle with how much to weigh the imperative to win that is so critical at the big league level. This is Nolan Ryan on the mound, April 30, 1989. Ryan is battling Roger Clemens and the Red Sox in a tough game and is losing 1-0 after seven innings. His pitch count is at 121. I'm going to assume points one and two are the same and that the points of consideration might go like this:

1. Positive self-report.

2. No one is picking up concerning signs of fatigue.

3. Ryan is 42 but has a truly exceptional aging profile and a proven level of high durability.

4. Ryan's already had a couple of 130+ games in two of his previous three starts (135, 103, 130), and it may be a little early in the season to be giving him three games of 130+ in four starts.

5. The long-term risks in pushing a pitcher with this kind durability and aging profile are not great. If I as the manager err in leaving him in, the negative impact will more likely tend to be short-term and maybe impact just one start.

6. We have a decent chance of coming back and winning this game (25 percent). If Nolan can give us another shut-out inning, we'll have almost a one out of three chance of winning this game.

I, the manager, am going to …

If you are playing along by pretending you are the manager, you probably would have concluded in the earlier example that it would be worth being cautious with Bobby Witt and decided not to send him out for another inning. I bet you find this one a lot tougher. If you are like me, you probably would leave Ryan in.

That's what actually happened, and the decision had mixed results. Ryan was able to give one more inning and it was a shutout inning, including retiring two of Boston's best hitters: Mike Greenwell and Jim Rice. In the bottom of the eighth inning the Rangers came back with a two-run homer by Rafael Palmeiro and ended up beating Clemens and the Red Sox two to one. (It's not relevant to this example, but it is interesting all the same to see that the game account suggests that the Red Sox might have lost because they tried too hard to get another inning out of Roger Clemens. His last batter in the seventh inning was a lineout to center field, and then he allowed four more hard-hit balls in the eighth, including the homer that won the game. Given that Clemens had pitched superbly for 26 batters and then given up five hard-hit balls to his last seven batters, he might have been gassed. It may have cost the Red Sox double, too, as Clemens also got knocked around in his next start.)

Anyway, as I said, the results of sticking with Ryan in this case got mixed results. He finished with 136 pitches, and in the context of the early stage of the season and his prior games, there was some potential for that to be a stressor. That may have had something to do with his next start being a disappointment (6.1 innings, 8 hits, a couple of home runs, and just three strikeouts in the 30 batters he faced). Texas ended up losing that next game by one run (seven to six). But given the same scenario again, I know I would have sent Ryan back out for that extra inning. Sometimes it just doesn't work out. As expected, the negative effect was short-lived. Nolan was back in peak form (11 strikeouts in a five-hit complete game) the next start after the bad one.

Let's do one more. So far, we've done a young pitcher in his formative years, and then a veteran pitcher with strong durability and a superb aging profile. Now let's do a pitcher with a compromised arm. Let's go back to Bobby Witt, but this time it's six years later. It's 1992; he has a negative aging profile, has been disabled at least twice for a sore shoulder in his career, including a rotator cuff tear, and he has exhibited actual symptoms of rotator cuff impingement and premature aging syndrome. It's May 28, he has a four to two lead after eight innings. He is having a very efficient game, allowing just three hits and a walk. His pitch count is at 104 pitches, he's working with an extra day of rest. He is pitching very strongly and has retired his last seven batters in a row with three strikeouts. Do you stretch him out and let him go for the complete game? Again, we'll assume No. 1 and No. 2 are the same, and in this case the factors go:

1. Positive self-report.
2. No one is picking up concerning signs of fatigue.
3. Witt has a compromised arm that can react sharply if a mistake is made in pushing him a bit too far.
4. Witt's profile also identifies him as a pitcher whose negative reactions to being pushed too far can last awhile, build and cascade though the season, making it especially costly if a mistake is made.
5. Though pitching with an extra day's rest, his previous start was a season-high 121 pitches and 112 before that. Even if he were to pitch well in the ninth his pitch count will likely be up around 120. He hasn't had back-to-back games over 112 yet this year, nor a streak of three games over 100, much less three straight of 112 or more.
6. With a four to two lead going into the ninth, we already have a 93 percent chance of winning the game.

I, the manager, am going to …

In this case, Witt was pulled. I don't actually think the decision to relieve Witt was about being careful with his workload. I suspect he was taken out largely because of a reason I left off the list. The team's ace closer, Jeff Russell, had three days of rest and was overdue for some work, and he closed out this game with a perfect ninth inning. Whatever the reasoning, this pitcher with a suspect shoulder was able to come out with a reasonably light outing. His actual pitch count was slightly below his seasonal average of pitches per start, and it appeared to be a game with even less strain than the pitch count suggests and might even qualify as a helpful "oasis" start. In Witt's next start he pitched well and tied his best game ERA for the whole year.

The decision in all of three of these examples would have been enhanced with a consideration of the different durability profiles of the pitchers involved. That would be my ideal recommendation for how these things should work. That kind of thing was not remotely possible during my career, and I'm not sure it is today. It takes a lot of cooperation to pull it off, and a lot of faith that the profiles would be done well enough to warrant being part of these decisions.

I do know that nothing like this is actually going on in the game today, and for the most part we instead have this ill-conceived quasi-substitute of pitch limits. Quite seriously, my recommendation for most teams is to eliminate their current practice of pitch limits and return to the old style of managing pitcher workloads—with the caveat of keeping the modern practice of lightening the workloads of pitchers in their formative years.

Again, to be perfectly clear on this point, I am not attacking the use of pitch counts. I am opposed to the *way* they are being used. It seems to me that the way pitch counts are used today is less about using them wisely and more about following a fad. They are used as insulation against being criticized for not being on board with the flavor of the month. With the vast majority of teams there is no more than a surface understanding and appreciation of what should be involved in monitoring pitcher workloads. The basic attitude seems to be: "If you can't give it to us quick and simple, then don't give it at all." There are some in the sabermetric field who feel it is better than nothing to acquiesce to that attitude, and in some instances I would agree. This is not one of them. When given that choice, I prefer the latter—don't use it at all—with the exception of a team's cautious work with immature pitchers.

I have no problem with counting pitches as one of the ways of loosely monitoring a pitcher's workload, as long as it is done in a reasonable, thoughtful manner—one that is responsive to what we have learned as being the most helpful in maximizing the return from that pitcher. I don't reject counting pitches; I reject the lazy stupidity of (A) setting a simple pitch limit that a pitcher is expected to press against in every start, and (B) using generic "one size fits all" pitch limits. For me, that's not "better than nothing," it is worse.

There is another element in the focus on pitch counts that disturbs me. The simple nature of counting pitches tends to lead folks to believe that a simple *application* will follow, that somewhere there is an answer in form of static levels of pitch counts. I see that path causing us to lose slight of and disengaging from the two key principles originally guiding this approach:

• We want our best pitchers working as much as they can, though within a level of reasonable risk in regard to their loss of effectiveness (both short and long-term).

• The greatest periods of vulnerability and risk are when a pitcher's arm is fatigued.

The higher the level of durability a pitcher can obtain, the longer he can go. That not only adds to his team's competitive edge, it also enhances the protection of his arm. Except for cases of extreme mismanagement, that added durability will reduce the number of times that competitive pressures push the pitcher's arm past his level of durability. It's not about pitch counts and pitch limits. The true issue revolves around the pitcher's envelope of durability. Our concern is with ways to better understand where it is, how to expand it, and how to do it with the least risk.

Pitch counts can be a part of that research and part of the applications arising from that research, but when you succumb to the siren song of the simplicity of pitch counts and allow them to become the focus, I guarantee you will end up taking backward steps. You will eventually find yourself in a place where you are uncomfortable letting certain pitchers throw 130 or 140 pitches in a game, and having no hesitancy about other pitchers throwing 90 pitches in a start.

That's exactly the wrong place to be. There are all kinds of cases where I would be very comfortable letting a certain pitcher throw 130 or 140 pitches, and have only mild concern at 150 pitches, while at the same time I would be hesitant to have another pitcher toss 90 pitches in his start. I'm quite sure that even in those extreme cases I would be exercising more wisdom than could be found in a system based on static levels of pitch counts.

Trivia Sidebar #2: Huh?

Alvin Greene became South Carolina's U.S. Senate nominee for the Democrats through no fault of his own, almost literally. Having just enough money to pay the filing fee, Greene ran no campaign of any sort; he continued to be unemployed and live with his father. Meanwhile, Vic Rawls campaigned extensively around South Carolina on the presumption of facing Sen Jim DeMint in November. But for a multitude of odd reasons—at least one Greene voter admitted she did so because he sounded like Al Green—the guy with no campaign received 59 percent of the vote, to the utter dismay of his party. If elected, his economic growth plans included selling action figures of himself.

1. Of the 16 franchises around in 1901, only the White Sox have failed to do this. The Phillies did it in 1980 and five expansion teams have done it, but Obama's favorite team still hasn't.

2. Two days after he turned 25, Mike Lehane debuted at first base for the 1890 Columbus Solons, becoming the first and so far the only player with this connection to the presidency. Though Howie Gregory, Luke Glavenich, Bob Grim and Craig Paquette can claim something similar, Lehane stands alone and, one hopes, always will.

3. In 1986, the Spartanburg, S.C. Phillies posted a 40-95 record in the South Atlantic League; this was one of three Single-A performances that year with affiliated teams under .300 on the season. It's happened at Single-A, Double-A or Triple-A only three times since then (once this year with the New Britain Rock Cats), but one was in 1998 with … the manager of Spartanburg in 1986! On top of that, he's been a major league coach for the White Sox and Blue Jays and continues to manage in the Phillies system that let him flounder in the first place. Who's the guy?

4. The career offensive leaderboards for South Carolina-born players are dominated by Joe Jackson, Willie Randolph and Jim Rice, but it's a fourth player, a deadball middle infielder, who leads in doubles.

5. On the topic of states, this state leads with a .537 winning percentage out of its native pitchers. If you think about the easiest way for a state to lead this category, you should get on the right track pretty quickly.

6. If you put Joe Niekro, Joe Hatten, Ice Box Chamberlain, Ricky Romero and Sidney Ponson in the same rotation, you'd have a serviceable front five, assuming they were alive and in their prime. Doug Corbett could do the closing. It was by democratic process that I decided to put this staff together. Why are these pitchers on my imaginary staff?

(Answers are in the back of the book.)

A Perfect Summer Dream

by Anna McDonald

"From the time that you played, til' the last time you prayed, it's been a simple matter of love."
—*Jack Buck*

Over the span of seven happy months, major league baseball brings us a wedding of sorts, one in which participants pledge from Opening Day onward that they will be part of both the merriment and melancholy. Each ball club, every player, each game, has for better or worse, an expectation of both. For every negative moment this year, we can find a positive.

For every naysayer who cites a decline in ticket sales, someone can rework the numbers and prove that just the right number of fans are purchasing tickets during a poor economy. The debate for more instant replay continued this year, but as people discussed what Major League Baseball should do, we saw a beautiful example of class and grace—extended from Armando Galarraga to Jim Joyce after one of the most infamous umpiring calls in sports history.

The contrasts make it seem that the baseball fairies are flitting about trying to make amends for all the confusion they've caused in recent years. There's more going on than a whimsical and irresponsible love for baseball. We're going to take a journey to discover why baseball will continue to be alive and well. Grab your glove and bat and let's begin.

The Youth Who Dream

Ted Hoehne had left something at home that he should have brought to school. The teacher had strict rules about being tardy, but it was his turn to bring the baseball bat and he forgot, so he had to run the two miles back home. In 1935, if you lived in the Midwest on a farm, you didn't start first grade until there were enough kids around to make a class of sufficient size, and the school certainly didn't supply bats and balls at recess to the kids who were in school. No one worried about leaving a child behind; they worried about feeding the children they had, but the Depression's hardships in these small German-American communities certainly didn't stop kids from playing ball at recess. Somehow they always found a way to get a game in.

Ted Hoehne grew up on one of those farms. The playground was a hill; a sloping hill that had woods wrapping all around it.

"Nobody had ball gloves, and home plate would be at the top of the hill," he recalled. "If you hit the ball down the third base line, the ball would land in the woods and you could get all the way around the bases."

"Antiover" was another favorite ballgame at recess. "We'd throw the ball over the school house roof and somebody on the other side would have to catch it, run around the school house, and tag someone on the other team." He laughed and said, "Now that I think about it, I'm not real sure what we were trying to do, or how a team would win, but it sure helped us learn how to throw hard."

"Sunday afternoons in the summer were my favorite. I loved playing in the pasture; it was level. All our cousins and the neighborhood kids would come over and we'd play until somebody called us home for dinner. Mom had a bell high on a post and she'd ring that and we knew it was time to head home."

As the kids in 1935 head in for dinner, we move forward three quarters of a century. Our excursion has landed us in the spring of 2010. We've put away our snowsuits, the scent of fresh green grass has reappeared and so has baseball.

John, a 13-year old who plays in a select league, is pitching and playing third base this year. His great-grandfather was Hub (Shucks) Pruett, a pitcher who played for the St. Louis Browns. John's parents said he genuinely loves baseball, "he's been given an intergenerational connect with the game."

John mentioned a time he forgot his bat for practice; he had left it in his grandparents' car. They were called on their cell phone and drove it back to his house, but meanwhile he had to borrow a teammate's bat. He said, "It ended up good though because sometimes it's good to try new things."

Every day at recess, John enjoys playing catch and when school is out he does long toss to develop his arm strength. He and his younger brother throw the ball as far as they can to each other. John talked about his favorite baseball memory: "Every year for my birthday we'll invite a bunch of friends, have cake, and go down to the beach and play baseball. That's always a really fun neighborhood time that everyone can get together and play baseball."

Does he think he'll have a lifelong love for the game of baseball? "Yes, baseball is an awesome game. It's America's game. It's always going to be a way to get exercise and a way to have relationships with the generation after me. There will always be something new about it; it's not going to be just something that you reach the limits of.

"There's always a new generation that's coming up, a new season, and new players who will come up and get better. There's always going to be older, talented players who will tail off and you will see new Hall of Fame inductions. There's always gong to be something new to discover about it."

Two kids, 1935 and 2010, who love playing baseball while dreaming of their future. Yet there are hiccups in baseball bliss.

Are Baseball Mortals Fools?

When I asked John if any of his coaches ever talked to him about steroids, his firm "no" was stunning. With all the news headlines about PEDs, the talk about their negative effects on the players, and the integrity of the game, surely someone is talking to a developing baseball player about steroid use?

Certainly John knows about the issue. "I do think about it a lot," he said, "when you read about it in the paper or watch it on 'Sports Center.' It's disappointing to me … I can understand why someone would do that; it really disappoints me though. They're trying to give themselves such an advantage … being so much more powerful than the other players."

I asked him again: No one ever mentions the topic? "Never." I expected him to say something like, "Every fourth Monday of the month we are required to attend the "Why steroids will kill you and your future" class, or at least, "Every year our coach hands us a pamphlet on why steroids are really bad." But nothing?

While we can assume that some bright person will figure out what to do with the steroid era, we cannot move forward if no one is talking to young ball players about it. In fact, there's movement toward doing that.

The best way to evaluate the quality of any company or organization, is to begin at the top. Be they good or bad, the standards, beliefs, actions and policies from the executives will trickle down, so I contacted The Office of the Commissioner of Major League Baseball.

Pat Courtney, principal spokesman for Commissioner Bud Selig, outlined a program that's designed to reach kids like John, teens and their parents. Major League Baseball has a partnership with Drugfree.org. This partnership is built around four pillars; research, media, grassroots education and celebration of clean competition and healthy lifestyles.

"In order to educate kids and their parents about the dangers of performance-enhancing substances, MLB and the Drugfree.org have built a first-of-its-kind online educational resource which explains in significant detail what performance enhancing substances are, and the dangers of their use. In turn, we have partnered with high school athletic associations to disseminate materials which reinforce the message sent through mass media. By the end of this year with this grassroots outreach, we will have covered each of the U.S. major league baseball markets, about 70% of the country, and Ontario."

This year, MLB and the partnership created the Play Healthy Education Module, a multimedia presentation for kids and parents. There's also an online campaign which features the "Parent Talk Kit," a coaches' blog and a listing of facts on performance-enhancing substances. This December, the Commissioner's Play Healthy Award was to be given to youth athletes and coaches whose work is extraordinary in promoting clean competition.

Major League Baseball also partners with The Taylor Hooton Foundation, which gives talks in stadiums and has enlisted Alex Rodriguez, who does appearances in communities, Boys and Girls Clubs, and high schools.

Still, Steve Pasierb, president and CEO of Drugfree.org., told me in a phone interview, "We don't think a lot of coaches are talking to kids, particularly at the Little League level. We do a lot of stuff through mass media. While that's not someone talking to a kid, we've been advertising in stadiums and we have an online site called PlayHealthy.org. It's the best steroid website out there. It's targeted at kids, parents, educators and coaches to give them the information they need.

"I think what may be happening is that the coaches of middle school age kids and elementary kids think the kids are too young to talk to them about steroids and PEDs, and they're not. Most kids start using illegal drugs in middle school. The programs we've done with MLB have reached millions and millions of kids, but it all comes down to the coach and the kids, a parent and their kids—whether or not the personal message gets to the kids."

John cares about the integrity of the game. I asked him if he would vote for someone under a serious suspicion of steroid use into the Hall of Fame, "No, I would not," he said. "What they did gave them an advantage over someone such as Hank Aaron, Babe Ruth or Whitey Ford. With the advantage the steroid players had they were able to perform at a much higher ability than they would have normally been able to. This is an unfair advantage."

To keep baseball alive and well, starting from the top down, there is a responsibility to educate. But following a clean path is up to the moral character and honor of each individual youth.

We Need Baseball

There are other complications in the future of major league baseball. It would be foolish to ignore the fact that kids today have many more choices for recreational activities then Ted Hoehne did in 1935.

For both children and adults, baseball competes with electronic devices. Most people in 2010 are controlled by a cell phone, allowing us to multitask while multitasking. We listen to the baseball game and email on the same device while standing in line at Starbucks. Or we check Twitter updates while riding the train to the game and catch up on Facebook while we wait in carpool lines or at soccer practice. We can get up-to-the-minute scores, highlights, articles and stats—any information we might need—anywhere.

We get frustrated by a cell phone that won't download an email instantly and yet, somehow, fans manage to sit through a ball game every night during the baseball season. While we watch baseball at the park, we email, check Facebook, text message, interact with the untouchable world on our cell phones—but we also do this at the dinner table or a wedding reception.

John, our 13-year-old, enjoys watching baseball from home, on TV. He likes the replays and having access to statistics and information. While there are many factors that play into attendance, such as the economy, time, and ease or difficulty of getting to the ballpark, we have to ask if the comforts of home will ultimately keep fans from enjoying a game in person.

John thought about that question: "Being around other fans, the noise, the atmosphere—I still enjoy going to a game. I enjoy being able to see wherever I want. I enjoy not being limited by the television screen, the way the director is filming the game and what they decide to put on television. It's being able to look at whatever I want, participating in the atmosphere—the smells and sights of the stadium, that's what I enjoy."

Modern technology hasn't stopped Ted Hoehne from enjoying baseball. He's 89 years old and still manages to annoy family members with the electronic device he carries with him at all times. While the teenagers are texting at family gatherings, he sits at the kitchen table with his small hand-held radio turned up loud. His family may wish that he would buy an iPhone (and some headphones), but he prefers to listen to the baseball games the way he always has; it's his way of keeping his favorite childhood memories close his heart.

Ted Hoehne has spent his entire life filling any free time he had with playing baseball or listening to the ballgames. He has passed on a love for baseball by bringing bats and balls to every family gathering and playing ball with the kids. Kids like John love baseball today because of family members like Ted Hoehne—people who have walked away from the television, or put down their cell phones, and stepped outside to play ball.

It's a wonderful thing to have access to every highlight of the year on tape, but it's even better to be watching in person. If you have baseball in your blood this will never change.

Being at the ballpark on a warm summer night with young and old, a cold beverage, the camaraderie of good friends (or complete strangers), talking about how the manager should have made the move to the bullpen, or if he'll use the hit and run—this is the beauty of baseball; keeping us calm, still and connected to each other in a busy world. Energetically catching a foul ball in the stands, sitting in the crowded bleachers, celebrating a walk-off home run with 40,000 other people, this is the game we love, the game that slows us down. We never know when a normal trip to the ballpark will give us an extraordinary chance to be part of history. Summer is baseball, it's every day; we live it, we need it.

When the Summer Dream Continues a Lifetime

As we draw our journey to a close, perhaps you were anticipating a storybook ending, one in which Hoehne played in the majors, in which his grandchildren and great-grandchildren love to hear his stories and play baseball and wish for a career in the baseball someday.

No, while John's baseball story is still unfolding, Ted Hoehne's path is known. He never became one of the farm boys of the '30s to be recruited for the majors. He never even had much of an opportunity to go and watch professional games, but he has remained a lifelong fan.

As I write this, the St. Louis Cardinals are having "Stand for Stan day." Stan Musial has the storybook ending we expect in baseball articles. I'm sitting here watching 38,000 Cardinals fans fill a stadium a few days after one of their most disappointing teams in recent history was eliminated from playoff contention. The baseball fairies have once again spread their magic dust, making fans do something that really makes no sense. The game has stopped in the bottom of the sixth inning on a cold, cloudy Saturday afternoon in St. Louis. The fans are on their feet, and both the St. Louis Cardinals and Colorado Rockies ballplayers are standing on the field acknowledging one of the great legends of the game. The children in the stands with their parents, watching an almost-90-year-old Stan Musial, will remember this day forever: the day they "stood for Stan."

I could have used Stan Musial's story, or that of other ballplayers with this ending. We've all read them before, but that's not the type of journey we are on. This one is about the common thread through generations—why we love baseball and why it will overcome the obstacles it faces.

Baseball is the perfect summer dream—as long as we are willing to interact with each other and are willing to go outside to play catch with our children, major league baseball will survive anything and give us lifelong memories. It changes, it grows, it bends, it's not perfect, but it does not break. It reaches into our past and delivers meaning for today. It will always be a source of dreams for young children. Baseball gives us fond memories of our favorite baseball players when we were kids, great pennant races we experienced (or hoped for), memories of collecting baseball cards and learning about the endless statistics of the game.

But ultimately, our love for baseball begins and continues with the feel of a ball glove on our hand and a simple game of catch in the backyard.

From the time we first learned how to throw the ball to our dad, to the day when we find ourselves tossing the ball to the little toddler across from us in the warm sunlight; our memories of baseball with loved ones will bind us to the game. When we drop our youngest child off at the college dorm, or we discover that our own parents can no longer play a game of catch with us, we realize what we'd give to have one more time together running around the yard playing baseball.

Entrenched in the memories we hold, we rise above the bumps in the baseball journey. When spring comes each year and we pull out the baseball bats and gloves and get ready for that first game of catch on the freshly mowed lawn, we feel baseball anew. We go through the stadium turnstiles every spring and summer to watch our favorite team play. Even though we turn on MLB Gameday while we email, Tweet and work on the laptop, even though professional baseball has its flaws and its struggles with right and wrong, we will always need baseball, because what we *really* want is one more game of catch in the backyard.

The Future of Fielding

Defense Matters

by Dave Cameron

Growing up as a Mariners fan in the 1980s, I wasn't exposed to much in the way of offense. The lineups regularly featured Alvin Davis and eight easy outs, so my formative years were spent being told how important it was to be fundamentally sound and good at playing defense. After all, the hometown announcers couldn't exactly tell me that the players were terrible, so they accentuated the few positives they could find.

So Harold Reynolds wasn't a guy who struggled to get on base and got thrown out stealing too often—he was a speedy second baseman with range who gathered up everything hit on the Kingdome turf. Henry Cotto didn't lack power, he played a mean left field. This was my indoctrination into baseball.

My parents broke down and got me Baseball Stars for the NES, where I found that a team of defensive wizards could easily beat the American Dreams lineup of Hank, Babe and Willie, and my conversion was complete. I was a believer in the value of defense.

At some point in the 1990s, our family got access to the Internet. While wending my way through the World Wide Web, I found a column called Chin Muzak on ESPNet SportsZone, written by some guy named Rob Neyer, whom you may have heard of. He didn't write about how great defense was. In fact, he wrote just the opposite and challenged nearly everything I believed about baseball.

Within a few years, Rob (and others who shared a similar viewpoint) had won me over. Walks matter, and so I should spend more time looking at on-base percentage than batting average. Wins aren't the ideal way of evaluating how good a pitcher is. As for defense, it is actually just a minor part of the game, far less important than hitting and pitching. Slow-moving sluggers win baseball games, and teams would be better off if they stopped giving so many at-bats to slap-hitting infielders.

Like any good teenager with an ounce or two of self-importance, I wanted to share these interesting new findings with anyone who would listen. During my senior year in high school in 1999, I landed a job shadowing Les Carpenter, then of the *Seattle Times*, who was nice enough to let me follow him around for an afternoon. The Mariners had a day game with the Tigers, so we wandered down to the Kingdome to cover the events of the day. The big story was the arrival of newly acquired leadoff man Brian Hunter, whom the team had acquired to add a spark to the offense.

Being someone who understood quite clearly that the primary goal of a leadoff hitter was to get on base, it did not take me long to let everyone around know that I thought Brian Hunter was absolutely terrible and giving him many at-bats would help ruin the team. Hunter's OBP the year before had been just .298, and while he was fast, outfield defense didn't really matter anyway. Hunter was going to cause the offense to grind to a halt. I told all of these things to various local writers and broadcasters, who listened, smiled, and then walked away.

Once the game started, I knew I would be vindicated, however. After all, Hunter was an out machine; he was everything that was wrong with the way the team was being run at the time.

The Mariners beat the Tigers 22-6 that day. Hunter racked up three hits and scored a couple of runs. The smirks in the press box couldn't be contained, and for the first time in my life, I found myself rooting for the hometown team to stop scoring so many runs. Humility had decided to punch me in the face.

I'm telling you this personal anecdote to illustrate the journey that the sabermetric community has taken in our appreciation of defense. Over the last 30 years, no other aspect of the game has seen such a prominent shift in perceived value. The tide of opinion has swung wildly from one side to the other as new data—and new opinions inspired by the data—have come to light. It has not been a smooth ride to the middle ground, if we are even there now.

As discussions about valuing defense still dominate conversation among the statistically inclined, that seems to be at the heart of the issue: Where is the state of fielding analysis today? We know where we've been; we can see the clear emphasis on glovework in the 1980s, followed by an overreaction in the 1990s that turned the game into a glorified softball contest. We think we know where we would like to be in the future; our minds dance at the thought of being able to capture the precise movements of every player on the field with a small army of cameras and databases.

We are not there yet, however, and legitimate questions remain about when we may see that kind of information become publicly available. So, for now, we make do with what we have, using tools that are often insightful but certainly not ideal. Thanks to the hard work of numerous leaders in the field, we have a bevy of options at our disposal that measure defensive ability in different ways. It is a testament to how far we have come in just 10 years.

However, numerous options often create confusion, as anyone who has ever watched my wife try to pack for a trip will attest, and defensive evaluation has not been immune. Disagreements between metrics attempting to measure defensive ability breed insecurity in the reliability of the field as a whole, and what look to be wild swings in performance from one year to the next by similar players also lead to skepticism about the validity of what is actually being measured.

The truth is that there is much that we still don't know about analyzing defensive ability, but we also know far more than we used to. To know where the state of fielding analysis currently is, we need to understand what we actually do know, allowing future research to focus on those things that we don't yet understand.

From my perspective, there are four primary things that we have learned about fielding analysis during this journey. Let's tackle each one individually.

1. Defense matters.

This is the point that most of us got very wrong for most of the last 20 years, including Major League Baseball itself. As we built measures that focused on offensive production, we began to value players who did things that were rewarded by the formulas. It didn't take long before most teams in baseball had a Giambi, or at least a reasonable facsimile of one, running around an actual position on the field. It became acceptable to play guys like Bobby Bonilla at third base, when in reality that should have been a felony in at least 47 states. Bernie Williams and Ken Griffey Jr. were allowed to roam center field long after their knees had lost all semblance of usefulness in large part because they both could still hit. Little thought was given to how many young pitchers were being discarded as overly hittable while being asked to pitch in front of teammates with the agility of a wounded rhinoceros.

Around the turn of the century, however, things started to shift. Voros McCracken published his seminal work on Defensive Independent Pitching Statistics in 2001, which helped establish baselines for expected pitcher performance in giving up hits. While his work focused on evaluating pitchers, there was inevitable spillover into the value of fielding.

What the work on DIPS theory actually showed was that outside factors have a large impact on how many hits a pitcher allows, and one of the main variables is the quality of the defense behind him. Once we were able to accept that the pitcher was a minimal player in the outcome of a batted ball, we were able to see that each fielder actually had enough opportunities to make a legitimate impact on his team's run prevention. Defense matters, and not just at catcher and shortstop.

By the time Michael Lewis was signing copies of Moneyball and converting the masses to the value of OBP, teams like the A's had already begun taking advantage of the "market's" under-appreciation of fielding. Oakland started both Chris Singleton and Terrence Long as outfielders in the year that Lewis' best-seller was published, and they won the AL West by holding opponents to just 613 runs, thanks in large part to preventing hits on balls in play.

In recent years, most of the major league organizations that could be described as statistically inclined have emphasized defense. The Boston Red Sox swapped out Nomar Garciaparra's bat for Orlando Cabrera's glove on their way to winning the 2004 World Series. The Tampa Bay Rays put together a roster full of athletes and rode a stellar defense to the AL pennant in 2008. The Mariners built a fantastic defense in 2009 and improved by 24 wins in a single season. This year, both Texas and San Diego reaped the benefits of better glovework.

The consensus now is that the truth lies somewhere between what was valued in the 1980s and the 1990s, and we're attempting to find the happy medium. There isn't one single way to create value—lumbering sluggers who pound the baseball can be good players, as can slap-hitting middle infielders who do back flips when they run onto the field. We may not know exactly how much defense matters in every context, but we've gotten past the point of minimizing its effects just because we don't understand them. That's progress.

2. Individual defensive contributions are not easy to measure.

While we've reached something of a consensus on the fact that the overall ability of a team to field its positions can have a significant impact on their record, there is less agreement on the relative value of each player. This is the byproduct of an inherent difference between measuring offense and defense—fielding is kind of a free-for-all. One ball can be chased by multiple players. On any given play, two or sometimes even three players may all have a chance at impacting the final result. Can you imagine if we had to try to judge Juan Pierre's ability to hit while Albert Pujols was simultaneously swinging at every pitch thrown from the other batter's box? We may not have any real-life examples at that kind of extreme level, but the issue of competition for opportunities is one that is simply a result of the structure of the game.

Likewise, the construct of a batting order means that we get decent offensive samples for most everyday players

Defense Matters

over the course of a full season. While teams can hit their better players at the top of the order, this doesn't result in a dramatic difference in opportunities. However, nearly every team aligns its defense in a way to maximize defensive opportunities for its best players. The shortstop is almost always the best defensive player on the field because that is the position with more opportunities than any other. Beyond the basics of hiding weak players in corner spots, teams can also align the strengths of their fielders to the tendencies of their pitching staff—focusing on infielders who can play their positions if the team is full of sinkerball starters, for instance.

These options create an inequity of opportunity that makes comparisons of simple statistics like putouts and assists heavily flawed. In general, every team's clean-up hitter is going to get a similar number of chances to hit, but the same is not true on the other side of the ball. The lack of something resembling an opportunity constant creates problems when attempting to compare players in different contexts.

This issue is compounded even further by the overall lack of chances for defenders to use their skills in the first place. A pitcher with a great defense (in a neutral park) behind him might have 73 percent of his balls in play converted into outs, while a pitcher with a terrible defense behind him in the same park would see 67 percent of those plays made. Only about 6 to 7 percent of all fieldable balls are in the margin where defensive ability truly makes a difference, which works out to about 300 plays per team per year.

When you factor in that those 300 plays are spread among seven positions or so, that leaves about 40 chances per year for a fielder to show what he's got. You don't have to be a math guy to know that 40 plays per season is a pretty small sample to be judging someone on, especially when compared to the 600 or more plate appearances for judging hitters.

These structural issues have nothing to do with the actual design of the fielding metrics currently in use. These are just the unchanging facts of how the game is played, and hurdles that we have to jump over to make accurate assessments of a defender's ability. Even a perfectly designed model will have to deal with these realities, and the truth is that they get in the way and make evaluations more difficult.

These problems are not insurmountable, but they require workarounds that can add their own problems to the mix. A lot of really smart people have spent large amounts of time working on these issues, and they've come up with ways to deal with the issues, but they will all admit that this is a complicated process. Measuring the defensive abilities of a single player is just difficult.

3. There is more agreement between scouts and stats than most people realize.

Whenever a player's defensive rating by any one system veers significantly from the public perception of his abilities, there is always a minor kerfuffle. People point to the result as proof that the system is broken or poorly designed, or they go the other way and say that the metric proves that subjective assessments of ability are too prone to human error. If you've been around the issue for any length of time, you've seen one of these flare-ups.

One of the more notable differences between scouting reports and defensive metrics came from Jacoby Ellsbury's 2009 Ultimate Zone Rating, which listed him at 10 runs below average, the third worst of any center fielder in baseball. However, he was a former top prospect in large part because of the expectation that he would be an elite fielder, and as a guy with speed, he seemingly had the range to back that up. The Red Sox publicly denounced the validity of the rating, with GM Theo Epstein stating that their internal metrics graded him out much better than what UZR was reporting.

Almost immediately afterwards, the Red Sox signed Mike Cameron to play center field, shifting Ellsbury to left to replace the departed Jason Bay. The big fight over Ellsbury's abilities turned out to be not such a big disagreement after all, as the Red Sox ended up making a decision that was in line with what metrics like UZR suggested was a prudent cause of action. I don't doubt that Boston's proprietary defensive system was more optimistic about Ellsbury's abilities, but in the end, there wasn't a large enough discrepancy to change the conclusion.

While the points of contention receive the headlines, the reality is that the measurements that systems like UZR are reporting are mostly in line with what the perceptions of the quality of defenders, both among fans and the teams themselves.

From 2008 to 2010, the players with the worst UZR ratings in baseball were Adam Dunn, Brad Hawpe, Jermaine Dye, Ken Griffey Jr. and Delmon Young. Dunn was moved to first base, Hawpe was released midseason before signing with an AL club where he could DH, Dye was unwanted as a free agent and forced into retirement, Griffey was made a permanent DH, and Young lost 40 pounds last winter in response to criticism about his work ethic.

On the opposite end of the spectrum, the metric is a big fan of Franklin Gutierrez, Chase Utley, Pedro Feliz, Omar Vizquel and Ryan Zimmerman. Those five are all universally accepted as premier defensive players, and are treated as such by major league organizations. The scouting reports for all five match the statistical profile. These guys can pick it, and that's obvious to scouts and statistical analysts alike.

There is not universal agreement on every player, of course, but then there wouldn't be any point to having a quantifiable metric if there was. As the old saying goes, if a statistic doesn't surprise you every once in a while, it's useless. While there will always be efforts to discredit either the stats or the scouting reports, the reality is that they work together nicely.

One of the challenges of the last few years was to move beyond a false dichotomy of having to choose between the subjective or objective; the most useful information combines the best of both. Fielding metrics were not created with the intention of displacing scouting reports, but enhancing them. The imperfections of both sides can be seen through the lens of the other, and this makes each one useful.

4. Humility is the bridge to acceptance.

The stats crowd had something of a Brian Hunter moment when it began to realize that we'd been very wrong about some of the favorite whipping boys of the 1990s. Despite all of the snark directed his way, Rey Sanchez really was a decent baseball player—we just didn't know it. Major league teams did, though, and kept employing him year after year in spite of his offensive futility. They saw value in his glove, and eventually, we came around and admitted that our dogmatic philosophies weren't entirely accurate.

While we know more now than we did a decade ago, we still don't know a lot of things. Over the next 10 years, as people continue to innovate and fill in holes with things like hang time data, we'll find out that some of the assumptions we've been making are wrong. That's okay—it's part of the process. We'll all just be better off if we anticipate those eventual shifts in thought, however, and temper our conclusions accordingly.

I would have benefited from a little more discretion back in 1999, even though Hunter eventually turned out to be a pretty bad player for a Seattle team that finished below .500. We all would have benefited from a little more skepticism of metrics that told us that Jeremy Giambi was a superstar in the making despite possessing the range of a wilting fern. Being insistent and wrong is a dangerous combination, especially when facing skeptics with legitimate questions.

I'm not saying that we should ignore the progress that has been made in sabermetric analysis over the last 10 years. We can be honest about what we know while also admitting that we don't fully understand all the places where we may have made mistakes along the way.

The sabermetric community should be proud of the work that has been done on evaluating defense. We haven't solved the puzzle yet, and we might not even yet have all the tools needed to put it together completely. However, important steps have been taken, and we have set ourselves up for breakthroughs in understanding that could bring an entirely new appreciation for those who specialize in making plays in the field.

We aren't there yet. We're getting there, though.

The Pitching and Defense Splits

by John Dewan

Analyzing defense using the main currency of baseball (i.e. runs) allows us to break down the number of runs each team allowed into two components: pitching and defense. For example, the Oakland A's allowed the fewest runs in the American League in 2010. Let's analyze why.

First, here are the eight teams that allowed the fewest runs in the American League:

Team	Runs Allowed
Oakland	626
Tampa Bay	649
Minnesota	671
Texas	687
New York	693
Seattle	698
Los Angeles	702
Chicago	704

As you can see in the Team Defensive Runs chart on the following pages, the Oakland A's team defense played a big hand in team run prevention. The A's had the best gloves and arms in the game, with their defensive prowess saving an estimated 74 runs compared to an average defense. The top eight American League defenses in 2010 were:

Team	Defensive Runs Saved
Oakland	74
Minnesota	54
Cleveland	50
Toronto	46
Tampa Bay	41
Seattle	37
Detroit	18
New York	0

One of the interesting byproducts of this analysis is that we can isolate the pitching component of a team's run prevention by estimating how many runs the team would have allowed with an average defense. For example, the A's allowed 626 runs to cross to plate in 2010. If they had an average defense, they would have allowed 74 more runs for a total of 700 runs.

By comparison, the Boston Red Sox, who allowed 744 runs, ranked 13th out of 14 defensively—their team defense cost them 56 runs during the year. That means that with an average defense, they would have allowed 744 minus 56, or 688 runs in 2010. That's fewer than Oakland's defense-independent runs-allowed total of 700.

By doing this calculation for all the teams, we can find out which teams had the best pitching staffs independent of their defense. Here are the top eight pitching staffs in the American League in 2010:

Teams	Total Runs Allowed	Defensive Runs Saved	Pitching Runs Allowed
Chicago	704	-30	674
Texas	687	-1	686
Boston	744	-56	688
Tampa Bay	649	41	690
New York	693	0	693
Los Angeles	702	-4	698
Oakland	626	74	700
Minnesota	671	54	725

If you ignore defense, the best pitching staff in the American League was the Chicago White Sox. The Red Sox were third. But these two teams had the second- and third-worst defenses in the AL, and neither team made the playoffs. In fact, two of the four playoff teams had average defenses (Texas and New York) while the other two had excellent defenses (Tampa Bay and Minnesota).

It is interesting that there were seven American League teams bunched quite closely together in Pitching Runs Allowed, all of them between 674 and 700.

Let's do a similar analysis for the National League. The San Diego Padres allowed the fewest runs in 2010:

Team	Runs Allowed
San Diego	581
San Francisco	583
Atlanta	629
Philadelphia	640
St. Louis	641
New York	652
Cincinnati	685
Los Angeles	692

100

Three of the top four teams in run prevention made the playoffs in the National League in 2010. The Padres just missed by one game while the fourth playoff team was seventh in run prevention. Here are the top defensive units:

Team	Defensive Runs Saved
St. Louis	61
San Francisco	54
San Diego	53
Atlanta	35
Cincinnati	33
New York	32
Colorado	30
Arizona	22

Three of the four playoff teams were in the top five in defense. The fourth team, Philadelphia, just missed the list with a fine team defense of 18 runs saved.

Let's look at the pitching staffs independent of defense:

Team	Total Runs Allowed	Defensive Runs Saved	Pitching Runs Allowed
San Diego	581	53	634
San Francisco	583	54	637
Philadelphia	640	18	658
Atlanta	629	35	664
Los Angeles	692	-21	671
New York	652	32	684
Florida	717	-23	694
St. Louis	641	61	702

San Diego remains on top of this chart. However, it is a notable that Padres pitchers have an advantage by pitching in the most extreme pitcher's park in baseball over the last three years. We estimate that the park itself is responsible for 50-60 fewer runs allowed for the Padres over the course of a season.

The Dodgers are of interest as well. Their pitching was fifth best in the National League, according to this measure, but their defense cost them 75 runs relative to the Giants. Using the rule of thumb that 10 runs is equivalent to a win, defense accounted for a difference of about seven or eight games in the standings between the Giants and Dodgers. The Dodgers still would have fallen short of the division title, since they were 12 games behind San Francisco overall, but this example highlights the importance of defense.

One more note from this past season's playoffs: The Braves beat the Padres by one game for the Wild Card. If the Braves had an average defense instead of a defense that saved 35 runs, it would have cost them three to four games in the standings, and it would have cost them the playoff berth. The same can be said about the Giants, who beat the Padres by only two games. Defense solidified their team and their playoff berth.

Description of the Team Defensive Charts

Defensive Runs Saved (Runs Saved, for short) is the innovative metric introduced in *The Fielding Bible—Volume II*. The Runs Saved value indicates how many runs a player saved or hurt his team in the field compared to the average player at his position. A player near zero Runs Saved is about average; a positive number of runs saved indicates above-average defense, below-average fielders post negative Runs Saved totals. There are eight components of Runs Saved, and you can view the leaders in each category in the table at the top of the next page (as well as in the *Bill James Handbook 2011*). The definition of each component is:

- Plus/Minus Runs Saved evaluates the fielder's range and ability to convert a batted ball to an out.
- Earned Runs Saved measures a catcher's influence on his pitching staff.
- Stolen Base Runs Saved gives the catcher credit for throwing out runners and preventing them from attempting steals in the first place.
- Stolen Base Runs Saved measures the pitcher's contributions to controlling the running game.
- Bunt Runs Saved evaluates a fielder's handling of bunted balls in play.
- Double Play Runs Saved credits infielders for turning double plays as opposed to getting one out on the play.
- Outfield Arm Runs Saved evaluates an outfielder's throwing arm based on how often runners advance on base hits and are thrown out trying to take extra bases.
- Home Run Saving Catch Runs credits the outfielder 1.6 runs per robbed home run.

In the top chart on each of the following pages, we break down each team's defense by Runs Saved at each position to isolate their strengths and weaknesses. As you can see, Washington Nationals third basemen (primarily Ryan Zimmerman) played the strongest defense of any position in baseball last year, while White Sox third basemen really hurt the club, costing the Sox 32 runs defensively.

The second chart on each page rates each team's performance in four categories. Plus/Minus is broken down into middle infield, corner infield and outfield. Ground DP tells

Component	Applicable Positions	2010 Leader	Top 2010 Runs Saved Total
Plus/Minus Runs Saved	All except Catchers	Brendan Ryan	24
Earned Runs Saved	Catchers	Yorvit Torrealba/ Yadier Molina/ Kurt Suzuki	6
Stolen Base Runs Saved	Catchers	Miguel Olivo	11
Stolen Base Runs Saved	Pitchers	Mark Buehrle/ Dallas Braden	5
Bunt Runs Saved	Corner Infielders	Todd Helton/ Casey McGehee	4
Double Play Runs Saved	Middle Infielders	Gordon Beckham	5
Outfield Arm Runs Saved	Outfielders	Shin-Soo Choo	12
Home Run Saving Catch Runs Saved	Outfielders	Ichiro Suzuki/ Franklin Gutierrez	5

you how often the team turned double plays given its opportunities (ground ball with a man on first and fewer than two outs). A team's overall handling of bunts is rated on the A through F grade scale. The throwing section rates how often outfielders gun out opposing baserunners and how often they prevent runners from trying for extra bases in the first place.

Team Defensive Runs by Position - 2010

Team	Pitcher	Catcher	First Base	Second Base	Third Base	Shortstop	Left Field	Center Field	Right Field	Total
Oakland Athletics	16	3	19	10	10	4	-5	1	16	74
St Louis Cardinals	11	11	0	-4	0	24	10	-1	10	61
Minnesota Twins	2	6	3	16	10	11	-4	10	0	54
San Francisco Giants	-2	7	7	1	5	-5	21	6	14	54
San Diego Padres	10	1	0	5	21	2	-1	14	1	53
Cleveland Indians	19	-3	5	13	9	-12	14	-8	13	50
Toronto Blue Jays	5	-2	11	16	4	13	2	-6	3	46
Tampa Bay Rays	-13	-5	0	29	10	8	11	-7	8	41
Seattle Mariners	-2	1	-1	-12	12	8	3	17	11	37
Atlanta Braves	4	0	-9	7	8	26	-3	-7	9	35
Cincinnati Reds	0	-4	0	1	0	-2	5	10	23	33
New York Mets	10	-1	16	-3	-7	-2	2	5	12	32
Colorado Rockies	8	11	0	-1	-6	28	8	-3	-15	30
Arizona Diamondbacks	-13	-6	2	3	0	-2	16	9	13	22
Detroit Tigers	-18	-4	-2	3	1	2	15	27	-6	18
Philadelphia Phillies	9	5	-17	16	-8	9	-7	7	4	18
Washington Nationals	-2	-1	-8	-9	31	-7	2	1	3	10
New York Yankees	-5	-10	-4	7	-1	-10	9	8	6	0
Texas Rangers	-11	-6	2	4	-16	0	4	13	9	-1
Baltimore Orioles	3	2	-3	-9	-9	1	11	3	-1	-2
Los Angeles Angels	0	-7	10	-14	11	-6	-7	14	-5	-4
Houston Astros	-1	5	6	-9	-17	-18	-13	15	12	-20
Los Angeles Dodgers	4	2	0	-2	12	0	-6	-19	-12	-21
Chicago Cubs	-2	-5	6	-10	-11	-3	-4	7	0	-22
Florida Marlins	-9	1	-4	-12	-11	-18	-1	2	29	-23
Chicago White Sox	4	6	-19	-5	-32	17	5	8	-14	-30
Milwaukee Brewers	-7	-5	-12	-10	-9	0	-2	12	-5	-38
Boston Red Sox	-13	-8	7	1	12	-14	-17	-15	-9	-56
Pittsburgh Pirates	2	-4	-6	-17	-13	-26	4	-20	-1	-81
Kansas City Royals	1	-4	-4	-12	-24	-20	-8	-4	-13	-88

Team Totals and Rankings - 2010

Team	PLUS/MINUS Middle Infield	Corner Infield	Outfield	Total	Rank	GROUND DP GDP Opps	GDP	Pct	Rank	BUNTS Opps	Score	Grade	Rank	THROWING Opps To Advance	Extra Bases	Kills	Pct	Rank
Oakland Athletics	+12	+45	+20	+77	1	316	133	.421	9	50	.473	C	27	361	179	14	.496	26
Tampa Bay Rays	+51	+14	+6	+71	2	273	117	.429	8	46	.559	B-	11	332	145	14	.437	8
San Diego Padres	+10	+23	+23	+56	3	295	120	.407	13	54	.606	B+	7	388	201	16	.518	29
Arizona Diamondbacks	-3	+2	+55	+54	4	306	124	.405	14	49	.532	C+	14	428	193	15	.451	11
San Francisco Giants	-3	+8	+45	+50	5	260	88	.338	28	44	.622	B+	4	339	146	20	.431	5
Seattle Mariners	-9	+22	+37	+50	5	312	124	.397	16	58	.441	C-	30	417	199	17	.477	21
Minnesota Twins	+36	+17	-16	+37	7	283	122	.431	7	41	.516	C+	18	419	204	27	.487	23
St Louis Cardinals	+19	+3	+15	+37	7	366	154	.421	10	40	.549	B-	13	409	183	13	.447	10
Cincinnati Reds	+1	-3	+38	+36	9	310	120	.387	19	32	.611	B+	6	413	171	15	.414	2
Atlanta Braves	+38	-5	+1	+34	10	344	141	.410	12	37	.514	C+	21	374	183	16	.489	25
Detroit Tigers	+2	0	+31	+33	11	326	147	.451	3	47	.507	C+	22	444	193	25	.435	6
Texas Rangers	+6	-8	+35	+33	11	299	119	.398	15	45	.442	C-	29	402	191	13	.475	20
Toronto Blue Jays	+25	+22	-15	+32	13	301	148	.492	1	25	.480	C	24	433	196	17	.453	12
New York Yankees	-8	-3	+28	+17	14	307	136	.443	4	36	.514	C+	20	356	178	23	.500	27
Washington Nationals	-14	+22	-4	+4	15	359	127	.354	25	53	.592	B	8	454	209	17	.460	14
New York Mets	-4	+8	-4	0	16	367	138	.376	23	62	.633	A-	3	432	168	23	.389	1
Cleveland Indians	-7	+20	-14	-1	17	365	159	.436	6	35	.476	C	26	468	204	25	.436	7
Colorado Rockies	+28	-10	-19	-1	17	351	155	.442	5	50	.619	B+	5	418	220	13	.526	30
Los Angeles Angels	-23	+31	-20	-12	19	248	96	.387	19	36	.517	C+	17	419	199	23	.475	19
Philadelphia Phillies	+26	-32	-10	-16	20	321	133	.414	11	55	.524	C+	16	373	160	17	.429	4
Chicago Cubs	-10	-3	-3	-16	20	326	118	.362	24	58	.476	C	25	442	206	15	.466	16
Houston Astros	-33	-21	+26	-28	22	305	116	.380	22	40	.649	A-	2	445	210	14	.472	17
Los Angeles Dodgers	+8	+14	-55	-33	23	306	104	.340	27	46	.552	B-	12	381	196	12	.514	28
Baltimore Orioles	-10	-14	-18	-42	24	302	117	.387	18	43	.528	C+	15	426	177	26	.415	3
Milwaukee Brewers	-14	-35	0	-49	25	299	114	.381	21	39	.690	A	1	454	199	17	.438	9
Florida Marlins	-37	-19	+7	-49	25	307	105	.342	26	50	.572	B	10	439	204	28	.465	15
Chicago White Sox	+8	-67	-8	-67	27	307	139	.453	2	46	.515	C+	19	459	223	11	.486	22
Boston Red Sox	-17	+25	-103	-95	28	297	116	.391	17	43	.581	B	9	402	185	23	.460	13
Kansas City Royals	-32	-33	-34	-99	29	328	109	.332	30	39	.467	C-	28	515	244	16	.474	18
Pittsburgh Pirates	-56	-23	-47	-126	30	304	102	.336	29	48	.491	C	23	466	227	22	.487	24

Team Defensive Runs by Position - 2009

Team	Pitcher	Catcher	First Base	Second Base	Third Base	Shortstop	Left Field	Center Field	Right Field	Total
Seattle Mariners	12	12	1	6	27	-6	8	36	14	110
Los Angeles Angels	-1	-3	10	14	28	-4	23	-1	-1	65
Tampa Bay Rays	-11	-4	-11	13	15	5	26	-1	25	57
Toronto Blue Jays	6	6	-1	22	11	14	-4	-10	8	52
Cincinnati Reds	12	1	-3	-3	-3	10	17	14	7	52
Texas Rangers	2	3	-8	20	-16	18	5	5	13	42
Detroit Tigers	-3	2	-2	5	8	4	13	15	-5	37
Arizona Diamondbacks	-5	3	-13	13	-4	9	15	4	12	34
San Francisco Giants	8	-4	11	-4	-6	-8	12	6	19	34
Pittsburgh Pirates	4	0	-1	-9	0	16	12	0	9	31
St Louis Cardinals	11	5	12	-8	-8	14	-5	4	6	31
Los Angeles Dodgers	0	5	3	8	15	5	-5	-3	2	30
New York Mets	13	-1	13	-12	-11	-6	5	11	8	20
Chicago Cubs	3	7	3	0	-4	2	-2	-1	8	16
Philadelphia Phillies	-5	2	-1	14	7	-5	-2	-6	12	16
Colorado Rockies	5	-2	-2	2	2	13	15	-10	-11	12
Atlanta Braves	4	2	7	-11	2	19	-11	-10	6	8
Washington Nationals	8	-1	-19	0	21	-3	-3	10	-6	7
New York Yankees	4	-7	1	6	-13	2	-1	3	7	2
San Diego Padres	5	2	12	-20	1	-14	0	17	-4	-1
Houston Astros	3	2	-2	-4	-12	-15	-3	10	19	-2
Cleveland Indians	-4	-9	5	2	-7	4	-7	-1	13	-4
Chicago White Sox	16	0	-4	1	-11	2	-8	5	-10	-9
Baltimore Orioles	7	-8	-12	-5	-5	14	0	-2	-3	-14
Oakland Athletics	1	2	-8	-10	-7	-32	19	12	8	-15
Milwaukee Brewers	-10	-7	-1	20	-8	2	-13	0	-5	-22
Florida Marlins	-12	-4	-8	-7	-5	4	-18	4	18	-28
Minnesota Twins	-4	-5	2	-22	9	-24	-1	17	-5	-33
Boston Red Sox	-17	-8	10	11	-18	-19	-2	-11	2	-52
Kansas City Royals	4	-5	-2	-13	-12	-17	6	-2	-21	-62

Team Totals and Rankings - 2009

Team	PLUS/MINUS Middle Infield	Corner Infield	Outfield	Total	Rank	GROUND DP GDP Opps	GDP	Pct	Rank	BUNTS Opps	Score	Grade	Rank	THROWING Opps To Advance	Extra Bases	Kills	Pct	Rank
Seattle Mariners	-8	+36	+79	+107	1	284	128	.451	3	31	.587	B	7	404	169	15	.418	4
Tampa Bay Rays	+28	+8	+55	+91	2	273	113	.414	11	39	.503	C+	24	418	181	24	.433	10
Arizona Diamondbacks	+29	-22	+49	+56	3	317	117	.369	25	51	.509	C+	21	457	220	10	.481	26
Los Angeles Angels	+1	+52	-2	+51	4	313	154	.492	1	31	.505	C+	22	452	196	19	.434	11
Texas Rangers	+40	-29	+38	+49	5	289	138	.478	2	28	.430	D+	29	434	208	17	.479	23
San Francisco Giants	-6	0	+42	+36	6	299	111	.371	24	72	.593	B	4	360	157	19	.436	12
Pittsburgh Pirates	+12	+1	+15	+28	7	342	140	.409	15	55	.537	C+	15	428	189	18	.442	14
Cincinnati Reds	+8	-12	+28	+24	8	336	135	.402	17	46	.620	B+	1	434	169	23	.389	1
Los Angeles Dodgers	+19	+19	-15	+23	9	299	114	.381	23	45	.593	B	3	369	177	16	.480	24
Toronto Blue Jays	+42	+27	-49	+20	10	345	145	.420	9	33	.342	F	30	456	181	16	.397	2
Detroit Tigers	+6	+14	-2	+18	11	319	140	.439	5	32	.433	D+	28	439	184	20	.419	5
San Diego Padres	-38	+18	+31	+11	12	318	117	.368	26	61	.588	B	6	428	236	15	.551	30
New York Mets	-17	+3	+24	+10	13	332	113	.340	30	46	.538	C+	14	460	208	15	.452	15
New York Yankees	+12	-12	+6	+6	14	290	112	.386	21	28	.511	C+	20	423	180	11	.426	7
Colorado Rockies	+21	-1	-16	+4	15	334	120	.359	28	57	.534	C+	17	440	213	18	.484	27
St Louis Cardinals	+5	+6	-15	-4	16	366	149	.407	16	43	.566	B-	8	425	182	13	.428	9
Cleveland Indians	-2	-2	-5	-9	17	337	150	.445	4	49	.541	B-	13	532	256	15	.481	25
Chicago Cubs	+8	-5	-14	-11	18	346	118	.341	29	65	.565	B-	9	374	175	16	.468	20
Atlanta Braves	+12	+5	-31	-14	19	354	138	.390	20	43	.592	B	5	418	195	14	.467	19
Washington Nationals	-3	-1	-15	-19	20	330	127	.385	22	54	.553	B-	11	455	207	16	.455	17
Philadelphia Phillies	+9	+6	-34	-19	20	271	108	.399	18	48	.558	B-	10	426	181	27	.425	6
Milwaukee Brewers	+24	-12	-33	-21	22	312	135	.433	6	45	.518	C+	19	424	202	9	.476	22
Minnesota Twins	-59	+17	+11	-31	23	281	116	.413	13	33	.480	C	27	447	222	11	.497	29
Oakland Athletics	-54	-20	+43	-31	23	301	129	.429	7	36	.504	C+	23	464	203	17	.438	13
Florida Marlins	-7	-19	-6	-32	25	319	115	.361	27	55	.525	C+	18	424	192	14	.453	16
Houston Astros	-26	-20	+7	-39	26	347	143	.412	14	40	.609	B+	2	472	202	21	.428	8
Boston Red Sox	-13	-11	-21	-45	27	251	98	.390	19	41	.537	C+	16	459	217	14	.473	21
Chicago White Sox	+1	-16	-46	-61	28	314	130	.414	10	45	.493	C	26	413	189	22	.458	18
Baltimore Orioles	+6	-23	-76	-93	29	312	132	.423	8	27	.544	B-	12	483	195	22	.404	3
Kansas City Royals	-46	-15	-42	-103	30	317	131	.413	12	40	.499	C	25	481	238	22	.495	28

Team Defensive Runs by Position - 2008

Team	Pitcher	Catcher	First Base	Second Base	Third Base	Shortstop	Left Field	Center Field	Right Field	Total
Philadelphia Phillies	1	-3	2	33	3	16	4	14	9	79
St Louis Cardinals	3	4	14	16	7	20	2	-8	18	76
Oakland Athletics	14	5	6	23	10	-17	-9	17	15	64
Toronto Blue Jays	9	1	5	3	29	-4	-7	-3	23	56
Milwaukee Brewers	8	10	-9	-3	3	17	11	14	2	53
New York Mets	13	-2	-6	-18	2	-4	25	21	13	44
Atlanta Braves	-2	7	5	-3	15	14	-2	7	-5	36
Cleveland Indians	1	-3	-6	7	-4	-3	12	3	24	31
Tampa Bay Rays	-8	-4	15	8	13	-13	14	1	0	26
Washington Nationals	2	1	-6	-13	11	12	12	-4	10	25
Houston Astros	-2	0	13	-19	3	8	3	7	11	24
Boston Red Sox	-5	2	2	9	12	1	0	0	-1	20
Seattle Mariners	-1	-3	0	-2	25	-13	-6	0	17	17
Florida Marlins	-8	-3	-21	6	-1	4	7	22	3	9
Chicago Cubs	13	0	4	-3	-6	4	8	-11	0	9
Los Angeles Dodgers	3	-2	0	-17	14	1	5	5	-5	4
Arizona Diamondbacks	0	-3	-12	6	-8	-1	11	7	-4	-4
San Diego Padres	-14	-2	0	-7	0	-6	6	7	11	-5
Los Angeles Angels	-13	-4	16	2	4	6	-8	4	-13	-6
San Francisco Giants	-12	3	5	-13	-6	1	7	-4	12	-7
Pittsburgh Pirates	9	4	-3	2	-3	10	-11	-17	2	-7
Minnesota Twins	4	-2	-2	-3	-15	-3	-14	17	9	-9
Colorado Rockies	9	1	-3	15	-6	6	0	-6	-25	-9
Cincinnati Reds	-1	-2	16	9	-25	-11	-12	18	-4	-12
Detroit Tigers	20	8	-8	9	-21	-13	-3	-3	-4	-15
Baltimore Orioles	-13	0	-7	-3	-13	-30	11	20	19	-16
Texas Rangers	-5	1	-1	-6	-26	-5	1	-4	18	-27
Chicago White Sox	-7	-9	-8	-7	6	1	3	-5	-8	-34
New York Yankees	-2	-1	-18	-13	-10	-10	10	12	-6	-38
Kansas City Royals	8	-5	-10	-6	-12	9	-7	-8	-11	-42

Team Totals and Rankings - 2008

	PLUS/MINUS					GROUND DP				BUNTS				THROWING				
Team	Middle Infield	Corner Infield	Outfield	Total	Rank	GDP Opps	GDP	Pct	Rank	Opps	Score	Grade	Rank	Opps To Advance	Extra Bases	Kills	Pct	Rank
Philadelphia Phillies	+70	+7	0	+77	1	338	127	.376	22	45	.559	B-	11	406	163	27	.401	2
St Louis Cardinals	+43	+26	-3	+66	2	330	135	.409	11	37	.634	A-	3	456	202	20	.443	8
Toronto Blue Jays	+4	+47	0	+51	3	293	111	.379	21	35	.499	C	24	373	167	21	.448	12
New York Mets	-21	-12	+79	+46	4	341	113	.331	29	47	.640	A-	2	446	203	20	.455	16
Oakland Athletics	-5	+26	+24	+45	5	273	142	.520	1	34	.529	C+	17	419	188	20	.449	13
Milwaukee Brewers	+25	-5	+25	+45	5	374	132	.353	25	68	.504	C+	23	389	175	15	.450	15
Washington Nationals	-1	+3	+35	+37	7	310	119	.384	19	39	.549	B-	14	465	227	12	.488	27
Tampa Bay Rays	-12	+33	+11	+32	8	303	134	.442	8	45	.622	B+	4	392	179	19	.457	17
Atlanta Braves	+22	+24	-19	+27	9	390	132	.338	28	34	.566	B-	10	416	187	13	.450	14
Boston Red Sox	+16	+18	-8	+26	10	299	119	.398	15	42	.577	B	7	422	202	14	.479	25
Florida Marlins	+17	-28	+36	+25	11	313	100	.319	30	54	.512	C+	20	448	207	20	.462	19
San Diego Padres	-16	-7	+46	+23	12	324	127	.392	17	53	.692	A+	1	424	216	14	.509	29
Houston Astros	-18	+24	+15	+21	13	296	120	.405	12	30	.532	C+	16	398	178	20	.447	11
Cleveland Indians	-10	-5	+33	+18	14	330	159	.482	2	47	.447	C-	27	489	203	23	.415	3
Arizona Diamondbacks	+6	-25	+30	+11	15	324	114	.352	26	52	.513	C+	19	415	199	13	.480	26
San Francisco Giants	-10	-8	+10	-8	16	283	104	.367	23	53	.607	B+	6	441	207	12	.469	22
Seattle Mariners	-23	+35	-20	-8	16	336	138	.411	10	44	.572	B	8	510	215	20	.422	4
Los Angeles Angels	0	+28	-41	-13	18	315	141	.448	4	31	.555	B-	13	407	206	16	.506	28
Los Angeles Dodgers	-11	+12	-14	-13	18	362	124	.343	27	50	.613	B+	5	452	210	19	.465	21
Baltimore Orioles	-38	-21	+37	-22	20	368	142	.386	18	44	.473	C	26	501	199	24	.397	1
Chicago Cubs	+6	-4	-26	-24	21	266	97	.365	24	49	.558	B-	12	361	161	17	.446	10
Cincinnati Reds	+2	-11	-24	-33	22	340	130	.382	20	50	.567	B-	9	442	187	18	.423	5
Chicago White Sox	-13	+3	-25	-35	23	311	138	.444	6	37	.435	D+	28	432	203	10	.470	23
Colorado Rockies	+21	-12	-48	-39	24	359	144	.401	14	43	.535	C+	15	519	241	15	.464	20
Minnesota Twins	-13	-21	-8	-42	25	327	142	.434	9	28	.511	C+	21	467	208	23	.445	9
Pittsburgh Pirates	+14	-4	-53	-43	26	391	157	.402	13	68	.524	C+	18	505	233	15	.461	18
Detroit Tigers	-8	-34	-22	-64	27	341	153	.449	3	36	.411	D+	30	503	237	14	.471	24
Texas Rangers	-22	-37	-7	-66	28	361	160	.443	7	44	.506	C+	22	549	240	19	.437	7
New York Yankees	-29	-33	-8	-70	29	280	110	.393	16	36	.419	D+	29	447	191	22	.427	6
Kansas City Royals	-4	-24	-49	-77	30	301	134	.445	5	31	.474	C	25	463	238	15	.514	30

The Next Frontier in Fielding Analysis

by Ben Jedlovec

Once upon a time, long before we got caught up in "medium line drives" and "hard fliner flies," there were ground outs and fly outs. Either you caught the ball on the fly, threw the guy out, or he reached base. There was nothing more, no statistics to judge fielders other than basic fielding average.

So Bill James designed "Range Factor," which used simple box score stats (put-outs, assists and errors) to estimate the number of plays a particular player made in a game. It wasn't perfect, and several analysts, including Tom Tippett and James himself, have made adjustments to compensate for Range Factor's shortcomings. However, these systems have limited accuracy—particularly in the short term—because they don't include any information about the ball's landing point or trajectory.

Somewhere along the way, data collectors starting manually recording hit locations and classifying velocities and trajectories: line drives, fly balls and pop ups, as well as Baseball Info Solutions' fliner liners and fliner flies. These descriptions gave us the tools to design smarter fielding systems, from Zone Rating and Revised Zone Rating to Ultimate Zone Rating and Plus/Minus.

These latest defensive statistics have been a revelation over the past decade. Now, we can estimate the value of a player's defensive performance to a reasonable degree of accuracy, and we can place it in the proper context to measure a player's total contributions on both sides of the ball.

The recent advancements due to batted-ball data aren't limited to defense either. J.C. Bradbury's PrOPS (published in the 2006 *Hardball Times Annual*) and Dave Studenmund's xFIP use batted-ball trajectory classifications to help us better evaluate hitters and pitchers, respectively.

However, the current classification of trajectories isn't ideal. Analysts have recently taken to dissecting batted-ball information from various sources, finding large park-to-park variation. Park-specific scorers have tendencies that carry over into the data they record, and while rotating scorers (which we do at BIS) eliminates one bias, there are still smaller inconsistencies and natural park effects. While we at BIS improve our quality control every year, there are

admittedly some imperfections that we can't always weed out.

Additionally, we lose a lot of valuable information by categorizing data in this way. While each batted ball is recorded as one of five trajectories and three speeds, there are an infinite number of trajectories a ball could take. Ideally, we'd have objective, non-discrete data to describe the trajectory of each ball in play of the entire season, and that's where BIS's hit timer data comes in.

An Intro to Hang Time Data

In 2009 Baseball Info Solutions began collecting timer data on all batted balls, from ground balls to line drives to fly balls. Two separate BIS Video Scouts record timer data for each ball in play in our charting software. If the two recorded values don't closely agree, we review the play a third time to record the most accurate possible time.

While the data are usually available exclusively to private clients, I wanted to take the data for a test drive and give you a glimpse of its potential. In this article, I'm going to focus on hang time for line drives and fly balls.

For the 2004 *Annual*, Robert Dudek performed the first notable study of hang time data. Dudek recorded hang time data for eight pitchers: four flyball pitchers and four ground-ball pitchers. Unfortunately, he lacked the resources to collect a more exhaustive sample of data.

Knowing the landing point and hang time of a fly ball allows us to reconstruct its entire trajectory, aside from atmospheric effects. The hit location tells us where the fielder needs to be in order to make the play, while the hang time tells us how long he has to get there before the ball drops in for a hit. The combination of hit location and hang time is an extremely powerful analytical tool.

Let's begin by confirming Dudek's results with BIS's 2010 data. First, Dudek looked at how often fly balls to the outfield were caught based on their hang time. He removed (as I do) home runs, balls that were in the air less than 1.5 seconds and balls that were caught by an infielder.

The comparative results are listed at the top of the next page.

Timer Group	BallsInAir	Outs	OutRatio	Dudek
1.5-2.0	4269	3	0.1%	0.8%
2.0-2.5	5338	192	3.5%	4.5%
2.5-3.0	5720	1734	30.3%	28.3%
3.0-3.5	5779	2925	51.1%	41.1%
3.5-4.0	5595	3507	64.6%	55.9%
4.0-4.5	5735	4108	75.0%	67.4%
4.5-5.0	5583	4642	86.8%	80.1%
5.0-5.5	5815	5364	94.2%	86.5%
5.5-6.0	5108	4924	97.0%	95.9%
6.0-6.5	3144	3049	97.3%	97.3%
6.5+	969	938	96.8%	96.4%

While the overall trend is very similar, I found an out ratio slightly higher than Dudek's in every group between 2.5 and 6.0 seconds, which could be attributable to one or more factors. The mostly likely cause stems from the fact that Derek Lowe and Pedro Martinez, two of the eight pitchers in Dudek's study, frequently pitched in front of Fenway's Green Monster, which often turns fly outs into base hits. Thanks to BIS's wall ball information, I'm removing unreachable wall balls from my data set, while 25 percent of the players in Dudek's sample could have been affected.

Here is a graph of BIS's data, with the points plotted continuously instead of being grouped:

No baseball player can hit a ball 300 feet in two seconds; most two-second line drives land just over the infield, if they make it that far. Balls generally take close to three seconds to make it far enough for outfielders to have a chance at a play.

Dudek then split his eight pitchers into a fly ball group and a groundball group and compared the characteristics of the two. I've taken all pitchers who allowed at least 150 balls in play, ranging from Sergio Santos' 150 to Mark Buehrle's 748, and compared their fly ball rates with the average hang time on their fly balls/line drives. Here's a graph of the results:

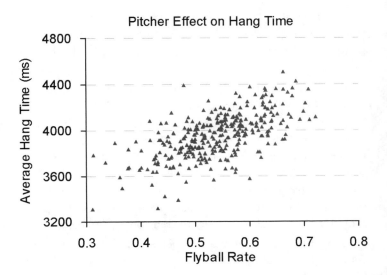

As you can tell from the graph, flyball rate and average hang time are significantly correlated, producing an r-squared value of .29. Major league pitchers who allow more fly balls also tend to give up higher fly balls. But are these high fly balls also more costly because they are hit deeper? Let's graph that data too:

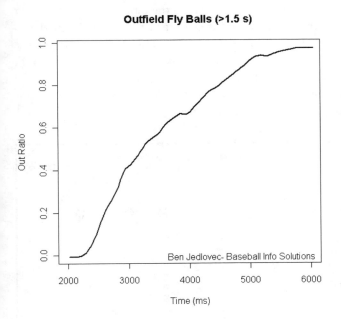

Notice how the curve isn't linear—it begins on a sharp slope and gradually flattens out. This is partially because a ball's hang time and distance traveled are somewhat related.

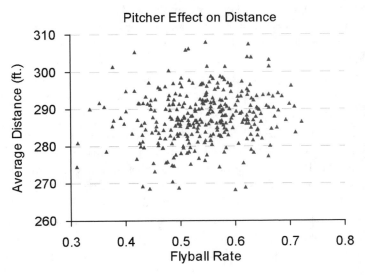

As it turns out, flyball rate does not also correlate well with how deep the ball is hit, producing an r-squared value of just .027. Dudek's small-sample observations hold up: Flyball pitchers who make the majors do give up softer fly balls. This confirms an important fact counter to defense-independent pitching theory: pitchers can "control" the characteristics of balls put into play, at least to some extent.

The Future of Hit Timer Analysis

Many of today's leading defensive metrics use trajectory and location information to approximate the difficulty of a play from the fielder's perspective. For example, all medium fliners that land at a certain coordinate are binned together. If we have large enough "buckets" of plays, we can add them up to determine how often we can expect balls in this bucket to be caught.

Say 72 out of 100 balls in a given bucket are caught for outs. In the Plus/Minus System, we call 72/100 = .72 the "Out Ratio." When a fielder fails to make the catch on this particular ball, he has failed to make a play that 72 percent of fielders make, so we penalize him -.72 "credits," or "plays." When the fielder does make the play, we award him 1 - .72 = .28 credits for making a play that 28 percent of fielders didn't. From there, we can easily translate plays into runs in order to properly value defensive contributions on a relatable scale.

Hang time data essentially replaces the information that velocity (hard, medium, soft) and trajectory (liner, fliner fly, fliner liner, fly ball) were giving us before. Perhaps the most obvious way to incorporate hang time into existing defensive metrics is to group hang times in clusters: 3.0-3.5 second fly balls in one category, 3.5-4.0 in the next, etc. This gives us a more consistent and objective way to group similarly hit fly balls together.

When we categorize similar plays into bins, we have to strike a delicate balance between sample size and precision. If we make the buckets too small, each bin will contain a handful of very similar plays, but we won't have enough plays to make reliable Out Ratio estimates. If we make the buckets too large, we'll have large enough sample sizes, but our collection of plays will be less similar. This tradeoff is one of the biggest challenges facing contemporary defensive metrics.

However, we can do better.

Hang time data is essentially continuous, meaning it can take any value between 0 and infinity. (In reality, we store the recorded time to the nearest millisecond, and very few fly balls make it past seven seconds, so we have something like 7,000 possible values—still many, many more than the 12 combinations of trajectories and velocities, excluding bunts and grounders.) Our hit locations, recorded to the nearest pixel, are also essentially continuous. Why should we forfeit accuracy from two continuous sets of data by categorizing and binning?

Shane Jensen was one of the first to utilize a continuous model to evaluate fielders, developing SAFE (Spatial Aggregate Fielding Evaluation) using BIS data in 2007. Jensen worked with continuous hit locations but was still limited to categorical batted ball trajectory classifications.

There are a variety of local regression models that work well with continuous data sets in one, two, or three dimensions. To avoid getting too technical, local regression models are like simple linear regression models that produce a best-fit straight line, except they aren't limited to straight lines and can work with multiple variables at once. Local regression models are often used to generate contour plots or heat maps like you might see in a weather forecast.

For example, I utilized a local regression model earlier when I plotted out ratio vs. hang time for outfield fly balls. Compare that graph to the preceding table where I grouped hang time in half-second intervals. The model can also return the out ratio for any given hang time, which you would otherwise need to interpolate from the table.

At the 2010 Sportvision Summit in San Francisco, Greg Rybarczyk proposed a graph to help evaluate fielders' range using Sportvision's FIELDf/x data. He put the distance between the fielder and the ball's eventual landing point on one axis, and on the other axis was the ball's hang time. He then plotted outs and safe hits on the graph.

Points closer to the top-left of the plot are balls that aren't in the air very long, and they're far away from the fielder—the type we wouldn't expect to be caught. Closer towards the bottom-right are the balls hit close to the fielder with a high hang time. Most fielders will make plays on the balls in the lower-right corner, but only the best fielders will be able to make plays towards the upper-left.

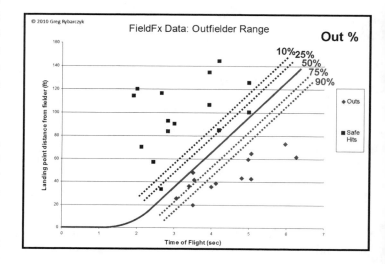

Along the diagonal of the distance versus time plot, there's a region where hits start to turn into fly outs. If Rybarczyk had more data points, we'd gradually start to see fewer base hits and more fly outs as we worked from the top left to the bottom right. At one point, in fact a full line of points, 50 percent of the balls are outs, meaning outfielders catch these balls half the time. In order to visualize the average outfielder's range, Rybarczyk sketched his own estimate of the 50 percent line and other contours in the gradient.

As Rybarczyk said, "That's the first step: to get a big set of data and figure out where those percent lines are. Once you know that, then you can turn this into a metric." So let's do that.

While Rybarczyk's sample was limited to just a few plays from AT&T Park, I'm utilizing the full 2010 season of BIS batted-ball timer data. Since we don't have full pre-pitch positioning data, I found the midpoint of all center-field put-outs and substituted that as the fielder's starting point. I'm also limiting the model just to center fielders for the time being.

The 50th percentile contour line (as indicated by the 0.5 label below) represents the average center fielder's range. It takes the median center fielder about 3.0 seconds to reach a ball hit 50 feet from the center-field midpoint. We can also determine that center fielders can reach a ball 75 feet away in the same three seconds about 10 percent of the time; in other words, the Out Ratio is .10. The model can also estimate Out Ratios between contour lines—for instance, a 3.7-second fly that falls 80 feet away from the center-field midpoint is caught about 34.5 percent of the time.

Center Fielder Range

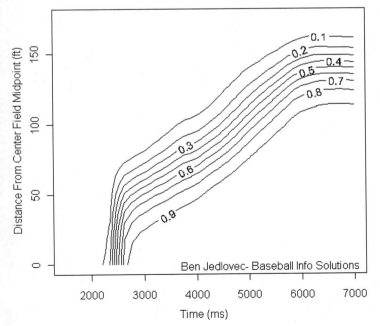

Note that the graph breaks down at the extremes—below about 2.75 seconds because there were no batted balls that made it to center field that quickly, and above 6.0 seconds because virtually every ball in the air that long is caught by some fielder.

However, there's at least one major flaw with this approach. The graph assumes that running in 50 feet for a fly ball is equivalent to running back 50 feet. I later ran the same model only on deeper-than-average fly balls; I'll spare you another graph, but the contour lines were shifted slightly down, meaning center fielders had a harder time going back than coming in. When I ran the model only on the shallower half of plays, the effect was the opposite—the contour lines shifted up.

This supports the notion that outfielders can range in further than they can range backwards. Of course, going directly back is also different than going back over one shoulder at an angle. Each direction might be different. By using distance as a variable, this approach loses the important directional aspect of a fielder's range.

Unlike Rybarczyk's model, Jensen's SAFE compensates for the directional differences by using separate parameters for "moving in" and "moving back". In doing so, Jensen reintroduces the same problem we're trying to avoid—categorizing balls in play into groups.

Instead, we might use a four-dimensional model, using hang time and the X and Y coordinates of the ball's landing point to predict Out Ratio. Because it's difficult to visually present a model with this many dimensions, let's instead compare two adjacent cross-sections of the data, one containing 3.5-4.0-second fly balls and the other containing those with 4.0-4.5-second hang times. You can see the graphical result of this approach at the top of the next page.

The ranges covered by all three outfielders expand when they have more time to get under the fly ball, as you would expect. In the 3.5-4.0 group, the 60th percentile ranges overlap between left and center. By comparison, the 90th percentiles begin to overlap in the 4.0-4.5-second cross-section.

We can use this multi-dimensional local regression to predict the Out Ratio difficulty of each play. This method doesn't have the small sample or binning issues that characterize contemporary systems. It's more complicated mathematically, but that's why we have computers. When we're striving for the most accurate defensive evaluations, why shouldn't we use a robust continuous model?

The next step is to refine the models presented here and compare the results to existing fielding evaluations. We also need to consider a fielder's environment to determine what kind of park adjustments, if any, are appropriate. Once we've established the defensive baseline, we can make true progress

Fly Balls (3.5-4.0 s)

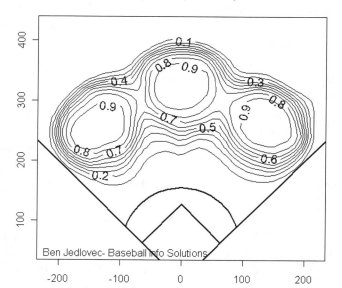

Fly Balls (4.0-4.5 s)

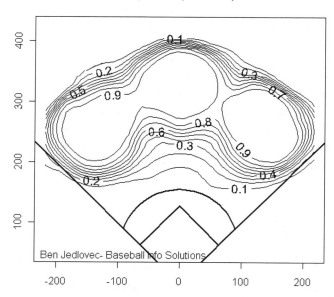

on defense-independent pitching statistics and make similar adjustments for hitting statistics. There's still a long way to go, but the introduction of comprehensive hang time data brings a challenge to develop new and improved brands of analysis.

A special thanks to the BIS Video Scouts who carefully record all of our hit location and batted-ball timer information, then double and triple check it until we're satisfied with its accuracy.

Everything is About to Change

by Rob Neyer

I've had my baseball mind blown exactly twice: in the fall of 1984, the first time I picked up a *Baseball Abstract*, and almost exactly 26 years later, when I attended the PITCHf/x Summit in San Francisco.

It's not that Sportvision's PITCHf/x technology is some state secret. For a few years, FanGraphs has been including a great deal of PITCHf/x-generated data in their statistical packages for pitchers. Before, if you wanted to know (approximately) how hard somebody threw, you had to dig up some book about what happened last year, or make a phone call to a friendly scout. Now the process is significantly faster and significantly more precise. PITCHf/x has, I would argue, drawn more of baseball's opinionators to sites like FanGraphs, The Hardball Times, and Brooks Baseball—and to the work of analysts like Dave Allen, Mike Fast, Jeremy Greenhouse, Harry Pavlidis, and John Walsh—than anything else could have. PITCHf/x also got a bright young man named Josh Kalk hired by the Tampa Bay Rays.

If PITCHf/x were to disappear tomorrow, it would already have justified its existence. Easily.

But it's not going to disappear. Well, it might sort of disappear. More on that later. For the *moment*, though, it's not going anywhere. And if you're already bored with me or you've got diapers to change or something, let me leave you with this: This technology and the people who know how to use it are going to change everything. Yeah. That's all.

Still with me? Come to think of it, I wish *I* had more time. And slightly more imagination. One could—and this might seem like hyperbole but it's not—one could literally fill this book entirely with *ideas* for how to use the data that Sportvision's technology will (or could) generate. Let alone the actual data and analysis.

This is where the my-mind-was-blown thing comes in. While the PITCHf/x data is still mostly unknown to everyone except guys who run baseball teams and guys like you, it's been around long enough that most of the PITCHf/x Summit—the third annual PITCHf/x Summit, I should mention—was actually devoted to the next tool created by Sportvision: FIELDf/x.

Now, you might not have heard much about FIELDf/x yet, and for a good reason: It's still just a baby, the technology installed in just one stadium (AT&T Park) and just a tiny dollop of data available to anyone who doesn't work for Sportvision or within Official Baseball.

What is FIELDf/x? You know that PITCHf/x essentially tracks the speed and direction of every pitch with great precision. FIELDf/x does the same thing for almost everything else that happens on the field.

Mind blown yet? Don't worry. I'm just getting started.

FIELDf/x will manifestly and forever revolutionize the evaluation of defense. In fact, I will venture that the defensive metrics in use today, whether by John Dewan or Sean Smith or David Pinto or Mickey Lichtman or anyone else, will in five years seem nearly as primitive as range factor does today. Because with FIELDf/x, we'll know not just (approximately) where the baseball went and whether it was caught and who caught it (or didn't). We'll know *exactly* where the ball went and *exactly* how long it took a fielder to arrive and *exactly* how he got there. All the talk about *range* and *getting a good jump* and *taking a good route*—it won't be just talk anymore. There will be cold, hard data for every bit of it.

At the Summit, I saw a graphical representation that (yes) blew my mind. Dave Allen took the limited data that's been released and plotted the actual paths that outfielders had taken to catch (or not) batted balls. Looking at Allen's work on the big white screen, I knew immediately that I was getting a glimpse into our future. Or somebody's future, anyway (again, more on that later). Just as we can now summon, with just a few keystrokes, the PITCHf/x data in myriad formats, someday those with access to the FIELDf/x data will be able to look at the average time it took an outfielder to start moving, at the exact path he took toward a fly ball at a key point in the game, at the efforts he made to back up plays in the infield. For the first time ever, everything a player does on the field will be measured. Everything.

But wait, there's more.

Some years ago, I was invited to speak to an organization's entire roster of scouts. I was then something of a public face for objective analysis, and scouts specialize in subjective analysis. It probably didn't much help my cause that *Moneyball* was still sitting on the bestseller charts. The other thing that didn't help my cause was when I suggested that someday there might not be a place in the sport for scouts. Because somebody would figure out a way to do all the things scouts do, but better (and probably more cheaply, though I didn't say that). Now, I hastened to add that I didn't actually *believe* that would happen. But it wasn't a polite or politic thing to say.

Of course I'd never heard of PITCHf/x or FIELDf/x because they hadn't been invented. Now they have. And

Greg Rybarczyk, in something of an aside, suggested an interesting (and scout-killing) idea. Once we know *exactly* what professional fielders do—essentially, how long it takes them to reach various spots on the field, once bat has met ball—we'll have baseline values; we'll know what it takes to be great, what it takes to be good, and what it takes to be adequate. From there, it's a relatively simple matter to apply those standards to amateur players being considered as future professionals. Instead of a grizzled old (or fresh-faced young) scout watching a college kid play a dozen games and giving him a 65 on the Range scale, some just-out-of-college kid with a machine can put the player through his paces, and conclude that he's got five percent more range than an average major leaguer.

Or whatever. You get the point. Have we just put scouts out of business? Of course not. But PITCHf/x and especially FIELDf/x and (yes) HITf/x are going to make the scout's job quite a bit different than it is today. The scouts who are good at what they do *and* are able to make some adjustments will thrive; the rest will try to simply survive.

And remember, it's not just fielding. The "field" in FIELDf/x refers (or should refer) not to fielding, per se, but rather to *the* field of play. Which baserunners are fastest from first to third? FIELDf/x will know. Which runners take the most efficient paths from first to third, or second to home? FIELDf/x will know. Which runners get the biggest leads off first base and the best jumps when trying to steal, or advance on batted balls? FIELDf/x will know.

Except that's not quite right. FIELDf/x won't *know* anything. Not until Skynet takes over Major League Baseball, anyway. It's the people who know how to use FIELDf/x who will know things. These things, and so many others.

What's not clear, what's not clear at all, is which people will be allowed to know how to use FIELDf/x.

To this point, the access that's been granted to PITCHf/x data is sort of phenomenal. At any point in the last few years, Major League Baseball could have stepped in and said to Sportvision, "We have allowed you to install your equipment in our stadiums, and now we'd like to keep all this data to ourselves. Of course we'll pay you handsomely for it. But we're tired of (among other things) guys who live in their mothers' basements using this data to make some of our umpires look incompetent. Actually, we know some of our umpires are incompetent. But we're trying to fix that, and it would be a lot easier if nobody knew about their incompetence except us. Also, some of the general managers are tired of those basement guys fixating on fastball speeds and saying pitchers are hurt when they're not. Anyway, we love the data, here's a big fat check, and stop sending everything to FanGraphs and Brooks Baseball."

Why hasn't that happened already? It's a good question. Sportvision loves to make the data available because it's great publicity. (And no, they don't make *everything* public; as I understand things, the teams do have access to things the rest of us don't.) And Major League Baseball hasn't stepped in because … Well, I think there are enough front-office types who are happy to see original (and cheap) research fomented by all this data that's floating around. Without the data being out there, the Rays never would have known about Josh Kalk. In a sense, having all that data available is like building a bunch of baseball fields in the Dominican Republic and just letting the kids play ball. You watch them for a while, and then you grab the best of them. I don't think Dave Allen and Mike Fast will be on the sandlots for much longer.

Of course, there's another possibility: Major League Baseball just doesn't realize how big this thing is. Also, if there have been any PITCHf/x-related controversies they've been mostly under the radar.

People love to argue about fielding, though. *Players* love to argue about fielding. We can assume the umpires despise PITCHf/x, but they haven't been able to do anything about it. Their union, though, while influential isn't anything as influential as the Players Association. It's easy for Raul Ibanez or Derek Jeter to point out potential flaws in Ultimate Zone Rating … but what are they going to do when their every movements are tracked, and suggest they're not getting to nearly as many balls as they (and their supporters) thought? Do they pressure their union to pressure Major League Baseball to suppress the data? And does Major League Baseball figure there are more important things to argue about?

Granted, now I'm navel-gazing. Public or not, all this data is going to fundamentally change baseball analysis. It's just not clear that it's going to happen where we can see it. The distinct possibility exists that some, most, or all of it will happen behind the closed-and-locked doors of the organizations smart enough to realize what's happening. Which will leave the rest of us in an awkward position, trying to analyze decisions made by teams with access to *significantly* better information than we've got.

Sort of like now, actually. But more.

This is where I have to point out that the PITCHf/x Summit—which was actually dominated by FIELDf/x discussions—was based mostly on ideas rather than data, a necessity, considering how little FIELDf/x data had actually been released. Greg Rybarczyk gave a highly entertaining presentation on "True Defensive Range," his proposed new metric based on the batted balls in the data that were hit in the air to the outfield. All 25 of them. The FIELDf/x system was installed in just AT&T Park, and Sportvision had released just a teeny, tiny percentage of the data they'd collected there.

Not that anybody's complaining. Sportvision didn't have to release any data at all and we'll take whatever little scraps we can get. But very little data has been released. So at this writing, all anyone can do is set up systems to analyze data; nobody can do any *actual* analysis, and it's not yet clear when anyone (outside of Major League Baseball's environs) will be able to. (Oh, and in a weirdly opposite problem, if comprehensive data ever *is* released, the set will be so massive that some teams will undoubtedly hire whole troops of engineers and analysts to tease out all the good stuff.)

So that's essentially where we're at. We know that Sportvision is collecting data, and will collect even more data, that will fundamentally change the whole world of baseball analy-sis. We don't know what the ramifications will be. We don't know how soon it's going to happen (though I would guess soon enough to surprise a lot of people). And we don't know if analysis based on this wonderful new data will appear inside these pages, a year or two from now, or will be as proprietary as the secret fielding metrics that so many teams have developed.

Most of all, we know that baseball's decision-makers, certainly four or five years from now, will have at their fingertips information that was scarcely imaginable just four or five years ago. Oh, and we know that those decision-makers will need a bunch of smart people to help them.

Do you know anybody who wants to work for a baseball team?

US BANKRUPTCY COURT, 2010

An Introduction to FIELDf/x

by Kate McSurley and Greg Rybarczyk

Sportvision first arrived on the baseball scene with the pitch-tracking PITCHf/x system, which allows viewers to identify the speed and trajectory of each pitched ball during a game. The technology moved beyond the limitations of the radar gun and allows fans a more robust knowledge of the ball's overall activity before and at the plate. It also provides a digital record of the pitch sequences for future evaluation and analysis.

By the end of the 2007 season, the system was installed in nearly every major league ballpark, and it was clearly becoming an important element of the baseball experience. Baseball enthusiasts were finally able to access supportive data to discuss the full breadth of a pitcher's performance, as well as exciting new offensive data for every major league game.

The PITCHf/x system continues to be well received by fans, but teams and coaches also recognize the value of objective data like accurate release points and movement trajectories when evaluating their players. Now minor leagues and baseball schools rely on Sportvision's system for informed roster decisions and strategies for player development. A coach's raw intuition can be supported with hard, comprehensive data from the PITCHf/x system.

In just a few seasons, the baseball community came to expect PITCHf/x data for every pitch and every game, but it also became clear that there was still a lot of untracked action left on the field. The natural next step in the tracking process was to record data from the other side of the pitch. HITf/x tracks and digitally records data for the contact point, speed off the bat, elevation angle and field direction.

Still, objective defensive data in baseball has always been somewhat of an enigma, or at least an unattainable dimension of the game. Sportvision had to respond with something just as telling, but, what's more, just as accurate as the PITCHf/x and HITf/x systems. This season Sportvision did respond with continued testing of the FIELDf/x tracking system in a few major league parks, and the baseball community is anxious to see how this new data will once again change the way we rank and evaluate player performance.

Soon people will be able to quantify new baseball statistics and unveil intriguing information about players. The FIELDf/x system identifies individual players and tracks player positions at a high enough resolution to understand granular movements like reaction times. This tracking technology reveals gripping new fielding data that may allow an explanation for the unexplainable. It is one thing to say that Derek Jeter is a great shortstop, but with FIELDf/x, his range can be directly compared with other players for an impartial assessment. It can also shed new light on fielding errors, which are traditionally subjective yet equally unyielding.

With FIELDf/x, we will be able to determine the percentage likelihood that a play was even possible to add validity to a called error. Sportvision's tracking technology can determine a third baseman's reaction time to a hit ball and even the path a base runner took to his base. The system also captures the who, when and where of ball events like pitches, hits, catches and throws for an all-inclusive record of the events on the field.

This new tracking system will certainly allow for fresh commentary and interesting player comparisons, but Greg Rybarczyk of Hit Tracker has identified one of the first pertinent applications for the FIELDf/x system. On the next few pages he explains the significance of being able to calculate defensive metrics with some interesting examples, and he alludes to ways the baseball community will be able to interact with this data.

People from all sides of the baseball community will be able to respond to FIELDf/x data in a unique way. Sportvision will also be able to apply FIELDf/x data to consumer applications so fans can see the defensive metrics illustrated on mobile devices as well as online applications and player analysis tools. Used in conjunction with Sportvision's PITCHf/x and HITf/x systems, FIELDf/x data will fill in the holes of what was once missing with meaningful information and revealing visuals.

FIELDf/x data will give fresh fodder for analysts and bloggers to chew on, encouraging new baseball statistics and engaging conversations. Sportvision's systems set up new and better analysis, since the human error element is diffused and replaced with hard, objective data.

It is an exciting thing to unleash baseball facts and figures that have been untapped for so long, and Sportvision is once again at the forefront. Yet, for every uncovered answer, baseball has a way of coming up with several new questions. Sportvision will continue to respond to the expected queries of the baseball community with innovative technology, humbled to know that we may never know all there is about the game.

A FIELDf/x Application: True Defensive Range

by Greg Rybarczyk

With the introduction of technology that permits the accurate tracking of the baseball and players throughout the entire play, across the entire field, Sportvision has created an opportunity to revolutionize defensive metrics by allowing the calculation of True Defensive Range, or TDR. This is a metric that will go beyond the current zone-based, event-counting methods, using continuous measurements of parameters such as fielder starting position, batted ball hang time and landing point to generate the most accurate, meaningful and transparent defensive metric ever.

Why we Should Move Beyond Zones

Many contemporary defensive metrics use "zones," discrete areas on the baseball field where all balls landing there are grouped and counted together. One prominent example of the use of zones is the Project Retrosheet Scoring System, which divides the fair territory on a standard baseball field into 55 zones. The average zone in the Retrosheet system covers just under 2,000 square feet, equivalent to an area 40 by 50 feet, but there is much variation: the zones go from tiny (zone 1, the pitcher's mound) to enormous (zone 8XD in deepest center field, spanning more than 130 feet corner to corner).

The size of the typical zones used in defensive metrics is one disadvantage; any system that requires balls landing 40 or 50 feet apart (or 130!) to be considered equivalent is clearly oversimplifying things. However, there is an even more troubling characteristic of the Retrosheet zones: They are not the same in every ballpark. The standard zones are defined for a field with 330 foot foul lines and a 405 foot center field fence, but for ballparks that do not match this standard, it is unclear whether the existing zones are to be extended, or stretched, or compressed to conform to the actual home run fences.

Perhaps the most serious drawback to zone-based systems is that by their very nature, zones mix together balls that were easy for fielders to reach with balls that were difficult or impossible to reach. Retrosheet zone 78S is a good example: Nearly every ball hit to the back left corner of 78S, located a few feet from the left fielder's typical starting position, will be caught, while nearly every ball hit to the opposite side of 78S, a spot more than 100 feet from the shortstop, left fielder and center fielder, will fall safely for a hit. Because any individual ball hit to this zone (and to others like it) can be simple to field, impossible to field or anywhere in between, metrics based on this zone are particularly susceptible to bias, and

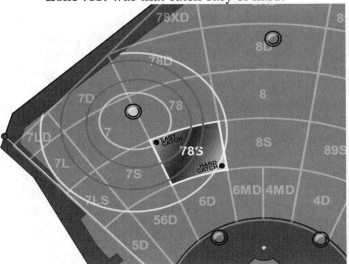

without any way to distinguish the easy chances from the difficult, there is little an analyst can do about it.

With so many important drawbacks, why are zones used in defensive analysis? The answer is that, for many years, no better alternatives came along. Precise tracking of the landing spots of batted balls by human eye is possible when the ball lands beyond the fence, among numerous easily located landmarks such as seats, aisles, access tunnels, etc., but it is much more difficult when the ball lands out in the middle of an unmarked expanse of green grass. The typical accuracy and precision in a "naked eye" estimate of a ball's landing point, when no landmarks are nearby, is poor. Zones came about as a way to group balls that landed near each other, upping the sample size and somewhat diminishing the importance of the poor measurement capability.

FIELDf/x is the Answer

The answer to all these zone-based problems is to know where the fielders were standing when the ball was hit, and to know exactly where the ball was throughout the play. FIELDf/x can deliver this.

FIELDf/x uses cameras mounted high above the field to track the position of the baseball and every human being on the field for the duration of each play. Fifteen times per second, position data are captured and archived, allowing analysts and color commentators to precisely reconstruct the movement of the ball, the fielders, the runners, and even the umpires and base coaches. For every batted ball, FIELDf/x can tell where the fielder started, where the ball landed (or was caught, or where it passed by a fielder), and how long the ball took to get there. Together these three factors describe the difficulty of any particular play, and enable the calculation of what I have named True Defensive Range, or TDR.

True Defensive Range is the Question

With complete data for all batted balls, it becomes possible to determine the relative difficulty of a play by looking at the outcomes of similar plays, with that similarity being based on flight time and the distance the fielder had to cover to reach it. If only 10 percent of all balls hit a certain distance from a fielder in a certain amount of time are caught for outs, then the fielder who makes this play has done something quite unusual, and deserves to be credited highly for having done it.

On the other hand, if a fielder does not convert this play, he will not be penalized greatly, since it was a very difficult play to make. The opposite is of course true: Fielders who make a play that is successfully converted into an out 90 percent of the time receive only a very small amount of credit, while fielders who fail to convert this same play will face a substantial penalty.

In the TDR system, the base amount of run credit awarded for plays is based on the area of the field where the ball is hit, and linear weights that assign a run value for each play category (single, double, triple, out, etc). Balls landing or being caught in front of an outfielder would be assigned the base value for the difference between an out and a single (-0.30 runs and 0.47 runs, respectively, in one model, for a difference of 0.77 runs), which would then be multiplied by either the league-wide out percentage for that distance/time or the quantity one minus that value. The result is the TDR for that particular play.

For example, suppose a ball is hit to shallow left field, and lands at a spot 55 feet from the left fielder's starting position after 2.75 seconds in the air. Suppose further that aggregated data from the entire league indicate that balls at that distance from the left fielder, for that time in the air, are caught 29 percent of the time (note: these values are not yet known, and will need to be calculated once FIELDf/x goes live across the major leagues, and a suitable volume of data have been captured).

If the left fielder did not catch the ball, the base value of 0.77 runs would be multiplied by 29 percent, and that value, 0.22 runs, would be subtracted from the left-fielder's TDR. If the left fielder did make the catch, the base value of 0.77 runs would be multiplied by (1-29 percent), and that value, 0.55 runs, would be added to the left fielder's TDR.

Because of the difficulty of the play, the fielder gets more credit for making the play than he would lose for missing it. This is not a new feature in defensive metrics, as zone-based metrics have previously incorporated different values for different zones and types of hits, but what is new is the fact

that the difficulty of the play will finally be *accurately* captured and built into the TDR metric.

We will no longer have to wonder if a player earned himself a sparkling zone-based metric by catching a lot of easy fly balls; nor will we have to rationalize away a weak metric by suggesting that a traditionally outstanding fielder must have had a lot of balls hit toward the outer edges of his zone while he was on the field. Every ball hit to a fielder will be individually measured, and individually scored. The TDR metric thus promises not only to be accurate, but also to be entirely transparent.

The key elements of the TDR metric, generated using the raw data that FIELDf/x provide, will obviously appeal to the sabermetrics crowd, but they will also resonate with the broader base of baseball fans, if presented in the right way. Imagine that during a baseball telecast, a hitter lines a double just beyond the outstretched glove of the left fielder, a slugger known more for his power than his defensive prowess. Within seconds, FIELDf/x can tell the audience that:

- 85 percent of all major league left fielders would have made that play
- The left fielder's failure to catch the ball cost his team, on average, 0.9 runs.
- The left fielder's TDR over the last week has been -3.2 runs.
- The left fielder's season total for TDR has been -8.7 runs over the first 95 games of the season, and projects his total defensive contribution over 150 games at -13.7 runs. This is the 26th best, or the fifth worst, total among major league left fielders.
- When the left fielder is replaced for a better defensive player late in the game, the screen could show the likelihood, in percentages, that a ball will be hit in the rest of that game that the first man would have missed, but the replacement would catch. The average run value could also be shown. For example, the FIELDf/x database of all batted balls might show a seven percent chance of a ball being hit in the eighth and ninth innings that would be missed by the original left fielder but caught by the substitute. This might work out to an expected run value of 0.1 runs (for example). This can provide a concrete way of showing how managers "play the percentages."

For a more visual presentation of FIELDf/x-generated information, a network televising the game could show a wide-angle shot of left field, with the left fielder's starting

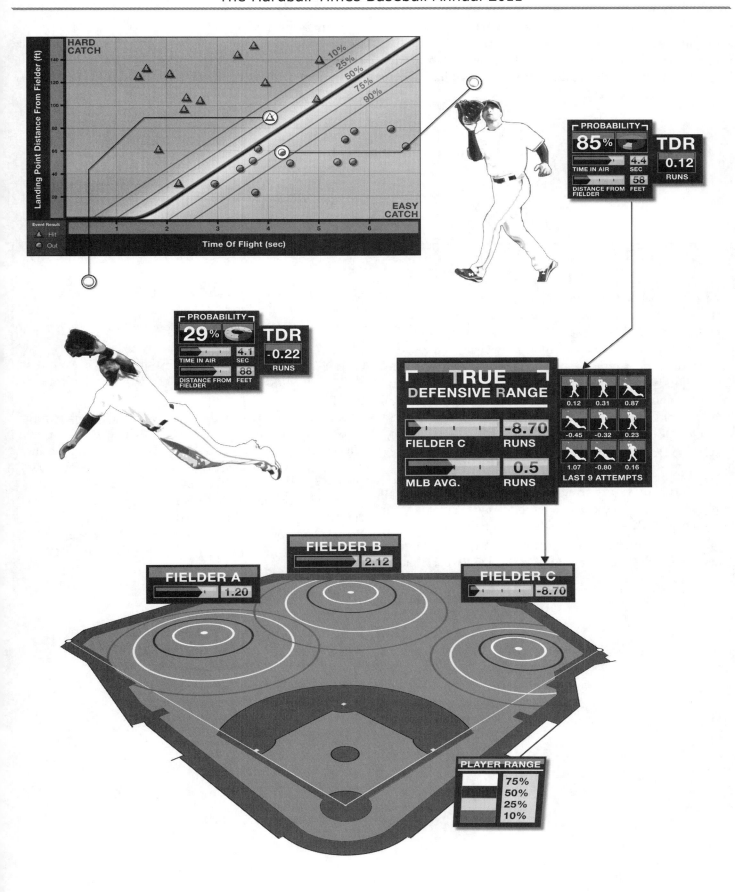

point marked, and then trace his path toward the ball, and show how he got there just too late. If a similar play has happened earlier in the game, it can be shown in an overlay, illustrating how the other team's left fielder, with his superior range, would have caught the ball.

There are many possible uses of FIELDf/x data, transformed into meaningful baseball information via the True Defensive Range metric, for all types of interested people: sabermetric analysts, television networks and viewers, and the baseball teams themselves.

Trivia Sidebar #3: Still?

The recession showed some signs of ending until it didn't, and terms that sound tastier than their meanings—double-dip recession chief among them—were bandied about frequently by an Associated Press that seemed to revel in the buffet of stories the recession provided. Many had to determine how to do without, and sacrifices seemed unending. Still, plenty of people kept their jobs and could lead their lives normally/as they were before the recession. (It all depends on the person, I suppose...)

Here lies trivia about sacrifices and doing without. Maybe this double-dip trivia will get you two scoops ahead.

1. Maybe this is surprising or maybe it isn't, but since 1920 only one major league game – a one hour and 12 minute affair on June 30, 1922 – has gone without this pair of events.

2. If the Mariners make it through 2011 without one of these, they will have matched the 1925-1927 Red Sox and by the looks of it no one else in AL history.

3. The 1982 Angels were the last playoff team without what?

4. The 2004 Brewers did without one of these; they are the only team after World War II to do so. The 2004 Angels would have gone without one of these, save for a game against the Brewers. What was missing?

5. Since Wes Parker's league-leading 19 sacrifice hits in 1965, Don Buford in 1966 and Coco Crisp in 2005 are the only players to do what?

6. Now to combine both themes of this challenge: In the expansion era (minimum 100 innings pitched), only one pitcher has gone two seasons without a successful sacrifice hit against him, and he managed to do it consecutively (1984-1985). Granted, his ERA was 5.09 over those two years, so small ball wasn't particularly necessary. (With minimum 200 IP in that time, only Jeff Russell, Dickie Noles and Matt Young were worse.) But unlike the guys in the parenthetical, our buntless wonder had 12 more seasons as a starter.

(Answers are in the back of the book.)

History

2010: Year of the Pitcher?

by Steve Treder

2010 is the Year of the Pitcher! How many times did we hear that this season? It was endlessly repeated by Baseball Tonight pundits, by sports columnists, and by drive-time talk radio personalities.

The evidence presented for this assertion? Sometimes it would be something relevant, such as, "Home runs are at their lowest rate since 1990-something!" But too often, it was something more along the lines of, "Ryan Howard's RBI total is way down!" Or, my favorite, "Just look at all the no-hitters!"

But is it true? Was 2010 actually a pitcher's year? To answer that we'll need to muster some more rigorous evidence than the anecdotal stuff. And, as we'll see, one question tends to lead to another.

First, let's consider something quite basic: what do we mean by a pitcher's year?

Putting it in Context

Major league teams scored 4.38 runs per game in 2010. In itself, does that make 2010 a year of the pitcher?

The key thing to bear in mind is that scoring rates in baseball are always fluctuating. Here's major league baseball's scoring rate for every season since 1920, when live ball conditions came fully into place:

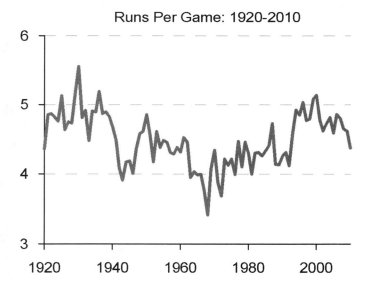

Runs Per Game: 1920-2010

Viewed from this long-term angle, it's clear that 4.38 runs per game isn't a particularly low rate historically; it's only moderately below the overall average for this 91-year period,

which is 4.49. We see that as recently as the late 1980s and early 1990s there were seasons with distinctly less scoring than 2010, and in the late 1960s, run production plunged to levels far below what we saw this year. So in historically absolute terms, 2010 didn't come close to being a pitcher's year, as it can't hold a candle to, say, 1968.

But it seems sensible that for any season to be considered a pitcher's year (or a hitter's year), we should be thinking of its status relative to the years closely leading up to it, not its grand historical status. After all, what got people's attention in 2010 wasn't how this year's run production compared to that of 1968—most fans and pundits today can't even remember 1968. It was how this year's run production compared to that of recent seasons, when general conditions can be considered more similar.

So let's view this data in a much tighter timeframe, say, since 1995:

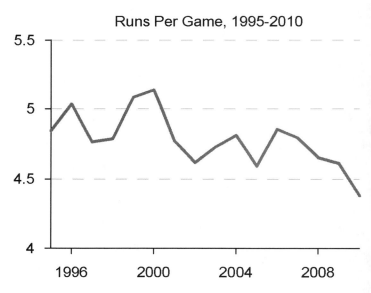

Runs Per Game, 1995-2010

Now it becomes clear that within this very modern context, 2010 was indeed a pitcher's year. But we also see that scoring in 2010 wasn't all that dramatically lower than that of 2009; instead what we notice is that 2010 was simply the latest in a sequence of four consecutive seasons of gradually declining run production, and that these four years are part of a decade-long trend toward lower scoring—or perhaps more accurately, toward less-high scoring.

We'll pick up on that point again. But first let's look a bit deeper at 2010 as an individual season and how it compares with other individual seasons throughout history on the "pitcher's year" scale.

An Operational Metric: SCS

As we've said, we understand a pitcher's year (or a hitter's year) as not so much a function of how it compares to all other seasons, but rather of how it compares to those seasons immediately preceding it. (And I'm careful to use the term "preceding," instead of "preceding and following," because in real time we never know what's going to happen next year; our frame of reference is always limited to the past.)

So let's create a metric for pitcher's and hitter's years. We'll take each season's rate of scoring and compare its increase or decrease from each of the five seasons immediately preceding it. (Five seasons seems a reasonable span of relevant comparability.) We won't weight the comparison to each of those five preceding seasons equally, though, as the most immediately preceding season is more relevant than the one five years ago. We'll weight the change from the immediately preceding season twice as much as two years ago, two years ago twice as much as three years ago, and so on.

Here's how it works: scoring in 2010 was 94.9 percent of the rate in 2009, 94.2 percent of 2008, 91.3 percent of 2007, 90.2 percent of 2006, and 95.4 percent of 2005. By applying this formula:

$$(((.949*16)+(.942*8)+(.913*4)+(.902*2)+(.954))/31) = .940$$

We get a figure of .940 to describe the weighted difference between 2010 scoring and that of the five preceding seasons. A season exactly equal to all the previous five would yield a score of 1.00, and a season higher in scoring than the previous five would yield a score greater than 1.00. So the .940 figure definitely indicates that 2010 was a pitcher's year.

We'll call this metric Scoring Change Score, or SCS.

Where does this place 2010 within the pantheon of pitcher's years? High, but not extremely high. 2010 ranks as tied for the twelfth-best pitcher's year since 1920:

Rank	Year	SCS
1	1968	0.882
2	1942	0.885
3	1963	0.888
4	1933	0.902
5	1952	0.903
6	1943	0.906
7	1988	0.911
8	1931	0.917

Rank	Year	SCS
9	1972	0.926
10	1981	0.928
11	1926	0.934
12T	2010	0.940
12T	1967	0.940
14	1941	0.941
15	2002	0.942

The most dramatic pitcher's year in absolute terms was also the most dramatic relatively speaking: the infamous 1968, when a half-decade of already low scoring suddenly plunged into deadball-era depths. That narrowly beat out 1942, the first season of the World War II-mandated "Balata Ball," and also 1963, the first season of the regrettable 1960s experiment with the enlarged strike zone. 2010 lags far behind such scoring free-falls.

Since I know you're curious, here are the top 15 hitter's years since 1920:

Rank	Year	SCS
1	1921	1.202
2	1920	1.164
3	1970	1.132
4	1969	1.124
5	1994	1.122
6	1930	1.118
7	1973	1.101
8	1977	1.099
9	1993	1.099
10	1922	1.098
11	1929	1.092
12	1948	1.087
13	1987	1.084
14	1950	1.076
15	1925	1.073

Here we encounter some usual suspects: 1921 and 1920, the first two years under cork-centered, spitball-outlawed "live ball" circumstances, and also 1970 and 1969, the first two years following the strike zone reduction and mound lowering in the wake of Mr. 1968.

And to put this into a more tightly modern perspective, how about the top 15 pitcher's years since 1969:

Rank	Year	SCS
1	1988	0.911
2	1972	0.926
3	1981	0.928
4	2010	0.940
5	2002	0.942
6	2001	0.946
7	1971	0.954
8	1989	0.955
9	1978	0.960
10	2005	0.962
11	1992	0.964
12	1976	0.965
13	1997	0.971
14	2008	0.972
15	2009	0.978

Emerging here is 1988, the season in which MLB forcefully cracked down on umpires to call the rule book strike zone, after several years of seeing it drift ever lower and smaller. We also see 1972, when the scoring advances of 1969-70 fully evaporated, prompting the American League to adopt the designated hitter rule the following year. And there's 1981, the year in which a prolonged work stoppage cancelled nearly all the games in the midsummer hot months, when weather conditions tend to produce the highest scoring.

And once again, for the sake of symmetry, the top 15 hitter's years since 1969:

Rank	Year	SCS
1	1970	1.132
2	1969	1.124
3	1994	1.122
4	1973	1.101
5T	1977	1.099
5T	1993	1.099
7	1987	1.084
8	1979	1.065
9	1996	1.058
10	1999	1.054
11	1995	1.041
12	2006	1.040
13	2000	1.038
14	1982	1.036
15	1975	1.034

What all this suggests is that although there have been more extreme pitcher's years, it was in fact correct for the pundits to call 2010 a "year of the pitcher." And the really interesting point is that 2010 is clearly not standing alone as a pitcher's year in the modern era: 2002, 2001, 2005, 2008, and 2009 all join it as seasons within the past decade among the 15-lowest SCS since 1969. Meanwhile, only 2006 and 2000 have been 21st-century seasons standing out as comparable hitter's years.

So, the deeper story isn't 2010 so much as it is the broader downward trend it represents, which is historically notable.

Causes?

While the chattering commentators basically got it right in identifying 2010 as a pitcher's year, they tended to be a whole lot less cogent when providing an explanation: almost always there would be something to the effect of "this proves that The Steroid Era is over."

In July of this year, on his website *The Diamond Appraised*, the iconic sabermetrician Craig Wright published an excellent article titled, "What is Behind the Offensive Decline?" Wright methodically considers various factors potentially causing scoring rates to decline over the past several years, including the crackdown on steroids. His take is that performance-enhancing drug testing is at most a minor explanation, for two good reasons:

- As best we can tell, pitchers have made at least as much use of steroids and other performance-enhancing drugs as hitters. Thus to the extent that drug testing has removed "enhanced" performance from the game, there's no reason to assume that the removal would necessarily result in a net reduction in scoring.

- The serious, penalty-laden drug testing regime was introduced in 2004—a season in which scoring increased. Then, following a decline in 2005, scoring climbed to even higher levels in 2006. There is no basis for concluding that the imposition of drug testing would somehow result in a time-released inhibition of offense, and definitely not one still slowly unfolding seven years down the road.

Wright assesses other issues as well: improved fielding, a less lively ball, and a wider strike zone. In each case, he dispassionately weighs the available evidence and dismisses them as meaningful factors.

His conclusion is that the gradual decline in offense can be traced to two interrelated causes: a general improvement in the tactical approach of pitchers attacking the strike zone and a lack of a corresponding general adjustment by hitters. Here's the money quote:

... let me just talk about the most common count, the one in every plate appearance, the 0-0 count, the first pitch. In the 20 years of data I have on this, there has been a fairly steady trend of the average batter taking more first pitches. The pitchers have wised up to this and starting around 2002 they began throwing more first-pitch strikes. That adjustment by the pitchers hasn't changed the mentality of the average hitter. In fact, the general response of batters has been to take even more of the first pitches. They have set a new record in that category—in that 20-year database—each of the last four years. And again, that is with the pitchers throwing even more first-pitch strikes than they did back in the 1991-2001 period.

For the first time in the 20-year history of the database, batters in 2010 are taking more than half of the first-pitch strikes thrown to them (.517). Twenty years ago it was .453. In a sample that covers the full variety of all hitters, a shift of 14.1% is a remarkable change.

That means there are more plate appearances going to an 0-1 count without a fight. As many of you know, an 0-1 count radically affects the ultimate effectiveness of a plate appearance. In 2009, the final result of plate appearances after reaching an 0-1 count was an OPS of .629 as compared to .860 in the other plate appearances. It is not hard to overdo the wisdom of taking a tough first-pitch strike, and the general trend for batters may have crossed that line.

I find this to be a penetrating insight on Wright's part. The never-ending battle between pitcher and hitter always revolves around each probing to see what the other is willing to give, and taking advantage accordingly. Wright's thesis is that through the 1990s batters were steadily gaining the edge by exploiting pitchers' cautiousness, but since the early 2000s pitchers have been effectively turning the tables on hitters in the same manner. He makes quite a compelling argument.

That said, I remain a bit skeptical that the picture is as simple as Wright paints it. I tend to believe that trends so deep that they're visible league-wide over a period of several years likely reflect changing underlying conditions beyond just the marketplace of competing tactical pitcher-batter approaches. In this case, given that first-pitch called strikes are the centerpiece of Wright's profound observation, I'm not nearly as willing as he is to remove the umpires from the equation. My guess is that the tactical trends that Wright has identified are being enhanced by a cultural shift in umpiring, with the men in blue increasingly inclined to give the pitcher the benefit of the doubt on a borderline first-pitch take (and likely on other takes as well).

I suggest this because history demonstrates that the strike zone is an immensely important factor in run production. Over the past half-century, nearly all of the biggest shifts in scoring, up or down, have been rooted in shifts in the manner in which balls and strikes are called:

- The offensive ice age of the 1960s was triggered by the enlargement of the rule book strike zone in 1963.
- It was ended in 1969 by the rewriting of the rule book to re-impose the pre-'63 zone.
- When the de facto zone had steadily drifted low and away in the mid-1980s, MLB cracked down on the umpires to start calling the strike above the belt again, resulting in 1988 in one of the most dramatic pitcher's years in history.
- When the umps then spent the 1990s paying less and less attention to the rule book zone, and offense climbed to historically high levels, MLB cracked down again, this time implementing the QuesTec system, resulting in back-to-back dramatic drops in scoring in 2001 and 2002.

I believe that unlike the 1988 crackdown, which the umpires began to ignore after about five years, the more recent one has (at least so far) shown staying power. Wright's data indicates that pitchers have steadily figured out how to work this to their advantage.

Roll out that Crystal Ball

So where is this dynamic likely to lead? The other thing that history clearly demonstrates is that every trend is arrested at some point. Not only are offenses and defenses selfishly motivated to figure out ways to effectively push back against one another, MLB has a business interest in maintaining a certain degree of historical normality in scoring levels. Fans tend to react less than favorably if they perceive that the product they're consuming is "unnatural" in comparison to that which they remember from a decade or two before; they tired of the pitching-dominated 1960s (and MLB responded), and they tired of the home run-happy "Steroid Era" 1990s (and MLB responded).

This suggests that if the decline in scoring we've witnessed in 2010 specifically, and in the last decade or so generally, continues in 2011 and beyond, MLB will probably intervene with some manner of rule change to counteract it—most likely by futzing with the strike zone again, given that it's the handiest and most demonstrably impactful tool.

Something else to consider in this regard isn't just the rate of scoring per se, but the shape of the events that are creating it. As we've seen, the level of run production in 2010 (4.38 runs per game) is completely in line with long-term historical norms. But the frequency of home runs, though slightly down from its decade-ago peak, remains very high historically, and most importantly, the rate of strikeouts continues to steadily climb, year after year, to record-setting high after record-setting high. (The strikeout rate of 7.06 per game in 2010 was 2 percent greater than the previous record set in 2009, which was 2 percent greater than the previous record set in 2008, which was—you guessed it—2 percent greater than the near-record rate of 2007).

In recent decades, hitters, hitting coaches, and managers/general managers correctly deduced that avoiding strikeouts in itself was not an optimal strategy, because the trade-off with power production meant that ever-higher scoring rates and ever-higher strikeout rates could go hand in hand. But just as Wright observes with taking first pitches, every approach eventually reaches a point of diminishing returns: there is a level at which ever-higher strikeout rates will choke off on-base percentage and thus choke off run production, even with lots of home runs. It may well be that we're finally reaching that point in today's MLB.

Consider the 1960s for a moment: even amid the trough in scoring that began in 1963, home run production was not at all low by then-historical standards. Through 1966, major league hitters were going deep nearly as frequently as they had in the 1950s and distinctly more frequently than they had ever done before the 1950s. But batting averages were sinking, and strikeout rates were soaring to unprecedented levels, and in 1967-68 the dynamic spun completely into the pitchers' favor.

We might be witnessing a similar dynamic today. Unless current patterns are structurally reversed, if we thought 2010 was The Year of the Pitcher, we ain't seen nothin' yet.

And Besides

I don't know. But purely from an aesthetic standpoint, even if run production stabilizes or increases again, the home run-centric, strikeout-saturated game we're watching these days leaves a bit to be desired. I continue to advocate for some of the rule changes Bill James suggested in his *New Historical Abstract* in 2001: move the batters' boxes a few inches back away from home plate, and impose an increased bat-handle-thickness minimum. These changes would make it a bit more difficult to hit for power, particularly to the opposite field, and thus would have the effect of motivating hitters to adopt a more traditional contact-oriented, batting average-centric approach.

More contact means (obviously) fewer strikeouts, and with more balls hit into play it also means a greater importance of fielding and throwing ability, and of baserunning ability. A greater balance between brawn and speed/agility would make for, in my humble opinion, a more entertaining game.

The Best and Worst Benches of All Time

by Chris Jaffe

Sept. 28, 2008 must have been a great day to be a Brewers fan. On that date, in the final game of the regular season, the Brewers clinched their first postseason appearance in more than a quarter-century by beating the Cubs 3-1. This victory pushed them one game ahead of the Mets (who lost that day) in the Wild Card race for Milwaukee's hard-fought, long-delayed return to October baseball.

Any time a team enters the promised land of postseason baseball by such a slender margin, many reasons can explain their achievement. A few reasons for Milwaukee's eking into the playoffs are obvious. On their pitching staff, they benefited from a strong season-long performance from Ben Sheets, and an amazingly fantastic stretch from mid-season acquisition CC Sabathia. On offense, the hitters crushed 198 homers, led by the dynamic duo of Prince Fielder and Ryan Braun.

However, another reason lurking in the background also helps explain Milwaukee's 2008 success: their bench. Of the four backups who compiled at least 100 plate appearances for the team, three posted an OPS+ of 119 or better (which means their park-adjusted OPS was 19 percent better than the league average). Aside from their eight starting hitters, Milwaukee's position players batted .253/.342/.404 in 1,144 plate appearances. For the record, the NL as a whole that year hit .260/.331/.413. That shouldn't happen. Benches are not supposed to hit about league average. By definition, backups should be worse than average.

In fact, the above stats arguably understate how effective the Brewers' reserve bats were on the year. Plugging their offensive numbers into Bill James' Runs Created formula, Milwaukee's bench produced 146 runs while tallying 772 outs. That put them on a pace to produce 5.11 runs per 27 outs—all while playing in a league that averaged 4.54 runs per game (and in a park that skewed a bit in favor of pitchers). That ain't too shabby. Meanwhile, the Mets' bench produced only 3.85 runs per 27 outs. Yeah, that would more than explain the one-game difference between the two teams that year.

Forget the Mets for a second—according to RC/27 outs, Milwaukee had the best hitting bench in the entire league that year. Their performance wasn't necessarily historic (the year before Philadelphia's bench produced 5.27 RC/27 outs), but Milwaukee's bench points out the importance of backup hitters. No one really expects much of bench players—again, they're supposed to be below average. For just that reason, if a bench does far better than one expects, it can make a

tremendous impact on a team's fortunes. As such, it's well worth finding out which teams had the best benches in baseball history, and which squads had the worst benches.

For this inquiry, I'll use Runs Created per 27 outs to determine which benches in baseball history were best and worst. Since James only intended Runs Created to be used from 1900-onward, I'll ignore the 19th century. I just have to make one or two little adjustments. To allow for offensive environment, I'll adjust each bench's RC/27 outs by park factor and their league's overall runs per game. (Minor nitpick: league runs per game isn't based on exactly 27 outs because MLB as a whole never averages exactly 27 outs per game due to extra innings, shortened games, etc—but ultimately it makes no difference to this exercise).

For example, if you adjust the benches from the 2008 Brewers by park and league, it turns out they batted 12.7 percent *better* than league average. That's amazing. Benches are not supposed to be superior. While impressive, as previously noted it wasn't necessarily historically brilliant. Among the 2,250 benches from 1900-2009, that Brewer bunch ranks as the 92nd best. But that just brings up the question: If the 2008 Brewers didn't have a historically great bench, who did?

Before getting to the fun stuff—the results—I should note that I have a simple definition of bench: all plate appearances by position players who aren't listed among the starting eight batters (or nine in a DH league) on Baseball-Reference. com's team page.

No point in beating around the bush any more. The following teams had the best benches of all-time ranked by how their park adjusted RC/27 outs compares to their leagues' R/G average.

Team	Year	Edge
NYM	1987	149.8%
CIN	1918	148.7%
CLE	1921	144.0%
NYG	1906	137.8%
PHI	2002	136.0%
NYG	1912	133.7%
NYG	1911	133.4%
BAL	1971	133.0%
CIN	1902	132.6%
ARI	1999	132.0%

The 1987 Mets, huh? Well, they shared essentially the same bench as the 108-win world championship 1986 Mets—who had the 19th best bench ever by this system. The four bench players on the 1987 Mets with the most plate appearances—Mookie Wilson, Tim Teufel, Dave Madagan, and Lee Mazzilli—all had an OPS+ of 119 or higher. Everyone but Mookie hit .300, and Mookie just missed, with a .299 mark. Those guys accounted for four-fifths of the bench's plate appearances.

What really sets the 1987 Mets apart was the over-his-head performance by Teufel. Normally an adequate hitter in a part-time role, Teufel that year was out of his mind. His .308 average was 46 points better than what he did in any other season he had over 100 plate appearances. He also tied his personal best in homers (14), and nearly did likewise in doubles. (His 29 doubles that year were one behind his 1984 season, when he had over 300 more plate appearances than his 1987 campaign.)

The success of the Mets bench in 1987 (and 1986) was partially due to how manager Davey Johnson deployed them. Teufel and Wilson both received plenty of playing time as platoon players. In what shouldn't be very surprising news, most of the best offensive benches of all-time engaged in platooning.

For example, the 1921 Indians, possessors of the best bench in American League history, featured three platoons. Manager Tris Speaker merged Doc Johnston and George Burns at first, Elmer Smith and Smokey Joe Wood in right and Charlie Jamieson and Joe Evans in left. Burns, Jamieson and Evans—the bench half of their respective platoons—combined to hit an BA/OBP/SLG of .352/.414/.498 on the year. Propelled by them, the entire 1921 Indians bench hit .341, which is easily the best ever (runner up: the 1930 Cardinals at .325). Sure it was a high offensive era—but .341 is amazing under any circumstances. Similarly, they also produced 7.51 runs per 27 outs, which is the best any bench has ever done without adjusting for environment.

John McGraw teams appear frequently at the top of the list. Not only are three of the top seven teams his, but the 1908 Giants came in 20th place. He was known as an innovator in using his bench. Baseball historian Peter Morris notes that McGraw was the main proponent for pinch hitting in the early century, when that practice really first caught on, McGraw was also the first manager to experiment with a pinch runner. By having a deeper pool of talent with his 1911-12 teams, McGraw succeeded in breaking the stranglehold on first the Cubs and Pirates shared from 1906-10.

Though he doesn't have as many teams at the top of the leaderboard as McGraw, Earl Weaver might be the true king of the bench. The 1971 Orioles, which had the eighth best bench ever, are only the tip of the iceberg. Under Weaver, the Orioles had the best bench in the league seven times. Not bad. In each season from 1968-73 their bench created runs at a better rate than the league average—not bench average, but overall offensive average. That isn't normal. The large majority of benches are, in news that shouldn't surprise anyone, offensively below average.

Tom Boswell, in one of his early 1980s books, marveled at Weaver's ability to take waiver-wire picks such as John Lowenstein or trade throw-ins like Gary Roenicke and turn them into consistently valuable offensive producers. In fact, Weaver was known for agonizing over his final roster slots every spring training. Those last slots were never filler for him—he had clear purposes for every player, and he would use each one in the appropriate role. Bill James noted Weaver never had players who were merely adequate, they were always really good at something. The 1971 Orioles might be the only bench listed above, but Weaver had many other fine units backing it up.

That just raises another question, though. If those teams had the best benches ever, who had the worst benches? Well, out of the 2,250 teams in the database, here are the bottom 10—team, year, and how their park-adjusted RC/27 outs compares to their leagues' average of runs per game.

Team	Year	Compares
OAK	1975	45.2%
STB	1923	47.0%
BOB	1905	48.6%
BOX	1901	53.1%
NYY	2005	53.6%
TOR	1994	53.8%
BRK	1902	53.8%
BOX	1921	54.6%
BOB	1901	55.1%
STB	1931	55.2%

The 1975 A's come in last, which is perfect, just absolutely perfect. You see, this team appeared at the end of a different bench-related article I wrote for my book (*Evaluating Baseball's Managers*). At that time I wanted to know which teams allocated the largest and smallest percentage of the team's plate appearances to their starting position players. Among all teams in a DH league, the 1975 A's gave the largest chunk of time to their starting nine: 88.3 percent.

Isn't that supremely appropriate? The team that relied so incredibly little on its bench was the team with the worst bench ever. Of course!

And man, did their bench ever stink. The bench player with the most playing time was backup catcher Ray Fosse with only 136 plate appearances. He hit .140 with five extra base hits and eight base on balls. The only other bench batters with over 100 plate appearances, Jim Holt and Angel Mangual, each hit exactly .220, and neither had any power or ability to draw walks.

In 723 plate appearances—less than many individual players have in a season, the 1975 A's bench hit .201 with 17 doubles, two triples and a half-dozen homers. Thanks to owner Charles Finely's fascination with the pinch runner, they stole 52 bases, but ultimately only produced 1.9 RC/27 outs, which is also the worst by any bench.

The next worst RC/27 (unadjusted for park or era) are the 1906 Braves and the 1905 Braves, both at 1.95. Sure there's an era bias as that was the bottom of the Deadball Era, but those benches just sucked. The 1905 Braves had exactly one player on their bench who hit over .200: backup catcher Tom Neeham at .218. At least he had the most plate appearances of anyone on the bench.

For my money, the most striking team on the worst benches list is the 1923 St. Louis Browns. In part, it's because of how dreadful their bench was. None of their backups hit over .244 and the entire bench hit .205/.264/.265. That would be bad in the Deadball Era, but in the 1920s AL it's staggeringly atrocious.

The main reason, however, I find the 1923 Browns bench so fascinating is because they had a tremendous bench in 1922. In fact, the 1922 Browns had the 18th best bench ever—one slot ahead of the 1986 Mets. Only instead of evolving into the bench best ever as the Mets did the next year, St. Louis's backups devolved into one of the worst units ever. The 1922 team nearly won the pennant, but the 1923 team didn't come close. The bench performance was one reason why that happened. It was—by far—the greatest comedown in history from one year to the next for a team's bench.

The 1922 unit—which hit .297/.375/.442 on the whole—had two players with considerable playing time whose batting averages topped .300: Eddie Foster (.306) and Pat Collins (.307). In 1923, both were still with the team, but this time Foster hit .180 (with only two extra base hits in 115 plate appearances), and Collins eked out a .177 batting average. Upshot: A team whose bench produced 6.35 runs per 27 outs one year created only 2.38 runs per 27 outs the next season.

The most surprising inclusion on the list of worst benches is the 2005 Yankees, possessors of the worst bench of any team since the mid-1970s. The Yankees are always so good and have such vast resources at their disposal, I wouldn't expect them to assemble a dreadful bench. They should be able to afford something better.

Actually, I think affording something was part of their problem. Their bench was made up of numerous high-profile batters, including Tony Womack, Ruben Sierra, Matt Lawton and Rey Sanchez. To a man, they were all really bad. They were almost all past their prime and having terrible seasons by any standard. For example, Sierra, a part-time DH, hit .229 with nine walks in 181 plate appearances. Lawton smacked out six hits in 21 games. Their non-stars were dreadful as well. Backup catcher John Flaherty hit .165. Bubba Crosby hit a respectable .276, but achieved the rare distinction of hitting zero doubles in over 100 plate appearances.

That said, they still won their division—and with a team-wide OPS+ of 115. For that matter, the 1975 A's won their division despite history's worst bench. Heck, they even had the most wins of any team in the league. Benches make a difference, obviously, but at least some of these teams had enough front line talent to not have to worry about it.

So far I've only looked at bench performance as a rate stat. That is a sensible way to look at them, but there is something to be said for volume as well. What teams had the largest number of raw Runs Created—not adjusted per outs, but just RC by itself? Here are the top five (there's an era bias clearly in play—as you'll see in a second—so I'll only give top five instead of top 10):

Team	Year	RC
DET	1993	354
HOU	2000	342
CIN	1997	308
PHI	1925	307
LAD	2005	307

The 1993 Tigers win—and with only one squad anywhere near them. They had two key qualities going for them: quality and quantity. In terms of quality, that Detroit bench produced 6.09 runs per 27 outs. After adjusting for park that was more than 30 percent better than league average, which is 13th best of any bench in history.

In terms of quantity, they had a pair of super-subs in Mickey Tettleton and Tony Phillips who each played over 150 games. It's pretty unusual for a team to have one bench player with that many games played, let alone two. Alongside them, the aging Alan Trammell played in more than 100 games. Each of these three key replacements had terrific years at the plate.

Looking at the top five overall, it's clear that recent teams are favored. That's partially because run scoring is higher in these days. It's also because the bench generally takes up a higher percentage of teams' overall plate appearances than they used to.

To that end, the 1925 Phillies really stand out. They are the only team in the top 22 not from the last two decades. They had six backups appear in at least 65 games, and each one hit between .304 and .326. Impressive.

The next-most RC for a pre-1990s bench belongs to the 1961 Dodgers, who tallied 261 Runs Created. They had four "backups" play in over 100 games each. That's probably happened other times in baseball history, but I have no idea when. (In a fitting bit of symmetry, the second most RC by a 1960s team was the other Los Angeles team, the 1961 Angels. Rather noteworthy given that they were an expansion team in their inaugural season).

Era bias also helps determine which benches accumulated the fewest RC:

Team	Year	RC
PHI	1908	25
CWS	1902	26
BOX	1901	27
PHI	1905	29
BRO	1902	36

The starting eight position players on the 1905 Phillies amassed 83.7 percent of the team's overall plate appearances, which is the most on any team since 1900. Their bench had only 415 plate appearances, which isn't very much. They didn't do much with it either—hitting .211 with 22 walks, 12 doubles, 3 triples and no homers. Even in 1905 you wanted to do a bit more than that. Then again, the 1908 Phillies would kill for a bench that good. That year's model hit only .186 with no power and not many walks.

The 1902 White Sox make the list in part because their bench had the fewest plate appearances of any since 1900:

only 308. It would be a couple more years until baseball lengthened the schedule to 154 games, which helps set them apart. That said, in the entire 20th Century only one other bench had fewer than 400 plate appearances in the season: the 1901 Boston Americans (now Red Sox) at 355.

The fewest RC by a post-deadball team was the 1938 Pirates, with 37. Fittingly, their starting eight hitters amassed the largest percentage of overall plate appearances by a team since 1920: 83.1 percent.

Actually, we should pause on the 1938 Pirates for another reason: They lived out the nightmare scenario of the 1975 A's and 2005 Yankees. While those other teams were good squads who overcame a lackluster bench to make the postseason, the Pirates were a quality squad done in by their bench, and ultimately blew a pennant in heartbreaking fashion.

In early September 1938, the Pirates appeared to be cruising to the pennant, sitting atop a seven-game lead. They proceeded to drop 16 of their last 28 decisions, finishing two games behind the surging Chicago Cubs. (It was in this pennant race that Cubs catcher Gabby Hartnett hit his famous "Homer in the Gloamin'"—against the Pirates—to help the Cubs clinch their final peacetime pennant.)

Pittsburgh's bench problem was two-fold. First, they stunk. It wasn't just a matter of minimal playing time. They hit .227/.290/.281 with the opportunities they were given. This, obviously, added considerably less to the team than rivals got from theirs. The Cub bench was no great unit (.249/.304/.355), but they still provided 105 Runs Created.

Second, because he couldn't trust his bench, manager Pie Traynor leaned a little too hard on his starters. Perhaps not-so-coincidentally, their offense grinded down as the season grinded on. Pittsburgh averaged 4.79 runs per game through Sept. 2, but afterwards only 4.04. A temperature curve can't explain all or even most of that.

A Gentleman Remembered

by Craig Wright

Gray Harwell loved the game of baseball and closely followed the career of major league pitcher Sherry Smith, one of his closest friends. Gray passed on his love of the game to his son, Ernie Harwell.

At age 8, Ernie heard his first baseball broadcast and was fascinated to hear the *live* account of Grover Alexander striking out Tony Lazzeri with the bases loaded in the clinching game of the 1926 World Series. As a boy his family could not afford a radio of their own, but their neighbor Thad Johnson built radios and was a fan of the local minor league team, the Atlanta Crackers. Harwell would listen to games at Johnson's home workshop, and if Johnson wasn't home, the boy would roam the neighborhood until he heard the broadcast coming through the open window of another house and he would settle in under the window listening to the game. When Ernie was still in elementary school, he had his first job in baseball, working as a bat boy for several of the visiting teams that played the Crackers. He was "paid" in trade, a used baseball for every game he worked.

As a boy Harwell struggled with a speech impediment that gave him a noticeable lisp. Despite hard financial times, Ernie's father was determined to get Ernie help in overcoming this handicap and paid for weekly lessons with an elocution teacher named Margaret Lackland. Working with an eager and bright pupil, she helped the boy eliminate his lisp and also taught him debate skills.

Ernie ended up winning a school medal as the best boy debater, and at the ceremony Ernie's father was in tears as he told Mrs. Lackland, "This is the happiest day of my life." As part of their work together, Mrs. Lackland had had Ernie practice reading out loud a poem by Sam Walter Foss titled: *The House by the Side of the Road*. Years later, Harwell's trademark description of a called strike three was, "He stood there like the house by the side of the road."

While in high school, Ernie talked *The Sporting News* into using him as its freelance correspondent in Atlanta, without mentioning that he was 16 and had never published a word before. In college, he prepared to be a sportswriter and did some part-time sports writing for the *Atlanta Constitution*.

When he graduated, there was a shortage of full-time newspaper jobs, and he decided to audition for an on-the-air position with WSB radio. Harwell was hired even though he had zero experience in radio. He started off doing interviews and sports reports but soon longed to follow in the footsteps of fellow southerner Red Barber and become a baseball broadcaster. During Atlanta Crackers games he would practice on his own "announcing" the play-by-play of the game.

In 1942, Harwell enlisted in the Marines, and while on furlough he got his first chance to broadcast some games for the Crackers. When the war was over he became their regular play-by-play announcer, and he was a hit. In 1948 Red Barber was seriously ill, and the Brooklyn Dodgers wanted to hire Harwell to fill in. In return for letting Harwell out of his contract, the Crackers received minor league catcher Cliff Dapper, making Harwell the only broadcaster to be acquired in a player trade.

In 1950, the New York Giants lured Harwell away to be their announcer. In New York, he broadcast the debut and early years of Willie Mays' career. For the 1951 playoff between the Dodgers and Giants, he broadcast the first nationally *televised* baseball series. His call on Bobby Thomson's famous pennant-winning home run was not recorded and was lost to posterity.

However, a fan did tape the *radio* call by Harwell's regular partner Russ Hodges, the one in which Hodges famously yells over and over, "The Giants win the pennant!" The fan sold the tape to Hodges for $10, and the radio sponsor, Chesterfield cigarettes, ended up putting Hodges' call on a record celebrating the Giants' amazing season. It became the most famous single broadcast tape in the history of American sports. Harwell thought he had the "plum assignment" with the historic TV job, but he enjoyed the humor of how it played out. He loved telling that story.

In 1954, Harwell moved on to Baltimore to broadcast the games of the newly arrived St. Louis Browns, renamed the Orioles. The next year he penned a poem called "Game for

---

You may have heard the story of how when Ty Cobb was a minor leaguer, sports writer Grantland Rice got several telegrams from a fan who was enthralled with how good this young player Cobb was, but that it was actually Cobb who had sent those telegrams. What you probably don't know is that it was Ernie Harwell who broke that story in 1958 after Cobb shared the details while they were attending the Masters golf tournament.

While Harwell felt Willie Mays was "... the best player I ever saw," he greatly admired Jackie Robinson, who stole home in the first major league game (Aug. 4, 1948) ever broadcast by Harwell. "He made the most of his ability. ... He was the most *exciting* player I ever saw."

"...once you start as an announcer, you have to decide what kind of approach you're going to have. I decided very early on that I was going to be a reporter, that I would not cheer for the team. I don't denigrate those who do it. It's fine. I think you have to fit whatever kind of personality you have, and I think my nature was to be more down the middle ... I've always said, 'Be whatever you are.' ... if you fake it, that's a lot of hard work for three hours."

— Ernie Harwell

America" that appeared in *The Sporting News* and today, over 50 years later, remains a revered part of baseball literature.

In 1957 George Kell was in his final season as a third baseman and while recovering from an ankle injury, worked briefly as a color commentator with Harwell on the radio. He was grateful for the insightful tips that Ernie gave him, and was impressed with Harwell's style. A few years later, Kell was working in Detroit, broadcasting the games of the Tigers. The station needed a new partner for Kell, and he recommended Harwell. The station made him an offer and when the Orioles wouldn't match it, the 42-year-old Harwell moved to Detroit. As the years went by, he came to appreciate that this had been the most important decision of his career, and that he had found his home.

Ernie and his wife, Lulu, fell in love with Michigan, its people, and especially the fans of the Tigers. He would live the rest of his life in Michigan and spent 42 years as the "Voice of the Tigers."

He valued blue collar commitment. "I had a job to do," he said, "and I did it all these years to the best of my ability. I'd like to be remembered as someone who showed up for the job. I consider myself a worker."

Harwell emphasized keeping the focus on the game. When giving advice to young broadcasters, he told them, "You can't give the score often enough. It is the key context for your listeners following the game. I actually tried to give the score every 60 seconds."

He was a wonderful story-teller, but he would not tell a story on the air if he could not fit it into the flow of an inning. When he was encouraged to tell longer stories that might carry over to the next inning, he refused: "No. The people tune in for the game. They never tune in for me."

On the air, Harwell made it seem effortless, and what you took away from listening to a game with Ernie Harwell was a sense of the game vividly described by a friend who exuded warmth, real love of baseball, and enjoyment in sharing the game. Harwell once said, "I love what I do. If I had my time over again, I'd probably do it for nothing."

The fans responded to his style with an affection rarely seen in the world of broadcasting. That affection was shared by those who knew him outside the radio booth. He was a gracious, gentle, extremely humble man of uncommon decency, and that allowed him to tell it like it was without offend-ing or alienating people. In the simplest of terms, he treated people well and had a gift for making them feel good.

Current Tigers manager Jim Leyland listened to Harwell on the radio growing up. Then as a minor leaguer with the Tigers, he got to meet Harwell in spring training. "When you met him, he was one of those guys you felt like you knew him all your life. And you felt like he knew you. ... Harwell treated me like I was a major league Tiger, and I was never a major league Tiger."

Eric Nadel, who has broadcast the games of the Texas Rangers for more than 30 years and is the voice of the radio show *A Page from Baseball's Past*, has fond memories of Harwell's kindness in mentoring him and other announcers:

"He was incredibly gracious to me and always was. ... He was humble to a fault, extremely giving. I don't think there's any announcer that has ever reached out as much as he did to young announcers, whether they be in the major leagues or minor leagues. He was always available for help and advice. ... [He treated me] as if I was an equal of his, which to me was totally ludicrous, but that's the way he treated people. He thought everybody was his equal even though he was this giant in the field of broadcasting. That didn't make him better than anyone else in his own mind."

> Because Ty Cobb, the greatest ballplayer from Georgia, was so identified with the Detroit Tigers, many youngsters in Georgia in the 1920s were fans of the Tigers. Harwell mentioned in a 2005 interview that he had been one of those boys, that the Detroit Tigers had always been one of his favorite teams.

In 1981, the former minor league bat boy from Georgia became the first announcer to be honored with the Hall of Fame's Ford C. Frick Award while still an active announcer. In the ensuing years the bond continued to deepen between Tigers fans and Ernie Harwell, and the story began to go beyond the simple theme of affection felt for a longtime baseball announcer.

A charming example came from the sister of a good friend of mine. She was a baseball fan, a Tigers fan, and in 1986 she moved from Michigan to Florida. Feeling perhaps a little homesick, she called her mother and had her lay the phone down on the kitchen table in front of the radio as Ernie shared another game with us.

"I listened to Ernie for an hour and half," she said. "Couldn't help it. Mom picked the phone up every 10 minutes and would ask, 'Have you had enough yet?' I felt lots better after I got to listen to him. I remember the call cost me about $11, and I considered it money well spent."

> "Ernie is probably the most beloved person who has ever been with ... the Detroit Tigers. He is loved by everybody and rightfully so. He's a great broadcaster but even a better person. That comes across on his broadcasts."
> — Al Kaline

> "If baseball could talk it would sound like Ernie Harwell."
> - Mitch Albom, *Detroit Free Press*

I surely felt it myself as someone who grew up listening to Ernie Harwell from the time I was seven years old. When I began working in baseball, I counted it a huge honor and absolute pleasure to get to meet and know Ernie in the 1980s and early '90s. When he signed my copy of his poem "Game for America," he so warmly obliged that it felt almost as if I had done *him* a favor. Like so many, I was struck by how genuine he was in his love of life, people, and baseball.

My grandfather was born in 1884 and literally had been rooting for the Tigers from the first game of their existence. He had heard all their announcers through the ages, but he never bonded with them the way he did with Ernie Harwell. I knew many Tigers fans who would turn down the volume when the Tigers were on TV and listen to Harwell on the radio. My grandfather was the first person I remember doing that.

My grandfather was excited when I told him about meeting Charlie Gehringer, an old teammate of his from their town ball days, and his favorite player from his favorite team, the 1935 Tigers. He was thrilled when I told him about meeting Al Kaline. But he was more excited to hear of my meeting Ernie Harwell than anyone else in baseball. I can still see his huge grin, and hear his delighted, "Imagine that."

But radio station WJR and Bo Schembechler, the president of the Detroit Tigers, did not fully appreciate what they had. When Harwell's partner Paul Carey decided that 1991 would be his final season, the 74-year-old Harwell was startled to learn from Schembechler that it was to be his last season as well.

The public outcry was incredible. You could not get 97 percent of a crowd to agree that the sun rises in the East, yet in a newspaper poll an incredible 97 percent of the respondents wanted Harwell to continue broadcasting the Tiger games. The day after the news broke, the headline over Mitch Albom's column on the front page of the *Detroit Free Press* read, "A GENTLEMAN WRONGED."

About a month after the announcement by WJR and the Tigers, I got to speak with Schembechler about this. He said there was no turning back from the decision, but admitted that he was totally caught off guard by the reaction. He had had no idea of how strongly the fans were attached to Harwell.

After a year of broadcasting CBS Radio's *Game of the Week*, Harwell was brought back to the Tigers in 1993 by Mike Ilitch, the new owner the Tigers. In 1998, at age 80, Harwell was inducted into the Radio Hall of Fame while still an active announcer. He was named Michigan Sportscaster of the Year a record 19 times before finally deciding to retire at the end of the 2002 season at the age of 84.

On Sept. 15, 2002, the Tigers honored him with Ernie Harwell Day. Stretching across the outfield were banners signed by tens of thousands of Tiger fans. The highlight was to be the unveiling of an Ernie Harwell statue that would greet the fans at the entrance to the ballpark, but the real highlight ended up being Ernie's humble and eloquent speech.

Infielder Damian Jackson said, "If I have a few positives I'm going to take out of this year, meeting Ernie is definitely going to be at the top. It was pretty emotional. (He) tugged at your heart when he was out there talking about the people who meant something to him, his lifetime commitment to his wife, his devotion to God. It was pretty touching. I got a little choked up."

In September of 2009, Ernie Harwell let the Tigers know that he had been diagnosed with terminal cancer. He made a brief public farewell address to Tigers fans, letting them know he was at peace.

He also addressed the team in a clubhouse talk that manager Leyland described as "fulfilling" and "priceless." Ernie

---

"... rather than say goodbye, please allow me to say 'thank you.' Thank you for letting me part of your family. Thank you for taking me with you to that cottage up north, to the beach, the picnic, your work place, and your backyard. Thank you for sneaking your transistor under the pillow as you grew up loving the Tigers. Now, I might have been a small part of your life, but you've been a very large part of mine."

— Ernie Harwell, at the close of his final 2002 broadcast

spoke simply about his thoughts on life and baseball, and his appreciation of the game they shared. Shortstop Adam Everett remembered being riveted, "I don't think anybody *blinked* the whole time. That's how intense it was." Catcher Gerald Laird said, "It was inspirational. It was unbelievable. That guy left his mark on this game, and he's definitely going to be remembered forever—as long as this game's going on."

On May 4, 2010, when the news of Harwell's passing reached the press box in Minnesota, where the Tigers were playing the Twins, rain began to fall over the ballpark. Then the sun broke through and a rainbow bent over the field. Tiger announcer Jim Price made the call, describing the rainbow and adding his view, "That was for Ernie Harwell."

And it went out on the air …

Notes

- When Ernie Harwell was a boy in Atlanta, one of the customers on his newspaper route was the most famous writer in the city, Margaret Mitchell, Pulitzer Prize winner and author of *Gone with the Wind*.

- Baseball is a hard, competitive game played by hard, competitive men, and profanity is common around the game. Harwell, the former Marine, was one of the shining exceptions. Denny McLain said, "I've known Ernie for nearly 50 years and I've never heard him curse once. I mean, not even a 'damn' or 'hell.'"

- Ernie would begin the first spring training broadcast by reading from the Bible, from the Song of Solomon (2:11-12): *"For lo, the winter is past, the rain is over and gone; the flowers appear on the earth; the time of the singing of birds is come, and the voice of the turtle is heard in our land."* (For those unfamiliar with the King James Version, the "turtle" is the turtledove.)

- Harwell loved music and he was delighted when the Tigers let him pick the singers for the national anthem in the three games played in Detroit during the 1968 World Series. His first two singers, including Marvin Gaye, did traditional versions that were well accepted, and then in the third game he went with the 23-year-old Puerto Rican artist, Jose Feliciano. Harwell had not known that Feliciano was going to do a stylized interpretation of the anthem, and many folks were outraged at the departure from the traditional performance. Harwell stood by Feliciano against the criticism and today stylized versions of the anthem are routinely accepted and appreciated.

- Harwell himself was a prolific songwriter and had over 50 songs recorded by various artists. Another songwriter from the baseball ranks, umpire Joe West, writes country

tunes and penned a song titled *Tribute to Ernie Harwell*. It ends, "That special place in Ernie's heart where the grass is always green. On the other side of memory's fence where the grass is always green."

- In a scene reminiscent of the passing of Babe Ruth, whose body lay in state at Yankee Stadium with the gates opened for visitation from thousands of fans, Comerica Park was open for the fans who wished to pay their respects to William Earnest Harwell. (Yes, that's how his parents chose to spell it.) Tiger GM Dave Dombrowski shook hands with many of the fans and was struck by how many of them expressed the sentiment, "I never met him, but I felt I knew him." On an online blog a Tigers fan shared: "I have cried more in the last 18 hours than I had any right to over a man I never met."

- Vin Scully got his start with the Dodgers when Harwell went over to the Giants. "(Ernie) was with the Dodgers in '48 and '49, then I sat in his chair. I didn't follow or succeed him. I just sat in his chair. He was so gracious and kind. Probably the best word is that he was a gentleman, and it came across. He just cared for people. He loved baseball. He was such a nice guy, so you can understand why the people of Detroit just loved him."

- When Jon Miller was informed he would be honored at the Hall of Fame with the Ford C. Frick award, he was deeply touched that Harwell, diagnosed just months earlier with terminal cancer, took the time to write him a warm congratulatory letter. Miller said, "It made me cry. It was very beautiful."

- Leyland paid the ultimate compliment to Harwell, one that I don't think many people understood. The professional baseball player tends to have a relationship with the media that goes like this: "Okay, you are part of the game, but don't ever get confused that you are one of us, a player." In trying to express his feelings for Harwell, the tearful Leyland said:

    "He was … the constant cleanup hitter for the Tigers. The constant leadoff man. The ever-ready defensive player. The ever-ready pinch runner. Most announcers aren't like that. Ernie was truly like that. This guy was the Tigers. He was looked upon as a player, not an announcer."

Craig Wright researches and writes "A Page from Baseball's Past," a popular subscription story series on the history of the game. Visit www.PageFromBaseballsPast.com to learn more.

Bully for the Yankee Clipper

by Jon Daly

San Francisco. Big city. Small world. New York. Bigger city. Small world. How are a paleontologist, a blonde bombshell, and a beatnik (among others) connected? And what does this have to do with baseball anyway?

The clipper was a fast ship for its time back almost two centuries ago. It was also graceful. The "Clipper" was also a long-range luxury flying boat built in the late 1930s for Pan Am's trans-Atlantic flights. Joe DiMaggio possessed what the author David Foster Wallace (when writing about Roger Federer) would later call kinetic beauty; "(A) human being's reconciliation with the fact of having a body." Hence, Arch McDonald[1] gave DiMaggio the nickname The Yankee Clipper. As most know, DiMaggio wed Marilyn Monroe after he hung up his spikes and glove. Soon after their wedding, Monroe traveled to Korea to entertain the troops. Upon reuniting with DiMaggio, Monroe commented: "I have never heard so much cheering." DiMaggio replied knowingly: "I have."

Baghdad by the Bay

Joltin' Joe DiMaggio grew up in the North Beach area of San Francisco. He also lived there while married to Marilyn Monroe. It was the mid-'50s. He probably ran into some of the Beats on the street. Jack Kerouac, Allen Ginsberg and Neal Cassady were all in the neighborhood. Kerouac was a baseball geek, inventing his own tabletop game. One wonders if he was aware of DiMaggio's presence nearby. But growing up in Lowell, Mass., his fandom may have lain elsewhere. Cassady would go on to become a bus driver, driving Ken Kesey's Merry Pranksters[2] around as they passed out LSD to all takers. The Grateful Dead had one of their first gigs at an Acid Test put on by Kesey.

Ginsberg befriended Timothy Leary, the Harvard prof. "Turn on, tune in, drop out." That's what Leary said at the Human Be-In on Jan. 14, 1967 in Golden Gate Park. The Dead, Quicksilver Messenger Service and Jefferson Airplane all performed.

DiMaggio was a coach for Charlie O. Finley's Oakland A's in 1968 and 1969. In the latter year, baseball was celebrating a centennial. An all-time team was voted upon and DiMaggio was named the Greatest Living Player. Why him over Mantle, Mays, Musial or Ted Williams? Many of those players were active recently and hadn't ascended to legendary status. And the voting panel was New York-centric.

Finley had just moved the A's from Kansas City to Oakland, which prompted Sen. Stuart Symington to opine that Oakland was the luckiest city since Hiroshima. The A's played in Oakland-Alameda County Coliseum, which they shared with the Oakland Raiders. This was one of those concrete ashtray multipurpose stadiums and was nicknamed The Mausoleum. The place was also home to rock concerts.

This was old hat to Finley. Like most men of his generation, his tastes ran more towards standards like "Sugartime." But he brought the Beatles to KC's Municipal Stadium during one of their tours. (And wound up paying the Fab Four more than he paid the Kansas City A's players that year.) The Rolling Stones played there a month before their free concert at Altamont. The Coliseum also played host to "Days On The Green"; big daytime outdoor concerts held there for almost 20 years starting in 1973. They were the brainchild of promoter Bill Graham. Graham was a San Francisco icon. Really promoted the San Francisco scene. He also got into the business of managing acts. One of these was the seminal psychedelic folk group Jefferson Airplane. Jorma Kaukonen was a founding member of Jefferson Airplane along with Marty Balin and Paul Kanter. He named the band after an imaginary blues musician named Blind Jefferson Airplane.

New York, New York

Marilyn and Joe's marriage would not last a year. She went on to marry Arthur Miller, the Pulitzer winning playwright. He wrote plays such as *Death of A Salesman* and *The Crucible*. Ostensibly about the Salem witch trials, *The Crucible* was really about Miller's experiences with the House Un-American Activities Committee. Miller played football at Abraham Lincoln High School in Brooklyn. That school is more known these days for being the alma mater of Stephon Marbury and Sebastian Telfair.

One of Miller's classmates from the class of '33 was Jerome Karle. Karle and Miller each took the subway from Brooklyn to City College. Miller supposedly read *War and Peace* on the subway back and forth to school. It was three hours round trip. Karle would do his homework on the subway. It worked. He worked on the Manhattan Project at the University of Chicago then went on to the Naval Research Laboratory in D.C. where he met Herbert A. Hauptman. The duo went on to win the 1985 Nobel Prize in Chemistry "for their outstanding achievements in the development of direct methods for

---

1   McDonald was a long time radio play-by-play guy who won the Ford C. Frick Award posthumously in 1999.

2   If you remember seeing the Merry Pranksters, you weren't really there.

the determination of crystal structures." Their x-ray scattering technique was a huge stride forward in crystallography.[3]

Hauptman was also from New York City. He went to Townsend Harris High School, which was sort of like an early version of a magnet school. One of his classmates was *another* Nobel Laureate. This was Julian Schwinger. Schwinger won the 1965 Nobel in Physics for his work in quantum electrodynamics; or how light and matter interact. He shared his prize with Richard Feynman (another contempo New Yorker) and Shinichiro Tomanga. NYC had very good schools in those days.[4] Schwinger worked at Harvard with Ed Purcell. He was a Nobel laureate as well, but he was from the prairies of Illinois.

A Band of Brothers

DiMaggio was one of three centerfielding brothers. There was Vince, who struck out as often as Joe didn't. Then there was Dom, yclept "The Little Professor." Dom played for the Red Sox; the Yankees' rivals to the north. He became a successful businessman in Massachusetts after his playing days. He manufactured seat padding for the automotive industry. He also formed a lifelong bond with teammates Bobby Doerr, Johnny Pesky, and Ted Williams. They were

---

3   X-ray crystallography was discovered serendipitously. Scientists wanted to see if x-rays were a form of high frequency light. They conducted experiments where they would bounce the rays off of crystals and see if they'd create interference patterns. The x-rays did, but more importantly x-rays provided a way to identify what kind of crystal they were being bounced off of by the patterns the rays created. Eventually, x-ray crystallography helped determine that DNA was in the shape of a double helix.

4   Incidentally, Feynman and Schwinger were opposites from a personality standpoint. Schwinger was reserved, while Feynman was one of America's foremost public intellectuals. He wrote books, gave lectures, appeared before Congress and played the bongos (though not at the Capitol).

four West Coast boys transplanted to Fenway. If you like double plays because they are the most democratic play in baseball, then you'll love Doerr. In 1949, he grounded into 31 of them while participating in 134 of them in the field. If that isn't a record, it is close.

Williams, of course, was the last .400 hitter. Noted paleontologist and public intellectual Stephen Jay Gould wrote an article 25 years ago for *Discover* magazine. It was titled "Entropic Homogeneity Isn't Why No One Hits .400 Anymore." Gould argued that it is harder to dominate today because the overall quality of play is better. From the article, "this decline (in variation) produces a decrease in the difference between the average and stellar performance. Therefore, modern leaders don't stand so far above their contemporaries." Thus, the .400 hitter is extinct.

Wrapping Things Up

Gould was actually a DiMaggio man, through and through. David Halberstam wondered why Gould wasn't more of a fan of Williams. The Kid approached the game like a scientist and was very candid. DiMaggio, on the other hand, was a harbinger of today's corporate, buttoned-down athlete. But Gould was smitten by DiMaggio's grace. Gould was friends with Ed Purcell at Harvard. The same year that Ted hit .406, DiMaggio had his hitting streak of hitting streaks. Purcell determined that for a streak of 56 games to be likely, there'd have to be four lifetime .400 hitters or 52 lifetime .350 hitters.

Gould did his undergrad work at Antioch College in Ohio. While he was there, Jorma Kaukonen was also at the school. But Gould's tastes ran more towards Gilbert and Sullivan, (Henry) Purcell and Handel. He was a member of the Cecilia Society; a Boston choral group.

Thus, the paths in this chapter converge. We go from DiMaggio to Gould via a few delightfully different paths. Hope you enjoyed the trip.

Analysis

Scouting by Numbers

by Jeremy Greenhouse

Our nationwide obsession with player evaluation went to a deeper level when Sportvision's PITCHf/x system debuted in 2006. At least it did for me—using PITCHf/x data to grade pitches has become my holy grail. We know that Roy Halladay has a great fastball, for instance, but that's because we already know that Halladay is a great pitcher. PITCHf/x data adds something else; it isolates a pitcher's process from his results. Essentially, PITCHf/x can be used to scout pitchers without ever laying eyes on them.

"Stuff" and "command" are the two most popular scouting terms in baseball ("wingspan" holds the title throughout major sports, and deservedly so), even though (because?) stuff and command remain largely undefined. On the next couple of pages, I intend to define them.

Before moving on, I should provide clearer explanations of those terms. I think of stuff as what a pitcher throws— the quality of force he exerts on the ball. In particular, that means spin and speed. Thanks to PITCHf/x, we can measure those.

Command is where he throws. You can't really fake "stuff," but command is harder to pin down. A pitcher can miss his spot and get the call, or he can locate perfectly and get hammered. So the options are to look at the location of every pitch in isolation or to attempt to divine a pitcher's intent given the situation. I'm going to give both of those approaches a try.

The goal is to objectively grade stuff and command. First, we need the data.

Pulling the Data Together

I took the data of more than two million pitches since 2007. Not only the usual data—pitcher/batter matchup, ball/strike count, pitch result—but also the advanced PITCHf/x data—velocity, movement, location at release and location crossing the plate. Still, I had to assign three additional values of my own to each pitch.

First and foremost I gave each pitch a value based on its result. In February 2008, Joe P. Sheehan and John Walsh developed a "run value" framework for individual pitches, and now FanGraphs carries that data for all major league pitchers.

Here's the concept: The average major league batter hit .258/.326/.404 in 2010. If he got to a 1-0 count, he went on to hit .273/.388/.437, but if he fell to 0-1, that fell to .229/.270/.349. By converting those lines to runs, we can esti-

mate that throwing a first-pitch strike decreases run expectancy by a bit over 0.04 runs, while throwing a ball costs a pitcher a bit less than 0.04. In addition, if a home run nets 1.4 runs on average, then allowing a home run on an 0-1 count is equivalent to allowing 1.44 runs, compared to allowing 1.36 runs on a 1-0 count. And so on.

Secondly, I classified each pitch into types. I predetermined the number of pitches in a pitcher's arsenal, and then I used a clustering algorithm to assign pitch types based on velocity and movement. There are eight main pitch types: four-seam fastball, two-seam fastball, cut fastball, slider, split finger, changeup, curveball, knuckleball.

Third and finally, I scaled each pitch's vertical location. PITCHf/x reports the height of the pitch relative to the ground, which isn't as useful as knowing how the pitch's height relates to the batter's strike zone. The batter's listed height generally gives a good idea of his strike zone. The bottom of the strike zone can be drawn at a quarter of his height, and the top at 56 percent. In addition, stringers who work at each game mark the borders of what they perceive to be the boundaries of each batter's strike zone. That data becomes useful given a full season of at-bats for a batter.

Measuring Stuff

I began this line of thinking back in 2008 as I was being introduced to sabermetrics. Here's a snippet of an e-mail I sent that August to Josh Kalk, a PITCHf/x pioneer and former THT writer.

> I have a question concerning fastball "rise." You hear anecdotally that a straight fastball is a bad thing, which I take to mean that a fastball with average "rise" will remain flat and be drilled. Some fastballs have been criticized for not having as much absolute vertical movement as the league average, but doesn't this just mean that they have more "sink"? My guess would be that as long as a pitcher has a difference of rise or sink a couple of inches from the mean, it may fool the batter.

I think I've finally found a solution to my question. There's really no such thing as "more" movement, since movement is a vector quantity. Movement is described by both magnitude and direction. In turn, when we talk about pitch velocity, we actually mean speed, which is scalar, since direction has no bearing.

We need to think of movement from the ball's point of view and not the batter's. Most pitches are thrown from off-center, so for the ball to move perpendicularly to the batter's swing plane as it crosses the plate, it would have to have tailed after it left the pitcher's hand. Hideki Okajima is virtually the only pitcher who throws from such an over-the-top arm angle that would allow a straight pitch to travel parallel on the pitcher-batter plane.

Let's try an exercise. The average fastball runs 91 miles per hour with six inches of horizontal movement and eight inches of vertical movement (as compared to a theoretically spinless pitch). Fastballs can move up and down, side to side, or somewhere in between. A pitch that has more upward vertical movement than average is called a rising fastball. The rising fastball has long stood as a baseball myth, since rise is a misnomer. It is physically impossible for a human to put enough backspin on a pitch for it to defy gravity. But people naturally throw baseballs with some backspin (eight inches of vertical movement), so we call that resulting movement "rise". Even sinking fastballs generally "rise" a bit in that sense, just not more than eight inches.

A tailing fastball runs more than half a foot back toward the pitcher's arm side. Finally, a cut fastball continues to move across a pitcher's body after he releases the ball, causing it to only move a couple inches horizontally. To generate rise or sink or tail or cut, pitchers try to hold the ball off-center or find a special grip.

The worst type of fastball is one that has no special movement. The only way to describe such a fastball is "average," because it falls directly in between all other fastballs. Therefore, a fastball with average movement—six inches of tail and eight inches of rise—is actually a substandard pitch.

To prove this, I took all fastballs with average velocity, average horizontal movement, and average vertical movement, and put them in a bucket. I also made buckets of similar average fastballs, holding two of the components constant while adjusting the third. Here is how each bucket ranks according to run value, and an example of a pitcher who throws such a fastball.

Rank	Trait	Example
1	Cut	Yovanni Gallardo
2	Rise	Johan Santana
3	Fast	Clay Buchholz
4	Tail	Trevor Cahill
5	Sink	Mike Pelfrey
6	Average	Carl Pavano
7	Slow	John Lannan

As you can see, the only way to make a fastball with average movement worse is by decreasing velocity. Any type of movement that deviates from the norm is beneficial.

Grouping similar pitches into buckets is called binning. A more sophisticated and efficient type of statistic is regression analysis. Because there's no linear relationship between run value and movement—again, the nature of movement being a vector quantity—I used local regression instead of a linear one. Local regression fits models on localized subsets of data to build up a function that describes the entire data set. Essentially, local regression creates all of the buckets necessary that would be used in binning, but it smooths them out, adding precision along the way.

But stuff ain't that simple. Left-handed pitchers in general don't throw as hard as right-handed pitchers, since being left-handed is an advantage in itself. If southpaws don't have to throw as hard as righties to achieve the same levels of success, then perhaps that shouldn't be held against them in a measure of stuff. The same tenet holds true for sidearmers and submariners.

Therefore, I made a second computation splitting left-handed pitchers and right-handed pitchers and also including arm angle as a variable. In addition, some pitches, like the sweeping slider, are filthy against same-handed batters, but to opposite-handed batters, they're eminently hittable. In my final calculation I split the data up by same-handed match-ups and opposite-handed matchups to adjust for the platoon advantage that exists in some types of pitches.

Measuring Location

Ever since I played Ken Griffey Baseball, I've loved the idea of batters having hot and cold zones. Dave Allen wrote an article in the Annual last year in which he graphed "heat maps"—the value of a pitch based on its location. I was looking at one of those heat maps and thought, Well, why not give each pitch that value? What I mean by that is that if a pitcher can hit that spot, then who cares about the result? He did his job, and just as a pitcher has no control over his defense, he also can't control the hitter. Again, using local regression, I predicted run values depending on the location of each pitch while controlling for the count, the pitch type, and the batter/pitcher handedness combination.

Still, a down-and-away fastball might be a bad pitch if it was meant to be thrown up and in. Fortunately, pitchers are creatures of habit. They repeat their delivery, their arm speed, their pitch grips, and more often than not, their intended locations. For every pitcher, I grouped all of his pitches based on the pitch type, the count, and the batter handedness. Then I measured the standard deviation in pitch locations. (Doing this gives us insight into the types of pitches that might be easiest to command. Curveballs and splitters have the largest spreads, while fastballs are the tightest.)

The resulting numbers from these analyses were expressed as runs and inches, which are meaningless to most people, so I'm not going to report those. Instead, I decided to put the numbers on the 20-80 scouting scale. What I did was Z-Score the values so that 50 was average, 60 was one standard deviation above the mean, and 20 was Daniel Cabrera. With that, I can at last turn to scoutspeak.

The Best Stuff on Earth

Here is a list of the 20 pitchers with the best stuff in the majors—the top ten score 80s in my system.

Best Stuff
Aroldis Chapman
Joel Zumaya
Daniel Bard
Matt Thornton
Henry Rodriguez
Jordan Walden
Kevin Jepsen
Stephen Strasburg
Jason Motte
Ryan Webb
Greg Holland
Jenrry Mejia
Neftali Feliz
Andrew Bailey
Brian Wilson
Evan Meek
Ronald Belisario
Brandon League
Billy Wagner
Chris Sale

Their stuff is *tripleplusgood*. The list more or less reads as a velocity leaderboard for the 2010 season. I touched on what makes an effective fastball earlier, but just to illustrate the importance of fastball velocity, I graphed the whiff rate of all fastballs by their velocity at the top of the next column. As you can see, the faster the fastball, the more unhittable it is.

A Star is Born

Strasburg is the only starter to score an 80 in stuff. He hits 98 mph with his four-seamer, while achieving plus command. His two-seamer at 97 mph has good life. His curveball is a visual marvel; baseballs aren't supposed to

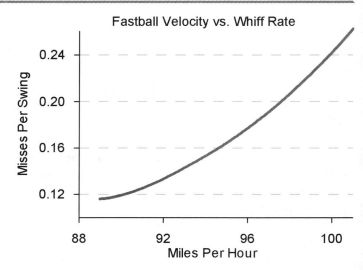

Fastball Velocity vs. Whiff Rate

bend that way. Candy Cummings would have accused Strasburg of sorcery.

And it's tough to call a changeup "nasty," since changeups tend to rely on deception. But his 90-mph changeup actually has negative vertical movement! That means the pitch is thrown with topspin, making it most physically similar to a Brandon Webb or Chad Qualls sinker, and there's no other off-speed pitch like it. Half the time a batter swung at Strasburg's change, he whiffed.

I'm not saying that Strasburg could have scrapped one of his four pitches and still have been one of the best pitchers in the game. I'm saying he could have scrapped two.

Chapmania

Before September 2010, no left-handed pitcher in the PITCHf/x era could say with confidence that he had ever thrown 100 miles per hour. Sure, David Price, Billy Wagner and Matt Thornton throw hard, and Chris Sale came up throwing gas. Randy Johnson used to hit triple-digits in his prime, but that was back when radar guns were the unstandardized standard. But Aroldis Chapman is playing a different game.

On Sept. 24, he hit 105 mph: The Fastest Pitch Ever Thrown. And his average fastball is four standard deviations above the mean for southpaws. I wouldn't even be comfortable using a 20-80 scouting scale on Chapman's heat.

The Chad Bradford All-Stars

LOOGY, short for Left-Handed One Out Guy, is a favorite acronym among seamheads. But what good is an acronym without an accompanying metric? I compared the stuff numbers on same-handed matchups to those on opposite-handed matchups to come up with expected platoon splits. Submariner Chad Bradford retired this year, but he was the perfect example, a pitcher whose stuff graded out as an 80 against righties and a 20 against lefties.

Left-handed relievers Joe Thatcher and Randy Choate jump out as the most obvious LOOGY candidates, while Brad Ziegler, Joe Smith, Darren O'Day, Justin Masterson and Fausto Carmona all have huge expected platoon splits, too. Masterson and Carmona are the only ones not currently in the 'pen. Their sinker-slider repertoires are neutralized by lefties.

The Best Location on Earth

Command is harder to nail down than stuff. Nobody rated 80 on command, though Carl Pavano, Mark Buehrle, Cliff Lee, Andy Pettitte and Wilton Lopez were at least 65s this year. Going back a couple of years, Mike Mussina, Curt Schilling and Greg Maddux topped the leaderboards.

Here's the current pitcher top 20:

Location
Carl Pavano
Mark Buehrle
Cliff Lee
Andy Pettitte
Wilton Lopez
Joel Peralta
Roy Halladay
Jered Weaver
Rafael Betancourt
Shaun Marcum
Kevin Slowey
Jason Vargas
Koji Uehara
Matt Belisle
Josh Johnson
Edward Mujica
Zack Greinke
Ricky Nolasco
Dan Haren
Matt Capps

All of those guys have (and had) great command, but to give you an idea of one issue in my rankings, Mariano Rivera, who unquestionably has the best command I've ever seen, scores only a 60. Mo is to command what Chapman is to velocity. In the same way that batters must choose whether to sit on a Chapman fastball or slider, they have to choose which half of the plate to concede against Mo. A picture of his 2010 pitch locations tells the story.

Where Mo Throws

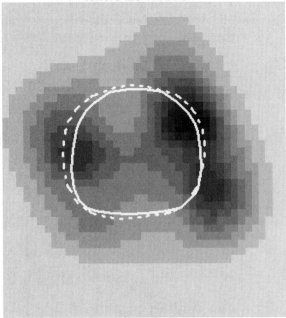

The darker points represent locations of higher frequency. The solid white line represents the league's strike zone, while the dashed line represents Mo's.

There are two flaws evident that reveal why my numbers underrate Rivera. First, he is able to expand the strike zone. Pitches on the corners are more valuable for Mo than pitches on the corners for anyone else, so comparing Mo's cutter locations to the league's averages undervalues him.

Secondly, it doesn't make sense to measure the overall variance in Mo's pitch locations since he obviously targets two distinct zones. Not many pitchers make it as clear as Rivera, but I can name a few other pitchers with outstanding "bimodal distributions." Jamie Moyer, David Huff, and Shaun Marcum locate their fastballs to both sides of the plate exceptionally well.

90>95?

Arm speed is not easily taught. So how can a pitcher compensate for a 5 mph difference in pure velocity via other means?

I found that pitchers cannot survive throwing 90 mph fastballs up in the zone. Their only recourse is to stay low and away. Ninety-five mph fastballs can thrive up and in, yet down and away, they are rendered no more effective than 90 mph fastballs. Furthermore, a 90 mph fastball with about half a foot of movement away from average is equivalent to a 95 mph straight fastball.

David Robertson and Joakim Soria are two guys who hit 90 mph regularly but have fastballs with electric movement.

And although he didn't pitch this year, Daniel Cabrera is the poster-boy for throwing an empty 95. He had good velocity, but that was all he had. Cabrera couldn't generate any movement, and saying he had 30 command would be generous.

Best and Worst Overall

Here are top 20 lists for the best and worst major league pitchers, based on a combination of their stuff and location scores:

Overall Best	Overall Worst
Matt Thornton	Dontrelle Willis
Josh Johnson	J.C. Romero
Andrew Bailey	Dan Meyer
Sean Marshall	Oliver Perez
Daniel Bard	Jeff Suppan
Justin Verlander	Kenekoa Teixeira
Heath Bell	Fu-Te Ni
Rafael Betancourt	David Riske
Mariano Rivera	Sean White
Grant Balfour	Jason Marquis
Joe Thatcher	John Maine
David Price	Will Ohman
Felix Hernandez	Francisco Rodriguez
Mat Latos	Billy Buckner
Joaquin Benoit	Scot Shields
Zack Greinke	Matt Palmer
Brian Wilson	Greg Smith
R.A. Dickey	Bob Howry
Bobby Parnell	Mike Ekstrom
Casey Janssen	Andrew Miller

Things Change

Over the course of an offseason, arms can improve or deteriorate. Many thought that Francisco Liriano's knock-out slider was lost after he underwent Tommy John surgery in 2006, but his slider returned to Brett Anderson levels of awesomeness this year.

Likewise, Tim Hudson, after recovering from injury, restored his fastball to 2007 levels. Hudson picked up the 1 mph that he had dropped over the 2008 and 2009 seasons, plus he added an inch of sink. His slider was also breaking across the plate by a couple more inches.

Other than recovering from injury, the easiest way to gain velocity is by going to the bullpen, where most pitchers add about 1 mph to their fastballs. Joba Chamberlain isn't like most pitchers. He lit the world aflame by throwing 97 mph as

a late-season call-up by the Yankees in 2007. The next year, having established himself as the team's setup man, he settled in at 95, still throwing a plus fastball. But he was moved to the rotation in 2009 where his velocity fell under 93, a precipitous decline. It bounced back to near-2008 levels when he made his return to the pen in 2010.

Finally, altering a pitch grip can do wonders. Roy Halladay changed his changeup from a straight change to a split-finger grip, and as a result, he added five extra inches of tumble. Batters are whiffing three times as often when they swing against Halladay's off-speed pitch as they did last year.

On the other hand, a couple of Dodgers who had 80 stuff a year ago fell to mere 75s this year. Although they still struck out more than a batter per inning, Jonathon Broxton and Clayton Kershaw saw their velocity diminish substantially. Kershaw gained fame through his curveball, which Vin Scully dubbed "public enemy No. 1," but Kershaw has wisely moved away from that pitch and gone to a dynamite slider. His slider is 10 percent faster than his curve, which means that it has less time in the air to move. Still, Kershaw's slider breaks more than his curve horizontally. His curve isn't a bad pitch, but his slider has crazy movement.

Fellow former phenom Tim Lincecum continued his downward descent in fastball velocity—he threw 94 mph when he came up but now throws 91.

Endurance

Pitchers can be compared from year to year, game to game, or better yet, within games. Who maintains their stuff throughout a game and who loses steam? Edwin Jackson and Jonathan Sanchez fastballs start out the game within a mile per hour of each other, but finish with a gap of 5 mph.

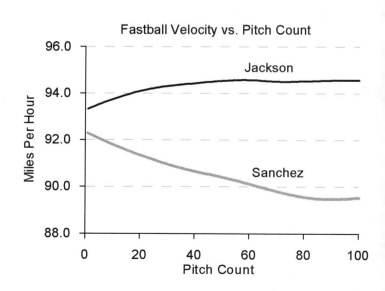

Justin Verlander and CC Sabathia can also push themselves to another level, whereas Zach Duke and James Shields have lesser stamina.

Rookies with the Stuff

Scouts are most useful in reporting on amateurs and minor leaguers, since there's no PITCHf/x data available at those levels. But with regard to rookies, PITCHf/x numbers stabilize quickly enough to draw some conclusions about them. We already know about Strasburg and Chapman, but there are other young rookies to discuss.

At the same time that Strasburg came up, Drew Storen burst upon the scene. Storen's slurve is the pitch most similar to Strasburg's curve, but he nonetheless prefers to throw a tighter slider. Jeremy Hellickson flashed great command, especially of his changeup. Jenrry Mejia's fastball grades out as an 80. It is not unlike Mariano Rivera's cutter, although the edge in velocity Mejia has on Rivera is insignificant compared to the difference in their command.

Also, PITCHf/x data was recorded at the Futures Game, providing an opportunity to grade the game's top prospects. Tanner Scheppers had the best stuff in that game, and he profiles as an A.J. Burnett 2.0 with an awesome fastball and curve.

What's to Come

2010: The Year of the Pitcher. We may never know what caused runs per game to fall from 5.14 in 2000 to 4.38 this year (though Steve Treder has some good observations in his article). But with another decade of PITCHf/x data, we'll be able to directly compare the stuff and command of pitchers from 2020 to the guys we so love watching today.

Postscript: What can Catchers' Gloves Tell?
by Nick Steiner

Measuring a pitcher's skill locating the ball is a dream of PITCHf/x analysts. The trouble is that we can't deduce a pitcher's intent from the data—we can only guess at it. As great as PITCHf/x data is, they do not tell us anything about the pitcher's intended location.

So, until the day Sportvision creates "MINDf/x," we're going to have to find alternate ways of guessing the pitcher's intent. Jeremy Greenhouse has taken a good stab in the "Scouting by Numbers" chapter, but I had another idea. We can see the position of the catcher's glove before the pitch is thrown, right? Aren't pitchers supposed to hit the catcher's glove as nearly as possible? Is it possible to measure this?

As far as I know, there are no such data available, so I decided to get it myself. I watched every pitch thrown in a Cardinals vs. Mets game on April 16 this year, choosing this particular game because it featured one great starting pitcher (Chris Carpenter) and one not-great one (Oliver Perez). Watching two such different pitchers gave me a diverse set of pitches to measure.

Also, as an unabashed Cardinals fanboy, I'm proud to say that the camera angle for St. Louis home games is perfectly dead-center, eliminating any parallax issues.

I experimented with different ways of measuring glove location. First, I entertained the idea of precisely measuring the exact location with a ruler or something, but I quickly found out this would be impractical due to the time constraints and the fact that the position of the camera often changed between innings. After watching several innings, I realized that there were really only a few distinct places where the catcher set up—five places across the horizontal, and four across the vertical.

Obviously, some of the pitches required a judgment call as to which "catcher glove bin" they fell into, but overall it was pretty easy to mark where the catcher was setting up.

There were 281 pitches thrown in the game, and I felt comfortable charting the catcher's glove in 271 of them. The pitches were thrown by eight different pitchers, each with a pretty distinct repertoire. Before we try to measure each of pitcher's command, let's look at how the two catchers, Yadier Molina and Rod Barajas, called the pitches. Below is the percentage of pitches out of the total that each catcher called in each bin (from the perspective of the pitcher):

Yadier Molina	Left	CenterL	Center	CenterR	Right
Letters	0.00	0.00	0.00	0.00	0.00
Waist	0.01	0.02	0.02	0.01	0.00
Knees	0.07	0.33	0.15	0.21	0.11
Below Knees	0.01	0.02	0.01	0.02	0.01

Rod Barajas	Left	CenterL	Center	CenterR	Right
Letters	0.00	0.00	0.01	0.01	0.00
Waist	0.00	0.01	0.01	0.09	0.02
Knees	0.01	0.20	0.13	0.25	0.04
Below Knees	0.01	0.08	0.04	0.07	0.00

At first glance there are some obvious differences between the two catchers. Molina stayed at the knees almost exclusively, and especially liked the first base side of the plate. Barajas was much more varied in his approach, calling a wide range of pitches up and down the strike zone. Molina also called for pitches out of the strike zone across the horizontal plane; Barajas often went below the zone.

Next I checked how the pitch type influenced the way the catcher set up, looking at the percentage of each pitch type thrown in each of the four vertical zones. Barajas' glove positioning seemed fairly typical of the average catcher. He called for off-speed pitches almost exclusively at or below the knees, and the four-seam fastballs higher in the zone than two-seam fastballs. Interestingly, the cutter was the pitch that he called for most often in the upper part of the zone, despite the fact that it often shares more attributes with a slider than a fastball.

Molina was downright weird in comparison. He called for 100 percent of the four-seam and two-seam fastballs at the knees, as well as 95 percent of the cutters. And while he frequently called for off-speed pitches below the knees, he did it at a far lower rate than Barajas.

Most interesting is the fact that he called for as many curveballs at the waist as he did below the knees. Curveballs are almost always best when thrown down in the zone, so perhaps Molina was going for the called strike, or he thought the movement of the curveball would take it out of the zone.

There is much more to be said about how the two catchers set up, especially regarding count, back-to-back pitches and batter tendencies. For now, however, I want to focus on pitcher command. First I want to share a startling statistic: Out of the 270 some-odd pitches thrown in the game, only 10 percent hit the catcher's glove. Of the total, 27 percent were one "box" away from the glove, 36 percent were two boxes away, 17 percent were three boxes away, and 10 percent were more than four boxes away. In other words, pitchers missed wildly as often as they hit their spot. Here are the breakdowns for each pitcher, including the number of pitches and the percentage that were hit:

Pitcher	Pitches	Hit	One	Two	Three	> Four
Chris Carpenter	105	11%	21%	37%	25%	6%
Oliver Perez	92	8%	29%	37%	11%	15%

Pitcher	Pitches	Hit	One	Two	Three	> Four
Blake Hawksworth	20	5%	30%	40%	20%	5%
Jenrry Mejia	18	17%	44%	17%	11%	11%
Raul Valdez	14	0%	7%	43%	36%	14%
Fernando Nieve	11	9%	55%	36%	0%	0%
Ryan Franklin	10	20%	30%	40%	10%	0%
Dennys Reyes	5	20%	20%	20%	0%	40%

To clarify on what each of the columns means in this context, remember that I split the strike zone into 20 boxes to mark where the catcher's glove was. PITCHf/x measures the location in a continuous fashion, but I simplified the locations in the same way. So "one" means that the pitch landed either one box vertically or horizontally away from the glove. "Two" means that the pitch landed either two boxes vertically, or two boxes horizontally, or one box vertically and one box horizontally away from the glove, and so on.

Some pitchers hit their spots better than others. Mejia was probably the best with Nieve and Franklin right up there with him. Valdez was absolutely awful, which might partially be the reason he gave up a grand slam to Felipe Lopez, although on that pitch, Valdez actually hit his spot pretty well—Barajas called for a slider right down the middle for some reason. Perez was surprisingly not terrible, at least in comparison to Carpenter.

The most accurate pitch, in any significant sample, was Carpenter's change-up, with a whopping 23.5 percent of them hitting the catcher's glove, and more than 40 percent within one box. Carpenter's cutter was the second best of the bunch, and his curveball was also very good. His sinker hurt him most: On those, he hit the glove only 5.8 percent of the time. Mejia's fastball/cutter was also very good, hitting the glove 20 percent of the time (with Mariano Rivera-like movement and 95-plus mph velocity to boot). The pitches thrown with the least command were Hawksworth's changeup, not hitting the glove a single time in 12 attempts, and Perez's fastball.

Of course all of this is simply representative of the game that I watched. Even if a pitcher's command is completely in his control, pitchers are humans and will have off days and on days. However, I think that systematically measuring catcher glove positioning has the potential to reveal a lot about how catchers call games and how well pitchers hit their spots. This is a topic that deserves a more detailed look. We here at The Hardball Times will be offering one in the near future.

Do Catchers Have an ERA?

by Sean Smith

"Hell of a situation we got here. Two on, two out, your team down a run and you've got the chance to be the hero on national television... if you don't blow it. Saw your wife last night. Great little dancer. That guy she was with? I'm sure he's a close personal friend, but tell me, what was he doing with her panties on his head?"

(Batter pops up)

—Jake Taylor, *Major League*

How much can a catcher help his pitcher's performance through game-calling, receiving and framing pitches? The conventional sabermetric wisdom, at least since Keith Woolner published "Field General or Backstop" for *Baseball Prospectus* in 1999, has been that catchers have no effect on pitcher performance, or at least so little that it is impossible to measure.

There are many who hold the opposite opinion, such as Craig Wright (whose article in this book two years ago highlighted Mike Piazza's impact on pitcher ERA, which we'll call "catcher ERA"). Japanese baseball teams, according to Wright, also believe that catcher ERA is an important statistic.

Baseball managers obviously believe that catcher's game calling is important. Consider Mike Scioscia, who plays Jeff Mathis and his woeful bat almost as often as he plays Mike Napoli—he of the .840 lifetime OPS. Unless you believe catchers have an impact on ERA, there is no reason to play Mathis as often as Scioscia does. I'll return to that combination in a few minutes.

For the past 10 years or so I have subscribed to Woolner's conclusions, but I can no longer do so. I believe his sample sizes were too small, and I think I've found a way to get around that and measure the unmeasurable. Before I get into the details, here are summaries of prior research on catcher game-calling skill:

In *The Diamond Appraised*, Wright introduced the Catcher ERA (CERA). Craig looked at matched innings, so if Mathis caught Ervin Santana for 150 innings, and Napoli caught him for 35, the Mathis innings would be pro-rated to 35. This was done for every pitcher on the staff, always using the lesser of the innings caught. He summed the pitcher/catcher pairs, and showed how many runs each catcher saved in comparison to other catchers on the staff. The chapter is well worth reading, since Craig (employed by the Texas Rangers at the time, with access to the players

themselves) investigates what the catchers were doing that helped or hurt their pitchers.

Framing a pitch is one thing catchers do. With enough skill, they can catch a pitch a few inches off the strike zone in such a way to make the umpires think it's a strike. This is not easy, because if you are obvious about it the umpire might even give you fewer breaks. The key is to catch it so naturally that the umpire doesn't think you're trying to sell a strike, he simply thinks it is a strike. The less catchers have to move for a pitch, the more likely it will be called a strike—if the catcher doesn't have to move then the pitch was going where it was supposed to.

On low pitches, catchers try to catch the pitch without turning the glove down. According to Wright, holding the glove closer to the body can help a catcher—the umpire is less able to see the glove, but if the catcher can receive the ball without much movement a strike call is likely. A bad habit is to drop the glove—give a sign, move the glove down, and bring it back up to catch the ball. This has two bad effects—the pitcher loses his target and the umpire sees too much movement.

The question that Craig does not answer is how much of the observed difference between one catcher and another is skill and how much is just luck. If Santana pitches an eight-inning shutout one start, and the next time out gives up seven runs in four innings, how much of that can we really attribute to the catcher? If there were no difference at all between catchers, pitchers would still have good and bad starts. Statistical methods can help us estimate how much we can trust the observed data.

An issue with catcher ERA is that it is a total contribution statistic. Yadier Molina can help his CERA in many ways: (1) Calling for the right pitch to the right hitter; (2) Receiving a borderline 3-2 pitch in such a way that it looks like a strike to the umpire, getting his pitcher out of the inning instead of loading the bases for Joey Votto; or (3) Throwing out base stealers, picking them off and blocking bad pitches in the dirt.

This last aspect of catcher defense is easy to measure. In fact, we have a good handle on who the best catchers are in blocking balls and controlling the running game. What we want to find out is how much the catcher, with his interaction with the pitcher, can influence the outcome of the pitcher/batter matchup.

To do this, Woolner looked not at catcher ERA, but at batter OPS with and without the catcher, for each pitcher.

He computed Z-scores, or standard deviations, to see if the observed differences in catcher/pitcher OPS were different from what one would expect by chance. He found the data looks almost identical to a bell curve; in other words, the differences observed among catchers appeared to be random.

My Method

Instead of looking at batter OPS, I am going to focus on statistics that a pitcher can control. Strikeouts, walks and home runs are the standbys of Defense Independent Pitching (DIPS), and I'm adding pop flies and line drives to the mix, as classified by MLBAM scorers and available in the Retrosheet event files. From these statistics I create an estimate for runs allowed that may differ from actual runs allowed, but is less dependent on the support of the rest of the defense. To estimate pitcher runs:

First, find out how many at-bats do not result in a strikeout, home run, line drive or pop-up. Call this AB1.

Second, plug in the following formula for runs:

AB1 *.05 + HR * 1.4 + LD *.38 + BB * .33 + HBP * .345 - SO * .105 - Pop * .096

Now, use matched innings to see how each pitcher did with and without each catcher, and pro-rate the "with" and "without" stats to the lower of the plate appearance totals.

Going back to our example, say Santana pitches 200 innings and allows 80 runs, and Jeff Mathis is his catcher for 150 of those innings, allowing 51 runs. Without Mathis, Santana therefore allows 29 runs in 50 innings. Prorate to the lesser of innings (actually in the real model I use plate appearances instead of innings, but never mind that). What we wind up with is 50 prorated innings with, and 17 runs allowed, and 50 without, and 29 runs, so Mathis saved Santana 12 runs.

Do this for every pitcher for whom the catcher is behind the plate, and total the runs saved. Do this for a multi-year period, splitting the results into even years (2004, 2006, 2008) and odd years (2003, 2005, 2007, 2009). If we are looking at a skill, then catchers who are good in even years should be good in odd years. Using multiple years grouped together in this way increases our sample size, and allows us to observe a correlation that was just too hard to detect when looking only at single consecutive years.

The Results

Looking at catchers who had at least 2,000 matched plate appearances in both odd and even years, I have 70 catchers, and find a correlation of 0.21. This group has an average of 4,343 plate appearance in each year category, which implies that you would have a correlation of 0.50 (where half of the observed difference is skill and half is luck) when you have

16,300 matched plate appearances, about three years of full-time catching.

So, to estimate the game-calling skill of a catcher, add 16,300 of average performance to his matched innings. This is what I've done in the results below. A catcher will see about 5,000 plate appearances in a typical season of 130 games caught, so I'll display the results per 5,000 plate appearances.

The best game-calling catchers, from 2003 to 2009:

Catcher	PA	Regressed Runs/5000 PA
Pratt, Todd	5,588	14.3
Snyder, Chris	9,375	13.2
Burke, Jamie	4,078	13.0
Castro, Ramon	8,829	13.0
Molina, Jose	13,241	12.9
Saltalamacchia, Jarrod	6,009	12.9
Lopez, Javier	6,525	12.8
Paulino, Ronny	6,695	12.1
Laker, Tim	3,158	10.9
Mirabelli, Doug	4,431	9.4

And these catchers were the worst:

Catcher	PA	Regressed Runs/5000 PA
Navarro, Dioner	10,509	-9.3
Montero, Miguel	5,074	-10.5
Schneider, Brian	13,773	-11.5
Wilson, Vance	7,199	-11.7
Greene, Todd	5,516	-12.4
Johjima, Kenji	7,177	-12.4
Hall, Toby	9,652	-14.0
Lieberthal, Mike	7,107	-14.8
Posada, Jorge	11,961	-14.8
Martinez, Victor	11,294	-15.0

Here's a list of other notable catchers:

Catcher	PA	Regressed Runs/5000 PA
Piazza, Mike	7,956	7.4
Rodriguez, Ivan	14,859	7.1
Kendall, Jason	10,226	4.8
Ausmus, Brad	7,788	4.3
Mathis, Jeff	6,921	4.1
Pierzynski, A.J.	11,154	2.4
Mauer, Joe	11,063	-0.9

Catcher	PA	Regressed Runs/5000 PA
Molina, Yadier	10,360	-1.3
Varitek, Jason	9,102	-2.1
McCann, Brian	8,061	-3.1
Napoli, Mike	9,030	-5.9
Molina, Bengie	13,633	-7.6

Napoli or Mathis?

Let's talk again about Mike Napoli and Jeff Mathis. When Bengie Molina left the Angels after the 2005 season, Mathis was handed the starting catcher job. After 12 games and batting only .103, Mathis was sent back to the minors and replaced by Napoli. Napoli homered off Justin Verlander in his first major league at bat, starting a two-month offensive tear. He finished the year in a slump, hitting .228 overall and striking out in a third of his at bats, but Napoli showed he could provide offensive value with his patience and power.

Since then, Napoli has played only a little more than half the time behind home plate, with Mathis reclaiming part of the job despite a .200/.277/.320 career batting line through 2009, and even worse numbers in 2010. It's not just a matter of injuries and keeping a catcher fresh throughout the season. Mathis even starts playoff games—six out of 16 from 2007 to 2009, though I can't complain about his 7-for-12, five-double showing against the Yankees last fall.

For their careers, Mathis is 30 batting runs below average per 500 plate appearances, and Napoli is 13 runs above average. On the easily measurable aspects of catcher defense (stolen bases and blocking wild pitches), Mathis is two runs below average per 1,200 innings caught, and Napoli is eight runs below average. They have virtually identical records against the stolen base, but Mathis does a better job at preventing wild pitches, and also picks off more runners from the bases than anyone not named Yadier Molina.

Add up offense and defense, and Napoli is 37 runs better than Mathis per 130 games caught. That is a lot of runs Mathis would have to save through game calling to justify playing ahead of Napoli. Looking at the regressed runs per season, Mathis is 10 runs better than Napoli. If you look at the unregressed total and give Mathis every benefit of the doubt (which is as wise as assuming that a rookie you've never seen before who comes up and hits .330 for two months is in fact a true .330 hitter, the next Wade Boggs) you'd have Mathis at +13.9 and Napoli at -16.6. That's 30 runs there, and comes close to making up the difference in batting/fielding runs, but still falls a bit short.

That does represent a little double counting though, since Mathis and Napoli represent so much of each other's with-out—the numbers say Mathis has been 13.9 runs better than the other catchers on the Angels staff, in other words 13.9 runs better than Napoli. There is almost no way you can make a reasonable case for Mathis to continue getting the playing time he has received. It is understandable that, given below-average defense (probably 15 runs below average all told), you want a better defensive catcher than Napoli, but Mathis costs you too many runs with the bat to justify his superior defense. He'd have to be the best defensive catcher on the planet to overcome his bat. Overall (counting game calling, blocking and throwing), Mathis is merely a slightly above average defender.

2010 Data

There were six situations in 2010 in which a team split their catching duties between a catcher who has ranked well in this metric and one who has rated poorly. In the case of the Red Sox catchers, Varitek does not rate well, but is substantially ahead of Martinez. I'll throw this in just to see how the ratings hold up outside of the years I used to test it.

I picked six pairs of catchers based on how they rated in this metric, before looking at any of their 2010 stats. Of the six pairs, in five cases the one pre-identified as the superior catcher had a lower catcher ERA than his teammate. I'll wait until after the season to do a full comparison controlling for matched pitchers and using defense independent stats, but this is an indication that the patterns identified persist in 2010.

Team	Good C	CERA	Bad C	CERA
Angels	Mathis	4.04	Napoli	5.07
Blue Jays	J. Molina	3.16	Buck	4.42
Yankees	Cervelli	3.72	Posada	4.05
Red Sox	Varitek	4.01	Martinez	4.29
Reds	Hanigan	3.27	Hernandez	4.70
Diamondbacks	Snyder	5.39	Montero	4.53

Rookie Catchers: Are They at a Disadvantage?

Next, I looked at catcher/pitcher matchups for the catcher's debut year, and compared the results to how that catcher/pitcher pair did in later years. There were 416 catcher/pitcher pairs, with more than 30,000 matched plate appearances, from 2003 to 2009. In their debut years, the catchers allowed 4.54 runs per game. In later years, they allowed 4.53, so there is apparently no disadvantage to having a rookie receiver. This conflicts with what was found by Tom Hanrahan and published in SABR's *By the Numbers* in November 2004, though that appears to be a result of different approaches to the study.

I tried another approach and found something that supports his study: I grouped the catchers by age, splitting them into approximate thirds. The first group was born before 1974, and were a run better than average per season. The catchers born between 1974 and 1979 were about average, and the catchers born after 1979 were 2.2 runs below average per 5,000 plate appearances. Game calling does appear to be a learned skill; catchers get better with experience.

Tom's study was different than mine. He looked at pitchers who threw at least 100 innings during a catcher's first season, and how those same pitchers did if they threw 100 innings in later years with that catcher as the starting catcher. From what I can tell, he looked at the pitcher's season ERA, not the ERA with that specific catcher. His sample included 26 catchers and 90 pitcher/catcher pairs.

Hanrahan found that pitchers performed better when that catcher was a veteran than when he was a rookie. His study is interesting, and if I don't get around to it myself I'd like to see it repeated with two changes: First, look at all rookie catchers, not a small sample (the 26 were from 1946 to 2003) and second, look at how these pitchers did while specifically pitching to that catcher.

Other Approaches

Dan Turkenkopf in April 2008 used the PITCHf/x data to see how often a pitch in a certain location was called a strike and how many extra strikes a catcher added. The effect was large, and he did find a strong correlation between performance in the first and second halves of the season. The study used data from the 2007 season.

Bill Letson added similar research in 2010. He used the PITCHf/x pitch location, batter height and handedness, and identity of the umpire to build a model that predicts the likelihood that a pitch will be a strike. Then he compared the catcher's actual record of strikes to the predicted total. As with Turkenkopf, he found a large effect, though he left open the possibility that some of that is related to the pitcher.

Studies like these are better for isolating one part of the catcher's contribution: framing pitches and gaining strike calls through receiving abilities. They don't tell the whole story though. Is the catcher calling for the right pitch in the right situation? Is he exploiting the hitter's weaknesses? Utilizing the pitcher's strengths? A results-based study like the one I have presented here will give a general sense of how well a catcher does for all of this, but can't break it down into details to tell you what a catcher does well or poorly.

Warnings

I think this study shows that there are repeatable differences in how pitching staffs perform with different catchers. There is a skill involved in either proper catching technique or game calling that impacts the scoreboard.

However this is not something that we can put a number on with the same reliability as, say, a hitter's batting contribution. This is merely a rough estimate; we should look for additional information before making judgments.

In an ideal world for an analyst, every catcher in the league would get to work with every pitcher in the league for a few thousand innings. From that it would be very easy to determine which catchers were the best. In reality, we are not comparing a catcher to a league average, but to only the other catchers on his team.

If one catcher has a few veteran defensive specialists as his backups, and another is backed up by sluggers who just happen to wear the mask, the first catcher is going to look worse than the second even if they are in fact equal. A dose of common sense is required to interpret a catcher's defensive record.

Another issue is that for whatever reason, a catcher who is good overall might not be the best catcher to work with a specific pitcher. The matched-inning samples for specific pitcher/catcher matchups aren't big enough to reliably pick this up—that's why Woolner wasn't able to detect a skill. A manager would have to use his discretion to make that call.

Conclusion

Catchers have a significant impact on the performance of the pitchers they catch. We need several years of data to have a reliable measure of this effect. In the future, studies like mine will probably be obsolete as the data available from PITCHf/x is more precise. Whatever the data source used, it is important that we recognize the value that outstanding game-calling catchers can provide, and to understand the spread of talent among catcher skill so decisions can be balanced between a catcher's defensive and offensive ability.

References:

Keith Woolner, "Field General or Backstop" (http://www.baseballprospectus.com/article.php?articleid=432)

Craig Wright, *The Diamond Appraised*

Tom Hanrahan, "Catcher ERA - Once More With Feeling" (http://www.philbirnbaum.com/btn2004-11.pdf)

Dan Turkenkopf: (http://www.beyondtheboxscore.com/2008/4/5/389840/framing-the-debate)

Bill Letson: (http://www.beyondtheboxscore.com/2010/3/26/1360581/a-first-pass-at-a-catcher-framing)

Retrosheet.org

Baseball-reference.com

That Was a Strike?

by John Walsh

You're watching a game on TV and after a close call on a pitch you are shown the replay along with the pitch-tracking graphic, which shows the actual location of the pitch with the strike zone overlaid. Often this K-Zone graphic, which is produced using actual data gathered by high-speed cameras for the pitch in question, clearly shows that the ump missed the call. Maybe a called strike was clearly outside, sometimes way outside. Or often a supposed ball is obviously shown to be within the strike zone. This happens a lot. Or does it? How often does the umpire miss the call? A few times a game, maybe three or four pitches?

Well, with the pitch tracking data known as PITCHf/x available to researchers (and normal people), we can answer these kinds of questions. The frequency of missed calls and other studies of the called strike zone have been researched quite a bit already. Do some Googling or refer to the resources listed at the end of this article. It's well known that the strike zone as called by major league umpires, on average, does not correspond precisely to the strike zone as defined in the rules of Major League Baseball. The called strike zone is a little wider and not as tall as the rulebook zone. It's also oval in shape, not rectangular, which is not too surprising if you think about it.

Strike Zone Versus Ball-Strike Count

One avenue of research that has not been fully explored is whether the strike zone as called by the umpires is influenced by external factors such as the ball-strike count or whether the home or visiting team is batting. I have previously looked into how the ball-strike count influences the umpires and I have found a very large effect. At the top of the next column is a picture of the strike zone as actually called by umpires when the count is three balls, zero strikes and when the count is zero balls, two strikes.

I told you it was a big effect: the strike zone is around 50 percent larger when the count is 3-0, compared to when the count is 0-2. This graphic appeared in the Hardball Times article, "The Compassionate Umpire." The idea is that the umpires felt sorry for the pitcher when the count stood at 3-0 and enlarged the strike zone to give him a break, with a corresponding shrinkage of the zone in favor of the batter when he was down 0-2. The title was supposed to be tongue-in-cheek: I don't truly believe that umpires are consciously siding with the underdog; my guess is that they do it unconsciously.

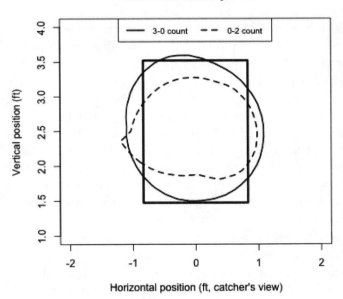

Strike zone comparison

Given that the ball-strike count can have such a large effect on the effective strike zone, you might wonder if other factors could have important effects as well. Pitch type would be one example; whether the home or visiting team is batting could be another. In the case of pitch type, you might imagine a particular pitch type to be inherently more difficult to call correctly—there's something about the pitch itself which causes the difficulty. In this case, the umpire might err more often, but you wouldn't necessarily expect a resulting change in the size of the strike zone. In other words, he would probably miscall balls and strikes with the same frequency.

On the other hand, whether the home or visiting team is batting is a little different. Here it's not any particular pitch that causes the problem, but a situation which may affect the psychology of the umpire causing him to subtly alter his calls. In this case, you might indeed expect the strike zone to change size—for example, the umpire might unconsciously give the home team a slight advantage by shrinking the strike zone while they are at bat.

Pitch Types and Speeds

With these preliminaries out of the way, let's get back to our original concern: the large difference in strike zone size depending on the count. After my article appeared several very smart people pointed out that perhaps I was really seeing different umpire performance on different pitch types (fastball, curveball, etc.) as well as on the ball-strike count. The reasoning goes like this: most 3-0 pitches are fastballs, while most 0-2 pitches are off-speed pitches. Maybe there is something about fastballs that lead to a larger strike zone than off-speed pitches do. I stated two paragraphs ago that while we might expect some pitch types to be more difficult to call correctly, we wouldn't necessarily expect the size of the strike zone to change as a result. But let's see what we can find in the data.

I gathered two years' worth (2008-2009) of PITCHf/x data, corresponding to roughly 1.5 million pitches. For all pitches that were called by the umpire (about half of the total), I determined if the pitch went through the rulebook strike zone. For each of these pitches, PITCHf/x contains loads of extra information: the names of pitcher and batter, the type of pitch, the pitch speed, the inning and so forth. That allows me to select a particular sample of pitches—for example, all pitches thrown on a 3-0 count.

If I have a large enough sample (maybe a few thousand pitches) I can determine the edges of the strike zone, as illustrated in the graphic on the next page. That edge is defined as the locations where a pitch has an equal chance of being called a ball or a strike. And given the edges, I can calculate the strike zone area. But the area is not the only way to investigate how umpires might be influenced when calling balls and strikes. I can also look at how often the umpire gets it wrong—that is, how often a true strike (as measured by PITCHf/x) is called a ball and how often a true ball is called a strike.

Okay, let's look at some results for the different pitch types. First, I select all pitches on a 0-0 count that are classified as a fastball (cutters not included), slider, change-up or curveball. I restrict myself to 0-0 pitches because I already know that the size of the strike zone will depend strongly on the count. So I confine myself to a single count; 0-0 happens to give the largest sample. (For the rest of this article, I require a 0-0 count for all pitches selected.)

Type	Pitches	Area	Strikes Wrong (%)	Balls Wrong (%)
All	147k	3.142	19.8%	12.9%
FB	91k	3.152	20.2%	14.2%
SL	24k	3.142	17.8%	10.8%
CH	12k	3.099	23.2%	10.0%
CU	15k	3.143	18.8%	10.1%

The first thing I noticed is that the size of the strike zone (reported as "Area" in square feet) depends very little on the type of pitch. It's a little smaller for change-ups (by about 1.5

percent), but that's nothing compared to the differences we saw for different ball-strike counts. To be explicit: the variation we saw at different counts isn't explained by the different mix of pitch types thrown on the different counts; it's not even close.

Another interesting thing is that umpires get (true) strikes wrong about 20 percent of the time, while they miss on true balls only about half as often. ("Strikes Wrong" is defined as the percentage of time that a true strike, one that passes through the rulebook strike zone, is called a ball, with an analogous definition for "Balls Wrong.") I think there are two reasons for this; first, many true balls are so far away from the strike zone that they cannot be possibly called strikes, while all true strikes, by virtue of passing through the relatively small area of the strike zone, are necessarily not too far from being a ball. Put another way, all true strikes are less than one foot from the edge of the zone, but many balls are more than a foot away. The second reason can be seen in the graphic at the top of the next page; umpires systematically do not call the lowest and highest parts of the strike zone. Pitches to those areas are generally called balls.

There are smaller areas (inside and outside) where the opposite holds: true balls are generally called strikes. The net effect is a slightly smaller strike zone and more missed calls on true strikes.

In any case, based on the numbers above it looks like umps will miss the strike call on change-ups somewhat more often than on other pitch types—maybe the batter is not the only one getting fooled.

So the different pitch types are all equally easy (or difficult) to call, with perhaps the change-up causing a few problems, but nothing major. What about the speed of a pitch? You might think that harder pitches are more difficult to get right. Here are the results for fastballs broken down by speed:

Speed	Pitches	Area	Strikes Wrong (%)	Balls Wrong (%)
> 95	6.5k	2.990	23.3%	12.1%
90 - 95	48.0k	3.131	20.6%	13.6%
87 - 90	26.0k	3.231	19.3%	14.9%
< 87	10.0k	3.337	18.4%	16.5%

Well, that's interesting: the harder a pitch is thrown, the more likely it is to be called a ball. This is the case both for true strikes (23.3 percent wrong) and true balls (only 12.1 percent missed). Note that the speed does not cause the ump to miss equally on pitches inside or outside the strike zone. On the fastest pitches the umps do worse than average on true strikes. But they actually call the blazing fastballs correct more often if they're outside the true strike zone. Curious!

Called strike percentage

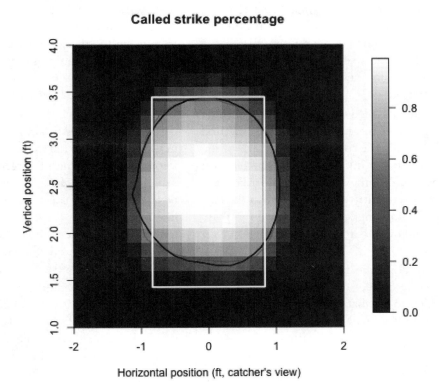

Horizontal position (ft, catcher's view)

Note that the trend holds perfectly as we move down the table to slower and slower pitches: the area of the strike zone increases, fewer strikes are missed and more balls are called incorrectly. The difference in strike zone size for the fastest and slowest pitches is fairly large, about 12 percent.

Pitch type and speed are inherent properties of the pitch, and while they may tell us something about the difficulty of calling balls and strikes, I think that investigating possible psychological factors is more interesting, or at least more fun. We have already seen the "compassion" umpires exhibit when the count leans heavily towards the batter or pitcher. Are there other situations causing the umpires to, consciously or not, shrink or enlarge the strike zone?

Rooting for the Home Team

How about home versus visiting team? In baseball, the home team wins around 54 percent of the time. Over the years, various hypotheses have been put forth to explain the home-field advantage. Among them: the strategic benefit of batting last, the psychological advantage of having the crowd on your side, greater familiarity of your own ballpark, the home team being specially tailored to play in a certain park, the benefit of "home cooking" and sleeping in your own bed and, last but not least, unconscious umpire bias towards the home team. Many studies have been done to try to nail down the origins of the home-field advantage; one of my favorites is still Craig Wright's seminal study on the subject, which

appeared in *The Diamond Appraised* in 1989. Craig addresses all of these possibilities, and though he cannot precisely quantify the various effects, he does get some handle on what's important and what isn't.

In any case, I don't believe I've ever seen a study that uses PITCHf/x data to see if, on average, ball-strike calling is biased towards the home team. So I divided my pitch sample (still only 0-0 pitches) into "visiting team batting" and "home team batting" sub-samples, and I restricted myself to the eighth inning or earlier (more on this in a minute). Here are the results:

Batting Team	Pitches	Area	Strikes Wrong (%)	Balls Wrong (%)	Extra balls (per game)
Visitors	66k	3.202	19.6%	13.4%	2.7
Home	67k	3.121	20.0%	12.3%	3.5

We can see here a very slight advantage for the home team, for which the strike zone is about 2.5 percent smaller than for the visiting team. Umpires have a slight tendency to turn more strikes into balls and fewer balls into strikes for the home team. I've added an extra column in this table: the number of extra balls per game (135 pitches) called by the umpire, compared to the rulebook strike zone.

The slightly smaller strike zone for the home team results in about one (0.8 to be precise) extra ball per game in favor of the home team, relative to the visiting team. That's nothing, right? Well, it doesn't sound like much, but let's have a closer look.

Imagine this scenario: two perfectly matched teams are playing on neutral turf (i.e. there is no home-field advantage), except that in each game the home plate umpire misses one call per game—he calls a true strike a ball. And he always gives this small advantage to the same team. How often would that team win the game?

To figure that out, you first need to know the relative value of a ball and a strike. What I mean is this: consider the first pitch of an at-bat. If it's a ball, the count moves in favor of the hitter, and he'll generally fare a little better than he does on average. On the other hand, if the first pitch is a strike, he'll do slightly worse. You can quantify the difference in the two results (ball or strike) by looking at how batters do in plate appearances when the count gets to 1-0 versus how they do when the count gets to 0-1.

I've actually already done the legwork on this (see the resources section if you're curious about the method) and it turns out that the value to the batter of miscalling a strike is 0.17 runs, averaging over all ball-strike counts. So in our hypothetical scenario, the home team is scoring 0.17 runs per game more than the visiting team. We can now apply the Pythagorean rule to convert runs scored and allowed into a winning percentage. If I assume a typical value of runs scored of 4.5, I get a home winning percentage of .519. Actually, though, I found the umpire bias to be 0.8 balls per game (not one, as I've been using in this example), or 0.14 runs, for a winning percentage of .515.

So, yeah, umpire bias in favor of the home team is pretty small, but it accounts for a little more than a third of the home-field advantage, which is not so small.

Let's Keep this Game Moving

Do you think umpires might call the strike zone differently depending on the inning? You might suppose that umps try to hurry things along a little more towards the end of games. One way to hurry things along is to enlarge the strike zone: fewer walks, more outs, quicker game. Maybe we'll see the strike zone growing gradually larger as the game progresses. In extra innings, though, you might see the opposite—after all, if you want to break a tie, you give the batter an advantage, right? Let's turn again to the PITCHf/x measurements.

Inning	Pitches	Area	Strikes Wrong (%)	Balls Wrong (%)	Extra balls (per game)
1-3	51k	3.172	19.2%	13.6%	3.1
4-6	49k	3.141	20.3%	12.4%	3.0
7-9	44k	3.140	20.2%	12.6%	3.1
>9	3k	3.253	21.4%	12.0%	3.7

Move along, folks, there's nothing to see here. I think the small differences that we see in this table are attributable to noise in the data. The area differs by less than 1 percent for the different inning samples, except for the extra-inning sample, which has low numbers. So, the umpires do not change their strike zone as the game progresses. Good for them.

There is another situation where you might wonder if the umpires are motivated to call a quick game: getaway day. You know, the last game of a series, where one or both teams usually pack up right after the game and head on to their next destination. You could imagine that everybody would like to get that last game over with quickly, if possible. Do the umpires enlarge their strike zones on getaway days, in the (subconscious, naturally) attempt to speed things up and get everyone on their way? Well, we can check that too.

I don't have scheduling information in a handy electronic form, but we can make reasonable guesses as to which games are the last game of a series. Firstly, Sunday games are essentially always getaway games. There is the odd four-game series that ends on a Monday, but they are very rare. That means that Mondays are not getaway days nearly 100 percent of the time; this is also true for Tuesdays, Fridays and Saturdays. That leaves Wednesdays and Thursdays, which tend to be a mixture. If a three-game series starts on Monday, Wednesday is the getaway day. But a good number are four-game series, in which case Thursday becomes the getaway day. After a few manual checks, I estimate that around half of Wednesday games and 70 percent of Thursday games are getaway games.

So let's make two groups: Mondays, Tuesdays, Fridays and Saturdays are days when there are no getaway games. Sundays, Wednesdays and Thursdays are days when a large majority of games are getaway games; I estimate about 75 percent. If there is an effect of strike zone shenanigans on getaway days, we should see it dividing the games up like this. But guess what? The umps call it straight on getaway days:

Day	NP	Area	Strikes Wrong (%)	Balls Wrong (%)	Extra balls (per game)
Sun,Wed,Thu	63k	3.138	20.3%	12.9%	3.3
Mon,Tue,Fri,Sat	84k	3.139	19.5%	12.8%	2.9

Remember, the top line is for the getaway days, when we might expect a slightly larger strike zone and, hence, fewer extra balls per game. Well, the strike zone area for the two sub-samples is virtually identical and the extra balls per game are quite close also. If you assume the 0.4 difference in extra balls is a real effect (I'm not sure that it is), it actually goes in the wrong direction, with the umps calling more balls on getaway days. I think this is probably an effect of noise, and the umps are not hurrying towards their post-game quaffs, at least not as regards calling the strike zone.

Summing Up

This has been an interesting exercise and I have certainly learned a few things (hopefully, you have too). The most important one is this: the umpires are really amazingly good. I found no umpire bias due to the inning of the game or to whether the game fell on getaway day or not. We have also seen that although the umpires do favor the home team in calling balls and strikes, it's a fairly small effect, contributing on average around 0.14 runs per game to the home team. I'd bet that referee bias in other sports is larger than we found here for balls and strikes.

I also found the umpires were remarkably consistent with different pitch types, which is pretty impressive considering the wide variety of pitches used in any given game. I did find that umps do vary their calls somewhat depending on the speed of fastballs, with faster pitches more likely to be called balls. I believe this is a real effect, although I don't have an explanation for it. That's probably a good place for further study.

Finally, the large difference in strike zone size in 3-0 counts and 0-2 counts remains, even after accounting for the different pitch types employed in the different counts. As I have said, I don't believe the umpires are consciously thinking, "Okay, it's 3-0, I'm going to expand my strike zone by 50 percent." I do think there is a psychological effect that is leading to the vast difference between the 3-0 and 0-2 strike zones. Maybe we need to get some research psychologists to have a look at this.

Related Resources

Studies on umpires' calls of the strike zone with PITCHf/x:

Walsh, J. "The Eye of the Umpire," (www.hardballtimes.com/main/article/the-eye-of-the-umpire/)

Hale, J. "A Zone of Their Own," (www.hardballtimes.com/main/article/a-zone-of-their-own/)

Allen, D. "Does the Umpire Know the Count?," (baseballanalysts.com/archives/2009/04/the_effect_of_t.php)

Walsh, J. "The Compassionate Umpire," (www.hardballtimes.com/main/article/the-compassionate-umpire/)

The run value of balls and strikes:

Walsh, J. "Searching for the game's best pitch," (www.hardballtimes.com/main/article/searching-for-the-games-best-pitch/)

Classic sabermetrics:

Wright, C. and House, T. (1989) *The Diamond Appraised*, Simon and Schuster.

The Curious Case of Barry Zito

by Max Marchi

When the Giants signed free agent Barry Zito to a seven-year, $126 million contract in December 2006—the highest figure for a pitcher in major league history at the time—four seasons had passed since he had won the Cy Young Award on the other side of the Bay.

After his stellar season in 2002, Zito had not been able to get close to the 2.75 ERA that brought him the hardware; on the contrary, every stat showed his decline. In four seasons his strikeout rate had diminished by one strikeout per nine innings (K/9) and his walks per nine innings (BB/9) had increased by one; as a consequence, his FIP, or Fielding Independent Pitching, had risen by a full run.

The budget-conscious Oakland A's had managed to stay on the positive side in the balance between Zito's value and the salary they were paying him. According to FanGraphs data, his production on the field was worth around $10 million each year from 2002 to 2005, when Zito was making, respectively, $300,000, $1 million, $3 million and $5.6 million. As the last season in his contract was coming to an end, they tried to trade him, but eventually he played out his contract in Oakland (this time his estimated value on the field, $7.9 million, exactly matched his salary).

Then he hit the free agent market and the San Francisco Giants went deep into their pockets, fascinated by his 16 wins and inattentive to his increasing walk and home run rates and decreasing strikeout rate. His 4.48 ERA in 2004 looked like an anomaly when compared to the 3.30 mark he posted in 2003 and the 3.86 and 3.83 marks of 2005 and 2006 respectively; but when you try to factor out luck and defense (looking at FIP), Zito's final season in Oakland was actually his worst and 2004 seemed the only one mirroring his real value.

The Fall of the Giant

In his first season as a Giant, while another Barry was pursuing history with his powerful lumber, Zito actually slightly improved both his strikeout-to-walk ratio and his FIP (his home runs allowed per nine remained the same). Unfortunately for him, for the second time in his career both his ERA and won-loss record mirrored his FIP—not exactly what the Giants thought they were paying for.

Then disaster came.

In 2008, though Zito's strikeout rate did not change from the previous year and he significantly dropped his home runs allowed rate, his walks per nine innings jumped from 3.8 to 5.1. He allowed a .305 Batting Average on Balls In Play (BABIP), a number in contrast with his habit of staying on the lucky side of BABIP year in and year out.

The result in the traditional stat line was 10 wins, a league-leading 17 losses and a dreadful 5.15 ERA.

The Rebound

After the disastrous 2008 campaign, it looked like Father Time had gained ground faster than expected on Zito; the former Big-Three ace seemed nearly done, and the word albatross was mentioned more and more often when his contract came up in conversation.

So 2009 came as a surprise to many.

Zito's Stats

Season	Team	W	L	IP	K/9	BB/9	HR/9	BABIP	ERA	FIP	Value*	Salary
2000	A's	7	4	92.2	7.6	4.4	0.58	.240	2.72	3.81		
2001	A's	17	8	214.1	8.6	3.4	0.76	.294	3.49	3.53		
2002	A's	23	5	229.1	7.1	3.1	0.94	.254	2.75	3.87	$11.5	$0.3
2003	A's	14	12	231.2	5.7	3.4	0.74	.248	3.30	4.05	$11.9	$1.0
2004	A's	11	11	213.0	6.9	3.4	1.18	.300	4.48	4.50	$9.8	$3.0
2005	A's	14	13	228.1	6.7	3.5	1.02	.252	3.86	4.34	$10.2	$5.6
2006	A's	16	10	221.0	6.2	4.0	1.10	.280	3.83	4.89	$7.9	$7.9
2007	Giants	11	13	196.2	6.0	3.8	1.10	.272	4.53	4.82	$6.9	$10.0
2008	Giants	10	17	180.0	6.0	5.1	0.80	.305	5.15	4.72	$6.4	$14.5
2009	Giants	10	13	192.0	7.2	3.8	0.98	.290	4.03	4.31	$10.0	$18.5
2010	Giants	9	14	199.1	6.8	3.8	0.90	.285	4.15	4.25	$8.6	$18.5

* Value equals WAR converted to a dollar scale based on what a player would make in free agency. Source: Fangraphs and Cot's Baseball Contracts

Control issues disappeared (he returned to the same 3.80 BB/9 of 2007) and suddenly Zito remembered how to strike people out—he actually posted a higher rate (7.22 K/9) than the one recorded by Cy Young Zito (7.14)!

The 10-13 record was still worse than what you expect from somebody making $18.5 million for the year, but his performance on the mound was similar (actually way better) to the one that convinced the Giants to give him big money.

Zito started 2010 on a roll, winning all his decisions in April, ending the month with a 4-0 record and a seven-inning no-decision in which he surrendered just four hits and one run. In one of his outings he even collected 10 strikeouts, and his final 1.53 ERA for the month, together with the perfect record, was already prompting Cy Young nominations from the mainstream media (apparently oblivious to the fact that a .208 BABIP is unsustainable for a whole season).

At the All-Star break Zito was 7-4, with a respectable 3.76 ERA coming from a BABIP of .287, a figure a tick higher than his career mark.

Following the midsummer classic, Zito threw an eight-inning, two-hit, 10-strikeout gem of a game in which the Giants scored just once—enough to get the win. After the July 16 masterpiece he got two losses (2-0 and 4-3 the final scores) and three wins (2-1, 3-2 and 5-4). Then, starting with an Aug. 17 game in Philadelphia, everything went wrong for number 75: in a series of seven consecutive losses (without even a no-decision!), he was crushed for nine earned runs in 3.2 innings one day, lost 1-0 while surrendering just one hit in 5.2 frames another day, and even relieved in a 12-inning affair against Cincinnati and conceded the winning run.

Despite the second half freefall (2-10, 4.70 ERA after the All-Star Game) Zito managed to post decent peripherals, not those expected from a top of the rotation ace, but better than the ones he produced in his final year in Oakland.

Looking for Changes (Lost and Found)

Probably we would not be far off the truth saying Zito's career curve is nothing exceptional. If we are not distracted by his deceiving won-loss records, we can see a drop in performance that is not very different from how other major league pitchers age. The dreadful 2008 could be labeled as an outlier and this article would end here.

But the rebound of the last couple of years, however small you might consider it, is enough to spur an analyst to investigate.

First, let's try to see what caused the drop (without which no rebound would have been possible).

Unfortunately PITCHf/x has been available for every MLB game only since 2008, so we have little information on how Zito used to throw the ball before getting worse.

Looking at BIS data from FanGraphs, we can point to what everybody was pointing to when Zito hit the skids—his velocity drop. All of a sudden the boy from Las Vegas lost more than a couple of miles per hour from his fastball; trouble is, since 2004 he has been throwing a two-seamer to complement his four-seamer, thus the drop might simply be due to differences in mixing those two pitches (BIS video scouts do not separate sinkers from regular fastballs).

Anyway Zito lost velocity on all his offerings, so the hypothesis that he was running out of gas is still plausible. Also it's not uncommon for pitchers to lose velocity as years pass by; in Zito's case the drop was somewhat abrupt, but it can be accepted as something not extraordinary.

What made people scratch their heads is what followed: In 2009, at age 31, Zito recovered a good dose of speed in his fastball, something unusual for pitchers not coming back from Tommy John surgery.

Zito's pitch speeds (source FanGraphs)

Season	Team	Fastball	Slider	Curve	Change-up
2002	A's	87.1		72.7	76.5
2003	A's	86.9		71.4	75.4
2004	A's	86.9		71.2	74.0
2005	A's	87.3	81.0	72.1	75.0
2006	A's	85.8	78.6	71.2	75.0
2007	Giants	84.5	77.8	70.4	73.0
2008	Giants	84.9	77.7	70.9	74.1
2009	Giants	86.5	79.7	73.1	73.6
2010	Giants	85.7	78.4	72.4	75.1

Let's dig deeper in the aging curve of fastball speed.

Josh Kalk in 2008 and Jeremy Greenhouse in 2009 wrote their preliminary findings on how pitchers' aging affects their velocity. Both used a couple of years of PITCHf/x data to track how fastball speeds changed as pitchers age. While Kalk reported an increase in speed from age 24 to 28, then a sharp decline, Greenhouse found velocity to remain constant in the first period, then the same decay detected by Kalk.

I replicated their work using fastball speeds from BIS—those you find on FanGraphs. By doing so I traded some consistency (since BIS only records speeds from TV telecasts) for a bigger sample of data (since they started collecting the information in 2002).

The results of the analysis I'm showing here are a couple of graphs.

The first graph shows the year-to-year variation in fast-ball speed. Values are reported for the median variation, for the first and third quartiles, and for the fifth and 95th percentile.

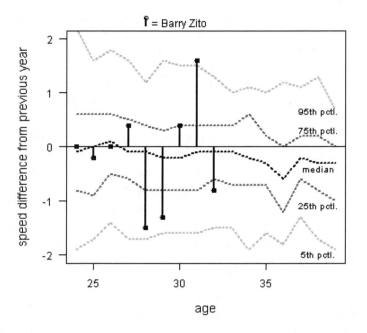

Barry Zito's career is superposed. At the ages of 28 and 29, he experienced two consecutive drops, both close to the fifth percentile line. Then, at age 31, Zito experienced an off-the-charts increase in velocity: As the graph shows, his improvement is over the 95th percentile line, meaning less than five percent of pitchers went through a higher gain between age 30 and 31.

Here's a graph showing the data in a different way:

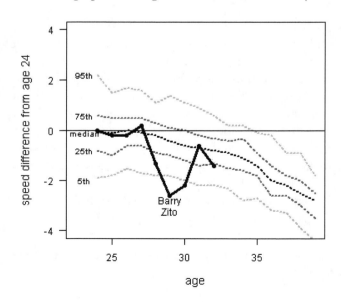

This graph shows the cumulative speed variation since age 24. Here it shows how Zito's career is anomalous between age 28 and 30, and how his recent resurgence brought him back on track with the average major league pitcher. Looking at this second graph, one wonders whether Zito had some minor physical problems during that period.

Did the Repertoire Remain the Same?

The Barry Zito who won the Cy Young Award in 2002 had a repertoire consisting of a fastball, a big looping curve thrown with an over-the-top motion and a good change-up. In 2005 he added a two-seamer and another pitch classified as a slider by BIS video scouts; Sven Jenkins, of the web site 60ft. 6in., considered it a "tighter breaking ball that he uses like a slider to [left handers]."

The Barry Zito who was considered done in 2008 had five arrows in his quiver and PITCHf/x data give us information about their movement.

Zito's pitch characteristics (PITCHf/x data, classification by the author).

Pitch Type	Season	Speed (mph)	Horizontal Movement	Vertical Movement
Four-seamer	2008	85.0	3.1	11.3
	2009	86.6	4.5	11.0
	2010	85.8	3.8	11.0
Two-seamer	2008	84.6	7.9	9.0
	2009	86.4	7.9	8.6
	2010	85.5	7.5	8.9
Change	2008	73.7	7.8	4.6
	2009	73.2	6.8	4.6
	2010	75.0	7.1	4.1
Curveball	2008	70.6	-1.6	-11.0
	2009	73.0	-4.5	-10.6
	2010	72.3	-4.4	-10.4
Slurve	2008	77.5	-2.8	0.6
	2009	79.7	-3.5	3.2
	2010	78.2	-3.8	1.7

I labeled the aforementioned fifth pitch as a slurve, both because of the Jenkins/BIS disagreement and because a pitch classification algorithm I am working on (you have surely read about it on our site) tags it that way.

In the 2008-2009 transition from rags (back) to (nearly) riches we can note a few things.

- The aforementioned comeback speed: Every pitch (except for the change-up) gained more than 1.5 mph (though some of that was lost again in 2010).
- A gain in lateral movement for the four-seamer.

- The transformation of the fifth pitch, which deserves some more discussion.

I decided to be conservative and classify the fifth pitch with the same name from 2008 to 2010, though my automatic classification algorithm tagged it as a slurve in the first year, then as a sharp slider.

As you can see looking at the pitch characteristics table, the slurve underwent a significant transformation a couple of seasons ago: Other than the increase in speed (a common trait with every Zito's weapon in that period) the pitch gained some lateral break and a good dose of carry.

The pitch selection tables show how Zito has gone to the slurve more frequently starting in 2009 both against right-handed batters and against lefties. He has especially increased the use of the pitch on hitter counts, as he has become less afraid to sneak one when behind 1-0 or 2-0.

Zito's Pitch Selection

	vs RHB			vs LHB		
Pitch Type	2008	2009	2010	2008	2009	2010
Two-seamer	32%	35%	30%	28%	28%	15%
Four-seamer	20%	14%	20%	29%	21%	36%
Curveball	15%	18%	20%	15%	17%	17%
Slurve	7%	15%	10%	24%	33%	31%
Change-up	26%	19%	20%	4%	1%	2%

Regarding the location of the pitch, the only distinction from 2008 to 2009 is that Zito threw it more frequently away from lefthanded batters, but the difference mitigated significantly in 2010.

Hoping that scoring biases do not play a big role here, we can note how, against righties, the slurve started to induce more ground balls beginning in 2009, taking away a share of line drives—it's always a healthy thing when you can trade screamers for worm killers.

Did he Alter Anything in his Delivery?

For the pre-PITCHf/x era we have to go with anecdotal evidence regarding Zito's pitching mechanics.

The day after Barry Zito reported to the Giants training camp for the first time, an article appeared on MLB.com website, and the news quickly made the rounds on the Internet: The recently acquired star was experimenting with a new delivery, which involved a big step back at the beginning of the windup and a longer stride at release point. According to the article, the pitcher was looking for an increase in velocity with the new style.

Unfortunately the radar gun continued to show figures lower than 85 mph on his fastball, as it had in 2006.

Instead, Zito picked up speed a couple of years later, and we can use two seasons of PITCHf/x data to look for changes in his delivery. Specifically, we can look at Zito's specific release point on every pitch.

The release point chart clearly shows a lowered arm angle starting in 2009 (2009 and 2010 data points nearly coincide on the chart, thus only those from the first year are visibly separate).

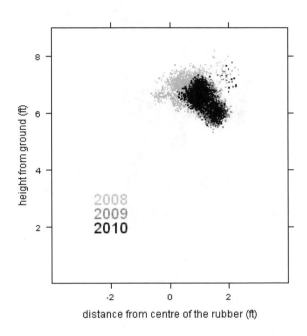

However caution is necessary when using PITCHf/x data to evaluate pitchers' arm slots; thus I performed a pair of further analyses to make sure that what the chart is showing is not an artifact of PITCHf/x camera calibration issues.

First, having the luxury of the Giants employing the same four starters (Zito, Tim Lincecum, Matt Cain and Jonathan Sanchez) for the period we are dealing with, I charted the release point for all of them. Nobody, other than Zito, showed a significant difference between 2009/10 and 2008; it seems unlikely that PITCHf/x cameras were differently set every fifth day when Zito was on the mound, both at AT&T Park and on the road.

Second, I went hunting for pictures around the web.

I found a couple of shots, one taken in 2008, the other in 2009, from virtually the same angle, both squarely facing home plate; also, the grips indicate that Zito was delivering the same type of pitch, and the elbow angle that he was at about the same point through the motion.

I'm not a wizard of graphic editing, but I did my best to extract a silhouette from both pictures and overlap them as you can see in the picture.

2009
2008

Where I live they say "three clues are evidence." Thus, I'm pretty confident that Zito did lower his release point in 2009.

The Effects of the Metamorphosis

Okay, so what came out of that change in the delivery? Let's start with the tight curve/slider/slurve. PITCHf/x gives us enough information to reconstruct the flight of the ball from the rubber to home plate.

From an aerial view (the first image below; pitcher's mound is on the right), we can see how the 2008 slurve had a much flatter trajectory than the one thrown in the subsequent two seasons. On the contrary, from a lateral angle (the second image), we see that the new delivery takes away some drop from the pitch.

The trade-off brings up an interesting story. After the mutation, the called-strikes-to-balls ratio (CS/B) of the slurve increased significantly (from 0.39 to 0.59 and 0.54 against right-handed batters and from 0.49 to 0.64 and 0.51 against left-handed batters). First explanation I thought of was that Zito started throwing the pitch in the zone more often, but that was not the case. The percentage of slurves in the zone (as defined by the rule book) remained the same during the three-year period. Another explanation could be that opposing hitters began chasing Zito's slurves out of the zone, but again it turned out that wasn't the case.

Obviously there was a third option which did not occur to me immediately: The official strike zone differs from the zone called by umpires. With the 2008 dropping version of the slurve, Zito tried to expand the zone vertically, hoping to get more calls on the lower border; unfortunately, several studies conducted since PITCHf/x data have been available have shown that umpires do not call the low strike. On the

The Bird's Eye View of Zito's Slurve

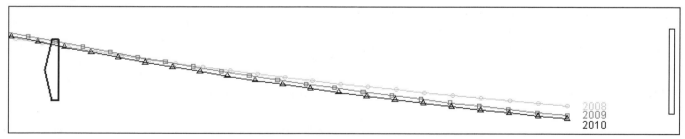

2008
2009
2010

The Lateral View of Zito's Slurve

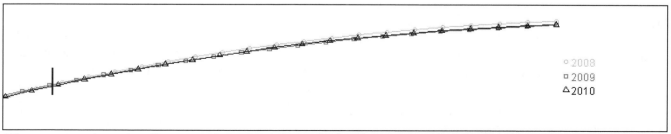

○ 2008
□ 2009
△ 2010

(Note: axes are intentionally not on the same scale, so the breaks are magnified; big thanks to Harry Pavlidis for the spreadsheet.)

other hand home plate umps concede more to pitchers on the horizontal plane, especially away from left-handed batters. The new version of Zito's slurve, as we said before, moves more on the horizontal axis, sacrificing some drop, thus exploiting the umpires' tendencies.

So, while in 2008 just five percent of the slurves thrown out of the theoretical strike zone were called strikes and 16 percent of slurves that crossed the rulebook zone were called balls, in 2009 the umps' mistakes favored Zito, with umps calling slurves outside the zone strikes 19 percent of the time versus calling slurves in the zone balls 10 percent of the time; in 2010, 10 percent of his slurves outside the zone were declared strikes and 11 percent of slurves in the zone did not satisfy the men in blues' tastes.

In his heyday, Zito's trademark pitch was the curve. The rainbow started from his high release point, dropping in the strike zone; it was what scouts, baseball writers and fans love to call a 12-6 curve. Describing his money pitch to *Sports Illustrated* as the reigning AL Cy Young winner during the 2003 spring training, Zito talked about sequencing: "If I can throw a curve that starts at (the batter's) eyes and drops in for a strike, the hitter processes that as a strike. Then I can throw a high fastball, and he thinks that's a strike too."

It's interesting to note how the success of the curveball, as reported by FanGraphs Pitch Type Values table, is strongly related to his fastball speed (apparently more than the success of the fastball itself); though I must admit I would have expected such correlation if Zito were using an opposite sequence than the one he described.

Here's a graph of the two values:

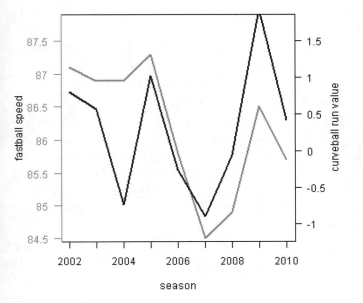

And here you can see how Zito's fastball speed affected the value of the fastball itself.

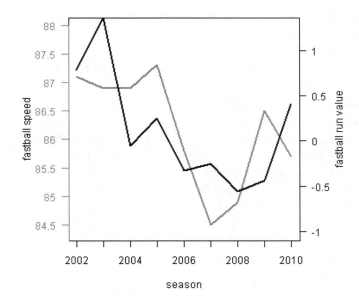

The 2008-2009 release point metamorphosis involved all of Zito's pitches, thus the curve is now more of the 11-5 variety. While there seems to be something romantic about the 12-6 version, Derek Carty, analyzing 2007 and 2008 PITCHf/x data for every major league pitcher, showed it is a good weapon only against same-handed batters, while it's a terrible pitch when the hitter has the platoon advantage. Given that Zito is a lefty, he is better served with a pitch he can throw to righties as well.

As was the case with the slurve, the looping curve has lost some of its drop, while gaining in lateral break. Starting from 2009, right-handed batters have been fed more often with the pitch inside, while lefties have seen a higher number of curves away. The effect has been an increase in swings, especially on balls out of the zone.

While all the talking was about the yakker, the young Zito got the best results with his change-up: From 2002 to 2007 it was the pitch with the highest run value in his repertoire, according to FanGraphs Pitch Type Values (table on the next page). The version he throws is the circle-change, sometimes holding the ball back in his palm; as for most southpaw hurlers, he uses it only against righty batters.

Of all the tools in Zito's bag, the change-up looks like the one ending on the losing side since the drop of the release point occurred. Contrary to the other offerings, it did not gain velocity, while surrendering a decent amount of tail away from batters. Zito seems to be conscious of the diminished quality of the pitch, because he has reduced its usage in the last couple of seasons, particularly on 0-1 and 1-2 counts.

This leaves us with the fastballs.

When facing lefties, Zito aims the four-seamer constantly on the outside part of the plate, while he tries to paint both corners with the two-seamer. Against righties the two-seamer is delivered prevalently away, while he goes either way with the four-seamer.

While a clear-cut difference between 2008 and 2009/10 can't be spotted for fastball behavior as it can for other pitches, it seems Zito is continuously making location adjustments. In 2008, he was trying to paint both corners with his four-seamer against righties, but he was leaving too many of them right down Broadway. In 2009 he concentrated mostly on the inside corner and in 2010 returned to pitch also to the outside part of the plate, having more success in staying away from the fat part of the dish. With the two-seamer he progressively accentuated the pounding of the outer border against right-handed batters.

According to FanGraphs' combined run value, his 2010 approach with the fastball was the most successful of the last three years.

Run value (per 100 pitches) by pitch type (source FanGraphs)

Year	Team	Fastball	Slider	Curveball	Change-up
2002	A's	0.79		0.80	2.44
2003	A's	1.36	1.04	0.56	1.62
2004	A's	-0.05		-0.74	1.28
2005	A's	0.25	1.87	1.02	1.54
2006	A's	-0.33	0.11	-0.26	1.96
2007	Giants	-0.25	-0.95	-0.90	2.53
2008	Giants	-0.56	0.81	-0.06	-0.21
2009	Giants	-0.44	2.50	1.93	-1.35
2010	Giants	0.32	0.47	0.48	0.01

What's Ahead?

After having dissected Barry Zito's career, especially the part covered by PITCHf/x, what should we expect from him?

If you are a subscriber of our Oliver projections, you can see what Brian Cartwright's forecasting system projects for every major and minor league player for the next six seasons. Zito is expected to steadily decline, becoming a replacement level player by 2014, when he is 36 and not a Giant anymore (unless the club decides to exercise its option for the year).

I feel you can divine the rest of his career by looking back at the velocity aging chart: He has aged as an average pitcher for all his career except for the two years when he inexplicably lost a lot of velocity; like Oliver, I expect him to decline as his velocity does. Does this win the Boldest Prediction Award for the year?

Reference, Resources and Acknowledgments

While writing this article I went back and forth to the *2009 Hardball Times Annual*, where, in "The Cliff Lee Turnaround," Mike Fast analyzed Cliff Lee's transition from barely fifth starter to Cy Young winner with the lenses of PITCHf/x.

Also by Mike Fast, "The Internet cried a little when you wrote that on it," appeared on our website (http://www.hardballtimes.com/main/article/the-internet-cried-a-little-when-you-wrote-that-on-it/) in June, was constantly on my mind as I tried to avoid many of the pitfalls he outlined (I'm not sure I always succeeded).

Finally, Mike helped me find pictures of Barry Zito's pitch grips around the web.

"On curveballs," by Derek Carty (http://www.hardballtimes.com/main/article/working-title-on-location-and-effectiveness-of-the-curveball/), analyzes the traits making an effective curveball, among them the delivery angle.

Josh Kalk first tackled the velocity aging issue in "Preliminary aging curve for fastball speed" (http://www.hardballtimes.com/main/article/preliminary-aging-curve-for-fastball-speed/), then Jeremy Greenhouse returned on the subject with the article "A quick take on velocity" (http://baseballanalysts.com/archives/2009/10/velocity_trends.php).

Rich Draper first reported on Zito's new delivery at MLB.com in 2007 (http://mlb.mlb.com/news/article.jsp?ymd=20070215&content_id=1803330&vkey=news_mlb&fext=.jsp&c_id=mlb).

One year later Paul Nyman (http://www.hardballtimes.com/main/article/crossing-the-bridge-a-closer-look-at-what-happened-to-barry-zitos-fastball/) dissected Barry's mechanics by looking at videoclips of him pitching.

Finally, every time I write about a pitcher (and his repertoire) I make sure to read his entry on the *Neyer/James Guide to Pitchers* (where I found the quote about his curveball-fastball sequencing), on Sven Jenkins' 60ft. 6in. website (http://www.60ft6in.com/), on FanGraphs (http://www.fangraphs.com/) and on Baseball Reference (http://www.baseball-reference.com/).

Big thanks to Sportvision and MLBAM for making PITCHf/x data publicly available.

Three Things I Wanted to Research

by Tom M. Tango

Have you heard of the Great Baseball DIPS Theory? The most extreme theorists of DIPS (Defense-Independent Pitching Stats) claim that pitchers tend to have consistent game impacts on strikeouts, walks and home runs—those things that don't involve the defense—but that pitchers have very little consistent impact on "balls in play" (batted balls that stay within the field of play).

The less extreme DIPS theorists claim that pitchers do have some impact on balls in play, but that you can't truly identify them based on one year, or even several years, of experience. One season contains too much randomness.

But I wonder—can we identify how pitchers might impact batted balls in specific games? Is there an angle we can pursue that helps us nail down this elusive aspect of the game?

1. The Secret to a Low Average on Balls in Play

Consider a couple of extreme outings …

On June 6, 2009, Jon Lester went through the Texas Rangers lineup twice, and was perfect. Not just run-of-the-mill perfect, but 10 strikeouts out of 18 outs perfect. The eight times he didn't strike out the opposition, five batters were put out by the outfielders, and three by the infielders.

On Aug. 22, 2000, Pat Mahomes had one of the worst performances imaginable by a starting pitcher. Of the first 18 batters he faced, he allowed three home runs, walked four batters, allowed four additional hits and struck out no one.

One would assume that a pitching line like Lester's would mean the pitcher was *on*, and nobody could touch him. And Mahomes' line would mean that just about anyone could get a hit off him.

Great and Poor Control games

Let's find out if this is true, starting off with some simple rules: We'll give a pitcher one point for every strikeout and subtract one point for every non-intentional walk and hit batter. We are going to look only at the first 18 batters a pitcher faced in a game. In the above games, Lester would be +10 and Mahomes would be a -4. Since 1993, there have been 623 games with pitchers having a score of at least +8. Let's call these Great Control games. There have been 693 games with pitcher scores of -4 or worse. These are the Poor Control games.

Now, this is not to say that every game of great control is captured in the Great Control group, nor that every Great Control game is in fact a game of "great control." But when you compare the groups of games, a much higher proportion of the true great control games will rest in the Great Control category. This is the reason we group games; to bias the results toward the kind of games we are interested in.

In the Great Control games, of the 18 batters faced, pitchers averaged 8.9 strikeouts and 0.3 walks. In the Poor Control games, also facing 18 batters, pitchers averaged 0.6 strikeouts and 4.9 walks. Again, you might think that it would be a lot easier to get a hit off pitchers with Poor Control than Great Control.

Typically, to figure the batting average on balls in play, we take the number of singles, doubles and triples, add them up, and divide by the number of balls in play. (Home runs are excluded. I'll get back to that shortly.) However, I am going to follow a more balanced approach, a weighted score that measures the relative impact of each hit. A single does not get a value of 1, but 0.9. And each double and triple won't get a value of 1, but 1.3. In this way, we achieve a better balance between the impact of all hits. (For justification, please Google wOBA.)

For the Great Control pitchers, their wOBA on balls in play was .293, which is not much better than the overall average of .299. How do you think the Poor Control pitchers fared? Would you believe .274? That's right, these pitchers, who couldn't strike anybody out, who were always pitching behind into hitter's counts, posted a better wOBA when hitters made contact.

Great and Poor Pitching Games

Let's try to get a sharper focus on Great and Poor Pitching games. In addition to the above score, we'll subtract four points for every home run allowed. In this way, we also capture how hard pitchers were being hit.

I've identified 1,078 Great Pitching games (score of +7 or better) and 1,095 Poor Pitching games (score of -10 or worse). In the Great Pitching games, pitchers averaged 8.1 strikeouts, 0.5 walks, and no home runs, over the first 18 batters. For the other 9.4 balls in play, the wOBA was .298, virtually equal to the overall league average of 0.299.

And for the Poor Pitching games, those that featured 1.5 strikeouts, 2.2 walks, and 2.7 home runs? Once again: .273. Adding home runs to the filter made no difference.

Let's try one more way. Pedro Martinez is a great pitcher, perhaps the greatest pitcher of all time. Surely, someone of his magnitude should betray some difference in batted ball impacts, no? Pedro has had only two (!) Poor Pitching games, so I had to go to the next level of Somewhat Poor Pitching games (score of -2 or worse).

Combining the two groups (for a total of 57 games), he has an average on balls in play of .287. In Martinez' 52 Great Pitching games, his average on balls in play was … .315. Same result.

How about Greg Maddux? With only two Poor Pitching games, we include his 88 Somewhat Poor Pitching games, where we see that he had a .309 average on balls in play. And in his nine Great Pitching games? .319.

We can do this all day if you'd like. How about this: Sixteen pitchers had at least four Poor Pitching games (average of 2.9 home runs, 2.2 walks, and 2.0 strikeouts) and at least four Great Pitching games (average of zero home runs, 0.3 walks, and 8.1 strikeouts). The simple average of their wOBA on balls in play was .282 in the Poor Pitching games and .296 in the Great Pitching games.

DIPS works?

So, what is going on? Well, it's possible that the bad pitchers are so bad that their pitches are doing one of two things: hanging in the middle of the plate and being crushed for home runs, or outside of the plate and resulting in a walk or a weak out if the batter swings. Basically, once you remove strikeouts, walks and home runs, you are left with a bunch of pitches that are, at best, indistinguishable between Great Pitchers and Poor Pitchers.

This may be the reason that DIPS theory works, in that great pitchers and poor pitchers have similar averages on batted balls that remain in the park. Is it so hard to believe that once you remove all the great pitches (those that lead to strikeouts) and bad pitches (those that lead to walks and home runs), that of the remaining pitches, the resulting outcomes of pitches thrown by major league pitchers are all basically similar, regardless of who throws them?

Breakdown by Strikeout, Walk, Home Run

Let's try to see if we can find some evidence for this in the data. Instead of splitting the data by some combination of strikeouts, walks and home runs, let's focus solely on the number of strikeouts. What kind of relationship is there between strikeouts and the other events?

In the 4,127 games in which there were no strikeouts to the first 18 batters, there were 1.69 walks. In the 308 games in which there were nine strikeouts, there was an average of 1.1 walks to the remaining nine batters, or an average of 2.27 walks per 18 non-strikeouts. Here's the

breakdown for walks, home runs, and average on balls in play:

K's	Walks per 18 Non-K	HR per 18 Non-K	wOBA on BIP
0	1.69	0.54	.299
1	1.74	0.55	.299
2	1.80	0.56	.301
3	1.86	0.57	.301
4	1.88	0.58	.297
5	1.95	0.56	.300
6	1.99	0.56	.297
7	2.03	0.61	.298
8	2.10	0.61	.300
9	2.27	0.62	.294

The more strikeouts a pitcher gets, the more walks and home runs he allows. Basically, a power pitcher does everything big. However, the one thing that is unaffected is the average on balls in play, which remains virtually constant around .300 regardless of the number of strikeouts.

Let's repeat this exercise, but let's focus on the number of walks per game:

BB's	Strikeouts per 18 Non-BB	HR per 18 Non-BB	wOBA on BIP
0	3.30	0.50	.297
1	3.29	0.51	.302
2	3.34	0.52	.302
3	3.41	0.52	.298
4	3.49	0.52	.289
5	3.61	0.48	.275
6	3.53	0.55	.272

Walks behave a bit differently. Pitchers who walk more batters also show a rise in strikeouts (but not as sharp as in the strikeout chart with respect to walks). And there is a slight rise to home runs as well. However, the average on balls in play drops with the four, fifth and sixth walk! This lends some support to the theory that pitchers who miss the plate a lot are probably not leaving other pitches over the plate—so when a batter makes contact, he's not making contact with a good pitch.

And what about home runs?

Home Runs	Strikeouts per 18 Non-HR	BB per 18 Non-HR	wOBA on BIP
0	3.14	1.56	.303
1	3.12	1.57	.295
2	3.11	1.60	.286
3	3.06	1.60	.278
4	3.02	1.44	.253

Ah! There is a very slight negative relationship between home runs and strikeouts, and almost no relationship to walks. However, the average on balls in play plummets substantially with every additional home run allowed. This lends support to the notion that a pitch that is crushed for a home run is one less good pitch for a batter to get a non-home run hit. That is, if this home run-centric pitch was just a half-inch off, it had a good chance to have been an extra base hit, and would have increased the pitcher's wOBA on balls in play.

Conclusion

What the last two charts show is that if you have a lot of walks or a lot of home runs, then of the remaining contacted pitches, there's nothing much left a batter can damage.

Indeed, if we focus on the 285 games with at least four walks and at least two home runs, we see the wOBA on BIP is just .267, while for all other games it's .300! Further limiting it to five walks and two home runs gives us 66 games with an average on BIP of just .238. So, the best way to lower your average on BIP is to pitch so poorly that all the damage is in the form of walks and home runs.

2. Yankees Without Mariano Rivera

Mariano Rivera pitched in 917 games through 2009. In his first two years, he was still establishing himself and his eventual role. Once John Wetteland left, Rivera was the undisputed ace of the Yankees bullpen. Let's break down his 837 games as ace reliever, and see how the rest of the Yankees bullpen has fared in comparison during that time.

Ninth Inning, Ahead or Behind

As we have shown in the past in *The Book*, a three-run lead heading into the ninth inning is a very safe lead. While an ace reliever will protect that lead 98 percent of the time, an average reliever will protect that lead 96 percent of the time. Basically, it's tough to add value when everyone else is finding success in the same situation.

So let's see what happened with Rivera and his backups.

Rivera was brought into a game to protect a three-run lead 124 times (116 times with no outs, four times with one out, and another four times with two outs). The Yankees won

122 of those games. The rest of the Yankees bullpen, when given a three-run lead, was even better. They protected that lead every single time. When a saberist says that just about anyone can save a three-run lead, well, this is what we are talking about.

Let's start keeping a running total:

Subtotal (three-run lead): Rivera, minus two wins.

In the ninth inning with a two-run lead, Rivera entered the game 141 times, and the Yankees won 139 of those games. Seems pretty impressive. The rest of the Yankees bullpen, however, never lost a game with a two-run lead!

Subtotal (two-run lead): Rivera, minus two wins.

How about a one-run lead? The Yankees won 122 of the 138 times Rivera entered such a game. If we focus on those in which there were no men on base and no outs when Rivera entered, he went 120 for 135. The rest of the Yankees bullpen faced only 19 one-run situations in the past 13 seasons, and the Yanks came away with the win 15 times. Prorating up to 135, that comes out to 108 wins. Big edge to Mariano.

Subtotal (one-run lead): Rivera, plus 12 wins.

With a four, or more, run lead in the ninth inning, Rivera was 130 for 131, a match for the rest of the bullpen.

Subtotal (four-plus runs lead): Rivera, no wins.

Rivera also came into a game with the Yankees trailing in the ninth 34 times, and the team eventually won five of those games, which is a bit better than the four that the rest of the bullpen delivered.

Subtotal (behind): Rivera, plus one win.

Ninth Inning, Tied Game

Now let's look at tied ballgames. The Yankees won 43 of the 76 tied games that Rivera entered. Of those, 61 games were in the top of the ninth at home, with the Yankees still having a chance to bat. They won 37 of those games. The rest of the Yankees bullpen won 16 of 30 similar games, which prorates to 32 wins, making Rivera plus five wins in this category.

Rivera came in to start the bottom of the ninth in tied games only eight times and the team won five of those. The rest of the Yankees bullpen won 35 percent of its games, which prorates to three wins, making Rivera plus two wins.

Rivera came in another seven times in tied games in the ninth inning under various other base/out configurations. The team won only one game. Prorating the rest of the Yankees bullpen onto Rivera's opportunities, and they won four times, making Rivera minus three wins.

Subtotal (tied): Rivera, plus four wins.

Overall, in the ninth inning, Rivera was 13 wins better than the rest of the Yankees bullpen.

Other Innings

What about the other innings? Repeating the exercise, and controlling for the various base/out/score configurations, here's how Rivera compares to his bullpen in total:

Extra Innings: Rivera minus one win

Ninth Inning: Rivera plus 13 wins

Eighth Inning: Rivera plus seven wins

Seventh Inning: Rivera minus one win

Total: Rivera plus 18 wins.

Here's a summary graph of all situations and Rivera's performance vs. the other Yankee relievers.

Inning	Score	G	W	W%	Wins vs other Yanks relievers
7th	Trailing	2	0	.000	0
7th	Tied	1	0	.000	-1
7th	Up By 1	0	0	.000	0
7th	Up By 2	0	0	.000	0
7th	Up By 3	0	0	.000	0
7th	Up By 4+	2	2	1.000	0
8th	Trailing	5	0	.000	0
8th	Tied	4	4	1.000	2
8th	Up By 1	56	50	.893	6
8th	Up By 2	39	35	.897	0
8th	Up By 3	29	28	.966	0
8th	Up By 4+	18	18	1.000	1
9th	Trailing	34	5	.147	1
9th	Tied	76	43	.566	4
9th	Up By 1	138	122	.884	12
9th	Up By 2	141	139	.986	-2
9th	Up By 3	124	122	.984	-2
9th	Up By 4+	131	130	.992	0
10th+	Trailing	0	0	.000	0
10th+	Tied	23	11	.478	-1
10th+	Up By 1	9	8	.889	0
10th+	Up By 2	1	1	1.000	0
10th+	Up By 3	4	4	1.000	0
10th+	Up By 4+	0	0	.000	0

Summary

Mariano Rivera has been 18 wins better than the rest of his bullpen over his career. That's fewer than two wins per year. I know it's a shockingly low figure, but that's what the method shows.

A measure such as Win Probability Added (WPA) gives Rivera an impact of plus 44 wins above the average pitcher from 1997-2009. However, WPA compares a player against the league average, and you can be sure that the Yankees bullpen would have been better than a typical major league bullpen, even without Rivera.

Also, the Yankees certainly would use a better pitcher in a close game than your typical major league reliever. This raises the bar against which Rivera is compared, turning the +44 wins that WPA gives him to +18 wins in the more detailed method offered here.

By the way, we are ignoring the fact that Rivera has been possibly the best pitcher ever in postseason history. That certainly counts for a great deal.

If the Yankees can keep finding arms, they should be able to weather Rivera's loss at an impact of under two wins a season. Two wins is plenty, something that teams pay an extra $10 million for. And, that's pretty much what's going to happen as the Yankees might go from a $15 million dollar ace to the typical $5 million next-best reliever.

Just as it was not the end of the world when the Twins lost Joe Nathan—a team that is currently (as I write this in late August) sixth in the majors in WPA for relievers, about 1.2 wins less than the Yankees bullpen—so too might the Yankees be able to absorb most of the loss of Mariano Rivera.

3. Does a Bad Season at an Old Age Mean More than at a Young Age?

Derek Jeter, at the age of 36, is having likely the worst season of his career. Just one year earlier, he had one of his best seasons. Each year, we can find many players having bad years following great years. If this happens to players in their 20s, we think "well, he can bounce back, maybe." If it happens to players in their mid-to-late 30s, we think "well, looks like he's finally lost it." But, is this true?

I'm going to use Wins Above Replacement (WAR), a framework I developed a few years ago on my blog. There are a few implementations around, versions where the creators of those systems added their own insights and research, notably at Baseball Reference (via Sean Smith's BaseballProjection.com) and at FanGraphs. I will be using Sean's version.

Let's look at players who follow this pattern: three good years followed by one bad year. Prior to this year, the most recent example was Marcus Giles. At the age of 25, Giles had an MVP-level season, and he followed that up with two excellent years at age 26 and 27. His age-28 season was a disaster, and he was soon out of baseball.

On the other hand we have Dale Murphy who had a great career, notably his age 27 through 29 seasons (which included one MVP and two top-10 finishes), which were followed by a terrible year at age 30. He bounced back in 1987 for another great year.

Of all players born since 1895 (Babe Ruth's birth year), I've identified 102 players who followed the three-good-one-bad seasons pattern. To qualify for a good season, a player had to have at least three Wins Above Replacement. A bad season was anything less than two wins, with at least 500 plate appearances.

I put the players into three buckets, based on their age. If the player entered that fifth season at age 30 or younger, he was "Young." If he entered that fifth season at age 35 or older, he was "Old." Guys between 31 and 34 were "Middle-aged." There were 30 Young, 37 Middle-aged, and 35 Old players. In their three good seasons, each group averaged between 4.5 and 4.8 wins per season. And in their bad season, their average wins were between 1.0 and 1.2.

Now, we are finally in a position to answer: What happens in that fifth season? The Young players averaged 2.4 wins, the Middle-aged averaged 2.6 wins, and the Old players averaged 1.3 wins. So, yes, if an old player has a bad season, that is an ominous sign.

But what do we think is going on here? Was the Old player's decline foreshadowed by the bad season? Or was he just an Old player losing his skills, period?

I ran another study. This time, the player had to have four good seasons in a row. There were 828 such players. These players averaged around eight wins per good season. What happened in that fifth season? The Young players averaged 5.2 wins, the Middle-aged players averaged 4.6 wins, and the Old players averaged 3.7 wins.

So let's recap: if you have a bad recent season, the Old player will have 1.1 fewer wins than the Young player, which is about 45 percent fewer wins. But if you have a good recent season, the Old player will have 1.5 fewer wins than the Young player, which is about 30 percent fewer wins.

As you can see, it's not a matter of the most recent/bad season having more impact because the player is old. It's simply the age of the player that is the ominous sign.

Running a regression, we find that each year of age will impact your performance by 0.15 wins. So, if you have two otherwise identical players in terms of past performance, one who is entering the season at the age of 27 and another at the age of 37, then expect the 37-year-old player to put up a performance that is 1.5 fewer wins than the 27-year-old. This is a fairly enormous finding, if the sample of players I chose is not somehow biased.

Ultimate Home Run Park Factors

by Greg Rybarczyk

In 2007, I published an article on the Hardball Times web site entitled "Home Run Park Factor: a New Approach," in which I outlined a method for calculating park factors for home runs not by counting four-baggers themselves (something that will always be hampered by the considerable limitations of small sample size), but by simulating an extensive, standardized set of test trajectories in each park, and analyzing the results for each park in comparison to the league average.

Since 2007, four major league ballparks (RFK Stadium, Yankee Stadium, Shea Stadium and the Hubert H. Humphrey Metrodome) have hosted their final games, and four new venues (Nationals Park, the new Yankee Stadium, Citi Field and Target Field) have opened. Several other parks have made minor revisions to their home run fences. Even the Hit Tracker analysis engine has undergone some revisions based on updated research on lift and drag coefficients, so it seems worthwhile to revisit this analysis.

The Hit Tracker Home Run Park Factor method runs a set of approximately 50,000 trajectories in each ballpark, first in 70 degree temperature and no wind, then in the average weather conditions for that ballpark. The park factor for each of five 18-degree wide field segments (left field, left-center field, center field, right-center field and right field) is calculated, based on the number of test trajectories that result in home runs, given each field's home run fence distances and heights. An overall park factor is also calculated, based on weighting factors for each of the five fields—this accounts for the preponderance of long flies to the left side versus the right side. At the end of the article, I'll provide approximate park factor adjustments for actual temperature and wind conditions.

Here are the results for each ballpark, along with some commentary on unique elements of the fence layout in each park.

---

1. Minute Maid Park, Houston Astros

Overall Home Run Park Factor: 119

Field HRPFs: LF: 141/LCF: 149/CF: 55/RCF: 118/RF: 118

Comments: The distant center field fence doesn't come close to balancing out the absurdly close fences in the other fields. A pull-hitter's paradise.

---

2. New Yankee Stadium, New York Yankees

Overall HRPF: 119

Field HRPFs: LF: 125/LCF: 88/CF: 87/RCF: 159/RF: 153

Comments: The close and short fences on the right side are well known, but the left field corner is relatively close also. Center and left-center are the place to encourage fly balls if you're a pitcher and can manage that.

---

3. U.S. Cellular Field, Chicago White Sox

Overall HRPF: 115

Field HRPFs: LF: 123/LCF: 120/CF: 112/RCF: 113/RF: 98

Comments: A relatively easy reach in all directions. The 2001 renovation that moved the fences in overdid it.

---

4. Great American Ball Park, Cincinnati Reds

Overall HRPF: 115

Field HRPFs: LF: 105/LCF: 112/CF: 116/RCF: 126/RF: 122

Comments: You don't have to be Adam Dunn to get one out of here. A great place for a hitter with all-field power (just ask Joey Votto).

---

5. Coors Field, Colorado Rockies

Overall HRPF: 112

Field HRPFs: LF: 137/LCF: 106/CF: 98/RCF: 117/RF: 90

Comments: Coors Field fences were set up deep to compensate for the thin, mile-high air, but even with the humidor in action it is still quite favorable for homers, particularly high fly balls. The 14-foot right field fence keeps a few balls in the park.

---

6. Citizens Bank Park, Philadelphia Phillies

Overall HRPF: 108

Field HRPFs: LF: 104/LCF: 121/CF: 95/RCF: 124/RF: 96

Comments: Citizens Bank Park has the kind of cozy dimensions that turned 18 of Jimmy Rollins' fly balls in 2007 into home runs, despite the fact that only three of them flew more than 400 feet. The 13-foot right field fence and 11-foot left field fence make the corners play close to average for homers, but the 90-degree angles between the foul lines and fences make the alleys great spots to hit one out.

7. Tropicana Field, Tampa Bay Rays

Overall HRPF: 108

Field HRPFs: LF: 131/LCF: 98/CF: 75/RCF: 122/RF: 111

Comments: Left field is very favorable due to the diagonal fence segment that angles in from the main outfield seating area, but left-center field gets quite deep out by the Power Alley Pub. Right-center field is similar to Citizens Bank Park; it is a little deeper, with a slightly shorter fence.

8. Progressive Field, Cleveland Indians

Overall HRPF: 105

Field HRPFs: LF: 98/LCF: 96/CF: 117/RCF: 107/RF: 117

Comments: The 19-foot left field wall limits home runs in that direction somewhat, but the rest of the park is eminently reachable. The Indians could probably leverage this asymmetry the way the Yankees have in the Bronx, by stacking their lineup with medium-power lefties and doing their best to hang onto any elite left-handed pitchers (e.g. CC Sabathia, Cliff Lee) who find their way to Cleveland.

9. Rogers Centre, Toronto Blue Jays

Overall HRPF: 105

Field HRPFs: LF: 115/LCF: 100/CF: 89/RCF: 96/RF: 106

Comments: 2010 saw a league-leading 227 home runs hit north of the border; Blue Jays hitters obviously played a big part in that, but the park is definitely a good one for long balls. Center field is slightly tougher than average, with a long arc of fence at 400 feet from home plate. One interesting note: Even though Rogers Centre is symmetrical on its left and right sides in the outfield, the park factors for the right and left sides are not the same. This is because each park factor for a field is computed against the league average for that field.

10. Oriole Park at Camden Yards, Baltimore Orioles

Overall HRPF: 103

Field HRPFs: LF: 94/LCF: 107/CF: 121/RCF: 101/RF: 93

Comments: Camden Yards comes in at slightly easier than average for home runs, but this is at the standard weather conditions of 70 degrees and no wind. During high summer, when temperatures in Baltimore routinely exceed 90 degrees, the ball will fly out at a much higher rate. Right field is close, but the 25-foot wall in front of the Flag Court keeps plenty of potential homers in play.

11. Fenway Park, Boston Red Sox

Overall HRPF: 102

Field HRPFs: LF: 102/LCF: 133/CF: 98/RCF: 69/RF: 104

Comments: Fenway Park is well known for its exceptionally tall and close Green Monster in left field, but the impact of the Monster is often overestimated. Its 37-foot height takes away quite a few line-drive type home runs, even as it bestows a trip around the bases for certain lofted fly balls that have no business landing outside the field of play. Right-center field is very deep, as is much of right field, but down the right field line the fence at Fenway is both close and short, making right field slightly easier than average for home runs.

12. Oakland Coliseum, Oakland Athletics

Overall HRPF: 99

Field HRPFs: LF: 101/LCF: 89/CF: 116/RCF: 91/RF: 98

Comments: Here we have another instance of the park factors for standard conditions not adequately describing the true situation. Oakland Coliseum is one of the coldest ballparks, on average, which means that for most games, the park factor for home runs will be lower than the listed values, which are accurate for 70 degrees and no wind. The vast foul territory also will knock down the effective home run park factor, since more foul flies will be caught in Oakland than elsewhere, leaving hitters in Oakland fewer opportunities to hit balls over the fence.

13. Safeco Field, Seattle Mariners

Overall HRPF: 99

Field HRPFs: LF: 79/LCF: 89/CF: 103/RCF: 122/RF: 120

Comments: Safeco Field is yet another ballpark that is strongly asymmetrical, and easier for home runs on the right side of the field. It is also a cold venue, on average, making it even harder for right-handed pull hitters to get the ball up and out.

14. Dodger Stadium, Los Angeles Dodgers

Overall HRPF: 98

Field HRPFs: LF: 95/LCF: 85/CF: 132/RCF: 90/RF: 91

Comments: I wrote extensively about Dodger Stadium and its unusual layout in the 2008 *Hardball Times Annual*. Dodger Stadium is deep in the corners and shallow in center field, sporting the highest park factor for center field in the majors. Overall, it plays as neutral for home runs, but its impact on elite sluggers would depend on where those hitters tend to place their long flies: pull hitters such as Paul Konerko would lose some home runs in LA, while guys who are comfortable hitting to center field (such as Jim Thome, Adam Dunn or Joey Votto) would fare particularly well here.

15. Sun Life Stadium, Florida Marlins

Overall HRPF: 98

Field HRPFs: LF: 120/LCF: 117/CF: 74/RCF: 91/RF: 66

Comments: Sun Life Stadium is a great place for right-handed pull hitters, where even the 22-foot height of the left field wall can't make up for how close that wall is to home plate. However, everyone else loses a lot of home run power when they come to South Florida. Center-, right-center and right field are deep, and on top of the unfavorable park factors for standard conditions, the frequent winds blowing in from right-center field knock down balls hit in that direction even more. It's a great place for a right-handed pitcher, though.

16. Target Field, Minnesota Twins

Overall HRPF: 96

Field HRPFs: LF:96/LCF: 104/CF: 89/RCF: 103/RF: 84

Comments: Target Field is a fair park if you consider only the field dimensions, but the cool temperatures will shave some distance off most homers hit in the Twins' new park. I suspect that after an adjustment period, home runs will settle in at Target Field at a level around 90 overall, based on the fence layout and the early and late-season temperatures.

17. PNC Park, Pittsburgh Pirates

Overall HRPF: 95

Field HRPFs: LF: 108/LCF: 65/CF: 109/RCF: 94/RF: 100

Comments: PNC Park plays fair everywhere except in its cavernous left-center field. Right field is close, but the 21-foot wall keeps the homers there to a reasonable total.

18. PETCO Park, San Diego Padres

Overall HRPF: 93

Field HRPFs: LF: 92/LCF: 99/CF: 98/RCF: 60/RF: 116

Comments: PETCO Park is a tough place to hit homers. The fences are deep everywhere except in the gimmicky right field corner, which employs the inexplicable "seats sticking out into the field" motif. Balls hit toward the reasonably fair left side often have to battle through a fresh breeze blowing left to right, and balls hit to center field are blown by that wind into the very deep right-center field.

19. Angels Stadium, Los Angeles Angels of Anaheim

Overall HRPF: 93

Field HRPFs: LF: 91/LCF: 72/CF: 130/RCF: 85/RF: 87

Comments: Center field at Angels Stadium is the place to hit the ball in the air, if one possesses the power to get one out. Everywhere else is difficult.

20. Miller Park, Milwaukee Brewers

Overall HRPF: 92

Field HRPFs: LF: 69/LCF: 88/CF: 122/RCF: 108/RF: 81

Comments: Center field at Miller Park is a comfortable reach for moderate or stronger power hitters, but the corners are difficult. The retractable roof means teams don't play in particularly cold or rainy conditions, which helps the home run numbers significantly. The AirTran picnic area is a field-level section added during a renovation prior to the 2006 season that needlessly brought the right-center field fence in.

21. Turner Field, Atlanta Braves

Overall HRPF: 91

Field HRPFs: LF: 96/LCF: 82/CF: 97/RCF: 75/RF: 105

Comments: The right field fence at Turner Field angles away from the foul line, creating the one favorable field for homers in Atlanta. Everywhere else is more difficult than average to clear. A solid pitcher's park, but not to excess.

22. National Park, Washington Nationals

Overall HRPF: 89

Field HRPFs: LF: 69/LCF: 88/CF: 122/RCF: 108/RF: 81

Comments: The Nationals' beautiful ballpark is deep in the corners, but shallow in center field, and somewhat so in right-center field. This combination makes it a bit tougher on less powerful hitters, who usually pull most of their home runs, but a bit easier on sluggers, who are more likely to blast homers out to center field.

23. Rangers Ballpark in Arlington, Texas Rangers

Overall HRPF: 87

Field HRPFs: LF: 81/LCF: 76/CF: 96/RCF: 95/RF: 97

Comments: The park factor numbers listed here will no doubt look too low, but remember that you have to separately adjust for temperature and wind. It is usually very warm in Arlington, which will add a few feet to most fly balls. The wind is also a factor, and a difficult one to model accurately. The winds outside the stadium tend to blow hard from the south, which translates to the wind blowing in from right field, but on the field, the wind swirls, and often blows out.

24. Comerica Park, Detroit Tigers

Overall HRPF: 87

Field HRPFs: LF: 86/LCF: 105/CF: 44/RCF: 107/RF: 98

Comments: The Tigers' home park is a tough one to get home runs out of, especially over the inappropriately distant center field fence. Only four balls made it over the center field fence at Comerica Park in 2010.

25. AT&T Park, San Francisco Giants

Overall HRPF: 87

Field HRPFs: LF: 74/LCF: 102/CF: 86/RCF: 66/RF: 110

Comments: The distinctive features of AT&T Park, in terms of home runs, are the huge right-center field, and the tall but close right field wall. Games in San Francisco are cold, but usually feature strong winds, often as not blowing out toward center or right field.

26. Chase Field, Arizona Diamondbacks

Overall HRPF: 87

Field HRPFs: LF: 94/LCF: 98/CF: 63/RCF: 98/RF: 78

Comments: Chase Field features a 25-foot wall in center field that is also quite far away from home plate, but the other fields play relatively fair. The humidity in Phoenix is the lowest of all MLB venues, and the Diamondbacks apparently have not been storing their baseballs in a controlled environment, so it is quite possible that dried out baseballs, which become lighter and smaller than properly stored balls, could explain the prevalence of home runs at Chase Field despite its overall low park factor for home runs. If the D-Backs do decide to install a humidor, we may see a very large drop in homers at Chase Field.

27. Busch Stadium, St. Louis Cardinals

Overall HRPF: 86

Field HRPFs: LF: 77/LCF: 85/CF: 109/RCF: 84/RF: 78

Comments: Busch Stadium is fairly nondescript in terms of its layout: symmetrical, a bit deep in the corners, and a bit shallow in center field. This relative arrangement tends to depress home run totals, as described in the Nationals Park section earlier. Temperatures are warm in St. Louis, and winds generally light.

28. Wrigley Field, Chicago Cubs

Overall HRPF: 86

Field HRPFs: LF: 51/LCF: 116/CF: 124/RCF: 89/RF: 47

Comments: Wrigley Field is exceptionally deep in the corners, more than 350 feet in both directions, but quite reachable in left-center field and center field. It plays very differently depending on the weather; on warm days, the wind blows out and the home runs come in bunches. When the weather is less favorable, the wind blows in and most fly balls stay in the park.

29. Kauffman Stadium, Kansas City Royals

Overall HRPF: 74

Field HRPFs: LF: 85/LCF: 65/CF: 75/RCF: 62/RF: 77

Comments: Kansas City's home park is truly unique, in that none of the five fields are even close to favorable to hitters. Kauffman Stadium has the most fair territory of all major league parks. Warm temperatures will give a foot or two of distance to fly balls, but the overall effect is to strongly suppress home run totals.

30. Citi Field, New York Mets

Overall HRPF: 70

Field HRPFs: LF: 70/LCF: 67/CF: 60/RCF: 64/RF: 96

Comments: There is just one spot at Citi Field that is relatively fair for home runs: the right field corner. Unfortunately for the Mets, that spot has been dubbed "Utley's corner," in honor of its most frequent visitor, Philadelphia's Chase Utley. Utley has hit this tiny target four times since the park opened, more than any other player—or the entire Mets roster. Citi Field's extremely deep and 16-foot-tall left field wall makes things tough for right-handed pull hitters, and the guys who hit home runs to all fields will have trouble doing so in Queens.

Weather Adjustments

The standard park factors listed for each park are the values that exist when the temperature is 70 degrees, and there is no wind. When the weather does not exactly match these values, a correction must be applied to get the correct park factor.

The adjustments were arrived at by repeating the standard analysis steps for each park with various wind and temperature values, and then analyzing the data to determine the values to be used for adjusting the park factors.

Temperature Adjustment Factor

For temperature, each degree of difference between actual temperature and 70 degrees results in a change in park factor of 0.26 per degree. Thus a temperature of 80 degrees will generate park factors equal to the standard values plus 2.6.

Wind Adjustment Factors

Wind is rather more complicated, but for any given wind speed and wind direction corrective values are known. Basically, when the wind blows in, it is bad for hitters, while a tail wind hampers the pitchers to a degree, turning some of their mistakes into short homers, rather than long fly outs.

To determine the proper park factor corrections for a given wind state, consult the following table, and for each 1 mph of wind, adjust the park factor for the field of interest by the amount listed for the wind direction:

	LF	LCF	CF	RCF	RF
Out to RF	0.0	0.5	1.4	1.7	1.9
Out to CF	1.4	1.7	1.9	1.7	1.4
Out to LF	1.9	1.7	1.4	0.5	0.0
R to L	1.4	0.5	0.0	-0.5	-1.4
In from RF	0.0	-0.5	-1.4	-1.7	-1.9
In from CF	-1.4	-1.7	-1.9	-1.7	-1.4
In from LF	-1.9	-1.7	-1.4	-0.5	0.0
L to R	-1.4	0.5	0.0	0.5	1.4

Example: A game is being played at Wrigley Field on a 45 degree day, with the wind blowing in from center field at 11 mph. What are the park factors?

Standard Factors: The standard park factors for Wrigley field are 51/116/124/89/47 for LF/LCF/CF/RCF/RF.

Temperature Adjustment: The temperature difference between the actual temperature of 45 degrees and the standard temperature of 70 degrees is -25 degrees. Adjust each park factor by the quantity $(0.26)*(-25) = -6.5$.

Wind adjustment: Adjust each field's park factor by the quantity $(11)*(adjustment factor)$.

- For LF, this is $11*-1.4 = -15.4$
- For LCF, this is $11*-1.7 = -18.7$
- For CF, this is $11*-1.9 = -20.9$
- For RCF, this is $11*-1.7 = -18.7$
- For RF, this is $11*-1.4 = -15.4$

Overall, Wrigley Field's Home Run Park factors for these weather conditions are 29/91/97/64/25 for LF/LCF/CF/RCF/RF. That's a tough day to hit one out of the "Friendly Confines"!

On an 85 degree day at Wrigley Field, with the wind blowing out to CF at 15 mph, the factors are 76/145/160/118/72. The ballhawks on Waveland Avenue live for days like this!

Acknowledgments

I would like to express my gratitude to those people who have helped me during the season, and in particular, I'd like to single out ESPN's Stats and Information group, Brenton Blair, Dave Davison and Alan Nathan, for everything they have done for me. Without all of your assistance, Hit Tracker would not be what it is today.

Many thanks also to the legion of "fans" who have taken the time to engage in discussion with me on the subject of home runs, and to those others who simply expressed their thanks for making the Hit Tracker data available. I am honored to have had an impact on your appreciation of the great game of baseball!

Home Run Park Factors Summary

Park	LF	LCF	CF	RCF	RF	Overall
Minute Maid Park	141	149	55	118	118	119
New Yankee Stadium	125	88	87	159	153	119
U.S. Cellular Field	123	120	112	113	98	115
Great American Ball	105	112	116	126	122	115
Coors Field	137	106	98	117	90	112
Citizens Bank Park	104	121	95	124	96	108
Tropicana Field	131	98	75	122	111	108
Progressive Field	98	96	117	107	117	105
Rogers Centre	115	100	89	96	106	104
Oriole Park at Camden Yards	94	107	121	101	93	103
Fenway Park	102	133	98	69	104	102
Oakland Coliseum	101	89	116	91	98	99
Safeco Field	79	89	103	122	120	99
Dodger Stadium	95	85	132	90	91	98
Sun Life Stadium	120	117	74	91	66	98
Target Field	96	104	89	103	84	96
PNC Park	108	65	109	94	100	95
PETCO Park	92	99	98	60	116	93
Angels Stadium	91	72	130	85	87	93
Miller Park	69	88	122	108	81	92
Turner Field	96	82	97	75	105	91
Nationals Park	77	84	125	81	81	89
Rangers Ballpark in Arlington	81	76	96	95	97	87
Comerica Park	86	105	44	107	98	87
AT&T Park	74	102	86	66	110	87
Chase Field	94	98	63	98	78	87
Busch Stadium III	77	85	109	84	78	86
Wrigley Field	51	116	124	89	47	86
Kauffman Stadium	85	65	75	62	77	74
Citi Field	70	67	60	64	96	70
Average	97	97	97	97	97	97

Statistics

As Much Fun as Doing Your Taxes

by Dave Studenmund

Bill James recently exclaimed on "The Simpsons," "I made baseball as much fun as doing your taxes." If you do find the next 140+ pages as dull as doing your taxes, that's okay. You've still got the first half of the book—the one filled with words—to read. The next half is filled with numbers. Baseball stats, actually. I think many of you will enjoy them.

Despite our progressive talk and our penchant for analysis, most of our statistics will be familiar to you. Hits, doubles, strikeouts, batting average, etc. are all here. The few exceptions, such as Base Runs (how many runs the hitter contributed to the offense) and Pitching Runs Created (the value of a pitcher, expressed in the same form as runs contributed by a hitter) are defined in our glossary.

However, the *Hardball Times Annual* also proudly displays statistics you won't find anywhere else: Batted Ball Stats. Even web sites like FanGraphs and Baseball Reference don't provide what you can find here. I like to think of them as a combination of statistics and scouting—numbers that quantify not only how well each player performed, but how he did it.

To give you a sense of how these numbers work, I'm going to review them in the context of 2010, the "year of the pitcher." In 2007, major league teams scored 23,322 runs. In 2010, they scored 21,308 runs. Two thousand runs have been lost in the past three years. Let's see where they went.

First, let's look at strikeouts and walks as a percentage of plate appearances for the last four years:

Year	K%	BB%
2007	17.1%	9.5%
2008	17.5%	9.6%
2009	18.0%	9.7%
2010	18.5%	9.3%

The 1.4 percent increase in strikeouts in just three years is huge. The walk rate had also been climbing, helping to offset the run-dampening effect of the strikeouts, but it dropped quite a bit in 2010. Forget home runs or ballparks—this little table explains over half of the decline in offense since 2007.

Our system applies a "linear weight" to each batting event, a weight that reflects the average impact each event has on run scoring. When you multiply the quantity of each event by its weight, you get a number that is roughly equal to the total number of runs scored each year. The system works pretty well.

So when you apply the appropriate weights to the total number of strikeouts and walks the past three years, you find that the net impact has been a decrease of about 400 runs, 20 percent of our total.

But there is another consequence of an increase in strikeouts: The total number of pitches put into play has decreased. Strikeouts and walks have grown from 26.6 percent of appearances to 27.8 percent. As a result, there were about 5,000 fewer balls put into play in 2010 compared to 2007. According to our linear weights, the net impact of this drop was about 700 fewer runs.

If you add the 400 and 700, you get 1,100 runs. Over half of the decrease in runs from 2007 to 2010 has been the result of more strikeouts and fewer walks.

Okay, so what happened when the ball was hit? Here's a list of the percentage of batted ball types for all balls put into play (ground balls, line drives and fly balls):

Year	GB%	LD%	FB%
2007	43.5%	18.6%	37.9%
2008	43.9%	20.2%	36.0%
2009	43.3%	18.9%	37.8%
2010	44.3%	18.2%	37.5%

I should tell you that our statistics partner, Baseball Info Solutions, has video reviewers watch every batted ball to classify it. They even have people review the video reviewers. Still, it's hard to tell the difference between a line drive and a fly ball, so there are certainly some judgment calls and biases in the data.

But when the overall data tell you that ground balls were up a full percentage point in 2010, you can believe the trend. And when the data tell you that line drives were down two full percentage points in just the last two years, you can believe that something was going on.

As you can imagine, the average ground ball generates fewer runs than the average line drive. I estimate that the movement toward grounders and away from liners has resulted in about 250 fewer runs.

The rest of the difference, about 650 runs, is the result of the outcome of each type of batted ball. Below you will find a few factoids about batted balls: Outs per ground ball and the average number of runs generated by each grounder (GBR); the average number of runs generated by each line drive (LDR); and three different facts about outfield flies:

home runs per outfield fly, outs per outfield fly and runs generated by the average outfield fly

Year	Out/GB	GBR	LDR	HR/OF	Out/OF	OFR
2007	73.9%	.046	.398	.103	82.9%	.181
2008	74.1%	.045	.386	.107	84.2%	.175
2009	74.7%	.041	.388	.109	83.0%	.189
2010	73.9%	.043	.383	.102	82.8%	.179

This mishmash of data accounts for 650 fewer runs during the three years under review.

- The out rate on ground balls had been trending up, and the subsequent run rate of grounders down, but they both came back to norms in 2010.
- The run impact of the average line drive has trended down. According to BIS, this is primarily due to fewer doubles and home runs off line drives. This trend could easily be a data classification issue, so we won't dwell on it here.
- The run impact of an outfield fly jumped up in 2009 but fell back again this past year. There were fewer outfield fly home runs, but the out rate (that's of outfield flies that aren't home runs) also stayed down, which helped negate the run impact of fewer homers. Again, this may partially be explained by the relative classification of flies and liners. Only partially, however.

Lots of info in just a few pages, huh? Let's recap. Run scoring has trended down the past three years primarily because there have been more strikeouts and fewer walks. In fact, the strikeout/walk differences account for more than half of the change in runs scored.

The rest of the change has been characterized by two things: a movement toward more weakly hit balls (fewer liners, more grounders) and weaker results from both line drives and fly balls.

Of course, these sorts of statistics can also be used for individual players. In our stats, you'll find 2010 batted ball stats for all batters with at least 100 plate appearances and all pitchers who faced at least 100 batters.

Using these numbers, you can pick apart a player's strengths and weaknesses the same way we just picked apart the last three years of major league baseball. For instance, check out the four-year batted ball profile of 2010's biggest breakout, Jose Bautista, in the table below.

The best way to read these tables is to start on the right and move to the left. There, you can see that Bautista created 48 runs above average on his fly balls. That's what you'd expect from a guy with 54 home runs, but it's not what you'd expect from a guy who totaled only *two* runs above average in the previous three years.

On balls not in play ("NIP"), or strikeouts and walks, Bautista was also much more productive due to striking out less and walking more often (you can see exactly how much on the left-hand side of the table).

What drove up his flyball run rate? Well, look at the rows labeled "% of Batted Balls." Bautista hit a lot fewer grounders and line drives and really concentrated on fly balls last year; 54 percent of his batted balls were fly balls, one of the highest totals in the majors.

He paid for all those fly balls. 15 percent of them were infield flies, a very high percentage. And 86 percent of the outfield flies that weren't home runs were caught for outs, also a high percentage.

But 25 percent of Bautista's outfield flies were home runs. That's, like, really, really good and results in an average run value per outfield fly of 0.36 runs, double the major league average.

On the next page is the other side of the ledger ... Back in 2008, we were all talking about Cliff Lee and how he had

Jose Bautista		% of PA		% of Batted Balls					Out %		Runs per Event				Total Runs vs. Avg.				
Year	PA	K%	BB%	GB%	LD%	FB%	IF/F	HR/OF	GB	OF	NIPR	GBR	LDR	OFR	NIP	GB	LD	Fly	Tot
2007	614	16	12	40	16	43	.12	.09	75	84	.08	.04	.41	.16	6	-2	-4	0	-0
2008	424	21	10	46	15	39	.08	.15	71	89	.03	.06	.38	.20	-1	1	-7	1	-6
2009	404	21	15	41	17	42	.10	.13	76	87	.08	.02	.48	.18	6	-3	-1	1	3
2010	683	17	16	31	14	54	.15	.25	75	86	.11	.03	.41	.36	17	-4	-6	48	55
TOT	2125	18	13	39	15	46	.12	.16	74	86	.08	.04	.42	.25	27	-9	-18	50	51
MLB Totals		18	10	44	19	37	.10	.11	74	83	.05	.04	.39	.18	--	--	--	--	--

come out of nowhere to become a superstar. Take a look at his batted balls table to see what happened then, and what has happened since.

For some reason, he learned how to do all the key things a pitcher should do, and he did them tremendously well. If anything, Lee was even better this year.

- He started striking out and walking batters at phenomenal rates. In fact, he walked only 2 percent of the batters he faced this year, compared to 10 percent just three years ago.

- Batters started hitting more grounders off him. There was a big rise in grounders in 2008, but he's been around the major league average the last two years.

- When fly balls have been hit off him, his home run rate has been below the major league average.

- As you can see from his "out" columns, the defense behind him has been about average each year. He did get a boost this year from having fewer runs scored off his line drives, though we don't know if that was pitching, fielding or the return of Halley's comet.

You can learn a lot from batted balls. Spend some time inside these pages and get to know your favorite players even better. I will also be posting four-year profiles at the Hardball Times website.

There are a few other background items you will want to know as you prowl through our stats.

Ballparks

How about them ballparks? A new one opened this year, Target Field in Minnesota, and we were once again reminded of how a beautiful ballpark can enhance the experience of watching a game … and how it can "enhance" the game itself. Target Field was the toughest park in which to hit a home run

last year, though Greg Rybarczyk thinks Target homers will increase next year—for more details, check out his "Ultimate Home Run Park Factors" chapter.

These things happen. Coors Field was known as an extreme hitters park for many years after it opened, so Rockies management took extreme measures a few years ago. The Rockies started placing all game baseballs in a humidor, hoping that a little extra humidity on the ball would dampen the bats.

It worked for a while, but it seemed to stop working this year. Here is the ratio of runs scored and home runs by both teams, at Coors games and at Rockies games away from home.

Season	Runs	Home Runs
2003	1.24	1.37
2004	1.42	1.23
2005	1.28	1.10
2006	1.15	1.17
2007	1.16	1.22
2008	1.13	1.30
2009	1.25	1.08
2010	1.36	1.50

See that big jump back up this year, particularly in home runs? The lesson is that you can't judge a park by a year. We use park factors in our statistics to adjust certain statistics, such as Base Runs, GPA (Gross Production Average) and Pitching Runs Created. (You know, the stats with the fancy names.) But we don't use one-year park factors.

For stadiums that have been open at least three years, we give 20 percent weight to 2008 data, 30 percent weight to 2009 data and 50 percent weight to 2010 data. For stadiums that have been open less than three years, we take the data available and regress it to the overall major league average.

We actually calculate three different park factors. One for total runs, one for home runs and one for all the runs not

Cliff Lee		% of BFP		% of Batted Balls					Out %		Runs per Event				Total Runs vs. Avg.				
Year	BFP	K%	BB%	GB%	LD%	FB%	IF/F	HR/OF	GB	OF	NIPR	GBR	LDR	OFR	NIP	GB	LD	Fly	Tot
2007	443	15	10	35	15	50	.09	.12	70	83	.07	.07	.48	.19	2	2	1	10	15
2008	891	19	4	46	19	35	.11	.05	73	84	-.03	.05	.36	.09	-18	1	-4	-21	-42
2009	969	19	5	41	22	36	.11	.07	74	85	-.02	.05	.40	.12	-17	-0	11	-16	-22
2010	843	22	2	42	18	40	.09	.07	71	83	-.07	.07	.33	.13	-26	4	-13	-10	-45
TOT	3146	19	4	42	19	39	.10	.07	72	84	-.02	.06	.38	.13	-59	7	-5	-37	-94
MLB Totals		18	10	44	19	37	.10	.11	74	83	.05	.04	.39	.18	--	--	--	--	--

scored off home runs (an invention of Bill James' called the "Park-S Factor." I have no idea why he called it that.).

Here's a table of the three park factors for every major league team. To use these, you simply divide your statistic of choice by the relevant park factor to derive a "normalized" statistic.

Team	Park Factor	HR Factor	Park-S
ANA	0.97	0.98	0.98
ARI	1.05	1.02	1.03
ATL	0.99	0.99	1.00
BAL	1.04	1.12	1.00
BOS	1.04	0.95	1.04
CHC	1.07	1.05	1.04
CHW	1.05	1.18	0.99
CIN	1.00	1.08	0.98
CLE	0.97	0.93	0.99
COL	1.13	1.16	1.06
DET	1.01	1.00	1.01
FLO	1.02	0.96	1.03
HOU	0.96	1.04	0.96
KC	1.01	0.93	1.03
LAD	0.95	0.97	0.97
MIL	0.98	1.05	0.97
MIN	0.99	0.88	1.03
WAS	0.99	0.99	1.00
NYM	0.96	0.93	0.99
NYY	1.04	1.16	0.99
OAK	0.98	0.92	1.00
PHI	1.00	1.03	0.99
PIT	1.00	0.95	1.01
SDP	0.92	0.90	0.96
SEA	0.94	0.90	0.98
SFG	1.00	0.97	1.01
STL	0.97	0.90	1.00
TB	0.95	0.96	0.97
TEX	1.05	1.08	1.01
TOR	1.00	1.07	0.98

If you think you truly understand park factors, you don't really understand park factors. A few years ago, we examined park factors for different types of batted balls (fly balls, grounders, etc.) and found that parks seem to have different effects on different types of batted balls. That's why we like the more detailed, nuanced approach in "Ultimate Home Run Park Factors," where you can see that some parks help right-handed home run batters but actually hurt left-handed home run hitters.

For more information about parks and park factors, pick up the latest *Bill James Handbook*.

Splits

There are other things to consider when pondering baseball players and their stats. For instance, the home team wins 54 percent of the time, regardless of the park. In "That was a Strike?," John Walsh discovers that umpires have some impact on this particular split, and there are certainly other, less identifiable, reasons too.

The home/road split impacts everyone on the ballfield. Last year, batters hit .254 at home and .240 on the road (that's in Gross Production Average, or GPA, my favorite all-around batting stat. GPA combines on-base percentage and slugging percentage, gives more weight to on-base percentage—which it should—and aligns its scale to the batting average scale so it is easy to interpret).

Or you could say the opposite: Pitchers pitched better at home so batters hit 14 points lower against them. The effect is some combination of batters hitting better at home, pitchers pitching better at home, fielders fielding better at home … umpires favoring the home team … and it all plays out in the home/road split.

Over time, most players will converge around that 14-point split in home and road performance (ignoring park factors), but they might have some wild splits in individual years. Take a look at the players who had the biggest difference between home and road production this year (H-A is the difference between the batter's Home GPA and Away GPA):

Player	Tm	H-A
Scott L *	BAL	.118
Gonzalez C *	COL	.117
Sandoval P +	SF	.107
Fowler D +	COL	.105
Konerko P	CHA	.092
Hamilton J *	TEX	.085
Bautista J	TOR	.085
Wells V	TOR	.083
Quentin C	CHA	.080
Castro S	CHN	.079

You're probably not surprised to see a couple of Rockies near the top of the list. If you read Greg's piece about home run park factors, you also aren't surprised that White Sox sluggers Paul Konerko and Carlos Quentin are there, too.

Yet I was surprised by the guy at the very top of the list, Baltimore's Luke Scott. According to previous *THT Annuals*,

Scott has had strong home differentials before (.039 in 2008 and .059 in 2009) but nothing approaching 100+ points.

Here are the pitchers who gained the most pitching at home. The stat is the same (difference in "GPA against" at home minus "GPA against" on the road) but, because they're pitchers, the leaderboard is negative—a lower GPA means that the pitcher did better at home.

Player	Team	H-A
Masterson J	CLE	-.069
Johnson J	FLA	-.062
Pelfrey M	NYN	-.056
Volstad C	FLA	-.056
Rodriguez W	HOU	-.056
Richard C *	SD	-.053
Weaver J	LAA	-.047
Carpenter C	STL	-.045
Bonderman J	DET	-.043
Sanchez A	FLA	-.042

No Rockies on this list. You'll find the home/away GPA splits for all batters and pitchers in our stats.

You'll also find the lefty/righty splits for all batters and pitchers there, too. Left/right splits are another fact of baseball life—they're often called "platoon splits." Right-handed batters had a .256 GPA against left-handed pitchers last year, but only a .240 GPA against right-handed pitchers.

The reverse is true, too. Lefties batted .260 against right-handed pitchers, but just .233 against southpaws (hence the left-handed bullpen specialist). Even switch-hitters typically show a slight split, and this year was no exception: .243 against righthanded pitchers and .240 against lefties.

Here are the batters who had the biggest platoon splits last year.

Player	Tm	L^R
Lind A *	TOR	.156
Ortiz D *	BOS	.143
Martinez V +	BOS	.143
Hamilton J *	TEX	.117
Ethier A *	LAN	.104
Choo S *	CLE	.101
Fielder P *	MIL	.096
Napoli M	LAA	.091
Mauer J *	MIN	.087
Weeks R	MIL	.085

Lefty Adam Lind posted a fine .276 GPA against right-handers and a woeful .117 GPA against lefties, a difference of

156 GPA points. Lind's platoon split wasn't nearly as extreme in 2009, so perhaps he'll find his same-side swing again.

The column at the top of the platoon split is labeled "L^R" because the exact math depends on the handedness of the batter (or pitcher). An asterisk means the batter was a lefty, so the math is: his GPA against righties minus his GPA against lefties. No mark means that the batter was a right-handed batter, so we reverse the math (GPA vs. lefties minus GPA vs. righties).

For switch-hitters (who are denoted with a plus sign), we treat them as right-handed batters (GPA vs. lefties minus GPA vs. righties) and for pitchers we simply reverse the calculations. The math is a little complicated, but the interpretation is relatively simple. Except for switch-hitters, you should expect a platoon split of 10 to 30 GPA points (positive for batters, negative for pitchers). A number much higher or lower than that deserves a little investigation.

Fielding

What, you haven't read enough about fielding stats already? The *Hardball Times Annual* is full of fielding stats and analysis. You should start by reading John Dewan's "The Pitching and Defense Splits," where you'll find fantastic detail on the strengths and weaknesses of each team at each position.

You'll find even more detail in the following pages of statistics. That's where we list the Revised Zone Rating (RZR) of every player who played at least 100 innings at a position in the field. A position's zone is defined as that portion of the field in which the average position player converts at least 50 percent of batted balls into outs. The Revised Zone Rating calculates the proportion of balls hit into each respective zone that the fielder successfully handled.

RZR percentages differ by position. For reference's sake, here are the average zone stats for all positions last year. BIZ is the number of balls hit into each zone; Plays is the number of balls in zone that were converted into outs; RZR is the Revised Zone Rating (Plays divided by BIZ) and OOZ is the number of plays that each position converted outside of its zone—the wide-ranging plays.

Position	BIZ	Plays	RZR	OOZ
1B	6027	4602	.764	1418
2B	12640	10380	.821	1072
3B	10159	7220	.711	1597
SS	12958	10354	.799	1865
LF	7938	6912	.871	2119
CF	11085	10086	.910	2449
RF	8282	7430	.897	2376

If you perused our other fielding articles, you read that zone-based analysis is on the way out. That may be, but in the meantime, we think you'll find them useful. We list each fielder's RZR relative to the position average (ZRDif), the number of plays he made out of zone (OOZ), and the number of plays made outside of zone compared to the major league average for that position per 1,000 innings played (Dif).

That concludes our introduction. You're mostly on your own now, though you'll run into some guides along the way. Each team section has a list of "Stats Facts" that might pique your interest (thank you, Steve Treder). We provide major league averages where there may be a question. There's also a glossary at the end of all the numbers.

Even a 1099 form includes instructions.

By the way, you can download several Excel spreadsheets of baseball stats, along with our coverage of the postseason, from a webpage created just for you. The URL of your page is http://www.hardballtimes.com/THT2011Annual/ (mind the capitals!). The username is "tht11" and the password is "blackbeard".

TAMPA BAY RAYS CAM 2010

American League Team Stats

Runs Scored and Allowed
(adjusted for ballpark)

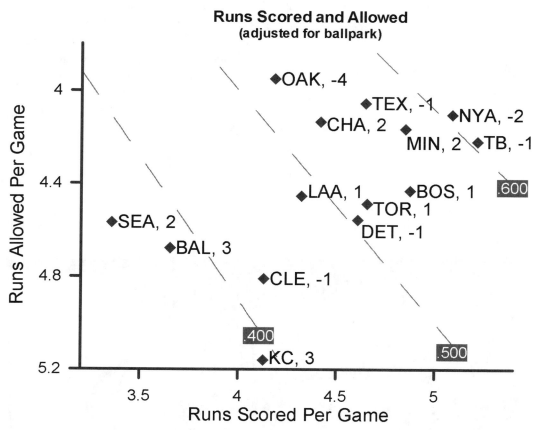

Notes: The dotted lines represent winning percentage based on run differential. The number after each team name represents the difference between the team's actual record and its run differential record.

Team	Team Record					Scoring Runs			Preventing Runs				Projection	
	W	L	RS	RA	RS-RA	AB/RSP	BA/RSP	HR	ERA	HRA	K	DER	PWINS	VAR
BAL	66	96	613	785	-172	1,336	.246	133	4.59	186	1,007	.694	63	3
BOS	89	73	818	744	74	1,396	.269	211	4.20	152	1,207	.696	88	1
CHA	88	74	752	704	48	1,355	.277	177	4.10	136	1,149	.682	86	2
CLE	69	93	646	752	-106	1,350	.248	128	4.30	147	967	.691	70	-1
DET	81	81	751	743	8	1,480	.256	152	4.30	142	1,056	.693	82	-1
KC	67	95	676	845	-169	1,428	.269	121	4.98	176	1,035	.682	64	3
LAA	80	82	681	702	-21	1,294	.242	155	4.04	148	1,130	.696	79	1
MIN	94	68	781	671	110	1,451	.285	142	3.95	155	1,048	.695	92	2
NYA	95	67	859	693	166	1,499	.258	201	4.06	179	1,154	.711	97	-2
OAK	81	81	663	626	37	1,433	.241	109	3.56	153	1,070	.714	85	-4
SEA	61	101	513	698	-185	1,266	.226	101	3.93	157	973	.709	59	2
TB	96	66	802	649	153	1,468	.266	160	3.78	175	1,189	.712	97	-1
TEX	90	72	787	687	100	1,482	.276	162	3.93	162	1,181	.708	91	-1
TOR	85	77	755	728	27	1,194	.246	257	4.23	150	1,184	.692	84	1
Average	82	80	721	716	5	1,388	.258	158	4.14	158	1,096	.698	81	1

Scoring Runs:
OBP and Power

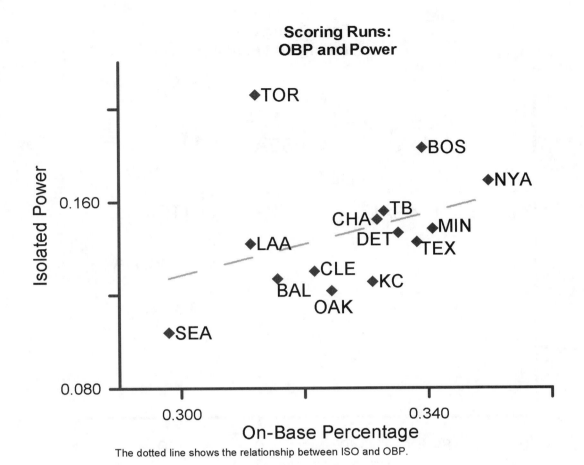

The dotted line shows the relationship between ISO and OBP.

Team	Runs	PA	H	1B	2B	3B	HR	TB	SO	BB	HBP	SH	SF	BA	OBP	SLG	GPA	ISO
BAL	613	6,109	1,440	1,022	264	21	133	2,145	1,056	424	54	31	45	.259	.316	.386	.239	.127
BOS	818	6,356	1,511	920	358	22	211	2,546	1,140	587	47	29	46	.268	.339	.451	.265	.183
CHA	752	6,118	1,467	1,006	263	21	177	2,303	922	467	79	50	38	.268	.332	.420	.254	.152
CLE	646	6,165	1,362	924	290	20	128	2,076	1,184	545	64	36	33	.248	.322	.378	.239	.130
DET	751	6,312	1,515	1,023	308	32	152	2,343	1,147	546	41	41	41	.268	.335	.415	.255	.147
KC	676	6,209	1,534	1,103	279	31	121	2,238	905	471	35	45	53	.274	.331	.399	.249	.126
LAA	681	6,089	1,363	913	276	19	155	2,142	1,070	466	52	42	37	.248	.311	.390	.238	.142
MIN	781	6,257	1,521	1,020	318	41	142	2,347	967	559	39	38	53	.273	.341	.422	.259	.148
NYA	859	6,379	1,485	977	275	32	201	2,427	1,136	662	73	33	44	.267	.350	.436	.266	.169
OAK	663	6,117	1,396	981	276	30	109	2,059	1,061	527	47	43	51	.256	.324	.378	.240	.122
SEA	513	5,989	1,274	930	227	16	101	1,836	1,184	459	39	42	40	.236	.298	.339	.219	.104
TB	802	6,270	1,343	851	295	37	160	2,192	1,292	672	57	39	57	.247	.333	.403	.251	.156
TEX	787	6,302	1,556	1,101	268	25	162	2,360	986	511	45	53	54	.276	.338	.419	.257	.143
TOR	755	6,072	1,364	767	319	21	257	2,496	1,164	471	55	16	34	.248	.312	.454	.254	.206
Average	721	6,196	1,438	967	287	26	158	2,251	1,087	526	52	38	45	.260	.330	.407	.250	.147

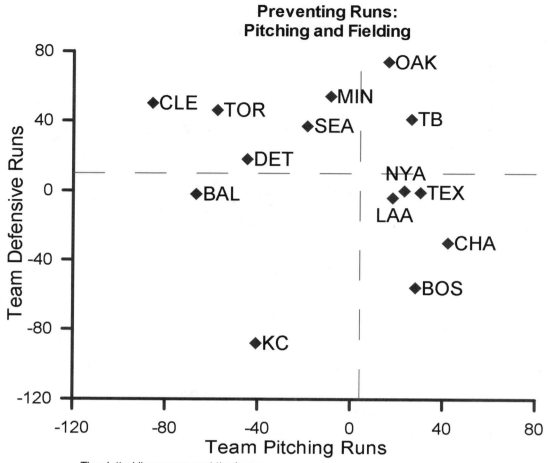

Preventing Runs: Pitching and Fielding

The dotted lines represent the league averages.
Positive numbers imply a positive performance on both fielding and pitching axes.
Refer to John Dewan's "The Pitching and Defense Splits" for more information.

Team	RA	IP	BFP	H	HRA	TBA	K	BB	ShO	Hlds	Sv	Op	Sv/Hld%	ERA	FIP	UERA	DER
BAL	785	1436.0	6,262	1,508	186	2,428	1,007	520	7	72	35	62	80%	4.59	4.51	0.33	.694
BOS	744	1456.0	6,267	1,402	152	2,216	1,207	580	9	65	44	66	83%	4.20	4.05	0.40	.696
CHA	704	1446.0	6,180	1,471	136	2,204	1,149	490	11	57	43	57	88%	4.10	3.75	0.29	.682
CLE	752	1433.0	6,224	1,477	147	2,283	967	572	4	73	34	50	87%	4.30	4.36	0.43	.691
DET	743	1444.0	6,198	1,445	142	2,200	1,056	537	5	60	32	45	88%	4.30	4.12	0.33	.693
KC	845	1436.0	6,333	1,553	176	2,448	1,035	551	3	64	44	65	84%	4.98	4.45	0.32	.682
LAA	702	1449.0	6,252	1,422	148	2,241	1,130	565	9	63	39	56	86%	4.04	4.08	0.32	.696
MIN	671	1452.0	6,106	1,493	155	2,335	1,048	383	13	75	40	58	86%	3.95	3.91	0.20	.695
NYA	693	1442.0	6,102	1,349	179	2,160	1,154	540	8	76	39	57	86%	4.06	4.30	0.26	.711
OAK	626	1431.0	6,011	1,315	153	2,040	1,070	512	17	65	38	51	89%	3.56	4.10	0.38	.714
SEA	698	1438.0	6,091	1,402	157	2,210	973	452	10	36	38	55	81%	3.93	4.14	0.44	.709
TB	649	1453.0	6,103	1,347	175	2,226	1,189	478	12	80	51	67	89%	3.78	4.05	0.24	.712
TEX	687	1455.0	6,213	1,355	162	2,152	1,181	551	8	83	46	66	87%	3.93	4.15	0.32	.708
TOR	728	1440.0	6,165	1,407	150	2,229	1,184	539	11	69	45	61	88%	4.23	4.00	0.33	.692
Average	716	1,443.6	6,179	1,425	158	2,241	1,096	519	9	67	41	58	86%	4.14	4.14	0.33	.698

Running and Miscellaneous Batting Stats

Team	SB	CS	SB%	GDP	P/PA	BABIP	H-A	L-R
BAL	76	34	69%	154	3.71	.296	.036	-.026
BOS	68	17	80%	131	4.02	.299	.032	.004
CHA	160	74	68%	148	3.77	.292	.001	.027
CLE	91	33	73%	118	3.86	.293	-.023	.004
DET	69	30	70%	118	3.80	.311	.019	.010
KC	115	50	70%	152	3.74	.305	.029	.004
LAA	104	52	67%	125	3.83	.281	.008	-.004
MIN	68	28	71%	159	3.79	.306	.014	.004
NYA	103	30	77%	124	3.92	.300	.012	.003
OAK	156	38	80%	129	3.80	.297	.006	-.012
SEA	142	39	78%	111	3.89	.282	-.000	.003
TB	172	47	79%	92	3.94	.293	.020	.006
TEX	123	48	72%	129	3.73	.307	.032	-.003
TOR	58	20	74%	114	3.72	.269	-.003	-.006
Average	108	39	74%	129	3.82	.295	.013	.013

Win Probability Added — Win Shares

Team	Bat	Start	Bullpen	LI	Bat	Pitch	Field	WSAge
BAL	-15.64	-0.01	0.65	1.06	79	80	39	28.2
BOS	0.18	5.44	2.38	1.17	139	87	41	29.8
CHA	0.11	3.74	3.15	1.05	118	105	41	29.9
CLE	-12.14	-3.72	3.86	1.04	102	70	35	27.0
DET	-1.11	-1.05	2.16	1.04	125	81	37	28.1
KC	-12.78	-5.00	3.79	1.10	109	61	31	28.6
LAA	-15.54	8.86	5.68	1.16	112	90	39	29.9
MIN	0.48	6.39	6.13	1.06	140	97	45	28.6
NYA	3.85	4.93	5.22	1.00	147	91	46	30.3
OAK	-10.89	8.41	2.48	0.99	100	96	47	26.9
SEA	-19.81	2.69	-2.89	1.07	59	83	41	29.0
TB	-0.58	6.14	9.45	1.02	154	90	44	27.3
TEX	-1.18	2.14	8.03	1.16	125	99	46	28.1
TOR	-1.87	4.76	1.11	1.01	131	85	39	29.1
Average	-6.21	3.12	3.66	1.07	117	87	41	28.6

Leverage Index (LI) for bullpen only.

Miscellaneous Pitching and Fielding Stats

Team	DER	Fld %	UER	SBA	CS	%CS	PO	E	TE	FE	DP	GIDP	H-A	R-L
BAL	.694	.982	52	110	27	25%	8	105	33	67	141	116	-.010	-.013
BOS	.696	.982	65	211	42	20%	15	111	56	53	132	116	-.015	-.007
CHA	.682	.983	46	144	39	27%	24	103	53	48	158	140	.001	-.014
CLE	.691	.982	68	183	58	32%	13	110	44	64	179	159	-.020	-.014
DET	.693	.982	53	151	50	33%	9	109	39	64	171	147	-.022	.001
KC	.682	.980	51	192	55	29%	16	121	48	71	138	109	.005	.011
LAA	.696	.981	51	174	41	24%	20	113	56	57	116	96	.003	-.029
MIN	.695	.987	33	119	37	31%	12	78	41	35	150	123	-.009	.003
NYA	.711	.988	42	155	23	15%	9	69	38	30	161	137	-.003	.004
OAK	.714	.984	60	120	32	27%	27	99	52	44	147	132	-.019	-.039
SEA	.709	.982	70	102	29	28%	9	110	42	67	145	124	-.016	-.014
TB	.712	.986	38	119	30	25%	11	85	43	40	134	115	-.022	.005
TEX	.708	.982	51	151	35	23%	10	105	44	60	133	119	.006	-.011
TOR	.692	.985	52	104	35	34%	7	92	57	35	172	148	-.022	-.006
Average	.698	.983	52	145	38	26%	14	101	46	53	148	127	-.010	-.009

Batted Ball Batting Stats

Team	% of PA		% of Batted Balls					Out %		Runs Per Event				Total Runs vs. Avg.				
	K%	BB%	GB%	LD%	FB%	IF/F	HR/OF	GB	OF	NIP	GB	LD	OF	NIP	GB	LD	FB	Tot
BAL	17	8	46	18	37	.10	.09	74	83	.03	.04	.38	.15	-24	1	-0	-37	-61
BOS	18	10	40	18	43	.09	.12	74	81	.05	.04	.39	.22	19	-10	7	110	127
CHA	15	9	46	18	37	.10	.12	74	84	.06	.04	.38	.19	16	4	2	21	43
CLE	19	10	45	18	37	.10	.09	75	83	.04	.04	.37	.16	6	-5	-14	-35	-48
DET	18	9	43	19	38	.10	.10	71	83	.04	.06	.39	.17	2	29	28	-2	57
KC	15	8	44	18	38	.09	.07	74	81	.05	.04	.38	.15	2	7	16	-24	2
LAA	18	9	46	17	37	.07	.10	77	82	.04	.03	.36	.18	-12	-19	-35	12	-54
MIN	15	10	46	19	35	.08	.09	75	81	.06	.03	.40	.19	28	-14	38	16	68
NYA	18	12	45	18	37	.09	.13	74	84	.07	.04	.40	.21	56	8	14	55	134
OAK	17	9	42	19	39	.11	.07	73	84	.05	.05	.37	.13	9	8	13	-70	-41
SEA	20	8	45	18	38	.11	.07	75	84	.02	.04	.37	.12	-33	-7	-34	-104	-177
TB	21	12	43	18	40	.10	.11	73	84	.05	.05	.39	.18	35	13	-23	11	37
TEX	16	9	45	19	36	.09	.11	74	83	.05	.04	.38	.19	10	8	28	17	62
TOR	19	9	40	17	43	.12	.15	75	84	.03	.04	.38	.24	-20	-22	-22	120	56
MLB Average	*18*	*9*	*44*	*18*	*38*	*.09*	*.10*	*74*	*83*	*.04*	*.04*	*.38*	*.18*	--	--	--	--	--

Batted Ball Pitching Stats

Team	% of PA		% of Batted Balls					Out %		Runs Per Event				Total Runs vs. Avg.				
	K%	BB%	GB%	LD%	FB%	IF/F	HR/OF	GB	OF	NIP	GB	LD	OF	NIP	GB	LD	FB	Tot
BAL	16	9	42	18	40	.09	.11	73	84	.05	.05	.41	.18	16	10	29	34	89
BOS	19	10	44	18	39	.10	.10	75	79	.04	.04	.36	.20	11	-14	-27	34	5
CHA	19	8	45	18	37	.08	.09	72	83	.03	.06	.38	.16	-19	30	6	-32	-15
CLE	16	10	48	17	35	.08	.10	74	81	.07	.04	.39	.20	42	-3	6	26	71
DET	17	10	44	18	38	.10	.09	74	82	.05	.04	.38	.17	19	-0	1	-8	12
KC	16	9	42	19	39	.08	.11	72	83	.05	.06	.40	.18	20	26	35	38	118
LAA	18	10	43	18	39	.08	.09	75	82	.05	.04	.38	.17	12	-5	2	9	19
MIN	17	7	45	18	37	.09	.10	75	83	.02	.03	.41	.18	-40	-12	35	1	-16
NYA	19	10	44	17	39	.09	.11	74	85	.04	.04	.36	.18	8	-1	-42	6	-29
OAK	18	9	46	17	37	.10	.11	77	83	.04	.02	.37	.18	-1	-34	-29	-11	-74
SEA	16	8	43	18	39	.09	.10	75	85	.04	.04	.38	.15	-10	2	7	-27	-29
TB	19	9	41	18	41	.11	.11	74	85	.03	.04	.38	.18	-25	-9	-17	6	-44
TEX	19	10	41	18	40	.11	.10	74	84	.04	.04	.36	.17	8	-4	-26	-13	-36
TOR	19	10	46	18	37	.09	.10	76	81	.04	.03	.41	.20	3	-30	10	23	7
MLB Average	*18*	*9*	*44*	*18*	*38*	*.09*	*.10*	*74*	*83*	*.04*	*.04*	*.38*	*.18*	--	--	--	--	--

National League Team Stats

Runs Scored and Allowed
(adjusted for ballpark)

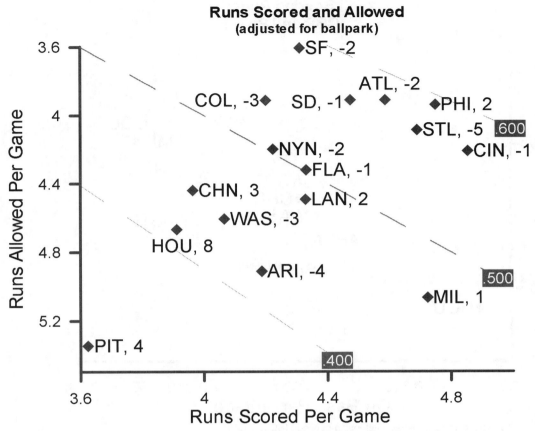

Notes: The dotted lines represent winning percentage based on run differential. The number after each team name represents the difference between the team's actual record and its run differential record.

	Team Record					Scoring Runs			Preventing Runs				Projection	
Team	W	L	RS	RA	RS-RA	AB/RSP	BA/RSP	HR	ERA	HRA	K	DER	PWINS	VAR
ARI	65	97	713	836	-123	1,339	.266	180	4.81	210	1,070	.692	69	-4
ATL	91	71	738	629	109	1,468	.262	139	3.56	126	1,241	.697	93	-2
CHN	75	87	685	767	-82	1,342	.262	149	4.19	154	1,268	.685	72	3
CIN	91	71	790	685	105	1,380	.278	188	4.01	158	1,130	.705	92	-1
COL	83	79	770	717	53	1,344	.269	173	4.14	139	1,234	.685	86	-3
FLA	80	82	719	717	2	1,401	.258	152	4.08	134	1,168	.685	81	-1
HOU	76	86	611	729	-118	1,299	.255	108	4.09	140	1,210	.681	68	8
LAN	80	82	667	692	-25	1,338	.256	120	4.02	134	1,274	.699	78	2
MIL	77	85	750	804	-54	1,445	.262	182	4.58	173	1,258	.680	76	1
NYN	79	83	656	652	4	1,326	.252	128	3.70	135	1,106	.695	81	-2
PHI	97	65	772	640	132	1,425	.260	166	3.67	168	1,183	.701	95	2
PIT	57	105	587	866	-279	1,266	.250	126	5.00	167	1,026	.675	53	4
STL	86	76	736	641	95	1,377	.270	150	3.57	133	1,094	.697	91	-5
SD	90	72	665	581	84	1,324	.263	132	3.39	139	1,295	.706	91	-1
SF	92	70	697	583	114	1,333	.248	162	3.36	134	1,331	.711	94	-2
WAS	69	93	655	742	-87	1,316	.253	149	4.13	151	1,068	.687	72	-3
Average	81	82	701	705	-4	1,358	.260	150	4.02	150	1,185	.692	81	0

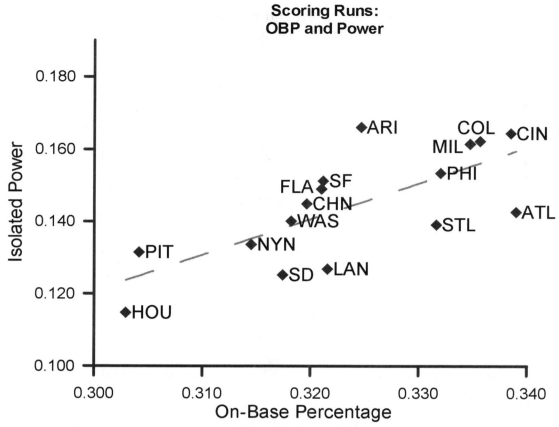

Scoring Runs: OBP and Power

The dotted line shows the relationship between ISO and OBP.

Team	Runs	PA	H	1B	2B	3B	HR	TB	SO	BB	HBP	SH	SF	BA	OBP	SLG	GPA	ISO
ARI	713	6,183	1,366	851	301	34	180	2,275	1,529	589	39	41	41	.250	.325	.416	.250	.166
ATL	738	6,252	1,411	935	312	25	139	2,190	1,140	634	51	69	35	.258	.339	.401	.253	.143
CHN	685	6,140	1,414	940	298	27	149	2,213	1,236	479	50	60	38	.257	.320	.401	.244	.145
CIN	790	6,285	1,515	1,004	293	30	188	2,432	1,218	522	68	66	50	.272	.338	.436	.261	.164
COL	770	6,265	1,452	955	270	54	173	2,349	1,274	585	47	56	47	.263	.336	.425	.257	.162
FLA	719	6,194	1,403	920	294	37	152	2,227	1,375	514	55	51	43	.254	.321	.403	.245	.149
HOU	611	6,005	1,348	963	252	25	108	1,974	1,025	415	33	75	29	.247	.303	.362	.227	.115
LAN	667	6,140	1,368	949	270	29	120	2,056	1,184	533	46	85	50	.252	.322	.379	.239	.127
MIL	750	6,304	1,471	963	293	33	182	2,376	1,216	546	81	35	35	.262	.335	.424	.257	.161
NYN	656	6,144	1,361	927	266	40	128	2,091	1,095	502	46	74	57	.249	.314	.383	.237	.134
PHI	772	6,291	1,451	961	290	34	166	2,307	1,064	560	63	44	43	.260	.332	.413	.253	.153
PIT	587	5,974	1,303	874	276	27	126	2,011	1,207	463	33	58	33	.242	.304	.373	.230	.131
STL	736	6,241	1,456	1,003	285	18	150	2,227	1,027	541	50	66	40	.263	.332	.402	.250	.139
SD	665	6,148	1,338	946	236	24	132	2,018	1,183	538	50	79	46	.246	.317	.371	.236	.125
SF	697	6,143	1,411	935	284	30	162	2,241	1,099	487	50	76	41	.257	.321	.408	.247	.151
WAS	655	6,100	1,355	925	250	31	149	2,114	1,220	503	60	71	47	.250	.318	.390	.241	.140
Average	701	6,176	1,401	941	279	31	150	2,194	1,193	526	51	63	42	.255	.324	.399	.246	.144

Preventing Runs:
Pitching and Fielding

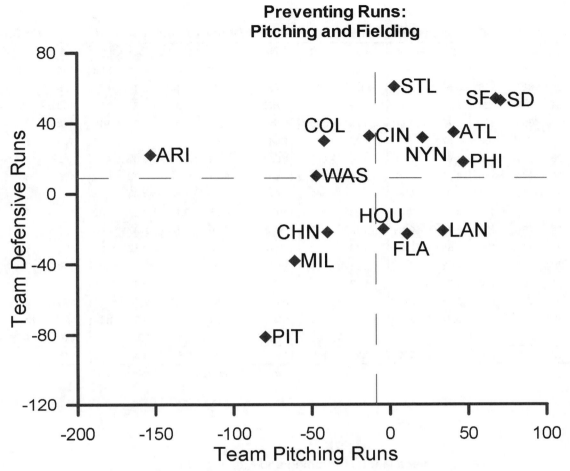

The dotted lines represent the league averages.
Positive numbers imply a positive performance on both fielding and pitching axes.
Refer to John Dewan's "The Pitching and Defense Splits" for more information.

Team	RA	IP	BFP	H	HR	TBA	K	BB	ShO	Hlds	Sv	Op	Sv/Hld%	ERA	FIP	UERA	DER
ARI	836	1432.0	6,260	1,503	210	2,481	1,070	548	3	48	35	59	78%	4.81	4.80	0.45	.692
ATL	629	1439.0	6,052	1,326	126	2,030	1,241	505	9	77	41	58	87%	3.56	3.63	0.38	.697
CHN	767	1436.0	6,298	1,409	154	2,198	1,268	605	14	68	40	54	89%	4.19	4.14	0.62	.685
CIN	685	1453.0	6,182	1,404	158	2,190	1,130	524	9	74	43	63	85%	4.01	4.17	0.23	.705
COL	717	1442.0	6,143	1,405	139	2,169	1,234	525	12	82	35	56	85%	4.14	3.83	0.34	.685
FLA	717	1438.0	6,217	1,433	134	2,187	1,168	549	17	86	39	64	83%	4.08	3.95	0.41	.685
HOU	729	1439.0	6,221	1,446	140	2,229	1,210	548	11	82	45	60	89%	4.09	3.92	0.47	.681
LAN	692	1441.0	6,141	1,323	134	2,047	1,274	539	16	70	41	59	86%	4.02	3.72	0.31	.699
MIL	804	1439.0	6,324	1,487	173	2,381	1,258	582	7	86	35	56	85%	4.58	4.24	0.44	.680
NYN	652	1453.0	6,245	1,438	135	2,179	1,106	545	19	62	36	52	86%	3.70	4.00	0.34	.695
PHI	640	1456.0	6,095	1,402	168	2,237	1,183	416	21	61	40	59	84%	3.67	3.96	0.28	.701
PIT	866	1411.0	6,300	1,567	167	2,498	1,026	538	6	67	31	48	85%	5.00	4.48	0.52	.675
STL	641	1453.0	6,137	1,412	133	2,133	1,094	477	16	59	32	42	90%	3.57	3.90	0.40	.697
SD	581	1456.0	6,058	1,305	139	2,006	1,295	517	20	111	49	64	91%	3.39	3.68	0.20	.706
SF	583	1461.0	6,159	1,279	134	2,007	1,331	578	17	65	57	73	88%	3.36	3.74	0.23	.711
WAS	742	1435.0	6,214	1,469	151	2,267	1,068	512	5	73	37	57	85%	4.13	4.12	0.53	.687
Average	705	1442.8	6,190	1,413	150	2,202	1,185	532	13	73	40	58	86%	4.02	4.02	0.38	.692

Running and Miscellaneous Batting Stats

Team	SB	CS	SB%	GDP	P/PA	BABIP	H-A	L-R
ARI	86	41	68%	115	4.01	.312	.032	.001
ATL	63	29	68%	136	3.89	.301	-.008	.002
CHN	55	31	64%	124	3.79	.304	.019	-.006
CIN	93	43	68%	113	3.73	.314	.020	.005
COL	99	41	71%	103	3.87	.310	.042	-.009
FLA	92	26	78%	108	3.91	.309	.014	-.011
HOU	100	36	74%	130	3.76	.285	.020	.012
LAN	92	50	65%	123	3.91	.299	-.011	.013
MIL	81	26	76%	116	3.81	.304	.003	.017
NYN	130	44	75%	101	3.78	.287	.012	.009
PHI	108	21	84%	121	3.85	.292	.010	.002
PIT	87	36	71%	119	3.82	.288	.031	-.010
STL	79	41	66%	124	3.76	.296	-.003	-.031
SD	124	50	71%	106	3.86	.290	-.026	-.011
SF	55	32	63%	159	3.74	.293	.025	-.006
WAS	110	41	73%	125	3.83	.294	.002	.008
Average	91	37	71%	120	3.83	.299	.011	-.001

Win Probability Added / Win Shares

Team	Bat	Start	Bullpen	LI	Bat	Pitch	Field	WSAge
ARI	-8.53	0.47	-7.95	1.03	105	56	34	26.4
ATL	6.20	1.10	2.70	0.99	128	102	43	29.2
CHN	-10.16	2.63	1.53	0.98	100	85	40	29.3
CIN	7.38	1.31	1.31	1.10	141	90	43	28.6
COL	-4.50	2.73	3.77	1.14	105	99	45	28.1
FLA	-4.59	3.57	0.02	1.07	115	87	38	26.6
HOU	-5.21	-0.77	0.98	1.02	105	86	36	29.6
LAN	-5.51	2.88	1.64	0.97	119	84	37	29.4
MIL	0.28	-3.11	-1.17	1.00	143	60	29	27.5
WAS	-11.00	-3.32	2.33	1.03	99	74	34	28.6
NYN	-10.36	4.54	3.82	1.09	105	89	43	28.8
PHI	1.97	10.12	3.91	1.07	139	103	49	31.5
PIT	-12.62	-10.70	-0.68	0.83	95	50	27	26.1
STL	0.41	2.19	2.40	0.95	125	91	42	28.9
SD	-4.04	3.96	9.08	1.04	120	102	48	28.7
SF	-1.73	7.19	5.54	1.11	110	114	52	29.0
Average	-3.87	1.55	1.83	1.03	116	86	40	28.5

Leverage Index (LI) for bullpen only.

Miscellaneous Pitching and Fielding Stats

Team	DER	Fld %	UER	SBA	CS	%CS	PO	E	TE	FE	DP	GIDP	H-A	R-L
ARI	.692	.983	71	151	36	24%	11	102	43	58	152	125	.006	-.012
ATL	.697	.980	60	146	44	30%	12	126	61	63	167	139	-.016	-.014
CHN	.685	.979	99	145	31	21%	8	126	56	70	137	119	-.004	-.017
CIN	.705	.988	37	105	34	32%	9	72	31	40	142	121	-.007	.003
COL	.685	.984	54	124	43	35%	16	101	50	50	182	155	.012	-.011
FLA	.685	.979	65	155	44	28%	7	123	65	57	130	103	.006	-.008
HOU	.681	.983	75	133	44	33%	6	103	42	60	135	113	-.016	-.004
LAN	.699	.984	49	136	39	29%	15	98	44	53	124	102	-.020	.002
MIL	.680	.983	71	131	31	24%	8	101	50	51	142	112	-.018	-.011
NYN	.695	.986	55	77	26	34%	7	87	45	41	159	136	-.028	-.001
PHI	.701	.986	46	115	31	27%	8	83	34	48	158	132	.001	.007
PIT	.675	.979	82	148	32	22%	16	127	57	68	120	102	-.031	-.009
STL	.697	.984	64	90	37	41%	12	99	42	56	172	152	-.013	-.023
SD	.706	.988	32	118	39	33%	19	72	36	35	141	118	-.048	-.023
SF	.711	.988	37	164	49	30%	12	73	38	35	110	91	-.019	.011
WAS	.687	.979	84	114	35	31%	9	127	61	65	148	126	-.025	-.019
Average	.692	.984	61	128	37	29%	11	101	47	53	145	122	-.014	-.008

Batted Ball Batting Stats

Team	% of PA		% of Batted Balls					Out %		Runs Per Event				Total Runs vs. Avg.				
	K%	BB%	GB%	LD%	FB%	IF/F	HR/OF	GB	OF	NIP	GB	LD	OF	NIP	GB	LD	FB	Tot
ARI	25	10	41	18	41	.10	.12	73	82	.02	.05	.41	.22	-27	-8	-6	52	11
ATL	18	11	45	19	37	.08	.09	74	83	.06	.04	.39	.17	38	-0	13	-17	34
CHN	20	9	44	19	37	.07	.10	74	82	.02	.04	.38	.18	-27	-6	6	6	-21
CIN	19	9	43	19	38	.09	.12	70	83	.04	.07	.38	.20	-4	40	17	42	96
COL	20	10	42	19	39	.09	.11	74	83	.04	.05	.41	.20	4	-4	29	34	63
FLA	22	9	45	18	37	.09	.11	72	82	.02	.06	.40	.20	-30	18	-6	8	-8
HOU	17	7	47	18	35	.10	.08	75	84	.03	.03	.37	.14	-32	-16	-16	-72	-136
LAN	19	9	45	20	35	.09	.09	74	84	.04	.04	.38	.15	-4	-9	29	-65	-49
MIL	19	10	45	18	37	.10	.12	73	83	.04	.05	.39	.21	9	17	7	38	71
NYN	18	9	43	18	40	.10	.08	75	83	.04	.04	.37	.15	-6	-12	-21	-29	-68
PHI	17	10	45	18	37	.08	.11	74	82	.06	.04	.37	.19	24	-6	-4	28	43
PIT	20	8	47	17	36	.10	.09	73	83	.02	.05	.38	.17	-35	7	-34	-40	-102
SD	19	10	45	18	36	.12	.09	76	82	.04	.04	.37	.16	-2	-16	-18	-48	-84
SF	18	9	45	18	37	.09	.11	75	82	.04	.04	.38	.19	-9	-19	-2	15	-15
STL	16	9	46	19	35	.09	.10	73	85	.05	.05	.37	.16	18	16	6	-25	14
WAS	20	9	47	17	35	.08	.11	75	84	.03	.04	.40	.18	-14	-4	-17	-17	-51
MLB Average	18	9	44	18	38	.09	.10	74	83	.04	.04	.38	.18	--	--	--	--	--

Batted Ball Pitching Stats

Team	% of PA		% of Batted Balls					Out %		Runs Per Event				Total Runs vs. Avg.				
	K%	BB%	GB%	LD%	FB%	IF/F	HR/OF	GB	OF	NIP	GB	LD	OF	NIP	GB	LD	FB	Tot
ARI	17	10	42	19	39	.10	.13	72	84	.05	.05	.37	.21	19	17	13	73	121
ATL	21	9	50	18	33	.09	.10	75	82	.03	.04	.39	.18	-19	-13	-16	-34	-82
CHN	20	11	43	19	38	.10	.10	72	82	.05	.05	.37	.19	18	8	-8	15	33
CIN	18	9	43	19	38	.10	.10	74	86	.04	.05	.37	.16	-0	4	-5	-32	-34
COL	20	9	46	19	34	.09	.10	75	82	.03	.04	.39	.19	-8	-13	15	-9	-16
FLA	19	10	44	18	38	.09	.09	71	83	.04	.07	.38	.16	5	40	-4	-29	12
HOU	19	9	44	19	37	.08	.09	72	83	.04	.05	.41	.16	-4	16	28	-21	20
LAN	21	10	45	18	37	.10	.09	76	82	.03	.03	.40	.17	-8	-21	-6	-29	-65
MIL	20	10	42	19	39	.08	.11	72	82	.04	.05	.39	.20	5	9	21	42	77
NYN	18	10	45	19	37	.10	.09	74	84	.05	.04	.39	.16	11	-2	10	-36	-17
PHI	19	8	47	17	37	.10	.12	75	81	.02	.04	.37	.21	-41	-6	-35	35	-48
PIT	16	10	44	19	37	.09	.11	71	81	.06	.06	.39	.20	24	47	41	42	154
SD	21	9	46	18	36	.08	.10	76	82	.02	.03	.36	.18	-29	-25	-42	-19	-116
SF	22	10	42	17	41	.13	.09	74	84	.03	.05	.38	.16	-5	-9	-37	-48	-98
STL	18	9	50	18	33	.07	.10	74	83	.04	.04	.38	.17	-13	-4	-6	-30	-52
WAS	17	9	44	19	36	.10	.10	74	83	.04	.04	.39	.18	2	-1	39	-6	34
MLB Average	18	9	44	18	38	.09	.10	74	83	.04	.04	.38	.18	--	--	--	--	--

Arizona Diamondbacks

Stat Facts:
- Stephen Drew's H-A was exactly .000
- Rodrigo Lopez led the majors in HRA
- Lopez allowed 22 SB in 24 attempts
- Barry Enright's FIP was far higher than his ERA
- Gerardo Parra tied for the ML lead in LF TE
- Justin Upton led the NL in RF TE
- Upton had 1 assist
- Adam LaRoche tied for the ML lead in 1B FE
- Chris Young tied for the ML lead in CF FE
- Kelly Johnson turned the most DP in the majors
- Mark Reynolds had 211 strikeouts, and 99 hits
- Dontrelle Willis walked 26% of his BFP

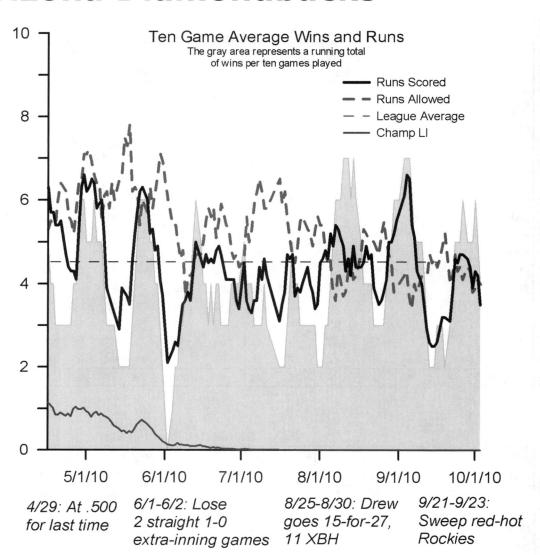

Ten Game Average Wins and Runs
The gray area represents a running total of wins per ten games played

— Runs Scored
- - Runs Allowed
- - League Average
— Champ LI

4/29: At .500 for last time

6/1-6/2: Lose 2 straight 1-0 extra-inning games

8/25-8/30: Drew goes 15-for-27, 11 XBH

9/21-9/23: Sweep red-hot Rockies

7/23: Johnson hits for cycle, but Dbacks lose

Sept/Oct: Reynolds hits .078 with 31 Ks in 64 AB

Team Batting and Pitching/Fielding Stats by Month

	April	May	June	July	Aug	Sept/Oct
Wins	11	9	11	7	16	11
Losses	12	20	16	18	13	18
RS/G	5.8	4.2	3.9	4.1	5.1	3.4
RA/G	6.0	6.3	4.6	5.8	4.3	4.1
OBP	.346	.318	.324	.328	.332	.303
SLG	.472	.401	.406	.398	.439	.385
FIP	5.04	5.41	4.26	4.70	4.66	4.76
DER	.687	.670	.692	.680	.716	.727

Batting Stats

Player	BR	Runs	RBI	PA	Outs	H	2B	3B	HR	TB	K	BB	IBB	HBP	SH	SF	SB	CS	GDP	H-A	L^R	BA	OBP	SLG	GPA
Johnson K *	96	93	71	671	438	166	36	5	26	290	148	79	1	2	3	2	13	7	12	.066	-.031	.284	.370	.496	.276
Young C	87	94	91	664	451	150	33	0	27	264	145	74	0	2	1	3	28	7	10	.067	.024	.257	.341	.452	.253
Drew S *	82	83	61	633	421	157	33	12	15	259	108	62	2	3	2	1	10	5	8	.000	.009	.278	.352	.458	.260
LaRoche A *	76	75	100	615	423	146	37	2	25	262	172	48	4	3	0	4	0	1	8	.011	.018	.261	.320	.468	.248
Reynolds M	70	79	85	596	412	99	17	2	32	216	211	83	7	9	0	5	7	4	8	.062	.071	.198	.320	.433	.240
Upton J	69	73	69	571	388	135	27	3	17	219	152	64	5	4	1	7	18	8	20	.010	-.001	.273	.356	.442	.258
Montero M *	37	36	43	331	229	79	20	2	9	130	71	29	3	2	0	3	0	1	10	-.015	.050	.266	.332	.438	.246
Parra G *	35	31	30	393	277	95	19	6	3	135	76	23	10	2	3	1	1	0	8	.045	-.009	.261	.308	.371	.220
Snyder C	27	22	32	234	155	45	8	0	10	83	61	36	6	1	1	1	0	0	5	.001	-.027	.231	.352	.426	.252
Ryal R	19	19	11	222	159	54	7	1	3	72	67	8	0	6	1	0	0	3	3	-.004	.028	.261	.308	.348	.214
Jackson C	15	19	11	172	120	36	11	0	1	50	18	20	2	0	0	1	4	1	4	.041	.074	.238	.326	.331	.218
Abreu T +	11	16	13	201	157	45	11	1	1	61	47	4	0	0	0	4	2	1	8	.066	.036	.233	.244	.316	.180
Gillespie C	10	11	12	113	83	24	8	0	2	38	29	7	1	1	0	1	1	1	2	-.038	-.075	.231	.283	.365	.208
Hester J	9	9	7	106	77	20	7	0	2	33	32	11	1	0	0	0	1	0	2	-.052	.019	.211	.292	.347	.208
Haren D	9	8	7	57	35	20	6	0	1	29	9	1	0	0	1	0	0	0	0	-.020	.005	.364	.375	.527	.286
Church R *	8	9	7	55	36	13	5	0	2	24	19	4	1	2	0	0	0	0	0	.018	.321	.265	.345	.490	.264
Allen B *	7	5	6	56	33	12	3	0	1	18	20	10	1	0	0	1	0	0	0	.125	.072	.267	.393	.400	.263
Roberts R	5	8	9	71	53	13	4	0	2	23	17	3	1	0	1	1	0	0	0	.081	-.133	.197	.229	.348	.181
Kennedy I	4	7	2	67	43	11	1	0	0	12	24	7	0	0	5	1	0	0	0	-.037	-.004	.204	.290	.222	.177
Ojeda A +	3	6	5	92	68	15	3	0	0	18	8	8	0	0	3	2	0	1	3	.019	.073	.190	.258	.228	.165
Enright B	2	1	6	37	25	8	1	0	0	9	9	0	0	0	3	1	0	0	0	.074	-.016	.242	.235	.273	.166
Jackson E	1	5	3	43	32	6	0	0	1	9	22	2	0	0	3	0	0	0	0	.153	.131	.158	.200	.237	.142

Only includes batters with at least one Base Run. Italicized stats have been adjusted for home park.

Batted Ball Batting Stats

Player	% of PA		% of Batted Balls					Out %		Runs Per Event				Total Runs vs. Avg.				
	K%	BB%	GB%	LD%	FB%	IF/F	HR/OF	GB	OF	NIP	GB	LD	OF	NIP	GB	LD	FB	Tot
Johnson Ke	22	12	41	21	38	.02	.16	73	79	.05	.06	.40	.28	4	2	5	20	31
Drew St	17	10	40	19	41	.09	.09	66	84	.06	.10	.42	.16	3	10	7	2	22
Young Ch	22	11	34	17	50	.12	.14	72	84	.04	.06	.42	.22	2	0	-1	13	15
Upton Ju	27	12	41	19	39	.09	.14	68	77	.03	.05	.37	.28	0	1	-2	11	10
LaRoche Ad	28	8	38	18	44	.05	.15	76	79	-.01	.03	.44	.28	-9	-4	0	20	7
Snyder Ch	26	16	42	12	46	.15	.17	72	86	.06	.05	.53	.26	3	-1	-3	3	3
Reynolds Ma	35	15	32	13	55	.16	.24	75	83	.03	.03	.38	.37	1	-6	-15	23	3
Montero Mi	21	9	38	19	43	.08	.10	78	77	.03	-0.00	.41	.23	-1	-5	2	7	3
Jackson Co	10	12	38	28	34	.13	.03	76	95	.13	.03	.36	-.02	3	-1	5	-8	-1
Hester Jo	30	10	35	19	46	.21	.09	68	86	0.00	.08	.44	.14	-1	0	-0	-2	-3
Gillespie Co	26	7	55	16	29	.14	.11	69	88	-.01	.09	.40	.14	-2	2	-1	-3	-3
Ryal Ru	30	6	45	16	39	.13	.06	56	89	-.03	.14	.53	.07	-5	6	1	-6	-5
Parra Ge	19	6	51	20	29	.02	.04	80	75	0.00	.01	.41	.17	-5	-4	4	-3	-8
Abreu Et	23	2	46	21	33	.10	.02	85	74	-.08	-.04	.39	.15	-7	-6	1	-3	-15
MLB Average	*18*	*9*	*44*	*18*	*38*	*.09*	*.10*	*74*	*83*	*.04*	*.04*	*.38*	*.18*	--	--	--	--	--

Only includes batters with at least one hundred Plate Appearances.

Pitching Stats

Player	PRC	IP	BFP	G	GS	K	BB	IBB	HBP	H	HR	DP	DER	SB	CS	PO	W	L	Sv	Op	Hld	H-A	R^L	RA	ERA	FIP
Kennedy I	80	194.0	810	32	32	168	70	2	10	163	26	13	.733	12	6	1	9	10	0	0	0	-.006	.018	4.04	3.80	4.41
Hudson D	65	79.7	301	11	11	70	16	1	4	51	7	8	.779	1	0	0	7	1	0	0	0	.000	.012	1.69	1.69	3.30
Lopez R	53	200.0	874	33	33	116	56	1	3	227	37	19	.693	22	2	3	7	16	0	0	0	-.008	-.018	5.67	5.00	5.31
Haren D	48	141.0	607	21	21	141	29	4	3	161	23	10	.647	15	7	1	7	8	0	0	0	-.006	-.023	5.04	4.60	3.91
Jackson E	40	134.3	587	21	21	104	60	2	5	141	13	19	.672	11	4	0	6	10	0	0	0	.023	-.026	5.36	5.16	4.31
Enright B	37	99.0	410	17	17	49	29	0	1	97	20	13	.743	6	3	1	6	7	0	0	0	-.034	.024	3.91	3.91	5.74
Heilman A	25	72.0	316	70	0	55	26	4	5	73	9	5	.710	4	1	0	5	8	6	14	12	-.002	.069	4.63	4.50	4.42
Saunders J *	23	82.7	358	13	13	50	19	0	4	97	11	11	.664	5	4	3	3	7	0	0	0	-.075	-.065	5.44	4.25	4.55
Gutierrez J	18	56.7	247	58	0	47	23	5	4	55	13	5	.738	8	0	0	0	6	15	17	8	-.116	-.073	5.24	5.08	5.68
Vasquez E	17	53.7	240	57	0	55	38	3	6	46	6	7	.704	3	4	1	1	6	0	2	6	-.036	.033	5.37	5.20	4.89
Boyer B	17	57.0	251	54	0	29	29	1	1	59	3	13	.683	4	0	0	3	2	0	4	5	-.064	-.100	5.05	4.26	4.39
Demel S	9	37.0	165	37	0	33	12	2	1	42	5	4	.658	1	0	0	2	1	2	2	4	-.044	.027	6.57	5.35	4.06
Rosa C	6	20.0	89	22	0	9	12	2	0	20	1	3	.716	1	0	0	0	2	0	1	1	.083	-.168	4.50	4.50	4.45
Carrasco D	6	22.7	98	18	0	20	12	2	1	18	1	4	.688	3	0	0	1	0	0	1	2	.114	-.013	5.96	3.18	3.46
Norberto J *	5	20.0	94	33	0	15	22	1	0	16	3	3	.759	1	1	0	0	2	0	1	3	-.035	-.013	5.85	5.85	6.80
Qualls C	5	38.0	190	43	0	34	15	4	1	61	5	4	.563	4	0	0	1	4	12	16	3	-.017	-.045	9.71	8.29	4.06
Willis D *	5	22.3	114	6	5	14	27	0	3	24	3	4	.687	6	2	1	1	1	0	0	0	-.115	-.220	6.85	6.85	7.72
Benson K	4	14.0	67	3	3	8	6	0	1	18	2	1	.660	4	0	0	1	1	0	0	0	-.094	-.035	5.79	5.14	5.41
Rosales L	3	16.3	80	16	0	12	9	2	0	25	2	2	.596	2	1	0	2	0	0	0	2	-.047	-.010	7.16	7.16	4.97
Valdez C	3	20.0	97	9	2	13	10	2	1	29	2	2	.606	1	0	0	1	2	0	0	0	.129	-.041	8.55	7.65	4.55
Howry B	1	14.3	67	14	0	6	6	1	0	18	6	0	.755	0	0	0	1	0	0	1	1	.046	.027	10.67	10.67	8.85
Buckner B	1	13.0	72	3	3	11	5	0	2	26	4	0	.560	1	1	0	0	3	0	0	0	.069	.241	11.77	11.08	7.12

Only includes pitchers with at least ten Innings Pitched. Italicized stats have been adjusted for home park.

Batted Ball Pitching Stats

Player	% of PA		% of Batted Balls					Out %		Runs Per Event				Total Runs vs. Avg.				
	K%	BB%	GB%	LD%	FB%	IF/F	HR/OF	GB	OF	NIP	GB	LD	OF	NIP	GB	LD	FB	Tot
Hudson Da	23	7	38	17	46	.18	.09	78	93	-.01	.02	.31	.09	-5	-3	-6	-8	-22
Kennedy Ia	21	10	37	19	44	.10	.12	75	90	.04	.04	.37	.16	-1	-4	-3	-2	-11
Heilman Aa	17	10	36	20	45	.13	.10	78	87	.05	.02	.44	.15	1	-2	4	-1	2
Boyer Bl	12	12	66	13	21	.15	.09	72	65	.12	.05	.29	.28	4	3	-4	-1	2
Vasquez Es	23	18	32	26	43	.15	.12	73	82	.09	.04	.24	.22	6	-1	-2	1	4
Gutierrez Ju	19	11	35	14	51	.13	.18	75	87	.05	.04	.38	.26	1	-1	-3	8	5
Demel Sa	20	8	53	16	31	.08	.15	76	66	.02	.03	.43	.38	-1	-0	0	6	5
Enright Ba	12	7	35	15	50	.12	.14	75	89	.06	.03	.44	.19	0	-2	1	8	6
Willis Do	12	26	46	26	28	.00	.16	77	88	.20	.01	.34	.22	8	-1	2	1	9
Saunders Jo	14	6	45	19	36	.05	.12	70	78	.03	.06	.35	.21	-2	3	2	6	9
Jackson Ed	18	11	50	19	31	.06	.11	73	79	.06	.06	.35	.22	4	4	-0	2	10
Haren Da	23	5	41	20	39	.08	.15	69	81	-.03	.07	.43	.25	-12	4	7	12	11
Qualls Ch	18	8	55	19	26	.00	.14	64	67	.03	.11	.42	.36	-0	7	2	6	15
Lopez Ro	13	7	38	21	41	.09	.14	72	85	.04	.06	.35	.23	-3	3	9	21	30
MLB Average	18	9	44	18	38	.09	.10	74	83	.04	.04	.38	.18	--	--	--	--	--

Only includes pitchers who faced at least one hundred batters.

Fielding Stats

Name	INN	SBA/G	CS%	ERA	WP+PB/G	PO	A	TE	FE
Catchers									
Montero M	658.3	0.86	25%	4.29	0.574	484	36	1	1
Snyder C	517.3	0.97	16%	5.38	0.505	411	32	1	0
Hester J	239.3	0.90	13%	5.04	0.940	189	10	0	0
Schmidt K	17.0	0.00	0%	4.24	0.529	12	0	0	0

Name	Inn	PO	A	TE	FE	FPct	DPS	DPT	ZRDif	OOZ	Dif
First Base											
LaRoche A	1239.0	1139	122	2	9	.991	15	1	-.001	46	5
Ryal R	140.0	127	9	3	1	.971	1	0	-.084	4	-1
Jackson C	26.0	27	2	0	0	1.000	0	0	--	0	--
Allen B	17.3	14	0	0	0	1.000	0	0	--	0	--
Reynolds M	9.0	7	1	0	0	1.000	0	0	--	0	--
Second Base											
Johnson K	1270.0	267	402	3	5	.988	34	68	.004	22	-9
Abreu T	88.3	16	18	0	3	.919	0	3	--	3	--
Ojeda A	63.0	10	19	0	0	1.000	2	0	--	2	--
Roberts R	8.0	3	4	0	0	1.000	1	1	--	0	--
Crosby B	2.0	0	1	0	0	1.000	0	0	--	0	--
Shortstop											
Drew S	1259.0	206	391	2	8	.984	42	40	-.009	58	4
Abreu T	112.0	16	33	3	3	.891	7	4	-.049	6	1
Ojeda A	60.7	8	15	0	0	1.000	2	1	--	2	--
Third Base											
Reynolds M	1214.0	101	250	8	10	.951	20	1	-.024	33	-12
Abreu T	129.0	11	33	0	1	.978	1	0	.054	3	-2
Ryal R	35.7	2	5	0	1	.875	2	0	--	0	--
Ojeda A	32.3	7	1	0	0	1.000	1	0	--	0	--
Crosby B	13.0	1	5	0	1	.857	1	0	--	1	--
Roberts R	8.0	1	1	0	0	1.000	0	0	--	0	--

Name	Inn	PO	A	TE	FE	FPct	DPS	DPT	ZRDif	OOZ	Dif
Left Field											
Parra G	569.3	146	6	3	0	.981	1	0	-.014	44	16
Jackson C	299.7	71	2	0	1	.986	0	0	.018	15	0
Ryal R	193.0	44	2	1	1	.958	1	0	.129	7	-2
Gillespie C	134.7	30	1	0	1	.969	0	0	.009	8	1
Allen B	103.7	27	0	0	0	1.000	0	0	.042	6	1
Roberts R	85.7	16	1	0	0	1.000	0	0	--	5	--
Church R	46.0	11	0	0	0	1.000	0	0	--	5	--
Center Field											
Young C	1350.0	418	10	1	6	.984	6	0	.012	86	10
Gillespie C	41.3	7	0	0	0	1.000	0	0	--	2	--
Parra G	24.7	9	1	0	0	1.000	1	0	--	1	--
Church R	16.0	9	0	0	0	1.000	0	0	--	2	--
Right Field											
Upton J	1117.0	265	1	3	1	.985	0	0	.034	61	-0
Parra G	255.0	65	2	0	0	.985	1	0	.015	13	-1
Gillespie C	59.0	10	0	0	0	1.000	0	0	--	2	--
Roberts R	1.0	0	0	0	0	0.000	0	0	--	0	--

Atlanta Braves

Stat Facts:
- Tommy Hanson led the NL in HBP and SB
- Tim Hudson induced the most GDP in the majors
- Hudson's FIP was far higher than his ERA
- Brian McCann caught the second-most innings in the majors
- McCann made the most TE of any C
- McCann tied for the most FE of NL C
- Melky Cabrera tied for the ML lead in CF TE, in 385 innings
- Yunel Escobar made 54 OOZ plays in 647 innings
- Billy Wagner struck out 39% of his BFP
- Jonny Venters and Peter Moylan both had a GB% of 68
- Christhian Marti-nez allowed 0 infield pop-ups
- Derek Lee hit 0 infield pop-ups

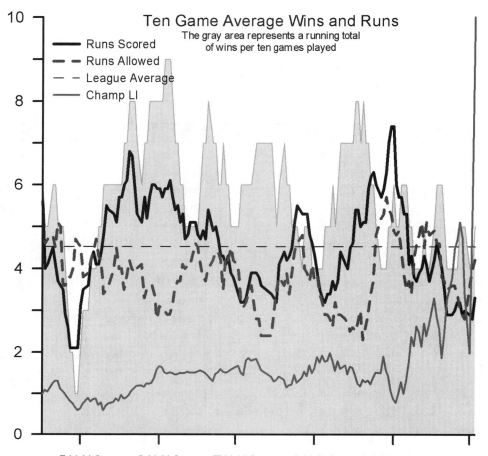

Ten Game Average Wins and Runs
The gray area represents a running total of wins per ten games played

— Runs Scored
- - Runs Allowed
— — League Average
— Champ LI

4/5: Heyward HR in debut

5/20: Conrad walk-off grand slam vs. CIN

7/22: ATL beats SD; 7-game lead

8/12: Chipper tears ACL and out for year

10/3: Cox's 2,504th win and last regular season game

Team Batting and Pitching/Fielding Stats by Month

	April	May	June	July	Aug	Sept/Oct
Wins	9	20	17	13	18	14
Losses	14	8	11	11	11	16
RS/G	3.7	5.8	4.5	4.2	5.4	3.5
RA/G	4.5	3.6	4.0	3.6	3.6	4.2
OBP	.326	.364	.346	.331	.341	.323
SLG	.342	.433	.391	.413	.454	.360
FIP	3.89	4.00	3.52	3.82	3.11	3.57
DER	.701	.701	.689	.703	.692	.681

Batting Stats

Player	BR	Runs	RBI	PA	Outs	H	2B	3B	HR	TB	K	BB	IBB	HBP	SH	SF	SB	CS	GDP	H-A	L^R	BA	OBP	SLG	GPA
Heyward J *	95	83	72	623	395	144	29	5	18	237	128	91	2	10	0	2	11	6	13	-.018	.046	.277	.393	.456	.293
Prado M	91	100	66	651	431	184	40	3	15	275	86	40	2	3	3	6	5	3	13	.046	-.029	.307	.350	.459	.274
McCann B *	81	63	77	566	364	129	25	0	21	217	98	74	10	9	0	4	5	2	12	.001	.021	.269	.375	.453	.284
Infante O	63	65	47	506	340	151	15	3	8	196	62	29	1	0	4	2	7	6	14	.023	-.051	.321	.359	.416	.267
Glaus T	57	52	71	483	329	99	18	0	16	165	100	63	2	4	0	4	0	0	16	.013	.015	.240	.344	.400	.257
Jones C +	53	47	46	381	243	84	21	0	10	135	47	61	6	0	0	3	5	0	10	.090	-.020	.265	.381	.426	.280
Cabrera M +	51	50	42	509	350	117	27	3	4	162	64	42	11	1	5	3	7	1	8	.011	-.012	.255	.317	.354	.233
Hinske E *	44	38	51	320	213	72	21	1	11	128	75	33	5	3	0	3	0	0	4	-.004	-.130	.256	.338	.456	.268
Diaz M	29	27	31	244	175	56	17	2	7	98	44	13	3	4	2	1	3	1	6	.075	.056	.250	.302	.438	.247
Gonzalez A	28	27	38	292	212	64	17	2	6	103	53	14	2	6	3	2	0	2	7	-.042	-.000	.240	.291	.386	.229
Conrad B +	27	31	33	177	118	39	11	1	8	76	45	16	0	1	4	0	5	1	0	-.007	.011	.250	.324	.487	.269
McLouth N *	26	30	24	288	201	46	12	1	6	78	57	33	2	5	6	2	7	2	3	.138	.095	.190	.298	.322	.216
Escobar Y	26	28	19	301	209	62	12	0	0	74	31	37	1	1	2	0	5	1	9	-.057	.027	.238	.334	.284	.223
Lee D	22	17	24	151	99	37	14	0	3	60	33	21	0	0	0	1	0	0	7	.034	.066	.287	.384	.465	.291
Ross D	22	15	28	145	92	35	13	2	2	58	28	20	0	1	2	1	0	1	5	.026	-.003	.289	.392	.479	.298
Ankiel R *	14	17	9	139	96	25	6	1	2	39	42	19	2	1	0	0	2	1	1	.040	.050	.210	.324	.328	.229
Blanco G *	8	9	3	66	44	18	1	1	0	21	15	8	1	0	0	0	1	2	2	.124	-.024	.310	.394	.362	.270
Hudson T	3	4	4	85	62	15	4	0	0	19	21	0	0	0	8	0	0	0	0	.028	-.003	.195	.195	.247	.150
Lowe D	2	6	3	69	46	8	4	0	0	12	14	5	0	0	11	0	0	0	1	-.050	.103	.151	.224	.226	.159
Medlen K +	2	2	2	33	22	5	1	0	0	6	14	3	0	1	2	0	0	0	0	-.296	-.194	.185	.290	.222	.188
Freeman F *	1	3	1	24	21	4	1	0	1	8	8	0	0	0	0	0	0	0	1	-.015	-.448	.167	.167	.333	.159
Hernandez D	1	5	1	10	8	1	0	0	1	4	4	0	0	0	1	0	0	0	0	.242	.290	.111	.111	.444	.162

Only includes batters with at least one Base Run. Italicized stats have been adjusted for home park.

Batted Ball Batting Stats

Player	% of PA		% of Batted Balls					Out %		Runs Per Event				Total Runs vs. Avg.				
	K%	BB%	GB%	LD%	FB%	IF/F	HR/OF	GB	OF	NIP	GB	LD	OF	NIP	GB	LD	FB	Tot
Heyward Ja	21	16	55	18	27	.08	.18	66	80	.09	.09	.41	.31	14	11	2	8	35
McCann Br	17	15	37	20	43	.09	.13	77	85	.10	.02	.42	.20	12	-3	7	8	23
Prado Ma	13	7	48	21	31	.09	.10	69	82	.04	.08	.38	.18	-2	11	11	-2	18
Jones Ch	12	16	38	18	44	.03	.09	75	83	.15	.03	.33	.16	12	-2	-1	4	13
Infante Om	12	6	47	19	34	.05	.06	65	85	.03	.09	.41	.09	-2	12	7	-8	9
Hinske Er	23	11	33	20	47	.08	.11	85	86	.04	-.02	.56	.19	0	-5	8	3	6
Ross Da	19	14	38	21	41	.08	.06	80	76	.08	-.00	.57	.17	3	-1	4	0	6
Glaus Tr	21	14	40	16	45	.06	.12	74	82	.07	.03	.36	.20	7	-2	-5	7	5
Lee De	22	14	43	23	34	.00	.09	74	83	.07	.04	.49	.16	2	-0	4	-0	5
Conrad Br	25	10	32	16	52	.14	.16	69	83	.01	.11	.34	.28	-1	2	-3	5	3
Diaz Ma	18	7	44	23	33	.00	.12	79	79	.02	-.01	.36	.24	-2	-4	3	4	1
Ankiel Ri	30	14	57	12	31	.17	.10	73	78	.03	.07	.39	.25	1	1	-3	-1	-3
Cabrera Me	13	8	49	19	32	.07	.03	73	84	.07	.05	.36	.07	2	3	2	-13	-7
Gonzalez Al	18	7	36	16	48	.15	.07	79	78	.01	.02	.35	.16	-3	-3	-3	0	-8
Escobar Yu	10	13	51	18	31	.11	.00	78	87	.14	.02	.36	.01	6	-2	0	-12	-8
McLouth Na	20	13	40	16	44	.11	.08	84	83	.07	-.02	.33	.14	3	-6	-5	-3	-11
MLB Average	18	9	44	18	38	.09	.10	74	83	.04	.04	.38	.18	--	--	--	--	--

Only includes batters with at least one hundred Plate Appearances.

Pitching Stats

Player	PRC	IP	BFP	G	GS	K	BB	IBB	HBP	H	HR	DP	DER	SB	CS	PO	W	L	Sv	Op	Hld	H-A	R^L	RA	ERA	FIP
Hudson T	110	228.7	920	34	34	139	74	8	9	189	20	36	.736	11	11	3	17	9	0	0	0	-.033	-.014	2.91	2.83	4.10
Hanson T	83	202.7	845	34	34	173	56	3	14	182	14	13	.709	33	4	2	10	11	0	0	0	-.014	.023	3.82	3.33	3.38
Lowe D	71	193.7	824	33	33	136	61	10	4	204	18	31	.674	10	11	1	16	12	0	0	0	-.019	-.014	4.09	4.00	3.85
Wagner B *	58	69.3	268	71	0	104	22	3	3	38	5	4	.746	3	1	1	7	2	37	44	0	-.018	-.097	1.82	1.43	2.09
Venters J *	42	83.0	350	79	0	93	39	2	8	61	1	13	.689	3	2	0	4	4	1	5	24	-.010	.006	3.25	1.95	2.74
Medlen K	41	107.7	438	31	14	83	21	1	3	108	13	17	.692	4	1	2	6	2	0	0	1	-.016	-.022	4.01	3.68	3.86
Jurrjens J	36	116.3	500	20	20	86	42	5	2	120	13	11	.695	6	3	1	7	6	0	0	0	.015	-.051	4.87	4.64	4.18
Kimbrel C	30	20.7	88	21	0	40	16	1	0	9	0	2	.688	3	0	0	4	0	1	1	2	-.101	-.053	0.87	0.44	1.50
Moylan P	29	63.7	271	85	0	52	37	6	2	53	5	13	.726	10	4	0	6	2	1	4	21	-.022	-.140	3.39	2.97	4.14
Saito T	27	54.0	221	56	0	69	17	2	0	41	4	3	.695	1	0	0	2	3	1	2	17	-.020	-.058	3.33	2.83	2.44
O'Flaherty E	23	44.0	181	56	0	36	18	2	1	37	2	8	.710	3	0	0	3	2	0	1	9	-.034	-.036	2.86	2.45	3.31
Kawakami K	21	87.3	391	18	16	59	32	10	1	98	10	6	.675	7	2	0	1	10	0	0	0	-.041	-.030	5.87	5.15	4.12
Dunn M *	15	19.0	88	25	0	27	17	2	0	15	1	2	.651	1	0	0	2	0	0	0	1	.060	-.058	1.89	1.89	3.41
Minor M *	10	40.7	185	9	8	43	11	0	1	53	6	1	.613	3	2	2	3	2	0	0	0	-.066	-.028	6.20	5.98	3.88
Chavez J	9	36.7	162	28	0	29	12	3	1	40	6	2	.693	0	0	0	3	0	0	0	0	-.015	-.019	5.89	5.89	4.56
Martinez C	8	26.0	110	18	0	22	6	1	0	28	3	2	.684	1	1	0	0	0	0	0	0	-.027	-.079	4.85	4.85	3.58
Farnsworth	6	20.0	82	23	0	25	7	1	0	15	2	0	.708	1	1	0	0	2	0	1	2	.034	-.155	5.40	5.40	2.90
Beachy B	4	15.0	67	3	3	15	7	3	0	16	0	2	.622	1	1	0	0	2	0	0	0	.001	.009	5.40	3.00	2.00

Only includes pitchers with at least ten Innings Pitched. Italicized stats have been adjusted for home park.

Batted Ball Pitching Stats

Player	% of PA		% of Batted Balls					Out %		Runs Per Event				Total Runs vs. Avg.				
	K%	BB%	GB%	LD%	FB%	IF/F	HR/OF	GB	OF	NIP	GB	LD	OF	NIP	GB	LD	FB	Tot
Hudson Ti	15	9	64	14	22	.06	.14	79	84	.06	.01	.38	.22	2	-10	-12	-8	-27
Hanson Th	20	8	42	17	42	.08	.06	72	83	.02	.06	.33	.13	-5	0	-11	-9	-25
Wagner Bi	39	9	38	18	44	.15	.10	75	93	-.02	.02	.40	.10	-7	-3	-5	-8	-23
Venters Jo	27	13	68	15	17	.12	.03	71	90	.04	.05	.35	.02	2	3	-6	-14	-15
Saito Ta	31	8	44	16	41	.20	.09	67	82	-.02	.09	.34	.18	-5	1	-5	-3	-11
O'Flaherty Er	20	10	57	20	23	.14	.08	80	77	.05	.00	.39	.16	0	-2	0	-4	-5
Medlen Kr	19	5	43	22	35	.06	.11	78	84	-.01	.02	.39	.19	-6	-4	5	1	-5
Moylan Pe	19	14	68	11	21	.05	.14	76	67	.08	.00	.40	.33	5	-4	-5	1	-4
Martinez Cr	20	5	59	16	26	.00	.14	73	78	-.01	.05	.40	.28	-2	1	-0	1	0
Lowe De	17	8	59	19	23	.04	.14	75	82	.04	.04	.38	.24	-2	2	4	-1	2
Chavez Je	18	8	29	21	50	.10	.11	65	81	.03	.10	.31	.20	-1	1	-1	4	3
Jurrjens Ja	17	9	40	18	42	.07	.08	74	82	-.0	.04	.48	.18	-0	-2	6	3	7
Minor Mi	23	6	35	17	48	.08	.11	64	73	-.01	.13	.39	.27	-3	4	-0	7	9
Kawakami Ke	15	8	40	22	38	.13	.11	75	85	.05	.05	.46	.18	0	1	11	1	13
MLB Average	*18*	*9*	*44*	*18*	*38*	*.09*	*.10*	*74*	*83*	*.04*	*.04*	*.38*	*.18*	--	--	--	--	--

Only includes pitchers who faced at least one hundred batters.

Fielding Stats

Name	INN	SBA/G	CS%	ERA	WP+PB/G	PO	A	TE	FE
Catchers									
McCann B	1109.7	0.93	27%	3.70	0.300	972	64	11	3
Ross D	328.7	0.68	28%	3.15	0.301	276	22	4	0
Boscan J	1.0	0.00	0%	0.00	0.000	2	0	0	0

Name	Inn	PO	A	TE	FE	FPct	DPS	DPT	ZRDif	OOZ	Dif
First Base											
Glaus T	936.3	977	46	2	6	.991	7	0	-.055	16	-15
Lee D	290.7	283	24	0	1	.997	0	1	-.039	12	2
Hinske E	167.3	179	10	0	1	.995	1	0	-.033	6	1
Freeman F	39.0	36	5	0	0	1.000	1	0	--	1	--
Prado M	6.0	7	0	0	0	1.000	0	0	--	--	--
Second Base											
Prado M	852.0	184	285	1	5	.987	26	39	.002	33	12
Infante O	555.7	110	195	4	3	.978	14	29	.008	12	-2
Conrad B	29.7	2	13	0	1	.938	0	0	--	2	--
Hicks B	1.0	0	0	0	0	0.000	0	0	--	--	--
Hernandez D	1.0	0	0	0	0	0.000	0	0	--	--	--
Shortstop											
Escobar Y	646.7	99	250	4	5	.975	36	26	.000	54	26
Gonzalez A	628.7	91	214	4	4	.974	31	12	.018	34	7
Infante O	156.0	29	69	1	4	.951	7	6	-.026	11	4
Hernandez D	6.0	3	1	0	0	1.000	0	1	--	--	--
Hicks B	2.0	0	0	0	0	0.000	0	0	--	--	--
Third Base											
Jones C	696.7	40	159	3	6	.952	9	1	.023	43	17
Prado M	369.7	29	84	1	4	.958	10	2	.019	22	8
Conrad B	227.0	17	48	4	3	.903	3	0	-.088	6	-2
Infante O	139.0	7	30	1	2	.925	1	0	-.023	5	-0
Hicks B	4.0	0	3	0	0	1.000	0	0	--	0	--
Glaus T	2.0	0	1	0	0	1.000	0	0	--	0	--
Hinske E	1.0	0	2	0	0	1.000	0	0	--	0	--

Name	Inn	PO	A	TE	FE	FPct	DPS	DPT	ZRDif	OOZ	Dif
Left Field											
Cabrera M	481.3	82	3	1	0	.988	1	0	-.044	15	-9
Diaz M	448.0	93	1	0	2	.979	0	0	.014	24	2
Hinske E	360.0	65	0	1	0	.985	0	0	.037	6	-12
Infante O	72.7	11	1	0	1	.923	0	0	--	5	--
McLouth N	52.0	8	0	0	0	1.000	0	0	--	2	--
Blanco G	13.3	2	0	0	0	1.000	0	0	--	0	--
Clevlen B	12.0	5	0	0	0	1.000	0	0	--	2	--
Center Field											
McLouth N	561.0	137	1	0	2	.986	1	1	-.016	28	-4
Cabrera M	385.0	95	4	3	0	.971	1	0	-.088	21	-1
Ankiel R	325.3	73	4	1	1	.975	1	0	.009	16	-2
Blanco G	168.0	40	1	1	0	.976	1	0	.061	7	-3
Right Field											
Heyward J	1196.0	235	5	2	4	.976	1	0	.023	64	-2
Cabrera M	197.7	36	1	0	0	1.000	0	0	-.030	10	-1
Infante O	45.3	12	0	0	0	1.000	0	0	--	4	--

Baltimore Orioles

Stat Facts:
- Cesar Izturis had the fewest Base Runs of any player with 400+ PA
- Izturis made the fewest TE of any regular SS
- Luke Scott had the highest H-A of any ML regular
- Brian Matusz allowed 17 SB in 20 attempts
- Matt Wieters had the lowest WP+PB/G of AL regular C
- Wieters made 0 FE
- Nick Markakis had the most innings of any RF with 0 TE
- Adam Jones led the majors in CF assists
- Koji Uehara walked 3% of his BFP
- Josh Bell walked in 1% of his PA
- 85% of Chris Tillman's GB were outs
- Jake Fox had 11 singles and 11 extra-base hits

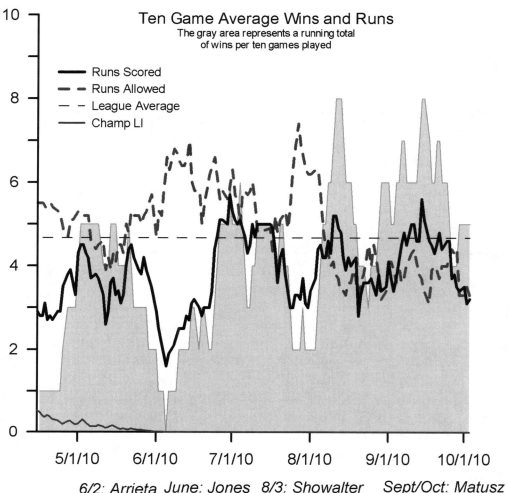

Ten Game Average Wins and Runs
The gray area represents a running total of wins per ten games played

- Runs Scored
- Runs Allowed
- League Average
- Champ LI

6/2: Arrieta debuts

June: Jones hits 8 HR, 21 RBI

8/3: Showalter takes over

Sept/Oct: Matusz posts 1.80 ERA

7/6: Atkins released

8/21: Bell goes 3-4, 2 HR off Lee

Team Batting and Pitching/Fielding Stats by Month

	April	May	June	July	Aug	Sept/Oct
Wins	5	10	9	8	17	17
Losses	18	18	17	19	11	13
RS/G	3.26	3.57	3.77	3.78	4.00	4.20
RA/G	5.13	4.82	6.04	5.85	3.57	3.90
OBP	.304	.318	.329	.308	.305	.327
SLG	.373	.369	.393	.396	.406	.379
FIP	4.36	5.11	4.79	4.92	4.05	4.35
DER	.670	.703	.673	.669	.715	.740

Batting Stats

Player	BR	Runs	RBI	PA	Outs	H	2B	3B	HR	TB	K	BB	IBB	HBP	SH	SF	SB	CS	GDP	H-A	L^R	BA	OBP	SLG	GPA
Markakis N *	86	79	60	709	462	187	45	3	12	274	93	73	9	2	0	5	7	2	18	-.007	-.049	.297	.370	.436	.266
Scott L *	78	70	72	517	329	127	29	1	27	239	98	59	4	4	0	7	2	0	9	.118	.053	.284	.368	.535	.289
Jones A	70	76	69	621	440	165	25	5	19	257	119	23	1	13	2	2	7	7	17	.044	-.045	.284	.325	.442	.248
Wigginton T	66	63	76	649	461	144	29	1	22	241	116	50	3	8	1	9	0	1	23	.013	-.013	.248	.312	.415	.236
Wieters M +	47	37	55	502	349	111	22	1	11	168	94	47	7	2	0	7	0	1	13	-.006	-.066	.249	.319	.377	.229
Patterson C	38	43	32	341	232	83	16	1	8	125	75	20	2	1	10	1	21	4	3	.051	.091	.269	.315	.406	.235
Tejada M	37	40	39	428	306	108	16	0	7	145	39	15	3	9	0	3	0	0	13	.047	-.008	.269	.308	.362	.221
Roberts B +	31	28	15	261	170	64	14	0	4	90	40	26	1	2	1	2	12	2	2	-.030	.025	.278	.354	.391	.248
Pie F *	30	39	31	308	221	79	15	5	5	119	52	13	0	1	3	3	5	2	10	.067	.015	.274	.305	.413	.232
Izturis C +	29	42	28	513	380	109	13	1	1	127	53	25	1	6	7	2	11	5	11	-.019	-.021	.230	.277	.268	.185
Lugo J	16	26	20	264	194	60	4	2	0	68	50	15	0	2	6	0	5	7	6	-.040	.077	.249	.298	.282	.198
Fox J	11	10	10	105	79	22	5	1	5	44	23	3	0	2	0	0	0	0	1	-.164	-.158	.220	.257	.440	.218
Tatum C	10	11	9	126	87	32	4	0	0	36	21	12	0	0	0	0	1	0	5	.033	-.078	.281	.349	.316	.228
Reimold N	9	9	14	131	98	24	5	0	3	38	26	12	0	1	0	0	2	0	6	-.131	.070	.207	.282	.328	.202
Atkins G	9	5	9	152	117	30	7	0	1	40	30	12	0	0	0	0	0	0	7	-.027	-.012	.214	.276	.286	.189
Moore S *	8	8	10	96	68	18	2	0	3	29	19	8	1	0	1	1	3	0	0	.001	.084	.209	.274	.337	.200
Bell J +	8	15	12	161	130	34	5	0	3	48	53	2	0	0	0	0	0	1	4	.019	.043	.214	.224	.302	.170
Andino R	8	6	6	66	47	18	4	0	2	28	13	3	1	0	1	0	1	1	3	.214	.031	.295	.333	.459	.256
Hughes R *	3	3	4	51	37	10	2	0	0	12	19	4	0	0	0	0	0	0	0	-.080	-.061	.213	.275	.255	.181
Snyder B	2	1	3	20	15	6	2	0	0	8	3	0	0	0	0	0	0	1	0	.100	.190	.300	.300	.400	.227

Only includes batters with at least one Base Run. Italicized stats have been adjusted for home park.

Batted Ball Batting Stats

Player	% of PA		% of Batted Balls					Out %		Runs Per Event				Total Runs vs. Avg.				
	K%	BB%	GB%	LD%	FB%	IF/F	HR/OF	GB	OF	NIP	GB	LD	OF	NIP	GB	LD	FB	Tot
Scott Lu	19	12	40	19	41	.13	.21	77	77	.07	.02	.41	.37	5	-4	4	26	30
Markakis Ni	13	11	46	18	36	.07	.06	68	83	.09	.08	.41	.13	8	10	7	-5	19
Jones Ad	19	6	46	17	37	.10	.11	70	83	-.01	.07	.43	.20	-8	9	3	3	7
Roberts Br	15	11	34	22	45	.09	.05	73	81	.08	.05	.37	.12	2	-0	3	-2	3
Fox Ja	22	5	31	13	56	.09	.13	75	82	-.03	.05	.46	.21	-2	-0	-1	3	-0
Wigginton Ty	18	9	47	16	37	.12	.14	74	85	.04	.03	.35	.23	-1	-1	-6	6	-2
Tatum Cr	17	10	52	22	27	.08	.00	77	78	.05	.01	.38	.07	0	-1	2	-4	-3
Patterson Co	22	6	43	18	38	.11	.09	68	86	-.01	.09	.44	.14	-5	5	1	-4	-4
Pie Fe	17	5	51	20	29	.06	.08	76	75	-.02	.03	.38	.21	-5	-2	2	0	-4
Wieters Ma	19	10	46	15	38	.06	.09	78	76	.04	.01	.40	.19	1	-5	-2	3	-4
Reimold No	20	10	49	12	39	.06	.09	82	77	.04	-.04	.30	.19	-0	-3	-3	1	-6
Atkins Ga	20	8	42	16	42	.09	.02	76	83	.02	.01	.37	.07	-1	-2	-2	-4	-9
Tejada Mi	9	6	48	19	32	.14	.07	74	92	.06	.04	.35	.06	-1	1	3	-13	-11
Bell Jo	33	1	57	17	26	.04	.11	68	75	-.10	.06	.29	.24	-7	1	-4	-1	-11
Lugo Ju	19	6	49	20	31	.05	.00	68	93	.00	.06	.43	-.05	-3	1	3	-14	-13
Izturis Ce	10	6	46	19	35	.13	.00	79	86	.06	.01	.33	.00	-1	-3	-2	-24	-31
MLB Average	18	9	44	18	38	.09	.10	74	83	.04	.04	.38	.18	--	--	--	--	--

Only includes batters with at least one hundred Plate Appearances.

Pitching Stats

Player	PRC	IP	BFP	G	GS	K	BB	IBB	HBP	H	HR	DP	DER	SB	CS	PO	W	L	Sv	Op	Hld	H-A	R^L	RA	ERA	FIP
Guthrie J	81	209.3	872	32	32	119	50	1	16	193	25	16	.737	5	2	0	11	14	0	0	0	-.036	-.042	4.00	3.83	4.46
Matusz B *	66	175.7	760	32	32	143	63	3	7	173	19	10	.697	17	3	4	10	12	0	0	0	-.018	-.052	4.51	4.30	4.03
Millwood K	56	190.7	842	31	31	132	65	2	6	223	30	20	.675	6	5	0	4	16	0	0	0	.003	-.023	5.48	5.10	4.86
Bergesen B	46	170.0	746	30	28	81	51	4	7	193	26	20	.695	9	3	0	8	12	0	0	0	.016	-.050	5.51	4.98	5.10
Hernandez D	30	79.3	347	41	8	72	42	4	4	72	9	8	.700	4	3	0	8	8	2	6	2	-.014	-.003	4.54	4.31	4.36
Arrieta J	30	100.3	449	18	18	52	48	3	4	106	9	11	.693	11	1	2	6	6	0	0	0	.007	-.094	5.11	4.66	4.71
Berken J	29	62.3	262	41	0	45	19	3	0	64	5	8	.684	2	2	1	3	3	0	4	7	.052	.038	3.47	3.03	3.48
Uehara K	26	44.0	175	43	0	55	5	0	0	37	5	1	.700	1	0	0	1	2	13	15	6	.030	-.092	3.07	2.86	2.43
Albers M	25	75.7	329	62	0	49	34	5	2	78	6	12	.681	8	2	0	5	3	0	2	7	.001	-.043	4.88	4.52	4.08
Hendrickson	22	75.3	339	52	1	55	20	4	3	97	9	7	.651	1	1	0	1	6	0	2	8	.028	.001	5.62	5.26	3.96
Simon A	15	49.3	222	49	0	37	22	2	2	54	10	4	.682	5	2	0	4	2	17	21	1	-.050	.073	5.47	4.93	5.58
Ohman W *	14	30.0	135	51	0	29	18	4	1	30	3	3	.679	2	1	0	0	0	0	1	15	-.005	-.096	3.60	3.30	3.98
Tillman C	13	53.7	236	11	11	31	31	1	1	51	9	7	.744	3	1	0	2	5	0	0	0	.083	-.065	6.20	5.87	5.87
Johnson J	12	26.3	117	26	0	22	5	1	1	32	2	2	.644	0	1	0	1	1	1	6	11	.060	.043	3.76	3.42	3.00
Gonzalez M *	11	24.7	106	29	0	31	14	4	0	18	1	2	.700	2	0	0	1	3	1	3	10	.045	.110	4.01	4.01	2.34
VandenHurk	5	16.3	67	7	1	17	7	0	2	13	2	4	.692	1	0	1	0	1	0	0	0	-.054	-.196	5.51	4.96	4.28
Meredith C	4	15.0	67	21	0	7	4	1	1	18	4	0	.725	2	0	0	0	2	1	2	3	.076	.008	5.40	5.40	6.45
Mata F	3	17.3	85	15	0	9	8	3	2	24	2	3	.625	3	0	0	0	0	0	0	1	-.074	-.022	8.31	7.79	4.78
Castillo A *	1	10.7	51	14	0	11	6	0	0	16	5	3	.586	0	0	0	1	0	0	0	1	-.108	.090	10.13	10.13	8.83

Only includes pitchers with at least ten Innings Pitched. Italicized stats have been adjusted for home park.

Batted Ball Pitching Stats

Player	% of PA		% of Batted Balls					Out %		Runs Per Event				Total Runs vs. Avg.				
	K%	BB%	GB%	LD%	FB%	IF/F	HR/OF	GB	OF	NIP	GB	LD	OF	NIP	GB	LD	FB	Tot
Uehara Ko	31	3	24	18	58	.08	.08	58	89	-.07	.14	.31	.13	-6	2	-3	-1	-9
Guthrie Je	14	8	42	14	43	.10	.09	76	86	.05	.04	.42	.15	-1	-2	-4	-1	-7
Gonzalez Mi	29	13	33	22	45	.12	.04	74	91	.03	.05	.49	.05	0	-1	1	-4	-3
Matusz Br	19	9	36	19	45	.12	.08	75	82	.04	.04	.41	.15	-1	-2	3	-2	-2
Berken Ja	17	7	47	16	37	.07	.08	67	93	.02	.08	.56	.06	-2	3	4	-7	-1
Johnson Ja	19	5	51	24	24	.10	.11	73	82	-.01	.06	.39	.17	-2	1	2	-2	-0
Ohman Wi	21	14	51	14	35	.07	.11	74	75	.07	.05	.41	.24	2	-0	-1	1	1
Albers Ma	15	11	56	15	29	.03	.09	74	80	.08	.04	.40	.18	3	1	-1	-1	2
Hernandez Da	21	13	28	21	51	.17	.07	71	89	.06	.06	.48	.10	4	-0	6	-6	3
Tillman Ch	13	14	43	22	36	.05	.16	85	88	.12	-.02	.35	.24	5	-5	2	4	6
Hendrickson Ma	16	7	43	22	35	.07	.11	69	81	.02	.07	.36	.20	-2	3	4	2	8
Simon Al	17	11	47	19	34	.11	.20	69	87	.07	.07	.34	.29	2	2	-0	5	9
Arrieta Ja	12	12	42	19	39	.13	.08	72	82	.12	.05	.35	.15	7	3	1	-2	9
Millwood Ke	16	8	37	22	41	.08	.12	75	82	.05	.04	.37	.20	0	-1	10	13	23
Bergesen Br	11	8	49	15	37	.07	.12	76	79	.08	.04	.44	.25	3	1	3	20	26
MLB Average	18	9	44	18	38	.09	.10	74	83	.04	.04	.38	.18	--	--	--	--	--

Only includes pitchers who faced at least one hundred batters.

Fielding Stats

Name	INN	SBA/G	CS%	ERA	WP+PB/G	PO	A	TE	FE
Catchers									
Wieters M	1060.3	0.63	28%	4.56	0.272	775	51	3	0
Tatum C	310.7	0.78	7%	4.55	0.406	222	17	2	1
Fox J	65.3	0.83	17%	5.37	0.276	49	6	0	0

Name	Inn	PO	A	TE	FE	FPct	DPS	DPT	ZRDif	OOZ	Dif
First Base											
Wigginton T	787.0	748	73	2	8	.988	10	1	.021	33	7
Atkins G	259.3	242	16	0	1	.996	2	1	-.122	5	-4
Scott L	158.0	153	11	0	3	.982	0	0	-.014	4	-1
Hughes R	98.0	98	3	0	1	.990	0	0	--	2	--
Fox J	66.0	58	4	0	1	.984	1	0	--	3	--
Snyder B	51.0	44	2	0	1	.958	0	0	--	3	--
Moore S	17.0	19	3	0	0	1.000	0	0	--	1	--
Second Base											
Roberts B	498.3	86	146	0	3	.987	16	21	-.017	11	-1
Lugo J	395.0	93	131	0	1	.996	9	17	-.008	15	5
Wigginton T	306.0	66	97	1	5	.964	0	12	-.017	8	0
Moore S	168.0	36	52	2	0	.978	1	8	.056	2	-2
Andino R	50.0	6	10	0	0	1.000	0	1	--	1	--
Turner J	19.0	4	4	0	0	1.000	0	1	--	1	--
Shortstop											
Izturis C	1250.0	212	382	1	8	.985	37	39	-.005	56	2
Lugo J	142.3	25	48	0	1	.986	9	2	.052	6	-0
Andino R	42.0	5	14	0	1	.950	1	2	--	2	--
Turner J	2.0	1	0	0	0	1.000	0	0	--	--	--
Third Base											
Tejada M	808.0	68	197	6	9	.946	21	0	-.038	30	0
Bell J	369.3	27	77	2	2	.963	6	0	.004	20	6
Wigginton T	166.0	13	33	0	4	.902	3	0	-.054	7	1
Andino R	50.0	6	4	0	0	1.000	1	0	--	3	--
Lugo J	18.0	0	1	0	0	1.000	0	0	--	0	--
Moore S	18.0	0	1	0	1	.500	0	0	--	0	--
Fox J	7.0	0	0	0	0	0.000	0	0	--	--	--

Name	Inn	PO	A	TE	FE	FPct	DPS	DPT	ZRDif	OOZ	Dif
Left Field											
Pie F	580.3	147	7	1	0	.994	3	0	.005	34	6
Patterson C	466.7	116	4	0	4	.960	1	0	-.039	32	9
Reimold N	175.0	42	1	0	1	.977	0	0	.044	10	1
Scott L	103.0	22	0	0	0	1.000	0	0	-.007	3	-2
Montanez L	89.3	23	1	0	1	.960	0	0	--	8	--
Fox J	13.0	4	0	0	0	1.000	0	0	--	0	--
Lugo J	9.0	1	0	0	0	1.000	0	0	--	0	--
Center Field											
Jones A	1298.0	422	12	2	5	.984	6	0	.011	60	-13
Patterson C	66.0	21	0	0	0	1.000	0	0	--	6	--
Pie F	64.0	15	1	0	0	1.000	0	0	--	0	--
Montanez L	8.0	4	1	0	0	1.000	0	0	--	0	--
Right Field											
Markakis N	1402.0	332	7	0	3	.991	1	0	-.001	57	-20
Pie F	12.0	5	1	0	0	1.000	1	0	--	0	--
Montanez L	10.0	1	0	0	0	1.000	0	0	--	--	--
Patterson C	9.0	1	0	0	0	1.000	0	0	--	--	--
Reimold N	3.0	0	0	0	0	0.000	0	0	--	0	--

Boston Red Sox

Stat Facts:

- Jed Lowrie had the most Base Runs of any player with <200 PA
- Josh Beckett allowed 18 SB in 19 attempts
- Victor Martinez had the second-highest SBA/G of any regular C
- Jon Lester had the highest H-A of any pitcher with 200+ IP
- Clay Buchholz's FIP was far higher than his ERA
- Jeremy Hermida tied for the AL lead in LF FE, in 349 innings
- J.D. Drew had 1 assist
- Marco Scutaro turned the fewest DP of any regular SS
- Adrian Beltre made the most OOZ plays of any 3B
- Felix Doubront's LD% was 10
- 23% of Hideki Okajima's FB were infield pop-ups
- Jason Veritek had 13 singles and 13 extra-base hits

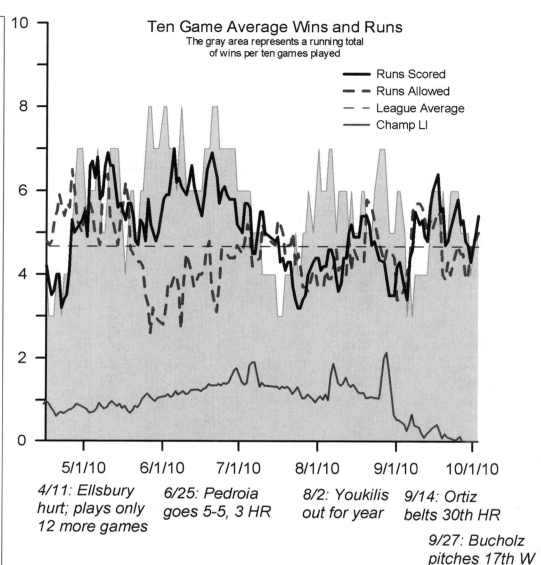

Ten Game Average Wins and Runs
The gray area represents a running total of wins per ten games played

— Runs Scored
– – Runs Allowed
– – League Average
— Champ LI

4/11: Ellsbury hurt; plays only 12 more games

6/25: Pedroia goes 5-5, 3 HR

8/2: Youkilis out for year

9/14: Ortiz belts 30th HR

9/27: Bucholz pitches 17th W

Team Batting and Pitching/Fielding Stats by Month

	April	May	June	July	Aug	Sept/Oct
Wins	11	18	18	12	15	15
Losses	12	11	9	13	13	15
RS/G	4.5	5.7	6.1	4.3	4.2	5.3
RA/G	5.2	4.6	4.3	4.3	4.4	4.9
OBP	.333	.350	.372	.331	.307	.340
SLG	.426	.466	.506	.439	.422	.443
FIP	4.38	4.41	3.80	4.14	4.11	4.02
DER	.693	.728	.693	.718	.692	.679

Batting Stats

Player	BR	Runs	RBI	PA	Outs	H	2B	3B	HR	TB	K	BB	IBB	HBP	SH	SF	SB	CS	GDP	H-A	L^R	BA	OBP	SLG	GPA
Beltre A	97	84	102	641	426	189	49	2	28	326	82	40	10	5	0	7	2	1	25	-.020	.013	.321	.365	.553	.292
Ortiz D *	91	86	102	606	391	140	36	1	32	274	145	82	14	2	0	4	0	1	12	.022	.143	.270	.370	.529	.288
Youkilis K	76	77	62	435	256	111	26	5	19	204	67	58	3	10	0	5	4	1	4	.007	.140	.307	.411	.564	.315
Scutaro M	73	92	56	695	475	174	38	0	11	245	71	53	1	3	4	3	5	4	13	.007	.011	.275	.333	.388	.238
Martinez V +	72	64	79	538	361	149	32	1	20	243	52	40	5	0	0	5	1	0	17	.067	.143	.302	.351	.493	.271
Drew J *	68	69	68	546	369	122	24	2	22	216	105	60	3	4	0	4	3	1	12	-.014	.077	.255	.341	.452	.257
Pedroia D	51	53	41	351	223	87	24	1	12	149	38	37	1	4	2	6	9	1	7	-.020	-.053	.288	.367	.493	.278
Hall B	48	44	46	382	264	85	16	1	18	157	104	34	0	1	2	1	9	1	4	.007	-.054	.247	.316	.456	.247
McDonald D	43	40	34	363	239	86	18	3	9	137	85	30	1	2	12	0	9	1	5	.023	.035	.270	.336	.429	.250
Lowrie J +	31	31	24	197	125	49	14	0	9	90	25	25	0	1	0	0	1	1	2	-.029	.064	.287	.381	.526	.292
Lowell M	22	23	26	244	175	52	13	0	5	80	34	23	1	0	0	3	0	0	9	.018	-.027	.239	.307	.367	.222
Cameron M	19	24	15	180	124	42	11	0	4	65	44	14	0	3	0	1	0	1	3	.015	.165	.259	.328	.401	.239
Nava D +	19	23	26	188	128	39	14	1	1	58	46	19	1	8	0	0	1	1	5	.113	-.020	.242	.351	.360	.239
Kalish R *	19	26	24	179	128	41	11	4	4	66	38	12	0	1	2	1	10	1	5	.004	.052	.252	.305	.405	.230
Varitek J +	15	18	16	123	87	26	6	0	7	53	35	10	2	0	0	1	0	0	1	.079	.029	.232	.293	.473	.241
Hermida J *	14	14	27	171	127	32	8	0	5	55	45	12	0	0	0	1	1	0	1	.029	.061	.203	.257	.348	.196
Patterson E	10	13	7	93	67	19	3	2	3	34	31	6	0	1	1	0	5	1	1	-.176	-.205	.226	.293	.405	.225
Ellsbury J *	5	10	5	84	64	15	4	0	0	19	9	4	0	1	0	0	7	1	0	-.094	.006	.192	.241	.244	.163
Reddick J *	3	5	5	63	51	12	3	1	1	20	15	1	0	0	0	0	1	0	1	.062	-.170	.194	.206	.323	.167
Anderson L *	3	4	4	43	29	7	1	0	0	8	8	7	0	0	0	0			1	.051	.058	.200	.326	.229	.197
Saltalamacch	3	2	1	25	16	3	3	0	0	6	4	6	0	0	0	0	0	0	0	-.025	-.013	.158	.360	.316	.233
Van Every J	2	6	1	21	15	4	1	0	1	8	9	2	0	0	0	0	0	0	0	-.261	.292	.211	.286	.421	.226
Lopez F +	2	2	1	16	11	4	0	0	1	7	4	1	0	0	0	0	0	0	0	.419	-.030	.267	.313	.467	.248
Cash K	1	1	1	68	54	8	1	0	0	9	16	6	0	1	1	0	0	0	2	-.048	.117	.133	.224	.150	.133
Brown D	1	0	2	12	10	3	1	0	0	4	2	0	0	0	0	0	0	0	1	.063	-.144	.250	.250	.333	.189

Only includes batters with at least one Base Run. Italicized stats have been adjusted for home park.

Batted Ball Batting Stats

Player	% of PA		% of Batted Balls					Out %		Runs Per Event				Total Runs vs. Avg.				
	K%	BB%	GB%	LD%	FB%	IF/F	HR/OF	GB	OF	NIP	GB	LD	OF	NIP	GB	LD	FB	Tot
Youkilis Ke	15	16	37	16	47	.09	.14	68	77	.12	.08	.45	.29	12	3	4	20	39
Beltre Ad	13	7	40	19	40	.11	.15	73	78	.05	.05	.40	.28	-1	1	10	26	36
Ortiz Da	24	14	38	17	45	.08	.20	78	76	.06	.02	.41	.36	6	-5	-2	31	30
Martinez Vi	10	7	41	17	42	.09	.12	73	81	.09	.04	.38	.22	2	1	4	14	21
Pedroia Du	11	12	39	22	39	.10	.13	80	88	.13	.01	.41	.19	6	-4	8	3	14
Lowrie Je	13	13	29	16	54	.01	.12	72	86	.12	.08	.42	.18	4	1	1	7	12
Drew Da	19	12	44	16	39	.10	.17	75	83	.06	.03	.36	.27	4	-2	-4	13	11
Hall Bi	27	9	38	18	44	.09	.18	75	81	.00	.04	.41	.29	-4	-2	-1	11	4
McDonald Da	23	9	42	19	39	.12	.10	70	75	.01	.07	.42	.25	-3	1	1	4	3
Scutaro Ma	10	8	41	17	42	.11	.05	70	86	.09	.07	.40	.08	4	7	5	-14	1
Nava Da	24	14	39	16	45	.00	.02	71	78	.06	.05	.56	.11	2	-1	1	-2	1
Cameron Mi	24	9	29	16	55	.11	.07	59	78	.02	.12	.40	.16	-1	2	-1	2	1
Varitek Ja	28	8	27	16	57	.09	.18	81	85	-.01	.02	.36	.27	-2	-1	-2	5	0
Kalish Ry	21	7	46	18	36	.18	.11	69	76	.00	.08	.32	.23	-2	2	-2	0	-1
Lowell Mi	14	9	31	18	51	.15	.06	86	78	.07	-.05	.37	.15	1	-7	0	1	-4
Hermida Je	26	7	38	20	42	.04	.11	81	80	-.02	.01	.28	.22	-3	-2	-3	2	-6
MLB Average	*18*	*9*	*44*	*18*	*38*	*.09*	*.10*	*74*	*83*	*.04*	*.04*	*.38*	*.18*	--	--	--	--	--

Only includes batters with at least one hundred Plate Appearances.

Pitching Stats

Player	PRC	IP	BFP	G	GS	K	BB	IBB	HBP	H	HR	DP	DER	SB	CS	PO	W	L	Sv	Op	Hld	H-A	R^L	RA	ERA	FIP
Lester J *	105	208.0	861	32	32	225	83	0	10	167	14	21	.703	22	7	6	19	9	0	0	0	.049	.007	3.50	3.25	3.16
Buchholz C	94	173.7	711	28	28	120	67	1	5	142	9	26	.720	8	6	3	17	7	0	0	0	.003	-.023	2.85	2.33	3.63
Lackey J	74	215.0	930	33	33	156	72	2	9	233	18	23	.670	26	10	2	14	11	0	0	0	-.001	-.032	4.77	4.40	3.85
Bard D	54	74.7	295	73	0	76	30	3	2	45	6	5	.773	8	1	0	1	2	3	10	32	-.082	.045	2.17	1.93	3.29
Matsuzaka D	53	153.7	664	25	25	133	74	1	8	137	13	10	.704	25	7	0	9	6	0	0	0	.009	-.057	4.92	4.69	4.06
Wakefield T	37	140.0	610	32	19	84	36	3	5	153	19	7	.693	24	5	3	4	10	0	0	0	.022	.004	5.91	5.34	4.49
Beckett J	34	127.7	577	21	21	116	45	3	8	151	20	12	.657	18	1	0	6	6	0	0	0	-.034	-.062	6.27	5.78	4.51
Papelbon J	27	67.0	287	65	0	76	28	4	2	57	7	2	.701	11	0	0	5	7	37	45	0	-.052	-.033	4.57	3.90	3.37
Atchison S	17	60.0	253	43	1	41	19	2	1	58	9	7	.716	6	2	0	2	3	0	0	7	-.015	-.065	5.55	4.50	4.60
Okajima H *	16	46.0	213	56	0	33	20	5	0	59	6	4	.649	1	1	1	4	4	0	4	11	-.108	-.059	4.70	4.50	4.35
Ramirez R	16	42.3	178	44	0	31	16	2	0	39	6	2	.736	3	1	0	0	3	2	2	2	.068	-.010	4.46	4.46	4.48
Delcarmen M	15	44.0	193	48	0	32	28	1	1	33	7	2	.784	0	0	0	3	2	0	2	8	.006	.076	4.91	4.70	5.63
Doubront F *	7	25.0	113	12	3	23	10	0	1	27	3	1	.645	1	1	0	2	2	2	3	1	-.047	-.119	5.76	4.32	4.15
Bowden M	6	15.3	66	14	0	13	4	0	0	20	2	3	.617	5	0	0	0	1	0	0	0	-.083	-.082	4.70	4.70	3.89
Richardson D	5	13.0	67	26	0	12	14	1	1	15	2	2	.658	4	0	0	0	0	0	0	2	.093	.139	4.15	4.15	6.50
Manuel R	4	12.7	54	10	0	5	7	1	0	10	5	0	.865	0	0	0	1	0	0	0	0	.177	.103	4.26	4.26	8.87
Schoeneweis	3	13.7	68	15	0	13	10	1	0	19	2	2	.605	3	0	0	1	0	0	0	1	-.103	-.014	7.90	7.90	5.09
Coello R	2	5.7	26	6	0	5	5	0	0	4	0	0	.750	1	0	0	0	0	0	0	0	.078	-.267	4.76	4.76	3.99

Only includes pitchers with at least ten Innings Pitched. Italicized stats have been adjusted for home park.

Batted Ball Pitching Stats

Player	% of PA		% of Batted Balls					Out %		Runs Per Event				Total Runs vs. Avg.				
	K%	BB%	GB%	LD%	FB%	IF/F	HR/OF	GB	OF	NIP	GB	LD	OF	NIP	GB	LD	FB	Tot
Lester Jo	26	11	54	17	30	.08	.09	79	77	.02	.01	.39	.20	-3	-8	-9	-8	-29
Buchholz Cl	17	10	51	18	31	.08	.06	79	79	.06	.01	.29	.14	3	-7	-9	-10	-23
Bard Da	26	11	47	15	38	.16	.10	81	88	.02	.01	.34	.13	-1	-4	-6	-7	-19
Papelbon Jo	26	10	38	18	44	.09	.10	75	76	.02	.05	.32	.21	-2	-1	-5	2	-5
Delcarmen Ma	17	15	46	16	39	.12	.16	81	84	.10	.01	.22	.24	4	-3	-5	2	-1
Matsuzaka Da	20	12	33	22	45	.09	.07	74	85	.06	.04	.34	.13	6	-2	0	-5	-1
Ramirez Ra	17	9	34	20	46	.10	.11	80	81	.04	.03	.30	.22	-0	-2	-2	4	0
Atchison Sc	16	8	48	11	41	.10	.13	69	80	.04	.07	.29	.24	-1	2	-6	5	1
Doubront Fe	20	10	47	10	42	.09	.10	57	74	.04	.16	.19	.27	-0	4	-4	3	4
Okajima Hi	15	9	35	23	42	.23	.12	72	74	.06	.05	.37	.24	1	1	3	2	7
Wakefield Ti	14	7	37	16	47	.14	.10	72	82	.04	.06	.42	.19	-2	3	3	9	12
Lackey Jo	17	9	46	18	36	.09	.08	75	74	.04	.04	.37	.22	0	1	2	10	13
Beckett Jo	20	9	46	19	35	.09	.15	77	76	.03	.04	.46	.30	-1	1	7	14	21
MLB Average	18	9	44	18	38	.09	.10	74	83	.04	.04	.38	.18	--	--	--	--	--

Only includes pitchers who faced at least one hundred batters.

Fielding Stats

Name	INN	SBA/G	CS%	ERA	WP+PB/G	PO	A	TE	FE
Catchers									
Martinez V	904.0	1.15	15%	4.28	0.408	778	44	5	0
Varitek J	275.3	1.37	19%	4.05	0.163	242	13	0	0
Cash K	181.0	1.24	8%	3.73	0.895	148	14	1	0
Saltalamacchia J	43.7	1.24	17%	4.33	0.000	38	2	0	1
Brown D	35.7	1.51	17%	4.04	1.262	26	4	0	0
Molina G	17.0	1.59	0%	6.88	1.588	15	1	0	0

Name	Inn	PO	A	TE	FE	FPct	DPS	DPT	ZRDif	OOZ	Dif
First Base											
Youkilis K	862.0	809	72	1	2	.997	4	0	.091	26	-2
Lowell M	324.0	310	24	0	2	.994	3	0	.070	9	-2
Anderson L	111.0	96	9	0	0	1.000	0	0	.146	4	0
Martinez V	106.0	95	14	1	1	.982	0	0	-.049	11	8
Ortiz D	26.7	23	1	0	0	1.000	0	0	--	0	--
Lowrie J	16.0	10	2	0	0	.923	0	0	--	1	--
Shealy R	5.0	5	0	0	0	1.000	0	0	--	0	--
Romero N	5.0	4	1	0	0	1.000	0	0	--	--	--
Salty	1.0	0	0	0	0	0.000	0	0	--	--	--
Second Base											
Pedroia D	667.3	137	212	1	2	.991	14	34	.040	13	-4
Hall B	353.3	72	100	3	3	.966	8	11	-.061	12	3
Lowrie J	209.0	44	77	0	3	.976	3	11	.074	4	-1
Scutaro M	132.3	17	46	0	2	.969	3	4	.009	2	-1
Patterson E	56.0	16	15	0	1	.969	1	2	--	0	--
Lopez F	19.7	4	6	0	0	1.000	0	0	--	1	--
Navarro Y	18.0	4	5	0	0	1.000	0	1	--	0	--
Romero N	1.0	0	0	0	0	0.000	0	0	--	--	--
Shortstop											
Scutaro M	1166.0	152	344	10	8	.965	33	20	-.024	50	-0
Lowrie J	176.7	26	46	1	0	.986	8	8	-.091	4	-4
Navarro Y	67.0	14	17	0	1	.969	1	3	--	2	--
Hall B	36.0	3	8	0	1	.917	3	0	--	2	--
Sanchez A	9.0	0	4	0	0	1.000	2	0	--	0	--
Lopez F	2.0	2	0	0	0	1.000	0	0	--	--	--
Third Base											
Beltre A	1342.0	138	285	9	10	.957	30	0	.029	74	24
Lowell M	32.0	2	6	0	0	1.000	1	0	--	1	--
Hall B	27.0	4	6	0	1	.909	1	0	--	2	--
Navarro Y	27.0	3	7	1	0	.909	0	0	--	2	--
Youkilis K	15.0	3	5	0	0	1.000	0	0	--	1	--
Lopez F	10.0	1	0	1	0	.500	0	0	--	0	--
Lowrie J	3.0	0	1	0	0	1.000	0	0	--	0	--

Name	Inn	PO	A	TE	FE	FPct	DPS	DPT	ZRDif	OOZ	Dif
Left Field											
Nava D	380.0	65	2	0	0	1.000	0	0	-.159	18	-1
Hermida J	348.7	84	3	0	4	.956	0	0	-.045	13	-4
Hall B	341.3	78	3	1	0	.988	0	0	-.066	16	-1
McDonald D	125.3	31	1	0	0	1.000	0	0	-.027	4	-2
Kalish R	96.0	21	1	1	0	.957	0	0	--	3	--
Patterson E	77.3	20	2	0	0	1.000	0	0	--	5	--
Ellsbury J	46.3	11	0	0	0	1.000	0	0	--	5	--
Reddick J	37.0	9	0	0	0	1.000	0	0	--	1	--
Van Every J	4.7	2	0	0	0	1.000	0	0	--	0	--
Center Field											
McDonald D	450.7	112	7	0	1	.992	1	0	-.046	17	-9
Cameron M	392.0	111	3	0	2	.983	1	0	-.053	15	-7
Kalish R	293.3	83	2	1	0	.988	1	0	.013	11	-6
Ellsbury J	104.7	33	0	0	0	1.000	0	0	.056	5	-1
Patterson E	78.7	13	1	0	1	.933	0	0	--	1	--
Hall B	48.0	18	0	0	1	.947	0	0	--	2	--
Van Every J	45.3	10	0	0	0	1.000	0	0	--	2	--
Reddick J	44.0	16	0	0	0	1.000	0	0	--	3	--
Right Field											
Drew J	1102.0	234	1	0	1	.996	1	0	-.002	55	-6
McDonald D	201.0	44	1	0	1	.978	0	0	-.064	9	-2
Reddick J	66.7	12	1	0	0	1.000	0	0	--	3	--
Hall B	40.3	8	0	0	2	.800	0	0	--	3	--
Hermida J	18.0	2	0	0	0	1.000	0	0	--	0	--
Van Every J	16.0	3	0	0	0	1.000	0	0	--	2	--
Kalish R	12.0	1	0	0	0	1.000	0	0	--	0	--

Chicago Cubs

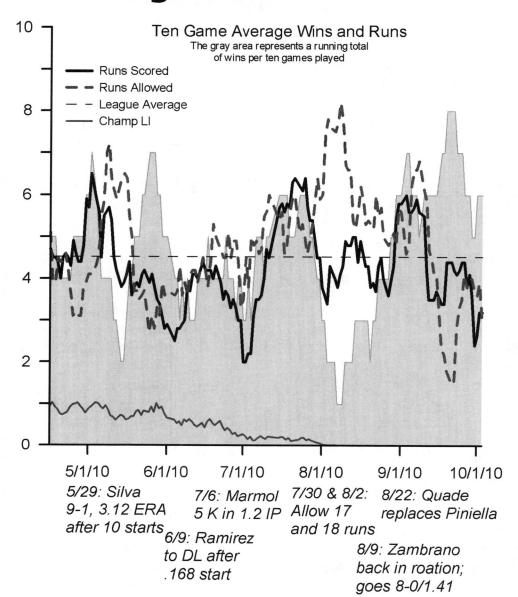

Ten Game Average Wins and Runs
The gray area represents a running total
of wins per ten games played

- Runs Scored
- Runs Allowed
- League Average
- Champ LI

5/29: Silva
9-1, 3.12 ERA
after 10 starts

6/9: Ramirez
to DL after
.168 start

7/6: Marmol
5 K in 1.2 IP

7/30 & 8/2:
Allow 17
and 18 runs

8/9: Zambrano
back in roation;
goes 8-0/1.41

8/22: Quade
replaces Piniella

Stat Facts:

- Ryan Dempster's R^L was exactly .000
- Geovany Soto had the highest SBA/G of any primary NL C
- Soto's LD% was 24
- Alfonso Soriano tied for the ML lead in LF FE
- Soriano had the highest ZRDif of any regular LF
- Tyler Colvin tied for the NL lead in RF FE, in 388 innings
- Kosuke Fukudome had the most innings of any RF with 0 FE
- Aramis Ramirez started the fewest DP of any regular 3B
- Ramirez had the lowest ZRDif of any regular 3B
- Carlos Marmol struck out 42% of his BFP
- Justin Berg struck out 7% of his BFP
- Jeff Samardzija walked 22% of his BFP

Team Batting and Pitching/Fielding Stats by Month

	April	May	June	July	Aug	Sept/Oct
Wins	11	13	10	12	10	19
Losses	13	15	16	14	19	10
RS/G	4.7	3.9	3.5	4.8	4.8	3.7
RA/G	4.5	4.5	4.1	5.8	5.9	3.6
OBP	.339	.319	.307	.327	.323	.305
SLG	.428	.386	.383	.443	.430	.343
FIP	3.67	4.12	3.89	4.73	4.29	4.08
DER	.704	.698	.695	.661	.676	.719

Batting Stats

Player	BR	Runs	RBI	PA	Outs	H	2B	3B	HR	TB	K	BB	IBB	HBP	SH	SF	SB	CS	GDP	H-A	L^R	BA	OBP	SLG	GPA
Byrd M	76	84	66	630	423	170	39	2	12	249	98	31	1	17	0	2	5	1	12	-.026	.062	.293	.346	.429	.247
Soriano A	72	67	79	548	381	128	40	3	24	246	123	45	3	3	1	3	5	1	12	-.023	.060	.258	.322	.496	.252
Soto G	58	47	53	387	238	90	19	0	17	160	83	62	4	0	0	3	0	1	5	.019	.091	.280	.393	.497	.282
Ramirez A	57	61	83	507	363	112	21	1	25	210	90	34	3	3	0	5	0	0	10	.073	.025	.241	.294	.452	.230
Fukudome K *	55	45	44	429	277	94	20	2	13	157	67	64	1	0	3	4	7	8	5	.024	-.002	.263	.371	.439	.259
Castro S	54	53	41	506	346	139	31	5	3	189	71	29	7	6	4	4	10	8	14	.079	.062	.300	.347	.408	.242
Colvin T *	53	60	56	395	274	91	18	5	20	179	100	30	2	6	3	1	6	1	6	-.024	.002	.254	.316	.500	.250
Lee D	52	63	56	475	332	105	21	0	16	174	101	52	1	2	0	3	1	3	16	.009	-.015	.251	.335	.416	.239
Theriot R	36	45	21	412	292	110	10	2	1	127	46	19	3	2	2	1	16	6	8	-.019	.008	.284	.320	.327	.212
Nady X	30	33	33	347	248	81	13	0	6	112	85	17	0	8	1	4	0	0	12	-.035	-.010	.256	.306	.353	.212
Baker J	24	29	21	224	156	56	13	2	4	85	50	16	0	1	0	1	1	0	6	.093	.204	.272	.326	.413	.234
DeWitt B *	20	18	22	204	139	46	9	1	4	69	37	17	4	1	0	2	1	0	1	.033	-.032	.250	.314	.375	.220
Fontenot M *	20	14	20	185	126	48	11	3	1	68	28	10	0	3	1	2	1	2	3	.104	.015	.284	.332	.402	.234
Hill K +	13	18	17	231	174	46	11	1	1	64	61	12	3	0	3	1	1	0	5	-.039	.058	.214	.254	.298	.177
Barney D	6	12	2	85	60	19	4	0	0	23	12	6	0	0	0	0	0	0	0	.011	.069	.241	.294	.291	.192
Tracy C *	4	6	5	49	33	11	2	0	0	13	15	5	0	0	0	0	0	0	0	.208	.231	.250	.327	.295	.207
Castillo W	4	3	5	21	14	6	4	0	1	13	7	1	0	0	0	0	0	0	0	-.231	-.115	.300	.333	.650	.293
Zambrano C +	4	5	6	57	40	12	0	0	1	15	15	2	0	0	2	0	0	0	0	.012	.020	.231	.255	.288	.175
Scales B +	3	4	2	20	9	4	0	0	0	4	5	7	0	0	0	0	1	0	0	-.081	.401	.308	.550	.308	.304
Hoffpauir M	2	5	5	57	46	9	3	0	0	12	15	5	0	0	0	0	0	0	3	.147	-.163	.173	.246	.231	.158
Snyder B *	1	1	5	28	22	5	1	0	0	6	12	1	0	0	0	0	0	0	0	.200	.178	.185	.214	.222	.143
Wells R	1	1	3	63	46	9	2	0	0	11	15	2	0	0	9	0	0	0	3	-.173	-.060	.173	.204	.212	.136
Samardzija J	1	0	1	7	3	1	0	0	0	1	2	2	0	0	1	0	0	0	0	.208	-.067	.250	.500	.250	.270

Only includes batters with at least one Base Run. Italicized stats have been adjusted for home park.

Batted Ball Batting Stats

Player	% of PA		% of Batted Balls					Out %		Runs Per Event				Total Runs vs. Avg.				
	K%	BB%	GB%	LD%	FB%	IF/F	HR/OF	GB	OF	NIP	GB	LD	OF	NIP	GB	LD	FB	Tot
Soto Ge	21	16	36	24	40	.08	.19	77	80	.08	.03	.37	.33	8	-2	5	14	25
Byrd Ma	16	8	52	17	30	.04	.09	72	77	.04	.06	.46	.19	-1	7	9	1	16
Soriano Al	22	9	29	16	54	.08	.13	75	75	.02	.03	.36	.27	-4	-5	-4	28	15
Fukudome Ko	16	15	49	16	35	.08	.13	73	82	.11	.05	.37	.23	10	2	-3	4	13
Colvin Ty	25	8	43	17	40	.09	.21	75	88	.00	.04	.47	.30	-4	-0	1	12	8
Castro St	14	7	51	20	29	.07	.03	71	78	.04	.06	.42	.12	-1	5	8	-7	5
Lee De	21	11	39	23	39	.02	.13	73	88	.05	.03	.33	.18	2	-3	1	3	3
Fontenot Mi	15	7	44	27	30	.02	.02	82	83	.03	-.01	.49	.06	-1	-3	10	-5	1
Ramirez Ar	18	7	27	16	57	.12	.13	74	87	.02	.03	.36	.18	-3	-4	-4	12	0
Baker Je	22	8	42	22	36	.05	.08	74	84	.00	.03	.48	.15	-2	-1	5	-2	0
DeWitt Bl	18	9	44	19	37	.16	.09	76	76	.04	.05	.26	.22	-0	1	-3	1	-2
Theriot Ry	11	5	56	20	24	.05	.01	69	89	.03	.07	.34	.00	-3	8	3	-17	-8
Nady Xa	24	7	47	20	33	.01	.08	71	79	-.01	.05	.31	.16	-5	-0	-3	-2	-11
Hill Ko	26	5	51	22	26	.03	.03	76	84	-.04	.03	.38	.07	-6	-1	-0	-8	-14
MLB Average	18	9	44	18	38	.09	.10	74	83	.04	.04	.38	.18	--	--	--	--	--

Only includes batters with at least one hundred Plate Appearances.

Pitching Stats

Player	PRC	IP	BFP	G	GS	K	BB	IBB	HBP	H	HR	DP	DER	SB	CS	PO	W	L	Sv	Op	Hld	H-A	R^L	RA	ERA	FIP
Dempster R	81	215.3	918	34	34	208	86	4	10	198	25	20	.698	16	6	0	15	12	0	0	0	.017	.000	4.60	3.85	4.05
Wells R	70	194.3	843	32	32	144	63	5	6	209	19	20	.671	14	4	2	8	14	0	0	0	-.001	.014	4.49	4.26	3.97
Zambrano C	57	129.7	571	36	20	117	69	0	6	119	7	19	.683	9	3	1	11	6	0	0	4	-.003	-.064	3.82	3.33	3.83
Marmol C	54	77.7	332	77	0	138	52	4	8	40	1	2	.699	10	1	0	2	3	38	43	0	.005	.010	2.67	2.55	1.97
Gorzelanny	50	136.3	604	29	23	119	68	4	2	136	11	14	.673	18	5	3	7	9	1	1	1	.011	.028	4.62	4.09	3.95
Lilly T *	47	117.0	480	18	18	89	29	3	2	104	19	7	.742	11	1	1	3	8	0	0	0	.000	.028	4.08	3.69	4.50
Marshall S *	43	74.7	307	80	0	90	25	5	2	58	3	6	.690	3	0	0	7	5	1	3	22	-.018	-.019	3.01	2.65	2.19
Silva C	42	113.0	480	21	21	80	24	2	7	120	11	10	.687	7	3	0	10	6	0	0	0	.018	.012	4.38	4.22	3.82
Coleman C	20	57.0	248	12	8	27	25	2	2	56	3	9	.696	1	2	0	4	2	0	0	0	.098	-.058	4.26	4.11	4.25
Cashner A	18	54.3	248	53	0	50	30	5	4	55	8	5	.686	5	2	0	2	6	0	1	16	.024	-.057	5.13	4.80	4.87
Russell J *	12	49.0	219	57	0	42	11	0	4	55	11	3	.675	3	1	1	1	1	0	2	6	.148	-.056	6.80	4.96	5.32
Berg J	9	40.0	187	41	0	14	20	1	3	45	3	5	.687	0	1	0	0	1	0	0	5	.006	.005	6.08	5.18	5.12
Maine S *	7	13.0	54	13	0	11	5	1	0	9	1	1	.730	0	0	0	0	0	0	0	2	-.041	.228	2.77	2.08	3.43
Diamond T	7	29.0	138	16	3	36	18	2	2	33	5	3	.623	1	0	0	1	3	0	0	0	.007	.049	7.14	6.83	4.82
Mateo M	6	21.7	93	21	0	26	9	1	1	20	6	1	.725	1	0	0	0	1	0	0	1	-.059	-.031	6.23	5.82	5.64
Grabow J *	4	25.7	126	28	0	20	13	0	1	35	5	1	.621	6	0	0	1	3	0	1	7	-.054	-.034	8.42	7.36	5.81
Stevens J	4	17.7	84	18	0	15	10	0	0	21	4	1	.691	1	0	0	0	0	0	1	1	.200	-.230	7.64	6.11	6.14
Howry B	3	20.7	101	24	0	8	7	1	0	29	2	1	.655	1	0	0	0	3	0	0	2	.021	.074	8.27	5.66	4.55
Atkins M	2	10.0	49	5	0	10	6	0	1	12	2	1	.633	0	1	0	0	0	0	0	0	.036	-.221	7.20	6.30	5.90
Samardzija J	2	19.3	100	7	3	9	20	1	2	21	4	2	.708	4	1	0	2	2	0	0	0	.050	.225	10.24	8.38	8.21

Only includes pitchers with at least ten Innings Pitched. Italicized stats have been adjusted for home park.

Batted Ball Pitching Stats

Player	% of PA		% of Batted Balls					Out %		Runs Per Event				Total Runs vs. Avg.				
	K%	BB%	GB%	LD%	FB%	IF/F	HR/OF	GB	OF	NIP	GB	LD	OF	NIP	GB	LD	FB	Tot
Marmol Ca	42	18	35	17	48	.06	.02	70	83	.03	.08	.35	.07	1	-1	-9	-10	-20
Marshall Se	29	9	52	23	25	.04	.07	80	73	-.01	-.00	.31	.22	-5	-5	-3	-4	-16
Lilly Te	19	6	30	19	51	.22	.12	68	95	.01	.08	.43	.12	-5	1	3	-7	-9
Dempster Ry	23	10	47	16	37	.07	.12	75	81	.03	.03	.41	.22	-1	-4	-7	6	-6
Zambrano Ca	20	13	44	20	37	.10	.06	71	80	.07	.05	.33	.13	6	-0	-3	-8	-5
Silva Ca	17	6	48	19	33	.08	.10	75	82	.02	.04	.37	.19	-4	1	2	-0	-1
Coleman Ca	11	11	49	17	34	.08	.05	71	84	.12	.05	.36	.09	4	2	-0	-5	0
Berg Ch	7	12	54	17	29	.07	.08	70	81	.17	.07	.27	.13	4	3	-1	-2	4
Cashner An	20	14	48	19	33	.04	.16	75	76	.07	.03	.33	.31	3	-1	-2	5	6
Gorzelanny Th	20	12	41	19	40	.10	.08	71	80	.06	.06	.37	.17	4	3	-1	-0	6
Diamond Th	26	14	29	25	46	.03	.14	65	83	.05	.08	.42	.23	1	0	2	3	7
Howry Bo	8	7	37	16	48	.13	.06	73	59	.10	.02	.38	.32	0	-0	0	7	7
Russell Ja	19	7	31	20	49	.15	.17	63	85	.01	.09	.40	.24	-2	2	2	6	8
Samardzija Je	9	22	30	17	52	.14	.13	76	89	.21	.02	.49	.19	6	-1	2	2	9
Grabow Jo	16	11	42	19	39	.15	.17	76	63	.08	.03	.33	.42	1	1	0	7	9
Wells Ra	17	8	47	20	33	.08	.10	71	83	.04	.07	.37	.18	-2	10	4	-2	10
MLB Average	18	9	44	18	38	.09	.10	74	83	.04	.04	.38	.18	--	--	--	--	--

Only includes pitchers who faced at least one hundred batters.

Fielding Stats

Name	INN	SBA/G	CS%	ERA	WP+PB/G	PO	A	TE	FE
Catchers									
Soto G	847.3	0.98	20%	4.29	0.297	762	45	3	1
Hill K	545.3	0.69	12%	4.16	0.330	493	29	3	1
Castillo W	44.0	1.02	40%	4.30	0.818	33	3	0	0

Name	Inn	PO	A	TE	FE	FPct	DPS	DPT	ZRDif	OOZ	Dif
First Base											
Lee D	916.7	784	92	4	2	.993	7	1	.055	25	-5
Nady X	423.0	389	36	1	0	.998	6	1	.014	15	1
Hoffpauir M	71.7	61	6	0	1	.985	0	0	--	2	--
Baker J	20.3	19	1	0	0	1.000	0	0	--	0	--
Tracy C	5.0	4	0	0	0	1.000	0	0	--	--	--
Second Base											
Theriot R	545.3	117	150	3	3	.978	10	20	-.069	22	8
DeWitt B	411.0	88	119	0	5	.976	11	19	.027	9	-1
Fontenot M	251.7	62	64	0	4	.969	6	7	-.058	8	2
Baker J	174.3	52	54	0	0	1.000	4	7	.015	2	-2
Barney D	54.3	13	17	0	2	.938	2	2	--	1	--
Shortstop											
Castro S	1073.0	183	334	11	16	.950	42	29	-.030	60	14
Theriot R	246.0	38	74	1	2	.974	6	7	-.069	11	0
Barney D	85.0	10	30	0	0	1.000	5	3	--	3	--
Fontenot M	32.0	7	9	0	0	1.000	1	1	--	1	--
Third Base											
Ramirez A	1003.0	56	190	6	10	.939	9	0	-.064	35	-2
Baker J	210.0	9	56	4	3	.903	1	1	.074	10	2
Tracy C	73.3	6	12	1	0	.947	2	0	--	2	--
Fontenot M	68.0	3	17	2	0	.909	1	0	--	2	--
Scales B	39.0	7	6	2	1	.813	1	0	--	2	--
Barney D	34.0	1	11	0	0	1.000	1	0	--	3	--
DeWitt B	8.0	0	2	1	1	.500	0	0	--	1	--
Hill K	1.0	0	0	0	0	0.000	0	0	--	--	--

Name	Inn	PO	A	TE	FE	FPct	DPS	DPT	ZRDif	OOZ	Dif
Left Field											
Soriano A	1111.0	204	6	1	6	.968	0	0	.057	37	-17
Colvin T	262.0	47	0	0	0	1.000	0	0	.004	12	-1
Nady X	33.0	6	0	0	0	1.000	0	0	--	1	--
Hoffpauir M	13.7	3	0	0	0	1.000	0	0	--	0	--
Fuld S	10.0	1	0	0	0	1.000	0	0	--	0	--
Snyder B	6.7	1	0	0	0	1.000	0	0	--	0	--
Center Field											
Byrd M	1261.0	371	6	1	2	.992	2	0	.008	80	9
Colvin T	128.0	31	1	0	1	.970	0	0	-.077	6	-1
Fuld S	47.0	22	0	0	0	1.000	0	0	--	4	--
Right Field											
Fukudome K	816.7	190	4	1	0	.995	1	0	.025	36	-9
Colvin T	388.3	96	3	1	4	.952	0	0	-.022	26	5
Nady X	153.0	24	2	0	1	.963	0	0	-.147	7	-1
Snyder B	41.7	11	0	0	0	1.000	0	0	--	2	--
Baker J	27.0	5	0	0	0	1.000	0	0	--	0	--
Hoffpauir M	10.0	2	0	0	0	1.000	0	0	--	0	--

Chicago White Sox

Stat Facts:

- Juan Pierre led the AL in HBP
- Carlos Quentin was second in HBP
- Pierre led the majors in CS
- Quentin led the majors in RF TE
- Pierre made the most OOZ plays of any LF
- Mark Buehrle had 1 HBP
- Buehrle led the majors in Pickoffs
- A.J. Pierzynski had the most innings of any C with 0 FE
- Paul Konerko tied for the AL lead in DP started by a 1B
- Alexei Ramirez turned the most DP of any SS
- Andruw Jones' LD% was 11
- Randy Williams and Lucas Harrell each had a LD% of 27

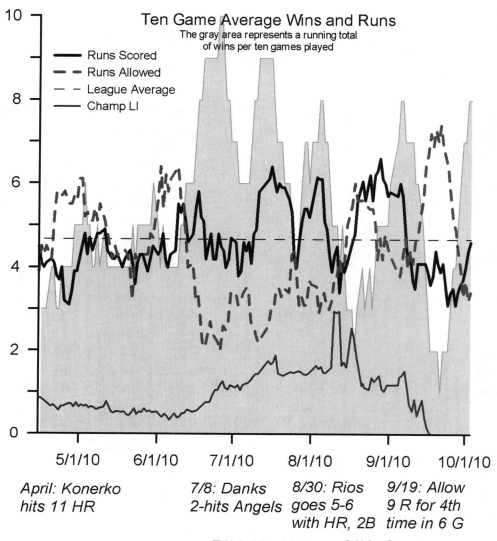

Ten Game Average Wins and Runs

The gray area represents a running total of wins per ten games played

- Runs Scored
- Runs Allowed
- League Average
- Champ LI

April: Konerko hits 11 HR

7/8: Danks 2-hits Angels

8/30: Rios goes 5-6 with HR, 2B

9/19: Allow 9 R for 4th time in 6 G

7/11: Hit 4 HR in one inning; take over 1st

8/10: Garcia shelled by MIN; drop to 2nd

Team Batting and Pitching/Fielding Stats by Month

	April	May	June	July	Aug	Sept/Oct
Wins	9	13	18	18	14	16
Losses	14	14	9	8	15	14
RS/G	4.0	4.4	4.6	5.4	5.3	4.1
RA/G	4.8	4.7	3.8	3.2	4.5	5.0
OBP	.308	.321	.335	.346	.354	.321
SLG	.390	.399	.415	.476	.460	.376
FIP	3.79	4.28	3.40	3.40	4.45	3.62
DER	.699	.686	.683	.706	.688	.657

Batting Stats

Player	BR	Runs	RBI	PA	Outs	H	2B	3B	HR	TB	K	BB	IBB	HBP	SH	SF	SB	CS	GDP	H-A	L^R	BA	OBP	SLG	GPA
Konerko P	111	89	111	631	387	171	30	1	39	320	110	72	7	5	0	6	0	1	9	.092	.052	.312	.393	.584	.307
Rios A	79	89	88	617	441	161	29	3	21	259	93	38	4	7	0	5	34	14	21	-.004	-.035	.284	.334	.457	.252
Pierre J *	76	96	47	734	498	179	18	3	1	206	47	45	0	21	15	2	68	18	8	.006	-.028	.275	.341	.316	.221
Ramirez A	71	83	70	626	440	165	29	2	18	252	82	27	2	2	7	5	13	8	12	.008	-.010	.282	.313	.431	.237
Quentin C	70	73	87	527	361	110	25	2	26	217	83	50	3	20	0	4	2	2	16	.080	-.016	.243	.342	.479	.260
Beckham G	50	58	49	498	347	112	25	2	9	168	92	37	0	7	6	4	4	6	9	.029	-.011	.252	.317	.378	.226
Pierzynski A	47	43	56	503	367	128	29	0	9	184	39	15	2	6	6	2	3	4	17	.025	.016	.270	.300	.388	.221
Jones A	44	41	48	328	231	64	12	1	19	135	73	45	0	3	0	2	9	2	15	.058	.047	.230	.341	.486	.262
Vizquel O +	37	36	30	391	264	95	11	1	2	114	45	34	0	2	7	4	11	7	8	-.054	-.052	.276	.341	.331	.225
Kotsay M *	34	30	31	359	261	78	17	2	8	123	36	32	3	0	0	0	1	3	9	-.033	.215	.239	.306	.376	.221
Teahen M *	26	31	25	262	186	60	13	2	4	89	61	25	0	0	2	2	3	5	8	-.016	.102	.258	.327	.382	.231
Castro R	18	18	21	128	86	32	2	0	8	58	26	9	0	0	3	1	1	0	3	-.006	.042	.278	.328	.504	.260
Viciedo D	15	17	13	106	77	32	7	0	5	54	25	2	0	0	0	0	1	0	5	.155	.065	.308	.321	.519	.261
Ramirez M	11	6	2	88	53	18	1	0	1	22	23	14	0	5	0	0	0	0	2	.052	.010	.261	.420	.319	.256
Lillibridge	8	19	16	101	81	22	5	2	2	37	36	3	0	0	0	0	5	3	2	-.060	.152	.224	.248	.378	.196
Morel B	7	9	7	70	52	15	3	0	3	27	17	4	0	0	0	1	2	0	2	.215	.132	.231	.271	.415	.215
Lucy D	4	2	2	18	10	5	3	0	1	11	3	2	0	1	0	0	1	0	0	-.292	.200	.333	.444	.733	.365
De Aza A *	4	7	2	32	22	9	3	0	0	12	4	1	0	0	1	0	2	1	0	.305	-.070	.300	.323	.400	.233
Nix J	3	3	5	57	42	8	1	0	1	12	12	7	2	0	1	0	0	0	1	.045	-.186	.163	.268	.245	.173
Flowers T	1	2	0	15	10	1	0	0	0	1	5	4	0	0	0	0	0	0	0	.240	-.219	.091	.333	.091	.164
Floyd G	1	0	0	5	3	1	0	0	0	1	2	1	0	0	0	0	0	0	0	-.243	-.008	.250	.400	.250	.231

Only includes batters with at least one Base Run. Italicized stats have been adjusted for home park.

Batted Ball Batting Stats

Player	% of PA		% of Batted Balls					Out %		Runs Per Event				Total Runs vs. Avg.				
	K%	BB%	GB%	LD%	FB%	IF/F	HR/OF	GB	OF	NIP	GB	LD	OF	NIP	GB	LD	FB	Tot
Konerko Pa	17	12	35	20	45	.08	.21	74	79	.08	.04	.42	.34	8	-1	10	39	55
Quentin Ca	16	13	37	14	49	.14	.16	76	87	.10	.02	.45	.24	9	-5	-2	15	18
Rios Al	15	7	45	17	38	.09	.13	69	86	.04	.07	.37	.19	-2	7	0	5	10
Jones An	22	15	44	11	44	.07	.22	79	79	.07	-.01	.32	.36	5	-5	-8	18	9
Viciedo Da	24	2	42	19	39	.16	.15	64	68	-.08	.08	.47	.35	-3	1	2	4	4
Ramirez Al	13	5	48	19	33	.12	.12	72	86	.01	.06	.37	.18	-6	7	3	-1	3
Castro Ra	20	7	42	20	38	.12	.23	71	87	.00	.06	.31	.32	-1	0	-1	4	2
Teahen Ma	23	10	47	23	30	.08	.08	79	80	.02	.00	.40	.19	-1	-3	3	-2	-4
Beckham Go	18	9	46	17	37	.12	.08	70	86	.04	.07	.40	.13	-1	4	-0	-7	-4
Lillibridge Br	36	3	36	25	39	.04	.09	76	80	-.08	.02	.35	.20	-4	-0	-0	-0	-5
Kotsay Ma	10	9	44	16	40	.05	.07	82	85	.10	-.00	.36	.13	3	-5	-2	-1	-6
Vizquel Om	12	9	46	21	33	.11	.02	70	88	.09	.07	.32	.01	3	5	2	-16	-7
Pierzynski An	8	4	49	16	36	.08	.06	79	82	.05	.01	.39	.13	-3	-6	1	-4	-13
Pierre Ju	6	9	59	19	23	.07	.01	75	82	.16	.05	.31	.04	9	7	-3	-26	-13
MLB Average	18	9	44	18	38	.09	.10	74	83	.04	.04	.38	.18	--	--	--	--	--

Only includes batters with at least one hundred Plate Appearances.

Pitching Stats

Player	PRC	IP	BFP	G	GS	K	BB	IBB	HBP	H	HR	DP	DER	SB	CS	PO	W	L	Sv	Op	Hld	H-A	R^L	RA	ERA	FIP
Danks J *	91	213.0	878	32	32	162	70	2	4	189	18	28	.710	6	6	4	15	11	0	0	0	-.016	.022	3.93	3.72	3.70
Floyd G	72	187.3	798	31	31	151	58	4	6	199	14	28	.663	7	4	1	10	13	0	0	0	.004	.034	4.42	4.08	3.43
Buehrle M *	71	210.3	897	33	33	99	49	1	1	246	17	22	.676	6	6	11	13	13	0	0	0	.015	-.004	4.49	4.28	3.92
Garcia F	51	157.0	671	28	28	89	45	5	3	171	23	19	.701	20	5	1	12	6	0	0	0	-.007	.010	4.87	4.64	4.70
Thornton M *	41	60.7	239	61	0	81	20	5	2	41	3	5	.714	3	0	0	5	4	8	10	21	.066	-.036	2.67	2.67	1.92
Peavy J	40	107.0	449	17	17	93	34	2	5	98	13	4	.717	12	3	3	7	6	0	0	0	-.037	-.026	4.63	4.63	3.99
Jackson E	36	75.0	315	11	11	77	18	2	1	73	8	5	.673	8	2	0	4	2	0	0	0	.021	.031	3.72	3.24	3.13
Putz J	32	54.0	219	60	0	65	15	2	1	41	4	2	.701	4	1	0	7	5	3	7	14	.047	-.082	3.00	2.83	2.45
Santos S	29	51.7	235	56	0	56	26	3	1	53	2	2	.649	4	1	1	2	2	1	3	14	-.037	.094	3.14	2.96	2.96
Pena T	28	100.7	445	52	3	56	45	6	1	108	10	15	.691	5	4	0	5	3	0	0	1	.025	.024	5.63	5.10	4.48
Linebrink S	21	57.3	249	52	0	52	17	0	3	59	11	5	.699	8	1	0	3	2	0	1	4	.048	-.068	4.87	4.40	4.84
Jenks B	20	52.7	231	55	0	61	18	1	1	54	3	3	.635	11	0	0	1	3	27	31	0	-.020	.018	4.78	4.44	2.56
Sale C *	20	23.3	92	21	0	32	10	0	0	15	2	3	.729	0	0	0	2	1	4	4	2	.049	.091	1.93	1.93	2.77
Threets E *	16	12.3	45	11	0	6	3	0	0	9	0	4	.750	1	0	0	0	0	0	0	0	.101	.130	0.73	0.00	2.87
Williams R *	7	25.0	132	27	0	22	21	6	3	37	2	4	.560	2	3	2	0	1	0	1	1	.028	-.056	6.12	5.40	4.55
Harrell L	5	24.0	119	8	3	15	17	1	0	34	2	3	.612	6	1	0	1	0	0	0	0	-.020	-.110	6.75	4.88	4.95
Hudson D	4	15.7	71	3	3	14	11	0	0	17	1	4	.622	2	1	0	1	1	0	0	0	.159	-.007	6.32	6.32	4.26
Torres C	2	13.7	71	5	1	13	9	1	0	23	2	1	.553	0	1	1	0	1	0	0	0	.028	-.008	8.56	8.56	4.87

Only includes pitchers with at least ten Innings Pitched. Italicized stats have been adjusted for home park.

Batted Ball Pitching Stats

Player	% of PA		% of Batted Balls					Out %		Runs Per Event				Total Runs vs. Avg.				
	K%	BB%	GB%	LD%	FB%	IF/F	HR/OF	GB	OF	NIP	GB	LD	OF	NIP	GB	LD	FB	Tot
Danks Jo	18	8	45	16	39	.10	.08	73	85	.03	.05	.39	.13	-3	0	-6	-11	-20
Thornton Ma	34	9	40	23	37	.12	.07	85	83	-.01	-.03	.41	.12	-5	-6	-0	-6	-16
Putz J.	30	7	49	13	39	.10	.09	71	81	-.02	.07	.39	.17	-5	1	-5	-2	-11
Peavy Ja	21	8	41	18	42	.06	.11	71	87	.02	.06	.32	.16	-3	3	-6	-0	-6
Jackson Ed	24	6	47	18	34	.07	.11	68	92	-.02	.08	.43	.12	-6	4	1	-5	-6
Jenks Ro	26	8	58	21	21	.03	.10	74	69	-.00	.05	.37	.26	-3	1	-0	-2	-4
Floyd Ga	19	8	50	18	32	.06	.08	71	83	.02	.06	.39	.14	-4	9	1	-9	-3
Santos Se	24	12	43	21	36	.06	.02	61	85	.04	.12	.39	.05	1	4	1	-7	-1
Linebrink Sc	21	8	32	19	49	.08	.14	73	81	.01	.04	.30	.25	-2	-1	-3	8	3
Buehrle Ma	11	6	46	16	38	.09	.06	72	76	.04	.05	.38	.16	-4	6	1	3	7
Pena Ad	13	11	49	18	33	.08	.10	72	87	.10	.05	.37	.14	5	5	1	-4	7
Harrell Lu	13	14	50	27	21	.11	.13	69	71	.13	.07	.36	.30	3	1	3	1	8
Garcia Fr	13	7	41	21	38	.10	.12	74	87	.05	.04	.39	.19	-1	-0	10	5	14
Williams Ra	17	18	37	27	36	.13	.07	59	72	.13	.12	.45	.21	5	3	5	1	14
MLB Average	18	9	44	18	38	.09	.10	74	83	.04	.04	.38	.18	--	--	--	--	--

Only includes pitchers who faced at least one hundred batters.

Fielding Stats

Name	INN	SBA/G	CS%	ERA	WP+PB/G	PO	A	TE	FE
Catchers									
Pierzynski A	1092.7	0.75	18%	3.95	0.428	865	61	4	0
Castro R	279.0	0.94	21%	4.48	0.226	214	14	0	1
Lucy D	43.0	1.05	0%	5.23	0.419	43	0	0	0
Flowers T	31.7	0.85	33%	4.26	0.568	30	1	0	0

Name	Inn	PO	A	TE	FE	FPct	DPS	DPT	ZRDif	OOZ	Dif
First Base											
Konerko P	1102.0	1069	83	2	5	.994	16	2	-.117	29	-7
Kotsay M	307.3	298	20	0	1	.997	1	1	.020	12	2
Viciedo D	28.7	30	0	0	0	1.000	0	0	--	0	--
Teahen M	8.0	5	0	0	0	1.000	0	0	--	--	--
Second Base											
Beckham G	1111.0	245	375	5	6	.981	36	61	-.034	31	3
Lillibridge B	171.0	34	56	4	0	.957	3	8	.042	2	-2
Vizquel O	151.0	22	41	0	0	1.000	5	4	-.001	3	-1
Nix J	13.0	5	2	0	0	1.000	0	0	--	0	--
Shortstop											
Ramirez A	1376.0	249	499	8	12	.974	46	53	.012	67	8
Vizquel O	61.0	13	15	0	0	1.000	2	4	--	2	--
Lillibridge B	4.7	1	0	0	0	1.000	0	0	--	--	--
Nix J	4.0	2	1	0	0	1.000	0	0	--	0	--
Third Base											
Vizquel O	582.3	31	110	1	2	.979	14	0	-.067	19	-3
Teahen M	411.0	32	82	6	4	.919	6	0	-.057	12	-3
Morel B	164.0	5	32	0	1	.974	1	0	-.036	2	-4
Viciedo D	162.0	8	27	1	3	.897	4	1	-.105	2	-4
Nix J	113.0	8	17	3	2	.833	2	0	-.111	2	-2
Lillibridge B	14.0	1	1	0	0	1.000	0	0	--	--	--

Name	Inn	PO	A	TE	FE	FPct	DPS	DPT	ZRDif	OOZ	Dif
Left Field											
Pierre J	1330.0	307	4	0	1	.997	1	0	.025	74	9
Jones A	101.0	21	2	0	0	1.000	0	0	.024	4	-1
Rios A	11.0	4	0	0	0	1.000	0	0	--	1	--
Lillibridge B	4.0	1	0	0	0	1.000	0	0	--	0	--
Center Field											
Rios A	1246.0	384	6	1	4	.987	3	0	-.005	99	28
Jones A	125.0	33	0	0	1	.971	0	0	-.004	4	-3
De Aza A	52.0	11	0	0	0	1.000	0	0	--	3	--
Lillibridge B	22.7	6	0	0	0	1.000	0	0	--	1	--
Right Field											
Quentin C	897.0	183	4	4	4	.959	1	0	-.052	30	-19
Jones A	397.3	82	6	2	0	.978	2	0	.013	20	-2
Teahen M	77.0	12	0	0	0	1.000	0	0	--	4	--
Kotsay M	48.0	9	2	0	0	1.000	0	0	--	2	--
De Aza A	19.0	6	0	0	0	1.000	0	0	--	1	--
Nix J	7.0	3	0	0	0	1.000	0	0	--	1	--
Lillibridge B	1.0	1	0	0	0	1.000	0	0	--	0	--

Cincinnati Reds

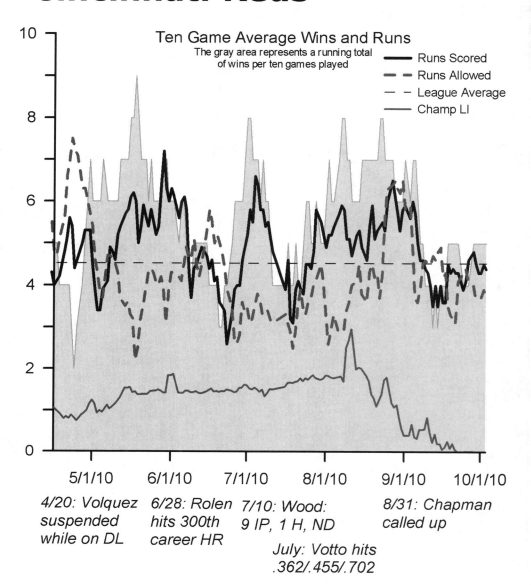

Ten Game Average Wins and Runs

The gray area represents a running total of wins per ten games played

Runs Scored — Runs Allowed — League Average — Champ LI

4/20: Volquez suspended while on DL

6/28: Rolen hits 300th career HR

7/10: Wood: 9 IP, 1 H, ND

July: Votto hits .362/.455/.702

8/31: Chapman called up

Team Batting and Pitching/Fielding Stats by Month

	April	May	June	July	Aug	Sept/Oct
Wins	12	18	14	14	19	14
Losses	11	11	13	12	8	16
RS/G	4.6	5.6	4.4	5.0	5.5	4.2
RA/G	5.5	4.0	4.3	3.3	4.7	3.8
OBP	.322	.366	.327	.326	.347	.337
SLG	.391	.507	.418	.423	.440	.424
FIP	4.56	3.92	4.67	4.31	4.31	3.44
DER	.680	.693	.695	.757	.699	.703

Batting Stats

Player	BR	Runs	RBI	PA	Outs	H	2B	3B	HR	TB	K	BB	IBB	HBP	SH	SF	SB	CS	GDP	H-A	L^R	BA	OBP	SLG	GPA
Votto J *	119	106	113	648	386	177	36	2	37	328	125	91	8	7	0	3	16	5	11	-.047	.073	.324	.424	.600	.339
Phillips B	78	100	59	687	480	172	33	5	18	269	83	46	1	8	6	1	16	12	14	.003	.014	.275	.332	.430	.256
Bruce J *	78	80	70	573	382	143	23	5	25	251	136	58	5	1	0	5	5	4	12	.047	-.019	.281	.353	.493	.281
Stubbs D	74	91	77	583	395	131	19	6	22	228	168	55	2	5	3	6	30	6	6	.029	.000	.255	.329	.444	.258
Rolen S	73	66	83	537	351	134	34	3	20	234	82	50	3	8	0	8	1	2	12	.025	.004	.285	.358	.497	.284
Gomes J	67	77	86	571	382	136	24	3	18	220	123	39	3	12	0	9	5	3	4	.007	.052	.266	.327	.431	.254
Cabrera O	47	64	42	537	379	130	33	0	4	175	53	28	0	3	5	7	11	4	11	.055	.070	.263	.303	.354	.224
Hernandez R	43	30	48	352	228	93	18	1	7	134	49	29	1	5	3	2	0	0	8	.025	.009	.297	.364	.428	.270
Hanigan R	32	25	40	243	148	61	11	0	5	87	21	33	4	4	1	2	0	0	6	.097	.073	.300	.405	.429	.288
Cairo M	27	30	28	226	146	58	12	0	4	82	30	17	0	4	2	3	4	0	4	.043	-.039	.290	.353	.410	.260
Heisey C	26	33	21	226	155	51	10	1	8	87	57	16	1	6	1	2	1	2	3	.007	-.124	.254	.324	.433	.253
Janish P	23	23	25	228	155	52	10	0	5	77	30	22	2	2	3	1	1	3	4	-.087	.059	.260	.338	.385	.247
Nix L *	21	16	18	182	123	48	11	2	4	75	39	15	4	0	2	0	0	1	5	-.075	-.032	.291	.350	.455	.270
Miller C	7	5	9	79	58	18	5	0	2	29	16	2	0	2	1	0	0	0	2	.063	-.089	.243	.282	.392	.224
Leake M	7	5	3	60	32	16	1	0	0	17	15	5	0	1	6	0	0	0	0	-.064	-.035	.333	.407	.354	.271
Francisco J	5	3	7	59	43	15	3	0	1	21	20	4	0	0	0	0	0	1	2	-.015	.101	.273	.322	.382	.239
Edmonds J *	5	6	3	32	23	6	2	0	3	17	7	3	0	0	0	0	0	0	0	-.340	.303	.207	.281	.586	.272
Valaika C	3	3	2	40	30	10	1	0	1	14	9	1	0	0	1	0	0	0	2	.112	.242	.263	.282	.368	.218
Wood T	2	1	3	42	30	7	2	1	1	14	15	0	0	0	5	0	0	0	0	.069	-.238	.189	.189	.378	.179
Dickerson C	2	9	0	45	36	9	1	1	0	12	19	1	0	0	0	0	3	0	1	-.074	.189	.205	.222	.273	.167
Sutton D +	2	1	4	3	1	2	0	0	1	5	1	0	0	0	0	0	0	0	0	--	1.100	.667	.667	1.667	.713
Bloomquist W	2	0	0	18	12	5	0	0	0	5	3	1	0	0	0	0	0	0	0	.162	-.354	.294	.333	.294	.223
Owings M	1	2	3	14	11	3	0	0	1	6	6	0	0	0	0	0	0	0	0	.407	-.238	.214	.214	.429	.203
Bailey H	1	1	2	39	27	7	0	0	0	7	15	2	0	0	4	0	0	0	1	.109	.047	.212	.257	.212	.168
Alonso Y *	1	2	3	29	24	6	2	0	0	8	10	0	0	0	0	0	0	0	1	-.034	.122	.207	.207	.276	.161

Only includes batters with at least one Base Run. Italicized stats have been adjusted for home park.

Batted Ball Batting Stats

Player	% of PA		% of Batted Balls					Out %		Runs Per Event				Total Runs vs. Avg.				
	K%	BB%	GB%	LD%	FB%	IF/F	HR/OF	GB	OF	NIP	GB	LD	OF	NIP	GB	LD	FB	Tot
Votto Jo	19	15	45	20	35	.00	.24	74	72	.09	.05	.40	.44	13	1	7	43	65
Rolen Sc	15	11	37	19	44	.08	.13	74	81	.08	.04	.38	.22	5	-1	4	14	21
Bruce Ja	24	10	36	20	44	.10	.17	70	83	.03	.06	.41	.28	-1	2	4	16	21
Hanigan Ry	9	15	48	21	31	.12	.10	72	82	.18	.06	.34	.18	8	2	3	-0	12
Stubbs Ro	29	10	44	16	40	.09	.18	61	85	.01	.13	.37	.27	-5	13	-9	9	8
Gomes Jo	22	9	29	21	50	.14	.09	64	85	.02	.10	.44	.14	-3	4	8	-1	8
Phillips Br	12	8	51	15	33	.04	.10	74	81	.07	.04	.38	.20	2	2	-2	7	8
Hernandez Ra	14	10	52	20	29	.09	.07	65	84	.08	.08	.40	.12	2	6	4	-6	7
Nix La	21	8	40	22	37	.02	.09	65	83	.01	.09	.46	.15	-1	2	4	-0	4
Cairo Mi	13	9	44	25	31	.09	.08	75	80	.08	.04	.35	.15	1	0	4	-2	4
Heisey Ch	25	10	35	19	45	.14	.13	67	89	.02	.09	.43	.18	-1	3	0	-1	2
Janish Pa	13	11	30	19	51	.16	.07	72	87	.09	.06	.40	.10	2	1	2	-4	1
Cabrera Or	10	6	45	18	37	.10	.03	70	88	.06	.08	.37	.03	-2	7	4	-20	-10
MLB Average	18	9	44	18	38	.09	.10	74	83	.04	.04	.38	.18	--	--	--	--	--

Only includes batters with at least one hundred Plate Appearances.

Pitching Stats

Player	PRC	IP	BFP	G	GS	K	BB	IBB	HBP	H	HR	DP	DER	SB	CS	PO	W	L	Sv	Op	Hld	H-A	R^L	RA	ERA	FIP
Arroyo B	78	215.7	880	33	33	121	59	5	6	188	29	22	.756	6	2	0	17	10	0	0	0	.011	-.070	3.96	3.88	4.66
Cueto J	74	185.7	780	31	31	138	56	5	9	181	19	17	.706	3	4	3	12	7	0	0	0	-.024	.012	3.83	3.64	4.01
Leake M	41	138.3	604	24	22	91	49	2	3	158	19	24	.667	5	3	1	8	4	0	0	0	.009	-.010	5.01	4.23	4.75
Wood T *	41	102.7	419	17	17	86	26	1	4	85	9	6	.728	0	0	0	5	4	0	0	0	.063	-.065	3.94	3.51	3.51
Bailey H	39	109.0	465	19	19	100	40	6	3	109	11	8	.682	10	6	1	4	3	0	0	0	.022	.029	4.54	4.46	3.69
Rhodes A *	35	55.0	217	70	0	50	18	0	1	38	4	2	.764	3	2	0	4	4	0	2	26	.068	.010	2.29	2.29	3.36
Masset N	35	76.7	322	82	0	85	33	3	1	64	7	8	.699	6	3	0	4	4	2	5	20	-.013	.028	3.64	3.40	3.38
Harang A	29	111.7	504	22	20	82	38	0	4	139	16	9	.659	3	4	1	6	7	0	0	0	-.038	.024	5.72	5.32	4.72
Cordero F	29	72.7	316	75	0	59	36	1	2	68	5	7	.701	12	1	0	6	5	40	48	1	-.043	-.048	3.96	3.84	3.99
Volquez E	24	62.7	275	12	12	67	35	0	3	59	6	8	.677	4	1	0	4	3	0	0	0	-.074	.013	4.31	4.31	4.12
Ondrusek L	23	58.7	240	60	0	39	20	1	0	49	7	5	.747	0	2	0	5	0	0	2	6	.005	.063	3.84	3.68	4.39
LeCure S	17	48.0	217	15	6	37	25	3	5	50	6	5	.694	7	1	1	2	5	0	0	0	-.094	-.074	4.50	4.50	4.97
Smith J	16	42.0	179	37	0	26	11	1	2	45	7	7	.692	1	1	0	3	2	1	2	2	-.008	-.074	3.86	3.86	4.98
Bray B *	11	28.3	117	35	0	30	10	1	0	21	4	0	.753	1	0	0	0	2	0	0	2	-.052	-.077	4.13	4.13	3.87
Owings M	10	33.3	153	22	0	35	25	0	3	28	3	1	.713	2	1	0	3	2	0	0	0	.113	-.157	5.40	5.40	4.79
Maloney M *	10	20.7	86	7	2	13	5	1	1	20	1	1	.723	0	1	0	2	2	0	0	0	-.012	-.040	3.05	3.05	3.92
Herrera D *	9	23.0	104	36	0	14	6	0	0	31	2	1	.646	0	0	0	1	3	0	1	9	.073	-.035	3.91	3.91	3.89
Chapman A *	8	13.3	51	15	0	19	5	0	0	9	0	2	.667	2	2	1	2	2	0	1	4	-.247	-.059	2.70	2.03	1.47
Fisher C	6	22.3	100	18	0	21	13	2	1	22	1	3	.672	5	0	0	1	1	0	0	0	-.089	-.040	5.64	5.64	3.51
Lincoln M	4	19.7	94	19	0	12	10	1	2	25	1	2	.652	0	0	0	1	0	0	0	3	.084	.094	7.32	7.32	4.47
Del Rosario	3	8.7	42	9	0	3	4	0	0	13	0	4	.571	0	0	0	1	1	0	2	0	-.109	-.012	4.15	2.08	3.89

Only includes pitchers with at least ten Innings Pitched. Italicized stats have been adjusted for home park.

Batted Ball Pitching Stats

Player	% of PA		% of Batted Balls					Out %		Runs Per Event				Total Runs vs. Avg.				
	K%	BB%	GB%	LD%	FB%	IF/F	HR/OF	GB	OF	NIP	GB	LD	OF	NIP	GB	LD	FB	Tot
Arroyo Br	14	7	43	16	40	.11	.12	77	91	.05	.03	.33	.15	-2	-5	-9	-5	-21
Wood Tr	21	7	31	21	48	.10	.07	79	87	.01	.02	.36	.10	-4	-5	0	-7	-16
Rhodes Ar	23	9	36	21	43	.10	.07	81	88	.01	.01	.30	.10	-2	-3	-3	-5	-13
Masset Ni	26	11	47	19	34	.15	.12	72	84	.02	.05	.34	.19	-2	-0	-4	-4	-10
Ondrusek Lo	16	8	48	14	38	.15	.12	78	84	.04	.02	.36	.20	-0	-2	-3	0	-5
Bray Bi	26	9	37	7	57	.12	.11	57	91	.00	.16	.31	.13	-1	3	-5	-1	-4
Cordero Fr	19	12	43	20	37	.09	.07	72	91	.07	.05	.39	.07	3	0	2	-9	-4
Cueto Jo	18	8	42	19	39	.09	.09	74	87	.03	.05	.40	.14	-2	-1	5	-6	-4
Fisher Ch	21	14	42	12	46	.10	.04	67	73	.07	.08	.27	.17	1	1	-3	0	0
Volquez Ed	24	14	54	15	31	.04	.12	70	88	.05	.08	.42	.18	3	3	-3	-2	0
Bailey Da	22	9	42	21	37	.10	.10	77	79	.02	.03	.38	.21	-2	-2	3	2	1
Owings Mi	23	18	31	20	49	.19	.09	70	84	.09	.08	.39	.13	4	-0	-0	-2	2
Herrera Da	13	6	43	26	31	.08	.08	75	91	.02	.06	.44	.08	-1	1	5	-2	2
Smith Jo	15	7	50	18	32	.09	.18	68	91	.04	.08	.33	.22	-0	3	-1	1	3
LeCure Sa	17	14	46	20	34	.12	.11	72	80	.09	.06	.32	.20	4	1	-0	0	5
Leake Mi	15	9	50	18	32	.07	.14	73	79	.05	.05	.38	.25	1	3	3	9	16
Harang Aa	16	8	37	22	41	.08	.11	69	86	.04	.08	.40	.16	-0	4	10	4	17
MLB Average	18	9	44	18	38	.09	.10	74	83	.04	.04	.38	.18	--	--	--	--	--

Only includes pitchers who faced at least one hundred batters.

Fielding Stats

Name	INN	SBA/G	CS%	ERA	WP+PB/G	PO	A	TE	FE
Catchers									
Hernandez R	732.0	0.60	29%	4.80	0.418	594	49	4	0
Hanigan R	525.7	0.68	30%	3.36	0.223	436	21	4	0
Miller C	195.3	0.51	27%	2.90	0.230	126	10	0	0

Name	Inn	PO	A	TE	FE	FPct	DPS	DPT	ZRDif	OOZ	Dif
First Base											
Votto J	1283.0	1132	128	2	3	.996	11	1	-.009	51	9
Cairo M	100.0	97	4	0	1	.990	0	0	-.049	3	-0
Alonso Y	30.0	24	4	1	1	.933	1	0	--	3	--
Hernandez R	22.0	19	0	0	0	1.000	0	0	--	1	--
Edmonds J	18.0	17	0	0	0	1.000	0	0	--	--	--
Second Base											
Phillips B	1311.0	281	419	1	2	.996	35	56	-.018	36	4
Valaika C	77.0	19	24	0	0	1.000	1	6	--	4	--
Janish P	34.0	7	7	0	0	1.000	0	1	--	0	--
Cairo M	26.0	3	8	0	0	1.000	0	1	--	0	--
Bloomquist W	3.0	0	0	0	0	0.000	0	0	--	--	--
Sutton D	2.0	0	1	0	0	1.000	0	0	--	0	--
Shortstop											
Cabrera O	1030.0	165	300	2	8	.977	24	32	.027	29	-15
Janish P	416.3	88	119	3	1	.981	17	13	.024	15	-3
Valaika C	3.0	0	2	0	0	1.000	1	0	--	0	--
Sutton D	2.0	0	1	0	0	1.000	0	0	--	0	--
Cairo M	1.0	0	0	0	0	0.000	0	0	--	--	--
Third Base											
Rolen S	1074.0	83	259	2	6	.977	25	0	.037	41	1
Cairo M	241.7	17	29	1	1	.958	3	0	-.056	8	-1
Francisco J	74.7	3	8	1	0	.917	3	0	--	2	--
Janish P	61.7	5	16	0	0	1.000	0	1	--	5	--
Sutton D	1.0	0	0	0	0	0.000	0	0	--	--	--

Name	Inn	PO	A	TE	FE	FPct	DPS	DPT	ZRDif	OOZ	Dif
Left Field											
Gomes J	1037.0	197	6	2	2	.981	1	0	-.016	38	-13
Nix L	269.0	52	2	0	0	1.000	1	0	.034	14	1
Heisey C	96.7	24	1	0	0	1.000	0	0	--	7	--
Dickerson C	33.3	7	0	0	0	1.000	0	0	--	1	--
Edmonds J	9.0	0	0	0	0	0.000	0	0	--	--	--
Bloomquist W	8.0	0	0	0	0	0.000	0	0	--	--	--
Center Field											
Stubbs D	1229.0	380	7	0	5	.987	2	0	.008	57	-13
Heisey C	143.0	38	0	0	0	1.000	0	0	.061	5	-3
Dickerson C	37.3	10	0	0	0	1.000	0	0	--	3	--
Edmonds J	26.0	7	0	0	0	1.000	0	0	--	0	--
Nix L	17.0	4	1	0	0	1.000	1	0	--	1	--
Right Field											
Bruce J	1199.0	343	7	0	3	.992	1	0	.041	84	18
Heisey C	189.0	44	1	0	2	.957	0	0	.073	11	1
Bloomquist W	27.3	6	0	0	0	1.000	0	0	--	2	--
Nix L	20.3	5	0	0	0	1.000	0	0	--	0	--
Cairo M	7.0	1	0	0	0	1.000	0	0	--	0	--
Dickerson C	7.0	3	0	0	0	1.000	0	0	--	2	--
Edmonds J	3.0	1	0	0	0	1.000	0	0	--	0	--

Cleveland Indians

Stat Facts:
- Luis Valbueña had the fewest Base Runs of any player with 300+ PA
- Valbueña's GPA was .194
- Fausto Carmona induced the most GDP in the AL
- Mitch Talbot had the highest H-A of any pitcher with 150+ IP
- Talbot allowed 4 SB in 15 attempts
- Lou Marson had the highest CS% of AL primary C
- Russell Branyan made 5 FE in 383 innings
- Jayson Nix led the AL in 3B FE, in 321 innings
- Shin-Soo Choo led the majors in OF assists
- Carlos Santana walked in 20% of his PA
- Carlos Carrasco allowed 0 infield pop-ups
- 87% of Jensen Lewis's GB were outs

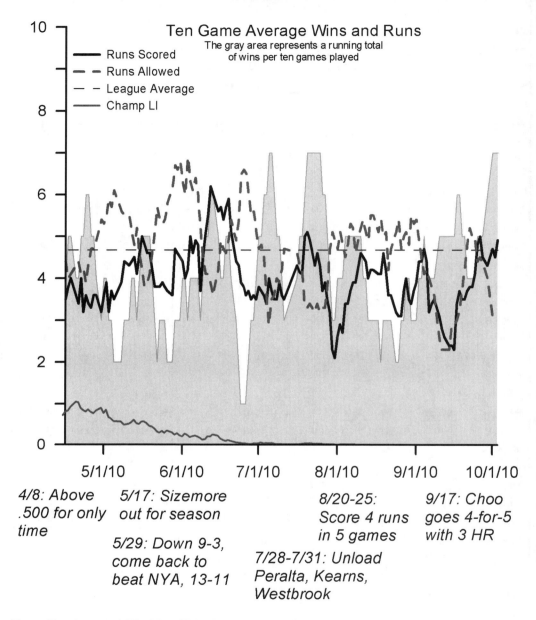

Ten Game Average Wins and Runs
The gray area represents a running total of wins per ten games played

- Runs Scored
- Runs Allowed
- League Average
- Champ LI

4/8: Above .500 for only time

5/17: Sizemore out for season

5/29: Down 9-3, come back to beat NYA, 13-11

7/28-7/31: Unload Peralta, Kearns, Westbrook

8/20-25: Score 4 runs in 5 games

9/17: Choo goes 4-for-5 with 3 HR

Team Batting and Pitching/Fielding Stats by Month

	April	May	June	July	Aug	Sept/Oct
Wins	9	9	12	13	10	16
Losses	13	18	16	14	18	14
RS/G	3.5	4.3	4.5	3.6	4.1	3.8
RA/G	4.7	5.7	4.8	4.1	5.0	3.6
OBP	.327	.325	.318	.323	.315	.323
SLG	.358	.366	.414	.379	.377	.372
FIP	4.71	4.86	4.07	4.37	4.95	3.83
DER	.715	.659	.697	.703	.683	.718

Batting Stats

Player	BR	Runs	RBI	PA	Outs	H	2B	3B	HR	TB	K	BB	IBB	HBP	SH	SF	SB	CS	GDP	H-A	L^R	BA	OBP	SLG	GPA
Choo S *	104	81	90	646	403	165	31	2	22	266	118	83	11	11	0	2	22	7	11	.048	.101	.300	.401	.484	.312
Hafner T *	66	46	50	462	289	110	29	0	13	178	94	51	10	12	0	3	2	1	2	.078	.048	.278	.374	.449	.291
Kearns A	43	42	42	342	232	82	18	1	8	126	78	34	2	5	0	2	4	1	12	-.037	-.026	.272	.354	.419	.273
Crowe T +	42	48	36	479	351	111	24	3	2	147	73	29	1	3	5	0	20	7	13	.004	-.058	.251	.302	.333	.227
LaPorta M	42	41	41	425	305	83	15	1	12	136	82	46	1	1	0	2	0	0	12	-.012	-.004	.221	.306	.362	.236
Cabrera A +	40	39	29	425	290	105	16	1	3	132	60	25	0	5	11	3	6	4	10	.008	-.015	.276	.326	.346	.242
Peralta J	40	37	43	373	259	82	23	2	7	130	69	32	1	1	0	6	1	0	7	-.057	.017	.246	.308	.389	.245
Donald J	35	39	24	325	225	75	19	3	4	112	70	22	2	3	4	0	5	1	3	-.018	.069	.253	.312	.378	.243
Nix J	34	29	29	306	223	66	14	0	13	119	75	13	0	7	2	2	1	2	5	.060	.066	.234	.283	.422	.241
Duncan S	31	29	36	259	180	53	10	0	11	96	76	26	2	3	0	1	1	0	4	.100	.057	.231	.317	.419	.256
Santana C +	30	23	22	192	114	39	13	0	6	70	29	37	2	1	0	4	3	0	3	-.068	-.131	.260	.401	.467	.308
Brantley M *	29	38	22	325	232	73	9	3	3	97	38	22	0	0	4	2	10	2	6	.035	.069	.246	.296	.327	.223
Branyan R *	28	24	24	190	128	45	9	0	10	84	49	16	1	1	1	1	0	0	2	-.082	.075	.263	.328	.491	.280
Marson L	21	29	22	294	219	51	15	0	3	75	55	26	0	3	2	1	8	1	7	-.005	.091	.195	.274	.286	.202
Marte A	19	18	19	188	136	39	7	2	5	65	35	17	0	0	0	1	0	3	2	.005	.034	.229	.298	.382	.238
Valbuena L *	19	22	24	310	229	53	12	0	2	71	61	28	1	3	2	2	1	2	5	-.079	-.133	.193	.273	.258	.194
Sizemore G *	10	15	13	140	104	27	6	2	0	37	35	9	0	2	0	1	4	2	1	.046	.117	.211	.271	.289	.201
Grudzielanek	9	10	11	119	84	30	0	0	0	30	10	8	0	1	0	0	2	0	4	-.029	-.013	.273	.328	.273	.223
Brown J *	6	9	2	92	70	20	7	0	0	27	10	4	0	1	0	0	0	0	3	.012	-.068	.230	.272	.310	.207
Gimenez C	6	6	8	67	48	11	5	0	1	19	22	8	0	0	1	0	0	0	1	.159	.050	.190	.288	.328	.219
Carlin L +	4	4	3	16	9	5	0	0	2	11	5	2	0	0	0	0	0	0	0	.038	.006	.357	.438	.786	.408
Hernandez A	4	6	2	63	48	15	3	0	0	18	9	2	0	0	0	0	1	0	2	-.074	-.103	.246	.270	.295	.202
Redmond M	3	7	5	68	52	13	4	0	0	17	10	2	0	1	2	0	0	0	2	-.087	.024	.206	.242	.270	.183
Sutton D +	3	4	4	39	29	8	1	0	1	12	12	3	0	0	0	0	0	0	1	-.218	.177	.222	.282	.333	.218

Only includes batters with at least one Base Run. Italicized stats have been adjusted for home park.

Batted Ball Batting Stats

Player	% of PA		% of Batted Balls					Out %		Runs Per Event				Total Runs vs. Avg.				
	K%	BB%	GB%	LD%	FB%	IF/F	HR/OF	GB	OF	NIP	GB	LD	OF	NIP	GB	LD	FB	Tot
Choo Sh	18	15	45	20	35	.03	.15	73	81	.09	.05	.40	.27	13	3	6	15	37
Hafner Tr	20	14	43	19	38	.06	.11	75	76	.07	.05	.45	.24	6	0	5	8	19
Santana Ca	15	20	35	21	44	.11	.13	86	86	.15	-.02	.41	.19	8	-2	2	2	10
Branyan Ru	26	9	39	15	47	.11	.20	72	80	.01	.07	.44	.32	-2	1	-1	8	6
Kearns Au	23	11	44	24	32	.08	.12	73	76	.04	.03	.31	.27	1	-2	1	4	4
Duncan Sh	29	11	29	16	56	.15	.15	73	81	.01	.04	.43	.25	-2	-2	-3	6	0
Marte An	19	9	35	15	50	.15	.09	72	81	.04	.07	.32	.17	-0	0	-3	1	-2
Donald Ja	22	8	48	21	30	.15	.07	69	86	.01	.08	.40	.13	-3	5	3	-7	-2
Peralta Jh	18	9	34	20	46	.06	.06	75	83	.04	.03	.39	.12	-1	-3	3	-2	-3
Nix Ja	25	7	37	15	48	.18	.16	65	84	-.02	.10	.30	.25	-5	3	-6	5	-3
Grudzielanek Ma	8	8	54	19	27	.11	.00	69	96	.10	.06	.33	-.07	1	2	1	-7	-4
Sizemore Gr	25	8	39	19	42	.08	.00	81	78	-.00	-.00	.38	.09	-2	-2	-1	-3	-8
LaPorta Ma	19	11	42	13	45	.09	.10	74	84	.05	.03	.30	.17	2	-2	-10	2	-9
Cabrera As	14	7	52	17	31	.08	.03	71	88	.04	.06	.38	.05	-1	5	-1	-13	-10
Brantley Mi	12	7	48	20	32	.13	.04	77	94	.05	.04	.36	.00	-1	0	2	-15	-13
Marson Lo	18	10	56	15	29	.10	.06	79	76	.05	.01	.28	.17	0	-3	-6	-4	-14
Crowe Tr	15	7	53	18	29	.10	.02	74	77	.03	.04	.34	.11	-3	-0	-3	-11	-16
Valbuena Lu	20	10	47	18	35	.11	.03	82	92	.04	-.00	.40	.00	0	-4	-1	-14	-20
MLB Average	18	9	44	18	38	.09	.10	74	83	.04	.04	.38	.18	--	--	--	--	--

Only includes batters with at least one hundred Plate Appearances.

Pitching Stats

Player	PRC	IP	BFP	G	GS	K	BB	IBB	HBP	H	HR	DP	DER	SB	CS	PO	W	L	Sv	Op	Hld	H-A	R^L	RA	ERA	FIP
Carmona F	73	210.3	880	33	33	124	72	0	9	203	17	34	.707	33	6	0	13	14	0	0	0	.011	-.012	4.19	3.77	4.14
Masterson J	52	180.0	802	34	29	140	73	4	11	197	14	21	.665	13	8	2	6	13	0	0	2	-.069	-.034	5.35	4.70	3.90
Talbot M	46	159.3	695	28	28	88	69	2	8	169	13	22	.685	4	11	1	10	13	0	0	0	.055	.017	4.97	4.41	4.48
Perez C	43	63.0	260	63	0	61	28	3	5	40	4	6	.765	9	0	0	2	2	23	27	9	-.050	-.100	2.14	1.71	3.43
Westbrook J	39	127.7	543	21	21	73	44	4	6	133	15	17	.691	11	7	0	6	7	0	0	0	-.027	-.009	4.79	4.65	4.58
Perez R *	26	61.0	273	70	0	36	25	4	0	72	3	11	.651	5	1	0	6	1	0	4	13	-.019	-.003	3.39	3.25	3.60
Sipp T *	25	63.0	266	70	0	69	39	3	2	48	12	7	.750	8	6	6	2	2	1	3	15	.015	.013	4.29	4.14	5.21
Tomlin J	23	73.0	301	12	12	43	19	3	3	72	10	8	.717	2	3	0	6	4	0	0	0	.024	.064	4.68	4.56	4.50
Lewis J	19	36.3	153	37	0	29	19	1	0	28	1	4	.740	0	0	0	4	2	0	0	1	-.114	-.062	2.97	2.97	3.36
Carrasco C	18	44.7	188	7	7	38	14	1	1	47	6	4	.674	5	6	0	2	2	0	0	0	-.049	.137	4.03	3.83	4.10
Laffey A *	16	55.7	253	29	5	28	28	1	2	62	1	7	.675	1	0	0	2	3	0	0	5	-.042	.011	4.85	4.53	3.90
Smith J	15	40.0	170	53	0	32	24	2	1	30	4	5	.752	6	1	1	2	2	0	1	17	-.047	-.153	4.05	3.83	4.54
Huff D *	15	79.7	369	15	15	37	34	1	3	101	14	9	.680	1	1	0	2	11	0	0	0	-.039	.056	6.89	6.21	5.82
Gomez J	15	57.7	265	11	11	34	22	3	2	73	7	5	.655	7	4	2	4	5	0	0	0	-.076	.072	5.62	4.68	4.60
Germano J	15	35.3	146	23	1	29	8	1	6	27	6	1	.763	2	2	0	0	3	0	1	2	-.030	.023	3.82	3.31	4.78
Herrmann F	14	44.7	189	40	0	24	9	0	2	48	6	4	.709	3	2	0	0	1	1	2	7	-.018	-.094	4.43	4.03	4.52
Ambriz H	13	48.3	224	34	0	37	17	1	1	68	10	6	.629	4	0	1	0	2	0	0	0	-.102	.068	5.77	5.59	5.33
Wood K	4	20.0	93	23	0	18	11	2	2	21	3	2	.678	3	0	0	1	4	8	11	1	.144	.073	6.75	6.30	4.91
Wright J	3	21.3	98	18	0	9	9	0	2	25	1	5	.662	5	0	0	1	2	0	0	1	.024	-.049	7.59	5.48	4.42
Pestano V	3	5.0	23	5	0	8	5	0	0	4	0	1	.600	1	0	0	0	0	1	1	0	-.158	-.155	3.60	3.60	2.91

Only includes pitchers with at least ten Innings Pitched. Italicized stats have been adjusted for home park.

Batted Ball Pitching Stats

	% of PA		% of Batted Balls					Out %		Runs Per Event				Total Runs vs. Avg.				
Player	K%	BB%	GB%	LD%	FB%	IF/F	HR/OF	GB	OF	NIP	GB	LD	OF	NIP	GB	LD	FB	Tot
Perez Ch	23	13	34	20	46	.10	.06	83	87	.05	-.03	.36	.10	1	-6	-2	-5	-12
Carmona Fa	14	9	56	14	31	.12	.09	76	78	.07	.03	.37	.21	4	-2	-9	-1	-8
Lewis Je	19	12	30	26	43	.05	.02	87	83	.07	-.06	.32	.07	1	-4	1	-4	-6
Smith Jo	19	15	56	16	28	.06	.14	84	80	.09	-.03	.38	.24	3	-4	-2	-0	-3
Germano Ju	20	10	40	17	42	.05	.15	83	88	.04	-.00	.35	.21	-0	-3	-2	2	-2
Herrmann Fr	13	6	36	20	45	.10	.08	76	88	.03	.04	.46	.12	-1	-1	4	-1	2
Sipp To	26	15	31	14	55	.11	.16	72	87	.06	.02	.44	.22	3	-3	-3	5	2
Tomlin Jo	14	7	28	21	50	.13	.10	82	83	.04	-.01	.36	.18	-1	-5	3	6	3
Perez Ra	13	10	55	19	26	.02	.06	75	79	.08	.03	.46	.12	2	0	5	-4	3
Laffey Aa	11	12	49	21	30	.13	.02	73	83	.12	.05	.39	.08	5	2	4	-6	3
Carrasco Ca	20	8	57	14	29	.00	.16	73	75	.02	.05	.48	.32	-1	1	-0	5	5
Masterson Ju	17	10	60	15	25	.05	.11	71	81	.06	.05	.42	.20	5	8	-1	-5	7
Westbrook Ja	13	9	53	18	28	.03	.12	77	80	.07	.03	.38	.23	3	0	3	4	10
Gomez Je	13	9	47	20	33	.06	.11	74	84	.08	.04	.45	.20	2	2	7	2	12
Talbot Mi	13	11	48	17	35	.07	.07	70	80	.10	.06	.35	.15	9	6	-1	-2	12
Ambriz He	17	8	42	16	42	.10	.16	72	70	.04	.04	.43	.36	-0	0	1	14	16
Huff Da	10	10	36	21	43	.14	.13	67	76	.12	.08	.27	.28	5	4	-1	14	23
MLB Average	18	9	44	18	38	.09	.10	74	83	.04	.04	.38	.18	--	--	--	--	--

Only includes pitchers who faced at least one hundred batters.

Fielding Stats

Name	INN	SBA/G	CS%	ERA	WP+PB/G	PO	A	TE	FE
Catchers									
Marson L	725.0	0.96	34%	4.33	0.372	504	44	2	2
Santana C	340.0	0.82	29%	4.42	0.529	245	22	1	2
Gimenez C	168.7	1.71	28%	4.54	0.480	109	14	1	0
Redmond M	162.3	1.50	7%	3.99	0.333	87	11	1	0
Carlin L	37.0	1.46	33%	2.68	0.000	34	4	0	0

Name	Inn	PO	A	TE	FE	FPct	DPS	DPT	ZRDif	OOZ	Dif
First Base											
LaPorta M	791.3	815	58	1	2	.997	7	0	.009	20	-6
Branyan R	383.3	426	44	0	5	.989	4	1	.044	28	15
Marte A	168.3	186	11	0	1	.990	0	0	-.014	4	-2
Brown J	73.0	70	2	0	0	1.000	0	0	--	1	--
Duncan S	17.0	15	0	0	0	1.000	0	0	--	0	--
Second Base											
Valbuena L	581.7	127	232	1	3	.989	23	35	.030	15	1
Donald J	356.7	61	128	2	1	.984	6	10	.042	12	3
Grudzielanek	228.3	54	86	0	2	.986	9	13	.018	5	-1
Nix J	213.3	53	80	0	1	1.000	7	14	.010	10	5
Sutton D	35.0	5	17	0	0	1.000	1	3	--	0	--
Hernandez A	18.0	3	6	1	0	.900	1	1	--	2	--
Shortstop											
Cabrera A	825.3	148	271	5	7	.972	35	33	-.030	43	7
Donald J	388.3	58	138	4	5	.956	20	11	-.075	13	-4
Hernandez A	127.3	25	43	0	0	1.000	4	8	-.042	7	2
Sutton D	50.0	11	16	0	0	1.000	2	0	--	3	--
Valbuena L	42.0	8	17	1	3	.862	1	4	--	3	--
Third Base											
Peralta J	780.0	61	194	3	2	.981	24	0	.009	32	3
Nix J	321.0	34	64	2	9	.899	4	0	-.026	9	-3
Marte A	264.3	21	55	2	6	.894	5	1	-.016	12	2
Valbuena L	66.7	3	12	1	1	.882	0	0	--	3	--
Hernandez A	1.0	0	2	0	0	1.000	0	0	--	0	--

Name	Inn	PO	A	TE	FE	FPct	DPS	DPT	ZRDif	OOZ	Dif
Left Field											
Kearns A	558.0	134	1	2	2	.971	0	0	.040	32	5
Crowe T	374.0	92	6	1	0	.990	1	0	.025	15	-3
Duncan S	309.0	66	6	0	0	1.000	1	0	-.018	14	-1
Brantley M	63.0	5	0	0	0	1.000	0	0	--	2	--
Brown J	57.0	17	1	0	0	1.000	0	0	--	4	--
LaPorta M	53.0	5	0	0	0	1.000	0	0	--	1	--
Nix J	14.0	2	1	0	0	1.000	0	0	--	0	--
Hernandez A	2.0	0	0	0	0	0.000	0	0	--	--	--
Gimenez C	2.0	1	0	0	0	1.000	0	0	--	0	--
Valbuena L	1.0	0	0	0	0	0.000	0	0	--	--	--
Center Field											
Crowe T	567.7	176	3	2	2	.978	0	0	-.024	36	4
Brantley M	562.7	156	0	1	1	.987	0	0	-.013	26	-6
Sizemore G	269.7	64	0	0	1	.985	0	0	.029	18	3
Kearns A	33.0	13	0	0	0	1.000	0	0	--	3	--
Right Field											
Choo S	1249.0	267	14	1	3	.986	3	0	-.028	62	-7
Kearns A	105.3	26	0	0	0	1.000	0	0	.103	8	2
Duncan S	50.0	9	1	0	0	1.000	0	0	--	3	--
Crowe T	27.0	6	0	0	0	1.000	0	0	--	1	--
Gimenez C	1.0	0	0	0	0	0.000	0	0	--	--	--

Colorado Rockies

Stat Facts:
- Carlos Gonzalez had the highest H-A of any NL regular
- Ubaldo Jimenez was second in the NL in PRC
- Jimenez was second in the NL in GDP
- Jeff Francis's H-A was exactly .000
- Jason Hammel's R^L was exactly .000
- Esmil Rogers' FIP was far lower than his ERA
- Miguel Olivo had the second-highest CS% of regular C
- Olivo had the most innings of any NL C with 0 FE
- Ryan Spilborghs tied for the NL lead in RF TE, in 402 innings
- Troy Tulowitzki started the most DP of any NL SS
- Tulo also turned the most DP of any NL SS
- 86% of Brad Hawpe's GB were outs

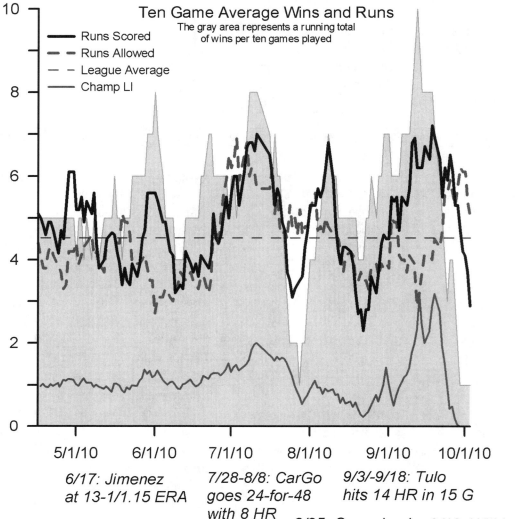

Ten Game Average Wins and Runs
The gray area represents a running total of wins per ten games played

— Runs Scored
- - Runs Allowed
— League Average
— Champ LI

6/17: Jimenez at 13-1/1.15 ERA

6/28-7/10: Take 10 of 12 from SD, SF and STL

7/28-8/8: CarGo goes 24-for-48 with 8 HR

8/25: Come back from 10-1 deficit to beat ATL

9/3/-9/18: Tulo hits 14 HR in 15 G

9/18: Within one game of 1st--will lose next 13 of 14

Team Batting and Pitching/Fielding Stats by Month

	April	May	June	July	Aug	Sept/Oct
Wins	11	16	14	13	15	14
Losses	12	12	13	13	12	17
RS/G	5.3	4.5	4.2	5.4	4.0	5.2
RA/G	4.1	3.9	4.6	5.0	4.1	4.7
OBP	.344	.330	.323	.365	.316	.337
SLG	.452	.392	.405	.478	.398	.428
FIP	3.94	3.62	3.83	3.93	3.54	4.16
DER	.701	.702	.681	.692	.655	.680

Batting Stats

Player	BR	Runs	RBI	PA	Outs	H	2B	3B	HR	TB	K	BB	IBB	HBP	SH	SF	SB	CS	GDP	H-A	L^R	BA	OBP	SLG	GPA
Gonzalez C *	105	111	117	636	407	197	34	9	34	351	135	40	8	2	0	7	26	8	9	.117	.027	.336	.376	.598	.282
Tulowitzki T	81	89	95	529	341	148	32	3	27	267	78	48	4	5	1	5	11	2	17	.052	.025	.315	.381	.568	.277
Fowler D +	55	73	36	505	338	114	20	14	6	180	104	57	0	2	7	0	13	8	5	.105	.003	.260	.347	.410	.229
Stewart I *	50	54	61	441	297	99	14	2	18	171	110	45	8	5	0	5	5	2	8	-.004	.031	.256	.338	.443	.232
Helton T *	48	48	37	473	306	102	18	1	8	146	90	67	3	2	0	6	0	0	10	.028	.010	.256	.362	.367	.225
Olivo M	47	55	58	427	298	106	17	6	14	177	117	27	5	1	2	3	7	4	6	.092	.024	.269	.315	.449	.225
Smith S *	46	55	52	398	276	88	19	5	17	168	67	35	1	2	0	3	2	1	5	.091	.144	.246	.314	.469	.229
Spilborghs R	45	41	39	388	258	95	20	2	10	149	83	39	0	5	2	1	4	5	7	.063	-.003	.279	.360	.437	.240
Mora M	39	39	45	354	236	90	12	5	7	133	53	31	2	5	2	0	2	1	9	.039	.014	.285	.358	.421	.235
Barmes C	35	43	50	432	303	91	21	0	8	136	66	35	10	5	2	3	3	2	5	.017	.045	.235	.305	.351	.199
Hawpe B *	34	24	37	300	198	66	21	2	7	112	68	36	4	1	0	4	2	1	4	.102	-.013	.255	.343	.432	.232
Giambi J *	25	17	35	222	138	43	9	0	6	70	47	35	5	6	0	5	2	0	5	.104	-.038	.244	.378	.398	.238
Herrera J +	24	34	21	257	163	63	6	2	1	76	36	25	1	0	7	3	2	2	2	.051	.005	.284	.352	.342	.216
Iannetta C	22	20	27	223	155	37	6	1	9	72	48	30	2	4	0	1	1	0	4	.075	.015	.197	.318	.383	.211
Young Jr. E	15	26	8	189	138	42	5	1	0	49	32	17	0	0	0	0	17	6	2	.063	-.017	.244	.312	.285	.187
Payton J	5	3	1	36	25	12	4	1	0	18	4	1	0	0	0	0	1	0	2	.089	-.145	.343	.361	.514	.257
Eldred B	3	4	3	27	18	6	1	0	1	10	10	2	0	1	0	0	0	0	0	.195	.218	.250	.333	.417	.225
Nelson C	2	7	0	27	19	7	1	0	0	8	4	1	0	0	1	0	1	0	1	.131	.143	.280	.308	.320	.193
Smith G *	1	2	2	16	9	4	2	0	0	6	1	0	0	0	3	0	0	0	0	-.039	-.229	.308	.308	.462	.224
Phillips P	1	4	1	25	18	5	0	0	0	5	7	2	0	0	0	0	0	0	0	.077	-.014	.217	.280	.217	.159
Belisle M	1	0	2	7	3	1	1	0	0	2	2	0	0	1	2	0	0	0	0	.305	--	.250	.400	.500	.270
Rogers E	1	2	1	21	15	3	2	0	0	5	7	0	0	0	3	0	0	0	0	-.042	.063	.167	.167	.278	.128

Only includes batters with at least one Base Run. Italicized stats have been adjusted for home park.

Batted Ball Batting Stats

Player	% of PA		% of Batted Balls					Out %		Runs Per Event				Total Runs vs. Avg.				
	K%	BB%	GB%	LD%	FB%	IF/F	HR/OF	GB	OF	NIP	GB	LD	OF	NIP	GB	LD	FB	Tot
Gonzalez Ca	21	7	43	21	37	.10	.22	67	74	-.00	.09	.45	.39	-7	11	14	33	51
Tulowitzki Tr	15	10	45	15	40	.16	.20	66	85	.07	.09	.44	.32	4	9	2	20	36
Spilborghs Ry	21	11	42	23	35	.04	.11	77	78	.05	.02	.37	.25	2	-3	3	6	9
Stewart Ia	25	11	37	22	41	.09	.17	72	89	.03	.05	.40	.23	-0	-1	4	6	9
Smith Ga	17	9	36	16	48	.05	.13	79	81	.05	.02	.34	.24	1	-4	-3	14	8
Mora Me	15	10	44	18	38	.07	.08	72	86	.07	.05	.46	.13	3	1	5	-3	7
Fowler De	21	12	45	22	33	.03	.06	73	83	.05	.06	.42	.14	3	3	6	-6	6
Giambi Ja	21	18	31	20	49	.05	.10	79	82	.10	-.00	.30	.18	7	-3	-2	3	4
Helton To	19	15	34	23	43	.03	.06	77	89	.09	.02	.42	.08	9	-4	8	-8	4
Hawpe Br	23	12	40	20	40	.03	.09	86	80	.05	-.02	.48	.21	2	-6	4	3	4
Olivo Mi	27	7	42	18	40	.14	.14	65	82	-.02	.10	.45	.24	-9	6	1	4	2
Herrera Jo	14	10	50	18	32	.03	.02	73	82	.07	.06	.38	.07	2	2	1	-6	-2
Iannetta Ch	22	15	41	13	45	.09	.16	83	88	.08	-.01	.32	.22	4	-4	-5	3	-2
Young Jr. Er	17	9	54	17	29	.15	.00	68	85	.05	.08	.38	.02	0	4	-1	-8	-4
Barmes Cl	15	9	30	21	49	.15	.06	77	87	.06	.02	.35	.08	1	-4	2	-9	-9
MLB Average	18	9	44	18	38	.09	.10	74	83	.04	.04	.38	.18	--	--	--	--	--

Only includes batters with at least one hundred Plate Appearances.

Pitching Stats

Player	PRC	IP	BFP	G	GS	K	BB	IBB	HBP	H	HR	DP	DER	SB	CS	PO	W	L	Sv	Op	Hld	H-A	R^L	RA	ERA	FIP
Jimenez U	129	221.7	894	33	33	214	92	7	9	164	10	35	.717	12	13	2	19	8	0	0	0	.030	.020	2.96	2.88	3.12
Hammel J	63	177.7	770	30	30	141	47	1	6	201	18	22	.658	18	5	2	10	9	0	0	0	.004	.000	4.91	4.81	3.80
Chacin J	60	137.3	583	28	21	138	61	5	9	114	10	18	.701	7	3	0	9	11	0	0	0	.024	-.034	4.19	3.28	3.55
Belisle M	49	92.0	365	76	0	91	16	5	2	84	7	12	.687	2	1	0	7	5	1	2	21	.018	.008	3.33	2.93	2.63
de la Rosa J	48	121.7	512	20	20	113	55	4	5	105	15	23	.704	6	3	1	8	7	0	0	0	-.021	-.027	4.59	4.22	4.32
Cook A	37	127.7	572	23	23	62	52	4	4	147	11	20	.679	4	0	2	6	8	0	0	0	-.019	-.075	5.43	5.08	4.57
Betancourt	34	62.3	248	72	0	89	8	2	0	52	9	1	.697	8	2	0	5	1	1	5	23	.096	-.099	3.61	3.61	2.51
Francis J *	33	104.3	441	20	19	67	23	3	2	119	11	14	.669	6	3	2	4	6	0	0	0	-.000	.016	5.26	5.00	3.91
Corpas M	23	62.3	274	56	0	47	22	5	2	66	7	7	.684	2	0	0	3	5	10	14	2	.081	-.109	4.76	4.62	4.06
Street H	21	47.3	187	44	0	45	11	4	2	39	5	6	.718	2	1	1	4	4	20	25	0	-.089	.034	3.99	3.61	3.24
Beimel J *	19	45.0	188	71	0	21	15	3	0	46	5	6	.714	3	0	3	1	2	0	1	20	-.066	-.075	3.60	3.40	4.51
Rogers E	17	72.0	333	28	8	66	26	2	5	94	5	8	.602	6	4	1	2	3	0	1	1	.002	-.052	7.38	6.13	3.47
Reynolds *	14	18.0	70	21	0	17	5	0	2	10	2	1	.795	0	1	1	1	0	0	0	2	.082	-.041	2.00	2.00	3.92
Flores R *	13	27.3	115	47	0	18	13	1	1	22	4	2	.747	0	1	0	2	0	0	1	4	-.018	.016	3.29	2.96	5.21
Smith G *	10	39.0	182	8	8	31	24	2	1	49	8	4	.653	1	1	1	1	2	0	0	0	.053	-.153	6.46	6.23	6.04
Daley M	10	23.3	108	28	0	18	10	1	3	27	2	1	.653	1	2	0	0	1	0	0	6	-.046	-.024	4.24	4.24	4.31
Morales F *	7	28.7	140	35	0	27	24	2	3	28	5	1	.716	1	0	0	0	4	3	6	1	-.146	-.089	6.91	6.28	6.20
Escalona E	4	6.0	26	5	0	2	4	2	0	4	0	0	.800	0	0	0	0	0	0	0	0	.114	-.259	1.50	1.50	3.53
Buchholz T	4	10.0	43	7	0	9	6	0	0	10	2	0	.692	0	3	0	1	0	0	0	0	-.031	.081	4.50	4.50	5.80
Delcarmen	2	8.3	41	9	0	6	4	1	0	12	1	1	.600	1	0	0	0	2	0	1	0	.011	.005	6.48	6.48	4.40

Only includes pitchers with at least ten Innings Pitched. Italicized stats have been adjusted for home park.

Batted Ball Pitching Stats

Player	% of PA		% of Batted Balls					Out %		Runs Per Event				Total Runs vs. Avg.				
	K%	BB%	GB%	LD%	FB%	IF/F	HR/OF	GB	OF	NIP	GB	LD	OF	NIP	GB	LD	FB	Tot
Jimenez Ub	24	11	49	16	35	.13	.06	78	77	.03	.01	.35	.16	0	-8	-14	-13	-34
Belisle Ma	25	5	46	20	33	.06	.09	80	84	-.04	-.01	.44	.16	-9	-4	3	-4	-15
Chacin Jh	24	12	47	22	32	.10	.10	76	86	.04	.02	.37	.15	2	-6	1	-10	-13
Betancourt Ra	36	3	26	22	52	.10	.13	76	87	-.08	.04	.46	.18	-11	-3	1	-0	-12
Street Hu	24	7	37	16	48	.07	.09	74	88	-.01	.02	.42	.12	-3	-1	-2	-1	-7
Beimel Jo	11	8	43	16	40	.10	.09	78	81	.08	.02	.43	.17	1	-2	1	1	1
Flores Ra	16	12	33	22	46	.11	.13	65	89	.09	.11	.23	.17	1	1	-2	0	1
de la Rosa Jo	22	12	52	19	29	.06	.17	77	86	.05	.02	.43	.25	2	-3	1	1	2
Corpas Ma	17	9	43	19	39	.16	.11	69	84	.04	.07	.40	.19	-0	2	2	0	4
Francis Je	15	6	47	21	32	.06	.10	74	84	.01	.05	.43	.16	-4	1	9	-1	4
Daley Ma	17	12	38	20	42	.13	.07	79	76	.08	.02	.53	.21	1	-1	3	1	4
Morales Fr	19	19	39	14	47	.10	.14	72	90	.12	.07	.41	.19	5	1	-1	1	5
Hammel Ja	18	7	47	20	33	.06	.10	73	78	.01	.06	.37	.21	-6	3	5	4	5
Cook Aa	11	10	58	17	25	.04	.10	75	74	.10	.03	.36	.23	6	-0	0	3	9
Rogers Es	20	9	52	21	27	.08	.09	66	81	.03	.09	.46	.19	-0	7	7	-2	12
Smith Gr	17	14	41	23	36	.14	.21	76	70	.09	.03	.36	.44	3	-0	2	10	15
MLB Average	18	9	44	18	38	.09	.10	74	83	.04	.04	.38	.18	--	--	--	--	--

Only includes pitchers who faced at least one hundred batters.

Fielding Stats

Name	INN	SBA/G	CS%	ERA	WP+PB/G	PO	A	TE	FE
Catchers									
Olivo M	935.0	0.72	40%	3.90	0.568	821	62	9	0
Iannetta C	443.0	0.83	15%	4.63	0.528	373	32	5	0
Phillips P	55.0	0.16	0%	3.93	0.982	43	2	1	0
McKenry M	9.0	0.00	0%	6.00	1.000	5	1	0	0

Name	Inn	PO	A	TE	FE	FPct	DPS	DPT	ZRDif	OOZ	Dif
First Base											
Helton T	947.7	932	77	0	8	.992	15	1	-.039	31	-0
Giambi J	270.0	267	8	2	2	.986	3	2	-.025	5	-4
Mora M	112.3	109	8	1	1	.983	0	0	-.049	3	-1
Hawpe B	52.0	42	4	0	0	1.000	0	0	--	3	--
Eldred B	46.0	52	3	0	0	1.000	0	0	--	1	--
Iannetta C	12.0	10	1	0	0	1.000	0	0	--	0	--
Phillips P	2.0	0	1	0	0	1.000	0	0	--	0	--
Second Base											
Barmes C	633.3	163	197	0	5	.986	21	31	.014	9	-7
Herrera J	425.3	91	149	1	3	.984	13	18	.011	14	3
Young Jr. E	257.3	44	94	2	4	.958	10	12	.031	8	2
Mora M	100.0	26	38	0	2	.970	2	3	.004	1	-1
Nelson C	26.0	8	7	1	1	.882	0	0	--	0	--
Shortstop											
Tulowitzki T	1065.0	211	389	3	7	.984	46	48	.034	51	5
Barmes C	361.0	50	141	3	2	.974	15	17	.047	25	9
Herrera J	16.0	1	1	0	0	1.000	0	0	--	0	--
Third Base											
Stewart I	925.3	59	212	7	3	.964	16	0	.015	39	5
Mora M	440.0	26	84	4	1	.957	7	0	-.044	11	-5
Herrera J	59.7	3	10	0	0	1.000	3	0	--	0	--
Nelson C	14.0	2	2	0	0	1.000	0	0	--	0	--
Iannetta C	2.0	0	0	0	0	.000	0	0	--	--	--
Barmes C	1.0	0	0	0	0	.000	0	0	--	--	--

Name	Inn	PO	A	TE	FE	FPct	DPS	DPT	ZRDif	OOZ	Dif
Left Field											
Smith S	512.3	107	3	1	1	.982	1	0	-.012	34	9
Gonzalez C	472.3	77	5	0	1	.988	0	0	.041	15	-8
Spilborghs R	297.7	46	2	0	1	.980	1	0	-.105	10	-5
Young Jr. E	65.0	11	0	0	1	.917	0	0	--	4	--
Payton J	64.0	11	0	0	0	1.000	0	0	--	3	--
Mora M	30.7	4	1	0	0	1.000	0	0	--	0	--
Center Field											
Fowler D	948.3	239	2	0	1	.996	0	0	-.001	39	-15
Gonzalez C	452.7	126	1	0	0	1.000	0	0	-.035	28	2
Spilborghs R	39.0	4	0	0	0	1.000	0	0	--	1	--
Payton J	2.0	1	0	0	0	1.000	0	0	--	0	--
Right Field											
Hawpe B	517.0	97	1	0	1	.990	0	0	-.033	14	-14
Spilborghs R	401.7	81	0	0	4	.953	0	0	-.016	14	-8
Gonzalez C	299.7	56	2	0	0	1.000	1	0	.005	10	-6
Smith S	223.7	48	1	0	1	.980	1	0	-.068	14	2

Detroit Tigers

Stat Facts:

- Miguel Cabrera was second in the AL in Base Runs
- Cabrera led the AL in GPA
- Cabrera tied for the ML lead in 1B FE
- Casper Wells had the most Base Runs of any player with <100 PA
- Brennan Boesch had the lowest L^R of any ML regular
- Boesch led the majors in RF FE, in 587 innings
- Boesch tied for the AL lead in LF FE, in 350 innings
- Austin Jackson tied for the ML lead in CF FE
- Jackson made the most OOZ plays of any CF
- Jackson had 4 HR, and 170 strikeouts
- Eddie Bonine struck out 9% of his BFP
- 86% of Enrique Gonzalez's GB were outs

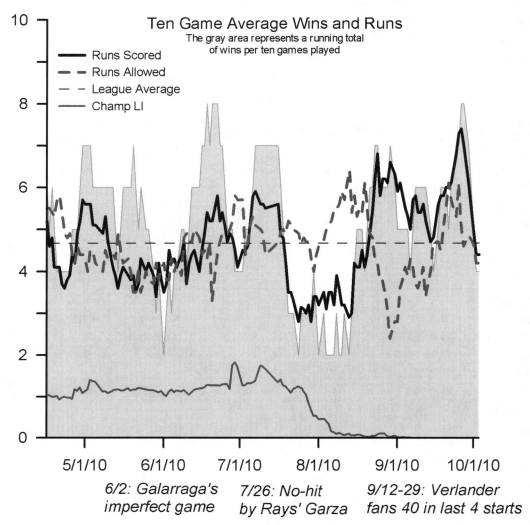

Ten Game Average Wins and Runs
The gray area represents a running total of wins per ten games played

- Runs Scored
- Runs Allowed
- League Average
- Champ LI

6/2: Galarraga's imperfect game

7/26: No-hit by Rays' Garza

9/12-29: Verlander fans 40 in last 4 starts

4/5-11: Cabrera starts 12-for-23 with 2 HR

7/3-10: Spend the week in 1st

8/13-19: Hit 17 HR in 7 G

Team Batting and Pitching/Fielding Stats by Month

	April	May	June	July	Aug	Sept/Oct
Wins	14	12	15	11	13	16
Losses	10	14	12	15	16	14
RS/G	5.0	3.9	4.7	4.1	4.8	5.3
RA/G	4.7	4.1	4.9	4.7	4.6	4.6
OBP	.364	.320	.338	.335	.339	.319
SLG	.435	.399	.419	.411	.414	.415
FIP	4.22	3.89	4.33	4.33	4.49	3.97
DER	.688	.704	.708	.671	.705	.703

Batting Stats

Player	BR	Runs	RBI	PA	Outs	H	2B	3B	HR	TB	K	BB	IBB	HBP	SH	SF	SB	CS	GDP	H-A	L^R	BA	OBP	SLG	GPA
Cabrera M	121	111	126	648	388	180	45	1	38	341	95	89	32	3	0	8	3	3	17	.023	-.006	.328	.420	.622	.342
Jackson A	84	103	41	675	448	181	34	10	4	247	170	47	4	4	3	3	27	6	5	.014	-.063	.293	.345	.400	.254
Damon J *	78	81	51	613	399	146	36	5	8	216	90	69	2	2	2	1	11	1	5	.022	.003	.271	.355	.401	.258
Inge B	63	47	70	580	402	127	28	5	13	204	134	54	4	5	0	7	4	3	12	.049	.037	.247	.321	.397	.242
Boesch B *	61	49	67	512	351	119	26	3	14	193	99	40	5	5	0	3	7	1	5	.076	-.091	.256	.320	.416	.247
Raburn R	56	54	62	410	277	104	25	1	15	176	92	27	0	8	1	3	2	2	8	-.007	.051	.280	.340	.474	.270
Ordonez M	52	56	59	365	239	98	17	1	12	153	38	40	0	0	0	2	1	0	14	.026	.122	.303	.378	.474	.287
Santiago R +	34	38	22	367	244	84	9	1	3	104	56	30	0	7	8	2	2	2	6	.026	.045	.263	.337	.325	.231
Guillen C +	30	26	34	275	196	69	17	1	6	106	41	21	2	0	0	1	1	2	10	-.034	-.050	.273	.327	.419	.250
Avila A *	30	28	31	333	241	67	12	0	7	100	71	36	0	2	1	0	2	2	12	.030	.050	.228	.316	.340	.226
Peralta J	26	23	38	242	166	55	7	0	8	86	34	21	1	0	0	4	0	0	4	-.050	.065	.253	.314	.396	.239
Rhymes W *	25	30	19	213	137	58	12	3	1	79	16	14	0	0	7	1	0	3	1	-.046	-.033	.304	.350	.414	.259
Kelly D *	24	30	27	251	181	58	4	0	9	89	42	8	0	2	1	2	3	0	1	.043	.045	.244	.272	.374	.215
Laird G	20	22	25	299	222	56	11	0	5	82	57	18	0	3	6	2	3	1	7	.022	-.034	.207	.263	.304	.193
Wells C	16	14	17	99	66	30	6	1	4	50	19	6	0	0	0	0	0	1	2	-.079	-.132	.323	.364	.538	.296
Sizemore S	14	19	14	163	115	32	7	0	3	48	40	15	0	0	4	1	0	0	4	-.022	.011	.224	.296	.336	.216
Worth D	10	10	8	115	81	27	5	0	2	38	13	6	0	3	0	0	1	2	0	.025	.072	.255	.295	.358	.221
Everett A	4	6	4	89	68	15	5	0	0	20	18	4	0	0	3	1	2	1	1	-.054	.094	.185	.221	.247	.160
Frazier J	1	3	1	24	20	5	1	0	0	6	6	1	0	0	0	0	0	0	2	.025	-.124	.217	.250	.261	.177
St. Pierre M	1	1	0	9	7	2	1	0	0	3	2	0	0	0	0	0	0	0	0	-.236	.275	.222	.222	.333	.182

Only includes batters with at least one Base Run. Italicized stats have been adjusted for home park.

Batted Ball Batting Stats

Player	% of PA		% of Batted Balls					Out %		Runs Per Event				Total Runs vs. Avg.				
	K%	BB%	GB%	LD%	FB%	IF/F	HR/OF	GB	OF	NIP	GB	LD	OF	NIP	GB	LD	FB	Tot
Cabrera Mi	15	14	39	19	42	.08	.20	71	76	.11	.05	.43	.36	15	2	11	39	66
Ordonez Ma	10	11	47	22	32	.08	.14	75	82	.12	.03	.35	.24	6	-1	6	6	16
Damon Jo	15	12	44	19	37	.13	.06	70	79	.09	.07	.38	.14	8	6	4	-5	12
Raburn Ry	22	9	39	18	44	.09	.13	65	85	.01	.09	.42	.23	-3	4	1	8	10
Jackson Au	25	8	48	24	27	.02	.03	64	78	-.01	.11	.41	.14	-9	15	12	-10	9
Boesch Br	19	9	45	15	40	.16	.11	72	82	.03	.07	.45	.20	-1	4	0	1	3
Rhymes Wi	8	7	44	23	33	.16	.02	72	78	.10	.07	.36	.10	1	3	4	-5	3
Guillen Ca	15	8	50	14	36	.06	.08	74	82	.04	.04	.45	.17	-1	0	0	1	1
Peralta Jh	14	9	35	25	40	.05	.11	74	89	.06	.03	.28	.13	1	-1	1	-1	-0
Worth Da	11	5	47	21	32	.14	.04	77	83	.03	.04	.37	.08	-1	1	1	-3	-2
Inge Br	23	10	38	17	45	.07	.08	70	83	.03	.07	.41	.15	-1	2	-2	-0	-2
Santiago Ra	15	10	49	21	30	.09	.04	70	92	.07	.08	.35	.01	2	7	1	-15	-4
Kelly Do	17	4	32	19	49	.13	.11	75	88	-.02	.05	.31	.13	-4	-0	-2	-1	-7
Sizemore Sc	25	9	38	22	40	.17	.09	87	77	.01	-.04	.36	.19	-1	-4	-0	-1	-7
Avila Al	21	11	43	22	35	.03	.09	80	87	.05	-.02	.36	.14	1	-6	1	-3	-8
Laird Ge	19	7	43	15	42	.09	.06	81	88	.01	.00	.34	.08	-3	-3	-6	-8	-19
MLB Average	18	9	44	18	38	.09	.10	74	83	.04	.04	.38	.18	--	--	--	--	--

Only includes batters with at least one hundred Plate Appearances.

Pitching Stats

Player	PRC	IP	BFP	G	GS	K	BB	IBB	HBP	H	HR	DP	DER	SB	CS	PO	W	L	Sv	Op	Hld	H-A	R^L	RA	ERA	FIP
Verlander J	106	224.3	925	33	33	219	71	0	6	190	14	11	.704	24	7	3	18	9	0	0	0	-.029	-.006	3.57	3.37	3.00
Scherzer M	85	195.7	800	31	31	184	70	1	7	174	20	27	.696	17	13	1	12	11	0	0	0	-.008	.019	3.86	3.50	3.73
Galarraga A	46	144.3	617	25	24	74	51	1	4	143	21	12	.730	6	3	0	4	9	0	0	0	-.064	-.012	4.68	4.49	5.10
Porcello R	45	162.7	700	27	27	84	38	2	7	188	18	20	.682	10	5	0	10	12	0	0	0	-.023	-.024	5.31	4.92	4.31
Bonderman J	44	171.0	754	30	29	112	60	1	10	187	25	19	.691	12	7	0	8	10	0	0	1	-.043	-.073	5.95	5.53	4.91
Valverde J	31	63.0	259	60	0	63	32	1	3	41	5	9	.756	3	1	0	2	4	26	29	0	-.015	-.042	3.43	3.00	3.76
Perry R	27	62.7	261	60	0	45	23	1	5	55	6	7	.725	8	1	0	3	5	2	5	19	-.053	.094	3.73	3.59	4.21
Coke P *	26	64.7	279	74	1	53	26	4	4	67	2	11	.655	1	0	0	7	5	2	4	17	-.082	-.010	4.04	3.76	3.08
Thomas B *	24	69.3	307	49	2	30	29	3	4	77	4	9	.688	0	2	2	6	2	0	0	3	-.039	-.075	4.02	3.89	4.29
Zumaya J	20	38.3	156	31	0	34	11	0	0	32	1	5	.700	4	0	0	2	1	1	3	11	-.014	-.013	3.05	2.58	2.54
Bonine E	19	68.0	303	47	1	26	22	2	3	84	7	10	.669	2	2	0	4	1	0	0	2	.035	.053	4.90	4.63	4.70
Willis D *	14	43.3	202	9	8	33	29	0	2	48	3	9	.659	3	1	0	1	2	0	0	0	.074	-.074	4.98	4.98	4.63
Gonzalez E	10	26.0	107	18	0	13	17	0	0	21	4	7	.767	0	1	0	0	1	0	0	0	-.004	-.070	3.81	3.81	6.07
Schlereth D	9	18.7	87	18	0	19	10	3	1	20	2	1	.673	5	0	0	2	0	1	2	1	-.064	.118	3.38	2.89	3.75
Weinhardt R	6	29.3	135	28	0	21	8	2	3	40	2	6	.594	1	2	0	2	2	0	2	5	-.034	.107	7.06	6.14	3.49
Ni F *	5	23.0	116	22	0	22	19	4	2	27	2	1	.620	1	2	2	0	1	0	0	1	-.019	.008	7.43	6.65	4.55
Oliver A *	3	22.0	102	5	5	18	13	2	2	26	3	5	.621	2	3	1	0	4	0	0	0	.021	.025	9.00	7.36	5.02
Figaro A	2	14.7	69	8	1	5	8	2	0	18	1	2	.673	1	0	0	0	2	0	0	0	-.010	.007	7.36	6.75	4.54

Only includes pitchers with at least ten Innings Pitched. Italicized stats have been adjusted for home park.

Batted Ball Pitching Stats

Player	% of PA		% of Batted Balls					Out %		Runs Per Event				Total Runs vs. Avg.				
	K%	BB%	GB%	LD%	FB%	IF/F	HR/OF	GB	OF	NIP	GB	LD	OF	NIP	GB	LD	FB	Tot
Verlander Ju	24	8	41	19	40	.12	.06	75	85	.01	.04	.40	.12	-9	-3	-1	-16	-30
Valverde Jo	24	14	55	13	32	.10	.11	81	76	.05	-.01	.31	.21	2	-5	-7	-1	-11
Scherzer Ma	23	10	40	20	40	.14	.11	76	81	.02	.03	.34	.20	-3	-3	-5	1	-11
Zumaya Jo	22	7	37	16	47	.14	.02	73	79	-.00	.03	.42	.10	-2	-1	-1	-3	-7
Perry Ry	17	11	44	15	41	.08	.09	71	87	.06	.06	.33	.13	2	1	-4	-3	-5
Coke Ph	19	11	35	21	43	.11	.03	78	78	.05	-.00	.44	.10	1	-4	5	-5	-2
Gonzalez En	12	16	47	14	39	.07	.14	86	88	.15	-.05	.46	.19	3	-3	0	1	1
Thomas Br	10	11	50	17	33	.12	.04	75	74	.13	.03	.39	.18	5	-0	1	-1	4
Willis Do	16	15	46	26	28	.13	.09	77	83	.11	.01	.37	.16	5	-2	4	-3	5
Porcello Ri	12	6	50	18	32	.08	.11	74	82	.05	.04	.38	.18	-2	2	4	1	6
Weinhardt Ro	16	8	56	20	24	.04	.09	61	62	.05	.12	.21	.29	0	5	-2	2	6
Oliver An	18	15	43	21	36	.04	.13	72	80	.10	.04	.49	.24	2	0	3	2	7
Galarraga Ar	12	9	37	14	49	.09	.09	73	85	.08	.05	.37	.16	4	2	-6	7	7
Ni Fu	19	18	33	24	43	.19	.08	79	74	.11	.01	.58	.19	4	-1	5	0	8
Bonine Ed	9	8	48	18	34	.16	.09	74	81	.11	.05	.43	.18	2	3	5	-1	11
Bonderman Je	15	9	45	16	39	.05	.12	72	87	.06	.05	.39	.18	3	8	-1	6	17
MLB Average	*18*	*9*	*44*	*18*	*38*	*.09*	*.10*	*74*	*83*	*.04*	*.04*	*.38*	*.18*	--	--	--	--	--

Only includes pitchers who faced at least one hundred batters.

Fielding Stats

Name	INN	SBA/G	CS%	ERA	WP+PB/G	PO	A	TE	FE
Catchers									
Avila A	756.7	0.75	32%	4.47	0.571	556	34	2	2
Laird G	670.7	1.10	29%	4.11	0.523	516	52	4	1
St. Pierre M	17.0	0.00	0%	4.24	0.000	12	1	0	0

Name	Inn	PO	A	TE	FE	FPct	DPS	DPT	ZRDif	OOZ	Dif
First Base											
Cabrera M	1285.0	1218	96	1	9	.990	12	1	-.016	37	-5
Kelly D	135.0	146	10	0	1	.987	4	0	.189	4	-0
Larish J	9.0	5	0	0	0	1.000	0	0	--	--	--
Raburn R	8.0	6	1	0	0	1.000	0	0	--	--	--
Peralta J	7.0	7	1	0	0	1.000	0	0	--	0	--
Second Base											
Rhymes W	412.7	89	150	1	3	.984	13	22	.011	16	6
Guillen C	393.3	86	138	3	0	.987	13	18	-.015	14	4
Sizemore S	314.3	59	90	2	5	.955	13	9	.018	1	-7
Santiago R	127.0	24	44	1	0	.986	5	6	.074	3	-0
Raburn R	120.0	27	43	0	1	.986	5	5	-.071	5	2
Worth D	77.0	14	31	0	0	1.000	5	3	--	0	--
Shortstop											
Santiago R	617.0	106	227	1	6	.979	21	30	.046	36	9
Peralta J	392.3	70	118	2	1	.984	12	13	-.008	16	-1
Everett A	229.3	48	74	0	1	.992	9	14	.026	11	1
Worth D	205.7	41	56	0	0	1.000	3	10	-.039	6	-3
Third Base											
Inge B	1226.0	119	267	3	5	.977	22	1	.022	30	-15
Kelly D	105.0	5	33	2	1	.927	5	0	.039	6	2
Peralta J	60.3	7	9	0	0	1.000	3	0	--	0	--
Sizemore S	38.0	7	7	1	0	.933	1	0	--	2	--
Worth D	11.0	0	2	0	0	1.000	0	0	--	--	--
Raburn R	3.3	1	1	0	0	1.000	0	0	--	0	--

Name	Inn	PO	A	TE	FE	FPct	DPS	DPT	ZRDif	OOZ	Dif
Left Field											
Raburn R	508.7	117	3	0	4	.968	0	0	.041	34	9
Boesch B	350.3	86	3	0	4	.957	1	0	-.082	30	13
Kelly D	255.0	57	2	0	0	1.000	0	0	.001	23	11
Damon J	239.3	51	2	1	1	.964	1	0	-.049	14	2
Wells C	39.0	5	1	0	0	1.000	0	0	--	1	--
Guillen C	28.0	6	0	0	0	.857	0	0	--	0	--
Frazier J	24.0	11	1	0	0	1.000	1	0	--	2	--
Center Field											
Jackson A	1256.0	383	9	0	6	.985	2	0	.019	109	38
Kelly D	90.0	33	2	0	0	1.000	0	0	--	10	--
Raburn R	44.0	11	0	0	0	1.000	0	0	--	2	--
Damon J	29.0	6	0	0	0	1.000	0	0	--	0	--
Wells C	25.0	6	1	0	0	1.000	0	0	--	1	--
Right Field											
Ordonez M	608.7	135	7	1	2	.979	3	0	-.052	26	-7
Boesch B	587.3	130	6	0	6	.958	1	0	-.017	23	-9
Wells C	151.3	24	2	0	0	1.000	0	0	-.030	11	3
Raburn R	94.0	22	1	0	1	.958	0	0	--	4	--
Kelly D	2.0	0	0	0	0	.000	0	0	--	--	--
Frazier J	1.0	0	0	0	0	.000	0	0	--	--	--

Florida Marlins

Stat Facts:
- Josh Johnson allowed 7 HR in 184 IP
- Ricky Nolasco allowed 24 HR in 158 IP
- Chris Volstad was second in the NL in SB
- Dan Uggla made the most TE of any 2B
- Jorge Cantu made 10 TE in 632 innings at 3B
- Hanley Ramirez had the lowest ZRDif of any regular SS
- 26% of Mike Stanton's FB were HR
- Stanton struck out in 31% of his PA
- Tim Wood struck out 8% of his BFP
- Andrew Miller's LD% was 28
- Emilio Bonifacio had 12 SB in 12 attempts
- Hector Luna had 2 HR, 1 2B, and 1 single

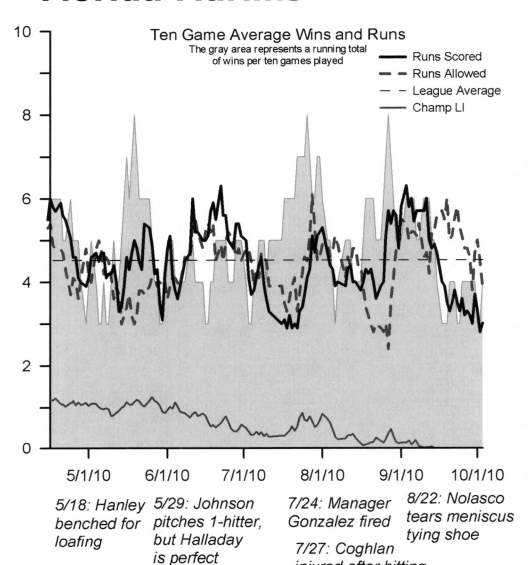

Ten Game Average Wins and Runs
The gray area represents a running total of wins per ten games played

— Runs Scored
- - Runs Allowed
– – League Average
— Champ LI

5/18: Hanley benched for loafing

5/29: Johnson pitches 1-hitter, but Halladay is perfect

7/24: Manager Gonzalez fired

7/27: Coghlan injured after hitting Helms with a pie

8/22: Nolasco tears meniscus tying shoe

Team Batting and Pitching/Fielding Stats by Month

	April	May	June	July	Aug	Sept/Oct
Wins	11	15	11	16	13	14
Losses	12	14	15	10	14	17
RS/G	4.7	4.5	5.1	3.9	4.3	4.2
RA/G	4.8	3.7	5.0	4.2	4.2	4.8
OBP	.330	.322	.344	.290	.317	.322
SLG	.388	.403	.433	.372	.418	.398
FIP	4.02	3.39	4.17	3.73	3.98	4.42
DER	.692	.702	.677	.694	.699	.674

Batting Stats

Player	BR	Runs	RBI	PA	Outs	H	2B	3B	HR	TB	K	BB	IBB	HBP	SH	SF	SB	CS	GDP	H-A	L^R	BA	OBP	SLG	GPA
Uggla D	105	100	105	674	431	169	31	0	33	299	149	78	2	2	0	5	4	1	10	-.031	.045	.287	.369	.508	.286
Ramirez H	92	92	76	619	404	163	28	2	21	258	93	64	12	7	0	5	32	10	14	.038	-.009	.300	.378	.475	.282
Sanchez G	84	72	85	643	430	156	37	3	19	256	101	57	2	5	3	6	5	0	14	.060	.059	.273	.341	.448	.259
Stanton M	56	45	59	396	275	93	21	1	22	182	123	34	6	2	0	1	5	2	7	-.125	-.081	.259	.326	.507	.267
Ross C	56	60	58	487	340	120	24	3	11	183	100	30	4	4	0	1	9	1	7	.078	.048	.265	.316	.405	.238
Coghlan C *	46	60	28	400	268	96	20	3	5	137	84	33	1	4	3	2	10	3	3	.035	-.003	.268	.335	.383	.240
Cantu J	45	41	54	410	287	98	25	0	10	153	76	23	1	6	0	7	0	0	11	-.001	-.004	.262	.310	.409	.236
Morrison L *	41	43	18	287	180	69	20	7	2	109	51	41	0	2	0	0	0	1	4	.087	-.053	.283	.390	.447	.280
Maybin C	33	46	28	322	229	68	7	3	8	105	92	24	1	5	1	1	9	2	4	-.004	-.028	.234	.302	.361	.221
Paulino R	32	31	37	344	245	82	18	0	4	112	51	25	4	0	0	3	1	0	11	.016	.101	.259	.311	.354	.223
Helms W	26	25	39	287	207	56	12	4	4	88	76	26	1	4	0	3	0	2	7	-.003	.139	.220	.300	.346	.216
Bonifacio E	21	30	10	201	134	47	6	3	0	59	42	17	0	0	1	3	12	0	1	-.133	.080	.261	.320	.328	.221
Davis B	12	8	16	123	87	23	7	1	3	41	37	9	2	1	1	3	2	0	1	.039	-.008	.211	.270	.376	.211
Tracy C *	10	5	10	111	79	25	6	0	1	34	21	6	0	2	0	1	0	0	2	-.058	-.095	.245	.297	.333	.212
Murphy D	10	9	16	47	30	14	6	1	3	31	19	2	0	0	1	0	0	0	0	-.014	.246	.318	.348	.705	.325
Carroll B	8	13	7	90	64	15	4	0	2	25	29	6	3	7	0	1	2	1	2	.072	.022	.197	.311	.329	.217
Hayes B	8	6	6	83	62	16	6	1	2	30	26	6	1	0	0	0	0	0	1	-.087	-.067	.208	.265	.390	.211
Martinez O	7	8	2	48	29	14	4	1	0	20	6	4	0	0	1	0	1	0	0	.107	-.047	.326	.383	.465	.282
Baker J *	6	7	6	88	66	17	3	1	0	22	18	9	1	1	0	0	0	0	5	.071	.134	.218	.307	.282	.204
Cousins S *	5	2	2	38	26	11	2	2	0	17	13	1	0	0	0	0	0	0	0	-.270	-.159	.297	.316	.459	.251
Lamb M *	2	2	4	40	31	7	1	1	0	10	6	2	0	0	0	0	0	0	0	-.102	.167	.184	.225	.263	.163
Nolasco R	2	3	3	55	40	8	3	0	0	11	16	2	0	0	6	0	0	0	1	-.056	.200	.170	.204	.234	.147
Luna H	2	2	4	30	26	4	1	0	2	11	13	0	0	0	0	1	0	1	0	.235	.041	.138	.133	.379	.151
Barden B	1	2	3	32	25	5	0	0	0	5	12	3	0	1	0	0	0	2	0	.092	-.045	.179	.281	.179	.167
Robertson N	1	2	1	35	23	5	1	0	0	6	6	2	0	0	7	0	0	0	2	-.048	.022	.192	.250	.231	.166
Mendez A	1	0	0	10	5	2	0	0	0	2	1	0	0	0	3	0	0	0	0	-.058	.058	.286	.286	.286	.195

Only includes batters with at least one Base Run. Italicized stats have been adjusted for home park.

Batted Ball Batting Stats

Player	% of PA		% of Batted Balls					Out %		Runs Per Event				Total Runs vs. Avg.				
	K%	BB%	GB%	LD%	FB%	IF/F	HR/OF	GB	OF	NIP	GB	LD	OF	NIP	GB	LD	FB	Tot
Uggla Da	22	12	40	18	43	.07	.19	65	82	.05	.09	.37	.29	4	7	-1	25	34
Ramirez Ha	15	11	51	16	33	.11	.16	68	83	.09	.08	.37	.27	8	12	-0	10	30
Morrison Lo	18	15	48	20	32	.08	.04	76	67	.10	.03	.50	.23	6	-1	6	2	14
Sanchez Ga	16	10	37	17	46	.08	.09	73	81	.06	.04	.38	.19	3	-0	-0	10	13
Stanton Mi	31	9	43	16	41	.20	.26	64	84	-.01	.12	.48	.39	-6	6	-1	12	12
Coghlan Ch	21	9	51	24	25	.06	.08	76	78	.03	.04	.40	.19	-1	2	7	-4	3
Ross Co	21	7	44	22	34	.10	.09	71	89	.00	.06	.43	.13	-5	3	9	-7	-0
Cantu Jo	19	7	39	21	41	.10	.09	78	82	.01	.02	.40	.17	-3	-4	4	0	-2
Davis Br	30	8	45	16	39	.17	.13	71	81	-.02	.06	.42	.23	-2	0	-1	-0	-4
Tracy Ch	19	7	38	21	41	.12	.03	84	86	.01	-.02	.49	.05	-1	-2	3	-4	-4
Bonifacio Em	21	8	52	22	26	.09	.00	67	80	.02	.10	.32	.09	-1	3	-1	-6	-5
Maybin Ca	28	9	53	14	33	.08	.14	68	84	-.00	.09	.31	.24	-4	7	-8	-0	-5
Paulino Ro	15	7	42	18	40	.06	.04	74	82	.04	.03	.43	.08	-1	-2	3	-6	-6
Helms We	26	10	44	18	37	.07	.06	73	83	.02	.06	.38	.14	-2	0	-2	-4	-7
MLB Average	18	9	44	18	38	.09	.10	74	83	.04	.04	.38	.18	--	--	--	--	--

Only includes batters with at least one hundred Plate Appearances.

Pitching Stats

Player	PRC	IP	BFP	G	GS	K	BB	IBB	HBP	H	HR	DP	DER	SB	CS	PO	W	L	Sv	Op	Hld	H-A	R^L	RA	ERA	FIP
Johnson J	*114*	183.7	744	28	28	186	48	2	5	155	7	13	.687	15	8	2	11	6	0	0	0	-.062	-.007	2.50	2.30	2.50
Sanchez A	76	195.0	841	32	32	157	70	5	7	192	10	18	.675	11	3	0	13	12	0	0	0	-.042	-.010	4.11	3.55	3.36
Nolasco R	55	157.7	665	26	26	147	33	1	2	169	24	11	.678	5	6	2	14	9	0	0	0	.035	-.005	4.68	4.51	3.96
Volstad C	54	175.0	758	30	30	102	60	5	8	187	17	17	.694	29	4	1	12	9	0	0	0	-.056	-.020	4.83	4.58	4.37
Hensley C	48	75.0	307	68	0	77	29	4	4	54	3	8	.716	5	1	0	3	4	7	10	22	-.017	-.033	2.40	2.16	2.82
Sanches B	35	63.7	254	61	0	54	27	0	1	43	7	6	.776	5	1	0	2	2	0	1	12	-.012	-.020	2.83	2.26	4.25
Nunez L	29	65.0	270	68	0	71	21	2	0	62	5	3	.665	2	4	1	4	3	30	38	5	.021	.075	3.74	3.46	2.89
Sanabia A	28	72.3	307	15	12	47	16	2	3	74	6	5	.689	4	4	0	5	3	0	0	0	.041	.066	3.98	3.73	3.68
Badenhop B	24	67.7	281	53	0	47	21	5	2	62	5	9	.714	1	2	0	2	5	1	3	8	.080	-.012	4.39	3.99	3.57
Robertson N	23	100.3	450	19	18	61	40	1	6	110	11	9	.678	5	3	1	6	8	0	0	0	-.006	-.032	6.28	5.47	4.75
Veras J	22	48.0	201	48	0	54	29	0	1	32	5	4	.750	4	1	0	3	3	0	2	19	.092	.030	3.75	3.75	4.18
Sosa J	10	36.7	165	22	2	19	18	4	0	39	4	3	.718	3	1	0	2	3	0	0	0	.031	-.097	5.40	4.66	4.72
Pinto R *	10	16.7	77	20	0	16	9	0	4	16	1	1	.681	3	1	0	0	0	0	0	4	.024	.161	2.70	2.70	4.40
Mendez A	7	24.7	109	5	5	11	12	0	2	28	7	5	.727	3	2	0	1	3	0	0	0	-.004	-.005	5.11	5.11	7.70
Wood T	6	27.7	129	26	0	10	15	1	0	33	2	3	.676	2	1	0	0	1	1	3	3	-.019	.049	6.18	5.53	4.93
Ohman W *	5	12.0	51	17	0	14	5	1	0	10	1	0	.710	0	0	0	0	2	0	0	3	-.145	.012	4.50	3.00	2.95
Miller A *	5	32.7	171	9	7	28	26	2	1	51	6	5	.564	4	0	0	1	5	0	0	0	-.047	.089	9.37	8.54	6.17
Leroux C	4	18.0	84	17	0	18	11	2	0	24	1	4	.574	2	1	0	0	0	0	1	3	.115	-.011	7.50	7.00	3.42
Ceda J	3	8.7	45	8	0	9	11	1	1	8	1	1	.696	0	0	0	0	0	0	0	0	-.029	-.114	5.19	5.19	6.43
Buente J	3	11.0	59	8	0	9	11	2	0	16	0	1	.590	1	0	0	0	0	0	0	0	.158	.094	6.55	6.55	4.01
Tankersley T	2	12.0	57	27	0	7	7	1	1	12	4	0	.763	2	0	0	0	0	0	3	6	-.188	-.162	8.25	7.50	8.11

Only includes pitchers with at least ten Innings Pitched. Italicized stats have been adjusted for home park.

Batted Ball Pitching Stats

Player	% of PA		% of Batted Balls					Out %		Runs Per Event				Total Runs vs. Avg.				
	K%	BB%	GB%	LD%	FB%	IF/F	HR/OF	GB	OF	NIP	GB	LD	OF	NIP	GB	LD	FB	Tot
Johnson Jo	25	7	46	21	34	.11	.05	75	80	-.01	.04	.37	.13	-12	-2	-1	-15	-30
Hensley Cl	25	11	53	15	32	.08	.05	75	81	.02	.04	.35	.12	-1	-1	-6	-7	-15
Sanches Br	21	11	33	15	52	.13	.09	76	91	.04	.02	.34	.11	0	-3	-5	-4	-11
Sanchez An	19	9	45	17	38	.10	.05	67	84	.04	.10	.38	.09	-1	14	-4	-17	-8
Veras En	27	15	40	23	37	.09	.13	83	91	.05	-.02	.31	.16	2	-3	-2	-3	-6
Badenhop Bu	17	8	57	14	29	.03	.09	71	88	.04	.06	.37	.14	-1	3	-3	-4	-5
Nunez Le	26	8	54	16	30	.13	.09	73	74	-.01	.05	.49	.23	-4	1	0	-1	-4
Sanabia Al	15	6	36	19	45	.12	.05	70	85	.02	.07	.42	.09	-2	3	3	-6	-2
Sosa Jo	12	11	40	17	43	.09	.08	64	87	.11	.08	.34	.12	2	2	-1	-1	2
Nolasco Ca	22	5	40	19	41	.07	.13	69	83	-.02	.08	.35	.23	-12	6	-2	12	4
Wood Ti	8	12	39	19	42	.12	.06	63	88	.16	.09	.40	.08	3	3	2	-2	5
Volstad Ch	13	9	48	18	34	.05	.09	73	84	.07	.05	.39	.15	4	2	4	-4	6
Mendez Ad	10	13	29	16	55	.09	.14	67	83	.14	.10	.33	.22	2	1	-1	5	7
Robertson Na	14	10	42	18	40	.11	.09	72	80	.08	.06	.39	.19	4	4	2	4	14
Miller An	16	16	38	28	34	.03	.17	69	73	.11	.06	.44	.32	5	1	7	6	19
MLB Average	*18*	*9*	*44*	*18*	*38*	*.09*	*.10*	*74*	*83*	*.04*	*.04*	*.38*	*.18*	--	--	--	--	--

Only includes pitchers who faced at least one hundred batters.

Fielding Stats

Name	INN	SBA/G	CS%	ERA	WP+PB/G	PO	A	TE	FE
Catchers									
Paulino R	740.3	0.90	28%	4.02	0.340	644	47	4	2
Davis B	278.0	0.84	27%	3.92	0.291	215	16	4	0
Hayes B	190.7	0.85	28%	4.01	0.519	142	13	0	0
Baker J	178.0	1.37	19%	4.04	0.303	152	9	2	0
Rivera M	28.7	1.26	0%	7.22	1.256	28	2	1	0
Hatcher C	22.7	0.40	0%	5.56	0.794	20	2	0	0

Name	Inn	PO	A	TE	FE	FPct	DPS	DPT	ZRDif	OOZ	Dif
First Base											
Sanchez G	1253.0	1115	70	3	7	.991	9	2	-.055	38	-3
Cantu J	125.0	109	10	0	0	1.000	0	0	-.171	7	3
Tracy C	36.0	46	3	0	0	1.000	0	0	--	3	--
Helms W	18.0	17	2	0	0	1.000	0	0	--	--	--
Lamb M	6.0	11	0	0	0	1.000	0	0	--	0	--
Second Base											
Uggla D	1392.0	312	415	8	10	.976	33	47	.002	23	-12
Bonifacio E	27.3	2	14	1	0	.941	3	0	--	1	--
Barden B	12.0	1	8	1	0	.900	0	0	--	0	--
Murphy D	3.7	2	1	0	0	1.000	0	0	--	0	--
Luna H	3.0	1	1	0	0	1.000	0	0	--	0	--
Shortstop											
Ramirez H	1217.0	200	342	9	7	.971	34	39	-.048	45	-7
Martinez O	86.0	10	22	0	0	1.000	2	0	--	3	--
Bonifacio E	71.7	11	11	0	0	1.000	1	0	--	2	--
Barden B	42.0	6	7	0	0	1.000	0	1	--	2	--
Murphy D	21.7	1	6	0	0	1.000	0	1	--	0	--
Third Base											
Cantu J	632.3	42	118	10	6	.909	11	0	-.050	24	1
Helms W	510.7	39	101	1	6	.952	8	0	-.035	23	4
Tracy C	181.0	13	42	2	1	.948	4	0	.028	8	1
Bonifacio E	37.0	3	10	0	0	1.000	1	0	--	3	--
Murphy D	31.3	1	7	0	0	1.000	0	0	--	2	--
Barden B	27.3	3	10	0	0	1.000	3	0	--	2	--
Luna H	18.7	2	5	0	0	1.000	0	0	--	0	--

Name	Inn	PO	A	TE	FE	FPct	DPS	DPT	ZRDif	OOZ	Dif
Left Field											
Coghlan C	770.0	160	7	1	0	.994	0	0	.001	31	-7
Morrison L	544.0	116	4	1	2	.976	0	0	-.043	25	-2
Carroll B	54.0	11	0	0	1	.917	0	0	--	2	--
Bonifacio E	48.3	8	1	0	0	1.000	0	0	--	1	--
Ross C	13.0	2	1	1	0	.750	1	0	--	--	--
Petersen B	9.0	1	0	0	0	1.000	0	0	--	0	--
Center Field											
Ross C	640.0	165	4	1	0	.994	1	0	.004	27	-9
Maybin C	634.3	215	4	0	4	.982	3	0	.001	51	15
Bonifacio E	130.0	40	2	0	1	.977	0	0	-.045	8	1
Cousins S	34.0	15	0	0	0	1.000	0	0	--	5	--
Right Field											
Stanton M	854.7	219	10	1	3	.983	1	0	.005	63	16
Ross C	391.3	101	1	0	2	.981	0	0	.050	30	9
Carroll B	132.7	22	2	0	0	1.000	0	0	.103	7	-0
Bonifacio E	40.7	7	0	0	0	1.000	0	0	--	2	--
Cousins S	11.0	3	0	0	0	1.000	0	0	--	1	--
Petersen B	8.0	1	0	0	0	1.000	0	0	--	0	--

Houston Astros

Stat Facts:
- Hunter Pence had the most PA of any player with 0 HBP
- Brandon Lyon issued 12 IBB in 78 IP
- Felipe Paulino's FIP was far lower than his ERA
- Jason Castro allowed .654 WP+PB/G
- Carlos Lee tied for the ML lead in LF FE
- Jeff Keppinger tied for the lowest K% of any regular
- Pedro Feliz had the lowest BB% of any regular
- 1% of Michael Bourn's FB were infield pop-ups
- Wilton Lopez walked 2% of his BFP
- Wesley Wright allowed 0 infield pop-ups
- One quarter of the FB allowed by Chris Sampson were HR
- Kazuo Matsui's GPA was .132

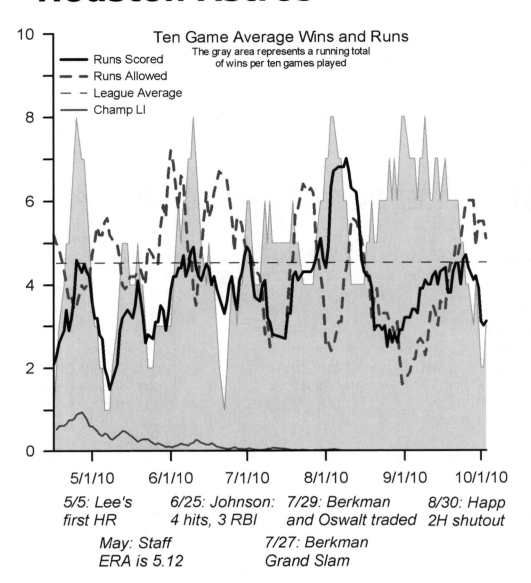

Ten Game Average Wins and Runs
The gray area represents a running total of wins per ten games played

- Runs Scored
- Runs Allowed
- League Average
- Champ LI

5/5: Lee's first HR

May: Staff ERA is 5.12

6/25: Johnson: 4 hits, 3 RBI

7/27: Berkman Grand Slam

7/29: Berkman and Oswalt traded

8/30: Happ 2H shutout

Team Batting and Pitching/Fielding Stats by Month

	April	May	June	July	Aug	Sept/Oct
Wins	8	9	14	13	17	15
Losses	14	20	14	11	12	15
RS/G	3.2	2.9	4.4	4.0	4.1	3.9
RA/G	4.5	5.4	5.2	3.9	3.6	4.4
OBP	.280	.284	.315	.318	.311	.305
SLG	.329	.322	.376	.403	.370	.371
FIP	3.85	4.31	3.87	3.36	3.74	4.32
DER	.693	.656	.657	.687	.719	.708

Batting Stats

Player	BR	Runs	RBI	PA	Outs	H	2B	3B	HR	TB	K	BB	IBB	HBP	SH	SF	SB	CS	GDP	H-A	L^R	BA	OBP	SLG	GPA
Pence H	95	93	91	658	461	173	29	3	25	283	105	41	2	0	0	3	18	9	11	.049	.014	.282	.325	.461	.271
Lee C	75	67	89	649	479	149	29	1	24	252	59	37	1	3	0	4	3	3	20	.034	.030	.246	.291	.417	.244
Bourn M *	75	84	38	605	411	142	25	6	2	185	109	59	5	3	6	2	52	12	6	.002	.054	.265	.341	.346	.249
Keppinger J	72	62	59	575	382	148	34	1	6	202	36	51	1	1	5	4	4	1	15	.006	.028	.288	.351	.393	.266
Johnson C	54	40	52	362	244	105	22	2	11	164	91	15	2	2	0	4	3	0	8	-.032	-.037	.308	.337	.481	.282
Berkman L +	51	39	49	358	239	73	16	1	13	130	70	60	4	0	0	0	3	2	12	.054	-.102	.245	.372	.436	.287
Michaels J	29	23	26	203	142	47	14	1	8	87	29	12	1	4	0	1	0	0	3	-.001	.054	.253	.310	.468	.266
Sanchez A	26	30	25	269	189	70	9	4	0	87	45	11	0	2	6	0	0	1	8	-.088	-.002	.280	.316	.348	.238
Blum G +	24	22	22	218	151	54	10	1	2	72	33	15	2	1	0	0	0	0	3	-.031	-.095	.267	.321	.356	.242
Quintero H	22	13	20	276	208	62	10	0	4	84	59	8	2	2	1	0	0	0	5	-.034	-.094	.234	.262	.317	.204
Feliz P	21	22	31	304	235	64	12	1	4	90	31	9	1	1	0	5	1	1	9	.035	.073	.221	.243	.311	.194
Manzella T	18	17	21	282	207	58	7	0	1	68	71	13	1	3	5	3	0	1	6	-.012	.072	.225	.267	.264	.193
Castro J *	17	26	8	217	159	40	8	1	2	56	41	22	2	0	0	0	0	0	4	-.005	.151	.205	.286	.287	.208
Wallace B *	14	14	13	159	115	32	6	1	2	46	50	8	3	7	0	0	0	0	3	.065	.012	.222	.296	.319	.221
Bourgeois J	11	16	3	136	105	27	4	1	0	33	16	13	0	0	0	0	12	4	5	.038	.010	.220	.294	.268	.207
Cash K	5	3	4	61	45	11	1	0	2	18	13	5	0	0	2	0	0	0	2	-.082	-.032	.204	.271	.333	.213
Hernandez A	5	7	1	56	40	9	2	0	0	11	10	8	0	0	0	0	2	0	1	-.081	.020	.188	.304	.229	.201
Sullivan C *	4	6	4	71	54	12	1	1	0	15	18	6	0	1	0	0	0	0	2	-.062	.182	.188	.257	.234	.181
Towles J	4	3	8	51	40	9	3	0	1	15	12	2	0	1	0	1	0	0	2	-.055	-.084	.191	.235	.319	.193
Paulino F	3	1	0	29	18	7	1	0	0	8	8	1	0	1	3	0	0	0	1	-.028	.052	.292	.346	.333	.248
Rodriguez W	3	4	4	74	51	12	2	0	0	14	23	1	0	0	9	1	0	0	0	-.025	-.022	.190	.200	.222	.151
Myers B	2	2	2	76	51	11	1	0	0	12	25	2	0	0	11	1	0	0	0	.051	.108	.177	.200	.194	.144
Bogusevic B	2	5	3	32	26	5	3	0	0	8	12	3	0	0	0	0	1	1	2	-.169	.201	.179	.258	.286	.195
Matsui K +	2	4	1	78	62	10	1	0	0	11	10	4	0	1	2	0	1	1	0	.101	-.133	.141	.197	.155	.132
Chacin G *	1	1	1	1	0	1	0	0	1	4	0	0	0	0	0	0	0	0	0	1.450	--	1.000	1.000	4.000	1.504
Norris B	1	2	2	56	38	7	2	0	0	9	13	2	0	0	10	0	0	0	1	.066	.147	.159	.196	.205	.144
Navarro O	1	2	0	25	19	1	0	0	0	1	4	5	0	0	0	0	0	0	0	-.060	-.032	.050	.240	.050	.125

Only includes batters with at least one Base Run. Italicized stats have been adjusted for home park.

Batted Ball Batting Stats

Player	% of PA		% of Batted Balls					Out %		Runs Per Event				Total Runs vs. Avg.				
	K%	BB%	GB%	LD%	FB%	IF/F	HR/OF	GB	OF	NIP	GB	LD	OF	NIP	GB	LD	FB	Tot
Pence Hu	16	6	53	15	32	.10	.15	68	85	.02	.08	.40	.25	-5	13	-2	9	15
Berkman La	20	17	47	17	36	.15	.19	78	81	.10	.00	.42	.32	9	-4	-0	8	12
Johnson Ch	25	5	41	24	35	.03	.13	70	80	-.04	.07	.44	.24	-8	3	9	5	9
Keppinger Je	6	9	51	20	30	.04	.04	77	87	.16	.02	.42	.08	8	-2	13	-13	5
Michaels Ja	14	8	34	18	48	.08	.11	85	82	.05	-.03	.42	.22	-0	-5	1	6	3
Blum Ge	15	7	44	21	35	.14	.04	75	80	.04	.04	.39	.10	-1	0	3	-5	-2
Bourn Mi	18	10	59	17	23	.01	.02	73	78	.05	.06	.38	.13	2	9	-2	-12	-3
Wallace Br	31	9	39	17	44	.12	.06	70	68	-.01	.06	.30	.23	-2	-0	-3	1	-4
Bourgeois Ja	12	10	45	18	37	.10	.00	79	83	.09	.00	.32	.05	1	-2	-1	-5	-6
Sanchez An	17	5	44	25	31	.02	.00	77	79	-.01	.01	.38	.07	-4	-3	5	-7	-8
Lee Ca	9	6	39	16	46	.12	.11	75	88	.07	.03	.29	.15	-1	-3	-8	3	-9
Castro Ja	19	10	41	22	37	.13	.04	81	85	.05	-.01	.32	.07	0	-4	-0	-6	-10
Quintero Hu	21	4	47	19	34	.13	.07	74	82	-.05	.04	.29	.14	-7	1	-4	-5	-15
Feliz Pe	10	3	43	13	44	.15	.04	72	88	-.00	.05	.35	.05	-4	1	-5	-10	-18
Manzella Th	25	6	53	18	29	.11	.02	71	89	-.03	.05	.38	.00	-6	1	-2	-13	-20
MLB Average	18	9	44	18	38	.09	.10	74	83	.04	.04	.38	.18	--	--	--	--	--

Only includes batters with at least one hundred Plate Appearances.

Pitching Stats

Player	PRC	IP	BFP	G	GS	K	BB	IBB	HBP	H	HR	DP	DER	SB	CS	PO	W	L	Sv	Op	Hld	H-A	R^L	RA	ERA	FIP
Myers B	94	223.7	936	33	33	180	66	3	3	212	20	18	.700	10	7	2	14	8	0	0	0	-.007	-.001	3.54	3.14	3.63
Rodriguez W	69	195.0	822	32	32	178	68	3	9	183	16	23	.672	13	11	2	11	12	0	0	0	-.056	-.025	4.38	3.60	3.58
Oswalt R	55	129.0	520	20	20	120	34	2	2	109	13	9	.712	10	2	0	6	12	0	0	0	.034	-.031	3.63	3.42	3.44
Norris B	43	153.7	683	27	27	158	77	3	6	151	18	15	.665	12	5	1	9	10	0	0	0	-.033	-.023	5.51	4.92	4.22
Lyon B	34	78.0	333	79	0	54	31	12	3	68	2	5	.720	6	0	0	6	6	20	22	19	-.042	.017	3.23	3.12	2.99
Lopez W	31	67.0	262	68	0	50	5	1	0	66	4	8	.685	1	3	0	5	2	1	3	14	-.056	-.027	3.09	2.96	2.66
Figueroa N	27	67.0	286	18	10	58	25	2	2	64	9	5	.703	6	3	0	5	3	0	0	0	.043	-.116	3.76	3.22	4.33
Happ J *	26	72.0	304	13	13	61	35	1	1	60	7	9	.725	1	2	1	5	4	0	0	0	-.006	-.063	4.13	3.75	4.22
Paulino F	22	91.7	411	19	14	83	46	4	3	95	4	5	.662	7	4	0	1	9	0	1	1	-.062	-.047	6.19	5.11	3.42
Lindstrom M	18	53.3	244	58	0	43	20	1	0	68	5	5	.631	6	1	0	2	5	23	29	4	.066	.020	4.39	4.39	3.87
Byrdak T *	16	38.7	170	64	0	29	20	0	0	40	4	4	.692	0	1	0	2	2	0	0	11	.034	-.109	3.49	3.49	4.59
Moehler B	15	56.7	249	20	8	28	26	1	1	66	5	13	.667	2	2	0	1	4	0	0	0	-.068	.009	5.08	4.92	4.73
Fulchino J	13	47.3	217	50	0	46	22	2	3	53	7	3	.662	2	1	0	2	1	0	1	5	-.059	-.024	5.70	5.51	4.63
Chacin G *	11	38.3	187	44	0	31	20	3	0	51	3	1	.632	4	0	0	2	2	1	1	5	-.028	-.005	5.17	4.70	3.93
Abad F *	9	19.0	76	22	0	12	5	0	0	14	3	0	.804	0	0	0	0	1	0	0	6	-.007	-.015	2.84	2.84	4.77
Melancon M	7	17.3	71	20	0	19	8	0	1	12	1	2	.714	0	0	0	2	0	0	1	8	-.050	.073	4.15	3.12	3.31
Wright W *	6	33.0	148	14	4	29	13	0	3	37	6	5	.670	1	1	0	1	2	0	0	0	-.086	-.083	7.36	5.73	5.26
Sampson C	6	30.3	139	35	0	16	8	0	1	43	7	4	.654	1	1	0	1	0	0	2	5	.034	.073	6.53	5.93	6.03
Villar H	2	6.0	27	8	0	3	3	0	1	5	0	1	.700	0	0	0	0	0	0	0	1	.194	.170	4.50	4.50	4.20
Daigle C	1	10.3	63	13	0	6	6	1	0	25	3	0	.542	4	0	0	1	1	0	0	3	-.142	-.256	11.32	11.32	7.26

Only includes pitchers with at least ten Innings Pitched. Italicized stats have been adjusted for home park.

Batted Ball Pitching Stats

Player	% of PA		% of Batted Balls					Out %		Runs Per Event				Total Runs vs. Avg.				
	K%	BB%	GB%	LD%	FB%	IF/F	HR/OF	GB	OF	NIP	GB	LD	OF	NIP	GB	LD	FB	Tot
Oswalt Ro	23	7	43	21	36	.08	.11	77	87	-.01	.03	.38	.16	-8	-4	1	-5	-15
Myers Br	19	7	49	16	35	.08	.09	74	84	.01	.04	.43	.16	-8	-1	1	-7	-15
Lyon Br	16	10	40	20	40	.12	.02	77	86	.06	.02	.39	.03	2	-1	1	-12	-11
Lopez Wi	19	2	56	16	28	.02	.07	73	87	-.07	.05	.42	.13	-7	2	-0	-4	-9
Happ Ja	20	12	40	18	42	.11	.08	75	81	.06	.03	.37	.15	2	-3	-2	-2	-4
Rodriguez Wa	22	9	48	20	32	.10	.09	70	81	.03	.06	.36	.19	-3	5	-1	-4	-3
Figueroa Ne	20	9	42	17	41	.13	.13	70	85	.03	.07	.35	.21	-1	1	-3	2	0
Byrdak Ti	17	12	29	18	53	.03	.07	71	84	.07	.05	.42	.12	2	-0	1	0	3
Paulino Fe	20	12	42	16	42	.05	.04	69	78	.06	.09	.47	.12	3	4	1	-4	4
Fulchino Je	21	12	40	22	38	.04	.13	67	91	.05	.09	.40	.15	1	2	2	-1	5
Lindstrom Ma	18	8	49	19	32	.05	.09	71	76	.03	.06	.40	.22	-1	2	2	3	6
Moehler Br	11	11	42	22	36	.12	.07	76	81	.11	.01	.43	.14	4	-3	7	-1	6
Chacin Gu	17	11	36	21	44	.07	.06	64	86	.07	.12	.48	.08	2	3	5	-3	7
Wright De	20	11	44	20	37	.00	.16	68	81	.05	.07	.34	.30	1	1	0	5	7
Sampson Ch	12	6	52	22	26	.03	.25	72	76	.05	.06	.32	.42	-0	2	1	6	9
Norris Bu	23	12	43	18	39	.10	.11	69	84	.04	.07	.49	.18	3	3	6	-1	11
MLB Average	18	9	44	18	38	.09	.10	74	83	.04	.04	.38	.18	--	--	--	--	--

Only includes pitchers who faced at least one hundred batters.

Fielding Stats

Name	INN	SBA/G	CS%	ERA	WP+PB/G	PO	A	TE	FE
Catchers									
Quintero H	653.7	0.72	33%	3.99	0.234	561	49	2	3
Castro J	509.3	0.85	35%	3.92	0.654	449	34	1	1
Cash K	156.7	1.03	17%	4.65	0.632	131	9	0	0
Towles J	116.7	0.85	27%	4.47	0.309	92	7	1	0
Esposito B	3.0	0.00	0%	9.00	0.000	2	0	0	0

Name	Inn	PO	A	TE	FE	FPct	DPS	DPT	ZRDif	OOZ	Dif
First Base											
Berkman L	739.0	696	72	1	0	.999	7	0	.045	27	3
Wallace B	375.3	327	32	1	2	.992	6	1	.052	14	2
Lee C	143.0	115	12	1	0	.992	0	0	.009	5	0
Feliz P	91.7	83	9	0	2	.968	0	0	--	5	--
Blum G	90.3	90	4	0	1	.989	0	0	--	1	--
Second Base											
Keppinger J	1070.0	217	351	1	5	.990	26	37	.025	13	-14
Matsui K	162.0	42	56	1	0	.990	2	10	-.037	2	-2
Sanchez A	71.0	14	19	0	0	1.000	0	4	--	2	--
Hernandez A	61.0	14	15	0	1	.967	2	3	--	3	--
Blum G	60.0	9	21	0	0	1.000	0	1	--	1	--
Downs M	11.7	2	0	0	0	1.000	0	0	--	0	--
Bourgeois J	3.0	2	2	0	0	1.000	0	1	--	0	--
Shortstop											
Manzella T	674.0	121	207	4	5	.973	23	16	-.026	29	-0
Sanchez A	484.0	79	128	2	3	.976	12	16	-.016	14	-7
Blum G	112.3	23	36	0	4	.937	2	3	-.015	3	-2
Keppinger J	87.0	14	19	1	0	.971	4	3	--	0	--
Navarro O	55.0	8	21	0	1	.967	0	3	--	4	--
Hernandez A	17.0	2	10	0	0	1.000	3	0	--	2	--
Downs M	10.0	2	2	0	0	1.000	0	1	--	0	--
Third Base											
Johnson C	790.0	42	135	9	9	.908	11	1	-.029	24	-5
Feliz P	529.7	28	103	3	5	.942	12	0	-.060	18	-2
Blum G	108.7	8	32	0	1	.976	1	0	.031	8	4
Downs M	11.0	0	3	0	0	1.000	1	0	--	2	--

Name	Inn	PO	A	TE	FE	FPct	DPS	DPT	ZRDif	OOZ	Dif
Left Field											
Lee C	1096.0	183	6	0	6	.969	1	0	-.021	47	-7
Michaels J	204.0	35	1	0	0	1.000	0	0	.058	9	-1
Bourgeois J	65.0	14	0	0	0	1.000	0	0	--	8	--
Sullivan C	45.0	9	0	0	0	1.000	0	0	--	3	--
Bogusevic B	29.0	11	0	0	0	1.000	0	0	--	4	--
Center Field											
Bourn M	1189.0	359	8	1	2	.992	2	0	.016	86	19
Bourgeois J	162.0	50	0	0	0	1.000	0	0	.040	12	3
Michaels J	69.0	14	0	0	0	1.000	0	0	--	5	--
Bogusevic B	17.0	4	0	0	0	1.000	0	0	--	1	--
Sullivan C	2.0	0	0	0	0	0.000	0	0	--	--	--
Right Field											
Pence H	1370.0	340	9	2	4	.983	2	0	.035	78	3
Michaels J	36.0	7	0	0	0	1.000	0	0	--	3	--
Sullivan C	23.0	5	0	0	0	1.000	0	0	--	4	--
Bogusevic B	9.0	3	0	0	0	1.000	0	0	--	2	--
Bourgeois J	1.0	1	0	0	0	1.000	0	0	--	0	--

Kansas City Royals

Stat Facts:
- Billy Butler led the majors in GDP
- Chris Getz had 15 SB in 17 attempts
- Kyle Davies allowed 17 SB in 20 attempts
- Luke Hochevar allowed 16 SB in 18 attempts
- Sean O'Sullivan allowed 15 SB in 16 attempts
- Jason Kendall had the most SBA/G of any regular C
- Kendall made the most TE of AL regular C
- Bruce Chen tied for second in the AL in Pickoffs
- Scott Podsednik had 0 assists
- Victor Marte allowed 0 infield pop-ups
- 24% of Marte's FB were HR
- 23% of Anthony Lerew's FB were HR

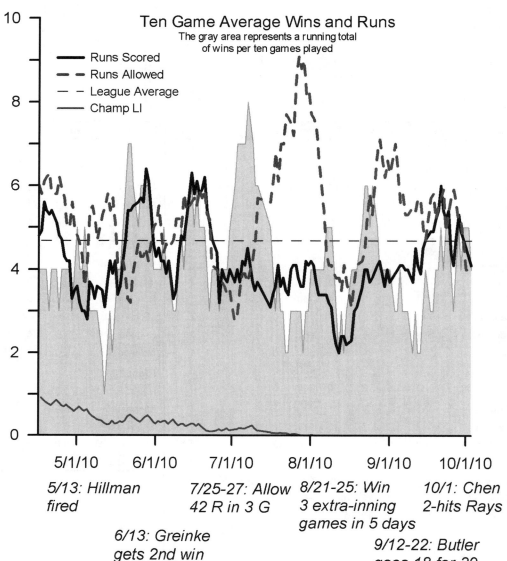

Ten Game Average Wins and Runs

The gray area represents a running total of wins per ten games played

— Runs Scored
- - Runs Allowed
– – League Average
— Champ LI

5/13: Hillman fired

6/13: Greinke gets 2nd win

7/25-27: Allow 42 R in 3 G

8/21-25: Win 3 extra-inning games in 5 days

9/12-22: Butler goes 18-for-39 with 4 HR

10/1: Chen 2-hits Rays

Team Batting and Pitching/Fielding Stats by Month

	April	May	June	July	Aug	Sept/Oct
Wins	9	12	13	10	12	11
Losses	14	17	14	15	16	19
RS/G	4.3	4.3	4.8	3.8	3.3	4.5
RA/G	5.6	4.6	4.6	6.9	5.0	4.9
OBP	.337	.336	.340	.326	.307	.340
SLG	.428	.397	.402	.377	.366	.427
FIP	4.84	4.66	4.15	5.34	4.07	4.32
DER	.687	.714	.704	.662	.659	.709

Batting Stats

Player	BR	Runs	RBI	PA	Outs	H	2B	3B	HR	TB	K	BB	IBB	HBP	SH	SF	SB	CS	GDP	H-A	L^R	BA	OBP	SLG	GPA
Butler B	90	77	78	678	438	189	45	0	15	279	78	69	8	5	0	9	0	0	32	.008	-.050	.318	.388	.469	.289
Betancourt Y	57	60	78	588	428	144	29	2	16	225	64	23	1	1	4	4	2	3	13	-.014	.042	.259	.288	.405	.228
Podsednik S	52	46	44	435	286	121	8	6	5	156	57	29	1	0	10	6	30	12	5	-.028	.022	.310	.353	.400	.256
DeJesus D *	51	46	37	394	253	112	23	3	5	156	47	34	2	4	3	1	3	3	10	.023	.044	.318	.384	.443	.280
Aviles M	51	63	32	448	313	129	16	3	8	175	49	20	0	1	0	3	14	5	13	.023	-.043	.304	.335	.413	.251
Guillen J	50	46	62	438	304	101	17	2	16	170	84	27	1	9	0	5	1	0	9	-.021	-.037	.255	.314	.429	.246
Betemit W +	49	36	43	315	197	82	20	0	13	141	74	36	2	1	0	2	0	0	3	.035	.020	.297	.378	.511	.295
Maier M *	44	41	39	421	280	98	15	6	5	140	68	41	2	0	4	3	3	2	3	-.011	.035	.263	.333	.375	.241
Callaspo A +	37	40	43	373	268	96	19	2	8	143	29	19	2	0	0	5	3	1	14	.003	-.026	.275	.308	.410	.239
Kendall J	37	39	37	490	342	111	18	0	0	129	45	37	2	6	6	7	12	7	12	.037	.061	.256	.318	.297	.215
Gordon A *	24	34	20	281	204	52	10	0	8	86	62	34	1	2	2	1	1	5	9	.008	-.008	.215	.315	.355	.228
Blanco G *	23	22	11	203	135	49	16	3	1	66	35	21	0	0	2	1	10	2	3	.006	.146	.274	.348	.369	.246
Ka'aihue K *	21	22	25	206	147	39	6	1	8	71	39	24	2	0	1	1	0	1	5	.053	-.009	.217	.307	.394	.234
Getz C *	19	23	18	248	176	53	9	0	0	62	28	19	1	2	3	0	15	2	3	.074	-.056	.237	.302	.277	.203
Bloomquist W	17	31	17	181	134	45	10	1	3	66	25	8	0	0	2	1	8	5	4	.012	.090	.265	.296	.388	.228
Pena B +	14	11	19	174	126	40	10	0	1	53	27	12	0	1	1	2	2	0	8	-.015	-.060	.253	.306	.335	.219
Ankiel R *	13	14	15	101	70	24	7	0	4	43	29	7	0	1	0	1	1	0	2	.106	.167	.261	.317	.467	.257
Dyson J *	8	11	5	65	48	12	4	2	1	23	16	6	0	0	2	0	9	1	2	.085	.175	.211	.286	.404	.227
Fields J	7	5	6	50	35	15	0	0	3	24	9	1	0	0	0	0	0	0	1	.025	.163	.306	.320	.490	.264
Miller J	6	5	4	60	42	13	3	0	1	19	23	4	0	1	0	0	1	0	0	-.000	.071	.236	.300	.345	.219
May L	1	3	6	39	32	7	1	0	0	8	10	0	0	1	0	1	0	1	1	.056	-.103	.189	.205	.216	.145

Only includes batters with at least one Base Run. Italicized stats have been adjusted for home park.

Batted Ball Batting Stats

Player	% of PA		% of Batted Balls					Out %		Runs Per Event				Total Runs vs. Avg.				
	K%	BB%	GB%	LD%	FB%	IF/F	HR/OF	GB	OF	NIP	GB	LD	OF	NIP	GB	LD	FB	Tot
Butler Bi	12	11	48	18	34	.04	.09	74	75	.11	.02	.43	.21	10	-2	11	10	29
Betemit Wi	23	12	40	15	45	.09	.16	67	71	.04	.09	.44	.32	1	3	-1	14	17
DeJesus Da	12	10	47	21	32	.06	.05	72	72	.09	.05	.37	.20	4	2	6	3	14
Podsednik Sc	13	7	52	19	30	.04	.05	65	78	.04	.10	.31	.12	-1	12	-2	-6	3
Maier Mi	16	10	39	17	44	.08	.04	71	83	.06	.06	.49	.08	2	3	5	-8	2
Aviles Mi	11	5	43	19	38	.10	.06	66	83	.02	.08	.34	.11	-3	8	2	-5	2
Ankiel Ri	29	8	48	17	34	.23	.24	74	85	-.01	.05	.60	.36	-2	0	2	2	2
Guillen Jo	19	8	41	17	42	.10	.13	76	82	.03	.03	.39	.21	-2	-3	-1	6	1
Blanco Gr	17	10	57	18	25	.03	.03	77	74	.06	.03	.44	.14	1	3	0	-3	1
Callaspo Al	8	5	42	17	41	.07	.06	72	84	.07	.04	.35	.12	-1	1	1	-1	-1
Ka'aihue Ki	19	12	35	15	49	.10	.13	82	91	.06	-.02	.41	.16	1	-4	-2	1	-3
Gordon Al	22	13	38	23	39	.08	.12	82	88	.06	-.02	.34	.17	2	-5	0	-1	-4
Bloomquist Wi	14	4	44	21	35	.18	.07	80	82	-.00	.01	.40	.15	-2	-2	3	-2	-4
Pena Br	16	7	45	16	39	.18	.02	76	80	.04	.02	.39	.10	-1	-1	-1	-4	-6
Getz Ch	11	8	52	18	30	.07	.00	73	82	.08	.06	.24	.02	1	4	-4	-9	-8
Betancourt Yu	11	4	40	18	42	.11	.09	80	82	.01	.01	.36	.16	-6	-8	1	1	-11
Kendall Ja	9	9	46	18	36	.09	.00	74	85	.11	.04	.32	.01	4	0	-2	-21	-19
MLB Average	18	9	44	18	38	.09	.10	74	83	.04	.04	.38	.18	--	--	--	--	--

Only includes batters with at least one hundred Plate Appearances.

Pitching Stats

Player	PRC	IP	BFP	G	GS	K	BB	IBB	HBP	H	HR	DP	DER	SB	CS	PO	W	L	Sv	Op	Hld	H-A	R^L	RA	ERA	FIP
Greinke Z	78	220.0	919	33	33	181	55	1	7	219	18	27	.676	12	11	3	10	14	0	0	0	.021	-.058	4.66	4.17	3.36
Soria J	55	65.7	270	66	0	71	16	1	2	53	4	4	.689	1	1	0	1	2	43	46	0	-.021	-.015	1.78	1.78	2.52
Davies K	51	183.7	817	32	32	126	80	1	2	206	20	22	.677	17	3	0	8	12	0	0	0	-.015	-.027	5.59	5.34	4.48
Chen B *	51	140.3	608	33	23	98	57	4	3	136	17	10	.709	5	7	8	12	7	1	1	0	.034	.013	4.36	4.17	4.49
Hochevar L	31	103.0	450	18	17	76	37	1	4	110	9	12	.673	16	2	1	6	6	0	0	0	-.064	-.029	5.33	4.81	3.94
Bannister B	29	127.7	581	24	23	77	50	0	3	158	23	8	.680	15	7	1	7	12	0	0	0	-.021	.066	6.49	6.34	5.49
Farnsworth K	26	44.7	185	37	0	36	12	0	4	40	2	3	.695	4	4	1	3	0	0	2	7	.003	-.030	2.62	2.42	3.16
Tejeda R	25	61.0	258	54	0	56	26	1	0	55	5	6	.690	4	1	0	3	5	0	6	12	.046	-.007	4.13	3.54	3.57
Hughes D *	19	56.3	252	57	0	34	24	0	5	59	3	7	.688	3	1	0	1	3	0	0	7	-.028	-.025	4.47	3.83	4.14
O'Sullivan S	16	70.7	319	14	13	37	27	0	1	83	14	6	.700	15	1	0	3	6	0	0	0	-.028	.053	6.37	6.11	5.83
Meche G	15	61.7	281	20	9	41	38	3	2	65	9	6	.696	17	4	1	0	5	0	0	6	-.005	.029	6.13	5.69	5.48
Wood B	15	49.7	220	51	0	31	22	5	1	54	3	3	.675	10	3	1	1	3	0	4	15	-.108	-.029	5.26	5.07	4.52
Texeira K	12	42.7	190	27	0	19	15	1	2	51	3	6	.662	3	3	0	1	0	0	0	1	.029	-.030	5.06	4.64	4.26
Bullington B	11	42.7	196	13	5	29	17	2	4	51	6	3	.664	7	4	0	1	4	0	0	0	.013	-.045	6.12	6.12	4.92
Humber P	8	21.7	94	8	1	16	7	2	1	22	1	1	.681	2	0	0	1	0	0	0	1	-.093	-.026	4.15	4.15	3.07
Chavez J	5	26.0	118	23	0	16	11	4	0	29	5	0	.698	1	1	0	2	3	0	1	6	.025	-.019	6.92	5.88	5.19
Holland G	4	18.7	87	15	0	23	8	0	0	23	3	1	.604	1	0	0	0	1	0	0	0	-.087	-.004	7.23	6.75	4.02
Lerew A	4	26.3	120	6	6	18	9	0	2	34	9	3	.695	1	1	0	1	4	0	0	0	-.212	.151	8.54	8.54	7.44
Thompson B	4	19.7	89	16	0	10	4	1	1	25	4	0	.686	1	0	0	0	4	0	0	1	-.019	-.169	7.32	6.41	5.35
Marte V	4	27.7	137	22	0	19	15	1	2	38	8	4	.667	1	0	0	3	0	0	0	1	.092	.024	9.76	9.76	7.23
Parrish J *	3	6.0	26	9	0	4	5	0	0	4	2	1	.867	1	0	0	1	1	0	2	2	.157	.118	3.00	3.00	8.61
Cruz J	3	5.3	28	5	0	7	4	0	0	9	0	0	.471	0	0	0	0	0	0	1	0	-.320	.034	3.38	3.38	2.74
Rupe J	3	9.7	49	11	0	8	7	0	0	14	1	2	.606	0	0	0	1	1	0	0	5	.068	.136	5.59	5.59	4.97

Only includes pitchers with at least ten Innings Pitched. Italicized stats have been adjusted for home park.

Batted Ball Pitching Stats

Player	% of PA		% of Batted Balls					Out %		Runs Per Event				Total Runs vs. Avg.				
	K%	BB%	GB%	LD%	FB%	IF/F	HR/OF	GB	OF	NIP	GB	LD	OF	NIP	GB	LD	FB	Tot
Soria Jo	26	7	48	17	35	.10	.07	66	86	-.02	.09	.31	.12	-5	4	-5	-6	-12
Greinke Za	20	7	46	18	36	.09	.08	73	78	.00	.04	.43	.18	-10	-3	5	-1	-8
Farnsworth Ky	19	9	43	24	34	.07	.05	77	85	.03	.03	.35	.09	-1	-1	1	-4	-5
Tejeda Ro	22	10	28	21	51	.14	.07	64	86	.03	.11	.37	.10	-0	2	0	-4	-2
Hughes Du	13	12	36	22	42	.05	.04	67	88	.10	.09	.34	.05	3	2	2	-6	2
Chen Br	16	10	34	18	48	.09	.09	74	83	.06	.04	.36	.15	3	-2	-1	3	4
Texeira Ka	10	9	55	16	29	.12	.08	68	77	.10	.08	.31	.19	2	5	-2	-1	4
Hochevar Lu	17	9	46	21	33	.12	.08	75	84	.05	.03	.46	.16	1	-1	10	-4	5
Chavez Je	14	9	42	13	45	.10	.14	65	84	.07	.12	.34	.25	1	3	-1	4	6
Wood Bl	14	10	51	15	34	.04	.11	74	75	.08	.04	.39	.24	2	0	-1	4	6
Bullington Br	15	11	46	17	36	.08	.13	70	86	.08	.08	.44	.19	2	3	2	1	8
Lerew An	15	9	41	14	44	.03	.23	62	90	.06	.12	.31	.31	0	3	-2	8	9
Meche Gi	15	14	45	18	38	.07	.13	76	87	.11	.05	.40	.19	6	0	1	3	10
O'Sullivan Se	12	9	40	18	41	.14	.16	72	87	.08	.06	.33	.23	2	4	0	6	12
Marte Vi	14	12	44	21	34	.00	.24	70	73	.10	.05	.31	.42	2	0	1	9	13
Davies Ky	15	10	41	17	42	.07	.08	71	83	.07	.06	.43	.15	5	5	5	2	18
Bannister Br	13	9	43	20	37	.07	.15	77	84	.07	.03	.42	.25	3	-1	10	14	27
MLB Average	**18**	**9**	**44**	**18**	**38**	**.09**	**.10**	**74**	**83**	**.04**	**.04**	**.38**	**.18**	--	--	--	--	--

Only includes pitchers who faced at least one hundred batters.

Fielding Stats

Name	INN	SBA/G	CS%	ERA	WP+PB/G	PO	A	TE	FE
Catchers									
Kendall J	1018.3	1.18	24%	5.13	0.362	721	68	10	1
Pena B	337.3	1.07	28%	4.75	0.427	269	24	1	2
May L	81.0	0.89	13%	4.00	1.000	60	3	0	0

Name	Inn	PO	A	TE	FE	FPct	DPS	DPT	ZRDif	OOZ	Dif
First Base											
Butler B	1102.0	1002	96	0	6	.995	7	0	-.015	35	-1
Ka'aihue K	290.3	277	21	1	1	.993	3	0	.070	19	9
Betemit W	35.0	33	0	0	1	.971	0	0	--	0	--
Bloomquist W	4.0	4	1	0	0	1.000	0	0	--	--	--
Gordon A	3.0	1	0	0	0	1.000	0	0	--	--	--
Maier M	2.0	1	1	0	0	1.000	0	0	--	--	--
Second Base											
Aviles M	755.7	183	258	4	7	.976	16	23	-.004	23	4
Getz C	535.0	113	164	1	2	.989	12	31	-.040	16	3
Callaspo A	99.0	19	30	1	0	.980	5	3	--	2	--
Bloomquist W	31.0	9	9	0	1	.947	1	1	--	0	--
Betemit W	16.0	1	4	0	1	.833	0	0	--	0	--
Shortstop											
Betancourt Y	1331.0	256	418	9	9	.974	41	31	-.018	49	-8
Aviles M	104.0	18	29	1	1	.959	5	0	-.122	10	6
Bloomquist W	1.0	0	0	0	0	0.000	0	0	--	0	--
Third Base											
Callaspo A	668.3	45	139	3	3	.968	12	0	.022	15	-10
Betemit W	455.3	30	75	1	7	.929	7	0	-.051	9	-8
Fields J	106.0	9	19	0	5	.848	0	0	-.031	2	-2
Gordon A	84.0	3	10	3	1	.765	0	0	--	2	--
Bloomquist W	79.0	5	18	1	3	.852	4	0	--	1	--
Aviles M	35.0	2	1	0	1	.750	0	0	--	0	--
Getz C	9.0	0	0	1	0	0.000	0	0	--	0	--

Name	Inn	PO	A	TE	FE	FPct	DPS	DPT	ZRDif	OOZ	Dif
Left Field											
Podsednik S	806.3	203	0	0	3	.985	0	0	-.006	37	-3
Gordon A	486.3	132	2	0	2	.985	1	0	.047	21	-3
Maier M	46.0	5	0	0	0	1.000	0	0	--	1	--
Bloomquist W	39.0	8	0	0	0	1.000	0	0	--	0	--
Miller J	23.0	7	0	0	1	.875	0	0	--	1	--
Betemit W	18.0	3	0	0	0	1.000	0	0	--	1	--
DeJesus D	10.0	2	0	0	0	1.000	0	0	--	1	--
Blanco G	8.0	0	0	0	0	0.000	0	0	--	0	--
Center Field											
Maier M	525.7	173	3	0	1	.994	1	0	.021	26	-4
Blanco G	347.0	95	3	0	0	1.000	1	0	-.033	18	-2
Ankiel R	209.0	68	1	0	2	.972	1	0	-.013	16	4
DeJesus D	155.0	48	1	0	0	1.000	1	0	.047	4	-5
Dyson J	129.0	48	2	0	2	.962	2	0	.041	9	2
Bloomquist W	69.0	20	1	0	0	1.000	0	0	--	2	--
Podsednik S	2.0	2	0	0	0	1.000	0	0	--	0	--
Right Field											
DeJesus D	597.3	133	4	0	0	1.000	0	0	-.007	28	-5
Maier M	355.0	81	1	1	3	.953	0	0	-.024	20	0
Guillen J	169.0	41	1	1	0	.977	0	0	.009	12	3
Bloomquist W	147.3	30	2	0	0	1.000	0	0	-.064	5	-3
Miller J	116.0	27	0	0	0	1.000	0	0	.055	7	1
Blanco G	27.0	4	0	0	0	1.000	0	0	--	0	--
Gordon A	25.0	5	0	0	1	.833	0	0	--	0	--

Los Angeles Angels of Anaheim

Stat Facts:

- Brandon Wood had the fewest Base Runs of any player with 200+ PA
- Torii Hunter had the lowest H-A of any ML regular
- Hunter was CS 12 times in 21 attempts
- Jered Weaver had the most IP of any pitcher with 0 HBP
- Weaver induced 7 GDP
- Weaver allowed 27 SB in 31 attempts
- Ervin Santana was second in the majors in SB
- Joe Saunders had more Pickoffs than SB
- Joel Pineiro had the lowest H-A of any pitcher with 150+ IP
- Jeff Mathis allowed .731 WP+PB/G
- Peter Bourjos had 10 assists in 450 innings
- Alberto Callaspo and Kevin Frandsen each struck out in 6% of their PA

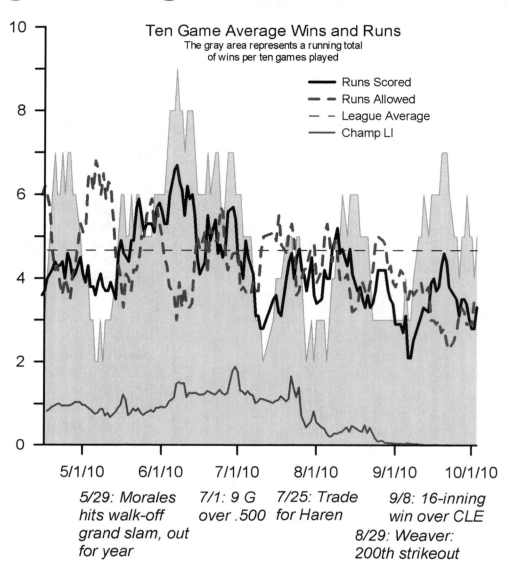

Ten Game Average Wins and Runs
The gray area represents a running total of wins per ten games played

— Runs Scored
-- Runs Allowed
- - League Average
— Champ LI

5/29: Morales hits walk-off grand slam, out for year

7/1: 9 G over .500

7/25: Trade for Haren

9/8: 16-inning win over CLE

8/29: Weaver: 200th strikeout

Team Batting and Pitching/Fielding Stats by Month

	April	May	June	July	Aug	Sept/Oct
Wins	12	14	18	9	11	16
Losses	12	15	9	17	16	13
RS/G	4.1	4.8	5.3	3.7	3.8	3.5
RA/G	5.1	5.0	4.4	4.4	4.0	3.2
OBP	.327	.305	.340	.296	.316	.286
SLG	.414	.391	.426	.376	.392	.348
FIP	4.90	4.21	3.84	4.32	4.12	3.76
DER	.699	.684	.690	.693	.716	.718

Batting Stats

Player	BR	Runs	RBI	PA	Outs	H	2B	3B	HR	TB	K	BB	IBB	HBP	SH	SF	SB	CS	GDP	H-A	L^R	BA	OBP	SLG	GPA
Abreu B *	95	88	78	667	450	146	41	1	20	249	132	87	3	2	0	5	24	10	13	.029	.071	.255	.352	.435	.275
Hunter T	91	76	90	646	446	161	36	0	23	266	106	61	6	7	0	5	9	12	22	-.069	-.023	.281	.354	.464	.283
Matsui H *	82	55	84	558	361	132	24	1	21	221	98	67	6	1	0	4	0	1	10	-.002	.069	.274	.361	.459	.285
Kendrick H	79	67	75	658	464	172	41	4	10	251	94	28	2	5	4	5	14	4	16	.030	-.021	.279	.313	.407	.250
Napoli M	70	60	68	510	362	108	24	1	26	212	137	42	2	11	0	4	4	2	15	.014	.091	.238	.316	.468	.266
Aybar E +	59	69	29	589	414	135	18	4	5	176	81	35	1	7	11	2	22	8	7	-.046	-.015	.253	.306	.330	.226
Rivera J	54	53	52	455	323	105	20	0	15	170	58	33	4	4	0	2	2	2	10	-.058	.015	.252	.312	.409	.249
Morales K +	31	29	39	211	143	56	5	0	11	94	31	12	3	5	0	1	0	1	5	-.002	-.142	.290	.346	.487	.285
Izturis M +	28	27	27	238	163	53	13	1	3	77	27	21	0	2	1	2	7	3	1	-.086	.014	.250	.321	.363	.242
Bourjos P	19	19	15	193	149	37	6	4	6	69	40	6	0	2	3	1	10	3	2	-.048	-.058	.204	.237	.381	.208
Callaspo A +	18	21	13	228	170	53	8	0	2	67	13	12	1	1	1	1	2	2	8	.027	-.070	.249	.291	.315	.215
Willits R +	18	23	8	182	123	41	7	0	0	48	26	19	0	1	3	0	2	4	1	.034	.000	.258	.341	.302	.235
Frandsen K	15	24	14	173	125	40	11	0	0	51	10	9	0	1	3	0	2	0	5	.056	-.017	.250	.294	.319	.218
Mathis J	13	19	18	218	168	40	6	1	3	57	59	6	0	1	3	3	3	0	3	.030	.031	.195	.219	.278	.173
Wilson B	12	12	15	106	77	22	6	0	4	40	23	8	0	0	2	0	0	0	3	-.003	.078	.229	.288	.417	.241
Wood B	6	20	14	243	196	33	2	0	4	47	71	6	0	2	8	1	1	0	3	.014	.014	.146	.174	.208	.134
Budde R	3	2	3	11	6	4	1	0	1	8	5	1	0	0	0	0	0	0	0	-.155	.576	.400	.455	.800	.416
Ryan M *	3	3	2	41	31	8	4	0	0	12	5	1	0	0	0	0	0	0	0	-.058	.180	.205	.220	.308	.181
Conger H +	3	2	5	34	25	5	1	0	1	8	9	5	0	0	0	0	0	0	1	.248	-.055	.172	.294	.276	.207
McAnulty P *	1	2	2	24	19	3	0	0	1	6	11	2	0	0	0	0	0	0	0	.358	--	.136	.208	.273	.166
Quinlan R	1	4	2	36	29	4	2	0	0	6	6	2	0	0	1	0	2	0	0	-.134	.157	.121	.171	.182	.126

Only includes batters with at least one Base Run. Italicized stats have been adjusted for home park.

Batted Ball Batting Stats

Player	% of PA		% of Batted Balls					Out %		Runs Per Event				Total Runs vs. Avg.				
	K%	BB%	GB%	LD%	FB%	IF/F	HR/OF	GB	OF	NIP	GB	LD	OF	NIP	GB	LD	FB	Tot
Hunter To	16	11	48	18	34	.08	.16	72	83	.07	.04	.39	.26	5	1	4	12	22
Matsui Hi	18	12	39	19	42	.03	.13	82	77	.07	-.00	.38	.25	6	-8	2	17	17
Abreu Bo	20	13	47	17	36	.03	.13	75	79	.07	.03	.36	.25	9	-2	-5	13	15
Morales Ke	15	8	48	21	31	.02	.20	79	83	.05	.01	.38	.31	0	-2	3	7	7
Napoli Mi	27	10	38	20	42	.04	.20	84	80	.02	-.03	.32	.34	-3	-11	-5	23	4
Rivera Ju	13	8	46	16	39	.13	.12	74	84	.07	.04	.32	.20	1	0	-4	3	0
Wilson Ro	22	8	40	12	47	.12	.13	76	85	.01	.03	.46	.20	-1	-1	-1	1	-2
Izturis Ma	11	10	42	18	40	.10	.03	73	83	.10	.06	.33	.08	2	1	-1	-5	-3
Kendrick Ho	14	5	53	19	28	.03	.07	76	75	.01	.03	.35	.20	-7	1	1	1	-4
Willits Re	14	11	35	20	45	.09	.00	67	84	.09	.09	.31	.02	2	2	-1	-7	-4
Frandsen Ke	6	6	56	15	28	.05	.00	78	84	.12	.03	.37	.03	0	2	-1	-6	-5
Bourjos Pe	21	4	51	10	39	.06	.13	79	88	-.04	.04	.42	.19	-4	1	-5	0	-8
Callaspo Al	6	6	49	19	32	.08	.03	82	82	.12	-.01	.33	.08	0	-4	1	-6	-9
Aybar Er	14	7	49	15	36	.09	.04	74	86	.04	.05	.40	.06	-2	7	-5	-18	-17
Mathis Je	27	3	39	13	48	.13	.05	75	86	-.06	.04	.43	.07	-7	-0	-4	-7	-18
Wood Ri	29	3	35	13	52	.09	.05	80	91	-.07	.01	.34	.03	-9	-3	-8	-10	-29
MLB Average	18	9	44	18	38	.09	.10	74	83	.04	.04	.38	.18	--	--	--	--	--

Only includes batters with at least one hundred Plate Appearances.

Pitching Stats

Player	PRC	IP	BFP	G	GS	K	BB	IBB	HBP	H	HR	DP	DER	SB	CS	PO	W	L	Sv	Op	Hld	H-A	R^L	RA	ERA	FIP
Weaver J	111	224.3	905	34	34	233	54	0	0	187	23	7	.709	27	4	3	13	12	0	0	0	-.047	.017	3.33	3.01	3.09
Santana E	83	222.7	954	33	33	169	73	2	12	221	27	16	.704	36	8	1	17	10	0	0	0	-.002	-.036	4.20	3.92	4.29
Pineiro J	58	152.3	634	23	23	92	34	6	1	155	15	14	.705	3	1	0	10	7	0	0	0	-.103	.013	3.90	3.84	3.76
Haren D	48	94.0	387	14	14	75	25	2	2	84	8	3	.726	4	2	1	5	4	0	0	0	-.056	-.010	2.97	2.87	3.42
Kazmir S *	35	150.0	682	28	28	93	79	2	12	158	25	16	.706	12	5	4	9	15	0	0	0	-.015	-.015	6.18	5.94	5.82
Saunders J *	33	120.7	522	20	20	64	45	1	1	135	14	17	.688	4	6	5	6	10	0	0	0	.012	-.017	5.22	4.62	4.68
Jepsen K	25	59.0	253	68	0	61	29	5	2	54	2	7	.673	5	2	0	2	4	0	4	27	.002	-.007	3.97	3.97	2.81
Rodney F	24	68.0	308	72	0	53	35	1	5	70	4	7	.673	13	1	1	4	3	14	21	21	.003	.004	4.37	4.24	4.04
Bell T	18	61.0	273	25	7	45	21	2	1	77	2	5	.623	10	2	0	2	5	0	0	1	-.028	-.011	5.16	4.72	3.05
Rodriguez F	17	47.3	209	43	0	36	26	3	1	46	5	7	.695	1	0	0	1	3	0	1	2	-.002	-.148	4.37	4.37	4.49
Fuentes B *	16	38.3	161	39	0	39	18	1	1	28	5	3	.714	3	1	2	4	1	23	27	0	-.008	-.130	3.99	3.52	4.18
Kohn M	15	21.3	96	24	0	20	16	1	0	17	0	0	.700	2	2	1	2	0	1	1	1	-.054	-.098	2.11	2.11	3.35
Thompson R	14	19.7	75	13	0	15	4	0	0	12	2	2	.778	1	0	0	2	0	0	0	0	-.041	.126	1.83	1.37	3.52
Shields S	12	46.0	217	43	1	39	34	1	2	45	6	1	.691	4	3	1	0	3	0	1	1	.019	.098	6.07	5.28	5.39
Walden J	11	15.3	65	16	0	23	7	0	0	13	1	1	.647	2	0	0	0	1	1	1	6	.016	.067	2.35	2.35	2.33
Palmer M	9	33.7	157	14	1	17	20	1	1	38	1	4	.661	1	1	0	1	2	0	0	1	.020	-.005	5.35	4.54	4.27
O'Sullivan S	8	13.0	49	5	1	6	4	2	0	7	1	1	.842	0	0	0	1	0	0	0	0	-.027	-.035	2.08	2.08	3.65
Bulger J	8	24.0	111	25	0	25	15	0	2	25	3	0	.667	2	2	0	0	0	0	0	2	-.028	-.051	5.25	4.88	4.78
Cassevah B	5	20.0	94	16	0	8	8	2	1	23	0	2	.649	0	0	0	1	2	0	0	0	-.223	-.166	4.95	3.15	3.36
Stokes B	2	16.7	90	16	0	16	16	1	1	26	4	3	.585	3	1	1	0	0	0	0	0	-.107	-.045	9.72	8.10	7.19

Only includes pitchers with at least ten Innings Pitched. Italicized stats have been adjusted for home park.

Batted Ball Pitching Stats

Player	% of PA		% of Batted Balls					Out %		Runs Per Event				Total Runs vs. Avg.				
	K%	BB%	GB%	LD%	FB%	IF/F	HR/OF	GB	OF	NIP	GB	LD	OF	NIP	GB	LD	FB	Tot
Weaver Je	26	6	36	16	48	.12	.09	75	82	-.03	.05	.37	.17	-19	-2	-13	1	-33
Haren Da	19	7	40	17	43	.07	.07	78	81	.01	.02	.33	.15	-4	-3	-5	-0	-12
Jepsen Ke	24	12	56	18	26	.08	.05	75	74	.04	.03	.39	.19	1	-2	-1	-4	-6
Pineiro Jo	15	6	55	16	29	.04	.11	80	73	.01	.02	.33	.27	-6	-2	-6	10	-4
Fuentes Br	24	12	22	21	57	.04	.09	73	86	.04	.07	.37	.14	0	-1	-0	0	-0
Rodriguez Fr	17	13	48	18	34	.10	.12	80	79	.08	.00	.43	.21	3	-3	1	0	2
Santana Er	18	9	35	22	43	.07	.09	75	86	.04	.04	.36	.14	-1	-2	7	-2	4
Bulger Ja	23	15	38	24	38	.08	.13	62	86	.07	.13	.33	.19	2	2	0	0	4
Rodney Fe	17	13	51	19	30	.10	.07	75	79	.08	.05	.40	.14	5	2	2	-4	4
Shields Sc	18	16	48	19	33	.02	.13	73	90	.10	.06	.36	.16	5	1	-0	-1	6
Palmer Jo	11	13	49	15	36	.05	.03	72	79	.14	.06	.47	.13	4	2	1	-1	6
Bell Tr	16	8	42	23	35	.10	.03	73	76	.04	.06	.46	.13	-0	2	8	-3	6
Saunders Jo	12	9	43	19	38	.07	.09	75	83	.08	.04	.43	.16	3	-0	8	2	12
Kazmir Sc	14	13	39	17	44	.08	.12	74	81	.11	.05	.36	.22	14	-1	-1	15	28
MLB Average	18	9	44	18	38	.09	.10	74	83	.04	.04	.38	.18	--	--	--	--	--

Only includes pitchers who faced at least one hundred batters.

Fielding Stats

Name	INN	SBA/G	CS%	ERA	WP+PB/G	PO	A	TE	FE
Catchers									
Mathis J	553.7	0.81	14%	3.67	0.731	433	36	5	2
Napoli M	525.0	1.11	20%	5.13	0.600	405	32	4	2
Wilson B	260.7	1.10	19%	3.63	0.414	217	12	1	0
Conger H	80.0	0.90	13%	1.91	0.113	63	3	3	0
Budde R	30.0	1.80	17%	1.20	0.900	35	2	0	0

Name	Inn	PO	A	TE	FE	FPct	DPS	DPT	ZRDif	OOZ	Dif
First Base											
Napoli M	586.3	502	44	2	4	.989	5	1	.036	27	8
Morales K	448.7	435	25	0	2	.996	3	0	.086	12	-3
Rivera J	107.0	98	12	0	1	.991	1	0	.125	6	2
Kendrick H	104.3	98	4	0	1	.990	0	0	.103	5	2
Quinlan R	65.3	71	1	0	1	.986	0	0	--	1	--
McAnulty P	37.0	45	0	0	1	.978	0	0	--	0	--
Trumbo M	33.0	38	4	0	0	1.000	0	0	--	4	--
Frandsen K	32.7	35	3	0	0	1.000	0	0	--	1	--
Ryan M	24.0	28	2	0	0	1.000	0	0	--	2	--
Wood B	9.0	11	0	0	0	1.000	0	0	--	0	--
Wilson B	2.0	4	0	0	0	1.000	0	0	--	--	--
Second Base											
Kendrick H	1251.0	259	366	4	5	.986	31	41	-.027	29	-2
Izturis M	176.3	30	52	1	0	.988	3	3	.016	2	-2
Frandsen K	20.0	3	6	0	1	.900	1	0	--	1	--
Callaspo A	2.0	0	0	0	0	0.000	0	0	--	--	--
Shortstop											
Aybar E	1179.0	198	344	9	12	.963	28	26	.008	61	10
Wood B	185.3	22	56	2	3	.940	5	2	-.094	9	1
Izturis M	55.3	5	24	0	0	1.000	0	3	--	2	--
Romine A	29.0	9	8	1	1	.895	2	1	--	1	--
Third Base											
Callaspo A	465.7	38	101	2	2	.972	10	0	.044	18	1
Wood B	412.7	33	76	4	1	.956	3	0	.098	14	-1
Frandsen K	346.3	28	73	4	1	.953	3	0	-.025	13	0
Izturis M	223.7	14	47	0	1	.984	6	0	.060	9	1
Quinlan R	1.0	0	0	0	0	0.000	0	0	--	--	--

Name	Inn	PO	A	TE	FE	FPct	DPS	DPT	ZRDif	OOZ	Dif
Left Field											
Rivera J	692.7	167	5	2	3	.972	0	0	-.071	47	13
Abreu B	349.0	71	1	0	0	1.000	1	0	-.037	16	-1
Willits R	226.7	53	0	0	0	1.000	0	0	.129	12	1
Matsui H	123.0	16	1	0	0	1.000	0	0	-.071	4	-2
Ryan M	48.0	11	0	0	0	1.000	0	0	--	1	--
Aldridge C	7.0	2	0	0	0	1.000	0	0	--	0	--
Quinlan R	1.0	0	0	0	0	0.000	0	0	--	--	--
Callaspo A	1.0	0	0	0	0	0.000	0	0	--	--	--
Frandsen K	1.0	0	0	0	1	0.000	0	0	--	0	--
Center Field											
Hunter T	828.3	252	2	0	1	.996	0	0	-.007	56	9
Bourjos P	449.7	149	10	0	1	.994	1	0	.020	29	4
Willits R	167.7	50	4	0	0	1.000	0	0	-.040	10	1
Evans T	2.0	1	0	0	0	1.000	0	0	--	0	--
Rivera J	1.0	0	0	0	0	0.000	0	0	--	--	--
Kendrick H	0.7	0	0	0	0	0.000	0	0	--	--	--
Right Field											
Abreu B	805.7	171	6	1	5	.967	1	0	-.003	36	-8
Hunter T	410.0	106	2	1	1	.982	0	0	-.001	20	-3
Rivera J	173.7	47	3	0	0	1.000	1	0	-.011	8	-2
Willits R	26.0	6	1	0	1	.875	0	0	--	2	--
Aldridge C	22.0	3	0	0	0	1.000	0	0	--	0	--
Trumbo M	7.0	1	1	0	1	.667	0	0	--	0	--
Quinlan R	5.0	1	0	0	0	1.000	0	0	--	0	--

Los Angeles Dodgers

Stat Facts:

- Clayton Kershaw led the majors in Sac Bunts
- Kershaw tied for the NL lead in Pickoffs
- Matt Kemp was CS 15 times in 34 attempts
- Hiroki Kuroda issued the most IBB in the majors
- Chad Billingsley allowed 8 HR in 192 IP
- James Loney had the most innings of any 1B with 0 FE
- Loney's LD% was 25
- Reed Johnson struck out 10 times as often as he walked
- Garrett Anderson's GPA was .168
- 13% of Hong-Chi Kuo's BFP got a hit
- Jamey Carroll's OBP was 40 points higher than his SLG
- So was Ryan Theriot's

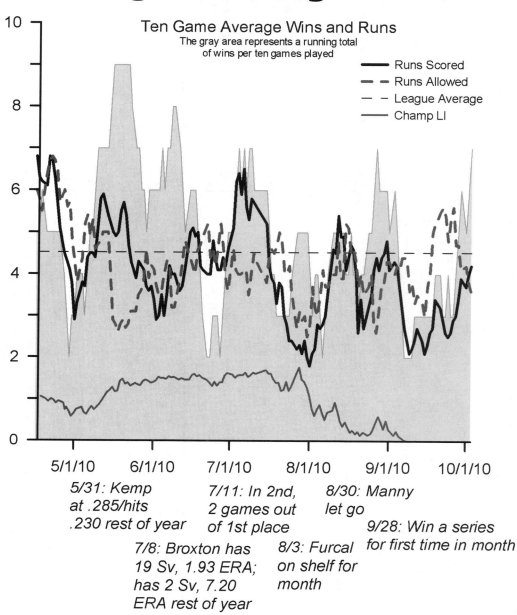

Ten Game Average Wins and Runs
The gray area represents a running total of wins per ten games played

Legend:
— Runs Scored
- - Runs Allowed
– – League Average
— Champ LI

5/31: Kemp at .285/hits .230 rest of year

7/8: Broxton has 19 Sv, 1.93 ERA; has 2 Sv, 7.20 ERA rest of year

7/11: In 2nd, 2 games out of 1st place

8/3: Furcal on shelf for month

8/30: Manny let go

9/28: Win a series for first time in month

Team Batting and Pitching/Fielding Stats by Month

	April	May	June	July	Aug	Sept/Oct
Wins	9	20	14	11	14	12
Losses	14	8	13	15	15	17
RS/G	5.1	4.7	4.4	3.5	4.1	3.1
RA/G	5.6	4.0	4.0	3.9	4.1	4.2
OBP	.343	.329	.341	.298	.334	.284
SLG	.424	.403	.390	.350	.380	.332
FIP	4.25	3.43	4.08	3.31	3.76	3.60
DER	.675	.697	.701	.689	.713	.689

Batting Stats

Player	BR	Runs	RBI	PA	Outs	H	2B	3B	HR	TB	K	BB	IBB	HBP	SH	SF	SB	CS	GDP	H-A	L^R	BA	OBP	SLG	GPA
Ethier A *	94	71	82	585	378	151	33	1	23	255	102	59	11	3	0	6	2	1	11	.021	.104	.292	.364	.493	.302
Kemp M	89	82	89	668	481	150	25	6	28	271	170	53	4	4	0	9	19	15	14	.021	.025	.249	.310	.450	.265
Loney J *	79	67	88	648	450	157	41	2	10	232	95	52	9	4	0	4	10	5	14	.001	.071	.267	.329	.395	.259
Blake C	70	56	64	571	395	126	28	1	17	207	138	48	3	8	3	3	0	4	8	.015	.077	.248	.320	.407	.259
Furcal R +	69	66	43	428	277	115	23	7	8	176	60	40	5	1	2	2	22	4	5	-.013	-.027	.300	.366	.460	.294
Carroll J	51	48	23	414	261	102	15	1	0	119	64	51	3	2	5	5	12	4	8	.011	.004	.291	.379	.339	.268
Martin R	43	45	26	387	258	82	13	0	5	110	61	48	7	4	1	3	6	2	7	-.008	.003	.248	.347	.332	.252
Ramirez M	41	32	40	232	140	61	15	0	8	100	38	32	4	1	0	3	1	1	4	-.009	-.012	.311	.405	.510	.326
DeWitt B *	35	29	30	292	193	69	15	4	1	95	49	30	4	3	2	1	2	2	4	.059	.062	.270	.352	.371	.264
Johnson R	22	24	15	215	154	53	11	2	2	74	50	5	0	4	2	2	2	2	3	.044	.081	.262	.291	.366	.234
Theriot R	20	27	8	228	158	48	5	0	1	56	28	22	0	2	5	1	4	3	5	.030	.050	.242	.323	.283	.227
Belliard R	17	24	19	185	133	35	10	1	2	53	35	18	1	1	2	2	2	2	4	-.057	-.048	.216	.295	.327	.226
Podsednik S	16	17	7	160	118	39	6	1	1	50	26	11	0	0	0	0	5	3	5	-.157	.073	.262	.313	.336	.236
Ellis A	13	6	16	128	83	30	5	0	0	35	18	14	1	1	4	1	0	0	5	.095	.012	.278	.363	.324	.257
Barajas R	13	9	13	72	47	19	3	0	5	37	15	5	3	2	0	1	0	0	2	-.051	-.074	.297	.361	.578	.323
Gibbons J *	12	11	17	80	57	21	2	0	5	38	14	4	0	0	0	1	0	1	2	.036	-.020	.280	.313	.507	.281
Paul X *	11	16	11	133	97	28	8	1	0	38	24	8	0	0	3	1	3	1	3	.105	-.006	.231	.277	.314	.214
Anderson G *	7	8	12	163	133	28	6	1	2	42	34	5	1	0	1	2	1	0	6	-.084	.014	.181	.204	.271	.168
Ausmus B	5	4	2	71	52	14	2	0	0	16	15	7	1	1	0	0	0	0	3	.019	-.032	.222	.310	.254	.213
Oeltjen T *	3	5	1	30	19	5	1	1	0	8	8	4	0	1	2	0	0	0	1	-.086	.258	.217	.357	.348	.260
Mitchell R	1	3	4	43	37	6	0	0	2	12	8	0	0	0	0	1	0	0	1	.034	.146	.143	.140	.286	.141
Padilla V	1	5	2	35	22	4	1	0	0	5	12	0	0	1	6	0	0	0	0	.198	.075	.154	.241	.192	.165
Billingsley	1	1	3	72	53	9	1	0	0	10	27	4	0	0	6	0	0	0	0	-.022	.002	.145	.197	.161	.136
Jansen K +	1	1	0	2	0	1	0	0	0	1	0	1	0	0	0	0	0	0	0	.250	--	1.000	1.000	1.000	.736

Only includes batters with at least one Base Run. Italicized stats have been adjusted for home park.

Batted Ball Batting Stats

	% of PA		% of Batted Balls					Out %		Runs Per Event				Total Runs vs. Avg.				
Player	K%	BB%	GB%	LD%	FB%	IF/F	HR/OF	GB	OF	NIP	GB	LD	OF	NIP	GB	LD	FB	Tot
Ethier An	17	11	39	22	40	.08	.15	69	83	.06	.08	.33	.24	4	6	3	13	25
Furcal Ra	14	10	47	20	33	.10	.09	71	77	.07	.07	.42	.20	3	6	7	1	18
Ramirez Ma	16	14	43	21	35	.04	.15	71	83	.10	.06	.44	.24	5	1	5	4	15
Kemp Ma	25	9	41	20	39	.02	.16	78	81	.00	.01	.39	.28	-7	-7	1	20	6
Carroll Ja	15	13	53	21	26	.08	.00	68	81	.09	.08	.41	.03	7	7	6	-14	5
Blake Ca	24	10	43	20	37	.12	.12	74	86	.02	.04	.46	.19	-3	-2	7	-2	1
DeWitt Bl	17	11	47	20	34	.16	.02	74	84	.07	.06	.48	.05	3	1	6	-10	-0
Ellis An	14	12	52	16	32	.14	.00	70	76	.10	.04	.43	.07	2	1	0	-4	-1
Loney Ja	15	9	43	25	32	.08	.06	80	88	.06	.01	.42	.09	1	-7	19	-15	-1
Martin Ru	16	13	51	21	28	.12	.07	76	87	.10	.03	.37	.10	7	-1	2	-9	-1
Podsednik Sc	16	7	47	18	34	.07	.03	73	81	.02	.04	.41	.08	-1	0	1	-4	-4
Theriot Ry	12	11	51	18	30	.04	.02	70	87	.10	.06	.28	.02	3	3	-2	-8	-5
Johnson Re	23	4	43	19	37	.13	.04	60	89	-.04	.13	.45	.04	-5	5	2	-8	-6
Belliard Ro	19	10	40	20	40	.12	.04	81	84	.05	.01	.33	.10	0	-2	-1	-4	-6
Paul Xa	18	6	41	23	36	.06	.00	72	85	.00	.07	.30	.03	-2	1	-0	-5	-6
Anderson Ga	21	3	42	20	38	.15	.05	85	82	-.05	-.05	.27	.12	-4	-5	-3	-4	-16
MLB Average	18	9	44	18	38	.09	.10	74	83	.04	.04	.38	.18	--	--	--	--	--

Only includes batters with at least one hundred Plate Appearances.

Pitching Stats

Player	PRC	IP	BFP	G	GS	K	BB	IBB	HBP	H	HR	DP	DER	SB	CS	PO	W	L	Sv	Op	Hld	H-A	R^L	RA	ERA	FIP
Kershaw C *	98	204.3	848	32	32	212	81	9	7	160	13	10	.708	8	8	8	13	10	0	0	0	.007	.013	3.22	2.91	3.11
Billingsley	75	191.7	817	31	31	171	69	7	10	176	8	19	.689	10	5	1	12	11	0	0	0	-.012	-.029	3.85	3.57	3.08
Kuroda H	73	196.3	810	31	31	159	48	13	5	180	15	15	.702	14	7	1	11	13	0	0	0	-.009	-.013	3.99	3.39	3.18
Kuo H *	62	60.0	229	56	0	73	18	0	1	29	1	3	.772	2	0	0	3	2	12	13	21	-.061	-.062	1.20	1.20	1.93
Jansen K	42	27.0	109	25	0	41	15	1	1	12	0	1	.769	5	0	0	1	0	4	4	4	.025	-.099	0.67	0.67	1.83
Lilly T *	34	76.7	305	12	12	77	15	1	3	61	13	5	.751	9	0	0	7	4	0	0	0	-.121	.149	3.52	3.52	4.06
Padilla V	33	95.0	389	16	16	84	24	4	7	79	14	8	.735	2	3	0	6	5	0	0	0	-.102	.048	4.36	4.07	4.20
Ely J	25	100.0	430	18	18	76	40	2	2	105	12	15	.680	4	3	1	4	10	0	0	0	.021	.031	5.67	5.49	4.44
Monasterios	25	88.3	399	32	13	52	29	3	4	99	15	5	.702	10	1	0	3	5	0	0	0	-.006	.046	4.89	4.38	5.38
Broxton J	23	62.3	271	64	0	73	28	5	2	64	4	5	.622	6	4	1	5	6	22	29	3	.002	.047	4.33	4.04	2.89
Troncoso R	16	54.0	234	52	0	34	18	5	3	55	7	10	.692	5	0	0	2	3	0	1	8	.033	-.040	4.67	4.33	4.51
Belisario R	15	55.3	233	59	0	38	19	4	3	52	6	9	.713	2	0	0	3	1	2	4	16	-.134	-.048	5.04	5.04	4.21
Weaver J	10	44.3	197	44	0	26	20	5	1	48	5	3	.703	6	2	1	5	1	0	1	5	-.048	-.059	6.09	6.09	4.57
Miller J	9	24.3	103	19	0	30	8	2	3	22	4	2	.690	4	2	0	0	0	0	0	1	-.070	-.038	4.44	4.44	3.98
Schlichting	9	22.7	98	14	0	14	10	2	0	20	0	1	.703	0	0	0	1	0	0	0	0	.008	.075	3.57	3.57	3.02
Dotel O	9	18.7	78	19	0	21	11	3	0	11	3	0	.814	4	0	0	1	1	2	2	3	-.012	-.091	3.38	3.38	4.32
Sherrill G *	7	36.3	180	65	0	25	24	4	1	46	4	2	.651	0	0	0	2	2	0	4	7	-.059	-.209	6.94	6.69	4.98
Ortiz R	6	30.0	135	16	2	21	16	2	0	33	5	5	.677	2	1	0	1	2	0	0	1	.004	-.188	6.60	6.30	5.36
Haeger C	4	30.0	151	9	6	30	26	0	1	36	4	3	.611	3	2	1	0	4	0	0	0	.080	-.048	9.60	8.40	5.63

Only includes pitchers with at least ten Innings Pitched. Italicized stats have been adjusted for home park.

Batted Ball Pitching Stats

Player	% of PA		% of Batted Balls					Out %		Runs Per Event				Total Runs vs. Avg.				
	K%	BB%	GB%	LD%	FB%	IF/F	HR/OF	GB	OF	NIP	GB	LD	OF	NIP	GB	LD	FB	Tot
Kershaw Cl	25	10	40	18	42	.12	.07	76	83	.02	.03	.41	.12	-4	-5	-5	-15	-28
Kuroda Hi	20	7	51	17	32	.17	.10	76	84	.00	.04	.42	.15	-9	0	-0	-15	-24
Kuo Ho	32	8	36	14	51	.19	.02	72	89	-.02	.05	.29	.02	-5	-0	-8	-11	-24
Billingsley Ch	21	10	50	18	32	.07	.05	79	76	.03	.02	.40	.16	-1	-6	-0	-8	-16
Jansen Ke	38	15	34	16	50	.16	.00	82	90	.02	-.01	.42	-.03	-0	-1	-3	-6	-10
Padilla Vi	22	8	40	18	42	.08	.13	75	92	.01	.04	.39	.14	-3	-0	-2	-3	-9
Lilly Te	25	6	29	16	55	.10	.13	81	85	-.03	-.01	.40	.22	-6	-5	-4	7	-8
Belisario Ro	16	9	61	17	22	.08	.18	83	68	.06	-.01	.36	.39	1	-5	-1	3	-2
Miller Ju	29	11	42	19	39	.08	.18	77	89	.01	.04	.44	.26	-1	-0	0	1	0
Broxton Jo	27	11	47	21	32	.06	.06	67	80	.02	.08	.47	.13	-1	2	4	-5	0
Troncoso Ra	15	9	53	14	33	.02	.12	72	80	.06	.04	.31	.22	1	1	-3	3	1
Weaver Je	13	11	36	20	44	.11	.09	78	86	.09	.03	.46	.14	2	-1	4	-1	4
Ortiz Ra	16	12	47	16	37	.23	.19	71	82	.09	.06	.49	.30	2	1	1	2	6
Ely Jo	18	10	46	20	34	.11	.13	74	83	.05	.04	.42	.23	1	-1	5	3	9
Monasterios Ca	13	9	42	20	38	.09	.14	75	86	.08	.04	.34	.21	3	-0	1	6	10
Sherrill Ge	14	14	40	20	40	.04	.09	73	70	.12	.05	.38	.26	4	0	2	5	11
Haeger Ch	20	18	41	21	38	.06	.12	74	72	.10	.05	.44	.29	4	1	2	4	12
MLB Average	18	9	44	18	38	.09	.10	74	83	.04	.04	.38	.18	--	--	--	--	--

Only includes pitchers who faced at least one hundred batters.

Fielding Stats

Name	INN	SBA/G	CS%	ERA	WP+PB/G	PO	A	TE	FE
Catchers									
Martin R	791.3	0.71	31%	4.03	0.444	681	59	9	1
Ellis A	308.7	0.99	24%	4.14	0.525	263	22	1	0
Barajas R	174.0	0.67	15%	3.52	0.207	165	6	0	0
Ausmus B	167.7	0.91	0%	4.24	0.215	168	5	1	0

Name	Inn	PO	A	TE	FE	FPct	DPS	DPT	ZRDif	OOZ	Dif
First Base											
Loney J	1338.0	1286	78	3	0	.997	13	2	.006	41	-3
Belliard R	53.3	46	6	0	1	.981	0	1	--	2	--
Mitchell R	20.0	22	1	0	1	.958	0	0	--	1	--
Gibbons J	15.3	16	2	0	0	1.000	1	0	--	0	--
Lindsey J	12.0	8	1	0	0	1.000	0	0	--	0	--
Blake C	1.3	1	0	0	0	1.000	0	0	--	--	--
Ethier A	1.0	0	0	0	0	0.000	0	0	--	--	--
Second Base											
DeWitt B	628.0	169	182	2	5	.980	14	25	-.026	18	2
Theriot R	447.0	103	125	0	1	.996	11	12	.044	12	1
Carroll J	219.0	48	78	0	0	1.000	3	8	.036	2	-3
Belliard R	127.7	38	37	0	1	.987	3	2	-.001	2	-1
Green N	20.0	4	9	0	0	1.000	1	1	--	1	--
Shortstop											
Furcal R	800.7	127	275	10	9	.955	24	20	.041	35	0
Carroll J	573.0	80	195	3	1	.986	16	12	.048	21	-4
Hu C	58.0	13	10	1	0	.958	2	1	--	1	--
Castro J	8.0	1	1	0	0	1.000	0	1	--	--	--
Green N	2.0	0	0	0	0	0.000	0	0	--	--	--
Third Base											
Blake C	1204.0	80	257	3	12	.957	17	0	.043	47	3
Belliard R	115.3	10	23	1	2	.917	3	0	.028	3	-1
Carroll J	73.3	5	14	0	2	.905	1	0	--	4	--
Mitchell R	49.0	4	13	1	1	.895	3	0	--	3	--

Name	Inn	PO	A	TE	FE	FPct	DPS	DPT	ZRDif	OOZ	Dif
Left Field											
Ramirez M	359.7	68	2	0	3	.959	0	0	-.047	12	-6
Podsednik S	272.3	61	0	0	1	.984	0	0	.057	10	-3
Johnson R	264.7	65	0	0	0	1.000	0	0	-.017	24	11
Anderson G	189.0	27	1	0	2	.933	0	0	.014	5	-4
Paul X	169.7	29	3	0	1	.970	1	0	-.071	9	1
Gibbons J	106.0	23	1	0	1	.960	0	0	-.102	3	-2
Carroll J	38.0	13	0	0	0	1.000	0	0	--	3	--
Oeltjen T	22.7	1	0	0	0	1.000	0	0	--	0	--
Mitchell R	19.7	2	0	0	0	1.000	0	0	--	0	--
Center Field											
Kemp M	1346.0	330	3	2	3	.985	2	0	-.005	43	-33
Podsednik S	34.0	9	0	0	1	.900	0	0	--	0	--
Johnson R	33.7	7	0	0	0	1.000	0	0	--	2	--
Oeltjen T	28.0	8	0	0	0	1.000	0	0	--	2	--
Right Field											
Ethier A	1151.0	223	6	0	1	.996	2	0	.018	50	-13
Johnson R	141.0	28	0	0	0	1.000	0	0	-.022	7	-1
Paul X	101.0	20	0	0	1	.952	0	0	-.015	5	-1
Anderson G	45.3	11	1	0	0	1.000	0	0	--	3	--
Gibbons J	3.0	2	0	0	0	1.000	0	0	--	1	--

Milwaukee Brewers

Stat Facts:

- Rickie Weeks led the NL in Outs
- Weeks led the majors in HBP
- Prince Fielder was tied for second in HBP
- Fielder had the highest BB% of any regular
- Fielder had the most innings of any 1B with 0 TE
- Alcides Escobar had the lowest GPA of any ML regular
- Escobar tied for the NL lead in SS TE
- Casey McGehee led the majors in 3B FE
- George Kottaras threw out 8% of base stealers
- Jim Edmonds's LD% was 28
- Carlos Villanueva's LD% was 27
- 85% of Trevor Hoffman's GB were outs

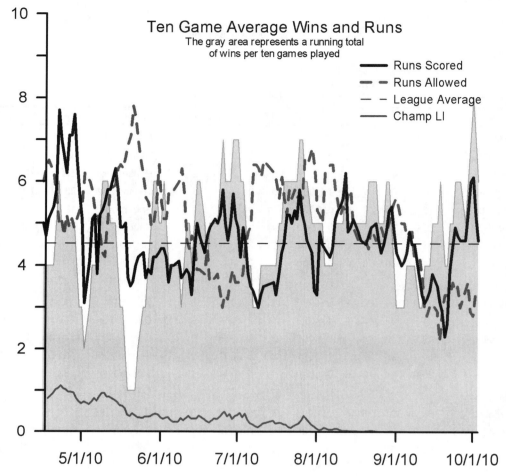

Ten Game Average Wins and Runs
The gray area represents a running total of wins per ten games played

Runs Scored
Runs Allowed
League Average
Champ LI

5/8: Gerut hits for cycle

5/20: Axford takes over as closer

6/24: Gallardo 12K Shutout

8/2: Braun & Fielder: 5 Hits each

9/7: Wolf 3H Shutout

6/3: Capuano's 1st game since 2007

Team Batting and Pitching/Fielding Stats by Month

	April	May	June	July	Aug	Sept/Oct
Wins	9	12	14	13	14	15
Losses	14	16	13	14	13	15
RS/G	5.5	4.7	4.5	4.0	5.3	4.1
RA/G	5.6	5.9	4.1	5.9	5.1	3.3
OBP	.355	.330	.323	.327	.348	.328
SLG	.454	.434	.423	.426	.422	.390
FIP	4.75	4.21	3.90	4.68	4.64	3.42
DER	.665	.637	.701	.681	.687	.721

Batting Stats

Player	BR	Runs	RBI	PA	Outs	H	2B	3B	HR	TB	K	BB	IBB	HBP	SH	SF	SB	CS	GDP	H-A	L^R	BA	OBP	SLG	GPA
Weeks R	111	112	83	754	485	175	32	4	29	302	184	76	0	25	0	2	11	4	5	.006	.085	.269	.366	.464	.286
Fielder P *	108	94	83	714	439	151	25	0	32	272	138	114	17	21	0	1	1	0	12	.042	.096	.261	.401	.471	.304
Braun R	104	101	103	685	451	188	45	1	25	310	105	56	1	6	0	3	14	3	17	-.046	-.033	.304	.365	.501	.296
Hart C	92	91	102	614	420	158	34	4	31	293	140	45	2	6	0	5	7	6	14	.057	.047	.283	.340	.525	.290
McGehee C	87	70	104	670	455	174	38	1	23	283	102	50	5	2	0	8	1	1	18	.047	.055	.285	.337	.464	.273
Escobar A	44	57	41	552	399	119	14	10	4	165	70	36	7	3	4	3	10	4	8	-.006	.007	.235	.288	.326	.216
Edmonds J *	36	38	20	240	157	62	21	0	8	107	53	21	0	1	0	1	2	0	2	-.006	.026	.286	.350	.493	.286
Gomez C	30	38	24	318	232	72	11	3	5	104	72	17	1	4	6	0	18	3	10	-.051	-.037	.247	.298	.357	.228
Kottaras G *	27	24	26	250	174	43	12	1	9	84	44	33	1	0	1	4	2	0	5	-.040	-.025	.203	.305	.396	.241
Lucroy J	24	24	26	297	218	70	9	0	4	91	44	18	1	1	0	1	4	2	9	.023	.037	.253	.300	.329	.221
Counsell C *	21	16	21	230	154	51	8	0	2	65	29	21	0	1	3	1	1	1	0	-.042	.033	.250	.322	.319	.229
Cain L	21	17	13	158	104	45	11	1	1	61	28	9	0	1	0	1	7	1	1	-.091	-.044	.306	.348	.415	.266
Inglett J *	19	15	8	160	107	36	8	5	1	57	34	15	0	2	0	1	1	0	1	-.057	.107	.254	.331	.401	.254
Zaun G +	13	11	14	117	81	27	7	0	2	40	12	11	0	3	0	1	0	0	6	-.011	-.095	.265	.350	.392	.261
Gallardo Y	11	7	10	72	47	16	4	0	4	32	17	5	0	2	2	0	0	0	0	.082	-.074	.254	.329	.508	.280
Narveson C *	5	3	7	59	34	16	1	0	0	17	15	2	0	1	7	0	0	0	1	-.141	.067	.327	.365	.347	.256
Gerut J *	5	7	8	74	59	14	4	1	2	26	17	3	0	0	0	0	0	1	1	.071	-.176	.197	.230	.366	.199
Wolf R *	5	11	5	83	60	19	4	0	0	23	24	1	0	0	4	1	1	0	2	.106	.150	.247	.253	.299	.192
Dickerson C	4	2	5	61	42	11	1	1	0	14	15	5	0	0	2	1	1	0	0	.100	.201	.208	.271	.264	.192
Parra M *	2	2	1	38	28	6	2	0	0	8	14	3	0	1	0	0	0	0	0	-.135	.275	.176	.263	.235	.181
Cruz L	1	2	1	17	14	4	0	1	0	6	2	0	0	0	0	0	0	0	1	.201	-.370	.235	.235	.353	.198
Gamel M *	1	1	1	17	13	3	1	0	0	4	8	1	0	1	0	0	0	0	1	-.069	-.172	.200	.294	.267	.203
Bush D	1	6	2	62	46	7	1	0	0	8	23	4	0	0	5	0	0	0	0	-.051	-.113	.132	.193	.151	.127

Only includes batters with at least one Base Run. Italicized stats have been adjusted for home park.

Batted Ball Batting Stats

Player	% of PA		% of Batted Balls					Out %		Runs Per Event				Total Runs vs. Avg.				
	K%	BB%	GB%	LD%	FB%	IF/F	HR/OF	GB	OF	NIP	GB	LD	OF	NIP	GB	LD	FB	Tot
Fielder Pr	19	19	42	18	40	.11	.21	80	79	.11	.01	.36	.34	24	-7	-3	25	39
Braun Ry	15	9	48	17	35	.11	.16	67	84	.06	.08	.46	.24	2	12	8	10	33
Weeks Ri	24	13	49	15	36	.10	.19	67	85	.05	.10	.45	.29	6	13	-3	13	29
Hart Co	23	8	38	18	44	.09	.18	70	85	.01	.07	.44	.29	-5	4	4	24	27
McGehee Ca	15	8	47	17	36	.09	.14	73	79	.04	.05	.37	.25	-1	2	-0	14	15
Edmonds Ji	22	9	30	28	42	.03	.12	80	78	.02	.02	.38	.24	-1	-2	6	7	10
Cain Lo	18	6	43	21	37	.12	.03	62	84	.01	.13	.44	.07	-1	5	3	-3	4
Zaun Gr	10	12	48	19	33	.07	.07	84	81	.13	-.05	.44	.16	2	-4	2	-0	0
Inglett Jo	21	11	34	20	45	.04	.02	73	80	.04	.07	.40	.12	0	0	1	-1	0
Kottaras Ge	18	13	43	12	45	.06	.13	73	89	.08	.05	.28	.17	4	0	-7	2	-1
Counsell Cr	13	10	42	19	39	.18	.04	76	80	.08	.04	.32	.09	2	-0	-1	-5	-5
Gomez Ca	23	7	48	16	36	.09	.08	75	86	-.01	.03	.49	.12	-5	3	-1	-6	-9
Lucroy Jo	15	6	44	19	38	.13	.05	75	85	.03	.03	.33	.09	-2	-2	-1	-7	-11
Escobar Al	13	7	44	21	34	.14	.03	76	88	.05	.04	.31	.05	-1	0	0	-19	-20
MLB Average	18	9	44	18	38	.09	.10	74	83	.04	.04	.38	.18	--	--	--	--	--

Only includes batters with at least one hundred Plate Appearances.

Pitching Stats

Player	PRC	IP	BFP	G	GS	K	BB	IBB	HBP	H	HR	DP	DER	SB	CS	PO	W	L	Sv	Op	Hld	H-A	R^L	RA	ERA	FIP
Wolf R *	70	215.7	936	34	34	142	87	6	9	213	29	24	.714	11	2	1	13	12	0	0	0	.019	.043	4.47	4.17	4.88
Gallardo Y	70	185.0	803	31	31	200	75	5	3	178	12	14	.661	11	6	1	14	7	0	0	0	-.010	-.056	4.33	3.84	3.06
Narveson *	49	167.7	724	37	28	137	59	3	5	172	21	14	.685	10	8	3	12	9	0	1	3	.021	-.064	5.15	4.99	4.28
Bush D	44	174.3	781	32	31	107	65	6	4	198	28	17	.685	22	6	0	8	13	0	0	1	.021	-.024	5.58	4.54	5.14
Axford J	35	58.0	238	50	0	76	27	3	1	42	1	5	.684	2	0	0	8	2	24	27	3	.046	-.070	2.64	2.48	2.09
Parra M *	34	122.0	560	42	16	129	63	3	3	135	18	11	.651	11	2	1	3	10	0	0	0	-.020	.068	5.61	5.02	4.55
Capuano C *	26	66.0	278	24	9	54	21	1	1	65	9	9	.710	1	0	0	4	4	0	0	1	-.036	-.029	3.95	3.95	4.29
Loe K	25	58.3	240	53	0	46	15	1	2	54	6	8	.713	2	0	0	3	5	0	2	22	.016	-.036	3.55	2.78	3.78
Villanueva C	19	52.7	231	50	0	67	22	1	4	48	7	4	.679	8	1	0	2	0	1	4	14	.086	-.038	4.61	4.61	3.80
Braddock Z *	19	33.7	151	46	0	41	19	0	2	29	1	1	.682	3	0	0	1	2	0	2	15	-.006	-.115	2.94	2.94	3.02
Coffey T	16	62.3	274	69	0	56	23	5	3	65	8	5	.685	3	1	0	2	4	0	2	13	-.083	-.054	5.78	4.76	4.08
Hoffman T	11	47.3	205	50	0	30	19	3	0	49	8	4	.723	1	0	0	2	7	10	15	2	.002	-.041	5.89	5.89	5.14
McClendon	11	21.0	84	17	0	21	7	0	0	15	2	2	.741	0	0	0	2	0	0	1	3	.004	-.008	3.00	3.00	3.43
Rogers M	8	10.0	36	4	2	11	3	0	1	2	0	0	.905	3	0	0	0	0	0	0	0	-.005	.127	1.80	1.80	2.20
Riske D	6	23.3	104	23	0	16	8	0	2	25	4	1	.697	2	0	0	0	0	0	0	0	-.094	.177	5.40	5.01	4.22
Davis D *	6	38.3	191	8	8	34	21	1	3	55	6	4	.591	3	2	1	1	4	0	0	0	-.032	-.079	8.45	7.51	5.26
Suppan J	4	31.0	148	15	2	18	12	1	1	50	4	7	.593	0	1	1	0	2	0	0	0	.107	-.033	8.42	7.84	4.87
Jeffress J	4	10.0	42	10	0	8	6	1	0	8	0	3	.714	0	0	0	1	0	0	0	0	-.193	-.041	3.60	2.70	3.10
Vargas C	4	19.7	94	17	0	18	10	0	0	28	3	3	.603	2	0	0	1	0	0	0	0	.092	.125	7.32	7.32	4.87
Hawkins L	3	16.0	74	18	0	18	6	1	2	21	2	2	.565	2	2	0	0	3	0	2	6	-.273	.068	8.44	8.44	3.88
Estrada M	1	11.3	58	7	1	13	6	0	1	14	3	0	.629	3	0	0	0	0	0	0	0	-.049	-.257	10.32	9.53	6.20

Only includes pitchers with at least ten Innings Pitched. Italicized stats have been adjusted for home park.

Batted Ball Pitching Stats

Player	% of PA		% of Batted Balls					Out %		Runs Per Event				Total Runs vs. Avg.				
	K%	BB%	GB%	LD%	FB%	IF/F	HR/OF	GB	OF	NIP	GB	LD	OF	NIP	GB	LD	FB	Tot
Axford Jo	32	12	48	19	33	.02	.02	73	80	.01	.05	.36	.10	-2	0	-3	-6	-11
Loe Ka	19	7	59	16	25	.09	.15	71	91	.01	.05	.30	.20	-2	2	-4	-3	-7
Gallardo Yo	25	10	43	24	33	.10	.08	70	84	.02	.07	.38	.14	-5	3	7	-12	-7
Braddock Za	27	14	30	22	49	.12	.03	73	81	.04	.06	.36	.10	1	-1	-1	-3	-3
Villanueva Ca	29	11	34	27	39	.08	.14	85	83	.02	-.02	.37	.21	-1	-4	2	1	-2
Capuano Ch	19	8	43	17	40	.15	.13	67	78	.02	.07	.29	.25	-2	2	-4	4	-0
Riske Da	15	10	31	21	49	.08	.06	67	91	.06	.10	.44	.05	0	1	2	-3	1
Coffey Ju	20	9	48	17	36	.16	.14	75	71	.03	.04	.38	.34	-0	-1	-1	7	5
Hoffman Tr	15	9	32	17	51	.13	.12	85	82	.06	-.03	.54	.20	1	-4	4	4	5
Narveson Ch	19	9	40	18	42	.10	.11	74	81	.03	.05	.39	.20	-2	1	1	8	8
Wolf Ra	15	10	39	19	42	.08	.11	75	82	.07	.03	.34	.19	7	-6	-2	11	10
Suppan Je	12	9	38	25	38	.07	.10	64	71	.07	.08	.44	.24	1	1	6	4	12
Davis Do	18	13	47	21	33	.05	.15	62	74	.08	.11	.38	.29	3	4	2	5	14
Parra Ma	23	12	47	18	34	.02	.15	72	80	.04	.06	.43	.27	2	3	2	10	16
Bush Da	14	9	39	18	42	.07	.12	71	85	.07	.06	.42	.19	3	4	9	13	28
MLB Average	*18*	*9*	*44*	*18*	*38*	*.09*	*.10*	*74*	*83*	*.04*	*.04*	*.38*	*.18*	*--*	*--*	*--*	*--*	*--*

Only includes pitchers who faced at least one hundred batters.

Fielding Stats

Name	INN	SBA/G	CS%	ERA	WP+PB/G	PO	A	TE	FE
Catchers									
Lucroy J	655.0	0.71	29%	4.40	0.563	614	44	2	3
Kottaras G	541.7	0.80	8%	4.45	0.382	434	20	3	1
Zaun G	242.3	0.85	17%	5.42	0.446	221	13	1	1

Name	Inn	PO	A	TE	FE	FPct	DPS	DPT	ZRDif	OOZ	Dif
First Base											
Fielder P	1411.0	1251	86	0	4	.997	5	0	-.105	48	2
Edmonds J	13.0	12	1	0	0	1.000	0	0	--	1	--
McGehee C	13.0	12	0	0	0	1.000	0	0	--	0	--
Kottaras G	2.0	1	0	0	0	1.000	0	0	--	--	--
Second Base											
Weeks R	1389.0	332	389	6	9	.980	24	65	.006	19	-15
Inglett J	35.0	6	10	0	1	.941	2	2	--	0	--
Counsell C	14.7	3	7	1	0	.909	0	2	--	1	--
Shortstop											
Escobar A	1151.0	174	358	13	7	.964	40	27	.010	55	5
Counsell C	253.7	30	79	1	1	.982	9	7	.006	9	-2
Cruz L	34.0	7	7	0	0	1.000	1	0	--	2	--
Third Base											
McGehee C	1326.0	81	268	4	13	.954	28	0	-.017	26	-23
Counsell C	99.0	7	20	2	1	.900	5	0	--	2	--
Gamel M	14.0	0	0	0	0	0.000	0	0	--	0	--

Name	Inn	PO	A	TE	FE	FPct	DPS	DPT	ZRDif	OOZ	Dif
Left Field											
Braun R	1326.0	279	6	2	1	.990	1	0	.030	53	-12
Inglett J	51.7	12	0	0	1	.923	0	0	--	5	--
Gerut J	30.7	9	0	0	0	1.000	0	0	--	1	--
Gomez C	12.7	2	0	0	0	1.000	0	0	--	0	--
Cain L	8.0	3	0	0	0	1.000	0	0	--	0	--
Gamel M	6.0	1	0	0	0	1.000	0	0	--	0	--
Escobar A	4.0	2	0	0	0	1.000	0	0	--	0	--
Center Field											
Gomez C	594.7	152	2	2	3	.969	0	0	.017	25	-9
Edmonds J	360.7	128	5	1	0	.993	3	0	.012	33	13
Cain L	306.3	96	2	0	2	.980	2	0	-.011	25	8
Dickerson C	95.7	25	0	0	0	1.000	0	0	--	3	--
Gerut J	70.7	20	3	0	0	1.000	1	0	--	3	--
Stern A	9.0	3	0	0	0	1.000	0	0	--	0	--
Escobar A	2.0	4	0	0	0	1.000	0	0	--	1	--
Right Field											
Hart C	1199.0	272	7	0	2	.993	1	0	.006	66	0
Inglett J	94.7	18	2	0	0	1.000	0	0	--	8	--
Edmonds J	77.7	18	1	0	0	1.000	0	0	--	4	--
Dickerson C	18.3	3	0	0	0	1.000	0	0	--	2	--
Gerut J	16.3	3	0	0	0	1.000	0	0	--	0	--
Gomez C	11.0	3	0	0	0	1.000	0	0	--	2	--
Escobar A	11.0	2	0	0	0	1.000	0	0	--	0	--
Cain L	9.0	2	1	0	0	1.000	0	0	--	1	--
Stern A	1.0	0	0	0	0	.000	0	0	--	--	--
Kottaras G	1.0	0	0	0	0	.000	0	0	--	--	--

Minnesota Twins

Stat Facts:
- Justin Morneau had the most Base Runs of any player with <400 PA
- Francisco Liriano's FIP was far lower than his ERA
- Brian Duensing's FIP was far higher than his ERA
- Delmon Young led the majors in LF assists
- Jim Thome walked in 18% of his PA
- 34% of Thome's FB were HR
- Joe Mauer's LD% was 24
- Mauer struck out at one-half the league-average rate
- Nick Blackburn struck out 10% of his BFP
- Carl Pavano walked 5% of his BFP
- Denard Span had 26 SB in 30 attempts
- Scott Baker allowed 3 SB in 9 attempts

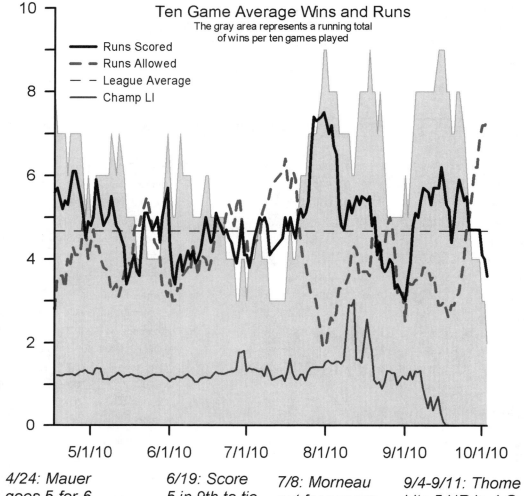

Ten Game Average Wins and Runs
The gray area represents a running total of wins per ten games played

— Runs Scored
- - - Runs Allowed
– – League Average
— Champ LI

4/24: Mauer goes 5-for-6

May: Blackburn is 5-0, 2.65 ERA; 5-7/6.11 rest of year

6/19: Score 5 in 9th to tie Phils and win 13-10 in 11

7/8: Morneau out for season

7/24-28: Score 53 runs in 5 games

9/4-9/11: Thome hits 5 HR in 4 G

Team Batting and Pitching/Fielding Stats by Month

	April	May	June	July	Aug	Sept/Oct
Wins	15	16	12	15	18	18
Losses	8	12	15	11	10	12
RS/G	5.1	4.8	4.3	5.7	4.3	4.9
RA/G	3.8	3.9	4.4	4.3	3.8	4.7
OBP	.357	.358	.325	.367	.328	.314
SLG	.421	.432	.403	.480	.417	.380
FIP	3.73	3.80	4.23	3.70	3.83	4.55
DER	.692	.690	.709	.683	.711	.695

Batting Stats

Player	BR	Runs	RBI	PA	Outs	H	2B	3B	HR	TB	K	BB	IBB	HBP	SH	SF	SB	CS	GDP	H-A	L^R	BA	OBP	SLG	GPA
Mauer J *	86	88	75	584	366	167	43	1	9	239	53	65	14	3	0	6	1	4	19	-.027	.087	.327	.402	.469	.300
Young D	86	77	112	613	420	170	46	1	21	281	81	28	5	6	0	9	5	4	16	-.006	.046	.298	.333	.493	.275
Cuddyer M	79	93	81	675	473	165	37	5	14	254	93	58	7	4	0	4	7	3	26	.018	.063	.271	.336	.417	.257
Span D *	76	85	58	705	479	166	24	10	3	219	74	60	0	4	10	2	26	4	12	.055	-.011	.264	.331	.348	.237
Morneau J *	71	53	56	348	200	102	25	1	18	183	62	50	7	0	0	2	0	0	6	-.077	.052	.345	.437	.618	.353
Kubel J *	69	68	92	582	406	129	23	3	21	221	116	56	5	3	0	5	0	1	16	-.001	.038	.249	.323	.427	.253
Thome J *	67	48	59	340	206	78	16	2	25	173	82	60	4	2	0	2	0	0	8	.044	.128	.283	.412	.627	.344
Hudson O +	62	80	37	559	381	133	24	5	6	185	87	50	0	4	5	3	10	3	14	.037	-.007	.268	.338	.372	.246
Valencia D	43	30	40	322	217	93	18	1	7	134	46	20	0	0	0	3	2	0	11	.104	.091	.311	.351	.448	.271
Hardy J	41	44	38	375	258	91	19	3	6	134	54	28	1	0	3	4	1	1	8	-.032	-.045	.268	.320	.394	.244
Punto N +	25	24	20	288	197	60	11	1	1	76	50	28	2	1	4	3	6	2	3	.023	-.001	.238	.313	.302	.218
Casilla A +	20	26	20	170	116	42	7	4	1	60	17	13	0	0	4	1	6	1	5	-.020	.042	.276	.331	.395	.249
Repko J	15	19	9	146	102	29	6	0	3	44	38	13	0	5	1	0	3	2	2	-.117	-.080	.228	.324	.346	.234
Tolbert M +	10	8	18	100	70	20	4	3	1	33	18	9	0	1	1	3	1	1	2	.166	-.188	.230	.293	.379	.228
Butera D	8	12	13	155	119	28	6	1	2	42	25	4	0	4	3	2	0	0	5	.009	-.046	.197	.237	.296	.182
Harris B	4	11	4	120	93	17	3	0	1	23	23	9	0	2	0	1	0	0	2	-.028	-.021	.157	.233	.213	.159
Ramos W	3	2	1	28	20	8	3	0	0	11	3	0	0	1	0	0	0	0	1	-.444	.294	.296	.321	.407	.248
Morales J +	3	4	7	44	31	7	2	0	0	9	14	6	0	0	0	2	0	0	2	.223	-.048	.194	.295	.250	.197
Plouffe T	2	7	6	44	35	6	1	0	2	13	14	0	0	0	2	1	0	0	0	-.002	-.004	.146	.143	.317	.144
Pavano C	1	0	0	8	3	3	0	0	0	3	2	0	0	0	2	0	0	0	0	-.350	.420	.500	.500	.500	.352
Hughes L	1	1	1	7	6	2	0	0	1	5	3	0	0	0	0	0	0	1	0	--	-.308	.286	.286	.714	.309

Only includes batters with at least one Base Run. Italicized stats have been adjusted for home park.

Batted Ball Batting Stats

Player	% of PA		% of Batted Balls					Out %		Runs Per Event				Total Runs vs. Avg.				
	K%	BB%	GB%	LD%	FB%	IF/F	HR/OF	GB	OF	NIP	GB	LD	OF	NIP	GB	LD	FB	Tot
Morneau Ju	18	14	33	22	45	.09	.19	65	72	.09	.10	.34	.37	7	4	3	23	37
Thome Ji	24	18	41	21	38	.04	.34	85	70	.08	-.04	.40	.58	9	-7	2	29	33
Mauer Jo	9	12	47	24	29	.03	.07	73	81	.14	.05	.39	.15	12	3	18	-2	31
Young De	13	6	45	15	40	.07	.11	73	77	.02	.04	.45	.23	-4	0	6	16	18
Cuddyer Mi	14	9	50	17	33	.10	.08	73	82	.07	.04	.42	.16	3	0	5	-4	5
Valencia Da	14	6	43	19	38	.11	.08	71	79	.03	.05	.40	.18	-2	2	4	2	5
Kubel Ja	20	10	38	19	43	.09	.13	79	81	.04	-.00	.33	.24	1	-9	-3	14	3
Casilla Al	10	8	50	13	37	.13	.02	76	80	.09	.03	.51	.11	1	2	-0	-3	-1
Hardy Ja	14	7	49	17	34	.10	.07	73	82	.04	.05	.40	.15	-1	2	1	-3	-1
Hudson Or	16	10	49	21	31	.10	.05	76	78	.06	.02	.39	.15	3	-4	6	-6	-2
Tolbert Ch	18	9	42	25	33	.04	.04	83	91	.04	-.02	.46	.04	-0	-2	3	-3	-2
Repko Ja	26	12	38	15	47	.15	.09	76	81	.04	.05	.33	.17	0	1	-3	-1	-3
Span De	10	9	54	18	28	.03	.02	76	85	.10	.04	.39	.06	6	2	3	-20	-8
Punto Ni	17	10	52	15	33	.08	.02	76	85	.06	.04	.41	.04	1	2	-2	-10	-9
Harris Br	19	9	58	15	27	.17	.05	80	100	.04	.01	.33	-.02	-0	-1	-2	-6	-10
Butera An	16	5	40	19	41	.06	.04	87	93	-.00	-.05	.41	.02	-2	-3	0	-6	-11
MLB Average	18	9	44	18	38	.09	.10	74	83	.04	.04	.38	.18	--	--	--	--	--

Only includes batters with at least one hundred Plate Appearances.

Pitching Stats

Player	PRC	IP	BFP	G	GS	K	BB	IBB	HBP	H	HR	DP	DER	SB	CS	PO	W	L	Sv	Op	Hld	H-A	R^L	RA	ERA	FIP
Liriano F *	90	191.7	806	31	31	201	58	0	10	184	9	19	.663	12	3	2	14	10	0	0	0	-.023	-.066	3.62	3.62	2.69
Pavano C	84	221.0	906	32	32	117	37	2	6	227	24	21	.715	31	8	2	17	11	0	0	0	.010	-.039	3.87	3.75	4.02
Duensing B *	65	130.7	535	53	13	78	35	5	3	122	11	16	.718	3	1	1	10	3	0	0	9	-.018	-.097	2.89	2.62	3.77
Baker S	61	170.3	725	29	29	148	43	0	6	186	23	14	.675	3	6	1	12	9	0	0	0	-.026	-.023	4.60	4.49	3.99
Slowey K	53	155.7	662	30	28	116	29	0	4	172	21	10	.687	6	4	0	13	6	0	0	0	-.040	.019	4.63	4.45	4.01
Blackburn N	39	161.0	692	28	26	68	40	1	4	194	25	23	.692	5	4	1	10	12	0	0	0	-.077	.001	5.65	5.42	5.09
Crain J	31	68.0	278	71	0	62	27	4	1	53	5	9	.732	7	1	1	1	1	1	4	21	.043	.010	3.57	3.04	3.30
Guerrier M	30	71.0	286	74	0	42	22	1	3	56	7	6	.764	1	2	1	5	7	1	7	23	.016	-.022	3.55	3.17	4.22
Rauch J	29	57.7	245	59	0	46	14	0	1	61	3	4	.674	0	1	0	3	1	21	25	2	.042	-.042	3.12	3.12	2.97
Capps M	17	27.0	106	27	0	21	8	1	0	24	1	5	.671	2	1	0	2	0	16	18	0	.093	-.011	2.33	2.00	2.82
Burnett A	14	47.7	211	41	0	37	23	3	2	52	6	8	.678	2	0	0	2	2	0	0	2	-.025	-.069	5.29	5.29	4.58
Mijares J *	14	32.7	139	47	0	28	9	1	1	34	4	3	.680	1	1	0	1	1	0	0	9	.089	.001	3.86	3.31	3.82
Mahay R *	14	34.0	141	41	0	25	8	0	0	33	5	4	.709	3	1	0	1	1	0	1	2	-.086	-.096	3.97	3.44	4.26
Manship J	7	29.0	124	13	1	21	6	0	0	34	3	2	.660	1	1	0	2	1	0	0	0	-.015	.065	6.21	5.28	3.63
Perkins G *	5	21.7	98	13	1	14	5	1	4	29	3	4	.611	2	1	1	1	1	0	0	0	-.025	-.129	6.65	5.82	4.73
Neshek P	3	9.0	43	11	0	9	8	0	1	7	1	0	.750	1	1	1	0	1	0	1	1	.038	-.029	5.00	5.00	5.56

Only includes pitchers with at least ten Innings Pitched. Italicized stats have been adjusted for home park.

Batted Ball Pitching Stats

Player	% of PA		% of Batted Balls					Out %		Runs Per Event				Total Runs vs. Avg.				
	K%	BB%	GB%	LD%	FB%	IF/F	HR/OF	GB	OF	NIP	GB	LD	OF	NIP	GB	LD	FB	Tot
Liriano Fr	25	8	54	19	27	.10	.07	75	75	.00	.04	.39	.20	-9	3	-2	-10	-18
Duensing Br	15	7	53	16	31	.09	.09	78	84	.04	.02	.38	.16	-2	-3	-3	-5	-13
Guerrier Ma	15	9	47	15	38	.10	.09	81	93	.06	.00	.42	.10	0	-4	-1	-6	-11
Crain Je	22	10	39	17	44	.06	.07	72	81	.03	.04	.30	.14	-1	-2	-5	-2	-10
Pavano Ca	13	5	51	18	31	.07	.11	78	85	.01	.03	.38	.19	-9	-3	4	-1	-9
Rauch Jo	19	6	38	18	44	.17	.04	65	84	-.00	.10	.40	.09	-3	3	1	-6	-5
Capps Ma	20	8	53	22	26	.11	.06	74	94	.01	.02	.43	.04	-1	-0	2	-4	-3
Mahay Ro	18	6	42	22	36	.11	.12	84	83	-.00	-.03	.44	.17	-2	-3	3	-1	-3
Mijares Jo	20	7	31	14	55	.13	.09	68	84	.01	.07	.58	.15	-1	1	1	1	1
Manship Je	17	5	44	19	37	.11	.10	62	96	-.01	.13	.46	.07	-2	4	2	-3	1
Slowey Ke	18	5	28	21	51	.10	.09	74	82	-.01	.04	.40	.17	-9	-3	9	8	5
Burnett Al	18	12	47	19	34	.08	.13	71	83	.07	.06	.40	.22	2	1	1	2	6
Baker Ti	20	7	36	21	43	.11	.11	75	81	.00	.04	.44	.21	-8	-3	12	10	11
Blackburn Ni	10	6	51	17	32	.07	.15	77	80	.07	.03	.42	.25	-0	-0	7	15	22
MLB Average	*18*	*9*	*44*	*18*	*38*	*.09*	*.10*	*74*	*83*	*.04*	*.04*	*.38*	*.18*	*--*	*--*	*--*	*--*	*--*

Only includes pitchers who faced at least one hundred batters.

Fielding Stats

Name	INN	SBA/G	CS%	ERA	WP+PB/G	PO	A	TE	FE
Catchers									
Mauer J	951.7	0.64	22%	3.82	0.293	696	34	3	0
Butera D	394.7	0.80	40%	4.10	0.388	301	26	3	1
Ramos W	63.0	0.57	0%	3.29	0.143	41	1	0	0
Morales J	43.3	1.04	20%	6.44	0.000	43	1	0	0

Name	Inn	PO	A	TE	FE	FPct	DPS	DPT	ZRDif	OOZ	Dif
First Base											
Cuddyer M	721.3	760	39	0	3	.996	4	2	-.021	18	-6
Morneau J	688.3	674	59	0	0	.999	12	0	.114	16	-7
Harris B	18.0	14	0	0	0	1.000	0	0	--	0	--
Morales J	17.0	19	2	0	0	1.000	0	0	--	0	--
Tolbert M	8.0	5	0	0	0	1.000	0	0	--	--	--
Second Base											
Hudson O	1067.0	255	374	4	4	.987	25	49	.005	36	10
Casilla A	159.0	34	51	0	1	.988	3	6	.048	3	-1
Tolbert M	131.7	21	41	0	1	.984	4	3	.016	2	-1
Punto N	77.0	15	29	2	1	.936	3	2	--	0	--
Plouffe T	9.0	2	4	0	0	1.000	0	1	--	1	--
Cuddyer M	8.0	3	3	0	0	1.000	0	0	--	0	--
Harris B	1.0	0	0	0	0	0.000	0	0	--	--	--
Shortstop											
Hardy J	858.3	150	289	8	3	.976	28	30	.053	34	-3
Punto N	258.0	48	80	1	4	.962	9	6	.042	14	3
Casilla A	189.3	30	69	3	1	.961	7	7	.031	11	3
Harris B	75.0	9	21	0	0	1.000	2	3	--	3	--
Plouffe T	68.0	13	20	0	1	.971	3	0	--	1	--
Tolbert M	4.0	2	2	0	0	1.000	0	1	--	0	--
Third Base											
Valencia D	709.3	46	171	4	2	.973	13	0	.055	22	-4
Punto N	344.7	29	93	0	0	1.000	6	1	.134	15	2
Harris B	183.7	11	40	0	0	1.000	3	0	.067	3	-4
Cuddyer M	107.0	3	21	0	1	.960	1	0	.020	1	-3
Tolbert M	73.0	8	21	0	1	.967	1	0	--	4	--
Casilla A	19.0	1	2	0	0	1.000	0	0	--	0	--
Hughes L	16.0	0	4	0	0	1.000	1	0	--	0	--

Name	Inn	PO	A	TE	FE	FPct	DPS	DPT	ZRDif	OOZ	Dif
Left Field											
Young D	1277.0	239	12	2	2	.984	2	0	-.006	48	-15
Kubel J	131.0	27	1	1	0	.966	1	0	.004	6	-0
Repko J	29.0	5	0	0	0	1.000	0	0	--	4	--
Revere B	15.0	5	0	0	0	1.000	0	0	--	0	--
Center Field											
Span D	1349.0	407	5	1	3	.990	3	0	.026	75	-1
Repko J	51.0	20	0	0	0	1.000	0	0	--	3	--
Revere B	38.0	9	0	0	1	.900	0	0	--	2	--
Cuddyer M	11.0	1	0	0	0	1.000	0	0	--	0	--
Casilla A	3.0	1	0	0	0	1.000	0	0	--	0	--
Right Field											
Kubel J	670.0	142	6	1	3	.974	2	0	-.038	32	-5
Cuddyer M	539.3	117	5	0	2	.984	0	0	-.018	15	-15
Repko J	226.0	62	5	0	0	1.000	1	0	.103	17	5
Revere B	16.3	4	0	0	0	1.000	0	0	--	0	--
Tolbert M	1.0	0	0	0	0	0.000	0	0	--	--	--

New York Mets

Stat Facts:
- David Wright tied for the major league lead in Sac Flies
- Wright tied for the most TE of any 3B
- Pedro Feliciano led the majors in appearances
- Jonathon Niese had the most IP of any pitcher with 0 SB
- Rod Barajas had the lowest SBA/G of any primary C
- Barajas threw out 12% of base stealers
- Barajas made 0 TE
- Johan Santana's H-A was exactly .000
- Mike Pelfrey had the lowest H-A of any pitcher with 200+ IP
- Ike Davis made 5 TE
- Jeff Francouer led the NL in RF assists
- Luis Castillo's GB% was 70

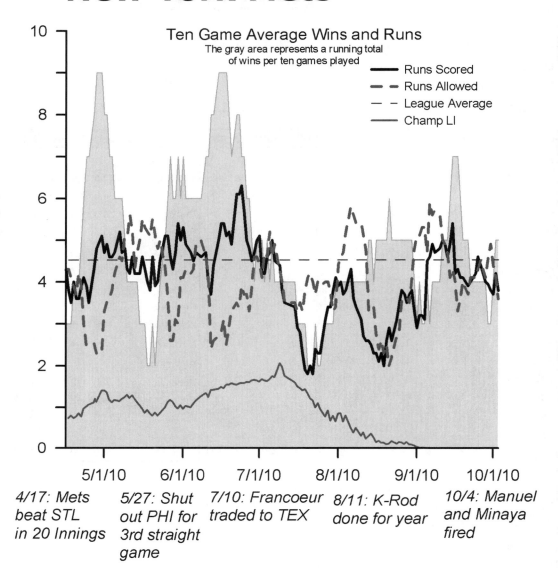

Ten Game Average Wins and Runs
The gray area represents a running total of wins per ten games played

— Runs Scored
-- Runs Allowed
- - League Average
— Champ LI

4/17: Mets beat STL in 20 Innings

5/27: Shut out PHI for 3rd straight game

7/10: Francoeur traded to TEX

8/11: K-Rod done for year

10/4: Manuel and Minaya fired

Team Batting and Pitching/Fielding Stats by Month

	April	May	June	July	Aug	Sept/Oct
Wins	14	12	18	9	12	14
Losses	9	17	8	17	16	16
RS/G	4.6	4.5	4.8	3.4	2.8	4.3
RA/G	3.2	5.0	3.6	3.8	4.1	4.2
OBP	.329	.324	.324	.293	.303	.316
SLG	.384	.401	.424	.353	.329	.402
FIP	3.73	4.80	3.78	3.65	3.77	4.19
DER	.703	.674	.698	.667	.699	.711

Batting Stats

Player	BR	Runs	RBI	PA	Outs	H	2B	3B	HR	TB	K	BB	IBB	HBP	SH	SF	SB	CS	GDP	H-A	L^R	BA	OBP	SLG	GPA
Wright D	102	87	103	670	444	166	36	3	29	295	161	69	9	2	0	12	19	11	12	.023	.082	.283	.354	.503	.297
Pagan A +	84	80	69	633	429	168	31	7	11	246	97	44	5	1	6	3	37	9	9	.041	-.035	.290	.340	.425	.270
Davis I *	80	73	71	601	400	138	33	1	19	230	138	72	6	1	0	5	3	2	13	.016	-.007	.264	.351	.440	.280
Reyes J +	76	83	54	603	422	159	29	10	11	241	63	31	4	2	4	3	30	10	8	.028	.008	.282	.321	.428	.262
Bay J	51	48	47	401	265	90	20	6	6	140	91	44	3	5	0	4	10	0	7	.047	.006	.259	.347	.402	.268
Francoeur J	44	43	54	447	315	95	16	2	11	148	76	29	8	7	0	10	8	2	7	-.027	.049	.237	.293	.369	.234
Beltran C +	33	21	27	255	169	56	11	3	7	94	39	30	5	1	0	4	3	1	4	-.035	.083	.255	.341	.427	.272
Barajas R	28	30	34	267	197	56	11	0	12	103	39	8	3	6	1	3	0	0	4	-.003	-.082	.225	.263	.414	.231
Thole J *	25	17	17	227	154	56	7	1	3	74	25	24	1	1	0	1	0	1	8	.001	.146	.277	.357	.366	.263
Castillo L +	25	28	17	299	198	58	4	2	0	66	25	39	1	0	11	2	8	3	6	-.004	-.007	.235	.337	.267	.228
Tejada R	20	28	15	255	174	46	12	0	1	61	38	22	3	8	6	3	2	2	2	.040	.066	.213	.305	.282	.217
Carter C *	20	15	24	180	127	44	9	0	4	65	17	12	1	0	0	1	1	2	4	.006	.146	.263	.317	.389	.250
Cora A *	12	14	20	187	139	35	6	3	0	47	16	10	1	4	2	2	4	1	4	.024	.047	.207	.265	.278	.197
Blanco H	11	10	8	144	103	28	5	0	2	39	26	11	2	0	0	3	1	0	1	.042	-.062	.215	.271	.300	.205
Duda L *	10	11	13	92	69	17	6	0	4	35	22	6	0	1	0	0	0	0	2	.060	.108	.202	.261	.417	.231
Feliciano J	8	12	3	119	86	25	4	1	0	31	12	6	1	3	1	1	0	0	3	-.024	.064	.231	.276	.287	.204
Tatis F	6	6	6	72	54	12	4	0	2	22	19	6	0	1	0	0	0	0	1	.163	.137	.185	.254	.338	.207
Hernandez L	5	4	6	47	34	11	1	0	2	18	7	2	0	1	0	0	1	0	1	-.113	.275	.250	.298	.409	.247
Evans N	5	5	5	37	26	11	3	0	1	17	10	1	0	0	0	0	0	0	1	-.083	.132	.306	.324	.472	.275
Dickey R	4	7	5	61	38	13	2	0	0	15	8	3	0	0	7	0	0	0	0	.088	-.169	.255	.296	.294	.216
Niese J *	4	3	4	66	43	10	2	0	0	12	27	0	0	0	5	0	0	0	0	.042	.115	.189	.295	.226	.198
Hessman M	4	6	6	65	50	7	2	1	1	14	23	8	1	2	0	0	0	0	2	.028	.138	.127	.262	.255	.189
Matthews Jr.	4	9	1	65	48	11	3	0	0	14	24	6	1	0	1	0	1	0	1	-.035	-.042	.190	.266	.241	.188
Jacobs M *	3	1	2	28	19	5	1	0	1	9	7	3	0	0	1	0	0	0	0	-.148	.236	.208	.296	.375	.237
Santana J *	3	2	1	67	51	11	3	0	0	17	22	0	0	0	5	0	0	0	0	-.023	-.009	.177	.177	.274	.155
Arias J	2	5	4	33	24	6	1	0	0	7	6	2	0	0	1	0	0	0	0	-.106	.213	.200	.250	.233	.178
Martinez F *	1	1	2	22	16	3	0	0	0	3	5	1	0	2	0	1	0	1	0	.041	--	.167	.273	.167	.171
Catalanotto	1	2	1	26	21	4	1	0	0	5	5	1	0	0	0	0	0	0	0	-.107	.142	.160	.192	.200	.142

Only includes batters with at least one Base Run. Italicized stats have been adjusted for home park.

Batted Ball Batting Stats

Player	% of PA		% of Batted Balls					Out %		Runs Per Event				Total Runs vs. Avg.				
	K%	BB%	GB%	LD%	FB%	IF/F	HR/OF	GB	OF	NIP	GB	LD	OF	NIP	GB	LD	FB	Tot
Wright Da	24	11	38	19	43	.05	.16	74	77	.03	.04	.42	.30	-1	-2	3	26	26
Davis Is	23	12	43	16	41	.08	.13	73	75	.05	.04	.41	.27	3	-1	-2	15	15
Pagan An	15	7	36	20	44	.11	.06	66	82	.03	.10	.35	.14	-2	12	2	-2	9
Bay Ja	23	12	36	19	45	.09	.06	67	77	.05	.07	.39	.17	2	1	1	2	6
Beltran Ca	15	12	42	19	39	.05	.10	71	90	.09	.05	.41	.13	3	1	2	-1	5
Reyes Jo	10	5	43	18	40	.14	.07	73	85	.04	.05	.43	.12	-3	6	7	-7	4
Thole Jo	11	11	44	23	33	.02	.05	73	87	.12	.04	.28	.08	3	0	1	-4	-0
Carter Wi	9	7	39	14	47	.10	.06	78	83	.09	.02	.46	.11	0	-1	1	-1	-1
Barajas Ro	15	5	21	14	66	.12	.09	77	83	.01	.02	.31	.15	-3	-3	-5	5	-7
Blanco He	18	8	34	15	51	.13	.04	69	87	.02	.08	.29	.06	-1	1	-3	-4	-7
Feliciano Je	10	6	62	14	24	.09	.00	85	76	.06	-.02	.38	.11	-0	-3	-1	-3	-8
Francoeur Je	17	8	41	14	46	.13	.08	71	88	.03	.07	.38	.12	-1	3	-6	-5	-9
Castillo Lu	8	13	70	14	15	.00	.00	78	85	.17	.02	.28	.04	7	-0	-6	-11	-10
Tejada Ru	15	12	41	23	36	.08	.02	85	82	.09	-.02	.30	.06	3	-4	-1	-8	-10
Cora Al	9	7	49	21	31	.09	.00	84	90	.10	-.02	.32	-.01	1	-3	0	-9	-11
MLB Average	18	9	44	18	38	.09	.10	74	83	.04	.04	.38	.18	--	--	--	--	--

Only includes batters with at least one hundred Plate Appearances.

Pitching Stats

Player	PRC	IP	BFP	G	GS	K	BB	IBB	HBP	H	HR	DP	DER	SB	CS	PO	W	L	Sv	Op	Hld	H-A	R^L	RA	ERA	FIP
Santana J *	93	199.0	817	29	29	144	55	2	2	179	16	18	.725	5	0	0	11	9	0	0	0	.000	.028	3.03	2.98	3.62
Dickey R	75	174.3	713	27	26	104	42	3	4	165	13	18	.715	9	3	1	11	9	0	0	1	-.033	.027	3.20	2.84	3.71
Pelfrey M	72	204.0	870	34	33	113	68	5	6	213	12	27	.689	12	5	2	15	9	1	1	0	-.056	-.026	3.88	3.66	3.87
Niese J *	52	173.7	770	30	30	148	62	3	9	192	20	18	.665	0	4	1	9	10	0	0	0	-.017	.019	5.03	4.20	4.16
Takahashi H	50	122.0	516	53	12	114	43	7	0	116	13	11	.694	3	4	0	10	6	8	8	3	-.034	-.067	3.76	3.61	3.60
Rodriguez F	39	57.3	236	53	0	67	21	4	2	45	3	1	.706	4	1	1	4	2	25	30	0	-.051	-.044	2.20	2.20	2.53
Feliciano P	27	62.7	280	92	0	56	30	6	6	66	1	13	.642	0	0	0	3	6	0	1	23	-.069	-.092	3.45	3.30	3.05
Acosta M	21	39.7	157	41	0	42	18	1	0	30	4	6	.720	2	3	0	3	2	1	2	2	.064	.084	2.95	2.95	3.67
Dessens E	21	47.0	194	53	0	16	16	6	3	41	4	7	.761	1	3	1	4	2	0	1	11	-.036	.014	2.68	2.30	4.45
Valdes R *	18	58.7	263	38	1	56	27	1	4	59	7	6	.675	1	1	0	3	3	1	3	1	.028	.087	5.06	4.91	4.37
Parnell B	16	35.0	149	41	0	33	8	2	0	41	1	6	.617	0	1	1	0	1	0	2	9	.028	-.058	3.34	2.83	2.20
Gee D	16	33.0	136	5	5	17	15	2	0	25	2	3	.765	0	0	0	2	2	0	0	0	.065	-.005	2.73	2.18	4.14
Mejia J	11	39.0	182	33	3	22	20	2	3	46	3	5	.664	3	1	0	0	4	0	1	2	-.026	.092	4.85	4.62	4.68
Misch P *	11	37.7	159	12	6	23	4	1	1	43	4	4	.685	1	0	0	0	4	0	0	0	-.080	.039	4.78	3.82	3.67
Nieve F	10	42.0	185	40	1	38	22	2	2	37	10	4	.761	1	0	0	2	4	0	2	6	-.161	-.066	6.00	6.00	6.05
Maine J	9	39.7	190	9	9	39	25	1	2	47	8	2	.655	5	0	0	1	3	0	0	0	-.031	.116	6.58	6.13	5.82
Perez O *	9	46.3	234	17	7	37	42	3	4	54	9	6	.669	1	0	0	0	5	0	0	0	-.072	-.028	7.19	6.80	6.91
Igarashi R	6	30.3	135	34	0	25	18	1	0	29	4	4	.705	1	0	0	1	1	0	0	2	-.179	-.058	7.12	7.12	4.94
Green S	3	9.3	48	11	0	12	8	3	4	7	1	0	.696	2	0	0	0	0	0	0	2	-.046	-.142	5.79	3.86	4.91

Only includes pitchers with at least ten Innings Pitched. Italicized stats have been adjusted for home park.

Batted Ball Pitching Stats

Player	% of PA		% of Batted Balls					Out %		Runs Per Event				Total Runs vs. Avg.				
	K%	BB%	GB%	LD%	FB%	IF/F	HR/OF	GB	OF	NIP	GB	LD	OF	NIP	GB	LD	FB	Tot
Santana Jo	18	7	35	20	45	.09	.07	77	88	.02	.02	.38	.09	-6	-8	3	-16	-28
Dickey R.	15	6	55	17	28	.10	.09	77	83	.03	.03	.34	.17	-4	-0	-5	-9	-18
Rodriguez Fr	28	10	42	18	39	.14	.06	74	83	.01	.05	.35	.13	-2	-0	-3	-5	-10
Acosta Ma	27	11	42	18	41	.18	.13	75	89	.02	.03	.37	.17	-0	-1	-2	-2	-6
Takahashi Hi	22	8	38	16	45	.08	.09	74	82	.01	.04	.42	.18	-4	-2	-2	3	-5
Gee Di	13	11	47	10	43	.12	.05	74	86	.10	.05	.28	.10	2	-0	-4	-2	-4
Dessens El	8	10	42	14	44	.10	.07	74	82	.14	.02	.32	.13	3	-2	-3	-1	-4
Parnell Ro	22	5	56	26	18	.21	.07	75	64	-.02	.03	.36	.26	-3	0	2	-3	-3
Misch Pa	14	3	52	15	33	.10	.11	70	79	-.03	.06	.35	.19	-3	2	-1	0	-2
Feliciano Pe	20	13	56	23	21	.10	.03	74	79	.07	.04	.38	.09	3	1	3	-8	-1
Pelfrey Mi	13	9	48	20	32	.07	.06	74	84	.07	.05	.40	.10	3	2	11	-16	-0
Igarashi Ry	19	13	38	18	44	.03	.10	76	91	.08	.02	.53	.13	2	-1	2	-0	3
Nieve Fe	21	13	37	18	45	.11	.21	82	87	.06	-.02	.38	.32	2	-4	-1	7	4
Mejia Je	12	12	61	13	26	.06	.09	74	81	.12	.05	.47	.19	3	2	0	-1	5
Valdes Ra	21	12	34	18	48	.13	.10	66	77	.05	.09	.37	.22	2	1	-1	5	7
Maine Jo	21	14	26	21	52	.08	.14	45	90	.07	.22	.36	.19	3	4	1	3	11
Niese Jo	19	9	48	21	32	.09	.13	72	81	.04	.05	.39	.23	-1	4	6	4	14
Perez Ol	16	20	35	19	46	.10	.15	71	84	.14	.05	.48	.23	9	-1	4	5	18
MLB Average	18	9	44	18	38	.09	.10	74	83	.04	.04	.38	.18	--	--	--	--	--

Only includes pitchers who faced at least one hundred batters.

Fielding Stats

Name	INN	SBA/G	CS%	ERA	WP+PB/G	PO	A	TE	FE
Catchers									
Barajas R	602.0	0.39	12%	3.98	0.299	516	21	0	3
Thole J	467.3	0.42	36%	3.56	0.385	341	29	3	0
Blanco H	361.0	0.55	50%	3.39	0.399	284	27	1	0
Nickeas M	22.7	1.19	0%	5.96	0.794	14	1	1	0

Name	Inn	PO	A	TE	FE	FPct	DPS	DPT	ZRDif	OOZ	Dif
First Base											
Davis I	1263.0	1239	105	5	3	.993	15	5	.029	58	17
Tatis F	72.3	67	5	0	0	1.000	1	0	--	1	--
Jacobs M	58.0	50	1	1	0	.981	1	0	--	0	--
Hessman M	53.0	50	1	0	0	1.000	0	0	--	1	--
Catalanotto F	5.3	0	0	0	0	.000	0	0	--	--	--
Cora A	1.3	1	0	0	0	1.000	0	0	--	--	--
Second Base											
Castillo L	576.7	122	176	0	2	.993	17	18	.002	13	-1
Tejada R	388.0	79	126	2	4	.972	8	21	-.067	10	0
Cora A	344.3	86	81	1	0	.994	8	19	-.117	3	-6
Hernandez L	75.0	17	32	0	0	1.000	2	5	--	1	--
Arias J	52.7	19	13	1	0	.970	1	2	--	3	--
Turner J	12.0	4	3	0	0	1.000	0	2	--	0	--
Tatis F	4.3	0	0	0	0	.000	0	0	--	--	--
Shortstop											
Reyes J	1171.0	179	362	5	10	.973	39	33	.002	43	-7
Tejada R	221.7	33	75	1	1	.982	7	6	-.021	12	2
Cora A	32.0	7	11	1	0	.947	1	3	--	2	--
Hernandez L	19.7	4	8	0	0	1.000	2	0	--	0	--
Arias J	8.3	1	0	0	1	.500	0	0	--	--	--
Third Base											
Wright D	1373.0	110	321	11	9	.956	30	2	-.023	52	1
Hessman M	57.0	4	13	0	0	1.000	3	0	--	2	--
Tatis F	18.0	2	1	0	0	1.000	1	0	--	0	--
Hernandez L	3.0	0	0	0	0	.000	0	0	--	--	--
Turner J	2.0	0	2	0	0	1.000	1	0	--	0	--

Name	Inn	PO	A	TE	FE	FPct	DPS	DPT	ZRDif	OOZ	Dif
Left Field											
Bay J	820.7	141	6	0	1	.993	1	0	-.041	34	-6
Pagan A	204.3	51	1	0	1	.981	0	0	-.045	13	3
Duda L	192.0	32	1	0	0	1.000	1	0	-.009	7	-2
Carter C	108.7	16	0	0	0	1.000	0	0	.004	2	-3
Feliciano J	46.0	7	0	0	0	1.000	0	0	--	1	--
Evans N	40.0	8	0	0	0	1.000	0	0	--	3	--
Martinez F	33.7	7	0	0	0	1.000	0	0	--	2	--
Matthews Jr.	4.0	0	0	0	0	0.000	0	0	--	--	--
Catalanotto F	2.7	0	0	0	0	0.000	0	0	--	--	--
Arias J	1.0	0	0	0	0	0.000	0	0	--	--	--
Center Field											
Pagan A	792.3	259	7	2	2	.985	3	0	-.010	62	17
Beltran C	517.7	146	4	0	0	1.000	1	0	-.009	19	-10
Feliciano J	72.7	17	0	0	0	1.000	0	0	--	6	--
Matthews Jr.	69.3	28	0	0	0	1.000	0	0	--	4	--
Evans N	1.0	1	0	0	0	1.000	0	0	--	--	--
Right Field											
Francoeur J	982.0	221	11	2	1	.987	5	0	-.044	58	4
Pagan A	259.7	58	2	0	0	1.000	0	0	.028	22	8
Feliciano J	99.7	28	1	0	0	1.000	0	0	--	7	--
Carter C	68.0	14	0	0	0	1.000	0	0	--	2	--
Matthews Jr.	22.7	3	1	0	0	1.000	0	0	--	1	--
Evans N	12.0	4	0	0	0	1.000	0	0	--	1	--
Martinez F	9.0	0	0	0	0	.000	0	0	--	--	--

New York Yankees

Stat Facts:
- C.C. Sabathia was second in the AL in PRC
- Sabathia allowed 15 SB in 18 attempts
- A.J. Burnett led the majors in HBP and SB
- Phil Hughes had 0 HBP
- Francisco Cervelli threw out 13% of base stealers
- Cervelli made the most FE of any C
- Jorge Posada threw out 12% of base stealers
- Mark Teixeira had the most innings of any AL 1B with 0 TE
- Robinson Cano made the most OOZ plays of any 2B
- Alex Rodriguez made the fewest FE of any regular 3B
- Derek Jeter made the fewest FE of any regular SS
- Jeter led the majors in Outs

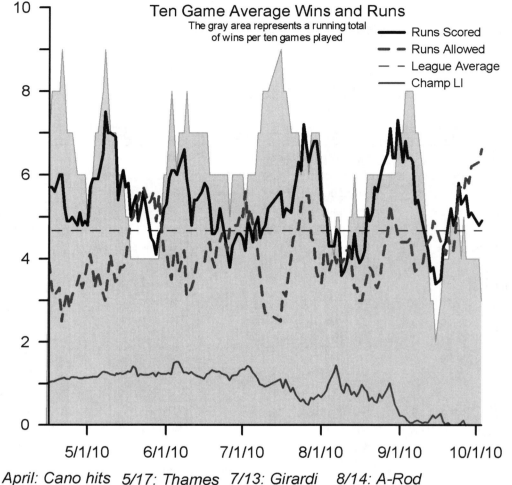

Ten Game Average Wins and Runs
The gray area represents a running total of wins per ten games played

- Runs Scored
- Runs Allowed
- League Average
- Champ LI

April: Cano hits .400/.436/.765

5/17: Thames walk-off HR off Papelbon

7/13: Girardi loses All Star game

7/31: Acquire Berkman

8/14: A-Rod goes 4-5, 3 HR

9/23: Vazquez hits 3 Rays in 10-3 loss

Team Batting and Pitching/Fielding Stats by Month

	April	May	June	July	Aug	Sept/Oct
Wins	15	16	16	19	16	13
Losses	7	13	10	7	13	17
RS/G	5.4	5.9	4.8	5.8	5.3	4.7
RA/G	3.6	4.6	4.3	3.8	4.1	5.0
OBP	.362	.371	.333	.347	.340	.346
SLG	.454	.451	.401	.463	.454	.398
FIP	4.01	4.44	4.15	3.97	4.81	4.78
DER	.729	.701	.707	.703	.714	.712

Batting Stats

Player	BR	Runs	RBI	PA	Outs	H	2B	3B	HR	TB	K	BB	IBB	HBP	SH	SF	SB	CS	GDP	H-A	L^R	BA	OBP	SLG	GPA
Cano R *	114	103	109	696	447	200	41	3	29	334	77	57	14	8	0	5	3	2	19	-.025	.033	.319	.381	.534	.292
Teixeira M +	105	113	108	712	463	154	36	0	33	289	122	93	6	13	0	5	0	1	15	.078	.048	.256	.365	.481	.273
Swisher N +	98	91	89	635	418	163	33	3	29	289	139	58	0	6	3	2	1	2	13	-.009	.010	.288	.359	.511	.278
Rodriguez A	90	74	125	595	391	141	29	2	30	264	98	59	1	3	0	11	4	3	7	.042	-.040	.270	.341	.506	.269
Jeter D	81	111	67	739	511	179	30	3	10	245	106	63	4	9	1	3	18	5	22	.049	.076	.270	.340	.370	.235
Gardner B *	81	97	47	569	360	132	20	7	5	181	101	79	1	5	5	3	47	9	6	.011	.016	.277	.383	.379	.256
Granderson C	74	76	67	528	356	115	17	7	24	218	116	53	3	2	4	3	12	2	3	.032	.064	.247	.324	.468	.252
Posada J +	64	49	57	451	295	95	23	1	18	174	99	59	3	7	0	2	3	1	6	.067	.003	.248	.357	.454	.263
Thames M	36	22	33	237	154	61	7	0	12	104	61	19	0	3	0	3	0	0	3	-.048	-.022	.288	.350	.491	.269
Cervelli F	33	27	38	317	202	72	11	3	0	89	42	33	1	6	8	4	1	1	7	-.007	.083	.271	.359	.335	.235
Berkman L +	12	9	9	123	85	27	7	0	1	37	15	17	3	0	0	0	0	0	6	.040	-.140	.255	.358	.349	.238
Kearns A	12	13	7	119	82	24	3	0	2	33	38	12	0	5	0	0	0	0	4	.062	.063	.235	.345	.324	.226
Johnson N *	11	12	8	98	63	12	4	0	2	22	23	24	0	2	0	0	0	1	2	.149	.016	.167	.388	.306	.241
Pena R +	9	18	18	167	124	35	1	1	0	38	27	6	0	1	4	2	7	1	4	.031	-.070	.227	.258	.247	.170
Miranda J *	8	7	10	71	51	14	2	1	3	27	12	7	0	0	0	0	0	0	1	.204	-.016	.219	.296	.422	.229
Winn R +	6	7	8	71	49	13	0	1	1	18	15	8	0	0	1	1	1	0	1	-.069	-.250	.213	.300	.295	.200
Nunez E	5	12	7	53	40	14	1	0	1	18	2	3	0	0	0	0	5	0	4	-.091	-.013	.280	.321	.360	.225
Curtis C *	4	7	8	64	48	11	3	0	1	17	15	4	0	1	0	0	0	0	0	.180	-.040	.186	.250	.288	.177
Russo K	3	5	4	54	40	9	2	0	0	11	9	3	0	1	1	0	1	0	0	-.097	-.002	.184	.245	.224	.160
Moeller C	2	2	0	15	11	3	3	0	0	6	4	1	0	0	0	0	0	0	0	-.176	.234	.214	.267	.429	.218
Golson G	1	3	2	23	19	6	2	0	0	8	3	0	0	0	0	0	0	2	0	.319	.276	.261	.261	.348	.196
Huffman C	1	1	2	21	16	3	0	0	0	3	5	2	0	1	0	0	0	0	1	-.216	-.174	.167	.286	.167	.163
Vazquez J	1	0	0	5	1	0	0	0	0	0	0	2	0	0	2	0	0	0	0	-.300	-.225	.000	.667	.000	.288

Only includes batters with at least one Base Run. Italicized stats have been adjusted for home park.

Batted Ball Batting Stats

Player	% of PA		% of Batted Balls					Out %		Runs Per Event				Total Runs vs. Avg.				
	K%	BB%	GB%	LD%	FB%	IF/F	HR/OF	GB	OF	NIP	GB	LD	OF	NIP	GB	LD	FB	Tot
Cano Ro	11	9	44	19	36	.09	.15	71	81	.10	.06	.39	.26	7	6	10	21	43
Teixeira Ma	17	15	36	19	45	.14	.17	80	82	.10	.00	.37	.28	15	-8	1	22	31
Swisher Ni	22	10	36	20	45	.08	.16	69	85	.03	.07	.44	.26	-0	2	7	20	29
Rodriguez Al	16	10	46	14	40	.09	.19	76	85	.06	.03	.44	.29	4	-2	-2	22	22
Gardner Br	18	15	53	19	28	.09	.05	69	82	.09	.08	.43	.12	12	11	3	-11	15
Posada Jo	22	15	43	19	38	.05	.16	80	82	.07	.01	.43	.28	7	-5	2	11	14
Granderson Cu	22	10	33	20	47	.07	.16	74	91	.03	.06	.39	.21	-0	-0	1	9	10
Thames Ma	26	9	32	16	52	.11	.17	70	76	.01	.06	.40	.30	-2	-0	-2	12	8
Berkman La	12	14	48	14	37	.18	.04	70	81	.13	.05	.30	.11	3	1	-2	-2	-1
Jeter De	14	10	66	16	18	.02	.09	74	86	.07	.04	.42	.15	5	7	2	-14	-1
Kearns Au	32	14	47	20	33	.05	.10	67	89	.03	.05	.46	.14	0	-0	0	-2	-1
Cervelli Fr	13	12	47	18	34	.05	.00	71	82	.11	.06	.36	.03	5	3	-0	-11	-3
Pena Ra	16	4	41	19	40	.10	.00	71	93	-.02	.04	.32	-.05	-3	1	-1	-10	-14
MLB Average	18	9	44	18	38	.09	.10	74	83	.04	.04	.38	.18	--	--	--	--	--

Only includes batters with at least one hundred Plate Appearances.

Pitching Stats

Player	PRC	IP	BFP	G	GS	K	BB	IBB	HBP	H	HR	DP	DER	SB	CS	PO	W	L	Sv	Op	Hld	H-A	R^L	RA	ERA	FIP
Sabathia C *	114	237.7	970	34	34	197	74	6	7	209	20	30	.710	15	3	2	21	7	0	0	0	-.029	.012	3.48	3.18	3.49
Hughes P	71	176.3	730	31	29	146	58	1	0	162	25	13	.725	10	5	0	18	8	0	0	0	.037	-.017	4.24	4.19	4.27
Pettitte A *	59	129.0	535	21	21	101	41	3	3	123	13	19	.698	2	1	2	11	3	0	0	0	.015	-.099	3.63	3.28	3.81
Burnett A	54	186.7	829	33	33	145	78	2	19	204	25	29	.671	37	5	4	10	15	0	0	0	-.008	-.002	5.69	5.26	4.83
Vazquez J	48	157.3	683	31	26	121	65	4	7	155	32	12	.729	4	4	0	10	10	0	0	1	.029	-.061	5.49	5.32	5.51
Rivera M	42	60.0	230	61	0	45	11	3	5	39	2	5	.772	8	0	1	3	3	33	38	0	-.039	-.038	2.10	1.80	2.70
Wood K	41	26.0	108	24	0	31	18	2	1	14	1	2	.772	6	0	0	2	0	0	1	10	-.009	-.119	0.69	0.69	3.19
Robertson D	29	61.3	274	64	0	71	33	6	3	59	5	5	.660	6	1	0	4	5	1	3	14	-.046	-.028	3.82	3.82	3.32
Chamberlain	28	71.7	305	73	0	77	22	2	1	71	6	6	.653	10	1	0	3	4	3	7	26	.046	-.013	4.65	4.40	2.93
Logan B *	23	40.0	169	51	0	38	20	3	1	34	3	5	.710	4	0	0	2	0	0	0	13	-.005	-.103	2.93	2.93	3.54
Mitre S	22	54.0	213	27	3	29	16	0	2	43	7	10	.767	9	0	0	0	3	1	1	1	.113	.031	3.83	3.33	4.72
Moseley D	20	65.3	278	16	9	33	27	0	2	66	13	11	.734	9	2	0	4	4	0	0	0	.038	-.034	4.96	4.96	6.02
Gaudin C	15	48.0	209	30	0	33	20	0	5	46	11	4	.743	0	0	0	1	2	0	1	0	-.053	-.043	5.06	4.50	6.28
Nova I	14	42.0	185	10	7	26	17	2	1	44	4	4	.708	3	0	0	1	2	0	1	0	-.017	-.016	4.71	4.50	4.25
Park C	9	35.3	157	27	0	29	12	0	1	40	7	3	.676	1	0	0	2	1	0	2	0	-.009	-.076	6.37	5.60	5.15
Marte D *	7	17.7	76	30	0	12	11	1	1	10	2	0	.820	3	0	0	0	0	0	2	9	.061	-.115	4.08	4.08	5.09
Albaladejo J	5	11.3	50	10	0	8	8	1	2	9	1	2	.742	2	1	0	0	0	0	0	0	.089	.065	3.97	3.97	5.23
Aceves A	4	12.0	53	10	0	2	4	1	1	10	1	0	.756	3	0	0	3	0	1	1	1	.144	-.027	3.75	3.00	4.86

Only includes pitchers with at least ten Innings Pitched. Italicized stats have been adjusted for home park.

Batted Ball Pitching Stats

Player	% of PA		% of Batted Balls					Out %		Runs Per Event				Total Runs vs. Avg.				
	K%	BB%	GB%	LD%	FB%	IF/F	HR/OF	GB	OF	NIP	GB	LD	OF	NIP	GB	LD	FB	Tot
Sabathia CC	20	8	51	15	34	.10	.09	73	82	.02	.04	.34	.17	-6	1	-14	-8	-26
Rivera Ma	20	7	51	15	33	.13	.04	90	81	.01	-.04	.40	.10	-2	-7	-2	-7	-19
Hughes Ph	20	8	36	16	47	.12	.11	72	90	.02	.05	.42	.14	-5	-1	-2	-2	-11
Pettitte An	19	8	44	18	38	.13	.10	74	79	.02	.03	.33	.18	-3	1	-4	-2	-8
Wood Ke	29	18	34	21	45	.08	.04	79	91	.06	.00	.24	.02	2	-2	-3	-4	-7
Mitre Se	14	8	51	17	32	.08	.14	80	88	.06	-.00	.27	.21	0	-3	-4	1	-6
Logan Bo	22	12	46	17	37	.03	.08	70	92	.05	.06	.33	.07	1	2	-3	-4	-4
Chamberlain Jo	25	8	46	17	37	.03	.08	66	84	-.01	.09	.41	.15	-4	4	-1	-2	-3
Nova Iv	14	10	51	18	30	.07	.10	73	89	.07	.05	.34	.15	1	1	-1	-2	-0
Robertson Da	26	14	40	25	36	.04	.09	71	76	.04	.06	.30	.20	2	-0	-1	-0	-0
Park Ch	18	8	45	15	40	.09	.14	71	86	.03	.07	.55	.21	-1	1	2	2	4
Gaudin Ch	16	12	40	13	48	.04	.16	69	91	.09	.07	.38	.20	3	1	-3	5	6
Moseley Du	12	10	49	16	35	.11	.20	80	87	.10	.00	.33	.29	3	-2	-2	7	6
Vazquez Ja	18	11	36	17	47	.10	.15	77	86	.06	.03	.39	.22	3	-4	0	17	17
Burnett Al	17	12	45	18	37	.10	.12	69	81	.07	.07	.36	.23	8	8	-2	10	25
MLB Average	18	9	44	18	38	.09	.10	74	83	.04	.04	.38	.18	--	--	--	--	--

Only includes pitchers who faced at least one hundred batters.

Fielding Stats

Name	INN	SBA/G	CS%	ERA	WP+PB/G	PO	A	TE	FE
Catchers									
Cervelli F	724.0	0.78	13%	4.04	0.460	579	45	8	4
Posada J	678.3	1.09	12%	4.13	0.531	562	22	6	2
Moeller C	40.0	1.13	0%	3.38	0.900	33	6	0	0

Name	Inn	PO	A	TE	FE	FPct	DPS	DPT	ZRDif	OOZ	Dif
First Base											
Teixeira M	1291.0	1227	80	0	3	.998	16	0	-.009	43	1
Berkman L	60.3	54	2	0	1	.982	0	0	--	1	--
Miranda J	50.3	53	5	0	0	1.000	0	1	--	2	--
Swisher N	21.0	19	2	0	0	1.000	0	0	--	1	--
Johnson N	17.0	18	0	0	0	1.000	0	0	--	0	--
Posada J	1.0	0	0	0	0	0.000	0	0	--	--	--
Huffman C	1.0	0	0	0	0	0.000	0	0	--	--	--
Second Base											
Cano R	1393.0	341	432	2	1	.996	48	64	.005	45	10
Pena R	44.0	12	17	0	1	.967	1	5	--	0	--
Russo K	4.0	2	1	0	0	1.000	0	0	--	0	--
Nunez E	1.0	0	0	0	0	0.000	0	0	--	--	--
Shortstop											
Jeter D	1303.0	182	365	4	2	.989	44	46	-.021	38	-18
Pena R	99.3	22	24	0	1	.979	4	3	--	4	--
Nunez E	39.3	7	16	0	0	1.000	3	1	--	3	--
Third Base											
Rodriguez A	1046.0	61	224	5	2	.976	23	0	.035	28	-11
Pena R	262.0	17	67	0	3	.966	3	2	.039	18	8
Nunez E	83.0	3	14	0	1	.944	1	0	--	2	--
Russo K	47.0	4	6	0	0	1.000	1	0	--	0	--
Cervelli F	3.0	1	0	0	0	1.000	0	0	--	--	--
Thames M	1.0	0	0	1	0	0.000	0	0	--	0	--

Name	Inn	PO	A	TE	FE	FPct	DPS	DPT	ZRDif	OOZ	Dif
Left Field											
Gardner B	906.0	200	9	1	0	.995	1	0	.028	49	5
Kearns A	144.0	36	1	0	0	1.000	1	0	.021	3	-4
Winn R	126.7	22	1	0	0	1.000	0	0	-.121	4	-2
Thames M	123.0	22	2	0	1	.960	1	0	-.081	7	1
Russo K	85.3	14	0	1	0	.933	0	0	--	7	--
Curtis C	26.0	5	0	0	0	1.000	0	0	--	0	--
Huffman C	24.0	9	0	0	0	1.000	0	0	--	4	--
Golson G	7.3	0	0	0	0	0.000	0	0	--	--	--
Center Field											
Granderson	1120.0	316	5	0	2	.994	2	0	-.001	55	-8
Gardner B	305.0	87	3	0	0	1.000	1	0	.026	29	12
Golson G	16.0	6	0	0	0	1.000	0	0	--	1	--
Swisher N	1.0	0	0	0	0	0.000	0	0	--	--	--
Right Field											
Swisher N	1102.0	265	10	1	3	.986	1	0	-.008	64	3
Kearns A	92.0	19	0	0	0	1.000	0	0	--	5	--
Curtis C	88.3	17	0	0	0	1.000	0	0	--	4	--
Golson G	52.0	19	1	0	0	1.000	1	0	--	9	--
Thames M	48.0	12	0	0	1	.923	0	0	--	1	--
Winn R	36.0	9	0	0	0	1.000	0	0	--	1	--
Huffman C	20.0	5	0	0	0	1.000	0	0	--	2	--
Pena R	4.0	1	0	0	0	1.000	0	0	--	0	--

Oakland Athletics

Stat Facts:
- Kevin Kouzmanoff's H-A was exactly .000
- Brad Ziegler led the AL in IBB, in just 61 IP
- Trevor Cahill had the highest DER of any AL starter
- Cahill's FIP was far higher than his ERA
- Dallas Braden allowed 1 SB
- Braden tied for second in the AL in Pickoffs
- Kurt Suzuki had the lowest CS% of AL regular C
- 20% of Suzuki's FB were infield pop-ups
- Cliff Pennington led the majors in TE
- Mark Ellis had the most innings of any 2B with 0 TE
- Ellis had the highest ZRDif of any regular 2B
- Daric Barton made the most OOZ plays of any 1B

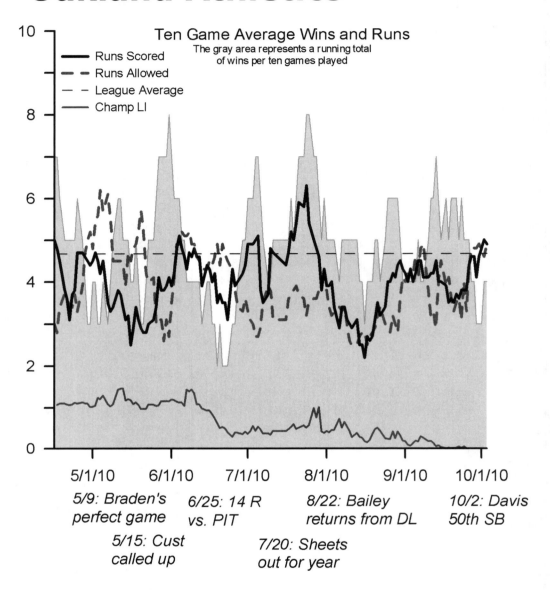

Ten Game Average Wins and Runs
The gray area represents a running total of wins per ten games played

- Runs Scored
- Runs Allowed
- League Average
- Champ LI

5/9: Braden's perfect game
5/15: Cust called up
6/25: 14 R vs. PIT
7/20: Sheets out for year
8/22: Bailey returns from DL
10/2: Davis 50th SB

Team Batting and Pitching/Fielding Stats by Month

	April	May	June	July	Aug	Sept/Oct
Wins	12	16	10	14	13	16
Losses	12	12	17	10	15	15
RS/G	4.4	3.5	4.3	4.6	3.5	4.3
RA/G	4.1	4.0	4.5	3.5	3.3	3.8
OBP	.322	.319	.332	.325	.309	.337
SLG	.373	.362	.412	.387	.342	.390
FIP	4.28	4.18	4.51	3.83	3.80	4.46
DER	.715	.724	.695	.721	.742	.717

Batting Stats

Player	BR	Runs	RBI	PA	Outs	H	2B	3B	HR	TB	K	BB	IBB	HBP	SH	SF	SB	CS	GDP	H-A	L^R	BA	OBP	SLG	GPA
Barton D *	94	79	57	686	415	152	33	5	10	225	102	110	2	3	12	5	7	3	8	.006	-.037	.273	.393	.405	.284
Davis R	66	66	52	561	397	149	28	3	5	198	78	26	0	4	1	5	50	11	10	-.015	.038	.284	.320	.377	.243
Pennington C	65	64	46	576	393	127	26	8	6	187	96	50	0	3	12	3	29	5	7	-.005	-.017	.250	.319	.368	.241
Cust J *	63	50	52	425	262	95	19	0	13	153	127	68	0	5	0	3	2	2	6	.012	.077	.272	.395	.438	.294
Ellis M	58	45	49	492	322	127	24	0	5	166	56	40	4	8	3	5	7	6	7	-.057	.041	.291	.358	.381	.262
Kouzmanoff K	57	59	71	586	436	136	32	1	16	218	96	24	2	6	0	5	2	1	20	.000	.023	.247	.283	.396	.231
Suzuki K	50	55	71	544	399	120	18	2	13	181	49	33	3	12	0	4	3	2	22	.046	-.037	.242	.303	.366	.233
Crisp C +	48	51	38	328	218	81	14	4	8	127	49	30	0	0	3	5	32	3	6	.072	.068	.279	.342	.438	.269
Sweeney R *	35	41	36	331	229	89	20	2	1	116	41	24	2	0	1	3	1	1	14	.054	.040	.294	.342	.383	.255
Rosales A	33	31	31	279	189	69	8	2	7	102	65	19	0	1	2	2	2	2	1	-.053	.037	.271	.321	.400	.250
Gross G *	19	27	25	244	175	53	11	1	1	69	39	17	2	0	2	2	5	1	5	.037	.012	.239	.290	.311	.213
Patterson E	12	13	9	111	83	21	5	2	4	42	31	7	0	0	1	0	6	0	1	-.004	.171	.204	.255	.408	.221
Powell L +	11	13	11	129	90	24	4	0	2	34	29	15	0	0	1	1	1	0	2	-.009	.011	.214	.305	.304	.218
Chavez E *	10	10	10	123	88	26	8	0	1	37	31	8	0	0	0	4	0	0	3	-.060	.117	.234	.276	.333	.212
Jackson C	7	6	5	69	46	13	2	0	1	18	9	11	1	1	0	0	2	0	2	-.062	-.089	.228	.362	.316	.247
Fox J	7	11	12	106	83	21	5	0	2	32	26	5	0	2	0	0	1	0	6	-.022	.070	.214	.264	.327	.205
Tolleson S	7	5	4	53	35	14	1	0	1	20	9	4	0	0	0	0	0	0	0	.197	.180	.286	.340	.408	.260
Carson M	7	7	9	83	65	14	2	0	4	28	23	2	0	0	0	2	4	0	0	-.075	.020	.177	.193	.354	.179
Larish J *	6	5	8	65	48	10	3	0	2	19	20	7	0	1	0	0	1	0	1	-.105	.173	.175	.277	.333	.213
Carter C	6	8	7	78	60	13	1	0	3	23	21	7	0	0	0	1	1	0	3	.182	-.003	.186	.256	.329	.202
Hermida J *	5	5	2	68	53	16	4	0	0	23	13	4	0	0	0	0	0	0	5	.079	.026	.250	.294	.359	.227
Buck T *	4	6	2	48	35	7	2	0	1	12	14	4	0	1	1	0	1	0	0	.087	.027	.167	.255	.286	.190
Watson M *	3	2	4	33	24	6	2	0	1	11	5	3	0	0	0	0	0	0	0	.147	--	.200	.273	.367	.219
Donaldson J	2	1	4	34	27	5	1	0	1	9	12	2	0	0	0	0	0	0	0	-.100	.256	.156	.206	.281	.167
Sogard E *	1	0	0	9	5	3	0	0	0	3	1	2	0	0	0	0	0	1	0	.087	-.500	.429	.556	.429	.365
Iwamura A *	1	3	4	36	27	4	1	0	0	5	10	5	0	0	0	0	0	0	0	-.041	.006	.129	.250	.161	.156

Only includes batters with at least one Base Run. Italicized stats have been adjusted for home park.

Batted Ball Batting Stats

	% of PA		% of Batted Balls					Out %		Runs Per Event				Total Runs vs. Avg.				
Player	K%	BB%	GB%	LD%	FB%	IF/F	HR/OF	GB	OF	NIP	GB	LD	OF	NIP	GB	LD	FB	Tot
Barton Da	15	16	39	21	39	.10	.06	70	85	.13	.07	.37	.11	20	3	6	-9	20
Cust Ja	30	17	40	22	39	.05	.16	74	74	.05	.04	.43	.31	6	-2	2	9	17
Ellis Ma	11	10	42	21	37	.13	.03	69	83	.10	.08	.39	.07	5	7	8	-12	8
Crisp Co	15	9	47	17	37	.07	.10	67	83	.06	.08	.31	.20	1	5	-3	3	6
Rosales Ad	23	7	38	28	34	.11	.09	67	85	-.01	.09	.36	.15	-4	2	6	-3	1
Sweeney Ry	12	7	52	20	28	.09	.01	74	79	.06	.03	.45	.08	-0	-1	8	-8	-1
Patterson Er	28	6	36	16	49	.15	.14	84	80	-.03	-.01	.47	.25	-2	-2	-1	2	-3
Chavez Er	25	7	49	19	32	.04	.04	76	80	-.02	.03	.45	.12	-2	-1	1	-2	-4
Davis Ra	14	5	48	16	37	.13	.03	63	83	.01	.12	.34	.07	-5	19	-4	-15	-5
Powell La	22	12	37	17	46	.08	.06	81	79	.04	.01	.28	.13	0	-2	-3	-1	-5
Fox Ja	25	7	48	12	40	.14	.08	71	87	-.02	.03	.46	.12	-2	-1	-2	-2	-6
Pennington Cl	17	9	36	21	43	.11	.04	76	84	.05	.04	.36	.09	1	1	3	-11	-6
Gross Ga	16	7	46	20	34	.06	.02	76	81	.03	.03	.31	.08	-1	-1	-1	-6	-9
Suzuki Ku	9	8	42	17	41	.20	.09	77	90	.11	.01	.36	.11	4	-6	-0	-10	-12
Kouzmanoff Ke	16	5	43	17	40	.08	.09	78	84	-.00	.01	.39	.16	-8	-7	1	1	-13
MLB Average	18	9	44	18	38	.09	.10	74	83	.04	.04	.38	.18	--	--	--	--	--

Only includes batters with at least one hundred Plate Appearances.

Pitching Stats

Player	PRC	IP	BFP	G	GS	K	BB	IBB	HBP	H	HR	DP	DER	SB	CS	PO	W	L	Sv	Op	Hld	H-A	R^L	RA	ERA	FIP
Gonzalez G *	95	200.7	851	33	33	171	92	1	4	171	15	18	.714	12	3	2	15	9	0	0	0	-.035	-.018	3.36	3.23	3.80
Cahill T	86	196.7	783	30	30	118	63	1	6	155	19	30	.752	15	5	5	18	8	0	0	0	-.028	-.012	3.34	2.97	4.20
Braden D *	73	192.7	781	30	30	113	43	0	5	180	17	19	.723	1	2	8	11	14	0	0	0	-.014	.022	3.88	3.50	3.83
Anderson B *	51	112.3	470	19	19	75	22	2	7	112	6	14	.692	8	5	4	7	6	0	0	0	-.029	.017	3.28	2.80	3.19
Bailey A	43	49.0	189	47	0	42	13	1	0	34	3	4	.748	3	1	0	1	3	25	28	0	-.011	-.019	1.47	1.47	2.93
Breslow C *	38	74.7	304	75	0	71	29	4	0	53	9	5	.759	4	1	1	4	4	5	7	16	-.014	-.021	3.13	3.01	3.78
Sheets B	37	119.3	511	20	20	84	43	2	0	123	18	7	.702	13	9	2	4	9	0	0	0	-.086	.005	4.90	4.53	4.70
Mazzaro V	36	122.3	537	24	18	79	50	0	4	127	19	13	.704	9	1	2	6	8	0	0	0	-.058	-.022	5.15	4.27	5.16
Ziegler B	26	60.7	257	64	0	41	28	9	3	54	4	10	.718	2	1	0	3	7	0	4	18	-.108	-.157	3.56	3.26	3.71
Blevins J *	22	48.7	220	63	0	46	18	1	1	54	7	0	.669	1	1	1	2	1	1	2	11	-.012	-.098	3.70	3.70	4.20
Wuertz M	14	39.7	171	48	0	40	21	5	0	35	6	4	.721	3	0	0	2	3	6	6	11	-.091	-.083	4.76	4.31	4.27
Duchscherer	12	28.0	116	5	5	18	12	0	1	26	3	7	.707	1	0	1	2	1	0	0	0	.028	.047	3.54	2.89	4.61
Ross T	11	39.3	169	26	2	32	20	0	0	39	4	6	.690	2	0	0	1	4	1	2	2	-.119	.051	5.49	5.49	4.33
Cramer B *	11	23.7	93	4	4	13	6	0	0	20	5	3	.783	0	1	1	2	1	0	0	0	.089	.050	3.04	3.04	5.52
Rodriguez H	9	27.7	121	29	0	33	13	0	1	25	2	1	.653	8	0	0	1	0	0	1	3	-.088	-.065	5.20	4.55	3.18
Bonser B	7	23.0	99	13	0	17	6	0	0	27	2	2	.662	3	1	0	1	0	0	0	3	.069	-.019	5.09	5.09	3.55
Kilby B *	6	8.3	32	5	0	8	0	0	0	7	2	0	.773	0	0	0	0	0	0	0	0	-.171	-.085	2.16	2.16	4.31
Wolf R	5	12.7	56	11	0	9	6	1	1	12	1	2	.692	0	0	0	0	0	0	0	0	.186	-.114	4.26	4.26	4.14
Bowers C *	4	14.0	62	14	0	18	6	1	1	12	4	0	.697	0	1	0	0	1	0	0	0	-.081	.196	5.79	4.50	5.54
Ramirez E	3	11.0	54	7	0	10	10	1	0	9	1	0	.697	0	0	0	1	0	0	0	0	-.026	-.073	5.73	4.91	4.93
Gaudin C	3	17.3	86	12	0	20	5	0	3	27	5	1	.566	3	0	0	0	2	0	0	1	-.129	.030	9.35	8.83	5.94

Only includes pitchers with at least ten Innings Pitched. Italicized stats have been adjusted for home park.

Batted Ball Pitching Stats

Player	% of PA		% of Batted Balls					Out %		Runs Per Event				Total Runs vs. Avg.				
	K%	BB%	GB%	LD%	FB%	IF/F	HR/OF	GB	OF	NIP	GB	LD	OF	NIP	GB	LD	FB	Tot
Cahill Tr	15	9	56	15	29	.05	.11	83	87	.06	-.01	.37	.15	1	-13	-8	-10	-30
Braden Da	14	6	41	18	41	.14	.08	80	82	.02	.00	.37	.14	-6	-8	1	-7	-20
Gonzalez Gi	20	11	49	15	35	.09	.08	75	83	.05	.04	.33	.15	4	-1	-13	-10	-20
Bailey An	22	7	39	16	45	.08	.06	77	80	-.00	.02	.24	.12	-3	-2	-5	-2	-12
Anderson Br	16	6	54	17	28	.08	.06	74	85	.02	.05	.38	.11	-4	3	0	-10	-11
Breslow Cr	23	10	30	15	56	.10	.09	78	86	.02	.01	.36	.15	-2	-4	-6	0	-11
Ziegler Br	16	12	54	19	27	.08	.09	80	78	.08	-.00	.34	.20	3	-3	-1	-2	-3
Duchscherer Ju	16	11	46	18	36	.03	.10	74	96	.08	.01	.41	.08	1	-1	1	-2	-1
Rodriguez He	27	12	39	17	44	.16	.08	68	79	.02	.10	.39	.14	-0	2	-1	-2	-1
Wuertz Mi	23	12	41	18	40	.17	.14	77	87	.04	.03	.46	.20	1	-1	0	-1	-1
Ross Ty	19	12	53	18	29	.03	.13	82	71	.06	-.01	.40	.28	1	-3	-0	2	0
Blevins Je	21	9	38	23	39	.10	.13	68	89	.02	.09	.37	.17	-1	2	2	-0	3
Mazzaro Vi	15	10	43	21	37	.08	.14	79	82	.07	.01	.32	.23	4	-4	0	8	8
Sheets Be	16	8	44	16	39	.11	.13	77	78	.04	.04	.45	.26	-0	-0	3	11	13
MLB Average	18	9	44	18	38	.09	.10	74	83	.04	.04	.38	.18	--	--	--	--	--

Only includes pitchers who faced at least one hundred batters.

Fielding Stats

Name	INN	SBA/G	CS%	ERA	WP+PB/G	PO	A	TE	FE
Catchers									
Suzuki K	1058.3	0.65	13%	3.29	0.349	825	35	7	1
Powell L	267.0	0.71	19%	4.45	0.169	198	8	5	0
Fox J	59.0	0.31	50%	4.58	0.305	37	2	0	0
Donaldson J	47.3	1.14	33%	3.99	0.380	44	3	1	0

Name	Inn	PO	A	TE	FE	FPct	DPS	DPT	ZRDif	OOZ	Dif
First Base											
Barton D	1333.0	1404	78	3	6	.993	9	0	.067	69	25
Larish J	45.0	41	5	0	0	1.000	1	0	--	3	--
Rosales A	38.0	34	1	0	0	1.000	0	0	--	2	--
Donaldson J	6.0	2	0	0	1	.667	0	0	--	--	--
Chavez E	5.0	7	0	0	0	1.000	0	0	--	--	--
Powell L	4.0	4	0	0	0	1.000	0	0	--	--	--
Second Base											
Ellis M	986.3	218	328	0	3	.995	30	44	.037	18	-6
Rosales A	393.3	72	126	0	0	1.000	14	16	.054	5	-5
Tolleson S	21.0	5	4	0	1	.900	0	2	--	0	--
Patterson E	16.0	6	4	0	0	1.000	0	0	--	0	--
Sogard E	15.0	4	5	0	0	1.000	2	2	--	0	--
Shortstop											
Pennington C	1304.0	218	496	14	11	.966	44	51	.016	53	-3
Rosales A	82.0	7	26	0	2	.943	1	2	--	2	--
Tolleson S	45.0	9	9	0	0	1.000	1	3	--	0	--
Third Base											
Kouzmanoff K	1231.0	90	278	8	4	.968	27	0	.052	49	4
Iwamura A	81.0	11	11	1	0	.957	0	0	--	2	--
Tolleson S	44.0	3	7	0	0	1.000	0	0	--	2	--
Rosales A	44.0	4	12	0	0	1.000	1	0	--	3	--
Larish J	28.0	3	5	1	1	.800	0	0	--	2	--
Fox J	3.0	0	1	0	0	1.000	0	0	--	0	--

Name	Inn	PO	A	TE	FE	FPct	DPS	DPT	ZRDif	OOZ	Dif
Left Field											
Davis R	320.3	57	1	1	0	.983	0	0	.063	15	-1
Gross G	229.7	42	1	0	1	.977	0	0	-.057	7	-4
Patterson E	191.0	45	1	1	0	.979	0	0	-.010	14	5
Carter C	156.0	25	0	0	2	.926	0	0	-.093	4	-4
Jackson C	133.3	24	1	0	0	1.000	0	0	.079	5	-2
Cust J	90.0	19	2	0	1	.955	0	0	--	7	--
Buck T	87.3	12	0	0	0	1.000	0	0	--	2	--
Watson M	74.0	6	0	0	0	1.000	0	0	--	1	--
Fox J	56.3	12	1	0	0	1.000	0	0	--	2	--
Larish J	44.0	3	0	0	0	1.000	0	0	--	2	--
Rosales A	27.7	4	0	0	0	1.000	0	0	--	0	--
Carson M	19.0	6	0	0	0	1.000	0	0	--	2	--
Hermida J	2.0	0	0	0	0	0.000	0	0	--	--	--
Tolleson S	1.0	1	0	0	0	1.000	0	0	--	0	--
Center Field											
Davis R	677.3	190	2	0	2	.990	1	0	-.013	33	-5
Crisp C	625.0	182	2	0	2	.989	0	0	.043	22	-13
Gross G	76.0	16	0	0	0	1.000	0	0	--	2	--
Patterson E	24.3	9	0	0	0	1.000	0	0	--	3	--
Carson M	21.0	6	0	0	0	1.000	0	0	--	1	--
Sweeney R	8.0	2	0	0	0	1.000	0	0	--	1	--
Right Field											
Sweeney R	659.3	147	4	0	0	1.000	1	1	.013	37	1
Gross G	245.3	54	5	0	0	1.000	0	0	.058	11	-2
Davis R	186.0	47	2	0	1	.980	1	0	.047	13	3
Carson M	154.0	33	2	0	0	1.000	0	0	.061	10	2
Hermida J	144.3	31	1	0	0	1.000	0	0	.020	9	1
Buck T	27.0	4	0	0	0	1.000	0	0	--	2	--
Cust J	15.3	10	1	0	0	1.000	0	0	--	3	--
Tolleson S	0.3	0	0	0	0	0.000	0	0	--	--	--

Philadelphia Phillies

Stat Facts:
- Roy Halladay led the majors in PRC
- Halladay led the NL in BFP
- Jamie Moyer had the lowest H-A of any pitcher with 100+ IP
- Carlos Ruiz had the lowest WP+PB/G of any regular C
- Ryan Howard made the most TE of any 1B
- 1% of Howard's FB were infield pop-ups
- Placido Polanco made the fewest TE of any regular 3B
- Shane Victorino led the NL in CF assists
- J.C. Romero walked 20% of his BFP
- 88% of Nelson Figueroa's GB were outs
- Jimmy Rollins had 17 SB in 18 attempts
- Wilson Valdez had 20 GDP in 363 PA

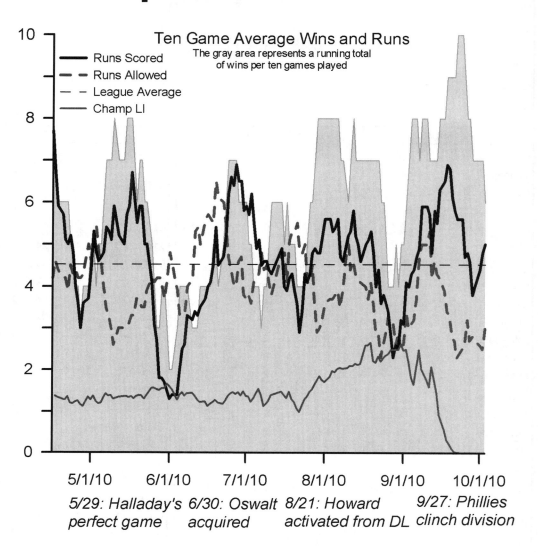

Ten Game Average Wins and Runs
The gray area represents a running total of wins per ten games played

Runs Scored · Runs Allowed · League Average · Champ LI

5/29: Halladay's perfect game 6/30: Oswalt acquired 8/21: Howard activated from DL 9/27: Phillies clinch division

Team Batting and Pitching/Fielding Stats by Month

	April	May	June	July	Aug	Sept/Oct
Wins	12	16	13	15	18	23
Losses	10	12	13	13	10	7
RS/G	5.2	4.3	5.0	4.4	4.2	5.6
RA/G	4.5	3.5	4.8	4.3	3.3	3.6
OBP	.339	.327	.325	.321	.312	.366
SLG	.417	.425	.408	.419	.355	.456
FIP	4.46	3.80	4.68	4.12	3.01	3.92
DER	.683	.737	.694	.698	.689	.702

Batting Stats

Player	BR	Runs	RBI	PA	Outs	H	2B	3B	HR	TB	K	BB	IBB	HBP	SH	SF	SB	CS	GDP	H-A	L^R	BA	OBP	SLG	GPA
Werth J	115	106	85	652	404	164	46	2	27	295	147	82	6	7	0	9	13	3	11	.045	-.010	.296	.388	.532	.307
Howard R *	95	87	108	620	413	152	23	5	31	278	157	59	11	8	0	3	1	1	14	.012	.019	.276	.353	.505	.284
Victorino S	89	84	69	648	448	152	26	10	18	252	79	53	5	7	0	1	34	6	7	.006	.072	.259	.327	.429	.254
Ibanez R *	86	75	83	636	425	154	37	5	16	249	108	68	11	0	0	7	4	3	15	.043	.035	.275	.349	.444	.267
Utley C *	81	75	65	511	314	117	20	2	16	189	63	63	3	18	0	5	13	2	4	.062	-.073	.275	.387	.445	.285
Polanco P	71	76	52	602	403	165	27	2	6	214	47	32	1	7	1	8	5	0	14	-.009	-.025	.298	.339	.386	.248
Ruiz C	65	43	53	433	268	112	28	1	8	166	54	55	13	6	0	1	0	1	8	-.036	.042	.302	.400	.447	.291
Rollins J +	48	48	41	394	270	85	16	3	8	131	32	40	2	1	0	3	17	1	4	.020	.043	.243	.320	.374	.237
Valdez W	32	37	35	363	267	86	16	3	4	120	43	21	7	2	7	0	7	0	20	-.014	-.023	.258	.306	.360	.227
Francisco B	27	24	28	197	137	48	13	0	6	79	35	14	1	2	1	1	8	0	6	.007	.072	.268	.327	.441	.256
Gload R *	20	16	22	138	93	36	8	0	6	62	15	8	3	1	1	0	1	0	1	-.037	.005	.281	.328	.484	.268
Schneider B	17	17	15	147	98	30	4	1	4	48	25	19	2	1	2	0	0	0	3	-.056	.220	.240	.345	.384	.250
Dobbs G *	14	13	15	176	134	32	7	0	5	54	39	12	1	0	1	0	1	1	2	.003	.054	.196	.251	.331	.195
Sweeney M	6	10	8	58	42	12	2	0	2	20	7	5	0	1	0	0	1	0	2	-.044	-.015	.231	.310	.385	.235
Castro J	6	7	13	136	103	25	5	0	0	30	23	7	0	0	1	2	0	1	1	.014	.020	.198	.237	.238	.166
Brown D *	6	8	13	70	51	13	3	0	2	22	24	5	1	0	0	3	2	1	1	.067	.192	.210	.257	.355	.204
Sardinha D	5	5	8	40	32	8	2	0	1	19	13	1	0	0	0	1	0	0	1	-.151	-.016	.205	.225	.487	.222
Ransom C	4	6	5	46	34	8	0	0	2	14	11	3	0	0	1	0	1	0	0	.123	-.173	.190	.244	.333	.193
Mayberry J	3	4	6	13	9	4	0	0	2	10	4	1	0	0	0	0	0	1	0	-.306	.180	.333	.385	.833	.380
Hoover P	1	6	2	25	20	5	2	0	0	7	5	3	2	0	0	0	0	0	3	-.299	.027	.227	.320	.318	.223
Figueroa N	1	1	0	4	2	2	1	0	0	3	1	0	0	0	0	0	0	0	0	.825	.717	.500	.500	.750	.411

Only includes batters with at least one Base Run. Italicized stats have been adjusted for home park.

Batted Ball Batting Stats

Player	% of PA		% of Batted Balls			IF/F	HR/OF	Out %		Runs Per Event				Total Runs vs. Avg.				
	K%	BB%	GB%	LD%	FB%			GB	OF	NIP	GB	LD	OF	NIP	GB	LD	FB	Tot
Werth Ja	23	14	37	18	45	.05	.14	66	76	.06	.10	.44	.28	7	6	3	25	42
Howard Ry	25	11	40	23	37	.01	.21	76	78	.02	.03	.34	.37	-1	-4	2	29	25
Utley Ch	12	16	41	20	39	.10	.12	73	88	.15	.06	.36	.18	16	3	3	3	25
Ruiz Ca	12	14	45	20	35	.07	.08	71	80	.13	.06	.40	.16	11	3	7	0	21
Ibanez Ra	17	11	45	18	37	.10	.10	73	81	.06	.04	.41	.21	4	-0	4	5	13
Victorino Sh	12	9	45	17	38	.15	.11	74	85	.09	.05	.35	.18	4	4	-1	1	8
Gload Ro	11	7	42	12	47	.06	.12	66	82	.06	.10	.26	.22	-0	2	-3	5	4
Polanco Pl	8	6	45	20	35	.06	.04	72	83	.10	.05	.34	.09	2	4	7	-10	3
Francisco Be	18	8	38	17	45	.08	.10	75	81	.03	.02	.42	.18	-1	-2	1	2	1
Rollins Ji	8	10	46	17	37	.10	.07	80	86	.14	.00	.43	.12	6	-5	4	-5	1
Schneider Br	17	14	45	17	38	.08	.11	80	84	.09	.01	.33	.19	2	-2	-2	1	-0
Valdez Wi	12	6	60	19	21	.07	.07	79	72	.05	-.01	.32	.23	-1	-4	-1	-3	-9
Dobbs Gr	22	7	33	14	53	.15	.09	83	84	-.01	.00	.33	.15	-3	-3	-4	-1	-10
Castro Ju	17	5	50	12	37	.03	.00	77	82	-.01	.05	.17	.03	-2	0	-5	-5	-13
MLB Average	*18*	*9*	*44*	*18*	*38*	*.09*	*.10*	*74*	*83*	*.04*	*.04*	*.38*	*.18*	--	--	--	--	--

Only includes batters with at least one hundred Plate Appearances.

Pitching Stats

Player	PRC	IP	BFP	G	GS	K	BB	IBB	HBP	H	HR	DP	DER	SB	CS	PO	W	L	Sv	Op	Hld	H-A	R^L	RA	ERA	FIP
Halladay R	142	250.7	993	33	33	219	30	1	6	231	24	29	.700	10	5	0	21	10	0	0	0	-.004	-.023	2.66	2.44	3.11
Hamels C *	105	208.7	855	33	33	211	61	5	8	185	26	23	.703	10	6	1	12	11	0	0	0	.013	-.013	3.19	3.06	3.71
Oswalt R	59	82.7	316	13	12	73	21	0	3	53	6	8	.770	5	4	1	7	1	0	0	0	.011	-.013	1.96	1.74	3.24
Blanton J	50	175.7	765	29	28	134	43	6	3	206	27	15	.658	11	2	2	9	6	0	0	0	-.018	.012	5.33	4.82	4.35
Kendrick K	48	180.7	771	33	31	84	49	4	3	199	26	23	.703	4	4	1	11	10	0	0	0	.019	-.062	5.13	4.73	4.93
Madson R	32	53.0	217	55	0	64	13	3	4	42	4	4	.705	4	0	0	6	2	5	10	15	-.046	-.019	2.72	2.55	2.55
Moyer J *	31	111.7	460	19	19	63	20	0	6	103	20	7	.758	12	1	0	9	9	0	0	0	-.105	.006	5.16	4.84	5.09
Durbin C	29	68.7	292	64	0	63	27	2	5	63	7	8	.700	3	1	2	4	1	0	1	15	-.036	-.110	3.80	3.80	4.00
Contreras J	26	56.7	233	67	0	57	16	2	4	53	5	9	.682	5	1	0	6	4	4	5	13	-.023	-.032	3.49	3.34	3.28
Lidge B	24	45.7	193	50	0	52	24	4	1	32	5	2	.748	7	0	0	1	1	27	32	0	-.008	-.047	3.15	2.96	3.72
Herndon D	16	52.3	232	47	0	29	17	4	2	67	2	11	.632	3	1	0	1	3	0	1	1	-.059	-.048	4.64	4.30	3.44
Romero J *	14	36.7	171	60	0	28	29	7	5	30	3	6	.736	2	0	0	1	0	3	6	9	.004	-.080	4.17	3.68	4.94
Worley V	12	13.0	51	5	2	12	4	0	0	8	1	1	.765	0	1	0	1	1	0	0	0	.097	.003	1.38	1.38	3.27
Baez D	12	47.7	216	51	0	28	23	2	3	55	6	8	.679	5	1	0	3	4	0	2	6	-.012	-.044	5.85	5.48	5.17
Figueroa N	11	26.0	104	13	1	15	9	2	0	20	1	1	.759	3	2	0	2	1	1	1	0	-.182	-.066	3.46	3.46	3.35
Happ J *	9	15.3	70	3	3	9	12	0	0	13	1	2	.729	0	1	1	1	0	0	0	0	.029	.007	2.35	1.76	5.22
Bastardo A *	8	18.7	86	25	0	26	9	0	2	19	1	0	.625	0	0	0	2	0	0	1	2	.046	-.017	4.34	4.34	2.87

Only includes pitchers with at least ten Innings Pitched. Italicized stats have been adjusted for home park.

Batted Ball Pitching Stats

Player	% of PA		% of Batted Balls					Out %		Runs Per Event				Total Runs vs. Avg.				
	K%	BB%	GB%	LD%	FB%	IF/F	HR/OF	GB	OF	NIP	GB	LD	OF	NIP	GB	LD	FB	Tot
Halladay Ro	22	4	51	19	30	.09	.12	76	81	-.05	.03	.34	.22	-25	-5	-6	-2	-37
Oswalt Ro	23	8	50	12	38	.09	.08	80	86	.00	.01	.41	.12	-4	-4	-7	-7	-21
Hamels Co	25	8	45	17	38	.11	.13	74	79	-.00	.05	.34	.25	-10	-2	-12	9	-15
Madson Ry	29	8	50	13	37	.08	.09	73	80	-.02	.06	.33	.16	-4	1	-6	-3	-11
Lidge Br	27	13	37	15	48	.13	.09	71	95	.04	.06	.56	.07	0	-1	-0	-6	-6
Figueroa Ne	14	9	42	20	38	.03	.04	88	74	.06	-.03	.23	.16	0	-3	-2	-0	-5
Moyer Ja	14	6	44	15	41	.09	.14	75	85	.02	.04	.24	.23	-4	-1	-11	11	-5
Contreras Jo	24	9	45	19	36	.07	.10	78	80	.01	.02	.41	.20	-2	-2	0	-0	-5
Durbin Ch	22	11	42	17	41	.06	.10	73	83	.04	.04	.47	.17	1	-1	1	-0	1
Romero Ju	16	20	61	12	26	.11	.12	72	77	.14	.04	.20	.23	7	0	-5	-1	1
Herndon Ke	13	8	57	17	27	.10	.05	70	73	.07	.06	.49	.16	1	4	4	-2	6
Baez Da	13	12	56	13	31	.10	.11	71	72	.11	.06	.43	.29	4	2	-1	4	9
Kendrick Ky	11	7	45	17	38	.08	.12	78	80	.06	.02	.39	.23	-0	-4	4	17	17
Blanton Jo	18	6	42	19	39	.10	.14	72	80	.00	.06	.38	.25	-8	5	6	16	19
MLB Average	18	9	44	18	38	.09	.10	74	83	.04	.04	.38	.18	--	--	--	--	--

Only includes pitchers who faced at least one hundred batters.

Fielding Stats

Name	INN	SBA/G	CS%	ERA	WP+PB/G	PO	A	TE	FE
Catchers									
Ruiz C	974.3	0.63	26%	3.33	0.157	814	60	5	1
Schneider B	333.0	1.03	21%	4.57	0.270	257	17	2	0
Sardinha D	87.0	0.41	25%	3.72	0.207	84	4	0	0
Hoover P	62.0	0.29	50%	4.50	0.435	42	2	1	0

Name	Inn	PO	A	TE	FE	FPct	DPS	DPT	ZRDif	OOZ	Dif
First Base											
Howard R	1229.0	1266	59	7	7	.990	5	1	-.064	29	-11
Sweeney M	103.0	104	6	1	1	.982	0	1	.083	5	2
Gload R	92.3	92	6	0	0	1.000	0	2	--	2	--
Ransom C	18.0	15	1	0	0	1.000	0	0	--	1	--
Dobbs G	12.0	14	1	0	0	1.000	0	0	--	0	--
Ibanez R	2.0	3	0	0	0	1.000	0	0	--	--	--
Second Base											
Utley C	1007.0	228	347	5	6	.981	40	41	.019	36	11
Valdez W	314.3	57	91	0	1	.993	6	13	.024	7	-1
Polanco P	82.0	15	37	0	0	1.000	5	2	--	5	--
Castro J	36.0	12	13	0	2	.926	0	5	--	1	--
Ransom C	17.0	5	6	0	0	1.000	1	1	--	1	--
Shortstop											
Rollins J	744.3	102	227	2	4	.982	28	18	.063	17	-15
Valdez W	458.0	83	148	2	0	.991	9	24	.015	16	-4
Castro J	239.0	31	78	0	3	.973	8	6	.004	11	1
Bocock B	15.0	3	2	0	0	1.000	1	0	--	0	--
Third Base											
Polanco P	1075.0	88	258	1	4	.986	30	1	.003	33	-7
Dobbs G	230.0	16	37	0	6	.898	2	0	-.088	6	-2
Ransom C	63.0	6	9	0	1	.938	2	0	--	0	--
Castro J	49.0	1	10	0	1	.917	1	0	--	2	--
Valdez W	39.0	3	12	0	0	1.000	0	0	--	2	--

Name	Inn	PO	A	TE	FE	FPct	DPS	DPT	ZRDif	OOZ	Dif
Left Field											
Ibanez R	1294.0	212	4	0	2	.991	1	0	.023	43	-20
Francisco B	160.0	30	3	0	0	1.000	0	0	.049	7	-1
Oswalt R	2.0	1	0	0	0	1.000	0	0	--	0	--
Gload R	0.3	0	0	0	0	0.000	0	0	--	--	--
Center Field											
Victorino S	1265.0	360	11	1	1	.995	4	0	.014	67	-5
Werth J	171.0	44	0	0	0	1.000	0	0	-.040	4	-6
Francisco B	13.0	2	0	0	0	1.000	0	0	--	0	--
Mayberry J	7.0	2	0	0	0	1.000	0	0	--	1	--
Right Field											
Werth J	1171.0	249	8	1	3	.985	2	0	.018	65	1
Francisco B	113.7	28	0	0	0	1.000	0	0	-.045	5	-1
Brown D	112.0	28	1	0	1	.967	0	0	-.040	4	-2
Gload R	43.7	10	0	0	1	.909	0	0	--	2	--
Mayberry J	10.0	0	0	0	0	0.000	0	0	--	--	--
Dobbs G	6.0	0	0	0	0	0.000	0	0	--	--	--

Pittsburgh Pirates

Stat Facts:
- Pedro Alvarez struck out in 31% of his PA
- Ross Ohlendorf allowed 16 SB in 17 attempts
- Ryan Doumit had the lowest CS% of any regular C
- Jeff Karstens had the lowest R^L of any ML starter
- Zach Duke had the lowest DER of any ML starter
- Neil Walker had the lowest ZRDif of any primary 2B
- Andrew McCutcheon had the lowest ZRDif of any regular CF
- Jose Tabata made 58 OOZ plays in 771 LF innings
- The Pirates had 6 players with 140+ PA and a GPA <.210
- The Pirates had 6 pitchers with 140+ BFP and a FIP >4.90
- Joel Hanrahan struck out 34% of his BFP
- Jason Jaramillo had 13 hits and 7 GDP

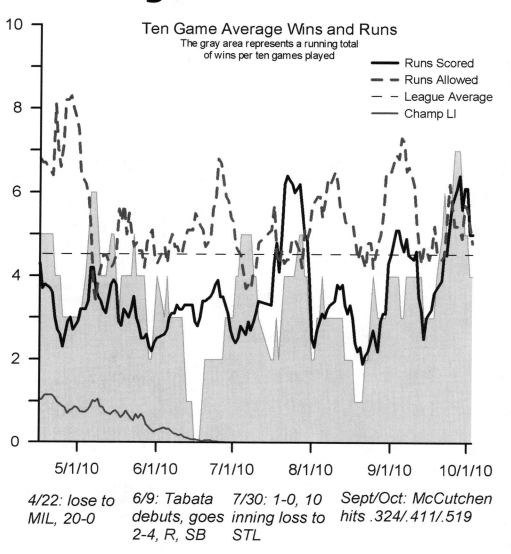

Ten Game Average Wins and Runs
The gray area represents a running total of wins per ten games played

Legend:
— Runs Scored
– – Runs Allowed
– – League Average
— Champ LI

4/22: lose to MIL, 20-0

6/9: Tabata debuts, goes 2-4, R, SB

7/30: 1-0, 10 inning loss to STL

Sept/Oct: McCutchen hits .324/.411/.519

Team Batting and Pitching/Fielding Stats by Month

	April	May	June	July	Aug	Sept/Oct
Wins	10	11	6	9	8	13
Losses	13	18	20	16	21	17
RS/G	3.6	3.0	3.2	4.3	3.4	4.3
RA/G	7.0	4.7	5.1	4.9	5.7	4.9
OBP	.312	.304	.297	.306	.293	.313
SLG	.365	.350	.355	.396	.378	.394
FIP	5.35	4.26	4.65	5.04	4.22	3.67
DER	.677	.678	.688	.707	.661	.675

Batting Stats

Player	BR	Runs	RBI	PA	Outs	H	2B	3B	HR	TB	K	BB	IBB	HBP	SH	SF	SB	CS	GDP	H-A	L^R	BA	OBP	SLG	GPA
McCutchen A	92	94	56	653	423	163	35	5	16	256	89	70	1	5	1	7	33	10	6	.050	.039	.286	.365	.449	.277
Jones G *	71	64	86	654	467	146	34	1	21	245	123	53	2	1	0	8	7	3	18	-.017	.052	.247	.306	.414	.241
Walker N +	63	57	66	469	307	126	29	3	12	197	83	34	1	3	2	4	2	3	4	.040	-.002	.296	.349	.462	.273
Tabata J	52	61	35	441	298	121	21	4	4	162	57	28	0	2	5	1	19	7	7	.065	-.028	.299	.346	.400	.256
Doumit R +	50	42	45	456	322	102	22	1	13	165	87	41	4	8	0	1	1	0	18	-.016	-.096	.251	.331	.406	.251
Alvarez P *	50	42	64	386	266	89	21	1	16	160	119	37	1	0	0	2	0	0	8	.051	.061	.256	.326	.461	.262
Cedeno R	49	42	38	502	361	120	29	3	8	179	106	23	4	2	7	2	12	3	10	.039	.040	.256	.293	.382	.227
Milledge L	43	38	34	412	284	105	21	3	4	144	62	28	3	3	2	3	5	3	7	.023	.106	.277	.332	.380	.244
Young D +	22	22	28	207	151	45	11	1	7	79	52	13	0	1	1	1	1	0	5	.087	.095	.236	.286	.414	.232
LaRoche A	18	26	16	271	204	51	8	0	4	71	43	19	0	2	2	1	1	1	7	.009	.067	.206	.268	.287	.192
Iwamura A *	14	18	9	193	140	30	6	1	2	44	31	26	0	0	1	1	3	1	4	-.066	.094	.182	.292	.267	.198
Crosby B	13	9	11	175	124	35	8	0	1	46	33	16	2	1	2	0	0	2	1	-.032	-.005	.224	.301	.295	.209
Church R *	13	16	18	183	142	31	11	1	3	53	46	12	0	1	0	0	1	0	3	.140	.040	.182	.240	.312	.186
Clement J *	12	11	12	154	117	29	3	0	7	53	37	6	3	1	1	1	0	0	2	-.173	-.051	.201	.237	.368	.199
Snyder C	9	12	16	142	109	21	1	0	5	37	33	16	4	1	0	1	0	0	6	-.025	.068	.169	.268	.298	.195
Bowker J *	7	7	13	77	57	16	5	0	2	27	10	8	1	0	0	0	0	1	3	.018	-.042	.232	.312	.391	.238
Pearce S	5	4	5	38	21	8	2	1	0	12	6	7	0	0	0	2	0	0	0	.114	.116	.276	.395	.414	.281
Jaramillo J	2	2	6	97	81	13	2	0	1	18	14	8	1	1	0	1	0	0	7	.053	.138	.149	.227	.207	.154
Diaz A	2	0	2	36	27	8	1	0	0	9	10	3	1	0	0	0	0	1	1	-.153	-.133	.242	.306	.273	.206
Ciriaco P	2	3	1	6	3	3	1	1	0	6	3	0	0	0	0	0	0	0	0	-.317	-.475	.500	.500	1.000	.475
Lincoln B *	2	0	3	18	9	6	0	0	0	6	3	0	0	0	3	0	0	0	0	.210	-.143	.400	.400	.400	.280
Presley A *	2	2	0	25	18	6	1	0	0	7	8	1	0	0	1	0	1	1	0	.170	-.293	.261	.292	.304	.207
Raynor J	1	1	0	11	8	2	0	0	0	2	3	1	0	0	0	0	0	0	0	.060	-.208	.200	.273	.200	.173

Only includes batters with at least one Base Run. Italicized stats have been adjusted for home park.

Batted Ball Batting Stats

Player	% of PA		% of Batted Balls					Out %		Runs Per Event				Total Runs vs. Avg.				
	K%	BB%	GB%	LD%	FB%	IF/F	HR/OF	GB	OF	NIP	GB	LD	OF	NIP	GB	LD	FB	Tot
McCutchen An	14	11	43	19	38	.10	.10	67	85	.10	.09	.37	.17	9	11	4	1	25
Walker Ne	18	8	36	22	41	.04	.09	66	83	.03	.10	.35	.17	-2	7	4	4	14
Alvarez Pe	31	10	46	15	40	.12	.19	71	71	-.00	.06	.42	.38	-5	1	-5	14	5
Tabata Jo	13	7	59	16	25	.00	.05	67	85	.05	.09	.42	.10	-1	12	2	-9	4
Milledge La	15	8	49	19	33	.16	.05	66	82	.04	.09	.36	.12	-1	9	1	-8	2
Doumit Ry	19	11	41	16	43	.09	.10	80	77	.05	-.01	.38	.21	2	-7	-2	7	-1
Young De	25	7	47	13	40	.09	.14	82	73	-.02	-.01	.52	.29	-4	-4	-1	6	-4
Jones Ga	19	8	44	17	39	.09	.12	77	84	.03	.02	.41	.19	-3	-4	-0	4	-4
Crosby Bo	19	10	52	14	34	.12	.03	76	86	.04	.04	.44	.04	0	1	-1	-6	-7
Iwamura Ak	16	13	56	13	31	.02	.05	80	85	.10	.01	.28	.11	3	-2	-5	-4	-8
Clement Je	24	5	46	20	33	.19	.24	92	91	-.04	-.06	.38	.32	-4	-6	-1	1	-8
Snyder Ch	23	12	42	19	40	.17	.17	79	100	.04	-.01	.23	.16	0	-3	-4	-2	-8
Cedeno Ro	21	5	49	16	35	.17	.07	66	83	-.03	.09	.44	.14	-9	10	-0	-9	-8
Church Ry	25	7	40	19	42	.06	.06	88	85	-.01	-.04	.38	.13	-3	-5	-2	-2	-12
LaRoche An	16	8	50	17	33	.18	.07	75	90	.04	.04	.31	.08	-1	-0	-3	-8	-13
MLB Average	**18**	**9**	**44**	**18**	**38**	**.09**	**.10**	**74**	**83**	**.04**	**.04**	**.38**	**.18**	--	--	--	--	--

Only includes batters with at least one hundred Plate Appearances.

Pitching Stats

Player	PRC	IP	BFP	G	GS	K	BB	IBB	HBP	H	HR	DP	DER	SB	CS	PO	W	L	Sv	Op	Hld	H-A	R^L	RA	ERA	FIP
Maholm P *	45	185.3	840	32	32	102	62	2	9	228	15	22	.660	8	2	2	9	15	0	0	0	-.026	-.065	5.78	5.10	4.26
Meek E	43	80.0	324	70	0	70	31	4	4	53	5	7	.748	10	2	0	5	4	4	10	15	-.068	.041	2.81	2.14	3.42
Ohlendorf R	37	108.3	475	21	21	79	44	2	6	106	12	6	.710	16	1	1	1	11	0	0	0	.009	-.031	4.49	4.07	4.51
Hanrahan J	34	69.7	294	72	0	100	26	0	4	58	6	2	.665	7	1	0	4	1	6	10	18	.056	-.051	3.62	3.62	2.74
Duke Z *	34	159.0	730	29	29	96	51	2	4	212	25	21	.643	10	3	2	8	15	0	0	0	-.032	.021	6.51	5.72	5.03
Karstens J	33	122.7	525	26	19	72	27	5	1	146	21	11	.681	8	6	1	3	10	0	0	0	.004	-.110	5.28	4.92	4.81
McDonald J	29	64.0	268	11	11	61	24	4	0	59	3	7	.678	2	3	1	4	5	0	0	0	-.010	.010	3.52	3.52	2.84
Carrasco D	22	55.7	232	45	0	45	22	1	4	50	4	5	.701	8	3	0	2	2	0	0	5	-.004	-.016	3.88	3.88	3.86
Burres B *	21	79.3	362	20	13	45	34	4	6	87	9	6	.690	4	1	1	4	5	0	0	0	-.060	.034	5.45	4.99	4.90
Lopez J *	17	38.7	166	50	0	22	18	3	2	39	2	7	.680	1	1	1	2	2	0	0	6	-.074	-.044	3.26	2.79	4.05
Resop C	15	19.0	77	22	0	24	10	0	0	10	1	0	.786	2	0	0	0	0	0	0	5	.043	-.103	1.89	1.89	2.93
McCutchen D	14	67.7	316	28	9	38	28	0	2	83	13	4	.681	8	1	2	2	5	0	0	0	-.024	-.030	6.38	6.12	5.90
Dotel O	14	40.0	173	41	0	48	17	2	3	35	5	1	.690	4	1	0	2	2	21	26	0	-.112	-.173	4.73	4.28	3.77
Morton C	11	79.7	382	17	17	59	26	3	7	112	15	6	.625	12	2	2	2	12	0	0	0	-.037	-.019	8.92	7.57	5.29
Park C	10	28.3	121	26	0	23	7	1	2	25	2	0	.724	1	0	0	2	2	0	1	1	-.027	.050	4.45	3.49	3.34
Lincoln B	9	52.7	240	11	9	25	15	0	5	66	9	4	.688	3	1	0	1	4	0	0	0	.077	-.010	7.18	6.66	5.61
Donnelly B	8	30.7	142	38	0	26	25	1	1	26	6	3	.750	7	0	0	3	1	0	0	9	-.138	-.138	6.16	5.58	6.49
Gallagher S	7	34.3	163	31	0	22	22	2	1	38	2	2	.672	1	0	1	2	1	0	0	3	-.021	.054	6.82	6.03	4.51
Taschner J *	5	19.3	88	17	0	17	8	0	2	22	3	0	.683	1	0	0	0	0	0	0	2	-.150	-.016	6.05	6.05	4.70
Ledezma W *	4	19.7	92	27	0	22	6	0	1	25	2	0	.607	0	1	1	0	3	0	0	3	-.105	.082	7.32	6.86	3.35
Thomas J *	3	13.0	62	12	0	5	5	1	0	21	3	2	.633	0	1	0	0	1	0	0	0	-.207	.134	6.23	6.23	6.35
Jackson S	2	11.3	55	11	0	7	6	0	0	17	4	1	.658	0	0	0	0	1	0	0	0	-.145	.109	8.74	8.74	8.14

Only includes pitchers with at least ten Innings Pitched. Italicized stats have been adjusted for home park.

Batted Ball Pitching Stats

Player	% of PA		% of Batted Balls					Out %		Runs Per Event				Total Runs vs. Avg.				
	K%	BB%	GB%	LD%	FB%	IF/F	HR/OF	GB	OF	NIP	GB	LD	OF	NIP	GB	LD	FB	Tot
Meek Ev	22	11	57	16	27	.15	.10	84	80	.04	-.01	.34	.20	0	-6	-5	-5	-16
Hanrahan Jo	34	10	42	18	40	.06	.08	65	88	-.01	.11	.48	.13	-4	3	-1	-5	-8
McDonald Ja	23	9	31	23	46	.10	.04	72	86	.02	.04	.44	.07	-2	-1	4	-7	-5
Park Ch	19	7	54	13	33	.07	.08	72	83	.02	.06	.35	.16	-1	1	-2	-1	-4
Carrasco Da	19	11	46	22	32	.08	.09	76	86	.06	.03	.37	.12	1	-1	1	-4	-3
Dotel Oc	28	12	31	16	53	.11	.10	65	79	.02	.13	.33	.22	-0	2	-3	3	1
Lopez Ja	13	12	60	15	24	.07	.07	72	73	.11	.05	.36	.21	3	1	-1	-1	2
Donnelly Br	18	18	44	13	43	.16	.19	72	92	.12	.07	.35	.23	5	0	-3	1	4
Gallagher Se	13	14	48	19	34	.11	.06	61	88	.12	.13	.31	.10	4	5	-1	-3	4
Ohlendorf Ro	17	11	31	22	46	.14	.09	75	84	.06	.05	.35	.17	3	-1	2	2	6
Lincoln Br	10	8	37	19	44	.05	.12	67	81	.09	.10	.31	.22	2	3	-0	7	12
Burres Br	12	11	42	19	39	.12	.10	82	72	.10	.01	.43	.26	5	-3	5	9	15
Karstens Je	14	5	42	18	40	.11	.14	67	84	.02	.10	.36	.22	-4	10	2	9	16
McCutchen Da	12	9	36	16	48	.09	.13	69	81	.09	.07	.44	.23	3	2	2	11	18
Morton Ch	15	9	47	24	29	.06	.18	65	88	.05	.09	.41	.26	1	7	10	6	25
Maholm Pa	12	8	51	19	30	.05	.08	71	78	.08	.06	.42	.19	4	9	12	1	26
Duke Za	13	8	48	20	33	.07	.15	70	81	.05	.06	.42	.25	0	10	13	15	38
MLB Average	18	9	44	18	38	.09	.10	74	83	.04	.04	.38	.18	--	--	--	--	--

Only includes pitchers who faced at least one hundred batters.

Fielding Stats

Name	INN	SBA/G	CS%	ERA	WP+PB/G	PO	A	TE	FE
Catchers									
Doumit R	790.3	0.97	7%	4.95	0.478	533	55	4	2
Snyder C	322.0	0.59	24%	4.81	0.363	268	26	0	3
Jaramillo J	222.0	0.97	25%	5.68	0.365	170	12	2	0
Kratz E	77.3	0.81	57%	4.42	0.349	56	9	0	0

Name	Inn	PO	A	TE	FE	FPct	DPS	DPT	ZRDif	OOZ	Dif
First Base											
Jones G	924.7	893	88	4	5	.991	5	0	-.031	29	-1
Clement J	293.3	295	18	0	2	.994	0	0	.070	12	2
Pearce S	75.7	78	7	0	1	.988	0	0	--	5	--
Crosby B	43.0	47	3	0	0	1.000	0	0	--	1	--
Bowker J	37.0	29	3	0	1	.970	0	0	--	0	--
Doumit R	23.0	23	2	0	1	.962	0	0	--	0	--
LaRoche A	15.0	15	0	0	0	1.000	0	0	--	1	--
Second Base											
Walker N	894.7	222	234	0	7	.985	27	31	-.072	11	-11
Iwamura A	341.0	75	94	0	3	.983	11	14	-.112	5	-3
Crosby B	88.0	18	21	0	0	1.000	1	1	--	3	--
Young D	52.0	5	11	0	0	1.000	0	2	--	1	--
LaRoche A	36.0	8	11	1	0	.950	0	1	--	0	--
Shortstop											
Cedeno R	1149.0	183	382	8	9	.969	32	34	-.014	48	-2
Crosby B	178.7	33	62	4	4	.922	3	4	-.099	6	-2
Diaz A	82.0	5	19	2	0	.923	2	1	--	0	--
Ciriaco P	2.0	1	2	0	0	1.000	0	1	--	0	--
Third Base											
Alvarez P	814.7	61	198	6	11	.938	16	0	-.057	34	4
LaRoche A	448.0	33	119	5	5	.938	6	0	-.001	12	-5
Young D	58.0	6	10	3	0	.842	1	0	--	2	--
Crosby B	51.0	1	11	0	0	1.000	0	0	--	2	--
Walker N	40.0	4	10	1	0	.933	0	0	--	4	--

Name	Inn	PO	A	TE	FE	FPct	DPS	DPT	ZRDif	OOZ	Dif
Left Field											
Tabata J	771.3	189	5	1	0	.995	1	0	-.015	58	20
Milledge L	515.3	110	5	0	0	1.000	1	0	-.034	33	8
Church R	95.0	25	2	0	0	1.000	0	0	--	7	--
Presley A	11.0	0	0	0	0	0.000	0	0	--	--	--
Jones G	8.0	3	0	0	0	1.000	0	0	--	1	--
Bowker J	6.0	0	0	0	1	0.000	0	0	--	--	--
Moss B	5.0	1	0	0	0	1.000	0	0	--	--	--
Center Field											
McCutchen A	1290.0	373	8	2	3	.987	2	0	-.021	78	5
Tabata J	91.3	22	0	0	0	1.000	0	0	--	3	--
Church R	18.0	6	0	0	0	1.000	0	0	--	0	--
Presley A	10.0	1	0	0	0	1.000	0	0	--	0	--
Raynor J	2.0	1	0	0	0	1.000	0	0	--	0	--
Right Field											
Jones G	397.7	98	4	1	2	.971	0	0	-.027	31	9
Milledge L	341.3	80	1	0	1	.988	1	0	-.113	29	10
Church R	205.7	45	3	0	0	1.000	1	0	-.081	14	3
Young D	153.7	29	2	1	0	.969	0	0	-.053	3	-5
Doumit R	146.0	38	1	0	3	.929	0	0	-.059	7	-1
Bowker J	113.0	30	0	0	0	1.000	0	0	-.045	7	1
Moss B	27.0	4	0	0	0	1.000	0	0	--	1	--
Presley A	24.0	2	0	0	0	1.000	0	0	--	1	--
Raynor J	3.3	1	0	0	0	1.000	0	0	--	0	--

San Diego Padres

Stat Facts:

- Adrian Gonzalez tied for second in the NL in Base Runs
- Gonzalez was second in the majors in IBB
- Wade LeBlanc tied for the NL lead in Pickoffs
- David Eckstein made 0 FE and 0 TE
- Eckstein struck out in 7% of his PA
- Kyle Blanks struck out in 38% of his PA
- Chase Headley made the most OOZ plays of any NL 3B
- Edward Mujica walked 2% of his BFP
- Ryan Webb's GB% was 62
- Ernesto Frieri's GB% was 25
- Joe Thatcher allowed 0 infield pop-ups
- 83% of Luke Gregerson's GB were outs

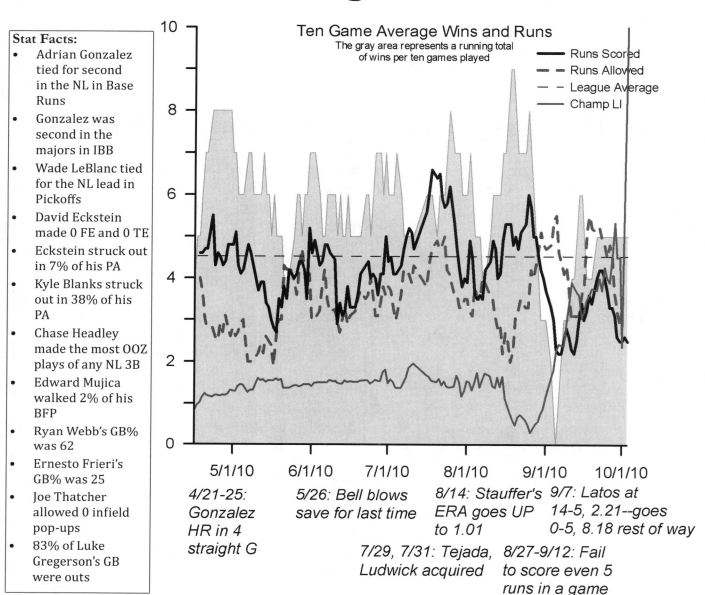

Ten Game Average Wins and Runs

The gray area represents a running total of wins per ten games played

— Runs Scored
- - - Runs Allowed
– – League Average
— Champ LI

4/21-25: Gonzalez HR in 4 straight G

5/26: Bell blows save for last time

7/29, 7/31: Tejada, Ludwick acquired

8/14: Stauffer's ERA goes UP to 1.01

8/27-9/12: Fail to score even 5 runs in a game

9/7: Latos at 14-5, 2.21--goes 0-5, 8.18 rest of way

Team Batting and Pitching/Fielding Stats by Month

	April	May	June	July	Aug	Sept/Oct
Wins	15	16	15	14	16	14
Losses	8	12	12	10	13	17
RS/G	4.6	4.1	4.0	4.8	4.5	2.9
RA/G	3.3	3.3	3.4	3.8	3.8	3.8
OBP	.325	.326	.303	.340	.317	.297
SLG	.387	.349	.369	.403	.385	.345
FIP	3.69	3.51	3.70	4.01	3.57	3.67
DER	.713	.725	.695	.714	.689	.679

Batting Stats

Player	BR	Runs	RBI	PA	Outs	H	2B	3B	HR	TB	K	BB	IBB	HBP	SH	SF	SB	CS	GDP	H-A	L^R	BA	OBP	SLG	GPA
Gonzalez A *	119	87	101	693	430	176	33	0	31	302	114	93	35	2	2	4	0	0	15	-.043	-.022	.298	.393	.511	.332
Headley C +	85	77	58	674	465	161	29	3	11	229	139	56	3	3	1	4	17	5	11	-.036	-.053	.264	.327	.375	.263
Venable W *	63	60	51	445	306	96	11	7	13	160	128	45	8	3	0	5	29	7	3	-.030	.076	.245	.324	.408	.270
Eckstein D	53	49	29	492	331	118	23	0	1	144	35	27	0	9	12	4	8	1	6	-.035	.006	.267	.321	.326	.246
Hairston J	52	53	50	476	336	105	13	2	10	152	54	31	2	5	4	6	9	6	5	.045	.013	.244	.299	.353	.243
Denorfia C	45	41	36	317	216	77	15	2	9	123	51	27	3	2	1	3	8	4	5	.026	.014	.271	.335	.433	.283
Torrealba Y	45	31	37	363	254	88	14	0	7	123	67	33	2	3	1	1	7	5	12	.069	-.007	.271	.343	.378	.271
Hairston S	37	34	36	336	237	62	10	0	10	102	69	31	1	6	0	4	6	1	3	.034	.006	.210	.295	.346	.239
Hundley N	37	33	43	307	218	68	18	2	8	114	66	25	0	1	2	6	0	5	8	.097	.058	.249	.308	.418	.265
Tejada M	34	31	32	253	175	63	10	0	8	97	28	15	0	2	1	0	2	0	3	-.091	.170	.268	.317	.413	.268
Gwynn T *	33	30	20	339	237	59	9	3	3	83	50	41	4	1	7	1	17	4	3	.013	-.097	.204	.304	.287	.228
Ludwick R	23	19	26	239	175	44	7	0	6	69	57	24	0	4	0	2	0	1	9	-.012	-.069	.211	.301	.330	.238
Cunningham A	19	17	15	147	100	38	12	1	1	55	28	7	1	3	2	3	1	3	3	-.011	.135	.288	.331	.417	.276
Cabrera E +	17	22	22	241	182	44	6	3	1	59	54	19	3	2	8	0	10	6	8	-.018	.020	.208	.279	.278	.213
Stairs M *	17	14	16	111	77	23	6	0	6	47	32	11	2	0	0	1	2	0	1	-.087	.149	.232	.306	.475	.280
Salazar O	15	19	19	148	106	31	4	0	3	44	23	16	1	0	0	1	1	2	4	.051	-.016	.237	.318	.336	.247
Blanks K	12	14	15	120	87	16	6	1	3	33	46	15	0	3	0	0	1	0	1	.110	.113	.157	.283	.324	.227
Garland J	5	6	2	69	44	12	1	0	0	13	18	6	0	0	6	1	0	0	0	-.067	.116	.214	.286	.232	.203
Durango L +	4	8	4	53	39	12	0	0	0	12	7	4	0	0	1	0	5	0	3	.001	.008	.250	.308	.250	.219
LeBlanc W *	4	2	1	49	31	13	0	0	0	13	12	1	0	0	4	0	0	0	0	.133	.079	.295	.311	.295	.233
Zawadzki L +	3	4	1	42	29	7	2	0	0	9	7	5	2	0	2	0	1	0	1	.079	.116	.200	.300	.257	.217
Stauffer T	2	2	2	21	14	3	2	0	0	5	12	2	0	0	2	0	0	0	0	-.199	.013	.176	.263	.294	.209
Richard C *	1	5	5	72	52	9	2	0	0	11	21	1	0	1	8	1	0	0	0	-.023	.080	.148	.172	.180	.133
Correia K	1	4	5	52	38	6	1	0	0	7	20	2	0	0	6	0	0	0	0	-.189	.043	.136	.174	.159	.129

Only includes batters with at least one Base Run. Italicized stats have been adjusted for home park.

Batted Ball Batting Stats

Player	% of PA		% of Batted Balls					Out %		Runs Per Event				Total Runs vs. Avg.				
	K%	BB%	GB%	LD%	FB%	IF/F	HR/OF	GB	OF	NIP	GB	LD	OF	NIP	GB	LD	FB	Tot
Gonzalez Ad	16	14	39	21	39	.05	.17	78	77	.10	.01	.39	.30	13	-5	9	28	44
Denorfia Ch	16	9	59	17	24	.11	.16	75	86	.05	.05	.44	.25	1	3	2	-1	5
Stairs Ma	29	10	38	18	44	.17	.24	77	84	.00	.03	.37	.37	-1	-1	-1	4	1
Tejada Mi	11	7	50	19	31	.09	.12	82	84	.06	-.00	.42	.19	-0	-3	4	-0	1
Torrealba Yo	18	10	55	20	25	.13	.13	76	78	.05	.03	.34	.22	1	1	0	-2	-0
Cunningham Aa	19	7	46	15	39	.15	.03	71	71	.01	.06	.44	.19	-1	1	-0	0	-1
Venable Wi	29	11	39	17	44	.16	.13	71	79	.01	.07	.39	.26	-3	2	-5	5	-1
Hundley Ni	21	8	41	19	40	.14	.10	74	78	.02	.04	.35	.22	-2	-1	-1	2	-2
Salazar Os	16	11	43	15	42	.15	.08	70	86	.07	.05	.32	.11	1	0	-2	-2	-3
Headley Ch	21	9	46	18	36	.06	.07	73	78	.02	.06	.39	.16	-3	3	0	-3	-3
Blanks Ky	38	15	41	14	45	.24	.16	83	81	.02	.02	.61	.25	-0	-1	-1	-1	-4
Hairston Sc	21	11	34	15	51	.21	.10	69	87	.05	.07	.41	.12	1	1	-3	-5	-6
Ludwick Ry	24	12	35	23	42	.08	.10	76	94	.04	.00	.34	.09	0	-3	0	-5	-8
Hairston Je	11	8	40	16	44	.13	.06	70	85	.07	.08	.25	.10	1	4	-9	-8	-12
Eckstein Da	7	7	48	20	32	.12	.01	76	88	.12	.04	.38	-.00	3	1	6	-22	-13
Gwynn An	15	12	46	19	35	.04	.01	85	88	.10	-.02	.42	.03	5	-6	0	-13	-13
Cabrera Ev	22	9	54	22	23	.15	.03	85	75	.02	-.03	.35	.16	-2	-6	-1	-6	-16
MLB Average	*18*	*9*	*44*	*18*	*38*	*.09*	*.10*	*74*	*83*	*.04*	*.04*	*.38*	*.18*	--	--	--	--	--

Only includes batters with at least one hundred Plate Appearances.

Pitching Stats

Player	PRC	IP	BFP	G	GS	K	BB	IBB	HBP	H	HR	DP	DER	SB	CS	PO	W	L	Sv	Op	Hld	H-A	R^L	RA	ERA	FIP
Latos M	89	184.7	748	31	31	189	50	3	2	150	16	10	.723	7	0	1	14	10	0	0	0	-.004	.015	3.07	2.92	3.07
Richard C *	71	201.7	861	33	33	153	78	6	4	206	16	27	.680	8	7	6	14	9	0	0	0	-.053	-.064	3.97	3.75	3.84
Garland J	71	200.0	837	33	33	136	87	9	6	176	20	28	.724	6	8	1	14	12	0	0	0	-.009	-.010	3.87	3.47	4.40
Stauffer T	53	82.7	326	32	7	61	24	5	2	65	3	11	.729	1	2	0	6	5	0	0	0	.001	.040	1.96	1.85	2.95
LeBlanc W *	48	146.0	625	26	25	110	51	5	2	157	24	12	.687	9	9	8	8	12	0	0	0	-.053	.014	4.25	4.25	4.81
Adams M	48	66.7	268	70	0	73	23	2	0	48	2	3	.718	6	1	0	4	1	0	4	38	-.003	-.009	1.89	1.76	2.34
Bell H	46	70.0	287	67	0	86	28	3	1	56	1	7	.667	3	3	0	6	1	47	50	0	.006	.013	2.19	1.93	2.04
Correia K	36	145.0	641	28	26	115	64	6	5	152	20	12	.691	11	5	0	10	10	0	0	0	.005	.005	5.52	5.40	4.71
Gregerson L	35	78.3	297	80	0	89	18	2	1	47	8	7	.779	7	0	0	4	7	2	7	40	-.055	-.012	3.45	3.22	2.90
Thatcher J *	34	35.0	137	65	0	45	7	2	1	23	1	0	.723	3	0	0	1	0	0	0	11	-.026	.037	1.29	1.29	1.51
Mujica E	28	69.7	268	59	0	72	6	0	0	59	14	6	.739	2	1	1	2	1	0	1	4	-.064	.030	3.75	3.62	4.00
Webb R	26	59.0	253	54	0	44	19	5	1	64	1	10	.654	10	0	0	3	1	0	2	9	-.086	-.091	3.20	2.90	2.69
Frieri E	23	31.7	128	33	0	41	17	3	0	18	2	2	.735	2	1	0	1	1	0	0	7	-.066	-.088	1.99	1.71	2.75
Young C	22	20.0	82	4	4	15	11	0	0	10	1	0	.818	2	0	0	2	0	0	0	0	.057	-.003	0.90	0.90	4.00
Luebke C *	7	17.7	76	4	3	18	6	0	1	17	3	0	.688	0	1	0	1	1	0	0	0	-.159	.041	4.08	4.08	4.55
Gallagher S	6	23.3	110	15	0	21	19	0	2	24	5	3	.698	1	1	1	0	0	0	0	0	-.041	.174	5.40	5.40	6.88
Russell A	5	15.7	63	12	0	18	5	0	0	14	0	3	.650	0	0	0	0	0	0	0	0	.029	.105	4.60	4.02	1.86

Only includes pitchers with at least ten Innings Pitched. Italicized stats have been adjusted for home park.

Batted Ball Pitching Stats

Player	% of PA		% of Batted Balls					Out %		Runs Per Event				Total Runs vs. Avg.				
	K%	BB%	GB%	LD%	FB%	IF/F	HR/OF	GB	OF	NIP	GB	LD	OF	NIP	GB	LD	FB	Tot
Latos Ma	25	7	45	15	40	.11	.09	73	85	-.01	.06	.34	.15	-13	1	-15	-9	-36
Gregerson Lu	30	6	48	15	37	.09	.13	83	87	-.03	-.02	.39	.18	-7	-7	-6	-3	-23
Adams Mi	27	9	41	20	39	.12	.03	74	84	-.00	.05	.27	.07	-4	0	-5	-9	-17
Stauffer Ti	19	8	55	15	31	.06	.04	82	74	.02	-.01	.31	.18	-2	-5	-7	-3	-16
Bell He	30	10	44	18	38	.06	.02	66	86	.00	.09	.46	.02	-3	2	-1	-11	-13
Thatcher Jo	33	6	41	21	38	.00	.03	82	90	-.04	.01	.37	.03	-4	-2	-2	-5	-13
Garland Jo	16	11	52	18	30	.09	.12	80	84	.07	.00	.37	.20	7	-10	-2	-3	-9
Mujica Ed	27	2	45	13	42	.04	.18	75	87	-.08	.03	.36	.28	-10	-2	-6	9	-8
Frieri Er	32	13	25	13	62	.12	.05	76	81	.02	.01	.43	.13	-0	-2	-3	-1	-6
Richard Cl	18	10	46	20	34	.05	.08	72	83	.05	.05	.34	.15	1	3	-1	-7	-3
Webb Ry	17	8	62	21	17	.10	.04	72	63	.03	.05	.34	.19	-1	3	1	-5	-2
Gallagher Se	19	19	35	18	47	.06	.17	78	79	.12	-.00	.36	.31	4	-2	-0	5	7
Correia Ke	18	11	49	21	30	.07	.16	80	77	.06	.01	.34	.30	4	-6	2	11	11
LeBlanc Wa	18	8	35	19	46	.11	.13	75	81	.04	.04	.40	.23	-1	-2	4	15	16
MLB Average	*18*	*9*	*44*	*18*	*38*	*.09*	*.10*	*74*	*83*	*.04*	*.04*	*.38*	*.18*	*--*	*--*	*--*	*--*	*--*

Only includes pitchers who faced at least one hundred batters.

Fielding Stats

Name	INN	SBA/G	CS%	ERA	WP+PB/G	PO	A	TE	FE
Catchers									
Torrealba Y	795.7	0.58	25%	3.14	0.215	681	45	2	1
Hundley N	659.7	0.71	21%	3.72	0.314	632	28	3	1
Stewart C	1.0	0.00	0%	0.00	0.000	1	0	0	0

Name	Inn	PO	A	TE	FE	FPct	DPS	DPT	ZRDif	OOZ	Dif
First Base											
Gonzalez A	1397.0	1324	127	2	6	.995	12	3	.053	36	-10
Salazar O	35.0	33	1	0	0	1.000	0	0	--	0	--
Blanks K	12.3	15	1	0	0	1.000	0	0	--	1	--
Stairs M	8.7	12	1	0	0	1.000	0	0	--	1	--
Venable W	1.0	1	0	0	0	1.000	0	0	--	--	--
Stewart C	1.0	2	0	0	0	1.000	0	0	--	0	--
Baxter M	1.0	1	0	0	0	1.000	0	0	--	--	--
Second Base											
Eckstein D	967.3	191	284	0	0	1.000	31	34	.010	15	-9
Hairston J	381.3	77	112	0	1	.995	10	16	.070	8	-1
Zawadzki L	54.0	9	18	1	1	.931	2	1	--	1	--
Cabrera E	44.0	7	15	0	0	1.000	2	1	--	3	--
Salazar O	9.7	1	4	0	0	1.000	0	0	--	0	--
Shortstop											
Tejada M	496.7	68	162	1	2	.987	20	19	.005	15	-6
Hairston J	489.7	87	162	6	0	.976	7	16	.017	30	9
Cabrera E	456.0	63	137	4	2	.966	15	13	-.025	18	-2
Zawadzki L	14.0	2	5	0	0	1.000	0	0	--	1	--
Third Base											
Headley C	1407.0	82	293	4	9	.966	20	1	.014	67	15
Hairston J	19.3	1	3	0	0	1.000	0	0	--	0	--
Tejada M	15.3	1	3	0	0	1.000	0	0	--	0	--
Zawadzki L	9.0	1	4	0	0	1.000	1	0	--	1	--
Salazar O	5.0	0	1	0	0	1.000	0	0	--	0	--

Name	Inn	PO	A	TE	FE	FPct	DPS	DPT	ZRDif	OOZ	Dif
Left Field											
Hairston S	487.7	94	0	0	3	.969	0	0	-.017	24	0
Blanks K	253.0	45	3	0	0	1.000	0	0	.024	11	-1
Denorfia C	208.3	41	2	0	0	1.000	0	0	.072	8	-2
Venable W	171.7	41	0	0	0	1.000	0	0	.055	16	8
Cunningham	141.7	25	0	0	0	1.000	0	0	.129	7	0
Salazar O	101.0	15	0	0	0	1.000	0	0	.052	3	-2
Stairs M	75.0	13	0	0	0	1.000	0	0	--	2	--
Hairston J	18.0	4	0	0	0	1.000	0	0	--	0	--
Center Field											
Gwynn T	701.3	160	5	0	0	1.000	0	0	-.007	48	8
Denorfia C	360.7	107	5	0	2	.982	2	0	-.017	15	-5
Venable W	164.3	56	0	0	1	.982	0	0	.049	9	-0
Hairston S	140.3	42	3	1	0	.978	1	0	-.031	13	5
Durango L	76.7	17	2	0	1	.950	0	0	--	0	--
Cunningham	13.0	3	0	0	0	1.000	0	0	--	1	--
Right Field											
Venable W	600.3	144	1	1	2	.980	1	0	.017	37	4
Ludwick R	488.0	117	2	1	1	.983	0	0	-.015	27	0
Cunningham	126.0	29	0	0	0	1.000	0	0	-.002	12	5
Denorfia C	116.0	23	1	0	0	1.000	1	0	.103	4	-2
Hairston J	51.0	12	0	0	0	1.000	0	0	--	4	--
Salazar O	43.0	2	0	0	0	1.000	0	0	--	1	--
Hairston S	27.0	5	0	0	0	1.000	0	0	--	2	--
Stairs M	5.0	0	0	0	0	0.000	0	0	--	--	--

San Francisco Giants

Stat Facts:

- Pablo Sandoval led the NL in GDP
- Tim Lincecum allowed 27 SB in 30 attempts
- Jonathan Sanchez's FIP was far higher than his ERA
- Juan Uribe and Edgar Renteria had 1 TE each at SS
- Nate Schierholtz had 7 RF assists in 542 innings
- Aubrey Huff had 6 RF assists in 244 innings
- Aaron Rowand had a .047 ZRDif in 695 CF innings
- Andres Torres had a .054 ZRDif in 656 CF innings
- Buster Posey hit 0 infield pop-ups
- 23% of Ramon Ramirez's FB were infield pop-ups
- 20% of Pat Burrell's FB were HR
- Santiago Casilla induced 11 GDP in 55 IP

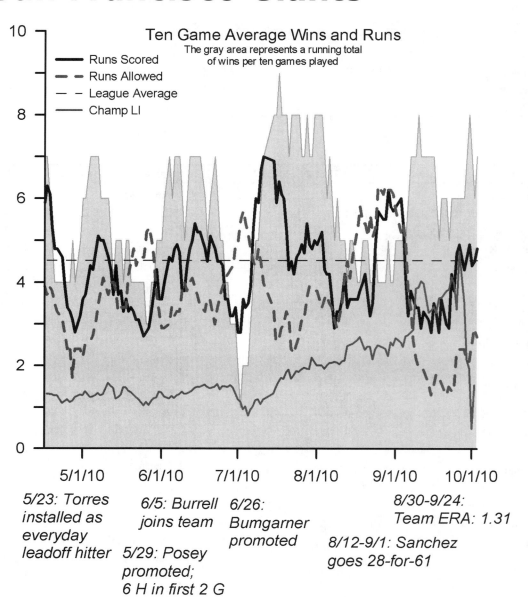

Ten Game Average Wins and Runs
The gray area represents a running total of wins per ten games played

Runs Scored
Runs Allowed
League Average
Champ LI

5/23: Torres installed as everyday leadoff hitter

5/29: Posey promoted; 6 H in first 2 G

6/5: Burrell joins team

6/26: Bumgarner promoted

8/30-9/24: Team ERA: 1.31

8/12-9/1: Sanchez goes 28-for-61

Team Batting and Pitching/Fielding Stats by Month

	April	May	June	July	Aug	Sept/Oct
Wins	13	14	13	20	13	19
Losses	9	14	14	8	15	10
RS/G	4.6	3.9	4.0	5.3	4.4	3.7
RA/G	3.0	3.9	4.0	3.6	4.9	2.1
OBP	.346	.312	.325	.328	.326	.295
SLG	.422	.378	.405	.423	.414	.410
FIP	3.46	3.95	3.99	4.04	4.07	2.91
DER	.737	.712	.681	.687	.668	.751

Batting Stats

Player	BR	Runs	RBI	PA	Outs	H	2B	3B	HR	TB	K	BB	IBB	HBP	SH	SF	SB	CS	GDP	H-A	L^R	BA	OBP	SLG	GPA
Huff A *	111	100	86	668	421	165	35	5	26	288	91	83	5	9	0	7	7	0	17	-.039	.004	.290	.385	.506	.300
Torres A +	87	84	63	570	388	136	43	8	16	243	128	56	2	2	5	0	26	7	10	.028	-.064	.268	.343	.479	.275
Uribe J	70	64	85	575	414	129	24	2	24	229	92	45	6	4	0	5	1	2	20	.042	-.016	.248	.310	.440	.250
Sandoval P +	69	61	63	616	440	151	34	3	13	230	81	47	12	1	0	5	3	2	26	.107	-.058	.268	.323	.409	.248
Posey B	68	58	67	443	296	124	23	2	18	205	55	30	5	4	0	3	0	2	12	-.088	.033	.305	.357	.505	.287
Sanchez F	58	55	47	479	315	126	22	1	7	171	68	32	1	3	8	5	3	1	9	.052	.062	.292	.342	.397	.254
Burrell P	55	41	51	341	219	77	16	0	18	147	77	47	4	0	0	5	0	2	5	.014	-.016	.266	.364	.509	.291
Rowand A	35	42	34	357	269	76	12	2	11	125	74	16	3	8	1	1	5	3	11	.014	.012	.230	.281	.378	.221
Renteria E	30	26	22	267	184	67	11	2	3	91	43	21	3	0	2	1	3	0	8	-.006	.036	.276	.332	.374	.244
Schierholtz	26	34	17	252	180	55	13	3	3	83	38	20	5	3	1	1	4	5	3	-.020	-.010	.242	.311	.366	.232
Molina B	20	17	17	221	157	52	6	0	3	67	19	14	4	3	0	2	0	0	7	.074	.138	.257	.312	.332	.224
Ishikawa T *	20	18	22	173	119	42	11	0	3	62	29	13	2	0	1	1	0	0	3	-.126	.161	.266	.320	.392	.242
Whiteside E	15	19	10	141	102	30	6	1	4	50	35	8	0	3	3	0	1	2	4	.050	-.082	.238	.299	.397	.234
Guillen J	14	9	15	139	102	34	5	0	3	48	29	5	0	5	0	1	0	0	8	.062	-.011	.266	.317	.375	.237
Ross C	12	11	7	82	55	21	4	0	3	34	21	7	0	1	0	1	0	1	2	-.091	.074	.288	.354	.466	.276
Downs M	10	6	7	88	60	19	7	0	1	29	18	8	0	1	0	1	0	0	1	-.048	.020	.244	.318	.372	.237
Bowker J *	8	9	8	90	66	17	3	0	3	29	23	6	1	0	0	2	0	0	1	-.092	.224	.207	.256	.354	.204
Fontenot M *	7	10	5	76	53	20	2	0	0	22	13	5	0	0	0	0	0	2	0	.052	.086	.282	.329	.310	.226
DeRosa M	5	9	10	104	83	18	3	0	1	24	16	9	0	2	0	0	0	2	6	-.045	.139	.194	.279	.258	.190
Velez E +	5	7	8	66	46	9	4	0	2	17	9	6	0	0	5	0	0	0	0	-.075	-.028	.164	.246	.309	.188
Bumgarner M	1	2	3	44	33	7	1	0	0	8	11	2	0	0	3	0	0	0	1	.043	-.039	.179	.220	.205	.150
Rohlinger R	1	1	1	18	13	3	0	0	0	3	5	2	0	0	1	0	0	0	1	-.158	.231	.200	.294	.200	.183
Burriss E +	1	3	0	5	3	2	0	0	0	2	1	0	0	0	0	0	0	0	0	.350	-.350	.400	.400	.400	.281

Only includes batters with at least one Base Run. Italicized stats have been adjusted for home park.

Batted Ball Batting Stats

Player	% of PA		% of Batted Balls					Out %		Runs Per Event				Total Runs vs. Avg.				
	K%	BB%	GB%	LD%	FB%	IF/F	HR/OF	GB	OF	NIP	GB	LD	OF	NIP	GB	LD	FB	Tot
Huff Au	14	14	45	18	37	.14	.17	76	78	.12	.02	.42	.31	15	-4	6	20	37
Posey Bu	12	8	49	18	33	.00	.15	74	76	.06	.04	.30	.31	1	1	-1	19	19
Burrell Pa	23	14	34	17	49	.14	.20	68	86	.06	.09	.43	.28	4	2	0	11	17
Torres An	22	10	39	22	39	.10	.11	71	85	.03	.08	.49	.19	-1	4	12	1	16
Sanchez Fr	14	7	44	22	34	.05	.06	72	85	.04	.05	.40	.10	-1	2	9	-7	3
Sandoval Pa	13	8	44	17	38	.11	.08	77	74	.06	.01	.37	.20	0	-7	1	7	2
Uribe Ju	16	9	40	15	44	.10	.13	72	90	.05	.04	.38	.17	-0	-1	-3	4	-0
Ishikawa Tr	17	8	42	25	32	.02	.07	82	84	.03	-.01	.38	.14	-1	-3	4	-2	-2
Whiteside Du	25	8	46	12	42	.16	.13	71	79	-.00	.05	.44	.24	-2	1	-2	1	-2
Renteria Ed	16	8	48	16	37	.07	.04	68	81	.04	.08	.38	.10	-1	4	-1	-4	-2
Guillen Jo	21	7	56	15	29	.14	.12	70	86	.01	.05	.39	.18	-1	1	-1	-2	-4
Schierholtz Na	15	9	44	18	37	.08	.05	76	85	.06	.04	.37	.09	1	-0	0	-5	-4
DeRosa Ma	15	11	44	19	36	.11	.04	82	79	.07	-.04	.23	.10	1	-3	-2	-2	-6
Molina Be	9	8	38	17	44	.09	.04	83	81	.10	-.02	.35	.09	1	-5	0	-3	-6
Rowand Aa	21	7	48	15	37	.06	.12	74	86	-.00	.04	.36	.19	-4	-1	-5	1	-9
MLB Average	18	9	44	18	38	.09	.10	74	83	.04	.04	.38	.18	--	--	--	--	--

Only includes batters with at least one hundred Plate Appearances.

Pitching Stats

Player	PRC	IP	BFP	G	GS	K	BB	IBB	HBP	H	HR	DP	DER	SB	CS	PO	W	L	Sv	Op	Hld	H-A	R^L	RA	ERA	FIP
Cain M	100	223.3	896	33	33	177	61	4	4	181	22	13	.741	19	10	3	13	11	0	0	0	-.032	-.010	3.39	3.14	3.71
Lincecum T	98	212.3	897	33	33	231	76	7	5	194	18	13	.686	27	3	0	16	10	0	0	0	.010	-.036	3.56	3.43	3.17
Sanchez J *	91	193.3	812	34	33	205	96	4	9	142	21	12	.736	17	9	5	13	9	0	0	1	.004	.004	3.44	3.07	4.05
Zito B *	70	199.3	848	34	33	150	84	7	7	184	20	20	.716	12	9	1	9	14	0	0	0	-.021	-.001	4.38	4.15	4.26
Wilson B	58	74.7	311	70	0	93	26	5	1	62	3	2	.681	0	1	0	3	3	48	53	0	.049	-.012	1.93	1.81	2.11
Bumgarner M	52	111.0	472	18	18	86	26	2	5	119	11	12	.677	8	2	1	7	6	0	0	0	.054	-.022	3.24	3.00	3.72
Romo S	41	62.0	247	68	0	70	14	2	4	46	6	3	.725	0	1	0	5	3	0	4	21	-.089	-.036	2.32	2.18	2.97
Casilla S	36	55.3	225	52	0	56	26	4	4	40	2	11	.715	2	3	0	7	2	2	3	11	-.011	-.041	2.28	1.95	3.05
Ramirez R	27	27.0	106	25	0	15	11	1	0	13	1	1	.810	2	0	0	1	0	1	1	4	-.045	-.032	1.00	0.67	3.68
Affeldt J *	18	50.0	228	53	0	44	24	5	3	56	4	6	.654	2	2	0	4	3	4	7	7	-.025	.014	4.50	4.14	3.80
Mota G	17	54.0	228	56	0	38	22	5	0	49	4	5	.726	7	1	0	1	3	1	3	8	-.050	-.037	4.83	4.33	3.70
Lopez J *	17	19.0	69	27	0	16	2	0	0	11	0	0	.784	0	0	0	2	0	0	0	5	.005	-.107	1.42	1.42	1.83
Runzler D *	16	32.7	144	41	0	37	20	3	1	29	1	4	.659	2	2	1	3	0	0	0	5	-.099	.001	3.31	3.03	2.98
Bautista D	15	33.7	157	31	0	44	27	4	3	25	4	0	.734	5	0	0	2	0	0	1	0	-.078	.003	3.74	3.74	4.44
Wellemeyer T	15	58.7	265	13	11	41	35	1	3	57	12	3	.736	5	1	0	3	5	0	0	0	-.164	-.108	5.68	5.68	6.35
Ray C	9	24.0	101	28	0	15	9	1	0	24	1	2	.697	2	2	0	3	0	1	1	2	.058	-.034	4.13	4.13	3.49
Martinez J	3	11.0	53	4	1	3	6	2	1	15	1	1	.667	3	0	1	0	1	0	0	0	-.106	.185	4.91	4.91	5.20
Medders B	3	15.0	73	14	0	8	6	1	0	26	3	1	.571	1	2	0	0	0	0	0	0	-.081	-.042	7.20	7.20	5.73

Only includes pitchers with at least ten Innings Pitched. Italicized stats have been adjusted for home park.

Batted Ball Pitching Stats

Player	% of PA		% of Batted Balls			IF/F	HR/OF	Out %		Runs Per Event				Total Runs vs. Avg.				
	K%	BB%	GB%	LD%	FB%			GB	OF	NIP	GB	LD	OF	NIP	GB	LD	FB	Tot
Cain Ma	20	7	36	17	47	.16	.09	76	87	.01	.04	.38	.14	-9	-5	-6	-10	-29
Lincecum Ti	26	9	49	20	32	.07	.11	74	85	.01	.06	.38	.17	-9	2	-3	-10	-20
Sanchez Jo	25	13	41	15	44	.13	.11	72	87	.04	.06	.33	.17	4	1	-17	-6	-18
Wilson Br	30	9	49	13	38	.11	.05	71	74	-.01	.07	.33	.19	-5	1	-8	-2	-13
Romo Se	28	7	35	14	51	.15	.09	76	81	-.02	.04	.39	.17	-5	-2	-5	-1	-12
Casilla Ja	25	13	51	21	29	.08	.06	80	88	.05	.00	.41	.06	1	-3	0	-8	-9
Ramirez Ra	14	10	39	11	50	.23	.03	81	93	.08	.01	.33	-.01	1	-1	-3	-5	-9
Zito Ba	18	11	36	19	45	.12	.08	76	85	.06	.03	.41	.14	5	-7	3	-5	-4
Runzler Da	26	15	52	21	27	.09	.05	71	79	.05	.05	.37	.16	1	0	-1	-3	-1
Bautista De	28	19	33	12	55	.21	.12	77	83	.07	.05	.45	.18	4	-0	-3	-1	-1
Mota Gu	17	10	38	17	44	.12	.06	78	84	.05	.01	.46	.15	1	-3	2	-1	-1
Ray Ch	15	9	40	19	40	.10	.04	76	80	.06	.05	.41	.12	0	-1	1	-1	-1
Bumgarner Ma	18	7	45	17	38	.10	.09	69	80	.01	.08	.34	.18	-4	6	-3	2	-0
Affeldt Je	19	12	56	19	26	.21	.13	69	73	.06	.07	.44	.28	2	2	2	-1	5
Wellemeyer To	15	14	34	17	49	.09	.15	77	85	.11	.02	.35	.23	6	-2	-2	7	9
MLB Average	18	9	44	18	38	.09	.10	74	83	.04	.04	.38	.18	--	--	--	--	--

Only includes pitchers who faced at least one hundred batters.

Fielding Stats

Name	INN	SBA/G	CS%	ERA	WP+PB/G	PO	A	TE	FE
Catchers									
Posey B	662.0	0.77	32%	3.18	0.313	615	41	4	2
Molina B	458.3	1.16	20%	3.50	0.609	396	36	1	0
Whiteside E	340.7	1.00	24%	3.54	0.687	334	26	2	0

Name	Inn	PO	A	TE	FE	FPct	DPS	DPT	ZRDif	OOZ	Dif
First Base											
Huff A	821.3	756	54	1	2	.996	2	0	.005	28	1
Ishikawa T	305.7	263	22	0	0	1.000	1	1	-.074	12	2
Posey B	248.0	196	17	0	1	.995	2	0	-.014	4	-4
Sandoval P	86.0	79	0	0	0	1.000	0	0	--	1	--
Second Base											
Sanchez F	943.0	198	256	3	1	.991	20	26	.022	17	-6
Uribe J	174.7	44	54	0	0	1.000	4	7	.051	6	2
Downs M	174.3	30	47	0	1	.987	6	5	.051	4	-0
Fontenot M	97.0	23	32	0	2	.965	3	2	--	2	--
DeRosa M	51.0	13	14	0	2	.931	0	3	--	1	--
Burriss E	12.0	3	1	0	0	1.000	0	0	--	0	--
Velez E	9.0	3	4	0	0	1.000	0	0	--	0	--
Shortstop											
Uribe J	864.0	134	233	1	5	.984	13	21	-.010	30	-7
Renteria E	553.0	80	149	1	3	.983	14	11	.057	8	-16
Fontenot M	29.0	4	7	1	0	.917	0	0	--	1	--
Rohlinger R	15.0	4	3	0	0	1.000	0	1	--	0	--
Third Base											
Sandoval P	1224.0	93	228	8	5	.961	21	0	.011	51	6
Uribe J	192.7	20	46	1	2	.957	2	0	.010	8	1
Fontenot M	26.7	1	5	0	0	1.000	1	0	--	3	--
Rohlinger R	17.0	0	2	0	0	1.000	0	0	--	0	--

Name	Inn	PO	A	TE	FE	FPct	DPS	DPT	ZRDif	OOZ	Dif
Left Field											
Burrell P	632.0	121	4	1	1	.984	0	0	.033	18	-13
Huff A	258.7	72	0	0	0	1.000	0	0	-.037	17	4
DeRosa M	163.3	31	0	0	0	1.000	0	0	.129	7	-1
Torres A	162.7	47	2	0	0	1.000	1	0	.060	20	12
Bowker J	103.3	25	1	0	0	1.000	0	0	.082	5	-0
Ross C	77.3	9	1	0	0	1.000	0	0	--	3	--
Velez E	63.7	16	0	0	1	.941	0	0	--	3	--
Center Field											
Rowand A	695.0	192	4	0	0	1.000	2	0	.047	36	-3
Torres A	655.7	193	1	0	1	.995	1	0	.054	32	-5
Ross C	77.3	15	0	0	0	1.000	0	0	--	3	--
Velez E	31.0	9	0	0	0	1.000	0	0	--	2	--
Ford D	2.0	0	0	0	0	0.000	0	0	--	--	--
Right Field											
Schierholtz N	542.3	118	7	1	0	.992	1	0	.049	31	1
Torres A	302.0	74	4	0	0	1.000	0	0	-.013	28	11
Guillen J	269.3	57	2	0	2	.967	0	0	-.045	11	-4
Huff A	243.7	53	6	0	0	1.000	2	0	-.064	13	-0
Bowker J	59.3	8	0	0	0	1.000	0	0	--	3	--
Ross C	41.3	9	1	0	0	1.000	0	0	--	3	--
Velez E	3.0	0	0	0	0	0.000	0	0	--	--	--

Seattle Mariners

Stat Facts:
- Jose Lopez had the fewest Base Runs of any player with 600+ PA
- Lopez tied for the lowest GPA of any AL regular
- Lopez had the highest ZRDif of any regular 3B
- Chone Figgins led the majors in 2B FE
- Felix Hernandez led the AL in PRC
- Hernandez led the majors in BFP
- Doug Fister allowed 2 SB
- Adam Moore allowed .682 WP+PB/G
- Michael Saunders tied for the ML lead in LF TE
- Josh Wilson led the AL in SS FE
- Franklin Gutierrez made 0 FE and 0 TE
- Ichiro made the most OOZ plays of any RF

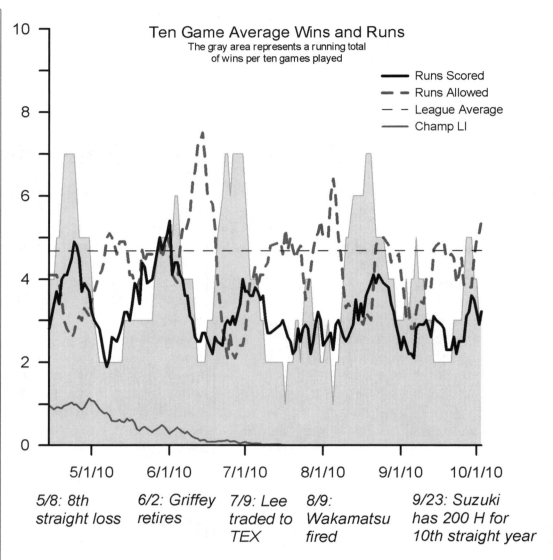

Ten Game Average Wins and Runs
The gray area represents a running total of wins per ten games played

— Runs Scored
- - Runs Allowed
– – League Average
— Champ LI

5/8: 8th straight loss

6/2: Griffey retires

7/9: Lee traded to TEX

8/9: Wakamatsu fired

9/23: Suzuki has 200 H for 10th straight year

Team Batting and Pitching/Fielding Stats by Month

	April	May	June	July	Aug	Sept/Oct
Wins	11	8	14	6	13	9
Losses	12	19	13	22	14	21
RS/G	3.6	3.7	3.2	2.7	3.1	2.8
RA/G	3.5	4.8	4.2	4.9	3.9	4.4
OBP	.312	.313	.304	.283	.295	.284
SLG	.342	.354	.354	.308	.349	.334
FIP	4.19	4.00	4.08	4.61	3.72	4.67
DER	.728	.700	.720	.690	.713	.735

Batting Stats

Player	BR	Runs	RBI	PA	Outs	H	2B	3B	HR	TB	K	BB	IBB	HBP	SH	SF	SB	CS	GDP	H-A	L^R	BA	OBP	SLG	GPA
Suzuki I *	90	74	43	732	478	214	30	3	6	268	86	45	13	3	3	1	42	9	3	-.017	.032	.315	.359	.394	.276
Gutierrez F	64	61	64	629	442	139	25	3	12	206	137	50	5	1	2	8	25	3	10	.022	.017	.245	.303	.363	.241
Figgins C +	63	62	35	702	481	156	21	2	1	184	114	74	0	3	17	6	42	15	20	-.009	.030	.259	.340	.306	.243
Lopez J	48	49	58	622	473	142	29	4	10	201	66	23	1	3	0	3	3	2	20	-.026	.034	.239	.270	.339	.219
Kotchman C *	36	37	51	457	339	90	20	1	9	139	57	35	6	3	0	5	0	0	15	-.016	.060	.217	.280	.336	.223
Saunders M *	34	29	33	327	232	61	11	2	10	106	84	35	0	0	2	1	6	3	1	.023	.032	.211	.295	.367	.238
Branyan R *	33	23	33	238	165	44	10	0	15	99	82	30	2	2	0	1	1	0	4	.018	.093	.215	.319	.483	.280
Wilson J	28	22	25	388	285	82	14	2	2	106	74	14	0	12	0	1	5	0	6	.075	.005	.227	.278	.294	.211
Bradley M +	28	28	29	278	198	50	9	1	8	85	75	28	2	3	1	2	8	2	2	-.050	.033	.205	.292	.348	.232
Wilson J	16	17	14	211	149	48	11	1	0	61	35	7	0	3	5	3	1	2	2	.075	.005	.249	.282	.316	.218
Sweeney M	15	11	18	110	76	26	3	0	6	47	14	9	0	1	0	1	2	0	3	-.021	-.058	.263	.327	.475	.282
Johnson R	15	24	13	209	150	34	10	0	2	50	46	25	2	2	1	3	1	1	5	-.110	.026	.191	.293	.281	.214
Langerhans R	14	16	4	132	87	21	2	1	3	34	51	24	1	0	1	0	4	1	0	.027	.154	.196	.344	.318	.248
Smoak J +	13	11	14	122	89	27	4	0	5	46	34	8	0	0	0	0	0	0	3	-.076	.150	.239	.287	.407	.245
Moore A	12	12	15	218	169	40	6	0	4	58	63	8	1	2	1	2	0	1	3	-.063	.048	.195	.230	.283	.185
Bard J +	11	9	10	126	92	24	7	0	3	40	27	10	0	0	3	1	0	0	4	-.126	.090	.214	.276	.357	.227
Tuiasosopo M	9	12	11	138	108	22	5	0	4	39	49	9	0	1	1	0	0	0	3	-.085	-.025	.173	.234	.307	.193
Griffey Jr.	4	6	7	108	83	18	2	0	0	20	17	9	0	0	0	1	0	0	3	.012	-.037	.184	.250	.204	.173
Carp M *	2	1	0	41	30	7	2	0	0	9	8	4	0	0	0	0	0	0	0	-.155	-.003	.189	.268	.243	.192
Alfonzo E	2	4	4	41	34	9	1	0	1	13	10	0	0	0	0	0	0	0	2	-.023	.000	.220	.220	.317	.189
Mangini M *	1	2	1	41	31	8	0	0	0	8	13	2	0	0	1	0	0	0	1	.054	.116	.211	.250	.211	.175
Byrnes E	1	1	0	38	30	3	2	0	0	5	9	6	0	0	0	0	1	0	1	.029	-.184	.094	.237	.156	.154
Woodward C	1	0	0	22	16	3	1	0	0	4	9	3	0	0	0	0	0	0	0	-.082	.082	.158	.273	.211	.186
Halman G	1	1	3	30	25	4	1	0	0	5	11	1	0	0	0	0	1	0	0	.096	.239	.138	.167	.172	.125

Only includes batters with at least one Base Run. Italicized stats have been adjusted for home park.

Batted Ball Batting Stats

Player	% of PA		% of Batted Balls			IF/F	HR/OF	Out %		Runs Per Event				Total Runs vs. Avg.				
	K%	BB%	GB%	LD%	FB%			GB	OF	NIP	GB	LD	OF	NIP	GB	LD	FB	Tot
Suzuki Ic	12	7	57	17	25	.06	.04	67	78	.05	.09	.39	.11	-1	23	6	-14	14
Branyan Ru	34	13	31	11	58	.10	.23	92	74	.02	-.07	.51	.40	-1	-6	-5	15	4
Sweeney Mi	13	9	40	10	50	.14	.16	71	97	.08	.05	.59	.16	1	0	-0	1	2
Langerhans Ry	39	18	38	20	43	.04	.13	67	95	.03	.10	.57	.14	1	1	0	-1	0
Smoak Ju	28	7	35	21	44	.20	.18	82	91	-.03	-.02	.49	.21	-3	-2	2	0	-3
Bard Jo	21	8	38	16	46	.10	.09	91	75	.01	-.07	.45	.19	-1	-5	-0	1	-5
Bradley Mi	27	11	37	18	45	.15	.11	77	88	.02	.03	.41	.16	-1	-1	-2	-3	-7
Wilson Ja	17	5	40	20	40	.23	.00	70	87	-.01	.08	.44	-.01	-3	3	3	-11	-8
Saunders Mi	26	11	36	16	48	.19	.13	80	82	.02	.02	.35	.23	-1	-2	-6	1	-8
Tuiasosopo Ma	36	7	44	19	37	.03	.14	79	79	-.04	0.00	.29	.26	-4	-2	-3	1	-8
Griffey Jr. Ke	16	8	34	15	51	.17	.00	71	97	.05	.03	.41	-.07	-0	-1	-1	-8	-10
Johnson Ro	22	13	52	12	36	.15	.03	80	85	.06	.01	.46	.07	2	-2	-4	-7	-10
Gutierrez Fr	22	8	42	16	42	.12	.07	68	85	.01	.07	.40	.13	-5	5	-4	-8	-12
Moore Ad	29	5	57	15	28	.05	.11	80	79	-.05	.01	.32	.23	-6	-2	-5	-2	-16
Figgins Ch	16	11	47	21	32	.05	.01	70	88	.07	.07	.34	-0.00	6	6	-0	-29	-18
Kotchman Ca	12	8	55	17	27	.07	.10	83	79	.07	-.01	.23	.20	1	-7	-10	-3	-19
Wilson Jo	19	7	35	20	45	.12	.02	75	86	.01	.04	.38	.03	-4	-2	2	-15	-19
Lopez Jo	11	4	43	18	38	.09	.05	82	86	.02	-.01	.36	.08	-6	-12	2	-13	-29
MLB Average	18	9	44	18	38	.09	.10	74	83	.04	.04	.38	.18	--	--	--	--	--

Only includes batters with at least one hundred Plate Appearances.

Pitching Stats

Player	PRC	IP	BFP	G	GS	K	BB	IBB	HBP	H	HR	DP	DER	SB	CS	PO	W	L	Sv	Op	Hld	H-A	R^L	RA	ERA	FIP
Hernandez F	133	249.7	1001	34	34	232	70	1	8	194	17	28	.724	15	5	0	13	12	0	0	0	-.031	-.011	2.88	2.27	3.06
Vargas J *	69	192.7	811	31	31	116	54	3	1	187	18	13	.711	9	1	1	9	12	0	0	0	-.027	-.062	4.02	3.78	3.93
Lee C *	57	103.7	408	13	13	89	6	0	0	92	5	7	.705	1	2	0	8	3	0	0	0	.008	.058	2.69	2.34	2.20
Fister D	54	171.0	720	28	28	93	32	2	6	187	13	18	.684	2	3	2	6	14	0	0	0	-.036	-.006	4.47	4.11	3.64
Pauley D	29	90.7	390	19	15	51	30	2	4	89	13	8	.726	8	0	0	4	9	0	0	0	-.027	.029	4.37	4.07	4.91
League B	27	79.0	326	70	0	56	27	6	2	67	7	13	.731	5	5	0	9	7	6	12	13	-.036	-.052	4.33	3.42	3.72
French L *	24	87.7	371	16	13	37	29	2	4	88	13	8	.733	2	3	3	5	7	0	0	0	-.040	.025	4.83	4.83	5.26
Aardsma D	23	49.7	202	53	0	49	25	5	2	33	5	5	.769	2	1	0	0	6	31	36	0	-.109	-.053	3.44	3.44	3.78
Rowland-Smit	17	109.3	510	27	20	49	44	2	7	141	25	13	.683	11	4	2	1	10	0	0	0	-.094	.005	7.74	6.75	6.53
Wright J	14	37.0	151	28	0	19	16	1	1	30	2	7	.752	8	0	1	0	1	0	1	8	.060	.089	3.65	3.41	4.08
Sweeney B	12	37.0	148	24	0	14	6	1	0	33	5	1	.764	1	1	0	1	2	0	1	1	.031	-.079	3.89	3.16	4.52
Olson G *	12	37.7	172	35	0	31	15	1	0	42	6	1	.675	2	0	0	0	3	1	1	1	-.013	-.036	4.78	4.54	4.65
Kelley S	10	25.0	112	22	0	26	12	2	1	26	5	2	.691	0	0	0	3	1	0	0	3	.037	.060	3.96	3.96	4.95
White S	9	34.3	150	38	0	15	11	4	0	45	4	8	.650	0	0	0	0	1	0	3	5	-.029	-.054	5.24	5.24	4.36
Snell I	9	46.3	227	12	8	26	25	0	1	60	10	1	.685	2	1	0	0	5	0	0	0	-.069	-.033	6.99	6.41	6.48
Seddon C *	6	22.3	95	14	0	16	10	0	0	21	4	3	.738	0	0	0	1	0	0	0	0	-.234	.019	5.64	5.64	5.35
Colome J	5	17.0	77	12	0	16	11	0	1	15	1	1	.708	2	0	0	0	1	0	0	0	.004	-.110	5.29	5.29	4.11
Texeira K	5	18.7	87	16	0	14	10	0	1	22	0	3	.645	1	0	0	0	1	0	0	1	-.098	.012	5.79	5.30	3.38
Lowe M	4	10.3	45	11	0	7	5	1	0	11	1	2	.688	0	0	0	1	3	0	0	4	.013	-.090	4.35	3.48	4.18

Only includes pitchers with at least ten Innings Pitched. Italicized stats have been adjusted for home park.

Batted Ball Pitching Stats

Player	% of PA		% of Batted Balls					Out %		Runs Per Event				Total Runs vs. Avg.				
	K%	BB%	GB%	LD%	FB%	IF/F	HR/OF	GB	OF	NIP	GB	LD	OF	NIP	GB	LD	FB	Tot
Hernandez Fe	23	8	54	16	30	.09	.08	77	84	.00	.02	.36	.14	-11	-5	-14	-19	-49
Lee Cl	22	1	42	17	41	.09	.04	69	85	-.08	.08	.34	.08	-13	5	-4	-11	-23
League Br	17	9	63	16	21	.04	.15	80	80	.04	-.01	.38	.25	-0	-7	-2	-2	-11
Aardsma Da	24	13	36	19	45	.08	.10	83	91	.05	-.02	.31	.12	1	-4	-3	-2	-8
Fister Do	13	5	47	18	35	.09	.07	72	86	.02	.06	.39	.10	-6	7	6	-13	-6
Vargas Ja	14	7	36	17	47	.14	.07	73	85	.03	.06	.40	.12	-4	4	1	-6	-5
Wright Ja	13	11	62	15	23	.15	.09	81	80	.10	-.03	.40	.20	2	-4	-1	-2	-5
Sweeney Br	9	4	37	16	47	.07	.09	72	92	.02	.07	.30	.08	-1	1	-2	-2	-5
Pauley Da	13	9	50	19	31	.05	.12	76	92	.07	.03	.34	.15	2	1	-0	-3	-1
Kelley Sh	23	12	23	16	61	.09	.13	75	82	.04	.05	.55	.20	0	-0	1	3	4
Olson Ga	18	9	37	22	41	.10	.13	72	88	.04	.06	.40	.19	-0	1	3	2	5
French Lu	10	9	32	16	51	.13	.09	68	88	.10	.08	.37	.13	3	4	-0	-0	6
White Se	10	7	45	23	32	.05	.11	72	82	.08	.04	.39	.20	1	1	4	2	7
Snell Ia	11	11	34	24	43	.11	.16	74	87	.12	.06	.37	.25	4	1	5	7	17
Rowland-Smith Ry	10	10	37	19	44	.06	.14	72	85	.12	.05	.48	.22	7	2	13	16	38
MLB Average	*18*	*9*	*44*	*18*	*38*	*.09*	*.10*	*74*	*83*	*.04*	*.04*	*.38*	*.18*	*--*	*--*	*--*	*--*	*--*

Only includes pitchers who faced at least one hundred batters.

Fielding Stats

Name	INN	SBA/G	CS%	ERA	WP+PB/G	PO	A	TE	FE
Catchers									
Moore A	514.7	0.73	17%	3.64	0.682	372	24	1	2
Johnson R	510.7	0.60	35%	4.00	0.564	347	35	4	0
Bard J	304.0	0.44	20%	4.29	0.385	202	12	0	2
Alfonzo E	91.0	0.30	33%	4.65	0.198	54	2	0	2
Quiroz G	17.7	1.53	33%	2.04	1.528	8	1	1	0

Name	Inn	PO	A	TE	FE	FPct	DPS	DPT	ZRDif	OOZ	Dif
First Base											
Kotchman C	966.7	946	74	0	1	.999	4	1	.019	27	-5
Smoak J	216.7	233	15	0	1	.996	0	0	-.044	9	2
Tuiasosopo M	66.7	65	2	0	1	.985	0	0	--	1	--
Carp M	66.0	65	4	0	0	1.000	1	0	--	2	--
Langerhans R	34.0	28	2	0	0	1.000	0	0	--	3	--
Branyan R	33.0	32	1	0	0	1.000	0	0	--	0	--
Wilson J	30.0	30	2	1	0	.970	0	0	--	1	--
Sweeney M	25.0	28	1	0	0	1.000	0	1	--	1	--
Second Base											
Figgins C	1417.0	274	414	1	18	.973	47	58	-.007	27	-8
Wilson J	13.0	6	5	0	0	1.000	1	2	--	0	--
Tuiasosopo M	8.0	0	1	0	1	.500	0	0	--	0	--
Shortstop											
Wilson J	839.0	124	304	7	13	.955	28	24	.006	31	-5
Wilson J	518.3	88	191	3	5	.972	16	17	.027	32	10
Woodward C	52.7	5	10	1	0	.938	1	0	--	0	--
Tuiasosopo M	28.0	6	11	1	1	.895	0	1	--	2	--
Third Base											
Lopez J	1252.0	107	322	10	8	.960	27	1	.055	56	10
Tuiasosopo M	91.7	8	24	1	1	.941	0	0	--	5	--
Mangini M	62.7	4	14	0	0	1.000	3	0	--	3	--
Wilson J	31.0	2	8	0	1	.909	1	0	--	1	--

Name	Inn	PO	A	TE	FE	FPct	DPS	DPT	ZRDif	OOZ	Dif
Left Field											
Saunders M	647.7	165	8	3	1	.977	4	0	-.015	40	8
Bradley M	323.3	87	3	0	1	.989	0	0	.049	18	2
Langerhans R	227.0	56	4	0	1	.984	0	0	.069	9	-2
Tuiasosopo M	122.0	21	1	0	1	.957	0	0	-.132	4	-2
Byrnes E	83.0	28	0	0	0	1.000	0	0	--	7	--
Halman G	31.0	7	0	0	0	1.000	0	0	--	2	--
Carp M	4.0	0	0	0	0	0.000	0	0	--	0	--
Center Field											
Gutierrez F	1277.0	413	2	0	0	1.000	0	0	.018	66	-6
Saunders M	108.0	32	0	0	0	1.000	0	0	.054	5	-1
Halman G	34.7	13	0	0	0	1.000	0	0	--	4	--
Langerhans R	16.0	5	1	0	0	1.000	0	0	--	0	--
Byrnes E	2.0	0	0	0	0	0.000	0	0	--	--	--
Right Field											
Suzuki I	1412.0	354	7	2	2	.989	1	0	.028	95	17
Langerhans R	18.0	6	0	0	0	1.000	0	0	--	2	--
Bradley M	7.0	1	0	0	1	.500	0	0	--	0	--
Halman G	1.0	0	0	0	0	0.000	0	0	--	--	--

St. Louis Cardinals

Stat Facts:

- Albert Pujols led the majors (yet again) in Base Runs, GPA, and IBB
- Pujols started the most DP of any 1B
- Colby Rasmus had the lowest H-A of any NL regular
- Rasmus had 1 assist
- Chris Carpenter allowed 3 SB in 12 attempts
- Kyle Lohse's FIP was far lower than his ERA
- Yadier Molina caught the most innings in the majors
- Molina had the lowest SBA/G of any regular C
- Molina had the highest CS% of any regular C
- Matt Holliday had the most innings of any LF with 0 TE
- Skip Schumaker led the NL in 2B FE
- Brendan Ryan had the highest ZRDif of any regular SS

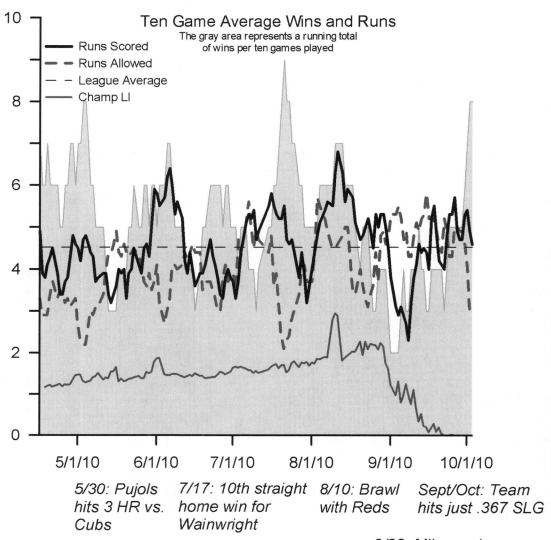

Ten Game Average Wins and Runs

The gray area represents a running total of wins per ten games played

- Runs Scored
- Runs Allowed
- League Average
- Champ LI

5/30: Pujols hits 3 HR vs. Cubs

7/17: 10th straight home win for Wainwright

7/31: Ludwick/ Westbrook trade

8/10: Brawl with Reds

Sept/Oct: Team hits just .367 SLG

9/28: Miles makes 2nd relief appearance

Team Batting and Pitching/Fielding Stats by Month

	April	May	June	July	Aug	Sept/Oct
Wins	15	15	13	15	11	17
Losses	8	14	13	11	15	15
RS/G	4.6	4.4	4.2	4.7	5.0	4.5
RA/G	3.2	3.8	4.0	3.8	4.7	4.3
OBP	.335	.342	.323	.339	.327	.324
SLG	.421	.398	.414	.418	.403	.367
FIP	3.47	3.76	4.32	4.26	3.76	3.83
DER	.726	.703	.698	.695	.693	.695

Batting Stats

Player	BR	Runs	RBI	PA	Outs	H	2B	3B	HR	TB	K	BB	IBB	HBP	SH	SF	SB	CS	GDP	H-A	L^R	BA	OBP	SLG	GPA
Pujols A	130	115	118	700	431	183	39	1	42	350	76	103	38	4	0	6	14	4	23	.020	.016	.312	.414	.596	.346
Holliday M	116	95	103	675	428	186	45	1	28	317	93	69	10	8	0	2	9	5	13	.015	.032	.312	.390	.532	.318
Rasmus C *	83	85	66	534	349	128	28	3	23	231	148	63	9	1	2	4	12	8	5	-.053	.019	.276	.361	.498	.296
Schumaker S	54	66	42	529	360	126	18	1	5	161	64	43	2	4	2	4	5	3	7	-.019	.046	.265	.328	.338	.240
Molina Y	50	34	62	521	366	122	19	0	6	159	51	42	6	7	2	5	8	4	19	-.033	-.050	.262	.329	.342	.241
Ludwick R	46	44	43	314	209	79	20	2	11	136	64	24	0	4	0	3	0	3	4	.069	-.054	.281	.343	.484	.284
Lopez F +	43	50	36	425	298	87	18	1	7	128	77	43	1	1	3	2	8	2	7	.053	.028	.231	.310	.340	.232
Jay J *	42	47	27	323	210	86	19	2	4	121	50	24	0	3	8	1	2	4	5	.042	.005	.300	.359	.422	.275
Ryan B	36	50	36	486	351	98	19	3	2	129	60	33	5	2	9	3	11	4	6	.040	-.000	.223	.279	.294	.205
Freese D	34	28	36	270	177	71	12	1	4	97	59	21	0	4	4	1	1	1	7	.119	.053	.296	.361	.404	.272
Winn R +	18	16	17	162	112	36	8	1	3	55	22	13	1	1	1	3	5	0	4	.056	-.053	.250	.311	.382	.243
Craig A	14	12	18	124	88	28	7	0	4	47	26	9	1	0	0	1	0	1	1	-.010	-.024	.246	.298	.412	.245
Miles A +	13	14	9	151	102	39	5	0	0	44	14	6	1	1	3	2	0	1	1	-.079	-.003	.281	.311	.317	.226
Greene T	12	14	10	122	82	23	3	1	2	34	24	13	4	4	0	1	2	0	1	.053	.018	.221	.328	.327	.237
Stavinoha N	10	11	9	126	95	31	4	0	2	41	28	4	0	1	0	0	0	0	5	.035	-.004	.256	.286	.339	.220
Pagnozzi M	7	4	10	44	26	14	2	0	1	19	8	2	0	1	2	0	0	0	1	.159	-.048	.359	.405	.487	.314
Feliz P	5	14	9	125	99	25	0	1	1	30	10	4	0	0	0	1	0	0	4	.032	-.018	.208	.232	.250	.172
LaRue J	5	3	5	63	48	11	1	0	2	18	7	5	0	1	1	0	0	0	3	.107	.105	.196	.274	.321	.210
Descalso D *	4	6	4	37	25	9	2	0	0	11	6	2	0	1	0	0	1	0	0	-.216	-.136	.265	.324	.324	.234
Wainwright A	4	4	6	96	72	14	5	0	0	19	23	7	0	0	5	0	0	0	2	.126	.070	.167	.231	.226	.166
Anderson B *	4	1	4	35	23	9	2	0	0	11	7	1	0	1	0	1	0	0	0	.047	-.195	.281	.314	.344	.235
Mather J	3	7	3	64	50	13	4	0	0	17	11	2	0	0	2	0	1	1	2	-.028	-.017	.217	.242	.283	.186
Garcia J *	2	8	2	60	45	10	1	0	0	11	13	2	0	0	4	0	0	0	1	.100	.045	.185	.214	.204	.152
Suppan J	1	1	1	23	17	4	1	0	0	5	5	1	0	0	1	0	0	0	0	.050	.037	.190	.227	.238	.167
Lohse K	1	2	3	37	29	6	2	0	0	8	8	0	0	0	2	0	0	0	0	-.023	-.162	.171	.171	.229	.139
Penny B	1	1	4	20	17	3	0	0	1	6	6	0	0	0	1	0	0	0	1	.205	-.158	.158	.158	.316	.155

Only includes batters with at least one Base Run. Italicized stats have been adjusted for home park.

Batted Ball Batting Stats

Player	% of PA		% of Batted Balls			IF/F	HR/OF	Out %		Runs Per Event				Total Runs vs. Avg.				
	K%	BB%	GB%	LD%	FB%			GB	OF	NIP	GB	LD	OF	NIP	GB	LD	FB	Tot
Pujols Al	11	15	38	17	44	.13	.21	71	88	.15	.05	.42	.30	21	2	7	32	63
Holliday Ma	14	11	42	17	41	.11	.15	68	79	.09	.08	.39	.28	9	8	3	24	45
Rasmus Co	28	12	32	19	49	.05	.16	62	80	.03	.14	.40	.27	-0	6	0	18	24
Ludwick Ry	20	9	30	22	48	.09	.10	59	84	.03	.13	.36	.18	-1	4	3	4	10
Jay Jo	15	8	49	19	32	.05	.06	66	78	.05	.10	.37	.15	0	8	1	-3	7
Freese Da	22	9	49	22	29	.02	.08	71	75	.02	.06	.37	.21	-1	1	2	0	2
Craig Al	21	7	38	22	39	.03	.12	82	77	.00	.02	.28	.23	-1	-1	-1	2	-1
Greene Ty	20	14	41	19	41	.06	.07	75	93	.08	.05	.39	.05	2	1	-0	-4	-1
Winn Ra	14	9	48	19	33	.02	.08	87	86	.07	-.04	.47	.12	0	-5	3	-2	-3
Miles Aa	9	5	54	13	34	.09	.00	69	79	.04	.09	.34	.04	-1	4	-2	-5	-4
Stavinoha Ni	22	4	48	20	33	.10	.07	68	88	-.04	.07	.35	.11	-3	1	-0	-3	-5
Schumaker Ja	12	9	59	22	20	.01	.06	77	85	.08	.03	.32	.11	3	0	3	-13	-7
Molina Ya	10	9	51	21	28	.04	.05	79	87	.11	.01	.35	.07	5	-5	5	-13	-8
Lopez Fe	18	10	48	18	34	.06	.07	75	85	.05	.04	.36	.12	2	-1	-2	-6	-8
Feliz Pe	8	3	49	13	39	.14	.03	69	94	.02	.07	.19	-.03	-1	2	-4	-7	-11
Ryan Br	12	7	47	18	35	.12	.02	73	92	.06	.06	.33	-.02	-1	3	-3	-25	-25
MLB Average	18	9	44	18	38	.09	.10	74	83	.04	.04	.38	.18	--	--	--	--	--

Only includes batters with at least one hundred Plate Appearances.

Pitching Stats

Player	PRC	IP	BFP	G	GS	K	BB	IBB	HBP	H	HR	DP	DER	SB	CS	PO	W	L	Sv	Op	Hld	H-A	R^L	RA	ERA	FIP
Wainwright A	128	230.3	910	33	33	213	56	2	4	186	15	27	.715	8	5	1	20	11	0	0	0	-.028	.010	2.66	2.42	2.95
Carpenter C	92	235.0	969	35	35	179	63	4	13	214	21	31	.706	3	9	0	16	9	0	0	0	-.045	.010	3.79	3.22	3.75
Garcia J *	69	163.3	695	28	28	132	64	4	3	151	9	21	.698	6	3	2	13	8	0	0	0	-.042	-.036	3.53	2.70	3.45
McClellan K	44	75.3	307	68	0	60	23	3	3	58	9	1	.755	8	2	1	1	4	2	3	19	-.122	.009	2.39	2.27	4.07
Motte J	34	52.3	208	56	0	54	18	3	0	41	5	5	.725	3	1	1	4	2	2	3	12	-.033	-.096	2.24	2.24	3.23
Westbrook J	30	75.0	317	12	12	55	24	0	2	70	5	9	.701	4	1	0	4	4	0	0	0	-.066	-.061	3.72	3.48	3.64
Franklin R	27	65.0	264	59	0	42	10	1	4	57	7	5	.736	2	1	0	6	2	27	29	0	-.059	-.045	3.46	3.46	3.90
Boggs M	26	67.3	285	61	0	52	27	2	4	60	5	10	.706	2	2	0	2	3	0	0	6	.036	-.035	3.88	3.61	3.91
Suppan J	23	70.3	304	15	13	33	25	0	1	80	9	9	.695	3	2	1	3	6	0	0	0	-.072	.053	4.09	3.84	5.03
Hawksworth	23	90.3	409	45	8	61	35	0	2	113	15	11	.662	4	2	1	4	8	0	0	4	.023	-.020	5.58	4.98	5.23
Penny B	20	55.7	232	9	9	35	9	1	3	63	4	10	.663	1	1	0	3	4	0	0	0	-.016	-.089	4.04	3.23	3.47
Lohse K	16	92.0	431	18	18	54	35	4	3	129	9	11	.627	1	3	1	4	8	0	0	0	-.074	-.039	7.34	6.55	4.47
Reyes D *	15	38.0	163	59	0	25	21	3	2	34	2	7	.699	1	1	2	3	1	1	4	6	.080	.120	3.55	3.55	4.14
Salas F	13	30.7	133	27	0	29	15	2	0	28	4	2	.706	2	0	0	0	0	0	1	1	.102	-.057	3.82	3.52	4.27
Miller T *	12	36.0	151	57	0	22	19	0	2	30	2	3	.734	1	3	0	0	1	0	1	11	-.059	-.065	4.25	4.00	4.20
Walters P	7	30.0	129	7	3	22	10	0	0	32	5	4	.696	1	0	0	2	0	0	0	0	-.012	-.029	6.00	6.00	4.90
MacDougal M	3	18.7	92	17	0	14	12	2	1	23	1	1	.641	1	0	0	1	1	0	1	0	.078	-.264	7.23	7.23	4.16
Ottavino A	3	22.3	110	5	3	12	9	1	0	37	5	4	.607	2	1	0	0	2	0	0	0	-.005	-.072	8.46	8.46	6.11

Only includes pitchers with at least ten Innings Pitched. Italicized stats have been adjusted for home park.

Batted Ball Pitching Stats

Player	% of PA		% of Batted Balls					Out %		Runs Per Event				Total Runs vs. Avg.				
	K%	BB%	GB%	LD%	FB%	IF/F	HR/OF	GB	OF	NIP	GB	LD	OF	NIP	GB	LD	FB	Tot
Wainwright Ad	23	7	52	18	31	.07	.08	79	82	-.01	.01	.40	.16	-15	-12	-5	-13	-45
Garcia Ja	19	10	56	19	26	.04	.08	75	80	.04	.02	.34	.15	0	-3	-4	-10	-17
Carpenter Ch	18	8	51	17	32	.07	.10	74	83	.02	.04	.38	.17	-5	1	-5	-7	-16
McClellan Ky	20	8	51	13	36	.05	.12	72	92	.03	.06	.30	.15	-2	2	-8	-3	-11
Motte Ja	26	9	39	13	47	.06	.08	75	83	.00	.02	.39	.14	-2	-2	-4	-1	-9
Westbrook Ja	17	8	62	15	23	.08	.10	75	84	.03	.04	.39	.17	-1	1	-2	-5	-7
Franklin Ry	16	5	45	17	39	.10	.10	82	83	.00	-.00	.40	.18	-3	-4	-1	1	-7
Miller Tr	15	12	41	21	37	.23	.06	77	90	.09	.03	.30	.09	2	-1	-1	-4	-4
Boggs Mi	18	11	53	16	31	.05	.09	72	83	.06	.05	.34	.17	2	0	-3	-2	-3
Reyes De	15	14	50	25	25	.00	.07	81	85	.11	-.01	.34	.12	3	-3	2	-3	-1
Penny Br	15	5	53	18	29	.08	.08	73	82	.00	.05	.42	.15	-2	2	2	-2	-1
Walters Ph	17	8	43	15	42	.10	.14	68	87	.03	.06	.43	.19	-1	1	-0	1	1
Salas No	22	11	33	18	48	.14	.11	76	84	.04	.03	.42	.19	0	-0	0	1	1
Suppan Je	11	9	42	19	39	.08	.10	76	84	.09	.04	.37	.17	2	0	3	2	7
Ottavino Ad	11	8	36	32	32	.04	.15	69	83	.08	.04	.49	.24	1	-0	9	3	12
Hawksworth Bl	15	9	51	17	31	.06	.17	66	85	.06	.09	.32	.25	2	10	-2	6	16
Lohse Ky	13	9	43	19	38	.09	.08	70	75	.08	.06	.49	.21	3	4	11	7	25
MLB Average	*18*	*9*	*44*	*18*	*38*	*.09*	*.10*	*74*	*83*	*.04*	*.04*	*.38*	*.18*	--	--	--	--	--

Only includes pitchers who faced at least one hundred batters.

Fielding Stats

Name	INN	SBA/G	CS%	ERA	WP+PB/G	PO	A	TE	FE
Catchers									
Molina Y	1138.0	0.50	44%	3.23	0.269	895	79	4	1
LaRue J	150.3	0.30	40%	5.45	0.479	96	6	0	0
Pagnozzi M	106.0	0.85	0%	3.06	0.594	77	4	1	0
Anderson B	55.0	0.82	0%	6.38	0.491	40	4	1	0
Hill S	4.0	0.00	0%	2.25	0.000	2	0	0	0
Stavinoha N	0.3	0.00	0%	27.00	0.000	1	0	0	0

Name	Inn	PO	A	TE	FE	FPct	DPS	DPT	ZRDif	OOZ	Dif
First Base											
Pujols A	1380.0	1458	157	3	1	.998	20	2	-.016	60	15
Hamilton M	21.0	23	1	0	0	1.000	0	0	--	2	--
Craig A	17.0	16	1	0	0	1.000	1	0	--	0	--
Mather J	11.0	14	0	0	0	1.000	0	0	--	0	--
Lopez F	10.0	11	0	0	0	1.000	0	0	--	--	--
Molina Y	7.0	7	0	0	0	1.000	0	0	--	--	--
Stavinoha N	3.0	3	1	0	0	1.000	0	0	--	0	--
Freese D	3.0	3	0	0	0	1.000	0	0	--	0	--
LaRue J	1.0	1	0	0	0	1.000	0	0	--	--	--
Second Base											
Schumaker S	1014.0	210	359	1	15	.973	23	50	-.052	33	8
Miles A	214.7	38	83	0	2	.984	6	6	.010	5	-0
Lopez F	147.7	35	51	0	0	1.000	3	11	-.005	0	-4
Greene T	76.0	7	22	0	2	.935	5	1	--	2	--
Craig A	1.0	0	0	0	0	.000	0	0	--	--	--
Shortstop											
Ryan B	1127.0	197	430	9	8	.974	43	45	.045	69	20
Lopez F	161.0	20	43	1	1	.969	0	4	-.010	6	-1
Greene T	145.3	22	49	4	1	.934	5	7	-.076	8	2
Miles A	19.0	9	5	0	0	1.000	1	2	--	0	--
Descalso D	1.0	0	1	0	0	1.000	0	0	--	0	--
Third Base											
Freese D	557.0	31	139	2	7	.950	20	1	-.019	18	-3
Lopez F	472.7	24	102	4	5	.926	8	0	-.026	9	-8
Feliz P	275.0	18	70	0	2	.978	4	0	.025	13	3
Descalso D	73.0	2	15	0	0	1.000	4	0	--	3	--
Greene T	40.0	1	12	0	1	.929	0	0	--	3	--
Miles A	25.0	3	4	2	0	.778	0	0	--	0	--
Craig A	10.0	0	0	0	1	.000	0	0	--	0	--
Mather J	1.0	1	0	0	0	1.000	0	0	--	--	--

Name	Inn	PO	A	TE	FE	FPct	DPS	DPT	ZRDif	OOZ	Dif
Left Field											
Holliday M	1341.0	261	8	0	3	.989	0	0	.016	65	-1
Craig A	28.0	7	0	0	0	1.000	0	0	--	1	--
Jay J	25.0	4	0	0	0	1.000	0	0	--	1	--
Winn R	20.0	4	0	0	0	1.000	0	0	--	1	--
Stavinoha N	13.0	1	0	0	0	1.000	0	0	--	1	--
Mather J	12.0	1	0	0	0	1.000	0	0	--	0	--
Schumaker S	6.0	2	0	0	0	1.000	0	0	--	0	--
Ludwick R	5.0	2	0	0	0	1.000	0	0	--	--	--
Lohse K	3.0	2	0	0	0	1.000	0	0	--	--	--
Center Field											
Rasmus C	1105.0	260	1	2	3	.981	0	0	-.005	50	-13
Jay J	195.0	63	2	0	0	1.000	0	0	-.035	14	3
Mather J	72.3	13	0	0	0	1.000	0	0	--	2	--
Winn R	56.0	12	0	0	0	1.000	0	0	--	3	--
Ludwick R	24.0	9	0	0	0	1.000	0	0	--	2	--
Schumaker S	1.0	0	0	0	0	.000	0	0	--	--	--
Right Field											
Ludwick R	562.0	132	2	0	0	1.000	0	0	.043	38	7
Jay J	381.7	70	3	0	1	.986	1	0	.001	17	-4
Craig A	175.7	32	1	0	0	1.000	0	0	.068	4	-6
Winn R	162.3	42	0	0	1	.977	0	0	-.002	8	-1
Stavinoha N	116.7	25	1	0	0	1.000	0	0	-.124	9	3
Schumaker S	39.0	16	4	0	0	1.000	1	0	--	3	--
Mather J	16.0	2	0	0	0	1.000	0	0	--	1	--
Lopez F	0.3	0	0	0	0	.000	0	0	--	--	--

Tampa Bay Rays

Stat Facts:

- Ben Zobrist tied for the major league lead in Sac Flies
- Carl Crawford and Carlos Peña tied for the fewest GDP of any regular
- Crawford had the most innings of any LF with 0 FE
- 24% of Peña's FB were HR
- Randy Choate led the AL in appearances
- James Shields led the AL in HRA
- Shields had the lowest DER of any AL starter
- Shields's FIP was far lower than his ERA
- Jeff Niemann allowed 21 SB in 23 attempts
- Evan Longoria started the most DP of any 3B, by far
- Kelly Shoppach struck out in 38% of his PA
- 86% of Joaquin Benoit's GB were outs

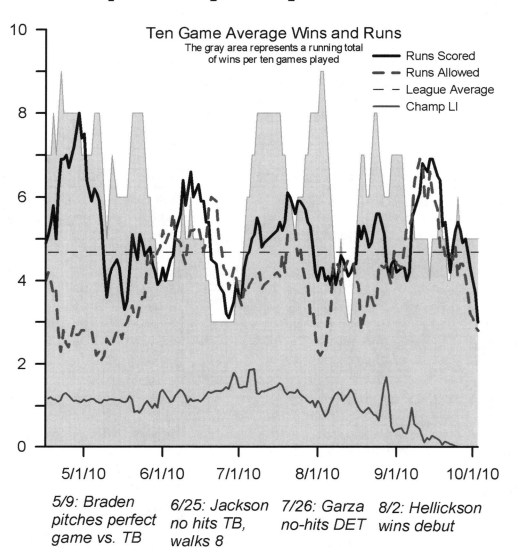

Ten Game Average Wins and Runs

The gray area represents a running total of wins per ten games played

— Runs Scored
- - Runs Allowed
- - League Average
— Champ LI

5/9: Braden pitches perfect game vs. TB

6/25: Jackson no hits TB, walks 8

7/26: Garza no-hits DET

8/2: Hellickson wins debut

Team Batting and Pitching/Fielding Stats by Month

	April	May	June	July	Aug	Sept/Oct
Wins	17	17	11	19	17	15
Losses	6	12	14	7	12	15
RS/G	6.3	4.2	5.0	5.1	4.6	4.8
RA/G	3.3	3.5	4.7	3.9	4.1	4.4
OBP	.350	.320	.347	.337	.328	.320
SLG	.447	.379	.392	.412	.387	.409
FIP	4.30	3.94	4.14	4.20	4.01	4.29
DER	.732	.732	.686	.719	.709	.706

Batting Stats

Player	BR	Runs	RBI	PA	Outs	H	2B	3B	HR	TB	K	BB	IBB	HBP	SH	SF	SB	CS	GDP	H-A	L^R	BA	OBP	SLG	GPA
Crawford C *	118	110	90	663	428	184	30	13	19	297	104	46	3	3	3	5	47	10	2	.001	.072	.307	.356	.495	.299
Longoria E	113	96	104	661	425	169	46	5	22	291	124	72	12	5	0	10	15	5	15	.037	.039	.294	.372	.507	.310
Upton B	87	89	62	610	431	127	38	4	18	227	164	67	1	2	1	4	42	9	13	.014	.081	.237	.322	.424	.264
Zobrist B +	84	77	75	655	425	129	28	2	10	191	107	92	1	3	7	12	24	3	10	-.024	-.002	.238	.346	.353	.257
Pena C *	79	64	84	582	392	95	18	0	28	197	158	87	4	7	0	4	5	1	2	.037	.024	.196	.325	.407	.261
Bartlett J	60	71	47	532	361	119	27	3	4	164	83	45	1	5	11	3	11	6	6	.006	.029	.254	.324	.350	.246
Jaso J *	56	57	44	404	258	89	18	3	5	128	39	59	1	2	1	3	4	0	8	-.091	.050	.263	.372	.378	.276
Rodriguez S	46	53	40	378	270	86	19	2	9	136	97	21	1	8	5	1	13	3	10	.010	.065	.251	.308	.397	.251
Joyce M *	43	30	40	261	168	52	15	4	10	103	55	40	2	2	0	3	2	2	2	-.084	.210	.241	.360	.477	.296
Brignac R *	37	39	45	326	233	77	13	1	8	116	77	20	3	3	0	2	3	3	6	-.033	.023	.256	.307	.385	.247
Aybar W +	33	22	43	309	212	62	13	0	6	93	61	30	1	3	2	4	0	0	4	.013	.020	.230	.309	.344	.237
Shoppach K	20	17	17	187	129	31	8	0	5	54	71	20	0	6	2	1	0	0	2	.028	.125	.196	.308	.342	.236
Johnson D *	20	15	23	140	90	22	3	0	7	46	27	25	0	1	0	3	1	0	1	-.042	-.043	.198	.343	.414	.272
Kapler G	11	19	14	140	102	26	4	0	2	36	24	11	0	3	1	1	1	1	3	-.046	-.035	.210	.288	.290	.213
Burrell P	9	9	13	96	69	17	5	0	2	28	28	10	0	1	0	1	0	0	0	.005	-.160	.202	.292	.333	.226
Navarro D +	9	11	7	142	104	24	5	0	1	32	20	12	0	1	5	0	0	1	3	.032	-.003	.194	.270	.258	.196
Blalock H *	8	8	7	69	49	16	3	0	1	22	15	6	0	0	0	0	1	1	1	-.122	.146	.254	.319	.349	.243
Hawpe B *	5	7	7	46	33	7	0	0	2	13	17	6	0	1	0	0	0	0	1	-.131	-.055	.179	.304	.333	.232
Jennings D	2	5	2	24	19	4	1	1	0	7	4	2	0	1	0	0	2	2	0	-.184	.149	.190	.292	.333	.226
Baldelli R	2	3	5	25	20	5	1	0	1	9	5	1	0	0	0	0	1	0	1	-.253	.267	.208	.240	.375	.213

Only includes batters with at least one Base Run. Italicized stats have been adjusted for home park.

Batted Ball Batting Stats

Player	% of PA		% of Batted Balls					Out %		Runs Per Event				Total Runs vs. Avg.				
	K%	BB%	GB%	LD%	FB%	IF/F	HR/OF	GB	OF	NIP	GB	LD	OF	NIP	GB	LD	FB	Tot
Longoria Ev	19	12	37	20	43	.07	.12	73	83	.06	.05	.46	.22	6	0	12	14	32
Crawford Ca	16	7	47	16	36	.09	.12	66	81	.03	.11	.40	.24	-2	18	2	12	30
Joyce Ma	21	16	33	18	49	.10	.14	81	77	.09	.00	.33	.29	5	-3	-2	10	10
Jaso Jo	10	15	46	17	37	.14	.05	74	84	.17	.05	.34	.11	12	2	-2	-5	8
Pena Ca	27	16	45	14	41	.10	.24	82	86	.06	-.00	.32	.35	8	-7	-13	18	6
Upton BJ	27	11	40	17	44	.09	.12	69	82	.02	.08	.39	.23	-2	3	-6	8	3
Johnson Da	19	19	38	15	47	.10	.19	82	93	.11	.01	.28	.23	4	-2	-3	3	2
Zobrist Be	16	15	44	18	38	.11	.06	74	91	.10	.04	.42	.06	13	2	2	-18	-1
Brignac Re	24	7	38	19	42	.09	.09	67	83	-.01	.09	.37	.16	-5	2	-1	-1	-4
Shoppach Ke	38	14	44	11	44	.10	.14	64	83	.01	.12	.49	.24	-1	2	-5	0	-4
Rodriguez Se	26	8	42	19	39	.09	.11	73	84	-.01	.04	.43	.18	-5	2	-0	-1	-4
Aybar Wi	20	11	42	18	39	.07	.08	81	83	.05	-.00	.41	.13	1	-4	1	-3	-5
Bartlett Ja	16	9	45	21	34	.10	.03	76	85	.06	.04	.41	.07	2	0	6	-15	-7
Kapler Ga	17	10	42	19	40	.25	.07	76	82	.06	.02	.26	.11	0	-1	-2	-4	-7
Navarro Di	14	9	47	16	37	.11	.03	79	82	.07	.02	.18	.08	0	-2	-5	-4	-10
MLB Average	18	9	44	18	38	.09	.10	74	83	.04	.04	.38	.18	--	--	--	--	--

Only includes batters with at least one hundred Plate Appearances.

Pitching Stats

Player	PRC	IP	BFP	G	GS	K	BB	IBB	HBP	H	HR	DP	DER	SB	CS	PO	W	L	Sv	Op	Hld	H-A	R^L	RA	ERA	FIP
Price D *	105	208.7	861	32	31	188	79	1	5	170	15	20	.716	13	7	3	19	6	0	0	0	-.037	-.027	3.06	2.72	3.44
Garza M	75	204.7	855	33	32	150	63	2	7	193	28	22	.720	9	4	1	15	10	1	1	0	-.017	-.005	4.13	3.91	4.42
Davis W	60	168.0	722	29	29	113	62	2	5	165	24	10	.722	13	5	2	12	10	0	0	0	.002	-.016	4.13	4.07	4.78
Niemann J	60	174.3	733	30	29	131	61	6	7	159	25	19	.727	21	2	2	12	8	0	0	0	-.010	-.017	4.44	4.39	4.54
Benoit J	56	60.3	217	63	0	75	11	1	0	30	6	4	.808	2	2	1	1	2	1	4	25	-.030	-.019	1.49	1.34	2.42
Shields J	56	203.3	899	34	33	187	51	2	5	246	34	16	.645	10	3	2	13	15	0	0	0	-.039	.017	5.67	5.18	4.24
Soriano R	44	62.3	237	64	0	57	14	2	1	36	4	3	.789	3	0	0	3	2	45	48	0	-.009	-.059	2.02	1.73	2.74
Balfour G	33	55.3	222	57	0	56	17	2	0	43	3	3	.726	2	2	0	2	1	0	1	16	.026	-.088	2.60	2.28	2.61
Sonnanstine	26	81.0	355	41	4	50	27	3	7	83	11	6	.719	6	0	0	3	1	1	1	0	-.004	.004	4.44	4.44	4.79
Cormier L	21	62.0	279	60	0	30	34	3	0	68	7	10	.692	3	2	0	4	3	0	0	4	.070	.066	4.06	3.92	5.11
Wheeler D	21	48.3	195	64	0	46	16	2	1	36	7	4	.752	2	1	0	2	4	3	6	9	-.018	.018	3.72	3.35	4.02
Hellickson J	16	36.3	149	10	4	33	8	2	2	32	5	2	.723	2	0	0	4	0	0	1	0	-.065	-.162	3.47	3.47	3.74
Choate R *	15	44.7	187	85	0	40	17	5	3	41	3	9	.669	1	1	0	4	3	0	2	18	-.059	-.210	4.63	4.23	3.20
Ekstrom M	7	16.3	68	15	0	10	9	1	2	12	0	2	.745	1	0	0	0	1	0	0	0	-.010	.009	3.31	3.31	3.72
Qualls C	5	21.0	91	27	0	15	6	0	1	24	2	4	.642	1	1	0	2	0	0	3	8	.002	-.178	6.43	5.57	3.92

Only includes pitchers with at least ten Innings Pitched. Italicized stats have been adjusted for home park.

Batted Ball Pitching Stats

Player	% of PA		% of Batted Balls					Out %		Runs Per Event				Total Runs vs. Avg.				
	K%	BB%	GB%	LD%	FB%	IF/F	HR/OF	GB	OF	NIP	GB	LD	OF	NIP	GB	LD	FB	Tot
Price Da	22	10	44	17	40	.10	.07	76	83	.03	.03	.37	.14	-2	-5	-8	-9	-24
Benoit Jo	35	5	39	12	49	.17	.11	86	91	-.05	-.02	.40	.13	-8	-5	-7	-4	-23
Soriano Ra	24	6	32	16	51	.17	.04	83	85	-.02	-.02	.38	.09	-4	-4	-4	-6	-18
Balfour Gr	25	8	31	20	50	.10	.05	67	92	-.01	.11	.44	.03	-3	1	1	-9	-10
Wheeler Da	24	9	35	20	45	.07	.13	80	83	.01	-.00	.29	.21	-2	-3	-3	3	-4
Niemann Je	18	9	44	16	39	.12	.14	75	88	.04	.03	.36	.20	0	-0	-7	3	-4
Hellickson Je	22	7	37	13	50	.08	.08	69	86	-.01	.07	.45	.12	-2	1	-1	-1	-4
Garza Ma	18	8	36	19	45	.11	.11	74	85	.03	.04	.32	.18	-3	-2	-5	7	-3
Choate Ra	21	11	60	15	24	.10	.11	76	71	.04	.03	.39	.27	0	-0	-2	-1	-2
Sonnanstine An	14	10	45	19	36	.16	.12	78	85	.07	.02	.38	.21	2	-2	3	1	4
Davis Wa	16	9	39	17	44	.13	.12	73	86	.06	.06	.36	.18	2	2	-3	3	5
Cormier La	11	12	50	19	32	.05	.11	74	86	.13	.04	.38	.18	5	1	2	1	9
Shields Ja	21	6	41	20	38	.07	.15	70	82	-.01	.07	.43	.25	-12	7	13	21	29
MLB Average	18	9	44	18	38	.09	.10	74	83	.04	.04	.38	.18	--	--	--	--	--

Only includes pitchers who faced at least one hundred batters.

Fielding Stats

Name	INN	SBA/G	CS%	ERA	WP+PB/G	PO	A	TE	FE
Catchers									
Jaso J	719.0	0.63	18%	3.87	0.463	611	30	3	1
Shoppach K	403.7	0.78	17%	4.35	0.446	324	18	1	1
Navarro D	331.0	0.71	27%	2.91	0.326	272	20	4	0

Name	Inn	PO	A	TE	FE	FPct	DPS	DPT	ZRDif	OOZ	Dif
First Base											
Pena C	1213.0	1074	83	1	5	.995	9	0	-.005	43	3
Johnson D	92.0	82	3	0	0	1.000	2	0	--	0	--
Zobrist B	79.0	77	8	0	0	1.000	1	0	--	1	--
Rodriguez S	21.0	23	1	0	0	1.000	0	0	--	0	--
Hawpe B	20.0	12	0	0	0	1.000	0	0	--	0	--
Aybar W	16.0	13	1	0	0	1.000	0	0	--	0	--
Blalock H	8.0	6	0	0	0	1.000	0	0	--	--	--
Jaso J	4.0	4	0	0	0	1.000	0	0	--	--	--
Second Base											
Rodriguez S	678.3	138	222	2	4	.984	17	34	.000	33	16
Brignac R	389.3	77	129	4	1	.976	6	10	.006	19	9
Zobrist B	371.0	74	116	0	3	.984	9	18	.037	16	7
Aybar W	15.0	2	5	0	0	1.000	0	0	--	0	--
Shortstop											
Bartlett J	1104.0	152	309	6	5	.977	28	25	-.018	45	-3
Brignac R	340.7	56	108	2	2	.976	7	12	-.044	23	8
Rodriguez S	9.0	0	3	0	0	1.000	0	0	--	1	--
Third Base											
Longoria E	1330.0	127	276	8	6	.966	40	5	.031	43	-6
Johnson D	40.0	5	6	1	1	.846	0	0	--	1	--
Rodriguez S	38.0	7	5	0	0	1.000	2	0	--	1	--
Aybar W	25.0	0	6	0	1	.857	0	0	--	0	--
Blalock H	10.0	1	3	1	0	.800	0	0	--	2	--
Zobrist B	10.0	1	0	0	1	.500	0	0	--	0	--

Name	Inn	PO	A	TE	FE	FPct	DPS	DPT	ZRDif	OOZ	Dif
Left Field											
Crawford C	1260.0	306	7	1	0	.994	0	0	.034	68	6
Joyce M	75.0	16	0	0	0	1.000	0	0	--	4	--
Kapler G	72.3	12	1	0	0	1.000	0	0	--	1	--
Rodriguez S	21.0	8	0	0	0	1.000	0	0	--	3	--
Jennings D	15.0	5	0	0	0	1.000	0	0	--	3	--
Johnson D	8.0	1	0	0	0	1.000	0	0	--	0	--
Zobrist B	2.0	0	0	0	0	0.000	0	0	--	--	--
Center Field											
Upton B	1301.0	397	3	0	5	.988	0	0	.017	67	-7
Zobrist B	83.3	22	0	0	0	1.000	0	0	--	6	--
Rodriguez S	42.7	8	0	0	0	1.000	0	0	--	1	--
Jennings D	16.0	10	0	0	0	1.000	0	0	--	4	--
Kapler G	10.0	0	0	0	0	0.000	0	0	--	0	--
Right Field											
Zobrist B	749.3	182	6	0	0	1.000	3	0	.015	58	17
Joyce M	397.0	99	4	1	2	.972	0	0	.033	20	-2
Kapler G	231.3	46	0	0	0	1.000	0	0	-.085	20	7
Jennings D	23.0	3	0	0	0	1.000	0	0	--	0	--
Baldelli R	22.0	6	0	0	0	1.000	0	0	--	2	--
Rodriguez S	19.0	6	0	0	0	1.000	0	0	--	2	--
Blalock H	5.0	1	0	0	0	1.000	0	0	--	--	--
Hawpe B	5.0	1	0	0	0	1.000	0	0	--	0	--
Brignac R	2.0	1	0	0	0	1.000	0	0	--	--	--

Texas Rangers

- Nelson Cruz had the most Base Runs of any player with <500 PA
- Elvis Andrus tied for the AL lead in Sac Bunts
- Andrus tied for the lowest GPA of any AL regular
- Andrus's GB% was 61
- Josh Hamilton was second in the AL in GPA
- Tommy Hunter's FIP was far higher than his ERA
- Matt Treanor made 1 TE
- Rich Harden walked 17% of his BFP
- Dustin Nippert's LD% was 27
- 35% of Doug Mathis's OF were HR
- 92% of Chris Ray's GB were outs
- Vladimir Guerrero struck out at one-half the league-average rate

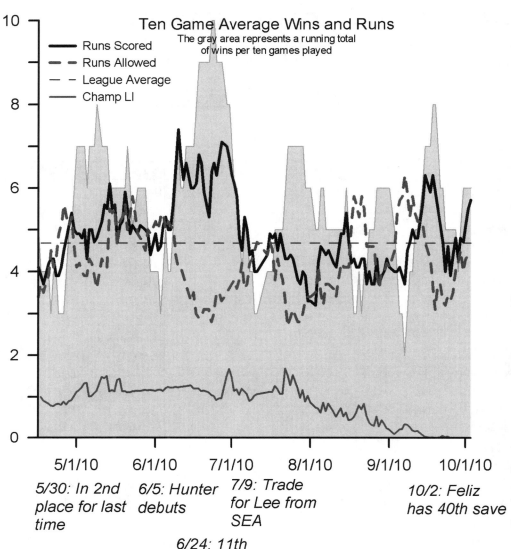

Ten Game Average Wins and Runs

The gray area represents a running total of wins per ten games played

- Runs Scored
- Runs Allowed
- League Average
- Champ LI

5/30: In 2nd place for last time

6/5: Hunter debuts

7/9: Trade for Lee from SEA

10/2: Feliz has 40th save

6/24: 11th straight win

Team Batting and Pitching/Fielding Stats by Month

	April	May	June	July	Aug	Sept/Oct
Wins	11	15	21	14	13	16
Losses	12	12	6	13	15	14
RS/G	4.4	4.9	6.6	4.1	4.3	4.8
RA/G	4.3	4.9	3.7	3.7	4.5	4.4
OBP	.313	.347	.372	.327	.321	.342
SLG	.369	.436	.481	.399	.415	.402
FIP	4.68	4.38	3.97	4.42	3.86	4.20
DER	.711	.707	.727	.735	.685	.718

Batting Stats

Player	BR	Runs	RBI	PA	Outs	H	2B	3B	HR	TB	K	BB	IBB	HBP	SH	SF	SB	CS	GDP	H-A	L^R	BA	OBP	SLG	GPA
Hamilton J *	114	95	100	571	344	186	40	3	32	328	95	43	5	5	1	4	8	1	11	.085	.117	.359	.411	.633	.328
Guerrero V	89	83	115	643	439	178	27	1	29	294	60	35	5	9	0	6	4	5	19	.025	.044	.300	.345	.496	.267
Young M	87	99	91	718	493	186	36	3	21	291	115	50	4	1	0	11	4	2	21	.060	.045	.284	.330	.444	.248
Cruz N	77	60	78	445	288	127	31	3	22	230	81	38	5	1	1	6	17	4	12	.093	.013	.318	.374	.576	.299
Murphy D *	65	54	65	471	305	122	26	2	12	188	71	45	2	0	0	3	14	2	6	.009	.046	.291	.358	.449	.261
Andrus E	63	88	35	674	453	156	15	3	0	177	96	64	0	5	17	0	32	15	6	-.006	-.001	.265	.342	.301	.219
Kinsler I	61	73	45	460	295	112	20	1	9	161	57	56	2	7	2	4	15	5	11	.067	.077	.286	.382	.412	.263
Borbon J *	43	60	42	468	329	121	11	4	3	149	59	19	0	2	8	1	15	7	5	.006	.016	.276	.309	.340	.214
Smoak J +	26	29	34	275	192	49	10	0	8	83	57	38	4	0	0	2	1	0	6	.005	-.105	.209	.316	.353	.221
Moreland M *	24	20	25	173	112	37	4	0	9	68	36	25	5	1	0	2	3	1	3	.017	.080	.255	.364	.469	.269
Treanor M	21	22	27	272	193	50	6	1	5	73	43	22	0	5	4	4	1	2	4	-.013	-.099	.211	.287	.308	.197
Blanco A +	18	17	13	185	122	46	10	1	0	58	24	11	1	3	3	2	0	2	0	-.003	-.070	.277	.330	.349	.225
Molina B	13	10	19	195	140	42	6	1	2	56	15	10	0	1	5	4	0	0	7	-.068	.061	.240	.279	.320	.197
Davis C *	10	7	4	136	100	23	9	0	1	35	40	15	3	0	0	1	3	0	3	.035	.066	.192	.279	.292	.190
Arias J	9	18	9	101	73	27	5	1	0	34	17	2	0	0	1	0	1	0	2	-.008	.039	.276	.290	.347	.208
Ramirez M	9	8	8	85	57	15	3	0	2	24	22	12	0	2	0	2	0	0	3	-.022	-.094	.217	.341	.348	.230
Francoeur J	8	9	11	56	38	18	2	0	2	26	5	1	0	1	0	1	0	1	2	-.096	.095	.340	.357	.491	.271
Cantu J	7	9	2	105	79	23	4	1	1	32	19	6	0	0	1	0	0	0	4	-.113	-.048	.235	.279	.327	.198
Teagarden T	7	10	6	85	60	11	1	0	4	24	34	8	0	2	4	0	0	0	0	-.036	.030	.155	.259	.338	.192
German E	2	5	1	16	11	3	0	0	0	3	2	3	0	0	0	0	4	1	0	-.159	.144	.231	.375	.231	.217
Gentry C	1	4	3	35	27	7	0	0	0	7	11	1	0	0	0	1	1	0	1	-.060	-.103	.212	.229	.212	.149

Only includes batters with at least one Base Run. Italicized stats have been adjusted for home park.

Batted Ball Batting Stats

Player	% of PA		% of Batted Balls					Out %		Runs Per Event				Total Runs vs. Avg.				
	K%	BB%	GB%	LD%	FB%	IF/F	HR/OF	GB	OF	NIP	GB	LD	OF	NIP	GB	LD	FB	Tot
Hamilton Jo	17	8	42	22	36	.04	.21	71	72	.04	.07	.41	.41	0	5	14	41	60
Cruz Ne	18	9	37	18	45	.06	.16	68	77	.04	.07	.44	.31	-0	2	5	24	31
Guerrero Vl	9	7	45	18	37	.11	.16	75	85	.08	.03	.40	.23	1	-1	9	14	23
Murphy Da	15	10	44	19	36	.05	.10	74	76	.06	.05	.40	.21	3	1	6	8	17
Kinsler Ia	12	14	40	18	42	.10	.07	71	81	.13	.05	.41	.14	11	1	4	-1	15
Young Mi	16	7	47	18	34	.03	.11	74	83	.03	.04	.37	.21	-4	0	3	9	8
Moreland Mi	21	15	40	23	38	.10	.24	84	93	.08	-.02	.39	.30	3	-3	2	5	7
Arias Jo	17	2	42	20	38	.16	.00	74	77	-.06	.04	.47	.09	-2	-0	2	-3	-3
Blanco An	13	8	44	22	34	.06	.00	69	89	.06	.10	.33	.01	0	3	1	-8	-3
Smoak Ju	21	14	39	24	37	.18	.15	84	87	.07	-.03	.31	.21	4	-6	-0	-1	-4
Cantu Jo	18	6	43	24	33	.23	.05	82	84	-.00	-.02	.33	.13	-1	-2	1	-3	-6
Davis Ch	29	11	42	22	36	.07	.04	82	88	.01	-.01	.41	.06	-1	-2	0	-5	-8
Molina Be	8	6	32	16	52	.09	.03	81	91	.08	-.02	.43	.02	-0	-4	1	-8	-12
Borbon Ju	13	4	56	13	31	.16	.03	71	81	.01	.07	.37	.08	-5	13	-7	-14	-13
Treanor Ma	16	10	43	19	38	.08	.07	86	86	.06	-.03	.31	.11	1	-6	-3	-5	-13
Andrus El	14	10	61	19	20	.05	.00	73	86	.08	.05	.34	.01	5	10	-2	-27	-13
MLB Average	18	9	44	18	38	.09	.10	74	83	.04	.04	.38	.18	--	--	--	--	--

Only includes batters with at least one hundred Plate Appearances.

Pitching Stats

Player	PRC	IP	BFP	G	GS	K	BB	IBB	HBP	H	HR	DP	DER	SB	CS	PO	W	L	Sv	Op	Hld	H-A	R^L	RA	ERA	FIP
Wilson C *	94	204.0	850	33	33	170	93	0	10	161	10	25	.728	21	8	1	15	8	0	0	0	.013	-.092	3.66	3.35	3.60
Lewis C	88	201.0	844	32	32	196	65	0	6	174	21	14	.709	13	4	0	12	13	0	0	0	.007	-.028	4.03	3.72	3.58
Hunter T	51	128.0	535	23	22	68	33	0	3	126	21	11	.734	5	2	1	13	4	0	0	0	-.018	-.025	3.87	3.73	5.03
Lee C *	43	108.7	435	15	15	96	12	2	1	103	11	6	.708	3	1	0	4	6	0	0	0	-.062	.021	4.39	3.98	2.96
Feliz N	43	69.3	269	70	0	71	18	1	5	43	5	5	.771	0	0	0	4	3	40	43	3	.104	.065	2.73	2.73	2.95
Ogando A	42	41.7	171	44	0	39	16	2	1	31	2	4	.726	6	1	0	4	1	0	2	7	-.001	-.065	1.30	1.30	2.94
O'Day D	42	62.0	240	72	0	45	18	2	5	43	5	6	.769	3	1	0	6	2	0	2	22	-.031	-.016	2.18	2.03	3.43
Oliver D *	36	61.7	244	64	0	65	15	4	2	53	4	8	.677	8	3	3	1	2	1	4	14	-.086	-.081	2.92	2.48	2.48
Feldman S	34	141.3	641	29	22	75	45	2	5	181	18	13	.655	16	8	1	7	11	0	0	0	-.005	.031	6.24	5.48	4.72
Harden R	26	92.0	430	20	18	75	62	0	9	91	8	10	.711	1	1	0	5	5	0	0	0	-.009	-.050	5.97	5.58	6.34
Francisco F	24	52.7	221	56	0	60	18	2	1	49	5	4	.672	9	1	0	6	4	2	6	15	.041	.052	3.93	3.76	3.04
Harrison M *	24	78.3	357	37	6	46	39	3	2	80	10	6	.708	5	1	0	3	2	2	3	3	-.006	-.014	5.17	4.71	5.05
Nippert D	22	56.7	262	38	2	47	34	3	5	61	7	5	.680	12	1	0	4	5	0	1	5	.068	-.050	4.45	4.29	4.96
Holland D *	21	57.3	253	14	10	54	24	0	4	55	6	5	.673	6	1	3	3	4	0	0	1	-.059	-.154	4.71	4.08	4.05
Kirkman M *	14	16.3	68	14	0	16	10	1	0	9	0	0	.786	0	0	0	0	0	0	1	2	.045	.064	1.65	1.65	2.81
Ray C	14	31.7	133	35	0	16	16	1	0	24	4	2	.794	3	0	0	2	0	1	3	7	.084	-.077	3.41	3.41	5.16
Mathis D	5	22.3	100	13	0	10	11	0	0	30	7	6	.681	1	2	0	1	1	0	0	0	-.150	.100	6.04	6.04	7.77
Strop P	1	10.7	60	15	0	11	11	0	1	17	2	2	.571	1	0	0	0	0	0	0	1	-.097	-.013	10.13	10.13	6.86

Only includes pitchers with at least ten Innings Pitched. Italicized stats have been adjusted for home park.

Batted Ball Pitching Stats

Player	% of PA		% of Batted Balls					Out %		Runs Per Event				Total Runs vs. Avg.				
	K%	BB%	GB%	LD%	FB%	IF/F	HR/OF	GB	OF	NIP	GB	LD	OF	NIP	GB	LD	FB	Tot
Wilson Ch	20	12	49	17	34	.04	.05	78	86	.06	.02	.35	.09	7	-5	-8	-20	-27
Feliz Ne	26	9	37	15	48	.17	.07	73	94	-.00	.04	.37	.06	-3	-2	-5	-10	-20
Lewis Co	23	8	38	17	45	.14	.10	73	84	.01	.04	.38	.17	-8	-2	-6	-2	-17
Lee Cl	22	3	42	18	40	.09	.09	73	81	-.06	.05	.33	.18	-12	1	-4	0	-16
O'Day Da	19	7	37	21	42	.18	.08	81	96	.01	-.00	.33	.05	-2	-3	-1	-9	-16
Ogando Al	23	10	44	18	38	.19	.06	71	94	.03	.04	.35	.04	-1	-0	-2	-7	-9
Oliver Da	27	7	48	20	32	.10	.09	70	77	-.02	.07	.31	.19	-4	1	-3	-3	-9
Francisco Fr	27	9	39	20	40	.15	.11	59	90	-.00	.13	.30	.15	-3	4	-3	-3	-5
Ray Ch	12	12	37	12	51	.10	.09	92	84	.12	-.06	.47	.15	2	-4	-1	1	-2
Hunter Ra	13	7	42	18	40	.12	.13	78	86	.04	.02	.35	.20	-2	-4	-1	6	-1
Holland De	21	11	42	15	43	.08	.09	68	74	.04	.08	.27	.23	1	3	-5	5	3
Harrison Ma	13	12	47	21	33	.07	.13	78	86	.11	.02	.33	.19	5	-0	1	1	7
Nippert Du	18	15	32	27	41	.10	.09	76	81	.10	.03	.32	.18	5	-1	3	1	8
Mathis Do	10	11	53	18	29	.13	.35	68	85	.13	.05	.26	.51	2	1	-1	6	9
Harden Ri	17	17	35	14	51	.09	.14	71	85	.11	.05	.46	.20	12	-1	-1	10	20
Feldman Sc	12	8	43	20	37	.09	.10	71	79	.07	.07	.41	.19	2	7	12	6	27
MLB Average	18	9	44	18	38	.09	.10	74	83	.04	.04	.38	.18	--	--	--	--	--

Only includes pitchers who faced at least one hundred batters.

Fielding Stats

Name	INN	SBA/G	CS%	ERA	WP+PB/G	PO	A	TE	FE
Catchers									
Treanor M	614.7	0.81	20%	3.92	0.307	512	22	1	1
Molina B	439.3	0.86	24%	3.93	0.369	355	24	4	1
Teagarden T	205.0	0.79	17%	4.30	0.571	171	9	1	1
Ramirez M	187.3	1.35	14%	3.56	0.577	154	7	2	0
Saltalamacchia J	9.0	1.00	0%	4.00	0.000	8	0	0	0

Name	Inn	PO	A	TE	FE	FPct	DPS	DPT	ZRDif	OOZ	Dif
First Base											
Smoak J	591.0	545	35	1	3	.993	2	1	.013	14	-5
Moreland M	320.7	289	16	1	1	.993	1	1	.055	7	-4
Davis C	298.7	269	22	1	1	.993	0	0	-.036	9	-1
Cantu J	177.0	158	11	0	0	1.000	2	1	.014	7	1
Arias J	35.0	34	2	0	1	.973	0	0	--	2	--
Garko R	33.0	17	6	0	0	1.000	1	0	--	0	--
Second Base											
Kinsler I	905.3	190	278	0	7	.985	20	42	.032	23	1
Blanco A	283.3	48	92	1	3	.972	12	7	.005	6	-1
Arias J	149.7	27	45	0	1	.986	5	7	.016	1	-3
Guzman C	77.0	12	21	0	1	.971	1	2	--	4	--
German E	20.0	5	6	0	0	1.000	0	1	--	0	--
Cora A	18.0	2	3	0	0	1.000	1	1	--	0	--
Cantu J	2.0	0	0	0	0	0.000	0	0	--	--	--
Shortstop											
Andrus E	1291.0	242	401	6	10	.976	42	41	.018	46	-10
Blanco A	128.0	16	37	1	1	.964	5	1	-.024	2	-4
Guzman C	22.0	4	4	1	0	.889	0	0	--	0	--
Arias J	12.0	5	6	0	0	1.000	1	1	--	0	--
German E	2.0	0	0	0	0	0.000	0	0	--	--	--
Third Base											
Young M	1370.0	95	265	9	10	.950	26	0	-.003	36	-15
Cantu J	48.0	2	6	0	0	1.000	0	0	--	1	--
Blanco A	33.0	1	5	0	1	.857	0	0	--	1	--
Cora A	2.0	1	1	0	0	1.000	0	0	--	0	--
Davis C	2.0	0	1	0	0	1.000	0	0	--	0	--

Name	Inn	PO	A	TE	FE	FPct	DPS	DPT	ZRDif	OOZ	Dif
Left Field											
Hamilton J	772.7	179	7	1	3	.979	1	0	.004	53	15
Murphy D	533.0	113	6	0	1	.992	0	0	-.012	28	2
Cruz N	88.7	22	0	0	0	1.000	0	0	--	7	--
Gentry C	28.0	7	1	0	0	1.000	0	0	--	3	--
Francoeur J	12.0	1	0	1	0	.500	0	0	--	0	--
Guerrero V	7.0	1	0	0	0	1.000	0	0	--	0	--
German E	7.0	0	0	0	0	0.000	0	0	--	--	--
Borbon J	6.0	2	0	0	0	1.000	0	0	--	1	--
Boggs B	1.0	0	0	0	0	0.000	0	0	--	--	--
Center Field											
Borbon J	1095.0	335	2	1	3	.988	0	0	.007	71	9
Hamilton J	262.0	75	2	0	0	1.000	1	0	-.016	16	1
Murphy D	53.7	13	0	0	0	1.000	0	0	--	2	--
Gentry C	44.0	9	0	0	0	1.000	0	0	--	3	--
Right Field											
Cruz N	799.3	228	3	1	4	.979	1	0	.036	60	16
Murphy D	381.3	80	3	0	0	1.000	1	0	-.026	26	5
Guerrero V	118.7	27	1	0	2	.933	0	0	-.051	5	-2
Francoeur J	88.0	19	0	0	0	1.000	0	0	--	5	--
Moreland M	45.0	10	0	0	1	.909	0	0	--	2	--
Boggs B	17.0	5	0	0	0	1.000	0	0	--	1	--
Gentry C	6.0	0	0	0	0	0.000	0	0	--	--	--

Toronto Blue Jays

Stat Facts:

- Jose Bautista led the AL in Base Runs
- One quarter of Bautista's OF were HR
- Bautista was second in the majors in RF assists
- Adam Lind had the highest L^R of any ML regular
- Shaun Marcum had the highest R^L of any ML starter
- Brandon Morrow's FIP was far lower than his ERA
- Edwin Encarnacion tied for the most TE of any 3B, in 841 innings
- Vernon Wells had the most innings of any CF with 0 FE and 0 TE
- Alex Gonzalez started the most DP of any SS, in 740 innings
- Jesse Litsch struck out 8% of his BFP
- Travis Snider's LD% was 24
- Aaron Hill had 26 HR, and a GPA of .220

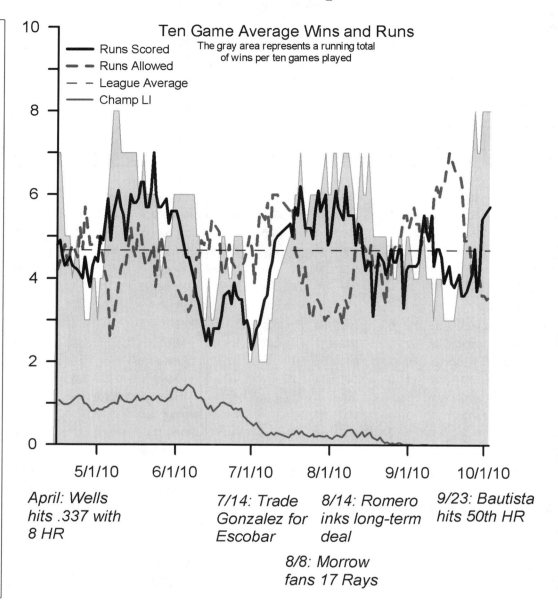

Ten Game Average Wins and Runs

The gray area represents a running total of wins per ten games played

Runs Scored
Runs Allowed
League Average
Champ LI

April: Wells hits .337 with 8 HR

7/14: Trade Gonzalez for Escobar

8/14: Romero inks long-term deal

9/23: Bautista hits 50th HR

8/8: Morrow fans 17 Rays

Team Batting and Pitching/Fielding Stats by Month

	April	May	June	July	Aug	Sept/Oct
Wins	12	19	9	14	15	16
Losses	12	10	17	11	13	14
RS/G	4.6	5.7	3.1	5.3	4.8	4.5
RA/G	4.5	4.0	4.7	4.1	4.8	4.8
OBP	.303	.318	.293	.331	.322	.304
SLG	.446	.493	.367	.501	.457	.452
FIP	3.90	3.58	4.31	3.94	4.65	4.12
DER	.702	.689	.696	.693	.720	.672

Batting Stats

Player	BR	Runs	RBI	PA	Outs	H	2B	3B	HR	TB	K	BB	IBB	HBP	SH	SF	SB	CS	GDP	H-A	L^R	BA	OBP	SLG	GPA
Bautista J	127	109	124	683	433	148	35	3	54	351	116	100	2	10	0	4	9	2	10	.085	-.058	.260	.378	.617	.324
Wells V	91	79	88	646	451	161	44	3	31	304	84	50	5	3	0	3	6	4	18	.083	-.074	.273	.331	.515	.278
Overbay L *	74	75	67	608	413	130	37	2	20	231	131	67	7	3	0	3	1	0	9	.025	.029	.243	.329	.433	.256
Lind A *	67	57	72	613	444	135	32	3	23	242	144	38	3	3	0	3	0	0	10	.045	.156	.237	.287	.425	.235
Buck J	58	53	66	437	300	115	25	0	20	200	111	16	1	6	0	6	0	0	6	-.026	.124	.281	.314	.489	.263
Hill A	58	70	68	580	430	108	22	0	26	208	85	41	2	8	1	2	2	2	8	.034	-.081	.205	.271	.394	.220
Lewis F *	57	70	36	480	331	112	31	5	8	177	104	38	1	9	1	4	17	6	9	-.017	.039	.262	.332	.414	.252
Encarnacion	48	47	51	367	260	81	16	0	21	160	60	29	1	2	0	4	1	0	9	-.066	.056	.244	.305	.482	.257
Gonzalez A	45	47	50	348	252	85	25	1	17	163	65	17	0	1	0	2	1	0	9	-.028	-.041	.259	.296	.497	.257
Snider T *	40	36	32	319	228	76	20	0	14	138	79	21	2	0	0	0	6	3	3	-.002	.026	.255	.304	.463	.252
Escobar Y	26	32	16	266	181	65	7	0	4	84	26	19	0	4	7	0	1	1	9	.015	.052	.275	.340	.356	.242
Molina J	18	13	12	183	133	41	4	0	6	63	36	9	1	5	2	0	0	0	7	.009	-.097	.246	.304	.377	.231
McDonald J	18	27	23	163	120	38	9	2	6	69	26	6	0	0	2	3	2	1	5	.028	.004	.250	.273	.454	.236
Wise D *	12	20	14	118	85	28	3	2	3	44	29	4	0	1	1	0	4	0	1	-.162	-.002	.250	.282	.393	.225
McCoy M	6	9	3	90	67	16	4	0	0	20	20	8	0	0	0	0	5	1	0	.010	.137	.195	.267	.244	.181
Arencibia J	3	3	4	37	30	5	1	0	2	12	11	2	0	0	0	0	0	0	0	.149	-.208	.143	.189	.343	.171
Hoffpauir J	2	1	0	37	28	7	1	0	0	8	5	2	0	0	1	0	0	0	1	-.051	.108	.206	.250	.235	.171
Reed J *	2	1	3	23	18	3	0	0	1	6	8	2	0	0	0	0	1	0	0	-.031	-.064	.143	.217	.286	.169
Ruiz R	2	3	1	40	34	6	2	0	1	11	11	0	0	0	0	0	1	0	0	-.076	.003	.150	.150	.275	.136
Marcum S	1	1	1	6	3	1	1	0	0	2	2	1	0	0	1	0	0	0	0	-.305	--	.250	.400	.500	.305

Only includes batters with at least one Base Run. Italicized stats have been adjusted for home park.

Batted Ball Batting Stats

Player	% of PA		% of Batted Balls					Out %		Runs Per Event				Total Runs vs. Avg.				
	K%	BB%	GB%	LD%	FB%	IF/F	HR/OF	GB	OF	NIP	GB	LD	OF	NIP	GB	LD	FB	Tot
Bautista Jo	17	16	31	14	54	.15	.25	75	86	.11	.03	.41	.36	18	-4	-4	48	58
Wells Ve	13	8	42	16	42	.19	.17	71	87	.06	.07	.42	.25	2	6	3	13	23
Overbay Ly	22	12	45	16	39	.04	.13	79	81	.05	.02	.45	.25	3	-5	0	12	9
Buck Jo	25	5	39	16	45	.11	.17	66	79	-.04	.10	.41	.28	-10	6	-2	14	8
Gonzalez Al	19	5	30	20	50	.15	.13	78	84	-.01	.01	.44	.23	-5	-4	6	9	6
Encarnacion Ed	16	8	32	17	51	.16	.18	77	88	.04	.00	.34	.25	-0	-5	-2	12	4
Snider Tr	25	7	41	24	35	.11	.19	71	78	-.02	.06	.28	.34	-5	1	-1	9	4
Lewis Fr	22	10	47	18	34	.16	.07	70	80	.03	.07	.41	.18	-1	5	1	-3	2
McDonald Jo	16	4	34	20	45	.12	.10	80	85	-.03	.02	.42	.16	-3	-2	2	0	-2
Escobar Yu	10	9	57	18	26	.09	.08	76	84	.10	.03	.34	.13	2	1	-1	-5	-3
Wise De	25	4	41	22	37	.10	.11	74	96	-.05	.06	.42	.11	-3	1	1	-2	-3
Molina Jo	20	8	43	22	35	.09	.15	82	80	.02	-.02	.29	.25	-1	-4	-1	2	-4
Lind Ad	23	7	41	19	40	.05	.13	79	83	-.01	.01	.35	.23	-10	-7	-4	11	-9
Hill Aa	15	8	35	11	54	.13	.12	80	88	.06	.01	.37	.17	0	-8	-13	8	-13
MLB Average	18	9	44	18	38	.09	.10	74	83	.04	.04	.38	.18	--	--	--	--	--

Only includes batters with at least one hundred Plate Appearances.

Pitching Stats

Player	PRC	IP	BFP	G	GS	K	BB	IBB	HBP	H	HR	DP	DER	SB	CS	PO	W	L	Sv	Op	Hld	H-A	R^L	RA	ERA	FIP
Marcum S	83	195.3	800	31	31	165	43	3	6	181	24	14	.710	7	8	0	13	8	0	0	0	-.003	.104	3.87	3.64	3.73
Romero R *	82	210.0	882	32	32	174	82	3	8	189	15	31	.698	4	5	3	14	9	0	0	0	-.021	.040	4.20	3.73	3.63
Cecil B *	60	172.7	726	28	28	117	54	2	1	175	18	26	.698	4	2	1	15	7	0	0	0	.017	-.060	4.53	4.22	4.03
Morrow B	56	146.3	629	26	26	178	66	0	9	136	11	13	.647	8	9	1	10	7	0	0	0	-.081	-.014	4.67	4.49	3.19
Downs S *	34	61.3	241	67	0	48	14	3	4	47	3	10	.727	3	0	1	5	5	0	2	26	.023	-.044	2.79	2.64	2.92
Camp S	34	72.3	298	70	0	46	18	5	4	71	8	12	.707	7	1	0	4	3	2	4	13	-.031	-.060	3.24	2.99	3.98
Janssen C	30	68.7	298	56	0	63	21	1	4	74	8	4	.673	4	1	0	5	2	0	0	2	.046	-.040	3.80	3.67	3.84
Gregg K	27	59.0	254	63	0	58	30	1	1	52	4	5	.702	2	0	0	2	6	37	43	3	-.048	-.018	3.66	3.51	3.55
Frasor J	26	63.7	279	69	0	65	24	6	4	61	4	8	.665	6	1	0	3	4	4	8	14	-.111	-.022	4.24	3.68	3.06
Rzepczynski	20	63.7	287	14	12	57	30	1	5	72	8	10	.647	5	3	0	4	4	0	0	2	.043	-.064	5.23	4.95	4.56
Tallet B *	16	77.3	356	34	5	53	38	3	4	84	20	7	.718	3	0	0	2	6	0	2	1	.087	-.152	6.98	6.40	6.62
Purcey D *	14	34.0	143	33	0	32	15	1	0	26	3	0	.742	0	1	0	1	1	1	1	3	.071	-.045	4.24	3.71	3.61
Litsch J	11	46.7	202	9	9	16	15	0	2	53	7	7	.716	2	0	0	1	5	0	0	0	-.063	-.017	5.79	5.79	5.47
Hill S	9	20.7	91	4	4	14	4	0	1	24	1	2	.662	1	0	0	1	2	0	0	0	.012	-.061	3.48	2.61	3.11
Eveland D *	8	44.7	213	9	9	21	27	1	2	57	4	6	.648	3	3	1	3	4	0	0	0	.027	-.011	7.05	6.45	5.22
Mills B *	6	22.3	98	7	3	18	12	1	1	20	2	3	.719	4	0	0	1	0	0	0	1	.192	.039	5.64	5.64	4.41
Drabek K	6	17.0	69	3	3	12	5	0	0	18	2	6	.640	2	1	0	0	3	0	0	0	-.087	.052	4.76	4.76	4.11
Carlson J *	4	13.7	59	20	0	8	5	2	1	13	3	1	.762	1	0	0	0	0	1	1	2	.118	-.170	4.61	4.61	5.67
Lewis R *	4	18.7	82	14	0	15	8	0	0	20	4	2	.709	0	0	0	0	0	0	0	0	.116	.013	6.75	6.75	5.58
Roenicke J	4	19.0	91	16	0	18	13	0	2	18	1	3	.667	0	0	0	1	0	0	0	2	-.088	.061	7.11	5.68	4.27

Only includes pitchers with at least ten Innings Pitched. Italicized stats have been adjusted for home park.

Batted Ball Pitching Stats

Player	% of PA		% of Batted Balls					Out %		Runs Per Event				Total Runs vs. Avg.				
	K%	BB%	GB%	LD%	FB%	IF/F	HR/OF	GB	OF	NIP	GB	LD	OF	NIP	GB	LD	FB	Tot
Romero Ri	20	10	55	18	27	.07	.10	78	79	.04	.02	.39	.20	1	-8	-0	-8	-15
Marcum Sh	21	6	38	18	43	.10	.11	77	86	-.01	.03	.41	.17	-11	-4	2	2	-12
Downs Sc	20	7	58	13	29	.04	.06	78	76	.01	.01	.27	.21	-2	-3	-7	-1	-12
Purcey Da	22	10	29	16	55	.18	.07	78	85	.03	.03	.37	.13	-0	-1	-2	-2	-5
Gregg Ke	23	12	42	17	40	.08	.07	75	79	.05	.03	.39	.18	1	-2	-2	-0	-2
Cecil Br	16	8	44	18	38	.09	.10	78	78	.03	.01	.40	.20	-3	-8	2	7	-2
Frasor Ja	23	11	46	19	35	.11	.07	68	79	.04	.07	.37	.17	0	2	-1	-2	-1
Camp Sh	15	7	52	17	31	.07	.12	79	85	.04	.01	.48	.19	-1	-3	3	0	-1
Janssen Ro	21	8	47	22	31	.05	.13	79	80	.02	.02	.38	.24	-2	-2	3	2	1
Morrow Br	28	12	40	18	42	.10	.08	69	78	.02	.08	.46	.19	-1	3	-0	0	1
Litsch Je	8	8	44	16	40	.09	.11	81	78	.12	-.00	.36	.24	2	-2	-0	6	5
Rzepczynski Ma	20	12	51	16	32	.02	.13	76	69	.06	.03	.40	.32	3	-1	-0	9	11
Eveland Da	10	14	52	16	32	.04	.08	71	76	.15	.06	.42	.18	6	4	1	1	12
Tallet Br	15	12	35	17	48	.16	.18	72	91	.09	.04	.45	.25	5	-0	4	10	18
MLB Average	18	9	44	18	38	.09	.10	74	83	.04	.04	.38	.18	--	--	--	--	--

Only includes pitchers who faced at least one hundred batters.

Fielding Stats

Name	INN	SBA/G	CS%	ERA	WP+PB/G	PO	A	TE	FE
Catchers									
Buck J	933.0	0.60	24%	4.46	0.415	733	40	5	0
Molina J	444.7	0.65	41%	3.72	0.688	417	37	2	0
Arencibia J	63.0	0.71	40%	4.43	0.286	48	3	0	0

Name	Inn	PO	A	TE	FE	FPct	DPS	DPT	ZRDif	OOZ	Dif
First Base											
Overbay L	1320.0	1309	101	3	3	.996	14	5	.034	40	-3
Lind A	76.0	70	9	0	0	1.000	0	0	--	3	--
Ruiz R	23.0	25	2	0	0	1.000	0	0	--	1	--
Bautista J	18.0	26	0	0	0	1.000	0	0	--	0	--
Reed J	3.0	2	0	0	0	1.000	0	0	--	0	--
Second Base											
Hill A	1188.0	236	383	5	5	.984	25	63	.017	35	6
McDonald J	150.0	32	50	1	0	.988	6	12	-.016	3	-1
McCoy M	74.0	10	31	0	0	1.000	2	5	--	6	--
Green N	18.7	3	8	0	0	1.000	0	0	--	1	--
Hoffpauir J	10.0	1	5	0	0	1.000	0	0	--	0	--
Shortstop											
Gonzalez A	740.0	104	272	8	3	.972	47	17	.009	40	8
Escobar Y	532.7	105	173	6	3	.969	23	23	-.002	18	-5
McDonald J	115.0	24	42	1	0	.985	6	7	.132	8	3
McCoy M	43.0	10	10	1	0	.952	0	0	--	5	--
Green N	10.0	3	2	0	0	1.000	0	0	--	0	--
Third Base											
Encarnacion	841.7	71	174	11	7	.932	12	1	-.001	34	3
Bautista J	393.0	26	100	2	2	.969	6	1	-.051	27	12
McDonald J	114.0	11	26	2	1	.925	3	0	-.005	2	-2
Hoffpauir J	87.0	6	25	0	0	1.000	3	0	--	4	--
McCoy M	5.0	0	2	0	0	1.000	0	0	--	1	--

Name	Inn	PO	A	TE	FE	FPct	DPS	DPT	ZRDif	OOZ	Dif
Left Field											
Lewis F	726.3	134	1	0	3	.978	0	0	-.051	34	-2
Snider T	433.7	88	2	1	2	.968	0	0	.057	24	3
Lind A	123.0	22	0	0	0	1.000	0	0	-.001	2	-4
Wise D	65.0	13	0	0	0	1.000	0	0	--	0	--
McCoy M	53.7	16	0	0	1	.941	0	0	--	5	--
Reed J	24.0	3	0	0	0	1.000	0	0	--	0	--
McDonald J	15.0	2	0	0	0	1.000	0	0	--	1	--
Center Field											
Wells V	1309.0	354	5	0	0	1.000	2	0	-.012	72	-2
Wise D	74.7	27	2	0	0	1.000	1	0	--	6	--
Lewis F	49.3	15	0	0	0	1.000	0	0	--	4	--
McCoy M	4.0	2	0	0	0	1.000	0	0	--	0	--
Bautista J	3.0	1	0	0	0	1.000	0	0	--	--	--
Right Field											
Bautista J	982.7	179	12	0	3	.985	5	0	.006	49	-5
Snider T	245.0	47	1	0	0	1.000	0	0	-.092	18	5
Wise D	100.0	20	1	0	0	1.000	0	0	-.002	3	-2
Lewis F	67.0	20	0	0	0	1.000	0	0	--	3	--
McCoy M	25.0	7	0	0	0	1.000	0	0	--	1	--
Reed J	21.0	8	0	0	0	1.000	0	0	--	1	--

Washington Nationals

Stat Facts:

- Mike Morse had the most Base Runs of any player with <300 PA
- Nyjer Morgan led the NL in CS
- Morgan tied for the fewest GDP of any regular
- Morgan tied for the ML lead in CF TE
- Livan Hernandez allowed 4 SB in 13 attempts
- John Lannan allowed 18 SB in 21 attempts
- Stephen Strasburg's H-A was exactly .000
- Ivan Rodriguez had the second-lowest WP+PB/G of regular C
- Ryan Zimmerman tied for the most TE of any 3B
- Ian Desmond tied for the NL lead in SS TE
- Desmond led the majors in FE
- Matt Capps walked 5% of his BFP

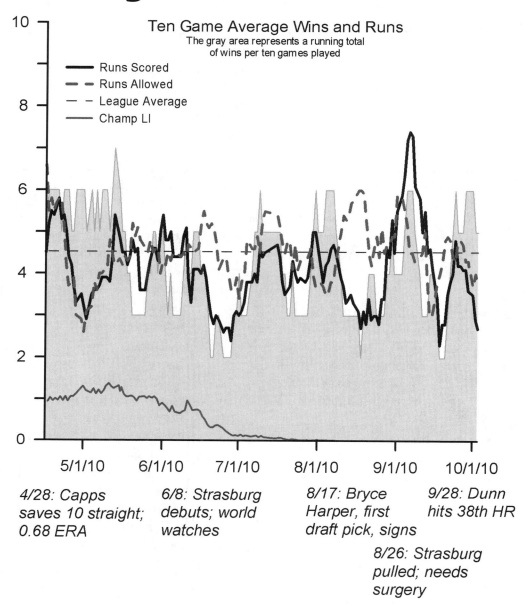

Ten Game Average Wins and Runs
The gray area represents a running total of wins per ten games played

- Runs Scored
- Runs Allowed
- League Average
- Champ LI

4/28: Capps saves 10 straight; 0.68 ERA

6/8: Strasburg debuts; world watches

8/17: Bryce Harper, first draft pick, signs

9/28: Dunn hits 38th HR

8/26: Strasburg pulled; needs surgery

Team Batting and Pitching/Fielding Stats by Month

	April	May	June	July	Aug	Sept/Oct
Wins	13	13	8	12	11	12
Losses	10	16	19	13	18	17
RS/G	4.3	4.5	3.4	4.3	3.8	4.0
RA/G	4.7	4.6	4.6	4.4	4.8	4.5
OBP	.336	.331	.308	.328	.301	.308
SLG	.413	.413	.361	.406	.391	.360
FIP	4.71	4.41	3.52	3.85	3.89	4.40
DER	.705	.707	.658	.692	.680	.700

Batting Stats

Player	BR	Runs	RBI	PA	Outs	H	2B	3B	HR	TB	K	BB	IBB	HBP	SH	SF	SB	CS	GDP	H-A	L^R	BA	OBP	SLG	GPA
Dunn A *	104	85	103	648	424	145	36	2	38	299	199	77	10	9	0	4	0	1	10	.003	.076	.260	.356	.536	.296
Zimmerman R	96	85	85	603	381	161	32	0	25	268	98	69	6	4	0	5	4	1	16	-.015	.036	.307	.388	.510	.304
Willingham J	68	54	56	451	279	99	19	2	16	170	85	67	3	9	0	4	8	0	8	.067	.026	.268	.389	.459	.292
Desmond I	62	59	65	574	398	141	27	4	10	206	109	28	3	5	9	7	17	5	9	-.014	.043	.269	.308	.392	.238
Morgan N *	54	60	24	577	399	129	17	7	0	160	88	40	1	10	15	3	34	17	2	.024	.045	.253	.319	.314	.223
Bernadina R	53	52	47	461	317	102	18	3	11	159	93	35	1	4	2	6	16	2	3	.018	-.024	.246	.307	.384	.236
Morse M	45	36	41	293	196	77	12	2	15	138	64	22	1	4	0	1	0	1	6	-.006	.055	.289	.352	.519	.290
Kennedy A *	38	43	31	389	269	85	16	1	3	112	44	37	1	5	1	4	14	2	10	-.007	-.066	.249	.327	.327	.230
Guzman C +	35	44	25	346	238	90	11	4	2	115	53	17	3	5	3	2	4	2	7	.067	.048	.282	.327	.361	.238
Rodriguez I	32	32	49	421	320	106	18	1	4	138	66	16	2	1	2	4	2	3	25	.049	.032	.266	.294	.347	.220
Harris W *	27	25	32	262	188	41	6	2	10	81	60	33	0	2	1	2	5	2	3	.021	-.043	.183	.291	.362	.223
Espinosa D +	13	16	15	112	83	22	4	1	6	46	30	9	1	0	0	0	0	2	0	.054	.043	.214	.277	.447	.238
Gonzalez A	13	19	5	198	148	46	8	1	0	56	30	7	0	1	3	1	0	0	8	.018	.008	.247	.277	.301	.201
Maxwell J	11	16	12	131	93	15	6	0	3	30	43	25	2	0	0	2	5	1	3	-.017	.112	.144	.305	.288	.211
Nieves W	10	10	16	172	132	32	8	0	3	49	29	8	2	1	4	1	0	0	6	-.012	.024	.203	.244	.310	.188
Ramos W	6	3	4	54	39	14	4	0	1	21	9	2	0	0	0	0	0	0	1	.070	.273	.269	.296	.404	.236
Stammen C	2	2	6	43	31	9	3	0	0	12	15	1	0	0	3	0	0	0	2	.189	.169	.237	.250	.316	.193
Maldonado C	2	1	3	12	8	3	0	0	1	6	2	1	0	0	0	0	0	0	0	--	-.317	.273	.333	.545	.288
Taveras W	2	7	4	37	30	7	0	1	0	9	6	2	0	0	0	0	1	2	0	-.047	.289	.200	.243	.257	.175
Hernandez L	1	2	3	71	54	9	1	0	1	13	13	1	0	0	9	0	0	0	2	-.056	-.140	.148	.161	.213	.127

Only includes batters with at least one Base Run. Italicized stats have been adjusted for home park.

Batted Ball Batting Stats

Player	% of PA		% of Batted Balls					Out %		Runs Per Event				Total Runs vs. Avg.				
	K%	BB%	GB%	LD%	FB%	IF/F	HR/OF	GB	OF	NIP	GB	LD	OF	NIP	GB	LD	FB	Tot
Zimmerman Ry	16	12	41	18	41	.07	.15	68	83	.08	.07	.44	.23	8	5	7	15	35
Dunn Ad	31	13	33	18	49	.07	.23	77	77	.03	.02	.45	.40	0	-6	-1	39	33
Willingham Jo	19	17	31	20	49	.14	.13	74	88	.10	.04	.45	.19	12	-2	7	4	20
Morse Mi	22	9	46	16	38	.05	.21	67	84	.02	.08	.43	.32	-1	4	0	12	15
Espinosa Da	27	8	46	8	46	.12	.21	82	83	-.01	.02	.48	.35	-2	-1	-3	5	-1
Kennedy Ad	11	11	43	20	37	.03	.03	78	82	.11	.01	.36	.07	5	-3	3	-8	-3
Maxwell Ju	33	19	35	16	49	.06	.10	77	92	.06	.03	.40	.11	2	-1	-3	-2	-4
Guzman Cr	15	6	51	20	29	.05	.03	73	81	.02	.06	.35	.09	-2	4	1	-8	-5
Desmond Ia	19	6	53	16	32	.09	.08	71	86	-.01	.06	.51	.13	-8	7	4	-10	-5
Bernadina Ro	20	8	47	13	39	.06	.09	71	85	.02	.07	.39	.16	-2	5	-7	-2	-6
Harris Wi	23	13	41	16	43	.04	.15	84	93	.06	-.01	.27	.20	2	-4	-7	1	-7
Gonzalez Al	15	4	55	14	31	.13	.00	72	86	-.02	.05	.41	.02	-3	1	-2	-9	-12
Nieves Wi	17	5	54	15	31	.08	.08	84	82	-.00	-.02	.33	.15	-2	-5	-3	-3	-13
Morgan Ny	15	9	53	22	25	.11	.00	75	83	.05	.06	.32	.05	1	6	-1	-20	-15
Rodriguez Iv	16	4	61	18	21	.09	.06	74	82	-.02	.03	.37	.14	-7	-1	1	-9	-16
MLB Average	18	9	44	18	38	.09	.10	74	83	.04	.04	.38	.18	--	--	--	--	--

Only includes batters with at least one hundred Plate Appearances.

Pitching Stats

Player	PRC	IP	BFP	G	GS	K	BB	IBB	HBP	H	HR	DP	DER	SB	CS	PO	W	L	Sv	Op	Hld	H-A	R^L	RA	ERA	FIP
Hernandez L	75	211.7	896	33	33	114	64	5	4	216	16	18	.705	4	9	3	10	12	0	0	0	.023	-.051	3.95	3.66	3.99
Clippard T	47	91.0	378	78	0	112	41	4	2	69	8	7	.707	5	1	1	11	8	1	11	23	-.028	-.038	3.26	3.07	3.16
Burnett S *	39	63.0	261	73	0	62	20	4	1	52	3	6	.697	4	0	0	1	7	3	4	20	-.022	.071	2.43	2.14	2.66
Lannan J *	38	143.3	643	25	25	71	49	3	4	175	14	21	.661	18	3	1	8	8	0	0	0	-.001	-.024	5.15	4.65	4.52
Strasburg S	35	68.0	274	12	12	92	17	0	0	56	5	4	.663	2	1	0	5	3	0	0	0	.000	-.048	3.31	2.91	2.20
Stammen C	34	128.0	562	35	19	85	41	4	1	151	13	17	.664	4	1	0	4	4	0	0	1	-.034	.040	5.48	5.13	4.08
Peralta J	33	49.0	189	39	0	49	9	4	1	30	5	2	.760	3	0	1	1	0	0	2	9	.001	-.051	2.20	2.02	2.89
Batista M	31	82.7	350	58	1	55	39	8	5	71	9	12	.731	8	3	0	1	2	2	2	1	.006	-.043	3.92	3.70	4.59
Storen D	23	55.3	232	54	0	52	22	3	3	48	5	6	.697	2	1	0	4	4	5	7	10	-.061	.012	3.90	3.58	3.21
Atilano L	19	85.7	385	16	16	40	32	5	2	96	11	6	.697	1	3	0	6	7	0	0	0	.014	-.034	5.88	5.15	4.95
Olsen S *	19	81.0	357	17	15	53	27	4	2	93	10	9	.679	3	2	0	4	8	0	0	0	-.032	-.022	6.00	5.56	4.42
Capps M	18	46.0	199	47	0	38	9	3	0	51	5	2	.653	1	1	0	3	3	26	30	0	-.019	.034	3.91	2.74	3.35
Slaten D *	16	40.7	174	49	0	36	19	2	4	34	3	1	.717	3	1	1	4	1	0	0	4	-.084	-.150	3.98	3.10	3.61
Walker T	14	35.3	145	24	0	30	8	2	0	35	5	3	.696	1	2	1	1	0	0	1	1	.040	.074	4.08	3.57	3.85
Balester C	13	21.0	89	17	0	28	11	1	2	15	2	2	.717	0	1	0	0	1	0	0	0	-.192	-.079	2.57	2.57	3.48
Martin J	12	48.0	212	9	9	31	11	1	1	56	9	4	.681	0	1	0	1	5	0	0	0	-.036	-.077	5.63	4.13	5.03
Marquis J	10	58.7	276	13	13	31	24	0	8	76	9	12	.647	9	2	0	2	9	0	0	0	-.024	-.060	7.21	6.60	5.77
Zimmermann	8	31.0	135	7	7	27	10	1	2	31	8	2	.716	3	1	0	1	2	0	0	0	.057	-.015	5.81	4.94	5.87
Detwiler R *	6	29.7	135	8	5	17	14	1	1	34	5	5	.673	4	2	1	1	3	0	0	0	.007	.094	6.67	4.25	5.66
Maya Y	5	26.0	118	5	5	12	11	1	2	30	3	3	.689	1	0	0	0	3	0	0	0	.058	-.033	6.23	5.88	5.16
Bruney B	2	17.7	93	19	0	16	20	1	0	21	1	2	.589	1	0	0	1	2	0	0	3	-.158	.111	9.17	7.64	5.35

Only includes pitchers with at least ten Innings Pitched. Italicized stats have been adjusted for home park.

Batted Ball Pitching Stats

Player	% of PA		% of Batted Balls					Out %		Runs Per Event				Total Runs vs. Avg.				
	K%	BB%	GB%	LD%	FB%	IF/F	HR/OF	GB	OF	NIP	GB	LD	OF	NIP	GB	LD	FB	Tot
Strasburg St	34	6	48	20	32	.08	.09	71	79	-.04	.06	.39	.19	-8	0	-2	-4	-13
Burnett Se	24	8	54	21	24	.07	.08	76	86	.00	.04	.31	.12	-3	-0	-2	-7	-12
Peralta Jo	26	5	26	18	56	.14	.08	67	93	-.04	.09	.38	.08	-5	-0	-2	-5	-12
Clippard Ty	30	11	28	17	56	.10	.07	73	85	.01	.03	.52	.12	-2	-4	-1	-5	-11
Storen Dr	22	11	40	20	40	.08	.05	68	90	.04	.08	.37	.06	0	1	-1	-7	-7
Hernandez Li	13	8	39	21	40	.10	.06	76	84	.06	.03	.38	.12	0	-6	10	-10	-6
Slaten Do	21	13	48	12	40	.22	.06	70	82	.07	.05	.36	.12	2	1	-3	-4	-4
Batista Mi	16	13	50	15	35	.10	.12	82	77	.09	-.01	.32	.24	5	-6	-5	4	-3
Walker Ty	21	6	42	13	44	.15	.13	66	91	-.02	.09	.47	.17	-2	2	-1	-0	-1
Capps Ma	19	5	48	18	34	.10	.11	72	75	-.03	.06	.43	.24	-3	1	1	2	1
Maya Yu	10	11	33	23	44	.08	.08	70	82	.13	.07	.32	.15	2	0	1	1	4
Zimmermann Jo	20	9	49	13	38	.06	.24	74	81	.03	.06	.27	.37	-0	1	-3	7	4
Detwiler Ro	13	11	43	20	37	.08	.15	67	93	.10	.06	.46	.17	2	1	3	0	6
Olsen Sc	15	8	46	19	34	.04	.11	74	86	.05	.04	.46	.17	0	-0	7	0	7
Martin J.	15	6	38	20	43	.10	.14	71	82	.02	.06	.36	.24	-2	1	2	6	7
Atilano Lu	10	9	41	21	38	.16	.11	78	76	.10	.02	.35	.25	3	-2	4	8	13
Stammen Cr	15	7	51	23	26	.05	.11	78	76	.04	.02	.40	.26	-1	-3	14	4	13
Marquis Ja	11	12	53	18	29	.05	.16	68	85	.12	.08	.36	.25	5	6	2	4	17
Lannan Jo	11	8	51	21	27	.06	.11	74	83	.08	.04	.42	.18	3	2	16	-2	19
MLB Average	*18*	*9*	*44*	*18*	*38*	*.09*	*.10*	*74*	*83*	*.04*	*.04*	*.38*	*.18*	*--*	*--*	*--*	*--*	*--*

Only includes pitchers who faced at least one hundred batters.

Fielding Stats

Name	INN	SBA/G	CS%	ERA	WP+PB/G	PO	A	TE	FE
Catchers									
Rodriguez I	884.0	0.62	31%	4.25	0.214	709	55	4	0
Nieves W	395.0	0.87	18%	4.01	0.205	290	20	5	0
Ramos W	129.3	0.49	14%	3.90	0.487	96	9	0	0
Maldonado C	25.7	0.70	0%	3.16	0.351	10	2	0	0

Name	Inn	PO	A	TE	FE	FPct	DPS	DPT	ZRDif	OOZ	Dif
First Base											
Dunn A	1246.0	1203	93	4	8	.990	6	0	-.014	28	-13
Kennedy A	113.0	105	7	0	1	.991	0	0	.036	4	0
Morse M	60.0	58	5	0	0	1.000	1	0	--	0	--
Gonzalez A	16.0	15	0	0	0	1.000	0	0	--	0	--
Second Base											
Kennedy A	628.3	143	207	4	3	.980	24	18	.007	14	-2
Guzman C	475.0	122	165	2	4	.980	10	17	-.016	15	3
Espinosa D	211.3	57	74	0	0	1.000	4	16	-.055	10	5
Gonzalez A	120.3	35	42	1	0	.987	6	10	-.016	2	-1
Shortstop											
Desmond I		221	382	13	21	.947	39	44	-.021	47	-5
Guzman C	130.3	23	52	1	1	.974	3	2	.001	9	3
Gonzalez A	78.7	9	26	1	0	.972	3	3	--	3	--
Espinosa D	18.0	2	9	0	1	.917	1	0	--	1	--
Third Base											
Zimmerman	1189.0	85	242	11	6	.951	22	0	.029	57	13
Gonzalez A	178.3	16	47	3	0	.955	3	0	.143	13	6
Kennedy A	45.3	2	6	0	1	.889	0	0	--	2	--
Harris W	22.0	1	8	0	1	.900	0	0	--	2	--

Name	Inn	PO	A	TE	FE	FPct	DPS	DPT	ZRDif	OOZ	Dif
Left Field											
Willingham J	880.3	164	7	0	1	.994	2	0	.007	42	-1
Bernadina R	318.0	58	2	1	0	.984	1	0	-.011	15	-1
Harris W	200.3	38	0	0	1	.974	0	0	.015	7	-3
Maxwell J	26.0	5	1	0	2	.750	0	0	--	1	--
Taveras W	5.3	1	0	0	0	1.000	0	0	--	0	--
Mench K	5.0	0	0	0	0	0.000	0	0	--	--	--
Center Field											
Morgan N	1124.0	339	2	3	2	.986	0	0	-.007	87	23
Bernadina R	177.7	45	2	0	1	.979	1	0	-.121	4	-6
Maxwell J	115.0	36	2	0	0	1.000	1	0	.002	5	-2
Taveras W	14.0	4	0	0	0	1.000	0	0	--	1	--
Harris W	4.0	2	0	0	0	1.000	0	0	--	1	--
Right Field											
Morse M	510.3	123	2	0	0	1.000	1	0	.037	23	-5
Bernadina R	492.3	104	5	0	2	.982	2	0	-.014	22	-5
Harris W	220.3	58	0	0	1	.983	0	0	-.028	18	6
Maxwell J	120.0	32	1	0	0	1.000	0	0	-.004	7	0
Taveras W	57.7	12	1	0	0	1.000	1	0	--	1	--
Guzman C	32.3	8	0	0	1	.889	0	0	--	3	--
Gonzalez A	1.7	0	0	0	0	0.000	0	0	--	--	--
Desmond I	0.3	0	0	0	0	0.000	0	0	--	--	--

The Hardball Times Glossary

A: Assists. The number of times a fielder makes a throw that results in an out.

AB: At-Bats

AB/RSP: At-Bats with Runners in Scoring Position (second and/or third base)

BA: Batting Average; Hits divided by At-Bats

BA/RSP: Batting Average with Runners in Scoring Position (second and/or third base)

BABIP: Batting Average on Balls in Play. This is a measure of the number of batted balls that safely fall in for hits (not including home runs). The exact formula we use is (H-HR)/(AB-K-HR+SF). This is similar to DER, but from the batter's perspective.

BR: Base Runs, a run contribution formula created by David Smyth, which quantifies the number of runs contributed by a batter. The fundamental formula for Base Runs is (baserunners * scoring rate) + home runs. Note that our Base Runs are adjusted for park effects.

BB: Bases on Balls, otherwise known as walks

BB/%: The percentage of plate appearances that result in a walk. In our batted ball statistics, this figure includes HBP.

BB/9: Number of walks allowed for every nine innings pitched.

BFP: Batters Faced by Pitcher; the pitching equivalent of Plate Appearances for batters

Champ LI: Championship Leverage Index, the importance of a game in terms of its impact on the team's chance of making the postseason. Please refer to the article "The Year in a Single Number" for more information.

CS: Caught Stealing

CWS: Career Win Shares

DER: Defense Efficiency Ratio. The percent of times a batted ball is turned into an out by the team's fielders, not including home runs. The exact formula we use is (BFP-H-K-BB-HBP-0.6*E)/(BFP-HR-K-BB-HBP). This is similar to BABIP, but from the defensive team's perspective.

Dif stands for Difference, and in the fielding stats it represents the difference between the plays made out of zone by a specific player and the major league average number of out-of-zone plays made at that position, per 1,000 innings.

DP: Double Plays

DPS: Double Plays Started, in which the fielder typically gets only an assist

DPT: Double Plays Turned, in which the fielder records both an assist and a putout

ERA: Earned Run Average. Number of earned runs allowed divided by innings pitched multiplied by nine.

ERA+: ERA measured against the league average and adjusted for ballpark factors. An ERA+ over 100 is better than average, less than 100 is below average.

ExpWS: Expected Win Shares. The number of Win Shares an average major leaguer would accrue, given a specific player's playing time.

FB: Fly ball, as categorized by BIS's scorekeepers. Includes both infield and outfield fly balls.

FE: Fielding Errors, as opposed to Throwing Errors (TE)

FIP: Fielding Independent Pitching, a measure of all those things for which a pitcher is specifically responsible. The formula is (HR*13+(BB+HBP)*3-K*2)/IP, plus a league-specific factor (usually around 3.2) to round out the number to an equivalent ERA number. FIP helps you understand how well a pitcher pitched, regardless of how well his fielders fielded. FIP was invented by Tom M. Tango.

FPct: Fielding Percentage, or the number of fielding chances handled without an error. The formula is (A+PO)/(A+PO+E).

G: Games played

GB%: The percent of batted balls that are grounders. GB% is a better way to measure ground ball tendencies than the more common Ground ball/Fly ball ratio (G/F), because ratios don't follow normal scales (a G/F ratio of 2 doesn't equal twice as many ground balls than 1) and definitions of fly balls can be inconsistent.

GIDP (or GDP): The number of times a batter Grounded Into Double Plays

GPA: Gross Production Average, a variation of OPS, but more accurate and easier to interpret. The exact formula is (OBP*1.8+SLG)/4, adjusted for ballpark. The scale of GPA is similar to BA: .200 is lousy, .265 is around average and .300 is a star.

GS: Games Started, a pitching stat.

H-A: Home minus Away, a stat for expressing the "home field advantage" enjoyed by each player. The exact formula is each player's GPA at home minus his

GPA on the road. This is calculated for both batters and pitchers; since both tend to perform better at home, H-A is generally positive for batters and negative for pitchers.

HBP: Hit By Pitch, an unfortunate consequence of batting

Holds: A bullpen stat. According to MLB.com, *A relief pitcher is credited with a hold any time he enters a game in a save situation, records at least one out and leaves the game never having relinquished the lead. A pitcher cannot finish the game and receive credit for a hold, nor can he earn a hold and a save in the same game.*

HRA: Home Runs Allowed, also a pitching stat

HR/Fly or HR/F: Home Runs as a percent of outfield fly balls. Typically, about 10% to 11% of outfield flies are hit for home runs.

IBB: Intentional Base on Balls.

IF/Fly or IF/F: The percent of fly balls that are infield flies. Infield flies are those fly balls caught within the infield baselines.

ISO: Isolated Power, which measures the extra-base prowess of a batter. The formula is SLG-BA.

K: Strikeouts

K/G: Strikeouts per Game, the number of strikeouts divided by total number of batters faced, times the average number of batters per game in that specific league (generally around 38 batters a game).

K/9: Strikeouts per nine innings pitched, a slight variation on K/G (and not as useful)

L: Losses

L^R: See R^L.

LD%: Line Drive Percentage. Baseball Info Solutions tracks the trajectory of each batted ball and categorizes it as a ground ball, fly ball or line drive. LD% is the percent of batted balls that are line drives. Line drives are not necessarily the hardest hit balls, but they do fall for a hit around 75% of the time.

LI: Leverage Index. Invented by Tom M. Tango, LI measures the criticality of a play or plate appearance. It is based on the range of potential WPA outcomes of a play, compared to all other plays. 1.0 is an average Index.

NIP: Not In Play; represents plays in which the batter didn't put the ball in play: strikeouts, walks and hits by pitch.

OBP: On Base Percentage, the proportion of plate appearances in which a batter reached base successfully, including hits, walks and hit by pitches.

OF: Outfield Flies. BIS categorizes each fly ball as an infield fly or outfield fly, using the infield baselines as the boundary, depending on where the ball would have landed if not caught.

OOZ: Plays made out of zone. A zone is defined as all areas of the field in which that fielding position successfully converts 50% of chances into outs, on average.

Op: Save Opportunities

OPS: On Base plus Slugging Percentage, a crude but quick measure of a batter's true contribution to his team's offense. See GPA for a better approach.

OPS+: OPS measured against the league average, and adjusted for ballpark factors. An OPS+ over 100 is better than average, less than 100 is below average.

Outs: Outs. Not just outs at bat, by the way, but also outs when caught stealing. Two outs are included when hitting into a double play.

P/PA: Pitches per Plate Appearance.

PA: Plate Appearances, or AB+BB+HBP+SF+SH.

Plus/Minus is a fielding system very similar to Ultimate Zone Rating. It was invented by John Dewan and is tracked by Baseball Info Solutions.

PO: Putouts, the number of times a fielder recorded an out in the field. First basemen and catchers get lots of these. From a pitching perspective, PO stands for pickoffs—the number of times a pitcher picks a base runner off a base.

POS: Position played in the field

PRC: Pitching Runs Created, a stat developed by THT's David Gassko. PRC measures the impact of a pitcher by putting his production on the same scale as a batter's Runs Created. PRC is calculated by inserting the number of runs allowed by a pitcher into a league-average context, and then using the Pythagorean Formula to estimate how many wins that pitcher/team would achieve. That win total is then converted into the number of offensive runs it would take to achieve the same number of wins. The impact of fielders is separated in the process.

Pythagorean Formula: A formula for converting a team's Run Differential into a projected win-loss record. The formula is RS^2/(RS^2+RA^2). Teams'

actual win-loss records tend to mirror their Pythagorean records, and variances can usually be attributed to luck.

You can improve the accuracy of the Pythagorean formula by using a different exponent (the 2 in the formula). In particular, a sabermetrician named US Patriot discovered that the best exponent can be calculated this way: $(RS/G+RA/G)^{.285}$, where RS/G is Runs Scored per Game and RA/G is Runs Allowed per Game. This is called the PythagoPat formula.

PWins: Pythagorean Wins. See the previous entry.

R: Runs Scored and/or Allowed.

R/G: Runs Scored Per Game. Literally, R divided by games played.

R^L (or L^R): The difference in GPA between a player's performance against left-handed and right-handed pitchers or batters. The order of subtraction depends on the player's natural platoon split—for right-handed batters, for instance, it's L-R. You can read more about R^L in "As Much Fun as Doing Your Taxes." Note that, for team stats, the formula is the more common L-R for batters and R-L for pitchers.

RBI: Runs Batted In

RISP: Runners In Scoring Position

RS: Runs Scored

Run Differential: Runs Scored minus Runs Allowed

RZR: Revised Zone Rating. RZR measures how often a fielder successfully fields a ball that is hit into his zone. A zone is defined as all areas of the field in which that fielding position successfully converts 50% of chances into outs, on average. RZR differs from the original Zone Rating by removing plays made out of zone and listing them separately.

SB: Stolen Bases

SB%: The percent of time a runner stole a base successfully. The formula is SB/SBA.

SBA: Stolen Bases Attempted.

SBA/G: Stolen Base Attempts per nine innings played.

ShO: Shutouts

SLG and SLGA: Slugging Percentage. Total Bases divided by At-Bats. SLGA stands for Slugging Percentage Against. It represents SLG from the pitcher's perspective.

SO: Strikeouts

Sv: Saves. According to MLB.com, *A pitcher is credited with a save when he finishes a game won by his club, is not the winning pitcher, and either (a) enters the game with a lead of no more than three runs and pitches for at least one inning, (b) enters the game with the potential tying run either on base, or at bat, or on deck, or (c) pitches effectively for at least three innings.*

Sv%: Saves divided by Save Opportunities

Sv/Hld%: Save/Hold Percentage. Saves and Holds divided by Saves, Holds and Blown Saves. Since a pitcher is given a Blown Save if he gives up a lead in a typical Hold situation, this is a more appropriate metric than Sv%.

TB: Total Bases, calculated as 1B+2B*2+3B*3+HR*4

TBA: Total Bases Allowed. A pitching stat.

TE: Throwing Errors, as opposed to Fielding Errors (FE)

UER: Unearned Runs

UERA: Unearned Run Average, or the number of unearned runs allowed for each nine innings pitched.

UZR: A fielding system invented by Mitchel Lichtman, it is similar to John Dewan's plus/minus system. Both systems calculate a fielder's range by comparing his plays made in various "vectors" across the baseball diamond to the major league average rate of plays made in those vectors. Both systems also look at other factors such as the effectiveness of outfield throwing, handling bunts and turning double plays.

W: Wins

WAR: Wins Above Replacement. A "win stat" that calculates the number of wins a player contributed to his team above a certain replacement level. WAR is calculated at Fangraphs and Baseball Reference. Though the two implementations vary a bit, they share a common framework that includes a "linear weights" approach to runs created, advanced fielding metrics, leverage for relievers and replacement levels that vary by position. The methodology was established over time at the *Book Blog* (www.insidethebook.com).

WHIP: Walks and Hits Per Inning Pitched, a variant of OBP for pitchers. This is a popular stat in rotisserie baseball circles.

wOBA: Introduced in *The Book*, this rate stat is similar to OPS and GPA, except that it is set to the scale of OBP.

WPA: Win Probability Added. A system in which each player is given credit toward helping his team win, based on play-by-play data and the impact each specific play has on the team's probability of winning. Read "The Year in One Number" for more details.

WPA/LI: Literally, the WPA of a play divided by its criticality (measured by LI). This stat takes WPA and effectively neutralizes the impact of the game situation. It's another approach for judging player impact on a game—removing the game context but leaving the player's impact on scoring. It can be thought of as "Situational Batting" (or Pitching).

WP+PB/G: Wild Pitches and Passed Balls per Nine Innings played. A fielding stat for catchers.

WS: Win Shares. Invented by Bill James. Win Shares is a very complicated statistic that takes all the contributions a player made toward his team's wins and distills them into a single number that represents the number of wins he contributed to the team, times three.

There are three subcategories of Win Shares: batting, pitching and fielding. We have tweaked James' original formula a bit.

WSAge: The average age of a team, weighted by each player's total Win Shares contribution.

WSAB: Win Shares Above Bench. WSAB is a refined approach to Win Shares, in which each player's total Win Shares are compared to the Win Shares an average bench player would have received.

Our research indicates that this is an important adjustment to Win Shares, because it gives greater context to the Win Shares totals. The impact is similar to adding "Loss Shares" for each player.

The bench player is defined as 70% of Expected Win Shares for all players except starting pitchers, for whom it is 50% of Expected Win Shares.

WSP: Win Shares Percentage is a rate stat, calculated as WS/(2*ExpWS). WSP is similar to winning percentage in that .500 is average, but WSP ranges above 1.000 and below .000.

xFIP: Expected Fielding Independent Pitching. This is an experimental stat that adjusts FIP and "normalizes" the home run component. Research has shown that home runs allowed are pretty much a function of flyballs allowed and home park, so xFIP is based on the average number of home runs allowed per outfield fly. Theoretically, this should be a better predictor of a pitcher's future ERA.

ZRDif is used in our fielding tables to show the difference between a player's Revised Zone Rating and the major league average Revised Zone Rating at that position.

Trivia Answers

Bye? (Page 6)

1. Denny Driscoll. Over his four seasons, his ERA+ postings were 64, 220, 81, and 90.

2. John Cassidy, who achieved his season of glory for Hartford in 1877.

3. Shortstop Archie Manning and quarterback Bill Buckner. Buckner never played in the NFL. Manning was drafted a few more times by MLB.

4. Pat Hentgen. Tom Underwood was the first to play for all three teams, but only Hentgen was bird-exclusive.

5. 1946, as the Dodgers' .718 and the Red Sox' .792 marks were franchise highs. The Red Sox tied their mark a few years later; the Dodgers broke in 1953, setting their current record at .779. Since 1910 the feat has happened only seven times.

6. Career visitor home runs at Coors Field. On the opposite end is Cesar Izturis, with 38 games at Coors and no homers.

Huh? (Page 90)

1. The White Sox have yet to appear in the World Series during a presidential election year.

2. Lehane was born on April 15, 1865, the day President Lincoln was shot; he is the only player to have born the day of a President's assassination. The others were born on a day a former President died: Gregory on the death of Chester Arthur; Glavenich on the death of Rutherford Hayes; Grim on the death of William Taft; and Paquette on the death of Dwight Eisenhower.

3. Roly de Armas. I have no idea why I'm not a manager if he still is; I could manage .300 in my sleep.

4. Del Pratt. Color me surprised.

5. Alaska, because it has Curt Schilling and only four other pitchers. Nebraska is a strong second at .533.

6. All six pitchers were born during a democratic process—Election Day in their given years. Outfielder Steve Behel, part of last year's Annual trivia, also was born on an Election Day. And the alliteration award goes to Ricky Romero for being born during Ronald Reagan's re-election.

Still? (Page 118)

1. Neither team walked or struck out. The closest occurrence since then was an A's-Browns doubleheader on Aug. 27, 1948, in which Browns hitters had no walks or strikeouts in game one and the A's did the same in game two. One team pulling this feat occurred only five times from 2000 to 2009.

2. A win by at least 10 runs. It is relatively common not to win by at least 10 runs in consecutive seasons, but three takes…well, a Mariners-type offense.

3. A pitcher with 10 saves. Doug Corbett, who managed to sneak himself into multiple challenges this year, had eight.

4. A left-handed reliever. Dusty Bergman's only major league appearance, a June 9 blowout versus Milwaukee, was the only southpaw reliever for the Angels that year.

5. Lead a league in sacrifice hits without playing primarily up the middle. Parker was a first baseman, Buford a third baseman, and Crisp a leftfielder.

6. Dennis Martinez. Four pitchers in the same criteria—expansion, 100 IP—have had two seasons without a sacrifice fly against them: Luis Tiant, Jerry Reuss, Shane Reynolds and Pat Rapp.

Who are These People?

Richard Barbieri lives in New York City. When not thinking about the current state of the Yankees or writing about baseball, he manages to squeeze in a little time for working and sleeping.

John Beamer works for a Bosten-based strategy consulting firm and is an avid supporter of the Atlanta Braves. He currently lives in Australia where baseball starts at 6am—a perfect pre-work tonic!

A graduate of Michigan State University, **Brian Borawski** is a CPA who owns his own small business consulting practice as well as other business ventures. A lifelong Tigers fan, Brian writes about his favorite team at Tigerblog (www.tigerblog.net) and he's a member of SABR's Business of Baseball committee.

Craig Calcaterra is the lead blogger for HardballTalk at NBC Sports.com, where he signed after being designated for assignment by the legal profession in late 2009. He believes no truer words were ever written than "You spend a good piece of your life gripping a wireless, optical mouse and in the end it turns out that it was the other way around all the time." He lives with his wife and two children—Mookie, 6 and Tyrus Raymond, 5—in a fortified compound on the outskirts of New Albany, Ohio.

Dave Cameron is the managing editor of FanGraphs and a co-founder of USSMariner. He also contributes regularly to ESPN and the *Wall Street Journal*, and he considers himself the sixth-best writer in this publication.

Jon Daly lives in Connecticut. He hopes to write the Great American Nonfiction Book some day.

For the past twenty-five years, Baseball Info Solutions owner **John Dewan** has collected, published and analyzed in-depth baseball statistics. He is the author of the award-winning *The Fielding Bible* and the *The Fielding Bible—Volume II*. He announces his annual Fielding Bible Awards on November 1 in The Bill James Handbook and at www.fieldingbible.com.

Joe Distelheim is a retired newspaper editor. He teaches English as a second language to immigrants after a career of preaching English as a first language to reporters. He hopes to see the Cubs in a World Series before Social Security goes broke.

Josh Fisher is a third-year law student at the University of Minnesota, and creator of DodgerDivorce.com.

Vince Gennaro is the author of *Diamond Dollars: The Economics of Winning in Baseball* and a consultant to MLB teams. Over his 30-year business career, he was president of a billion dollar division of PepsiCo and he currently teaches in the Graduate Sports Management programs at Columbia University and Manhattanville College.

A journalism student at Duquesne University, **David Golebiewski** is a writer for The Hardball Times, Fangraphs and *Heater Magazine*. His research for Inside Edge Scouting Services has appeared on ESPN.com and Yahoo.com, and he has also contributed to Rotoworld and Baseball Daily Digest. When's he not writing about baseball, you can find him taking in a game at PNC Park.

Larry Granillo is a lifelong baseball fan living in Milwaukee and rooting for the Brewers. He is the proprietor of the websites Wezen-Ball.com, where subjects like Charlie Brown's win/loss record and the history of the batting helmet are explored in depth, and TaterTrotTracker.com, where each and every major league home run trot is timed and recorded.

Jeremy Greenhouse's other work can be found at BaseballAnalysts.com. He graduates from Tufts University in December 2010 and hopes to avoid unemployment.

Carolina Bolado Hale is a food writer by day and a THT copy editor by night. She roots for her hometown Marlins, despite living in New York City with her Mets fan husband. When not watching baseball, she spends her time swimming, cooking, and weaving her little blue bicycle in and out of traffic in Manhattan.

Brandon Isleib exists in Alabama but lives on the Internet. He browses large databases for relevant, interesting information. This pays him as a lawyer but rewards him as a baseball historian.

Chris Jaffe is the author of *Evaluating Baseball's Managers, 1876-2008*, from McFarland Publishers. In his normal life, he is a history instructor.

Ben Jedlovec, a research analyst for Baseball Info Solutions, lived in the South for the first 21 years of his life. Somehow, he escaped with just the slightest trace of a southern accent.

Brad Johnson is a 23-year-old baseball addict currently residing in the DC Metro area. He may have left his playing days behind him when he graduated from Macalester College in 2009, but the need to be around the game will never leave him.

Max Marchi is a baseball nut in a country where a lot of people can't tell a cowhide from a pigskin. Despite the big pond between Europe and America, he has experienced the following thrills in the last couple of years: becoming a regular contributor for The Hardball Times; being at AT&T Park the night Jonathan Sanchez tossed his no-hitter; consulting for an MLB team and delivering a presentation at the 3rd PITCHf/x Summit.

Anna McDonald is a member of both SABR and the Jane Austen Society of North America. She finds nothing odd about that combination. In her spare time she relishes in writing for The Hardball Times, has contributed to ESPN.com and writes about everything from baseball to Jane Austen at her website.

Kate McSurley is a Technical Writer for Sportvision, the inventors of PITCHf/x, as well as a lifelong White Sox fan. She holds an MA in English from DePaul University.

Rob Neyer has written more words for ESPN.com than any other human, dead or alive. Also, there are six baseball books with his name on the spine.

Jeremiah Oshan is a former editor and writer of things that used to be called "newspapers." The apex of his prestigious writing career was covering the Single-A High Desert Mavericks where he once interviewed such legends as pitcher Javier Lopez and slugger Bill Hall. A graduate of The San Jose State University, he's now plying his trade in Seattle.

Oliver is The Hardball Times' projection system, developed by Brian Cartwright.

Harry Pavlidis is a software and web consultant and a partner in Complete Game Consulting. The New Jersey native and Syracuse grad has lived in Chicago, with a Cub obsession, since 1993.

Greg Rybarczyk is a reliability engineer, and the creator of *Hit Tracker*, a system designed to accurately measure home run distances. Since 2006, if a major leaguer hit a ball over the fence, or legged out four bases the hard way, Greg can tell you "How Far It Really Went!" Greg is an ESPN contributor, a three-time Sportvision PITCHf/x Summit presenter, and offers his 5th and 6th *Hardball Times Annual* articles this year. He lives outside Portland, Oregon with his wife and two children.

Sean Smith has been a fan of baseball and the Angels since 1982. He lives in Maryland with his wife, two cats, one daughter, and a baby to be named later (sometime before spring training).

Nick Steiner is a student living in Los Angeles who happens to be an avid Cardinals fan for some reason. When he's not busy ruining other peoples enjoyment of the game by overanalyzing baseball to a disgusting degree, he enjoys listening to music and complaining about how much it sucks to be a teenager.

Dave Studenmund has been told that he could pass for Bill James' younger brother. Dave is not sure what to think of this.

By day, **Tom Tango** works in the development of computer systems. By night, he is co-author of *The Book: Playing the Percentages In Baseball*, runs the Tangotiger.net website, blogs at InsideTheBook.com, and consults with pro teams in MLB and the NHL. By weekend, he is a stay-at-home dad. He prefers his weekends.

Steve Treder has been a writer for The Hardball Times since its founding in 2004. He's also been a frequent presenter/contributor to other forums, such as the SABR national convention, the NINE Spring Training Conference, and the Cooperstown Symposium. He roots for the Giants from his home in Sanata Clara, California.

TUCK's toons—commenting on sports, pop culture, politics, and life's other necessities—have appeared at or on or in an array of websites, publications, and other venues for the last 20-mumblemumble years. Having just completed his third full season at Hardballtimes.com, this is his fourth *THT Annual*.

John Walsh is a research physicist by day, baseball researcher by night. Despite living four thousand miles from Fenway Park, he remains an avid Red Sox fan.

Craig Wright worked 21 years in major league baseball pioneering a career that integrated science and baseball. He is the primary author of the book *The Diamond Appraised* and currently writes a baseball column under the same name at diamondappraised.com. Subscription information can be found at the site. Craig also researches and writes *A Page from Baseball's Past*, one of the longest running pre-game radio shows in baseball history. A delightful text version of these stories, delivered to your email inbox, can be subscribed to at pagefrombaseballspast.com.

Geoff Young is the founder of Ducksnorts, one of the world's first baseball blogs. Since 1997, he has written countless articles and published three books under that name. He is a regular contributor to The Hardball Times. He is a proud alum of the University of San Diego and still lives in that fine city with his wife, Sandra.

Free Bill James Daily Match-Ups
E-mailed to You
Every Day of the Season

ACTA Sports is offering our customers a free subscription to ***The Bill James Daily Match-Ups***. Each day you'll receive a PDF file in your e-mail inbox showing lifetime batter vs. pitcher statistics for your favorite team against your team's next opponent. These match-ups are updated daily throughout the season.

If you would like to receive a free subscription to ***The Bill James Daily Match-Ups*** for the 2011 season, please send an email to **matchups@actasports.com** with your name and favorite team and where you usually buy your sports books. Limit one team per customer.

Thanks for your patronage.

Play ball!

Greg Pierce
Co-Publisher